In Her Own Time

Maggie Siggins

In Her Own Time
A class reunion inspires
a cultural history of women

HarperCollins*PublishersLtd*

www.harpercanada.com

HarperCollins books may be purchased for
educational, business, or sales promotional use. For
information please write: Special Markets Department,
HarperCollins Canada, 55 Avenue Road,
Suite 2900, Toronto, Ontario, Canada M5R 3L2.

First HarperCollins hardcover ed. ISBN 0-00-255431-3
First HarperCollins trade paper ed. ISBN 0-00-638629-6

Canadian Cataloguing in Publication Data

Siggins, Maggie, 1942–
In her own time:
a class reunion inspires
a cultural history of women

ISBN 0-00-255431-3

1. Women – Canada – Social conditions – 20th century.
2. Women – Canada – History – 20th century.
3. Women – Social conditions.
4. Women – History.
I. Title.

HQ1453.S533 2000   305.42'0971   C99-932143-9

00 01 02 03 04 RRD 6 5 4 3 2 1

Printed and bound in the United States
Set in Bembo

To the next generations: Alla, Shoshana, Carrie-May, Yaya and Samantha

Table of Contents

Acknowledgements   ix
The Reunion   1

1. Relationships
Jane   7
Lovers   18
Daphne   46
Daughters   57
Mary G.   81
Sons   91

2. The Married State
Elizabeth   115
The Family   125
Ursula   148
Class   158
Sandra   177
Breakdown   187
Dale   208
Frances   215
The Single Life   223

3. The Body
Gail   243
Health   255
Pat   269
Care-givers   279
Judy   296
Physiology   307
Gwen   321

Physical Activity   331
Lynne   347
Beauty   355

4. The Mind
Danielle   377
Education   388
Mary B.   407
Intellectualism   416

5. The Soul
Mary L.   437
Spirituality   450
Betty   467
Consecrated Women   478
Gay   494
Winnie   504
The Chosen   513

6. The Imagination
Adèle   529
Creativity   537
Noreen   549
Musicians   558
Louise   573
Visual Artists   587
Marjorie   601
Writers   620

Notes   639
Bibliography   663
Permissions   677
Index   679

Acknowledgements

I am greatly indebted to the researchers who assisted me in this book: Leanne Sywanyk, who so diligently transcribed interview tapes; Shoshana Sperling, who arranged the interviews; David Leeson, who so expertly weeded out factual and spelling errors and put the footnotes in order; and Brenda Geil, whose perseverance, skill and good humour contributed so much to this manuscript.

I would also like to express my appreciation to the staff of the library of the University of Regina for their unstinting time and effort.

Thanks to Iris Tupholme, the publisher of HarperCollins, for seeing the potential in this book, and my editor Jocelyn Laurence, for giving it shape.

My gratitude, as always, goes to my husband Gerald B. Sperling, who remains as always my first and best editor.

Finally my thanks to the Canada Council for its generous support.

The Reunion

The Dogfish Bar & Grill is pretty ordinary as such pubs go. There are the usual plain wooden tables and chairs, fake fishermen's lanterns and signs advertising Sleeman's beer. Its location in Bluffer's Park in Scarborough overlooking Lake Ontario is appropriate, though. It was here, among these sloping woods, that so many of us relished our first thrilling rendezvous with a real date—and where, a few years later, some nervously lost their virginity.

It wasn't billed as a reunion, but as a celebration of the 50th birthday of the youngest member of our high-school gang. That Mary (Beattie) Thompson, class of '61, R. H. King Collegiate, had lived up to her reputation as the Brain by becoming an eminent professor of mathematics set just the right tone for the occasion.

The vivacious Adèle Koehnke—"our Jackie Kennedy," as one classmate described her—stood at the door, greeting each arrival, handing out the name tags. After all, it had been 33 years since graduation. Weight had been gained, hair had greyed or gone missing, wrinkles had become entrenched. Yet within half an hour, the years melted away, and there was the same gang up to its old tricks. The clique of beautiful girls gossiped away, the sports addicts demonstrated some basketball play of a long-ago triumph and the music-lovers were gathered in adoration around Mr. McKinlay, the former conductor of the school orchestra.

For the most part, it was a prosperous, healthy, good-looking group. Many lived in the same area in which they had grown up, although their houses tended to be bigger and grander than their parents'. Many were professionals, most had well-paying jobs. While everyone had suffered some misfortune or other, there had been no wars, famines, plagues to ruin their lives. The women had been particularly lucky.

Those of us who were born during the war and came of age in the early 1960s are part of what is called the cusp generation. We were carried along, pushed forward, given a huge shove by that enormous, overpowering wave of the women's liberation movement that burst on the scene in the 1970s. The majority of us now believe in easy, cheap divorce, freedom of choice in

deciding whether or not to terminate a pregnancy and that living with a man
before actually marrying him is a good thing. But having been teenagers
during the 1950s, we were still very much a part of that staid, decorous era.
We once wore girdles and white gloves, sported false eyelashes, purposely lost
tennis games to our boyfriends so as not to damage their manhood. Few of
our mothers worked and, after we married, most of us (not all) quit our jobs
as soon as our children arrived; the accumulated pension money was used to
buy washing machines or trips to Bermuda. That all except two women
returned to careers after a few years in the home indicates how profoundly
affected we were by the second wave of feminism.

My contemporaries have stood in the forefront of a revolution so
profound, so sweeping—the emancipation of half the human race, no less—
that the magnitude of it has still not sunk into the consciousness of those
living in the Western world, even though the signs are all there.

While for eons the female was less healthy than the male, primarily because
of the danger of childbirth, work-related diseases such as tuberculosis and
poor nutrition (the T-bone always went to the head of the household),
women now live years longer than men, at least in the developed world.
While only 130 years ago women were barred from universities, now they
make up over 60 percent of the student body. While men still make more
money than their female counterparts, women's wages are increasing at a
faster rate than men's. The next millennium, say the wise, will belong to the
female sex.

In this context, my peer group seems all the more interesting, and I
decided to write the life stories of a sampling of the cusp generation, my
high-school classmates. But it was more than superficial profiles I was after. I
wanted to understand what made these women tick. What historical and
contemporary forces formed them as women? How deep, how secure was
their belief that the female is just as capable, just as worthwhile as the male?

The *modus operandi* soon presented itself. In the interviews I conducted, it
became apparent that a major thread ran through each woman's narrative, a
leitmotif that coloured her life. These themes could involve relationships:
sons, daughters, lovers. Or cultural interests: beauty or athletics or religion. Or
careers. Among this group were teachers, nurses, artists, physicians, professors,
ministers. Why not, I thought, peer back into the historic past and, through a
discussion of these topics, try to chart the up-and-down progress of the so-
called second sex? What emerged is not only a collection of contemporary life

stories but a cultural history of women in the Western world from antiquity to the present.

For centuries, women lived under a black cloud of misogyny; lies about their inferior nature permeated society. Geoffroy, the abbot of Vendôme Monastery, could feel perfectly free to write in 1095, "Woe unto this [female] sex, which know nothing of awe, goodness or friendship, and which is more to be feared when loved than when hated."[a] Such insidious and immensely damaging stereotyping has hobbled and denigrated women since antiquity.

Yet women have always lived productive and worthwhile lives. Century after century they have overcome the misogyny that stained their existence, and some have managed to soar far above it. It is these ancestors who must not be forgotten by contemporary women. We, who are positioned on the cusp, our feet in two very different worlds, understand the historical conflict more than our mothers or our daughters. In the major themes that run through our lives can be heard echoes of women's struggles and victories, beginning from antiquity and running, pell-mell, through the ages. We, who are so lucky to live when we do, have a duty to understand and acknowledge our history. There must be no complacency, no backsliding by the next generations.

On that lovely September evening, the class of '61 sang "Happy 50th Birthday" to Mary Thompson, cut the cake and then, late in the evening, waved each other goodbye. As Mary stepped outside, whether accidentally or on impulse, she let her birthday balloon go and it soared off towards the stars, a symbol, it is to be hoped, of where women of the future are headed.

1. Relationships

Jane

In 1957, my second year of high school, my family moved into the upper duplex of a lovely old house in a neighbourhood called Birch Cliff. It was tree-lined and well lived-in, not unlike the place where I had spent my childhood. It stood on what is known as The Bluffs, those ragged cliffs that dominate a portion of Toronto's shoreline, arching over Lake Ontario. Birch Cliff was a half-hour streetcar ride from downtown Toronto and had been a comfortable, middle-class enclave for years, part of Scarborough that had been settled as a suburban community as far back as the 1910s.

My family life was in chaos by this time—my mother's second marriage was finally disintegrating beyond repair—and to live on Kingsbury Crescent in Birch Cliff was to provide me with a much-need patina of respectability.

In September I enrolled in my new school, R. H. King Collegiate, and much to my amazement was told I had been placed in 10A, the "brainers" class where academic excellence was a given. More happiness that day when I found out Jane Sanderson lived nearby.

Everyone liked Jane. Little and small-boned, she had fine, curly blonde hair, lovely eyes the colour of forget-me-nots—she often wore a wool skirt of the most exquisite pale blue that matched them perfectly—and a grin full of mischievous glee. She was gregarious, funny and warm, surrounded always by an army of admiring friends. While I never became part of her inner circle, I was happy simply being on the periphery. To me, she represented the side of our teenage years that was wholesome and safe and fun.

Jane's father, Ted Sanderson, had grown up in a big, rambling house in Toronto's Beaches area, not far from The Bluffs. While attending Malvern Collegiate he had met Eleanor Beer, the eldest daughter of a well-known family doctor who practised in the Beaches area.

The lovely Eleanor would not prove an easy catch. For one thing, she was considered better educated, more refined and more of an intellectual than Ted. She attended Victoria College at the University of Toronto, and worked for a short time as a social worker investigating the families of abused children.

There had been a terrible disappointment in Eleanor Beer's young life. She had been going out with a medical student, the son of a prominent, upper-class doctor—the Beers were dazzled by the family's pedigree—but he had lost interest. Meanwhile, she, with her broken heart, was approaching 30, nearly on the shelf, and there was Ted Sanderson, still pursuing her, still proclaiming his undying love. They were finally married when both were in their early thirties. By that time, Ted had graduated from law school and set up his own practice in downtown Toronto. An old friend describes him this way: not very literate, not too bright, but sweet, faithful, patient—and he would do anything for his "Nor."

Through all his married life, Ted Sanderson remained passionately in love with his wife. Jane remembers how, as a young child, she'd excitedly wait for her Dad to come home from work. He'd walk in the door, wouldn't say hello or even look at her, just demand, "Where is your mother?"

He was a man of contradictions. While he would give Eleanor anything she wanted, wouldn't hesitate for a moment if she wanted to go to New York to take in the theatre she loved so much, he had very rigid views of a woman's proper place in life. It was having babies, looking after the house and being gracious to guests. Every afternoon, in honour of Ted's arrival home from work, Eleanor put on a pretty dress and did up her hair.

Years later, after Women's Liberation had raucously proclaimed a new era, Jane, who was pregnant with her second child, and her sister Mary were sitting around the dinner table with their father. A discussion ensued about which sex the baby might be.

"You want a girl, you certainly want another girl," said Ted.

"Why?" Mary and Jane asked in surprised unison.

"Being a boy is so hard. All a girl has to do is be pleasant and good-looking and get married."

The two sisters looked at each other and thought to themselves, "We've been raised by this man?" Yet, Jane adds, a heavy burden was imposed on men in those days. Her father, a man full of optimism and good humour, saw himself as the great provider and protector. He never much challenged his vivacious daughter Jane, never pushed her, and in the end neglected to teach her the skills that would make her existence easier. Always she would be dependent on the men, often lovers, who would shape her life.

From her early thirties, Jane's mother Eleanor suffered from arthritis that grew progressively worse as time went on. Ted did everything he could to make her comfortable: a cleaning woman came once a week, and the Sandersons were one of the first families in the neighbourhood to purchase an automatic washing machine because Eleanor couldn't handle the wringer on the old one. Jane never once heard her mother complain about the painful disease that would eventually cripple her. Her condition was a kind of "elephant in the dining room"—nobody ever talked about it.

Jane was closer to her mother than her father. Eleanor was always at home for her girls, and Jane remembers spending hours in the kitchen just yakking to her. Jane feels her mother was probably lonely—she didn't have a lot of friends—and reading was her refuge.

Jane was such a happy child, so extroverted, inquisitive and smart, that she sailed through elementary and high schools. She did all the right things: she was elected to the Student Administrative Council; she was a girl prefect, that hand-picked elite who made sure students put their lunch trays away; she was on the badminton team. She developed lots of anguished crushes on football players and other hunks, but she never had a steady boyfriend. She was so cute and bubbly, lots of the guys gave her pet names and invited her to their parties, but they were after the *femmes fatales*, the beauty queens, and Jane was never that. She resented this a little; as she grew older, getting her hands on a boyfriend, a lover, became ever more important.

Unlike many of us who barely managed the torment of Grade 13, Jane easily made the honour roll with 83 percent, languages and math being her two outstanding subjects. University was certainly in the cards for her, and in the yearbook, she brightly told the world she wanted to become a lawyer.

While growing up, Jane would often beg her father to talk about his legal cases. The two would sit after dinner and debate the details of a particular court proceeding until Jane's sister Mary, who hated arguments of any kind, would quit the kitchen table in disgust. Ted would compliment Jane on her sharp logic, but at the same time he made it very clear: the "law business," as he called it, was not for her. Ted Sanderson had a habit of ridiculing women lawyers and he made a point of not hiring female articling students for his firm. (Years later, he, like everyone else in the profession, finally relented on this particular prejudice.) What Jane now considers pathetic is that neither she nor her sister, or, for that matter, her mother, challenged him about this. It was supposed to be a joke, but it left an indelible scar on Jane's psyche. The idea of law school vanished quickly.

Jane was presented with another chance to break from tradition. She was accepted at York University, which had been founded only two years before to accommodate Toronto's burgeoning population. Jane thought it would be a thrill to be there at the beginning, when the professors would be keen and the atmosphere charged. But in the end, she took her parents' advice and enrolled in Victoria College at the University of Toronto, where both her mother and her aunt had studied. It was another example, she says, of not searching for her bliss, not striving for the gold ring.

Jane's high-school marks were high enough for acceptance into an honours program, and she chose English language and literature. By this time she was convinced that becoming a lawyer was impossible, and without a career in mind, she did not enjoy her courses. Though she kept slugging away, she failed her second year and transferred into general arts. The women in this stream, it was said, were after only one thing: their MRS. degree.

Jane's summers, which she spent in Montreal, were more interesting. The rebellious 1960s were just starting to heat up, and some of the university's formerly staid institutions were flexing their left-wing muscles. The Student Christian Movement was one of these. Established in 1921 as a reaction to the perceived conservatism of the YWCA and YMCA, it was regarded as the thinkers' group; there was always some important issue being debated— peace, poverty, politics.

Jane wasn't involved in the SCM's activities on campus, but she found the idea of their summer work camps intriguing. Ten to 25 students lived co-operatively during the summer months, often in a church basement or parish hall. They pooled their wages, sharing daily expenses, and at the end of the summer, divvied up the accumulated savings according to each individual's needs. There were Mental Health Camps, and Industrial Camps, where students supposedly learned all about the proletariat by working in factories. Although the camp program had begun in 1945, by the 1960s there was a definite Marxist flavour to it.

One summer in particular was special because Jane finally became serious about a man—the director of the work camp. David Laurent L'Esperance was 11 years older than she was, dark and bespectacled, not very good-looking but embodying what 1960s idealism was all about. He was brilliant, a Marxist, a trained theologian, a philosopher and musician—he had taught himself flamenco guitar and played wonderfully. He was also married.

This was not Jane's only involvement with a married man; there were several affairs while she was at university, including a brief, mad encounter with a

United Church minister. She loved the excitement, the sneaking around, the drama, the satisfaction of pleasing these men who were sometimes close in age to her father. That the wives could be badly hurt by such deception bothers her now, of course, but it didn't back then in the passionate, devil-may-care '60s. Her romance with David, however, turned out to be anything but a fling.

David's mother was American, his father French-Canadian, a crackerjack insurance salesman who made lots of money. The family home was located in fashionable Outremont, a suburb of Montreal—Mrs. L'Esperance often had tea with Mrs. Trudeau, the mother of Canada's future prime minister. Like all the other males in the family, David was supposed to follow in his father's entrepreneurial footsteps. He dutifully enrolled in business administration at McGill University but quickly realized he loathed it. He failed his year, and began looking around for something else.

The L'Esperances were not a religious family, but in his early twenties, David had embraced the Anglican Church. He was enchanted by its symbols, its liturgy, its pomp and circumstance, and its humanitarianism. In 1958, he joined the worker-priest movement in England.

By the time he returned to Montreal three years later, he had married. His wife enrolled in library science and he in religious studies at Sir George Williams University (which later joined with Loyola College to become Concordia University), a hotbed of student radicalism during the 1960s. Eventually he would earn both his Bachelor of Divinity and STM, Master of Sacred Theology, but he was never ordained a priest. The hierarchical structure of the church did not appeal to him; he was turned off by what he perceived as a lack of intellectual brilliance among the divinity students. Later, though, he would regret his decision.

By the time he met Jane in the early 1960s, he was over 30 and his marriage was in serious trouble. Jane always thought David and his first wife were an odd couple: she was a strong feminist, a professional career woman who did not want children; David's values were centred in the family.

After her summer in Montreal, Jane returned to university in Toronto, but she and David kept their love affair going. One of them would say, "This is ridiculous" and call it off, but a few months later letters would start flying: "I love you, I miss you." By the time Jane graduated in 1966, David had obtained a divorce.

Jane and David were married in a small wedding two years later with Jane's parents happily in attendance. At first they had been shocked at the idea of their daughter being involved with an older married man, but Eleanor, at least, quickly came to adore David. He was sophisticated and cultured and charming to her—all the things her husband wasn't. When she was dying, it was David who sat talking with her for hours.

Jane was supposed to move to Montreal but, as she says, she wimped out on yet another challenging experience; David came to Toronto instead. Both found jobs with the Ontario government's correctional services, she as an after-care worker, counselling young girls who had been in training school, he as a probation officer. They considered their work as a kind of joint ministry.

Jane says David was a wonderful husband, so responsible, so loving and appreciative of her, yet looking back, she understands that there was a shadow over the marriage. Because David was so much older than she, and so capable, he took charge of the household, paying the bills, renovating an old home, making the important decisions. And she always deferred to him. He was so knowledgeable and well read, in a conversation or argument, she felt she could never win. She says she did a lot of play-acting and didn't grow much during her time spent with David.

The year after Jane was married, her mother died of cancer at age 62. Gone was the one person Jane most loved to talk to, and she was devastated. Eleanor suffered from two diseases, arthritis and cancer, which Jane believes often result from emotional repression, from closing doors on life, from seldom saying yes. Jane can still hardly talk about her mother without becoming teary-eyed—she now feels Eleanor's life was so wasted.

The L'Esperances' first child, christened Eleanor Ruth but called Norah by everybody, came along four years later. By that time David was moving up the ladder—he was a supervisor of probation officers—and Jane didn't hesitate to quit work. She gloried in being pregnant, loved the physical experience of childbirth, the breast-feeding. She submerged herself in research, studying all the latest books on motherhood, attending lectures. It was one area, she says, where she didn't have any competition from David.

Joseph was born three years later. By that time, the L'Esperances were settled into a comfortable, middle-class life, fixing up their house, having other couples in for dinner. Neither had given up on their social activism: David started a program working with people on probation, and he was still involved with the Anglican Church, serving as a warden at nearby St. Aidan's. Jane was a volunteer teacher at her kids' school, and joined Zero

Population Growth, a movement that believed the world's numbers were spinning dangerously out of control. To prove her point, she underwent a tubal ligation after Joseph's birth and scolded anybody who dared to become pregnant with their third child. She now thinks of herself then as being "totally obnoxious."

When both children were finally in school, Jane, now in her mid-thirties, began thinking about going back to work. She found a law-clerk course that appealed to her, but her father once again dampened her enthusiasm by insisting it wasn't an interesting enough job for his daughter. She began taking library-science courses, and in the newspaper want ads found a position in a law library working three days a week. It was a flunky's job, she says, but she loved it, and even considered going back to university to get a library science degree. But in late 1982, all plans came to an abrupt halt. David was diagnosed as having cancer and given six weeks to live.

Jane says he was remarkable during his illness. He held court. All day long people would visit him, often coming away with tears in their eyes. He was so brave and inspiring, talking about the act of dying and death as part of life. Jane thought it was sad that only as his end approached did he finally find his true ministry. He died February 15, 1983 age 50, one day before their 15th wedding anniversary.

The children were devastated, of course. The way Jane coped with the tragedy was to get involved with another man.

John Teal (a pseudonym) admired and loved David so much, he tried to emulate him—he even looked like him a little. He was the sexton at St. Aidan's Church where David was a warden. Both men worked in the same office. John had three daughters, but he was divorced and had been on his own for seven years. Jane recognized he was lonely and very needy, and always welcomed him to her house. It was John who helped Jane take David to the hospital the first time, before they knew what was wrong with him. And it was John who took charge when David died.

Jane realizes now that if she and the two kids had clung together and grieved together, they would have slowly recovered. But she was benumbed, the family was in total disarray and there was John hovering in the wings. And Jane had always been so dependent—David had been this huge rock of security—she simply didn't believe she could look after the children herself.

John moved into high gear and before Jane knew what had happened, they were married. Their relationship was not a happy one. John had grown up in a very traditional family and expected to be treated in the same way his mother had treated his father. When John came home from work, there was no chitchat over a drink. He sat waiting at the kitchen table for his meals to be served. David, who had been a strong feminist, had always been considerate towards Jane, and she deeply resented John's attitude.

They argued fiercely about everything from disciplining the children to financial matters. John's way of striking back was to threaten to leave Jane. Sometimes he made good on this intimidation and would disappear for days. Jane's kids remember her running outside on a cold winter night, pleading, "Come back! Forgive me!" as John's car pulled away. Sometimes he would ensconce himself in the basement; "I'm not going to spend the night with you because I'm so mad at you," he'd say. Jane had such a fear of being abandoned that she would go down and sleep on the floor beside him, even though he refused to speak to her.

Joseph was the one family member who adored John, went fishing with him, shared jokes. Norah, on the other hand, was furious that another man had replaced her father so quickly. It took her a long time to forgive her mother for allowing it to happen. But Jane knows what drove her: desperation. Desperation and fear and a feeling of inadequacy.

In the spring of 1985, six months after her marriage to John, Jane was buying cheese at Pasquale Brothers delicatessen near Toronto's St. Lawrence Market when she ran into an old flame from her first-year university days. When she had dated Harry Watson, before she met David, she had thought him a gorgeous dreamboat. He was not only good-looking, red-headed and blue-eyed with a husky build, but he wasn't studying engineering or one of those boring, all-male courses. He was an English major. He played football for the Varsity Blues but he also wrote poetry. Nothing serious had resulted from their dating, but Jane still remembered the heart-throbbing crush she had had on him.

The two were delighted to see each other and went for a cup of coffee. Harry told Jane he had been a high-school English teacher for years, but had grown tired of the job. He and his wife travelled around Europe for four years and when they returned to Canada, Harry turned himself into a successful management consultant. By the time he ran into Jane in 1985, he was making over $100,000 a year. Like Jane, Harry had been married twice and was unhappy in his current relationship.

Something incredible happened when Jane ran into Harry. Even today, she gets goose bumps thinking about it. They fell madly in love, and within six months, both had left their spouses and were living the Great Romance.

They went out together for two years before Harry finally moved into Jane's cozy Blantyre Avenue house on July 1, 1987. Neither of Jane's marriages had been particularly joyful: David was a serious man, a father figure to Jane; John was a needy child. Harry was fun, her playmate, her soul mate. They had everything in common. They both loved good food, and Harry had the kitchen renovated so they could create ever more elaborate meals. They enjoyed the same movies and going to the theatre. They liked books and then talking about what they had read. They took great trips, travelling twice to England and twice to Jamaica. Their sex life was wonderful.

However, there was a dark side to Harry Watson, and he didn't hesitate to lay it on the table for Jane. He was a serious alcoholic. His problem began when he became a management consultant. Every afternoon was spent drinking with his business associates at a favourite watering hole. His drinking had wrecked one marriage, so when Harry became involved with Jane, he was determined to overcome his addiction. He went for extensive treatment at Toronto's Bellwood Clinic, a private hospital with an admirable record of success. Jane says Harry passed with flying colours, and she never saw him take another drink. Nonetheless, she now wonders why the Bellwood staff did not give him more support once his treatment was finished, insisting, for example, that he join Alcoholics Anonymous. He was a man who thought he could tame the ferocious beast all by himself and for a long time, Jane thought he had done just that.

Neither Harry nor Jane had recovered from the bad experiences of their second marriages and they felt living together was just fine. Jane believes they eventually would have married, since they came to feel more committed to each other than they had to anyone else in the past. Indeed, there was a lot of love and respect within the entire family.

They lived full lives and June 1989 was particularly hectic. Joseph was graduating from high school and Norah was involved in mounting a puppet show that would be performed at the opening of the Canadian Museum of Civilization. Harry was extremely busy at his job, travelling a lot, and Jane was worried because he seemed so exhausted. He was attending business meetings near Ottawa, and Jane thought it would be a great idea if they could all meet in the capital, attend the opening of the museum and then travel to the family cottage for a much-needed vacation.

On Thursday, June 29, Harry drove to Ottawa in the morning and phoned Jane as soon as he arrived. They talked about how the second anniversary of his moving in with her was drawing near and how happy they had been. Three years before, Harry had lost his license for drunken driving, but the restriction had just about come to an end, and he told her how overjoyed he was at the thought of being at the wheel again. He had already leased a brand new Honda Prelude.

Jane had intended to call Harry later—she telephoned him every evening he was away—but she was so busy getting ready to travel the next day, she didn't get around to it. It was an oversight for which she never forgave herself.

The following morning, Jane and Joseph drove to Ottawa to meet Harry and Norah, who was already there rehearsing her puppet show. They were supposed to meet Harry in the lobby of the Château Laurier Hotel where he was staying, but when they arrived, he wasn't there. This surprised Jane, because considerate Harry never keep her waiting. She finally went to the reception desk, identified herself and asked if he had left a message. The manager told her there had been an accident and the police were waiting to talk to her. She got back in her car with Joseph and somehow found her way to the police station. She was ushered into a small room—Joseph remained outside—and there she learned Harry was dead. He had hung himself from the shower of his hotel room the previous midnight.

It was his alcoholism, of course. Unbeknownst to Jane, he had begun drinking when he was on the road, and in fact he was probably drunk when he killed himself. He had looked into a hole so dark and so deep, he had been swallowed by it. He couldn't fight his addiction any longer and he couldn't stand the shame of disappointing Jane and humiliating the kids.

Jane believes it was loneliness. When he had stopped drinking, he had been shunned by his friends; all the camaraderie had gone. For a man who was on the road so much, who was so sociable, it became intolerable. The worst of it was that Jane blames herself for not contacting him that night. He was drowning, and a phone call might have provided a life raft. If only he had made it through that one terrible, dark time. Jane is sure he hadn't planned on killing himself—there was no suicide note, and she found the packages of cigarettes he had bought for the next day.

Somehow Jane managed to survive the funeral and the terrible grief that followed. This time she was determined to be as strong as she could, to become independent, and she has managed rather miraculously to rebuild her life. Since both David and Harry had insurance policies, she was not left destitute, although she is far from being rich. When she was living with Harry, her job at the law library came to an end, much to her disappointment, and she ended up volunteering as a secretary at the nearby St. Bede's Anglican Church. Fortunately, a new minister, a woman, insisted Jane be given an honorarium—the fact that she was a paid secretary looked good on her résumé when she finally went hunting for a full-time job.

She is the now the secretary of St. John, York Mills, an old Anglican church that has an eminent and conservative congregation. Situated in wooded parkland in an affluent part of Toronto, it smacks of Old England and the Family Compact. Jane, who does everything from administering the business of the church to calming down the distressed, says she loves her job. But she knows that none of her tasks are very difficult and she is not taxing her skills and talents. The problem was that when everybody else was going back to school to upgrade their skills, Jane was burying husbands.

Over the years Jane has sought, and found, a sense of herself. Her Anglican religion has remained important in this voyage of discovery, but she has also been deeply influenced by feminist writers: Simone de Beauvoir, Betty Friedan, Gloria Steinem. But it is Erica Jong, with her great appetite and appreciation of men, with whom she identifies the most. While Jane still longs for, and often has, men in her life, her concept of the male-female relationship has changed dramatically. She enjoys someone with a religious faith, a sense of humour, a passion about his work, but she also wants freedom, a chance to live her own life on her own terms. Within any relationship, no matter how loving, she will now insist on her independence.

Lovers

I should say the majority of women (happily for society) are not very much troubled with sexual feeling of any kind.... She submits to her husband, but only to please him; and, but for the desire of maternity, would far rather be relieved from his attentions.
William Acton, British physician and moralist, 1857

If God made anything better, he kept it to himself. It's wonderful... We both come every time. It's the most important thing in the world.
A Cincinnati housewife and mother of three in a sociological survey, 1960

During one spring semester, the girls in my high-school class spent a lot of time arguing over who was sexier, who the more gorgeous hunk, Heathcliff in Emily Brontë's *Wuthering Heights* or Edward Rochester in Charlotte Brontë's *Jane Eyre*. I was part of the Heathcliff contingent. Dark, unruly, a gypsy kid who had mysteriously arrived in the Earnscliffe household, Heathcliff was, for me, the very embodiment of unbridled, unquenchable passion. Rochester was more refined than Heathcliff, cool and controlled, although he, too, brooded a lot. But did Rochester throw all prudence to the wind, abandon himself completely to his love as Heathcliff did? Those among us who considered ourselves "artistic" or "bohemian" thought it only natural that we should adore the wild Heathcliff while the more prissy girls fell for Rochester.

Whatever camp we were in, we were obsessed with sex, never mind that the awkward boys with pimples and big ears who we dated were hardly passionate and handsome Heathcliffs or Rochesters. Although we were deeply mired in the dreary domesticity of the 1950s, we knew, with as much ferocity as cats in heat, that the lovers in our lives would also be our destinies.

I

It's hard to imagine what sort of sex life the ordinary housewife could have had in ancient Athens, given that eroticism was so warped, at least from a woman's point of view. Her lowly position in society reflected this. The orator Demosthenes summed it up: "Mistresses we keep for pleasure, concubines for daily attendance upon our person, wives to bear us legitimate children and be our faithful housekeepers."[1]

A woman of antiquity was a perpetual child. While her sons came of age at 18, she was forever at the mercy of a male guardian. If her father, husband or other male relatives weren't available, the state would take over, controlling both her property and her person. She was married in her early teens to a man usually 20 years older who had been selected by her father, most likely without her knowledge, never mind her consent. Female infanticide was endemic, childbirth mortality rates were high and her general health was not as good as a male of the same age so that her life span was five to ten years less than his.[2] She lived in the dark secluded recesses furthest away from the busy courtyard. Her life, as described in Plutarch's *Dialogue on Love*, consisted of "drudgery of housework, sordid account-keeping and day-long bickering."

She was not permitted to partake in the sociable world of the market place, to participate in the great debates of the day or even to visit the famous perfume shops—the slave was sent to get the equivalent of Chanel Number Five. She probably wasn't allowed to go to the theatre; she couldn't attend the funeral of anybody but a close relative. In Euripides' play *Trojan Women*, Andromache, the wife of the great Trojan hero Hector, says:

> Fault them or not, there is
> one prime source of scandal
> for a woman, when she won't stay indoors.
> I longed to go out, but no! I stayed at home
> and indoors I didn't practise saucy speech,
> like some women. My mind, sound by nature,
> was my teacher. I needed no more.
> I offered my husband a silent tongue
> and gentle looks. I knew when to have my way and
> when to let him have his.[3]

Yet Andromache's cloying words reveal something else going on here. There must have been women who escaped the confines of their home, women who possessed sharp tongues, women who scolded their husbands and bossed them about, or why would she bother to criticize them? All the same, respectable wives were expected to spend their days spinning and weaving in the women's quarters, not flitting about. They were also expected to be modest and circumspect about their sex lives.

Athenian men, on the other hand, were anything but. As the historian Eva C. Keuls writes, "As foreigners were astonished to see, Athenian men habitually displayed their genitals, and their city was studded with statues of gods with phalluses happily erect."[4] Vase paintings are replete with birds whose heads are male organs, plants shaped like penises, phalluses with eyes, creatures with not one but two huge, extended members.[5]

The fascination with erect penises seems to have had everything to with the pleasure of men and little to do with satisfying women. This presents an interesting paradox. In antiquity, women were considered "sexually voracious and incapable of such control." Confined to her home, hard at work at the loom and spindle, a woman was nonetheless supposed to have a perpetual longing for orgiastic release.

However, the ancient Greeks were obsessed with controlling promiscuity. As the scholar Margaret Williamson put it, "... since she came as an outsider to her husband's household, there would always be doubts about her loyalty, and hence about the legitimacy of her sons: so her sexuality had to be vigilantly watched."[6] Adultery by women, certainly not by men, was considered a crime in Athens and severely punished. The job of the wife was to produce legitimate heirs; anything that might interfere with this, her primary function, was curtailed.

Because women were considered so intellectually inferior to men, the relationship between husband and wife, according to philosophers like Aristotle, would always be unequal. Living their separate lives—they didn't even dine together—married couples were basically strangers. The husband's pleasure lay in the camaraderie of men, close friends who had lots to talk about since they participated in the political and economic business of their society; the wife's in the warmth and sympathy of her female companions.

It's hard to picture how there could have been much erotic horseplay between spouses. During marital sexual intercourse, women might not even have taken off their clothes.[7] In fact, sexual fulfillment seems to have occurred far from the conjugal bed. The husband had his high-class call girl, the *hetaerae* or companions to men, who were not only talented singers and dancers but whose sexual expertise was renowned. And the wife? She was supposed to quietly accept her unfulfilled lot in life, her position as a second-class citizen.

Yet a puzzling irony lies at the heart of antiquity. As Virginia Woolf has pointed out, despite ordinary women being kept in seclusion like "odalisques or drudges," the most powerful and vivid characters dominating the great Greek tragedies are the heroines.[8]

Moreover, the female Olympian divinities are anything but simpering hand-maidens. Hera, Athena, Artemis, Demeter are all powerful and determined characters. And the great Aphrodite, the goddess of sexual passion, seduction and beauty, has little to do with begetting children, and her feminine charms are anything but ladylike. The goddess whose only task was to make love and inspire others to do the same was supposedly born of man, not woman. In one version of her birth, her father Uranus, the sky god, was castrated by Cronus, ruler of the universe, and his genitals thrown into the ocean. Aphrodite was said to have sprung from the divine sea foam thus generated.

She, the most beautiful of all goddesses, was married to the ugliest immor-tal, the lame Hephaestus, god of fire and metalwork. This part of the myth may have resulted from wishful thinking on the part of the funny-looking men of antiquity, or it may have provided an excuse for her infidelity for, of all the goddesses, she is the only one who engages in adultery.[9] Her sexual appetite was legendary, and one of her most lustful liaisons was with Ares, god of war, the father of three of her children.

Aphrodite has been frowned on over the centuries as being the ultimate frivolous and irresponsible sex object. But she has also been admired for the amazing power she wielded. In finding pleasure everywhere except in her marriage bed, she broke all the rules. Did the wives of Athens look at her with envy or with abhorrence? The great poet Sappho hints at the sex goddess's sway in this description of a young girl's longing:

> Truly, sweet mother, I cannot do my weaving:
> I am overcome with desire for a boy, because of slender Aphrodite.[10]

The sensuous goddess of sexual passion is not the only erotic image that has vibrated down from antiquity. The bodies of beautiful Greek boys are on display in all the world's great museums. Divisions were not made in classi-cal Greece between homosexual or heterosexual. Both types of sexual expe-rience were considered part of the natural order of things although, according to Plato, relations with boys were considered a more spiritual, more "heav-enly" kind of love. Since it need not concern itself with such vulgar, down-to-earth functions as reproduction, boy love could evoke ideas, philosophy and great art.

And what about women? How ardently did they pursue same-sex love? Plato in his *Symposium* admits there are women "who ... direct their affections towards women and play little attention to men; Lesbians belong to this category."[11]

Who knows what went on in the dark, damp houses where women of antiquity were cruelly secluded? We know from Homer's *Hymn to Demeter* that they liked to indulge in ribald jokes. Some women gloried in their collection of leather dildos, sometimes decorated with the most ludicrous caricatures of the male private parts. Women lived and played with women—certain religious festivals allowed them time off their jobs as heir-producers to drink and frolic as they wished. Young girls were initiated into the pleasures of sex in the company of adult women. In the phallus-dominated world of ancient Greece, it would be surprising if women hadn't loved their own sex. The most moving and intense eroticism that echoes down from antiquity was written not by a man but by a woman on contemplating her beloved—another woman. It is the glorious Sappho, of course.

> ... and the thrill of your laugh, which have so stirred the heart
> in my own breast, that whenever I catch
> sight of you, even if for a moment,
> then my voice deserts me
>
> and my tongue is struck silent, a delicate fire
> suddenly races underneath my skin,
> my eyes see nothing, my ears whistle like
> the whirling of a top
>
> and sweat pours down me and trembling creeps over
> my whole body, I am greener than grass;
> at such times, I seem to be no more than
> a step away from death.[12]

II

Woman is a fragile thing, steadfast in nothing but crime and always harmful. Woman is a voracious flame, the utmost folly, man's intimate enemy, who learns and teaches every possible way of doing harm. Woman is a vile *forum,* a public thing, born to deceive, for whom success is the ability to commit crime. All-consuming in vice, she is consumed by all. A predator of men, she becomes in turn their prey.[13]

This denunciation was written by the archbishop and poet Hildebert of Lavardin (1055–1133), but he certainly wasn't the only devoted misogynist of the Middle Ages. This was the age when women were harangued by men telling them what to do; fathers, husbands, sons, preachers, confessors, philosophers all felt free to castigate and pontificate. As the historian Carla Casagrande points out, "It is hard to define precisely what women were doing that was so strange and so different than that of their counterparts in previous centuries to produce such an outburst from the self-proclaimed moral trustees of society."[14]

It all had to do with sex, of course. To be more precise, the male terror of Eve, the eternal seductress. It was Eve who, in the Garden of Eden, listened to the serpent/Satan and then enchanted Adam with the apple of desire. The early Church fathers had grabbed onto the Genesis story and firmly placed the tragedy of man's mortality at the feet of Eve, who was Everywoman.

With the concept of original sin firmly rooted, the separation of the body and soul was complete. Woman, the vile temptress, was the body; man, the rational being, was the soul. Sex became something dark, dangerous, malignant, associated with death and putrefaction—something to be avoided if at all possible. St. Paul put it succinctly: "... it is good for a man not to touch a woman."[15]

Given this distaste for the erotic, it's not surprising that the woman placed on the highest pedestal was the Virgin. Asserted Saint Cyprian, "... in them [the virgins] is the flower of the church, the honour and masterpiece of spiritual grace, a happy blossoming of nature ... the most brilliant portion of Christ's flock ..."[16] The virgin had an enormous obligation: it wasn't just that her hymen must remain intact, she must be free forever of all lustful, unsavoury thoughts. But then, she could expect far greater rewards in heaven than the married woman since she had overcome the curse of Eve.

The obsession with virginity reached new heights in the 12th century as the adoration of Mary, the queen of all virgins, strengthened. The pitying Mother of God, smiling benignly, her head tilted in supplication, became the image of ideal womanhood. Her elevation to a cult figure undoubtedly raised the status of women, but since her virtue was impossible to emulate—what woman remained free of all sin?—she was also a font of guilt and oppression. As the writer Marina Warner puts it, "Her freedom from sex, painful delivery, age, death, and all sin exalted her *ipso facto* above ordinary women and showed them up as inferior."[17] The most powerful erotic image, which permeated all of society, was of a woman who gave birth without experiencing either the sublime pleasure or exquisite pain of sexual intercourse.

However, there was the little matter of reproducing the species. How could a society survive without mothers begetting children? In religious teachings, a wife could be virtuous, too, although on a lower plain than a virgin, as long as her love-making was for the express purpose of giving pleasure to her husband and producing babies. Adultery would bring down the wrath of God. A widow could also find a place in heaven, as long as she was chaste, not just because of the stroke of fate that ended her sexual life but also because her thoughts were permanently pure.

The sexual neurosis and erotic contradictions of this period are vividly illustrated in one of the most celebrated of love affairs: the pathetic, passionate tale of Héloïse and Abélard.

Peter Abélard, born in 1079 in Brittany, was a brilliant philosopher and teacher, much admired and beloved by his students. By his mid-thirties he had established his own school in Paris and had gained great renown as an original thinker. He admits in his memoir that his fame went to his head: not only was he too proud of his work but, as a vigorous young man, he took to hanging out with "harlots."

Then he caught sight of the beautiful Héloïse. Much beloved by her guardian and uncle, Fulbert, a canon of Notre Dame in Paris, she was one of the few women of her time to be given a first-rate education. Tutored at home and at the Saint Benedictine Convent at Saint-Argenteuil near Paris, she was well versed in Latin as well as classic and Christian literature. Abélard was smitten with her and set out to seduce her. He talked his way into the uncle's household promising to tutor the young woman. But "there was more kissing than teaching; my hands found themselves at her breast more often than on the book."[18] Héloïse was soon pregnant. A desperate Abélard spirited her off to his sister's house in Brittany where she gave birth to a son.

Meanwhile, the uncle found out about the affair and was "mad with grief and rage." There wasn't much he could do, though, since his niece was ensconced in the Abélard family home. Abélard promised to marry Héloïse, which seemed to appease the old man a little, but Héloïse refused the offer. Marriage she insisted would bring "disgrace" and "humiliation" on so great a scholar as Abélard. How could a man bent on philosophical reflection "bear the wailing of babies, the silly lullabies of nurses ... the noisy horde of servants, both male and female ... the constant degrading defilement of infants." [19] Abélard insisted, and Héloïse finally gave in, but both agreed to keep the marriage secret forever to protect his reputation as a teacher.

The uncle, trying to salvage something of the family's name, decided to let the world know about the union. Abélard's response was to carry Héloïse off to the convent at Argenteuil where she had been educated. Fulbert believed Abélard simply wanted to shunt his niece aside, and his revenge was a particularly gruesome one. While Abélard was sleeping in his chambers one night, two henchmen broke in and castrated him. According to Abélard, the entire population of Paris went into mourning. "When morning came, the whole city flocked to me and it is hard, yes impossible, to describe the astonishment which stunned them, the wailing they uttered, the shouting which irritated me and the moaning which upset me.... I felt the embarrassment more than the wound and the shame was harder to bear than the pain."

The lovers never met again, at least not on this earth. Eventually, Héloïse became one of the great abbesses of her time at Paraclete Convent, which became a centre of learning and scholarship for nuns. Abélard continued the struggles of an original and controversial theologian. His castration, however, had entirely reversed his thinking about sex. God, by allowing the brutal act, had "cut him off from the dirt in which he had been immersed." He had "cleansed rather than deprived him." He no longer craved "miserable, obscene pleasure."

An inspiring story of a strong, clever woman and a passionate, brilliant man, but what does it tell of eroticism and love? Héloïse, who believed in the natural inferiority and intemperance of women, felt that the more one indulged in sex, the more sinful it became. Abélard came to consider intercourse as "sordid and worthless." For a man who was once a wandering minstrel proclaiming the beauty of love, this was a neurotic about-face indeed.

These two star-crossed lovers were repudiating their passion just as a profound sexual revolution was unfolding, one of those cycles of surprise that constantly overtake history. In the late 12th century, relationships between the sexes underwent a remarkable reversal, coded in a particular kind of literary creation called courtly love. Literature beloved by generations would form this tradition—the epic tales of Lancelot, Tristan and Isolde, the Arthurian legends and the epic poem *Le Roman de la Rose* were all part of it. It began with the Provençal poets of southern France writing in the colourful local dialect called *langue d'oc*. Troubadours travelled from castle to manor house singing out their message until it had spread to the great princely courts of Champagne, Normandy, Touraine and Flanders, and then to countries beyond.

The themes are similar. A dashing young knight catches sight, perhaps in a church or at a jousting tournament, of a beautiful lady. She is always married, the mistress of the local castle or manor house. He is smitten and can think of nothing but possessing his beloved. He suffers, mortifying himself for her sake, willingly becoming her slave. Kneeling before her, he pledges his love forever. Now the ball is in her court. Should she encourage his advances or spurn them? Since she probably has a tyrant and a boor for a husband, she naturally gives in to desire.

But that's not the end of the story, not by a long shot. The courtier mustn't rush his advances. He must write adoring love poems, perform valiant deeds. And he must find some place for the lovers to meet. This was not such an easy task; medieval castles provided almost no privacy, and male eyes had been trained since childhood to ferret out any threat to female chastity.

When the gallant at last arranges their *tête-à-tête*, they meet in a "secret garden," usually in balmy spring under a bower of beautiful flower. First she allows him to kiss her on the cheek, then on the lips. They passionately embrace. Finally comes the great trial, the *assaig*, as the troubadours called it. The two lovers lie naked together. They kiss, they embrace, they fondle, but consummation never comes. Keeping his passion bridled, he must pull away just before the exquisite moment. The ultimate pleasure is thus postponed forever.

Why this strange impasse? Some critics suggest the brave knight was terrified of the "unfathomable mystery of the female orgasm."[20] Women, it was thought, were driven by an insatiable lust. Better not to try at all than face the shame of not satisfying them.

It was all make-believe, erotic fantasy, but the values it embraced spread like wildfire. All over Europe, well-born gentlemen were urged to treat their women as Sir Lancelot did Queen Guinevere. Men must now win their ladies' hearts, not merely knock them over for a quick snatch. The poet Octavio Paz saw enormous significance in this:

Courtly love conferred upon women the most highly prized dominion: that of their own bodies and souls. The raising of woman was a revolution not only in the realm of the ideal but also in social reality. It is clear that love did not confer political rights on women, that it was not a judicial reform: it was a change in the vision of the world. The traditional hierarchical order was upset, and woman's social inferiority was counterbalanced by her superiority in the realm of love. In this sense it was a step toward the equality of sexes.[21]

And indeed women's status in society was enhanced during the later Middle Ages. The idealization of the female perpetrated by the cult of the Virgin Mary and the proper manners insisted on by courtly love had something to do with it, but the changing economic and cultural environment probably had more influence. Despite political chaos and religious fanaticism, the 12th and 13th centuries were a period of affluence and spiritual quest. The great Gothic cathedrals were constructed during this time—Abélard was connected both with the Great Abbey of Saint Denis and the Cathedral of Notre Dame. The feudal estate was thriving as an independent economic entity. An urban economy was taking shape, which meant artisans were flourishing. The powerful merchant-bankers, especially the Italians, were travelling to the Middle East and the Orient, returning not only with exotic goods but with a bagful of new ideas.

Women at all levels of society benefited. A nobleman was often absent on Crusades for years on end, during which time his wife was left in charge of his vast estates. If he died, she inherited the fiefdom, and although she would likely marry again, there was a tacit understanding that she would be a principal player in managing her affairs. For artisans or merchant families, the wife was equally important. It was often her business acumen that guaranteed the family prosperity. Even the laws of the High Middle Ages granted women more power. She was deemed mistress of the house, given "power of the keys," even allowed some official say in the family's business dealings. And if literature is any indication, she often held her own within the marriage and certainly enjoyed her conjugal bed.

Despite their aversion to the female body, the moral arbiters of the Middle Ages had never denied women enjoyed sex. They were like moist wood, they said, slow to take flame but apt to burn for a long time.[22] Even the most severe of the spiritual tyrants had never been able to extinguish this relishing of the bawdy, and by the late 13th and early 14th centuries, there was a flourishing of erotica. From the wondrous new printing presses spewed sex manuals of all kinds. One, at least, recommended that the overt part of the female's private parts (the clitoris was not named) be "rubbed until she swoon." There was even some suggestion that women perform the deed themselves.

III

In the early modern age (1500–1800), the forces of Puritanism squelched the erotic energy of the Middle Ages. At the core of the Protestant Reformation and the Catholic Counter-Reformation was a loathing of the body, a distaste for the sexual. The containment of women's primal urges and their "hungry" wombs became an obsession.

It began with a campaign in the 16th century against nudity. The lower part of the body became an off-limits zone, never to be seen in public and certainly not talked about. Nightgowns and bathing costumes became de rigueur—refined ladies would certainly faint if they caught sight of naked male buttocks diving into the Seine or the Thames. When a lady did undertake her occasional private bath, the water would be clouded with milk or bran just in case a servant, or perhaps even the lady herself, happen to glance at an unmentionable body part. Nightgowns fell severely from neck to ankles. Artists, who had fought hard for the privilege of portraying the human form, found themselves covering the private parts of their nubile figures with all manner of drapery, leaves or shrubs.[23]

Sexual bliss could not be denied, but it was strictly in the service of making babies. Erotic pleasure as an end unto itself became sinful and evil. Naturally, it fell on female shoulders to uphold the all-important virtue of chastity. Women, after all, represented "insidious temptresses whose primary object in life was to seduce unsuspecting men and deliver them to Satan."[24] It was up to them to harness their voracious sexual appetites. For if a man and woman thought too much of each other, surely that would diminish their love of God.

In England, certain parts of Europe and in the American colonies, Puritan morality became all-pervasive, colouring every aspect of female decorum and appearance. Take the simple matter of hair. Pamphleteer Philip Stubbes, one of a whole assortment of moral policemen propagating their Puritanism, wrote that a wife's long locks were a God-given "signe of subjection" before her husband and master. Like her sexuality, her hair must be strictly controlled, neatly combed and covered with a cap. Long, unruly tresses that had broken free of confinement were symbolic of woman as sexual hussy.[25]

The Catholics meddled even further into the sex lives of their followers. Aberrant practices such as sodomy or oral sex were considered monstrous sins, but other sexual customs also came under attack by the moralizers. The *more canino* or backward, spoon-shaped coupling was disgusting because it was reminiscent of animals. A woman atop a man was certainly not to be condoned, because it, too, went against nature—the female playing an energetic, even superior role, in the sex act. There were also many occasions on which sex was prohibited altogether—from 120 to 140 holidays, including Sundays, Christmas, Good Friday and Easter, not to mention the hot months of summer.[26]

The sex act itself could not have been much fun, especially for the female. For one thing, there was always the threat of violence. "He threw me on the ground, stuck a handkerchief in my mouth, and lifted my skirts" was a kind of stock phrase used by women instigating paternity suits, but many married women complained of similar rough treatment.[27]

By the late 16th century, the constricting of the erotic went beyond the religious into the secular realm. Governments began to police "devious" sexual behaviour. Official brothels that had been encouraged for a century were closed down and prostitutes punished. Premarital sex of any kind became subject to fines and imprisonment. In Hertfordshire, a woman was sentenced to a year in jail for giving birth to a bastard and her child was taken from her. In Maryland, an unmarried couple who had enjoyed sex could be sentenced to 20 lashes and fined a whopping 500 pounds of tobacco.

This increasing fear and denigration of the sex act could be partly traced to the sudden appearance of syphilis in the late 15th century. The worst of the epidemics had abated by the 1550s, but the metaphor—venereal disease as a punishment for lust—had imprinted itself on the collective psyche of the Western world and would remain firmly lodged there until the 19th century, only to reappear with the AIDS epidemic of the late 20th century.

That much of society was paying close attention to the Puritans is reflected in one telling statistic: the number of illegitimate children fell to a record low from the 16th to mid-18th centuries. During this same period, primarily because of economic reasons, the age at which young people married kept rising until it reached somewhere around 28 years. Sexual intercourse was therefore denied for at least a decade after physical maturity. It was an intolerable situation, and parents realized it. A charming, albeit curious exercise called bundling in English, *maraîchinage* in French, was practised all over Europe and in the American colonies. There were different versions, but basically, a young couple was allowed to share the same bed for the entire night—in the dark, by themselves. Petting and cuddling and cooing were permitted, but sexual intercourse was not supposed to happen. In Savoy, the young man had to swear on the Bible to respect his girl's virginity. In Scotland, the girl's thighs were tied together, if only symbolically. In England and the colonies, a bundling board was sometimes placed between the couple.

Surprisingly few pregnancies resulted from these nights of petting, and if an accident did happen, marriage almost always followed. Bundling was first a safety valve, allowing pent-up urges to escape, and secondly, a means to test the young lovers' affection for each other.

High society, on the other hand, paid almost no attention to Puritanism. Sex within marriage was meant to produce a male heir; pleasure was a mistress. Even the aristocratic wife, once she had given birth to sons, felt free to take lovers. In the mid-17th century, when Puritanism finally blew itself out, the sexual peccadilloes of the Court became even more extravagant. The outstanding female Restoration playwright Aphra Behn, in one of her many farces, felt quite free to refer to the vagina as

> That fountain where delight still flows
> And gives the universal world repose.[28]

The Age of Enlightenment, that heady time when an abiding faith in the power of human reason gained credence, when ideas held for centuries by church and philosophers were examined and found wanting, and when "the laws of nature" became the important catchwords, changed the relationship between the individual and society. With the American Revolution and Declaration of Independence, freedom of choice became not merely a hypothetical ideal but a real possibility. Naturally, sexual relations were very much part of this "pursuit of happiness."

Romance flourished in both literature and real life. Women expected to be wooed by their suitors, and a whole web of intricate practices grew in connection with the courting game. The young apprentice as well as the aristocrat's son were required to express their sentiments by stumbling out words of affection or reciting lofty poetry to their betrothed. The historian Lawrence Stone writes that there had always been two "archetypes" of sexual conduct: sex in marriage, which had a single aim of producing a male heir, and sex outside marriage, for "love, companionship and sexual pleasure." In the 18th century, the two archetypes fused for the first time; affection became necessary to marriage.[29] Interestingly, it was the lower classes who enjoyed the new mating rituals the most—the aristocracy still arranged marriages based on wealth and power. As William Alexander in his 1779 *The History of Women* insisted, "The poor are the only class who still retain the liberty of acting from inclination and from choice."[30]

The Age of Enlightenment could also be called the Age of Eroticism.[31] Robust sexuality thrived in literature, particularly magazines and periodicals, illustrations, cartoons and paintings. John Cleland's licentious novel *Memoirs of a Woman of Pleasure*, commonly known as *Fanny Hill*, is a prime example.

The portrayal of Fanny Hill, the most famous "loose" woman of her time, is very revealing. Even after gamboling in many beds, Fanny does not suffer the terrible nemesis that would have been required a few years earlier. Indeed, she prospers both financially and emotionally and, after many adventures in and out of brothels, attains the quiet, respectable, middle-class life she always wanted. (It helps that Fanny, an orphan, was hoodwinked into a life of prostitution.) What is fascinating in this fiction is the very explicit description of a young woman's sexual awakening, from innocence, to curiosity, to real lust.

Fanny Hill was fictional, but this new revolutionary attitude towards sex— and women—did spill over into daily society. Indeed, some writers consider the mid-18th century as a golden era for women. Simone de Beauvoir, pointing to fascinating and powerful women of the time—in particular Mme de Pompadour and Mme du Barry, who presided over the great French salons of the day—wrote in *The Second Sex*:

The democratic and individualist ideal of the eighteenth century ... was favorable to women; to most philosophers they seemed to be human beings equal to those belonging to the stronger sex. Voltaire denounced the injustice of woman's lot. Diderot felt that her inferiority had been largely *made* by society.... Condorcet wanted women to enter political life, considering them equal to man if equally educated.[32]

However, modern historians, looking at society as a whole and not just at the intelligentsia, question if the Age of Enlightenment really did much for the middle-class woman. She still had not come close to achieving independence;

it was still almost impossible for her to earn her own living. She remained a child both legally and by social convention, and to survive, she needed the protection of men. Catching and keeping a husband remained the central issue in her life.

The social code that dictated this pursuit was complex and dominated by the male establishment, so that a girl had to be exceedingly clever and strong-minded to act in her own interest. No one portrayed the rules of the court-ing game with such humour or insight as the great British writer Jane Austen. In *Mansfield Park*, the reprobate and womanizer Henry Crawford has decided to toy with the affections of the heroine Fanny Price. He tells his sister Mary that he can't believe Fanny is truly indifferent.

Why did she draw back and look so grave at me? I could hardly get her to speak. I never was so long in company with a girl in my life—trying to entertain her—and succeed so ill! Never met with a girl who looked so grave on me! I must try to get the better of this. Her looks say, 'I will not like you, I am determined not to like you,' and I say, she shall.

His sister replies:

Foolish fellow! And so that is her attraction after all! This it is—her not caring about you—which gives her such a soft skin and makes her so much taller, and produces all these charms and graces! I do desire that you will not be making her really unhappy; a *little* love perhaps may animate and do her good, I will not have you plunge her deep, for she is as good a little creature as ever lived, and has a great deal of feeling.[33]

The complicated mating game, full of pitfalls and artifice, will continue for another 100 years or so. It will hem women in, turn them into foxy, devious plotters. Humiliation and disappointment will often be their lot. When their very survival depends on their snaring a husband, by necessity, sexual attrac-tion, the heat of eroticism, must take a back seat.

IV

As industrial capitalism developed during the 19th century, it became more and more the prerogative of the man, the head of the household, to struggle all day in the business and industrial jungle while the woman was confined to the home, creating his private place of peace and security. Even those who could not afford such domestic bliss—the vast majority of women, who laboured at cottage industries or were being exploited in the "satanic mills" of the Industrial Revolution, whose homes were crowded, poorly heated and unsanitary—aspired to this ideal of domesticity. Women who managed the household became "specialists in emotion or spiritual life, protecting tradition and providing a stable refuge from the harsh, impersonal public sphere that men now entered in increasing numbers."[34]

The critic and social philosopher John Ruskin summed up society's new-found attitude towards women in his *Sesame and Lilies,* a collection of essays written in 1865.

There is not a war in the world, no, nor an injustice, but you women are answerable for it; not in that you have provoked, but in that you have not hindered.... There is no suffering, no injustice, no misery, in the earth, but that the guilt of it lies with you. Men can bear the sight of it, but you should not be able to bear it. Men may tread it down without sympathy in their own struggle; but men are feeble in sympathy, and contracted in hope; it is you only who can feel the depths of pain, and conceive the way of its healing.[35]

A woman might be the "angel in the house" but she remained a non-person under law. During the early Victorian era, a woman could not dispose of her own income without her husband's permission; she could be left destitute by a mere flick of her husband's pen; and under common law, her husband was allowed to subject her to corporal punishment as long as it was "moderate correction." An innocent in mind and body, sheltered from the poverty and misery of the real world, the upholder of society's rigid moral code, the middle-class Victorian woman developed a most peculiar personality. For one thing, it became her job to promote and uphold the prudery that rippled with ever greater intensity through her society.

Victorian priggishness reached preposterous heights. The word "pregnant," for example, was never spoken in mixed company; expectant mothers had "interesting" conditions. Legs were forbidden; women never revealed theirs, and if for some reason they had to mention them, they were called "limbs." Books authored by males and females were carefully separated on the shelves.

A girl was kept pure by ensuring she remained absolutely ignorant about sex and the reproductive system. She seldom saw her father without his tie, never mind naked. As one woman put it, "I'd never seen a man in bed and at home smalls would never be seen on the [washing] line, and underwear would certainly never be mended in front of father."[36]

It's hard to imagine how this much-coveted modesty could have allowed for much passion and creativity in bed. The new science of ovology that flowered in mid-century had established once and for all that orgasm in women was not a prerequisite for fertilization. A woman's sexual pleasure was suddenly irrelevant, and the male experts began chatting about the intriguing notion of female frigidity. Many physicians (all male) writing at the time, as well as some female advice-givers, insisted women were passionless creatures. Others conceded women did often seem to be having a good time in bed, but they insisted this had only to do with her instinct for making babies.

It was not only self-proclaimed male experts who pronounced on women's sexual desire, or lack of it. Many women themselves considered having intercourse with their husband one of the great burdens in life. Lady Hillingham, a member of the English upper crust, wrote in 1912:

I am happy now that Charles calls on my bedchamber less frequently than of old. As it is, I now endure but two calls a week and when I hear his step outside my door I lie down on my bed, close my eyes, open my legs and think of England.[37]

And the men themselves? The Victorian male perceived sex as a kind of game or competition; women were to be conquered or subdued like primitive people in the rest of the British Empire. It can't have allowed for much gentle foreplay.

Some writers and historians have recently suggested that 20th-century ideas of Victorian prudery are mistaken.[38] The Victorians, they claim, were far more sexy, passionate and uninhibited than they have been given credit for. For one thing, the entire society was larded with euphemistic, erotic images. The small waists nipped in by steel-ribbed corsets highlighted the swelling breasts and derrières so beloved by Victorian males. The blushes, heaving bosoms, the wilting looks were all signs of woman in heat. The pearl, so prominent in 19th-century romantic fiction, symbolized not only the spiritual union of man and woman but also the clitoris.[39]

Diaries and letters left by 19th-century men and women certainly reveal passionate affairs. Novelist Nathaniel Hawthorne wrote to his wife of 14 years:

Oh, dearest, dearest, interminably and infinitely dearest—I don't know how to end that ejaculation. The use of kisses and caresses is, that they supersede language, and express what there are no words for. I need them at this moment—need to give them and to receive them.[40]

Like much in the discordant Victorian society, the images of eroticism swung from one extreme to another. On the one hand, the sentimental valentine came into its own. These were created of gold and silver leaf, lace, satin ribbon, tiny silk flowers with pearlized leaves. The messages sighed on the page: "I Love But Thee," "Accept My Heart," "I Worship, Adore and Honour Thee, My Beloved." On the other hand, hard-core pornography, brutal in its depraved portrayal of women, gained a huge following. In yellow-papered, cheap porn or glossy art books, women were stripped naked and their bare buttocks were whipped with birch rods; they were savagely raped in trains; they were brutally flogged by pirates. In one bestseller, *The Lustful Turk,* which quickly went into three editions, an "Eastern Potentate" specialized in forcibly deflowering virgins. When, in 1888, in London's Whitechapel district, Jack the Ripper began stalking and then murdering prostitutes, many believed it was simply a real-life culmination of the brutality that was playing in the pages of popular literature.

Indeed, a world of hypocrisy, of prostitution, sado-masochism and homosexuality thrived as the underbelly of the respectable bourgeois world of Europe and North America. In the 1850s, about 6,000 prostitutes, one for every 64 men (some historians claim it was much more), worked the streets of New York. In London, the number was about 10,000, and in Paris, the women of ill-repute were so numerous as to defy counting. As the 19th century refused to provide the jobs and income independent women needed to survive, they naturally turned to the one occupation that yielded some real money. Said a former domestic servant turned "sport": "I'd rather do this than be kicked around like a dog in a kitchen by some woman who calls herself a lady."[41]

The "angels" at home watched the wicked mayhem being played out on the streets and brothels with increasing disgust. Since women had been elevated to the ethical and spiritual overseers of society, it naturally fell on their shoulders to do something about the degradation. In the process, they, at last, came from under the shadow of their husbands and fathers and inaugurated the first great feminist movement.

The Female Moral Reform Society, founded in 1834 in New York, was dedicated to reforming "fallen women." Members took to noisily descending on brothels early Sunday morning, singing hymns, reading the Bible and jotting down the names of any men they recognized trying to sneak out the doors. In fact, their attitude towards the males who frequented prostitutes was quite different than the usual hypocrisy of the day, which blamed the trade entirely on the women. The Society's founding document states, among other things, "Resolved.... That the licentious man is no less guilty than his victim, and ought therefore to be excluded from all virtuous female society."

Given that most recruits to the Female Moral Reform Society were staunch members of the new bourgeoisie, where the natural order of things was female acquiescence, they were surprisingly strong and militant in their anti-male opinions, blaming men for the greed and decadence that had led to the exploitation of women, to the terrible poverty undermining the cities and to the break-up of families.[42]

Gradually, the American Female Moral Reform Society expanded its advocacy beyond prostitution to other women's issues such as work and education. Early on, the Society and *The Advocate*, the mouthpiece of the Society, established a policy of hiring women only, not just as clerks and writers but also as subscription agents, bookkeepers and editors. The organization never formally established ties with the growing women's rights and suffragette movement, but the two had much in common and bolstered one another. As the historian Carroll Smith-Rosenberg points out:

Both groups found women's traditionally passive role intolerable. Both wished to assert female worth and values in a heretofore entirely male world. Both welcomed the creation of a sense of feminine loyalty and sisterhood that could give emotional strength and comfort to women isolated within their homes— whether in a remote farmstead or a Gramercy Park mansion. And it can hardly be assumed that the demand for votes for women was appreciably more radical than a moral absolutism which encouraged women to invade bordellos, befriend harlots, and publicly discuss rape, seduction and prostitution.[43]

A similar link between moral outrage at society's double standard and the battle for women's rights that followed this outrage developed in almost every European country, in particular Great Britain, France, Germany and Italy. As one historian put it, "Slowly but steadily—and ever so discreetly— woman's consciousness began to drift away from its traditional moorings."

The Victorian era might be nearing its end, but the battle of the sexes was only beginning to heat up.

V

Something strange happened to sex on its way into the 20th century. In the name of scientific advancement, experts of all kinds—psychologists, physicians, moralists, legal authorities—began dissecting it, categorizing it, labelling it, until it became full of prohibition. Whenever erotic symbols are tinkered with by men, women lose out. The birth of sexology was no exception.

Richard von Krafft-Ebing, a professor of psychiatry at the University of Vienna, was the first of the sexologists. His job was to examine sexual offenders for any "degeneracy" or "morbidity." The result was a categorizing of all sex acts into "normal" and "abnormal." Not surprisingly, Krafft-Ebing's "normalcy" dictated that the male was aggressive and dominant, the female passive and subservient, the "eternal victim." His labelling would cause great damage: the "mannish lesbian" was one example. She was supposedly the aggressive, independent woman who was prone to dressing in men's clothes, wearing her hair short, engaging in male sports and, for some reason, taking up the career of opera singer. She was a dangerous individual, a male soul trapped in a female body. After his bestselling *Psychopathia Sexualis*, a compilation of case studies of "perverted behaviour," mostly homosexual, was published in 1886, Krafft-Ebing was deluged by letters from people who had been scarred in one way or another by their sexual relations. Sex as an acknowledged, widespread problem was born.

The most influential of the new sex researchers was the British psychologist Havelock Ellis. A hero to liberals and non-conformists, he set out to shatter Victorian prudishness, insisting sex was "the chief and central function of life ... ever wonderful, ever lovely."[44] He advocated birth control, felt women were *not* entirely without passion and promoted the idea of trial marriages. He defended homosexuals, claiming they were mentally ill, not criminals. Yet it now appears Ellis did an enormous disservice to the emancipation of women.[45]

In his first of five volumes of *Studies of the Psychology of Sex*, published in 1897, Ellis analyzed what was called "sexual inversion," that is, homosexuality, a good example of which was the educated "New Woman." Place her in an unwholesome environment—a boarding school or college for females, a woman's club or political organization—and she might very well fall prey to the advances of the "congenital homosexual." What Ellis provided was a tar brush to blacken the reputation of the newly liberated woman, turning her into a sexual deviant, a social outcast, a corrupter of innocent young girls.

The male elite grabbed hold of this weapon and put it to work. When she wasn't being portrayed in literature by male writers such as James Joyce and D. H. Lawrence as a mannish seducer of younger women, she was labelled a withered school marm. By the 1920s, an easy way to discredit the female professionals, artists, educators and reformers trying to live economically independent lives was to label them as lesbians or old maids. The next generation of educated young women naturally wanted nothing to do with these depressing images. Enrollment in graduate and professional schools dropped; many more college-educated women took the traditional route, giving up their careers to marry and have families. Once again the male establishment had dictated that the proper place for women was in the home.

At the same time as the embattled New Woman was being chopped down to size, the ordinary female seemed to sprout wings. Joan Crawford, dressed in the scantiest of chemises, cutting loose with the Charleston in the 1928 movie *Our Dancing Daughters,* became a symbol of new-found freedom. The flapper lived for jazz clubs, petting parties, Hollywood scandals. Corsets and woollen vests were tossed aside and women donned chiffon frocks, which provocatively revealed their slim, boy-like bodies. They cropped their hair and took to smoking cigarettes and drinking martinis in smoky bars. Edna St. Vincent Millay famously wrote,

> My candle burns at both ends;
>   It will not last the night;
>   But, ah, my foes, and oh, my friends—
>   It gives a lovely light!

This new defiance wasn't all frivolity; there were remarkable feats performed by the flapper-era women. In 1926, 19-year-old Gertrude Ederle swam the English Channel in a shorter time than any man had to that point. In 1932, Amelia Earhart flew across the Atlantic Ocean alone. Mary Pickford, the darling of the silver screen, was reported to earn the astounding salary of $1-million a year.

But most importantly, the mating game itself was transformed. Flappers flaunted their eroticism, daring their young men to make love to them with passion and finesse. As Alfred Kinsey would discover, the age of linking sex with reproduction had suddenly vanished; sexual bliss for its own pleasure, even if it happened before marriage, was a prerequisite to a happy relationship.

Meanwhile, avant-garde writers and artists, the Futurists, Dadaists and Surrealists, were demolishing the barriers of propriety. The experimental poet Mina Loy outraged New York when her poem "Pig Cupid" was published in 1916. It was not only a daring evocation of female sexual desire but also a disturbing use of a phallic symbol. And there were no punctuation marks, the spacing was odd—hardly poetry written by a lady.

> Spawn of Fantasies
> Silting the appraisable
> Pig Cupid his rosy snout
> Rooting erotic garbage
> 'Once upon a time'
> Pulls a weed white star-topped
> Among wild oats sown in mucous-membrane
>
> I would an eye in a bengal light
> Eternity in a sky-rocket
> Constellations in an ocean
> Whose rivers run no fresher
> Than a trickle of saliva[46]

And yet the flashy eroticism of the Roaring Twenties was as superficial, as meaningless, as transparent as the raincoats worn by the chorus line tapping away to "Singin' in the Rain" in the musical extravaganza *The Hollywood Review*. As soon as adversity struck, flapper power evaporated.

The Dirty Thirties was a terrible time for many people, but it was especially hard on a female with a thought of liberation in her head. Ironically, in the first years, the number of women in the workforce actually went up, partly because they were hired to replace laid-off men—at lower wages, of course. Most were employed as non-union workers and their wages fell drastically as the economic disaster deepened.

For married working women, the Depression was even more of a disaster. The economic crisis was blamed on them—they were preventing men from earning their families' bread and butter—and female teachers, bank clerks, textile workers were abruptly fired. When government relief was provided for the destitute, it went to men. Women, whether single or married, were supposed to be looked after by their families, and, when that wasn't possible, by some charitable organization. The dream of independence completely vanished.

Once again, as the constraints on women tightened, erotic images in society as whole dampened down. Hollywood was forced to listen to moral crusaders such as the National Legion of Decency and enforce the strict Motion Picture Industry Code; even the irrepressible Mae West was censored. By the mid-'30s, gone were the exuberant, sexy Hollywood singing and dancing shows such as *Glorifying the American Girl* or *Happy Days* or *The Jazz King*. They were replaced by the misogynist sarcasm of W. C. Fields, the silliness of the Marx Brothers, the poignancy of Charlie Chaplin or the social realism of films such as *Dead End* or *The Grapes of Wrath*.

While women certainly did their part in the struggle, particularly as munitions workers, World War II actually reinforced traditional attitudes towards them. Those few who served in the armed forces might have worn the uniforms of their respective countries, but they kept on doing women's work as clerks, telephone operators, cooks, laundresses, and they earned less than men of the same rank. The once-proud Women's Division of the Royal Canadian Air Force was quickly humbled when the recruits found their job was to scrub the floors of Rideau Hall, the posh Governor-General's residence in Ottawa.[47] When peace was declared, it was assumed by almost all men that the "little misses" would quietly give up their jobs and return to the kitchen where they belonged. Dorise Nielsen, one of the few Canadian parliamentarians of the time, sarcastically reflected on the male attitude: "Well, girls, you have done a nice job: you looked very cute in your overalls and we appreciate what you have done for us; but just run along; go home; we can get along without you very easily."[48] And that is exactly what women in North America did.

After the deprivation of the Great Depression, after the fear and uncertainty caused by a terrible war, with the threat of the Cold War lurking, what ordinary people craved was the permanency of a loving relationship, a few creature comforts and a predictable daily routine. They hankered after the ordinary, and in the suburbs, they found it. Separate spheres—the private realm of home and children for women, the public domain of factory or office for men—became just as marked as in the late Victorian period.

The huge number of advice-givers who flourished during the 1950s, espe-cially in the women's magazines, advocated regular sexual intercourse, within marriage of course, and the birth rate did soar. But it was an uninspiring, innocent kind of sex. Erotic images were off-limits in the neat streets of the suburban maze. *Father Knows Best* and *Leave It to Beaver* on television and Hollywood comedies such as *Pillow Talk* and *That Touch of Mink*, starring the rambunctious but marriage-loving Doris Day, set the mood.

Advertisers discovered what a great seller eroticism was; sex was served up in many mysterious and subtle ways. In one full-page magazine ad, a lovely woman is dressed in a glamorous, strapless cocktail dress, her hair done in an elegant French roll, her diamond earrings sparkling. She is holding a spatula that is pointed at the true beauty in the picture—an electric frying pan on which sausages sizzle away. The caption reads: "The surest way to a man's heart! The wonderful G-E frypan makes sure it turns out right every time."

Yet by the middle of the decade, it was obvious that all was not well in the suburban marriage bed. For one thing, couples tried too hard to achieve the sexual bliss promised them by advertisers, novelists and the media. As one man put it: "I have a sense of guilt when I have relations with her [his wife] and feel she does not enjoy them as much as I do. The fact that she's not getting orgasm takes the pleasure of intercourse away from me."[49] Eustace Chesser, whose *Love Without Fear* was one of the most popular advice manu-als in the United States, told her readers, "Success comes to those who consciously and deliberately will to achieve.... Both partners should, in coitus, concentrate their full attention on one thing: the attainment of simultaneous orgasm." Hardly the natural flowering of a beautiful passion.

It was Betty Friedan who pointed out with such directness and unrelent-ing bluntness the link between the lonely, alienated, frustrated suburban housewife and her dysfunctional sexual relations. Friedan herself was a woman of her era. She had graduated *summa cum laude* from Smith College in 1942, then married and moved to the suburbs, had children, led a typical, affluent, middle-class life. In the mid-1950s she began freelancing for maga-zines. The deal she had with her husband was that her earnings would pay for the family maid. In 1957, *McCall's* asked her to do a story on the 15th reunion of her college class. She dutifully prepared questionnaires asking things such as "What are the chief satisfactions and frustrations of your life today?" The replies were not what she or anyone expected, particularly the editors at the magazine.

In the wilds of suburbia, wrote Friedan, there was "a strange stirring, a sense of dissatisfaction, a yearning.... Each suburban wife struggled with it alone. As she made the beds, shopped for groceries, matched slipcover materials, ate peanut butter sandwiches with her children, chauffeured Cub Scouts and Brownies, lay beside her husband at night, she was afraid to ask even of herself the silent question—'Is this all?' "[50] Advertisers were interested in happy consumer-housewives, not angry, frustrated complainers, and so *McCall's*, along with all the other women's magazines, turned down Friedan's article. It made a better book anyway. Published in 1963, *The Feminine Mystique* eventually sold three million copies and jump-started the women's liberation movement.

In the ten years from 1957 to 1967, the U.S. Supreme Court ruled on a series of obscenity cases, gradually determining that sex was acceptable for public consumption, that sex and obscenity were not synonymous. Sexy Fanny Hill reappeared to scandalize a new generation of readers. It was she who won the final battle when, in 1966, Justice Brennan ruled that "A book cannot be proscribed unless it was found to be *utterly* without redeeming social value," and *Memoirs of a Woman of Pleasure* was hardly without worth. Even Hollywood lightened up; the production code of the early 1960s was a great deal more liberal than the one instituted in the 1930s. Magazines—*Playboy* and *Cosmopolitan* were the most blatant—and popular novels put eroticism on display. Some of it was pornographic, much of it involved the selling of the female body, and yet, in the wake of this new libertinism, the status of women spiralled upwards.

"Love, Love Me Do" the Beatles sang seductively in 1962, a civilized version of the messages the Animals, the Stones, the Fugs, the Trogs were hammering into the minds of North America's youth. As the writer Lynne Segal puts it, "Whether screaming, swooning and fainting at Beatles concerts, or lining up to compete with other groupies and score a fuck with Rolling Stones (and then write about it), it was sexual excitement ... that so many young women were after."[51]

The 1960s sexual revolution was a rude reaction to 1950s prissiness. Suddenly there were singles bars everywhere, as well as weekend sex orgies, chaperone dating services (in reality, bureaus of prostitution), love shops where the most fantastic gadgets could be bought (or fingered). Scientific research got into the act. One sexologist admitted: "Now, after the toing and froing of the last 50 years, we can safely say there is no biological difference between the sexuality of the human female and the human male. The clitoris and the penis respectively are the 'seat' of genital release, the orgasm."

The double standard took a beating. Advised Helen Gurley Brown, in her runaway bestseller of the early 1960s, *Sex and the Single Girl*, "It's a question of taking married men, but not taking them seriously. Use them in a perfectly nice way just as they use you.... One married man is dangerous.... A potpourri can be fun."[52]

But what truly freed women from the traditional fear and even loathing of sex was the birth-control pill. By end of the '60s, millions of women world-wide were using it. Feminist and fashion designer Mary Quant wrote about its impact:

Now that there is the pill, women are the sex in charge. They, and they only can decide to conceive.... She's standing there defiantly with her legs apart saying, 'I'm very sexy, I feel provocative, but you're going to have a job to get me. You've got to excite me and you've got to be jolly marvellous to attract me. I can't be bought but if I want you I'll have you.'[53]

This time the sparks ignited by the sexual revolution set the whole of society afire.

The civil-rights movement, the anti-war movement, the protests of the New Left all profoundly affected the emancipation of women, but ironically, only after a revolution within a revolution had exploded. Young female activists glanced around the grungy offices of this or that altruistic leftist cause and discovered they were being as exploited as ever. In an early feminist essay, the poet Marge Piercy wrote about this predicament:

Fucking a staff into existence is only the extreme form of what passes for common practice in many places. A man can bring a woman into an organization by sleeping with her and remove her by ceasing to do so. A man can purge a woman for no other reason than that he has tired of her, knocked her up, or is after someone else.... There are cases of woman excluded from a group for no other reason than that one of its leaders proved impotent with her.[54]

When women complained that their ideas were not being listened to, or asked why so few women were in positions of leadership, or griped that they were tired of making the coffee, the male reaction was typical: "All those bitches need is a good screw." Or "The place of women in the movement is prone." Not surprisingly, women began abandoning these male-dominated organizations to follow their own star. By the early 1970s, thousands of feminist groups had taken root in the United States, Canada and Europe.

They quickly decided sex was at the heart of their oppression. At the beginning, it was not the act itself but the sexual objectification that they identified as the enemy. As one woman put it, "Married or not, our bodies had ownership by many: men, doctors, clothes and cosmetic manufacturers, advertisers, churches, schools, everyone but ourselves."[54a] In her famous essay "The Myth of the Vaginal Orgasm," Anne Koedt wrote: "Women have been defined sexually in terms of what pleases men." Anger and rage were suddenly palpable.

In 1968, American women staged the "burial of traditional womanhood" with a torchlight parade at Arlington National Cemetery; they threw their bras, girdles and false eyelashes into a "freedom trash can." In San Francisco, the National Bridal Fair was disrupted by WITCH (Women's International Terrorist Conspiracy from Hell) and on Wall Street, businessmen and construction workers were shocked when hundreds of women began whistling at their cute, sexy bodies. In France in 1970, women laid a wreath to "the Unknown Wife of the Unknown Soldier" at the Arc de Triomphe in Paris. In Britain, feminists created the clenched fist inside the female sex sign, which became the international talisman of the women's liberation movement.

Once the blame for female oppression had been connected to men's penises and the violence of male sexuality, an alternative to the traditional love relationships had to be found. For some, celibacy became the answer, shades of the New Woman of the late Victorian period. Many others embraced lesbianism, and did so with a sigh of relief and passion.

In the 1980s and '90s, it is the preoccupation with gay culture that is moving the sexual discourse forward; lesbian and homosexual sensibilities have imprinted on North American society no matter how hard the Far Right fights them. But the change in sexual attitudes goes beyond simply an acceptance of gay rights. There have been signs for decades that gender barriers are crumbling. Everything from cross-dressers—Sarah Bernhardt, Greta Garbo, Marlene Dietrich, Michael Jackson, Boy George, k.d. lang, the list goes on and on—to unisex beauty salons to identical his-and-her nose rings indicates that the distinct attributes marking gender are disappearing. On the scale that ranges from most feminine to most masculine, everyone can now find a place.

It's the same note that has sounded down through the centuries: women's emancipation comes with sexual freedom, and sexual license depends on the liberation of women.

Daphne

We would have gladly given up a week's worth of cherry Coke and fries for an invitation to join the Clique. These were the popular girls, the charmers, who wore lilac-coloured cashmere sweater sets and expensive wool skirts, whose hair was always beautifully styled and who were never without a date—or so we believed.

Among this dazzling group of butterflies was one dark-haired girl with an intriguing (we thought sexy) accent, who seemed particularly exotic. A Spanish background was talked about, and I always heard an echo of castanets and the roar of bull-fight fans when I was in sniffing distance of her Carmelita *eau de cologne*. Only her name disappointed. I would have expected something like Milvita Maribona or Carmen Calena. Instead she was plain old Daphne Griffin.

In fact she was as much a WASP as any of us. Her family on both sides had been part of the mass British migration to Argentina at the turn of the century. Daphne's grandparents had settled in Bahía Blanca, a bustling port city 90 kilometres south of Buenos Aires.

Daphne's paternal grandfather had been an engineer who died when his four children were young, and her father Lionel decided to follow in his footsteps, eventually graduating as a mechanical engineering. He was a handsome young man, over six feet tall, strong and athletic, with dark, wavy hair. Having absorbed the passion of the Latin Americans he grew up with, rather than the sobriety of his dour British ancestors, he was full of life and machismo.

The Anglo-Saxon émigrés still stuck together to some degree, and the highlight of the season was a lavish ball given by the British Embassy in Buenos Aires at carnival time. It was at this festive event in 1939 that Lionel met Mabel Atkinson, a beauty with dark hair and dark eyes.

Despite having an independent mother (her father killed himself when she was eight), Mabel was very much a product of her male-dominated Hispanic environment. A woman had only one job that mattered—as wife and mother—so when handsome, well-educated Lionel Griffin with his great prospects before him rolled into her life, she was happy indeed. In the years to come, her traditionalist views on male and female roles would irritate her daughter.

Mabel and Lionel Griffin began their married life in Bahía Blanca, and Daphne was born there in 1940, her brother David a year later. Lionel was working as an engineer for the railway—an important industry in Argentina at the time—and, as he made his way up the corporate ladder, he was transferred from one city to another. In her adult life, Daphne would uncannily follow a similarly peripatetic lifestyle when she, too, married an engineer whose job required that the household move constantly.

English was most often spoken at family gatherings, but almost everybody was fluently bilingual. They had to be: Spanish was the *lingua franca* in use outside the home and was, of course, the language taught in the schools. Daphne was always a good student, seldom achieving anything less than B-plus.

By 1952, Lionel Griffin was worried about his future in Argentina. Spiralling inflation had badly damaged the country's economy, but more alarming was the growing conflict between the Argentinean dictator Juan Domingo Perón and factions of the military as well as the Catholic Church. Lionel could see civil war looming, and decided Argentina was not a safe place to bring up his children. Lionel's elder sister, who had already immigrated to Canada, wrote that she would sponsor them and help them get settled. Their house and all their possessions were quickly sold, and in September 1954, the family boarded a ship in Buenos Aires and set sail for New York. Lionel had just turned 41 and Mabel was 40.

Lionel had been in such a hurry to leave Argentina, he had not paid much attention to the details of the Canadian immigration procedures. He was shocked when he was told his degree in mechanical engineering was not valid in his adopted country. He ended up selling socks at Simpson's department store.

The move to Canada was a painful experience for everyone in the family. Lionel's sister had found the Griffins an apartment in Scarborough. A suburb with growing pains, with ugly, wide roadways, few trees, houses that all looked the same and utilitarian strip malls, it had none of the charm of a Buenos Aires or Bahía Blanca. To make ends meet, Mabel had to take a job for the first time in her married life. Every day she travelled back and forth by bus and streetcar to Simpson's in downtown Toronto where, like Lionel, she was a sales clerk.

But it was more than having to work. The frantic pace, the isolating car-culture deeply disturbed Mabel. Remembers Daphne, "When we came from Argentina, my mom was a very beautiful, slim person, and within two years, she was this frumpy, fat person. It just killed her being in Canada." Mabel started to smoke. "She developed this ability to put the cigarette in one side of her mouth, ashes hanging down, and talk out of the other side. I thought it was disgusting."

It took several years, but the Griffin family slowly began to adjust to Cana-dian life. Lionel put his nose to the grindstone, studied every moment he could and within two years, passed the exams that would give him back his professional status as a mechanical engineer. He was quickly hired on by Massey-Harris-Ferguson, the large manufacturer of farm machinery whose head office was located in Toronto. The company was expanding its opera-tion in Central and South America, and Lionel, with his Spanish, his knowl-edge of local customs and farming methods, and his amazing ability with machinery, was just the man to establish their service bureaus in the region. He travelled to cities and towns in Ecuador, Argentina and Bolivia to demonstrate the tractors and combines. Lionel was very good at his job and would work for Massey Ferguson (as it was later called) for the rest of his life.

By 1960, the Griffins were able to buy a house on Midland Avenue in Scarborough. It was not grand by any means, nothing like the house in Argentina, but it was a nice bungalow with three bedrooms and a basement that was converted into a study and drop-in centre for David and his friends.

Once Daphne entered high school, she blossomed. When she was in Grade 9, she wrote her Grade 13 exams in Spanish, which gave her an acad-emic leg-up. She joined all the right activities and clubs: she was a deadly badminton player, a Girl Prefect and a member of the Senior Girls' High Y. In her last year she astonished everyone by winning a tough race for vice-president of the Student Administrative Council.

Her mother, whose beautiful sewing was one of her greatest achievements, made her lovely outfits, and Daphne, with her black hair and high complex-ion, was very attractive. Yet she says she did not have the social life everyone thought she did. For one thing, a curfew was imposed: 9:30 p.m. in Grade 9, creeping up to 11 p.m. only by Grade 13.

It was her father who imposed these rules, punished his kids, spanked them if he thought it necessary, but there was no resentment on Daphne's part. "He was very strict, but he was also very kind and was always doing nice things for us…. If we were feeling sad or upset, we were allowed to phone him, no matter where he was. And he always comforted us."

Lionel always treated her as an equal with her brother, but her mother did not, and Daphne resented this. "I had to iron my brother's shirts, I had to do the laundry and help with the cooking. He didn't have to do anything in the house because that was woman's work. I would say to her, 'I thought we were equal!' My mother would reply, 'That's how it is. Boys are boys and girls are girls.'" Even though it was Daphne who was getting the good marks in school and David was not a brilliant scholar, it was her brother whom her mother earmarked for university. In later life, Daphne would have daughters and not sons. Even so, she knows she would never have treated boys and girls differently.

During Daphne's fourth year in high school, an event occurred that shook the Griffin family to the core. Mabel discovered Lionel was having a passionate love affair. In his job with Massey Ferguson, he would be away from home for as long as six months at a time, and during one of these sojourns, he had met a younger, very attractive woman. Mabel was devastated, and the Griffins were soon locked in crisis. However, Lionel had no intention of giving up his family for his new love. "My dad took me for a long drive," remembers Daphne. "He said he had made a mistake and he hoped I wouldn't think badly of him. I think he was lonely, being away from his family for so long. But I was shocked. My brother and I didn't know what was going to happen. My mother was so upset."

They all forgave Lionel, but the upshot was Mabel Griffin decided from that moment on, she'd better be by her husband's side. The children were asked if they, too, would move to Puerto Rico, headquarters of Massey Ferguson's Central and South American operation, but both wanted to finish their high school in Canada. The Griffins solved the problem by asking Mabel's mother to move in to the Midland Avenue house.

By this time Daphne was close to writing her Grade 13 exams. Because she had excelled at sciences and math, her goal was to study microbiology at the University of Toronto. She managed the marks to gain admission to the necessary courses: physics chemistry, biology and math. Then she abruptly changed her mind.

There were several reasons for her sudden decision. Her family had never encouraged her to think about a serious career; her mother always made it clear university was for males only. Daphne was still unsure whether she might move to Puerto Rico after high-school graduation and the University of Toronto would not accept credits from a college there. More to the point, she had fallen in love.

In the summer of 1958, the Griffin family had gone camping at Lake St. Peter, near Cornwall, Ontario. David had run into his scout master, Bill Omerod, whose family had a cottage nearby, and had brought Bill back to the campsite to meet Daphne. They knew of each other since both attended R. H. King Collegiate, although Bill was a grade ahead. They got to talking, and Daphne challenged Bill to a game of badminton. She trounced him, but he didn't seem to mind and kept showing up for more humiliation. It took a while, but by the following year, they were dating steadily. "I don't know what attracted me to him," says Daphne. "He was tall and skinny and not very handsome. But there was something special about him. He was nice. And he was into sports and the outdoors, which I loved." By their last year of high school, they were engaged.

Daphne's family didn't like him much at first, this thin, blond kid who not only looked like Jimmy Stewart but had the same drawl. At first, Daphne's parents thought Bill rude because he didn't say much, just sat and watched television. "But that was because they were all speaking Spanish," says Daphne, "even though they all knew English. I kept saying to them, 'Don't you know you're in Canada now? You're being rude.'" Eventually the Griffins came to accept and grow very fond of Bill Omerod. Lionel took to bringing him gifts from South America: rum, Cuban cigars, gold cufflinks.

Bill's family didn't like Daphne much either. The Omerods were sixth-generation Canadian, originally of British and Scandinavian origin. The family were strict Presbyterians. If you happened to be caught humming at the table, that old gloomy proverb would be thrown at you: "Sing while you eat, cry before you sleep." If you objected, you were apt to get a whack across the head. Children were not allowed to contradict their parents.

The Omerods were not exactly liberal in their attitudes. Says Bill, "My grandfather, who was a justice of the peace, was well known for his opinions about Indians—thieving, lying, drunken, and the only good Indian was this and that. So I grew up in a pretty intolerant household."

Despite her Anglo-Saxon name, Daphne was considered a foreigner and therefore not the kind of wife the Omerods had wanted for their son. Even after they were engaged, Bill's mother would call Daphne "Bill's friend," wishfully thinking the whole thing would soon be called off. In fact, Catherine

Omerod made such a scene that Bill and Daphne postponed their wedding for a year. "I was really ticked off, because we had made all these wedding plans and he came and said, 'We can't do it. My mom won't let me.'" Catherine Omerod was to be the only source of real friction during their entire married life.

Still, both the Omerod and Griffin families were present for the wedding at St. Nicholas Anglican Church on May 9, 1964, with a reception following at the Scarboro Golf and Country Club. There was no honeymoon. Bill was still an undergraduate, studying electrical engineering at the University of Waterloo in Ontario. A course requirement was a six-month apprenticeship with an engineering firm, and Bill was assigned a job at Honeywell Ltd. in Montreal. Daphne joined him there, and with her superb command of French, had a wonderful time.

After their Montreal sojourn, they lived separately for a year. Bill was completing his course at Waterloo and Daphne was working in Scarborough and living in her parents' home. Although she hadn't gone to university, she had taken a two-year medical lab-technician course at Ryerson Polytechnical Institute. After she graduated, she was taken on at East General Hospital, but then found a more interesting, higher paying job in the microbiology lab at Eli Lilly, testing antibiotics meant for cattle and pigs.

Once Bill graduated, the couple resumed their married life and, with two pay cheques coming in, had a wonderful time. They moved into a large apartment, both had sporty cars and they bought a 19-foot sailboat and joined the National Yacht Club. Their swingers lifestyle came to an abrupt end, though, when Bill's company, Leeds & Northrup, transferred him to Temagami, Ontario.

Daphne found a job at a hospital in the small town of Haileybury where they lived, and rather enjoyed her two years in Ontario's north. But it marked the beginning of a wandering existence for the Omerods. They would just settle into yet another house in another community when Bill's job would require they uproot themselves again.

Once back in the Toronto area, Daphne went to work in the chemistry lab at Peel Memorial Hospital. She and Bill were still sailing, giving dinner parties and enjoying their affluence. Four years later, when Daphne finally got pregnant, they were on the move again. This time to Ottawa.

Their first child was born there in May 30, 1970. It was an easy birth and Stephanie a lovely baby and so easy to look after that Daphne decided to have a second child right away. Shelley was born in June, 1972, and by that time, the family had moved again, back to their spacious home located in the Toronto bedroom community of Georgetown.

A few months later, Daphne experienced the first tragedy in what had been an otherwise sunny life. Her father died, suddenly and unexpectedly. She had loved Lionel Griffin so much that for five years after, she couldn't bring herself to speak his name. Twenty-two years later, she still breaks down in tears when she talks about him. Mabel Griffin moved into Daphne's home for several months, finding her two little granddaughters a great comfort in her grief. Mother and daughter grew closer during this trying time.

Bill and Daphne had planned to have four children, spaced exactly two years apart. But their second daughter was such a handful, they postponed the next baby. Unlike her sister, Shelley never slept through the night, or much during the day, for that matter. She cried all the time. Daphne thought she might be colicky or that her milk was not satisfying her, so she stopped breastfeeding. By the time Shelley was ten months, she was so rambunctious she would fling herself out of her crib. "I had to take her to the hospital so many times, with her teeth through her lip, cuts to her chin, rips to her knees," says Daphne.

By 1976, Shelley had calmed down and Daphne felt she was ready for her third baby. Bill loved his two little girls and he was rather reluctant to have another child who might interfere with the relationship, but Daphne badly wanted a son. "I said to Bill, 'Let's try for a boy.'" On October 8, 1976, Elizabeth Kelly was born in Ottawa.

She was a lovely baby, happy and independent, and, about a year after her birth, Daphne felt it was time to try again for a son. "Bill just ran the other way. 'Three strikes and you're out,' he said." Some time later, Daphne came home to find her husband resting on the couch, an ice pack on his private parts. "He had gone and had a vasectomy. Much to my disgust I was mad at him and said, 'How could you? You didn't even tell me!'" She still feels a fourth child would not only have been a playmate for Elizabeth but a curb on the excessive affection that was bestowed on the baby of the family.

Up until the birth of her third daughter, Daphne had continued working as a lab technician with a hospital or private laboratory, depending on where they were living. Usually on call, Daphne would be phoned in the middle of the night if there were an emergency, an accident or an appendix, and she would rush over to the hospital to do the necessary blood work. "I didn't want to lose touch with my profession," she says. "I loved my babies, but I wanted to be more than just a mom. I wanted to be my own person as well." But within a few years of Elizabeth's birth, the family moved from Ottawa to Mississauga, a suburb of Toronto, then to Ottawa and back to Mississauga. Daphne decided to give up her job and become a full-time mother. It might not have been the wisest choice.

The problem was the youngest child, Elizabeth. Daphne says her two older daughters lavished attention on Elizabeth, treating her like a doll, always wanting to dress her up and take her everywhere. "I think that's why she's so spoiled. Anything she wanted, she got." But her daughters see it a different way. It was Daphne, they say, who coddled and pampered Elizabeth. "My mother did so much for her," says Stephanie, the eldest. "I think that's why Elizabeth is so demanding today. She expects that people will always do everything for her."

When Elizabeth was 12, she fell in love with horses and began taking riding lessons, eventually developing into a first-rate competitor, especially in the hunter and jumper classes. Says Daphne, "A lot of the time I would sit in the car in the cold while she was having her lessons, because what was the point of me driving 45 minutes back to our house when I would have to immediately turn around and drive back to get her." The Griffins didn't complain about the huge expense—private lessons, costumes, vet bills, boarding and feeding fees piling up alarmingly. Then one day, Elizabeth simply quit. It marked the beginning of an open rebellion and conflict with her mother that would shake the entire family.

Indeed, much of the 1980s was a time of tension and worry for the Omerods. For one thing, Bill quit his long-time job with Digital Equipment Corp. over a conflict with his boss. He joined another company started by two former employees who had become as disenchanted with Digital as Bill. But after a ferocious row between the engineers and the board of directors, the company collapsed. Bill found himself again at loose ends.

Daphne had been upset when Bill decided to leave Digital, but she supported her husband through his trying times, bolstering his ego and trying to keep alive his enthusiasm. If that weren't enough, her two youngest daughters were going through equally difficult times as they hit their rebellious teens.

After years of living the life of executive gypsies, the Omerods finally settled in a lovely, four-bedroom house in Mississauga. With its huge kitchen, spiral staircase and family room for the kids, it was Daphne's dream home. As a suburban mom, she got involved in the usual things: raising money for computers for the local public school, tutoring children with learning disabilities and, of course, keeping an eye on her daughters' progress at school.

After Grade 7, the girls attended Woodlands Secondary. "The school was horrible for cliques," says Shelley Omerod. "There were the preppies and the rockers, the jocks and the nerds. Some were poor, lower-middle-class kids, others very wealthy, at 16 driving Mercedes or BMWs to school. They lived in mansions and threw wild house parties. They'd go shopping for clothes and spend $3,000 on their parents' credit cards without blinking." It was a formula for disaster, and many of the students floundered badly. Drugs became a serious problem, as did drunken driving and dropping out of school. Violent fights were not unheard of and the police were sometimes summoned. "The kids just got worse and worse every year," says Elizabeth.

Stephanie, the Omerods' eldest girl, sailed through high school, almost oblivious to the chaos swirling around her. Shelley was different. "I was always picked on," she says, "because I was the biggest, the tallest kid, and I had red hair and wore glasses." She managed good grades until she hit her senior years at Woodlands and became involved with the group who had the money to buy drugs and booze. "It was fun for a year but it drove my parents nuts, the coming home drunk and taking the car out after curfew. But it wasn't for an extended period of time. I knew what it was like to be a party girl and what it was like to be an achiever. I chose to be an achiever." By Grade 13, though, her marks had slid to a C average and she was turned down at all the universities to which she had applied. She took part-time jobs, studied at night, and the following year went to Sheridan College. She got straight As and entered Wilfred Laurier University in Waterloo, Ontario in 1993.

Elizabeth, the baby of the family, was the model child at first. She was tall, beautiful and smart, achieving marks in the 90s with little or no studying. After a battery of IQ tests, she was placed in the enriched program for gifted students. Says Daphne, "She told me one day when she was in Grade 10 that only geeks were in enrichment and she was dropping out of the program. I said, 'You can go ahead if you finish your year.' Letting her do that was my big mistake."

Elizabeth's marks started to slip towards the end of Grade 11 and by the following year, she was spinning out of control. "It was hard for me to accept that Elizabeth had actually done drugs because, of course, at our house, we never thought this would happen," says Daphne. "Almost overnight, Elizabeth changed from being the girl we all knew and loved to someone entirely different." She dropped out of school—her father calls her "a heartache of talent wasted."

She was taken to child psychologists and pediatricians, but Daphne says her daughter wouldn't co-operate. "She would just look out the window, and say, 'He [the doctor] is the problem, not me.'" To top it all off, Elizabeth and Shelley began doing battle. "For years they had been rivals for my attention," says Daphne, "and as they got into their teenage years, they began fighting and it got worse and worse."

"Elizabeth took her aggression out on me," says Shelley. "I ended up in the hospital three times and had to have reconstructive surgery. I couldn't breathe because she smashed in my nose so badly. I had a plastic surgeon fix my eye where she hit me." Shelley feels her sister needs therapy and to be put on medication. Elizabeth, of course, doesn't agree.

All of this took a toll on Daphne. Her family says she gets too emotionally involved, she can't keep a lid on her feelings. "My mother is very Latin and hot-blooded," says Shelley. "She thinks the louder you scream, the better you're going to be heard." Yet there is something admirable about Daphne expressing disapproval and standing up for values she believes her daughters should adopt. Even Elizabeth concurs. "She is a good mom. She nags a lot, but she means well. I know it, and even though I do some bad things, she is always there. I'm her daughter and she still loves me. I truly love my mom."

In December 1989, Daphne went back to work. The family needed the income—for one thing, there was now no medical plan available to them—but also, she says, "I was sick and tired of all these little causes I was fighting for. I was tired of playing bridge every afternoon and evening. I had decorated my house to the point where I couldn't change one more thing. I had sewn every curtain I could sew, I had gardened until it was perfect." She started out working as a technician at MDS Laboratories in Brampton, Ontario, but in a short time her department was shut down. In 1991, she began working full time as an internal customer-service agent, providing doctors with information on procedures or test results. "I love this position, the trouble-shooting," she says. She admits, however, it's still a technical job, and she sometimes dreams of what it would be like to be a real scientist. "To this day, I regret not going to university," she says.

In 1994, the Omerods sold their Mississauga house and bought a smaller but elegant New England-style home near Orton, Ontario, 60 kilometres from Toronto, which has a sweeping view of the Caledon Hills. This is Bill's dream home. He still works under contract for various computing companies, but he has left the rat race behind and what he enjoys most is puttering about his property. He and Daphne bought each other a tree for their 33rd wedding anniversary.

Daphne considers her daughters, along with her successful marriage, her great accomplishment. Stephanie is an elegant, self-confident young woman who attended the University of Western Ontario in London, studying urban development, and now works for Laidlaw Waste Systems as a customer-service representative. Shelley graduated from Wilfred Laurier in the spring of 1997 with an honours degree in English, and she hopes to take a graduate degree so she can teach at college level. She's desperate for a career. "I'm not an at-home mom, that's for sure," she says. She remains very close to Daphne, very open about her affection for her mother

All through the screaming matches and fights with her family, Elizabeth never left home. She once told her mother that Daphne would have to call the police to get her out of the house. It's as though she knows deep within her that she can't let go of the love and security offered by her family. Eventually, she began opening up more readily to her family, communicating better. She also applied for admittance to the veterinarian-technicians course at several community colleges. While Daphne is glad of this, she is still disappointed that she didn't go to university. "She is so brilliant and so beautiful."

Daphne knows all her daughters have engaged in sexual intercourse—Stephanie and Shelley have both gone on trips with their boyfriends—but the idea still shocks her. She remembers how strict her own parents were, and how much she loved them anyway. Still she understands she is "old-fashioned" in her attitudes and will not allow this to cloud her relationship with her girls. "I love them to pieces," she says. "They are my all."

Daughters

"I have no children, sir; I have only daughters."

Breton farmer, 1849

The catastrophe of [giving birth to a daughter] was a bore, but what can't be cured must be endured and never mentioned.

Lady Westminster, in a letter to a friend, 1834

Oh, my darling, how I wish I could see you, if only for a moment, to hear your voice, to embrace you, just see you pass by, if nothing more!

Mme de Sévigné, in a letter to her daughter, 1671

One of my classmates often travelled to New York to visit an aunt. One day, after her annual Easter visit, she shoved several books towards me. "My aunt gave me these," she said. "Don't much interest me, but you'll probably find something in them." A gold mine! Six novels by the famous French writer Colette, recently translated into English. In three weeks I gobbled my way through them all and was never quite the same afterwards. They were, as I breathlessly told everybody, "*So utterly obsessed with sex.*"

These were not simply literary bonbons, though. They said much of youth and poignant longing. They stayed with me. When the translated version of Colette's autobiography, *Earthly Paradise*, was published in the mid-'60s, I could hardly wait to get my hands on it. It was not at all what I expected.

For one thing, the rebellious, bohemian Colette utterly adored, indeed worshipped her mother. Yet Sidonie Colette was very much her own person, as a letter she wrote to Colette's second husband makes clear.

Sir,

You ask me to come and spend a week with you, which means I would be near my daughter, whom I adore. You who live with her know how rarely I see her, how much her presence delights me, and I'm touched that you should ask me to come and see her. All the same I'm not going to accept your kind invitation, for the time being at any rate. The reason is that my pink cactus is probably going to flower. It's a very rare plant I've been given, and I'm told that in our climate it flowers only once every four years. Now, I am already a very old woman, and if I went away when my pink cactus is about to flower, I am certain I shouldn't see it flower again.

So I beg you, sir, to accept my sincere thanks and my regrets, together with my kind regards.

Sidonie Colette, née Landoy.[55]

What astounded me was Colette's response to the letter. I would have been a little hurt if my mother had preferred her cactus to a visit from me, but not Colette; she understood. "Whenever I feel myself inferior to every-thing about me," she wrote, "threatened by my own mediocrity, frightened by the discovery that a muscle is losing its strength, a desire its power, or a pain the keen edge of its bite, I can still hold up my head and say to myself: 'I am the daughter of the woman who wrote that letter.'"[56]

During the 1950s it was de rigueur not to talk about one's admiration or love for a mother. We didn't want the lives our mothers had led. Mother didn't soar in the outside world as father did. She was the protector of the status quo, someone to do battle with. Yet I adored my mother, who, like Sido, broke all the rules. I know she was fond of me, and later on even admired me, but she made no bones of the fact that there were other things in her life besides her children.

It was only on reading Colette's work that I came to appreciate this rela-tionship with its astonishing passion and complexity—sometimes full of love, and sometimes full of hate. When my daughter was born years later, the significance of this strongest of all family bonds was doubly reinforced.

I

Girls in ancient Greece led cloistered lives; the outside world intervened almost not at all. Through the eyes of the early poets and painters of vases, their daily life seems idyllic. We catch sight of them plucking irises, roses and, of course, narcissus beside a river or in a lovely meadow, or carrying water jugs or plaiting their sisters' hair. We see them dancing and singing and play-ing the lyre at festivals and mysterious cult worship. Most of all we glimpse them gambolling at weddings, by far the most important event in their lives.

But there was a dark side to this seemingly bucolic existence. From early childhood, a girl of antiquity lived with a sense of danger. To begin with, she was lucky to be alive; her father had every right to have his infants killed by exposure, and perhaps several of her sisters had perished this way.

In adolescence, a girl faced an even greater hazard—the loss of her virginity, her most valuable attribute by far. Since it was often her job to fetch the family's supply of water, the well was a focal point of her daily life. And it was considered a dangerous place. In Greek literature, girls were always being seduced, abducted or molested there. One of the commonest themes that weaves through Greek tragedy is the girl who conceals her pregnancy—often after she has been raped—and then exposes the infant to the elements.

The real threat to a girl's happiness, however, was marriage. Daughters of classical Greece were usually handed over to their husbands at puberty. They were so young that on leaving home, many of them dedicated their dolls and other toys to the family gods. In aristocratic circles, where important alliances were formed through marriages, brides could be sent so far from home they would seldom, or perhaps never, see their families again. The choice of mate was entirely their fathers' affair; often their mothers weren't even consulted. That this painful rupture of the mother and daughter bond wasn't always passively accepted can be sensed in Homer's *Hymn to Demeter*, probably composed somewhere between 650–550 BC.

Homer's poem tells of the dramatic story of the rape and abduction of Persephone by Hades, god of the underworld, and the fierce anger of her mother Demeter. Zeus, Persephone's father, arranged her marriage to Hades without consulting her mother. Persephone is in a meadow somewhere playing with the daughters of Ocean when she reaches for that most sensuous of flowers, the narcissus. The earth opens and Hades appears in his golden chariot to whisk away the young girl.

> ... the lord Host to Many [Hades] rose up on her
> with his immortal horses, the celebrated son of Kronos;
> he snatched the unwilling maid into his golden chariot
> and led her off lamenting. She screamed with a shrill voice ...[57]

When Demeter finds out Persephone is missing, "Sharp grief seized her heart, and she tore the veil/on her ambrosial hair with her own hands./She cast a dark cloak on her shoulders/and sped like a bird over dry land and sea,/searching."[58] Demeter finally learns the truth: Zeus has arranged for the

abduction of his own daughter. The goddess of the harvest falls into a deep
depression and refuses to make the grain grow. Not wanting the human race
destroyed, Zeus finally relents, and convinces Hades to part with his bride for
eight months of the year. The reunion of mother and daughter is appropri-
ately emotional. Persephone is brought by Hades' horses to the place

> ... where rich-crowned Demeter
> waited before the fragrant temple. With one look she darted
> like a maenad down a mountain shaded with woods.
> On her side Persephone, seeing her mother's radiant face,
> left chariot and horses, and leapt down to run
> and fall on her neck in passionate embrace.[59]

A mother has dared to rebel and is remarkably successful in doing so. As one
scholar puts it, "Demeter directly challenges the patriarchal reign of Zeus and
comes within a hair of entire success."[60] Honours are heaped on both mother
and daughter, and Demeter ends up becoming a more powerful goddess.

Persephone's abduction came to symbolize the symbolic death of all young
girls who left their families before emerging into married life and fertility. For
some, it echoes the resurrection of Christ from the dead, only in decidedly
female terms.

II

Few heroic mother-daughter stories have emerged from the Middle Ages,
perhaps because women's voices generally were silenced. With so few
options available for any female, life seems to have been ruled by the nitty-
gritty of domesticity. The *Handbook of Good Customs*, written around 1360 by
the Florentine family man and entrepreneur Paolo da Certaldo, gives this
advice to parents.

If you have a female child, set her to sewing and not to reading, for it is not suitable for a female to know how to read unless she is going to be a nun.... Teach
her to do everything about the house to make bread, clean capons, sift, cook,
launder, make beds, spin, weave French purses, embroider, cut wool and linen
clothes, put new feet onto socks, and so forth, so that when you marry her off
she won't seem a fool freshly arrived from the wilds.[61]

This essay nicely illustrates the attitude of the Middle Ages towards daughters: they were difficult to control, capricious and lacking in discipline. Above

all, they were lots of trouble. The main objective of any mother or father was to round up enough dowry to get them married and out of the house as quickly as possible.

It wasn't that they weren't loved. Obviously they were, since church moralizers were always warning parents against lavishing too much attention on their daughters, claiming it wasn't good for their souls. Smiling too much at a little girl was particularly harmful, they insisted.[62] The problem was that the worth of a daughter rested so much on her virginity that protecting her from scandal became a major headache. Frankish legal codes of the early Middle Ages give some idea of the precise value placed on a girl's purity.

If any free virgin [as opposed to a servant] on her way between two farms is stopped by someone and he violently uncovers her head, he shall make amends by paying six solidi. And if he lifted her dress up to the knee, he must pay six solidi. And if he uncovered her genitals or backside, he shall pay twelve solidi. But if he raped her, he must pay forty solidi in compensation.[63]

The recompense, of course, went not to the girl but her family.

Among the aristocracy, a daughter spent almost no time at home with her mother, and it must have caused considerable heartache. If she was deemed marriageable, she was often sent away the moment the contract was signed with her future's husband family. As the Middle Ages progressed, the age at which a young girl could be spoken for became younger and younger. By the time of Alexander III, pope from 1159 to 1181, canon law specified a girl could be betrothed at age seven and married at 12, but there were many examples of girls as young as four being spirited away from their homes. Their brothers, meanwhile, were still playing on their rocking horses.

If she weren't handed over to her husband's family, a daughter could be sent to a nunnery to be educated, or to serve at a nobleman's court "to receive instructions of proper manners." From either court or convent, she would most likely never return to her mother's care but would be handed over directly to her future in-laws.

There was always the threat that she would be sent to a nunnery for good. For one thing, the Church fathers thought the younger a girl was when she became a novice, the more submissive she would be in accepting the harsh discipline of the order. No wonder mothers were such dedicated matchmakers, expending all their ingenuity and energy on finding appropriate husbands for their daughters. Unless a girl had a definite spiritual calling, marriage was a better alternative than the cloistered life.

A girl who was also a substantial heiress was constantly at the mercy of predators. If she were to be left a major fief, sometimes the king himself stepped in and arranged her marriage. It was very much to his advantage to do so: large sums would be handed over to him from the vassal to whom he awarded the plum prize. A monarch could hardly resist such a windfall, and marrying off rich heiresses as soon as possible became a kind of royal crusade.[64] Her mother usually had absolutely no say in the matter.

In many ways, daughters of artisans or peasants were better off than their upper-class sisters. Very early on, poorer girls began helping with the household tasks—almost all girls looked after younger children—and as they grew older, they worked in the fields or in their fathers' shops. The result was that they didn't marry as young as their aristocratic sisters, and therefore probably enjoyed a closer, more nurturing relationship with their mothers.

On the other hand, they suffered terrible disadvantages. Sometimes girls of artisans had to wait for the death of a parent before they could get their hands on their dowry and marry. And if the poverty of a farmer's family was too grinding, hunger always gnawing, few children received loving care. After all, when a woman worked like a mule, suffered through one pregnancy after another, saw the majority of children die in infancy and lived in a hovel, how could she be a tender, doting mother?

During the Middle Ages, the mother's main chore was to safeguard the purity of her daughters. As the historian Silvana Vecchio writes, "The control of her daughters' sexuality seems to have been a mother's exclusive privilege, one of the only areas where she [alone] was responsible...."[65] Her job was to rear her daughter to the feminine ideal of modesty, gentleness, reserve.

One of the first things taught a girl was what to do with her eyes. They must either be lowered or raised to heaven; certainly no flirtatious glances were allowed. In about 1420, the writer Christine de Pisan described a daughter's appropriate demeanor thus:

At parties or gatherings, let them [girls] not venture in among the men but hang back with their mothers and other women, and let them have a sedate expression and be sober of speech, bearing and smile; moreover, let their glance be reluctant, decided, neither wandering or unsure but direct and simple.[66]

As in all times, there were rebellious girls, but the stories that have come down to us are the protestations of the do-gooders, the girls who were determined to sanctify their virginity to God. One of the most gruesome of these struggles for freedom involved a pious young girl called Ode d'Espérance.

Close by her family's huge manor was located the abbey of the Order of Prémontré. At a young age, Ode became entranced by the idea of spending her life there in the service of God. She asked a close cousin to tell the abbot of her desires. Shocked, the cousin ran directly to her parents. An extended-family council ensued, and an appropriate suitor, one from a rich and powerful family, was chosen.

The manor house was decked out for the wedding, and friends and relatives were invited from all over. The historian Philippe de Harvengt describes what happened at the ceremony:

... the priest asks Simon [the groom] three times if he consents freely to unite with Ode. He answers yes and then Ode is asked the same question. She lowers her head and gives no response. Same question, same silence. An intimate friend of the family tries to persuade her. She is silent. The third question, again silence.[67]

Simon was deeply offended and galloped off, and the wedding party, needless to say, was thrown into a frenzy. Ode's parents were beside themselves. Her father kept grumbling, "Whether she wants to or not, she will marry." In the confusion, Ode escaped, ran home and locked herself in her mother's bedroom. After seizing "a sword that hangs at the head of the bed," she attempted to hack off her nose. De Harvengt describes what happened next: "The relatives arrive, search for her, hear her talking to herself and praying aloud. They knock at the door, order her to open it, then with an ax and hammer they finally succeed in breaking it down. They find the young girl lying in a pool of blood, almost dead, her once beautiful face disfigured.... Everyone cries but her."

Two monks from the nearby abbey were sent for. The father still tried to impose his wishes, babbling on about "the riches of the groom's family and all the material advantages," but the young girl remained adamant. Finally, her parents could do nothing but relent. Sister Ode de Bonne-Espérance died in that same convent in 1159.[68]

An interesting aspect of this tale is that a modern historian, Jean Leclercq, uses it to illustrate his conviction that during the Middle Ages, a female, even if she were betrothed at seven, could of her own free will reject her parents' choice of husband. However, as the historian Paulette L'Hermite-Leclercq rightly asks: "How many women were willing to pay such a price for freedom?"[69]

III

During the early modern period, it was the mother's job to ease her daughter's way into a society that was all too ready to victimize her. It was often a terrible struggle. There were strong forces aligned against a mother's natural love for a daughter, not the least of which came from the religious moralizers. The case of Isabella de Moerloose living in 16th-century Holland is an example.

Isabella had the misfortune to be born with a caul over her head. Some people regarded this as lucky, others felt it was a sign of the devil. Her mother's confessor was particularly worried, and although the little girl seemed healthy and happy, he instructed her mother to watch out for any traces of "evil" behaviour. Not surprisingly, Isabella developed a rather odd personality: at times she was shy and withdrawn; at others she was talkative and outgoing. The priest decided the devil was within sight and ordered the little girl to be beaten. Isabella's mother followed her confessor's advice, albeit halfheartedly, but she drew the line when the clergyman insisted the child be locked by herself in a dark room for several days without food. Isabella's mother would have only herself to blame, admonished the religious, if her daughter turned into a witch. Isabella was not only not possessed of the devil but, in adulthood, would write an influential autobiography in which she exposed the priest and chastised her mother for following his advice.[70]

With the advent of the Protestant Reformation, not even the choice of convent life was available to a young woman in non-Catholic countries. Her future depended entirely on marriage, and that meant somehow accumulating enough of a dowry to attract a husband. In this, her mother could prove invaluable.

In a farm family, the mother might collect money from the sale of eggs and honey, or she might hide the runt of a litter, the "peppermint pig," raise it to a fat hog and eventually sell it. A mother and daughter might rear rabbits. A girl might, under her mother's guidance, be trained in fine needlework, making exquisite French purses that the aristocracy loved. All of these funds were set aside for the girl's dowry.[71]

Sometimes godparents played an important role by contributing some hens or even, if the girl were really lucky, a couple of lambs. Sometimes the family was so poor that all a girl could bring to a marriage was a cow or pig and perhaps the conjugal bed. Whatever the circumstances, a daughter's future happiness—her authority in the marriage, her prestige in her community—depended on the nest egg that she and her mother had struggled long and hard to accumulate.

Among the aristocracy, a daughter's dowry took on weighty symbolism, actually determining the social status of a family. These marriage portions represented an incredible expense, not only in land but in jewels, clothes, furniture and, most important, hard cash. As the early-modern era progressed, dowries spun even further out of control. They became so large that many noble families could afford to marry off only one or two of their female children. By the 18th century, more than a third of the daughters of the Scottish aristocracy and almost the same number among the British peerage were doomed to permanent spinsterhood, whether they liked it or not.[72] In Catholic countries, the spiralling cost of dowries meant the lower-cost convents were crowded. In Milan, three-quarters of the aristocracy's female children were sent to nunneries, there to spend the rest of their lives. In Spain, at the end of the 18th century, legislation was enacted that forbade the amount of a dowry to be more than 12 times the annual income of the head of the household.[73]

When a girl handed over her marriage portion, she was often guaranteed a jointure, a sum that would be returned to her if her husband died. The problem was, the dowry was most often much larger than the jointure: in England, in the mid-16th century, a family had to hand over £400 or £500 for every £100 of jointure; by the end of the 17th century, the ratio had become ten to one.[74]

There was always a huge number of girls for whom no marriage portion at all was available. These were the daughters of the very poor, the large part of the population who fought a daily battle against pauperism. Their girls were sent out to earn their own dowries. By the mid-17th century, 80 percent of country girls would leave home to work by the time they were 12. As the historian Olwen Hufton writes, "From the moment of her departure, the average European girl began a ten to 12-year phase of her working life upon the success of which the future depended. The prospect may have been daunting and frightening, and the pitfalls were known to be many."[75]

Fortunately, servant girls were almost always in great demand. It's estimated that maids of one sort or another made up 12 percent of the total population of any European town in the 17th and 18th centuries.[76] In New France, girls from poor families were sometimes bonded into service as young as four years old, their contract stating they would remain with their master until they were married.[77]

The servant's job was to do dishes, scrub floors, light fires, fetch water, coal and slops, and manage her master's chamber pot. If she were lucky and hardworking, she might, after years of drudgery, be raised to the exalted position of chambermaid or even lady's maid. Always in mind was the thought of the husband she could attract with the nest egg she was methodically building.

Domestic service wasn't the only work available to girls. In 1739, *Gentleman's Magazine* urged mothers and fathers to avoid teaching their daughters the "ornamental accomplishments" and apprentice them to "suitable 'genteel and easy' trades such as 'Linnen or Woollen Drapers, Haberdashers of Small Wares, Mercers, Glovers, Perfumers, Grocers, Confectioners, Retailers of Gold and Silver Lace, Buttons etc.'"[78]

The jobs many girls were forced to take were anything but genteel, but they could lead to some independence. After a gruelling 14-year apprenticeship, a young woman could become a highly skilled silk worker, if she had not contracted tuberculosis, which killed many of her number. It made her marriage prospects bright indeed. She could not only accumulate a dowry large enough for a young apprentice to pay for his master status, she could help out her future husband in the running of a workshop he might set up.[79]

There were terrible pitfalls for a working girl, though, not the least of which were the sexual advances of her employer and others whom she was required to please. Servant girls enjoyed almost no privacy, and often slept in the corner of a room so the master of the house could call on them whenever they were needed. In 17th-century New England, one-third of the victims of recorded rape were maids. Outright rape might not be part of a girl's daily life, but sexual harassment and assault certainly were. William Byrd of Virginia recorded the following in his diary: "I sent for the wench to clean my room and when I came [in] I kissed her and felt her, for which God forgive me."[80] She would not, of course, have dared to complain.

Often a girl had three strikes against her even before she was born. It was widely believed a female child inherited her moral character from her mother. Whores begat whores, stupid women had silly daughters, incompetent housekeepers produced lazy children. For girls born into unfortunate circumstances, it meant their lives were crippled from the start.

Mothers taught their daughters the usual things: how to manage a household, milk the cows, accomplish fine needlework and, if the mother herself were able, how to read—an invaluable skill in the days of widespread illiteracy. If she lived within reasonable distance, a mother was expected to be at her daughter's side during childbirth, and when a mother was old or ill, the daughter was required to attend to her. Reneging on this tradition was considered a disgrace.

All of this meant mothers and daughters often enjoyed a mutually agreeable, symbiotic bond, even if they lived far away from each other. The obsessive love Mme de Sévigné held for her daughter, Mme de Grignan, is one well-known example. Virginia Woolf wrote of their relationship that it was "a passion that was twisted and morbid." It certainly was extraordinary.

Mme de Sévigné was one of the fantastic, glittering creatures who whirled around the court of France's Sun King, Louis XIV. Although orphaned at ten, she was a fortunate individual. Hers was a cultured, affectionate family, full of aunts and uncles who adored her. She was extraordinarily beautiful, witty and clever, with a wonderful gift for making and keeping friends. Maybe most lucky of all: her father, who was killed in a duel in 1633 when she was seven years old, left her a well-to-do heiress.

She was married off at 18 to a Breton nobleman, Henri, Marquis de Sévigné, a handsome aristocrat who owned a great deal of land, most of it encumbered with debt. The Marquis was also a rake and a terrible philanderer. Fortunately for Mme de Sévigné, in 1651, he, too, was killed in a duel, fighting not for the honour of his wife but of his mistress.

Mme de Sévigné was left with two children, Françoise-Marguerite and Charles, huge estates, much debt and a high place in French society. A biographer Frances Mossiker describes her thus: "Renowned for her verve and beauty, the young widow of the Marquis de Sévigné soon achieved prominence in the Parisian pleasure-round, shining as one of the brightest stars of the capital's social firmament—sought after, paid court to, made much over."[81] What astounded everyone was that, although she had a string of suitors a mile long, some of them very illustrious indeed, she never married again. She made it clear she thought being a widow was just fine—she could be independent, conduct her own financial affairs and suit herself in her daily life.

The person on whom she poured all her effusive and passionate love was her daughter, a beauty, a dancer of note and a social snob. In 1669, Françoise-Marguerite married the twice-widowed Count François Adhémar de Monteil de Grignan, an aristocratic name famous throughout France. Among his many prestigious jobs was that of Lieutenant-Governor of Provence, which meant he spent most of this time in the south of France, administering to the region's affairs. His bride's place was at his side, which left Mme de Sévigné devastated. When the Grignans left Paris, she began a correspondence with her daughter. Over the years, it totalled over 1,500 letters, some as long as 30 pages, and has long been regarded as an invaluable source for historians, a witty, insightful portrayal of French aristocratic society laced with interesting gossip and literary references. As Mossiker points out, "No love letters ever written to a man could surpass in fervor the Marquise de Sévigné's letters to her daughter."[82]

In February 1671, shortly after her daughter left Paris, Mme de Sévigné wrote:

I look in vain for my dear daughter; I no longer see her, and every step she takes increases the distance between us. Still weeping, still swooning with grief, I went over to Sainte-Marie [the convent attended by Mme de Grignan in her youth]. I felt as if my heart and soul were being torn out of me … oh! What a cruel separation it is! I asked to be left alone. I spent five hours there, sobbing incessantly; my thoughts were mortal wounds.[83]

Three years later, she was still inconsolable:

This is a terrible day, my dear daughter. I confess to you that I can go on no longer…. My heart and mind are full of you. I cannot think of you without weeping, and since I think of you constantly, I am in a dreadful state.[84]

What is interesting about the Sévigné-Grignan relationship is that, according to Frances Mossiker, the two women had little in common and if they hadn't been mother and daughter, probably wouldn't have liked each other very much. "Where Mme de Sévigné was warm, open, approachable, expansive, Mme de Grignan was cold, aloof, uncommunicative, undemonstrative—a classic example of extrovert versus introvert."[85] The mother meddled continuously in the affairs of her daughter. She advised her on how to raise her children and how to manage her household. She harangued her son-in-law about his sexual demands on her daughter: "My dear Grignan," she

wrote in 1676. "You say that my daughter should do nothing but have children because she acquits herself so well of that function. Oh, my Lord God,
does she do anything else? But I warn you if you do not give that pretty
machine a rest—whether you do it out of love or out of pity—you will
assuredly destroy it, and that would be a shame." (To be fair to Mme de Sévigné, her daughter had at that point endured six pregnancies in six years.) And
Mme de Sévigné constantly meddled in the couple's financial affairs, expressing shock and dismay at their gambling and profligate lifestyle.

Not surprisingly, Mme de Grignan began to feel smothered by all this. Her
letters were destroyed, but it's obvious from Mme de Sévigné's responses that
Mme de Grignan was embarrassed by the extravagant public displays of affection, and she grew increasingly irritated at her mother's obsessive, almost
morbid worry about her health. The result was a sad and terrible tension that
grew between the two of them. Their reunions were so stormy, they had to
be separated because, as a family friend, wrote, "You two are killing each
other." Yet after the death of Mme de Sévigné in 1696, her daughter would
write to a family friend:

You are well aware, Monsieur, of the terrible misfortune which has befallen me.
You know what a fond association, what an intimate union was broken off, what
bonds were severed. No separation could be more cruel; its impact on me as
strong today as on the first, seeming—if possible—even crueller, even bitterer.
My mind now dwells longer on every circumstance connected with my loss, and
it seems to me that I am racked by pain even sharper than before. A loss so
irreparable allows for no hope of solace save in tears and regrets....[86]

Mme de Sévigné's letters remain a testament to the incredible love that can
form the heart of the mother-daughter relationship, even as it is fraught with
personality conflicts and overwrought emotions.

IV

In the 19th century, girls were not so much victimized as simply neglected,
both emotionally and physically. They were constantly told they were second
best, they weren't worth much. In their letters, journals and diaries, girls
themselves told of their deep feelings of inferiority, of failure. Since higher
education and therefore most professions were still closed to them, many
expressed a sense of uselessness. Stéphanie Jullien, a young Parisian, wrote the
following to her father in 1836:

Is it astonishing that since any work that I could do would be *null* and *useless* for others as well as for myself, since it would not lead to anything, that I let myself be lazy, that I try to prolong my sleep to escape life? This laziness that you seem to reproach me for is really a means of discharging an excess of energy that has no outlet. If you believe that this *laziness* prevents me from doing anything, you are mistaken. I would quickly find courage and ardor again if I had some mission to fulfill or if some goal was proposed to me.[87]

Charlotte Brontë understood the deep-down neurosis that afflicted young girls. In just a few poignant lines in her great classic *Jane Eyre*, she reveals the most disturbing aspect of a Victorian girl's psychology: her acceptance of her inadequacy. At the monstrous Lowood School for the daughters of the deserving poor, one of the students has contracted tuberculosis and, as she lies dying, she matter-of-factly tells Jane, "I leave no one to regret me much: I have only a father, and he is lately married, and will not miss me. By dying young I shall escape great sufferings. I had not qualities or talents to make my way very well in the world: I should have been continually at fault."

In the Victorian period, the physical well-being of girls was neglected as well. Among the middle and upper classes this negligence arose out of the prevalent philosophy that girls were hot-house flowers, with constitutions so delicate as to disable them from any energetic activity. As the historian Carroll Smith-Rosenberg puts it: "Puberty, the nineteenth century never doubted, brought strength, vigor, and muscular development to boys; to women it brought increased bodily weakness, a new found and biologically rooted timidity and modesty, and the 'illness' of menstruation."[88]

Menstruation was considered particularly tricky because it was thought to cleanse the poisons from the system. Since a female's one important function in life was to give birth, she and her womb must be coddled. Dr. Marc Colombat, a Parisian professor of obstetrics and gynecology, gave this advice in 1850:

When a young girl shows, by the unfolding of her physical faculties, that she is approaching the completion of her full development, she needs the closest watching, and a management having a different object from that towards which her childish constitution tended. Whereas before puberty she existed but for herself alone, having reached this age, the spring time of life, she now belongs to the entire species which she is destined to perpetuate, by bearing almost all the burthen of reproduction.[89]

This coddling, and "management" did not mean fattening up a girl to make her healthy. In fact, it resulted in serious deprivation. Meat, for example, wasn't supposed to be good for girls. Their diets should consist of "light and easily digestible substances,"[90] a recipe that sometimes led to malnutrition.

Exertion of any kind was also supposed to be bad for the supposedly delicate female teenager. Writes historian Yvonne Knibiehler: "The principles of proper upbringing required young women to be confined inside dark apartments, deprived of fresh air, sunshine and exercise, and required to devote long hours to needlework."[91]

Delicacy, of course, depended on one's station in life. Girls of the working class—the vast majority of the population—were treated nothing at all like hot-house flowers. Instead, they became fodder for the savage engine that was the Industrial Revolution, performing work that was physically exhausting, horribly underpaid, dangerous and environmentally poisonous. In the sparsely populated Canada of 1891, over 7,000 girls younger than 16 laboured in factories under the most dreadful conditions. They earned about 55 percent of a man's wages for performing the same job.[92]

If they weren't part of the industrial machine, girls maintained the society it created. Huge numbers of them worked as servants in the houses of the demanding and difficult *nouveaux riches*. They also hawked fish, kept boarding houses, did laundry, were shop girls, made jewellery, artificial flowers and matchboxes, and sold flowers. Muck-raking journalist Henry Mayhew interviewed a little girl of eight who survived on selling watercress. She was proud of her entrepreneurial skills. "I'm a capital hand at bargaining," she bragged.

When, in the 1830s and 1840s, ready-to-wear clothing became the rage, thousands of young women flocked to sweat shops, labouring for wages so low they could hardly feed themselves. Job security was nonexistent—they were simply laid off when business got slow. Agricultural workers were even worse off. Carla Lee wrote that when she was eight years old, she was forced to leave school in Lincolnshire to join a gang of 50 child farm workers. She worked 14 hours a day, and "We were followed all day long by an old man carrying a long whip in his hand which he did not forget to use. For four years, summer and winter, I worked in these gangs—no holiday of any sort, with the exception of very wet days and Sundays—and at the end of that time it felt like Heaven to me when I was taken to the town of Leeds and put to work in a factory."[93]

If there was one compensation in all this, it was the comfort and guidance of one's mother. "I do not believe a child ever loved her mother as much as I love you," wrote the Canadian writer Margaret Marshall Saunders from her Halifax boarding school in the 1870s. "I would be willing to die to ensure your happiness, my darling. I hope the dear Lord Jesus will keep you safely till I come back."[94]

The 19th century was a time when the mother-and-daughter bond was at its most intimate, a time of hugs and kisses and heart-to-hearts. Pictures and photographs of mothers and daughters were all the rage. In Mary Cassatt's painting *The Bath* (1891–1892), a half-naked, pudgy little girl sits on the knee of her mother, who is washing the child's feet in a basin. There is an intense closeness, both physical and emotional, between the two as this mundane chore is carried out. As the historian Carroll Smith-Rosenberg says: "At the heart of this [19th-century] world lay intense devotion and identification between mothers and daughters. Mothers and daughters took joy and comfort in each other's presence. They often slept with one another throughout the daughters' adolescence, wept unashamedly at separation, and rejoiced at reunions."[95]

If, for whatever reason, a daughter didn't experience a mother's strong support, she deeply resented it. The French writer George Sand felt her flighty, irresponsible mother who was so often absent had betrayed her, abandoned her. "You have inflicted a wound that will bleed all my life. You have soured my temper and warped my judgement," she wrote in her journal.[96]

In upper-class families where nursemaids and governesses ruled with iron fists, mothers were seen as ethereal figures who wafted in occasionally to kiss their children goodnight. Queen Victoria's mother, the Duchess of Kent, was infamously cold and obtuse towards her daughter. "To miss a mother's friendship—not to have her to confide in—when a girl most needs it, was fearful," the Queen later complained with much bitterness. "I dare not think of it—it drives me wild now."[97]

One of women's major jobs was to teach their daughters the facts of life. They weren't very good at it. Writes Yvonne Knibiehler, "Mothers brought up to despise their bodies and to be ashamed of their sexuality could hardly be expected to teach anything other than blind, rote passivity. Many girls had no idea what awaited them on the wedding night."[98]

For teenage girls, sex was supposed to be kept in abeyance until the great event—her wedding night. Since, as the century progressed, girls married later and later, this was a bit much to ask. As well, young girls began to admit they possessed their own inner fantasy life in which love and sex starred. What a scandal! Long hours spent deep in romantic novels only fuelled such imaginings, leading to the famous dictum "An honest [meaning pure] girl does not read books about love." Thus began the long tradition of girls locking themselves in the family bathroom and poring over romances.

"Boys should go everywhere and know everything, and a girl should stay home and know nothing," the father of British writer Molly Hughes told her, and it was a sentiment expressed by many. No wonder the daughter of the family began to rebel.

All of sudden girls were riding bicycles all over the place, taking grand tours of Europe, joining strange religious sects that allowed an outpouring of emotion and passion never permitted in their families' sombre pews. Most important, they began banging at the doors of colleges and universities. One such ambitious woman was M. Carey Thomas, the daughter of a wealthy Quaker family in Baltimore and the future president of Bryn Mawr College. She kept a diary as an adolescent, and it reveals the anger and frustration many young Victorian girls suffered:

October 1 [1871] Oh I think it's cruel when a girl wants to go to college and learn and she can't and is laughed at and absolutely kept from it while *a boy* is made to go whether he wants to or not. I don't see why the world is made so unjust and I don't see why all unjustness should be turned against girls in general and me in particular.[99]

That the days of the dainty hot-house flower were nearing their end was signalled loud and clear by two remarkable fictional characters who danced across the Victorian landscape. The first was the charming and inquisitive Alice of *Alice in Wonderland*. What is extraordinary about her is not only that she is clever and adventurous but that she longs for independence and eventually earns it. The second is the major character in Louisa May Alcott's *Little Women*, the rambunctious Jo March, who has served as a role model for generation after generation of spirited girls. *Little Women* is a sentimental tale, full of moral pronouncements, but in its time, it was considered a radical statement on the status of women. Far from the usual whimpering, saccharine sissies found in the juvenile literature of the day, Jo is the ultimate tomboy, full of life and with a burning ambition to become a writer.

The task of the novel is to suppress the boyish side of Jo and transform her into a proper, selfless young woman, which happens via two baptisms of fire. The first test she fails miserably. She loses her temper after her younger sister Amy spitefully burns a manuscript Jo had completed and hoped to have published. Jo turns her back on the young girl, even though she knows she is skating on the dangerously thin ice of a nearby pond. Amy almost drowns and Jo cannot forgive herself. She tells her mother, "I *shall* do something dreadful some day, and spoil my life, and make everybody hate me."

The second test she passes with flying colours. Jo gives up her independent life as a writer in New York to come back to Massachusetts to nurse her tubercular sister Beth. On her death bed, Beth pleads, "You must take my place, Jo, and be everything to father and mother when I am gone. They will turn to you—don't fail them." Jo takes up her duties as housekeeper, but with a heavy heart: "What could be harder for a restless, ambitious girl than to give up her own hopes, plans and cheerfully live for others?"

Jo is rewarded, of course. She sensibly rejects a proposal of marriage from a handsome and wealthy young neighbour, Lawrence—"I shouldn't like elegant society and you would, and you'd hate my scribbling,"—and marries Professor Friedrich Bhaer a stocky, middle-aged foreigner with whom she knows she can live an independent life. "I'm to carry my share, Friedrich, and help to earn the home. Make up your mind to that, or I'll never go."

In the end, Jo seems to have everything: a happy marriage, children and two careers—she runs a progressive boarding school and writes books for children. However, a closer reading shows she has made only a partial leap to independence. She does not pursue what had been the most important thing in her life: serious writing. Gone are the passionate, creative and original stories she had once produced. Nearly 20 years later, in *Jo's Boys*, she calls herself a "literary nursery-maid who provides moral pap for the young." It would take another century before women could believe their artistic and intellectual work need not be sacrificed to their role as wife and mother.

Marmee, Jo's mother, is a patient and dutiful wife who uses common sense in advising and comforting her girls. Her biggest job is subduing the wild, "coltish" Jo. There's little friction between the two because Jo doesn't rebel too much against society's norms; she is willing to give up her literary ambition for a good man and children. In the 20th century, daughters did mutiny, mothers reacted and the relationship became full of conflict and tension.

V

Sigmund Freud's theory of girls and their perverse sexuality formed a dramatic backdrop for the 20th century, a tapestry woven through and through with threads of neurosis. Freud postulated that female sexual development was entirely subordinated to that of the male; once again, she was considered the lesser of the species. "We might lay it down," he wrote, "that the sexuality of little girls is of a wholly masculine character."[100] What he meant was that everything revolved around the phallic organ, which, in a little girl, meant the clitoris, certainly not the powerhouse that was the mighty penis.

Indeed, according to Freud, the great disappointment of a little girl's life is the discovery she does not have the same apparatus as her brother. He wrote, "She makes her judgement and her decision in a flash. She has seen it and knows that she is without it and wants to have it." This so-called penis envy scars her for life. She begins to feel more and more inferior to the male, and grows more contemptuous of the women in her life, particularly her penis-less mother. The great, overwhelming love she once had for her mother gradually erodes, shifting invariably to the father. At the same time, the primary erotic zone of the little girl shifts from the clitoris to the vagina. As the scholar David Willbern puts it, Freud theorized that

From being a little girl who is sexually a 'little man' with a little clitoris-penis, the young woman becomes a 'castrated' female with a newly discovered vagina who wants a penis for herself—[which means] a baby from her father. That is, her wish for a penis becomes normally the wish for a baby, and if she later bears a child (especially a son), its unconscious significance reverses the prior symbolic equation, so that the baby represents a penis and not merely an Oedipal 'gift' from the father.[101]

If decades later, girls would laugh at this psycho-babble, the ridiculous idea of penis envy and incestuous passion for their fathers, Freud's theories wormed their way into the collective psyche of the Western world in the earlier half of the century. In 1949, after decades of debate, Simone de Beauvoir wrote, "Even if the young girl has no serious penis envy, the absence of the organ will certainly play an important role in her destiny.... Because she is a woman, the little girl knows that she is forbidden the sea and the polar regions, a thousand adventures, a thousand joys: she was born on the wrong side of the line."[102] Freud's theories provided one more blunt instrument to

remind girls they were biologically and intellectually inferior to their brothers, that from babyhood they were condemned to unfulfilled and unaccom-
plished lives. No wonder the history of young girls in the 20th century is full
of neurosis and outright rebellion.

At the turn of the century, young women were still excluded from influence or power in society. As usual, Virginia Woolf put it wonderfully: "It
was with a view to marriage that she tinkled on the piano, but was not
allowed to join an orchestra; sketched innocent domestic scenes, but was not
allowed to sketch from the nude; to read this book, but was not allowed to
read that."[103]

It was World War I that finally opened doors for young women. For the
first time, middle-class girls worked outside the home, earned their own
money, perhaps as typists or telephone operators, met their friends after work
without being shadowed by a chaperone, went to intellectually stimulating
lectures and joined in hiking trips, scandalizing the world by wearing shorts.
They engaged in love affairs all the more passionate because their darling was
leaving for the Front.

The recently emancipated girl with her newfangled ideas and shocking
behaviour was bound sooner or later to bring down the condemnation of her
seniors. In many instances it was her mother who scolded in the loudest and
most aggressive voice. In Virginia Woolf's *To the Lighthouse*, even the placid
and accomplished Mrs. Ramsay seems to sigh with envy when she thinks of
her daughters. "... Prue, Nancy, Rose—could sport with infidel ideas which
they had brewed for themselves of a life different from hers; in Paris, perhaps;
a wilder life; not always taking care of some man or other...."[103a]

As the century progressed, conflict between daughter and mother became
endemic, and the battle raged on many fronts. The call to tradition, for
instance, was a heavy weapon used against young women. Emma Goldman
often recalled the occasion of her first menstrual period. She told her mother
who promptly slapped her across the face. It was an old Russian folk custom
to remind all women of the pain they would suffer in childbirth. "This is
necessary for a girl, when she becomes a woman, as a protection against
disgrace," said her mother.[104] No wonder Goldman could hardly wait to
leave home.

But it was mothers who lived vicariously through their daughters, those
who would stop at nothing to shape them into their own image, who caused
the greatest pain and suffered the most heartache. The poet Mina Loy did

battle with her tradition-bound mother until the two finally became estranged. What Loy particularly found distasteful was her mother's penchant for turning herself into a sickly martyr and expecting her three daughters to feel guilty about it. "Seeing my mother fall by the fender purposely, hearing her sob at will, served merely to render more complex the initial imposition of filial duty. Behind her tantrums loomed the collective maternal heart given into the keeping of the doctor of that era. He pronounced it so weak the slightest emotional stress must cause a devoted mother's instantaneous decease."[105] Julia Lowy lived until she was 82 years old.

Nowhere is the heartbreaking conflict between mother and daughter so painfully and precisely chronicled than in the work of novelist Doris Lessing. In 1918 Lessing's mother Emily had been offered the matronship of St. George's, a famous teaching hospital in London, a singular honour, especially for someone so young. At the same time, she received a proposal of marriage from a man she had been nursing. Alfred Tayler was a war veteran with an amputated leg and a bad case of shell shock. After agonizing over the choice, she said yes to Alfred, and at age 35, married him. In 1924, the family moved to Southern Rhodesia (now Zimbabwe), and thereafter Emily spent all of her considerable energy managing the lives of her two children.

Doris Lessing grew up in what she called a "white-heat of hatred" for her mother. In her autobiography *Under My Skin*, she writes, "I was in nervous flight from her ever since I can remember anything, and from the age of four-teen I set myself obdurately against her in a kind of inner emigration from everything she represented." Lessing admits "my mother was conscientious, hard-working, always doing the best as she saw it. She was a good sort, a good sport. She never hit or even slapped a child. She talked about love often...."[105a]

Why then the hostilities? In many amazing ways, the mother meddled in the daughter's life, conducting an unrelenting crusade to shape her into what she perceived was a proper young woman, and all the while complaining bitterly about her job as mother. "I remember very well," recalls Lessing, "... my mother chatted on and on in her social voice to some visitor about her children, how they brought her low and sapped her, how all her own talents were withering unused, and how the little girl in particular (she was so difficult, so naughty!) made her life a total misery. And I was a cold flame of hatred for her, I could have killed her there and then."[106]

Desperate to leave the poverty-stricken farm and the terrible battles with her mother, Lessing quit school at 14. She subsequently married and divorced twice. When she finally fled to England in 1949 to pursue a writing career, she left behind her widowed mother and two of her three children.

What is interesting is for both Loy and Lessing, the conflict with their mothers served as a fertile source of energy and inspiration in their writing. It's hard to imagine how Lessing could have created the following marriage scene in *Martha Quest* if she hadn't lived through something similar.

Mrs. Quest waited anxiously immediately behind Martha's left shoulder, and at the crucial moment when the ring must be put on she grasped Martha's elbow and pushed forward her arm, so that everyone was able to see how Martha turned around and said in a loud, angry whisper, 'Who's getting married, me or you?'[107]

With such resentment in the air, no wonder the mother-daughter relationship was criticized in the later part of the century. In the 1950s and '60s, the upbringing and socialization of little girls came under intense attack. Feminists came to abhor that narcissistic, passive creature in a frilly dress, dragging along baby dolls, told not to get herself dirty or play too strenuously, who was not required to do much at school since marriage was her only goal, and who wouldn't anyway because she was so insecure. It was all blamed on mothers, who became society's most pathetic scapegoats. If a mother worked, which was rare, she was blamed for not spending enough time with her children; if she were a full-time mom, she was said to live vicariously through her daughters, to suffocate her son, to dominate her husband. In *The Second Sex*, Simone de Beauvoir painted one of the most extreme and cruel portraits of the mother:

... the daughter is for the mother at once her double and another person, the mother is at once overweeningly affectionate and hostile toward her daughter; she saddles her child with her own destiny; a way of proudly laying claim to her own femininity and also a way of revenging herself for it. The same process is to be found in pederasts, gamblers, drug addicts, in all who at once take pride in belonging to a certain confraternity and feel humiliation by the association: they endeavor with eager proselytism to gain new adherents.[108]

By the 1960s, the idea of mother as a grotesque had threaded its way through mass culture. A spate of movies portrayed older women in a variety of vile and demonic characterizations. In the 1967 classic *The Graduate*, for example, Mrs. Robinson is depicted as a kind of praying mantis who lusts after young men. It became a *cause célèbre* among the young and one of the biggest box-office hits in Hollywood's history at that time.

The portrayal of the abusive mother reached its apotheosis in the 1981 film *Mommie Dearest*. Based on the book by Christina Crawford, the daughter of movie star Joan Crawford, it depicts Crawford as a psychopath, a woman who on the surface is a model of maternity, but who underneath is cruel and vindictive. In one famous scene, she finds one of the child's expensive, frilly dresses has been hung on a wire, rather than a wooden, hanger and she savagely beats the little girl for this offense. Writes the critic Suzanna Danuta Walters, "The wire-hanger scene … has come to signify to daughters everywhere the violence behind the façade of maternal nurturance."

Yet by the time *Mommie Dearest* was produced, the furious struggle between mother and daughter had played itself out. It was time for reconciliation. It was the poet Adrienne Rich who re-established the link in her classic book *Of Woman Born*. The bond, both emotional and physical, between mother and daughter was primeval and permanent, she insisted, and there was no advantage in denying it. She wrote as though whispering in a confessional:

There was, is in most of us, a girl-child still longing for a woman's nurture, tenderness, and approval, a woman's power exerted in our defense, a woman's smell and touch and voice, a woman's strong arms around us in moments of fear and pain.… The cry of that female child in us need not be shameful or regressive; it is the germ of our desire to create a world in which strong mothers and strong daughters will be a matter of course.[109]

Any doubt that this vital relationship was on the mend was dispelled in the writings of the Chilean novelist Isabel Allende. Her amazing, unflinchingly honest memoir *Paula*, published in 1995, is a paean to the love a mother can hold for a daughter.

In 1991, Allende's beloved daughter Paula, living in Madrid at the time, was seized by convulsions and fell into a coma. The 27-year-old was afflicted by porphyria, a metabolic disease that is seldom fatal. Isabel Allende was told her daughter would awake in a week or two. Months passed and Paula remained unconscious, until finally it was understood that a hospital error had resulted in permanent brain damage. A year later, Paula died in her mother's arms.

During the long months Allende sat at her daughter's bedside, she scribbled her life's story on yellow notepads. "I had a choice," she said. "Was I going to commit suicide? Sue the hospital? Or was I going to write a book that would heal me?"[110] It is the story of the novelist's turbulent life, full of eccentric, fantastical characters, especially the women—there was a great aunt "who at the end of her life begins to sprout the wings of a saint"—offered up as a gift to a suffering daughter. When Allende finally understood that death would be better for Paula than a permanent state of Sleeping Beauty, her moment of grief was overwhelming. She drove to a forest and plunged herself into the dark woods.

My feet are heavy with mud and my clothes are dripping and my soul is bleeding, and as it grows dark, and when finally I can go no farther after walking and stumbling and slipping and getting up to flounder on, I drop to my knees, tear my blouse, ripping off buttons, and with my arms opened into a cross and my breast naked, I scream your name, Paula.... I bury my hands in the muck, claw out wet clods of dirt, and rub them on my face and mouth, I chew lumps of saline mud, I gulp the acid odor of humus and medicinal aroma of eucalyptus. 'Earth, welcome my daughter, receive her, take her to your bosom; Mother Goddess Earth, help us,' I beg Her, and moan into the night falling around me, calling you, calling you. Far in the distance a flock of wild ducks passes, and they carry your name to the south. Paula... Paula...[111]

Mary G.

We may have dreamed of belonging to the popular clique, but in reality, we were quite comfortable with our group of less glamorous classmates. What we dreaded was somehow being ostracized from our gang and thereafter having to seek the company of the outsiders. These were the girls who never aspired to the A class, who took bookkeeping instead of Latin, who may have piddled about in intramural basketball but who never made the school team. Yet, looking back, they seemed happy enough, surviving the insidious snobbery of high school as a closely knit pack. Mary Gray, for one, was petite, dark-eyed and bright. Although you couldn't tell by her accent—she had quickly rid herself of it—we knew she was Scottish. I thought she was lovely, and could see her frolicking through the highlands just like Katie in *Brigadoon*.

To this day, Mary doesn't know why her parents emigrated to Canada. In Glasgow, they owned a nice, suburban home and a family car, which was considered something of a luxury at the time; her father Harry had a secure job; they had a large circle of family and friends.

Like most working-class kids in Britain at the time, Harry Gray's prospects of higher education had been dim and he was forced to leave school at 15. He found a job in an aircraft factory, assembling the massive engines for bombers and other planes readying for World War II. Mary says he became "a mechanic of sorts" and, when the war was over, worked for a company that specialized in installing and servicing large air-conditioning units.

Mary's mother Jessie was as outgoing as Harry Gray was quiet and reticent, and he fell for her at once. Mary says he remained utterly devoted to her for his entire life.

As the oldest girl, Jessie was sent out to work as a helper to the milkman when she was barely a teenager. She went into domestic service, and eventually got a good job looking after a wealthy dowager, whom she rather liked. Jessie enjoyed earning her own money, developed a taste for fashionable clothes and other small luxuries, and she would have been content to continue as nursemaid to rich old ladies—there were even whispers she might have inherited a significant amount—if she hadn't fallen in love with Harry.

They were married in 1938, and Mary's sister Betty was born a year later. Unlike most of his mates, Harry did not go off to war. It had to do with a dark secret that he would keep throughout his life. He was an epileptic, a disease that, in those days, carried a stigma, never to be mentioned, even in the bosom of the family. After the war, the family prospered. Harry made a decent wage as an air-conditioner repair man and Jessie was an efficient housekeeper, carefully supervising the family's bank account. The two girls were doing well, even if Betty was a bit rebellious, and both seemed destined to get a good education. So everybody was astounded when, in the spring of 1956, the Grays announced they were emigrating to Canada. Jessie was already 48 years old and Harry 47.

The transition to their new life was not difficult. An apartment on Kingston Road in Scarborough had already been rented for them by Mary's aunt and uncle, who lived in the same building. Harry quickly found a job installing and servicing refrigerator systems for Loblaws grocery stores, a company he worked for until his retirement 18 years later. Jessie, never one to sit at home, also took outside work, as a dietitian's assistant, in charge of all the cold foods—salads and so on—at Bell Canada's employees' cafeteria. Mary's sister Betty suffered from the move—in fact she never got over it— but Mary was another story. "I simply put on my duffel coat and got on the bus," she says.

Since she had managed good grades in the half year she had spent at Scottish high school, she was placed in Grade 9 at R. H. King Collegiate, a year ahead of most kids her age, but she felt like someone from outer space. "The clothing was so completely strange. I had worn a tunic at school, bloomers, a white blouse, black stockings and shoes, a little beret, a navy overcoat and a school tie, for God's sake, and here were these ridiculous crinoline skirts and flowing scarves. The girls curled their hair and they wore makeup. My mother said they looked like they were dressing for Hallowe'en. I was just a lost little soul bumping around those halls. I was right out of it."

She made friends, but with those girls who felt just as awkward as she. By the end of Grade 9, the so-called outsiders had woven themselves into a tightly knit group. They spent a lot of time at the Bo Peep restaurant, drinking Coke and eating french fries and talking about how they were going on diets. "I remember one of the girls' mothers saying, 'If you have to go to that slop shop, don't take any cigarettes from strangers unless they're brand name.' She was petrified someone was going to seduce us with dope. Here we were, as homely as hedgehogs, who wouldn't know marijuana if we stumbled over it."

They may not have been regarded as the belles of the ball, but Mary says she, for one, enjoyed school. She was pretty and, unlike most of the others in her group, had no trouble finding boyfriends; the most important thing about them was whether they had a car or not. Then, in Grade 13, she met Steve Nichols.

By that time, Mary and her parents were living in a nice fourplex on Glen Manor Drive in the Beaches area, close to Lake Ontario. Steve's grand-mother owned the apartment next door and he often stayed with her. Since his parents had divorced when he was 16, he didn't see his father often, and his mother, who worked at the Toronto Stock Exchange, was involved with a stockbroker. He'd had trouble at school—Mary believes he has a learning disorder—and had been directed into the vocational stream. At Danforth Technical School he studied architectural graphics, and just before he met Mary had landed a job at the Ontario Land Surveying Department, working as a draftsman. He was a bit of a wild boy, but awfully good-looking in the chip-on-the-shoulder, James Dean mode. There was instant chemistry, says Mary. He was her date for her graduation dance.

All through high school Mary had done well academically, especially in English and French. Even though her marks were more than adequate, attending university was not given a thought. She had considered a career in medicine, but not medical school. "Being anything beyond a nurse—an assistant to a man—that wasn't in the cards for most of us. We thought secretary, nurse, teacher. And it's been one of my real regrets that I didn't go to university."

She did attend Toronto Teacher's College for a year, got superb marks and knew at once she had found her vocation. In September 1962, she began teaching Grade 3 at Norway Public School in Toronto. Mary liked trying out new ideas: unstructured classrooms, a more creative approach to reading, emphasis on the oral. "Anything to get them to love reading," she says.

She had gone out with several young men while she attended teacher's college but Steve was always in the background, and by 1962, they were dating steadily. In April 1966, they finally got engaged. "When Steve told my father he thought we should get married, Dad said, 'Well, it's about time.' I guess he'd been a fixture around the house for God knows how many years."

Everything about the wedding was traditional: the ceremony at Fallingbrook Presbyterian Church, the reception at the posh Ascott Inn, a honeymoon at Niagara Falls. Many of Mary's schoolmates were in attendance.

In 1962, Steve had taken a job as a salesman at Bell Canada, where he quickly found his niche. The newlyweds rented one of the apartments in the fourplex that Steve's grandmother owned. When it came time for her to move into a nursing home, she offered to sell it to the young couple for $42,000, but they felt they couldn't afford it. The man who did buy it jacked their rent up, and they decided they would have to buy after all. They found a pretty, three-bedroom house that faced onto a park and decided to go for it.

Mary still remembers with real resentment what happened when they approached their bank. "Our salaries were identical, I was making about $3,800 a year and so was Steve. But the bank manager said my salary didn't count because I could get pregnant at any time. I said I was on the Pill. He said, 'No way. I won't count a nickel of it.' So Steve's Dad had to co-sign the mortgage. I'm still angry about it." During that summer's break, Mary took a part-time job as a doctor's secretary to help make the payments.

They bought the Glen Manor house in 1967 for $31,500. Everybody told them the price was too high, that they were crazy to shoulder such a debt load. "We weren't very kind to ourselves in taking on such a financial hardship—every cent had to be counted. Steve ended up spending a lot of time fixing the place. But it was the best thing we could have done," says Mary. Nine years later, it sold for $95,000. "It really set us up well financially." In fact, taking advantage of spiralling house prices was a major factor in propelling Mary's generation into a higher financial bracket.

By the late 1960s, Steve felt he had gone just about as far as he could at Bell Canada. In 1969, Bache & Company stockbrokers in Toronto offered to send him to New York to train as a commodities broker. He jumped at the chance. However, it meant he was absent during Mary's first pregnancy, although he was back in time for the birth in November 1970. Mary was weeks overdue and her labour had to be induced. Forceps were used, and the baby, Melissa, was not a pretty sight, although she was perfectly healthy.

Mary had quit her teaching job at Norway Public School—she and Steve spent her pension money on a fabulous vacation in Barbados—but she continued part-time work, mostly as a supply teacher, filling in when the regular teacher was sick or needed time off.

In 1974, Mary became pregnant again. It was Steve who thought there was something odd about the way she looked. "She had this humungous belly. She would come around the corner and it would take five minutes." He'd feel the baby and say, "There's an awful lot of things sticking out." The doctor noticed, too, and two months before the due date, Mary was sent to be X-rayed. (Ultrasound was not available at the time.) "The doctor phoned and said, 'Are you sitting down? You're going to have twins.' I burst into tears."

Even though she was huge, and had to wear elastic stockings because of the pressure on the lower part of her body, Mary wasn't ill at all. She was on her way to an evening reception given by Steve's employer, dressed to kill and nicely made up, when she went into labour. They detoured to the hospital. Two hours later she gave birth.

The first baby arrived easily enough, but, says Mary, "I was aware there was a general lack of jubilation. They [the doctors and nurses] were very quiet. They were having problems because the other baby was way up under my ribs—in fact one of his hands or feet was entangled in the ribs. And he was a breech presentation, so it was a very difficult delivery for them."

What the doctors told Mary later was that it wasn't so much the position of the child that caused the concern—although the second baby could easily have been still-born—but the fact that the first one weighed so much. If the first twin is big, the second one often is seriously deprived of nourishment and doesn't develop properly. There was great rejoicing when the second child finally emerged. Mary, who is five feet and usually carries about 118 pounds, had given birth to two sons, Kyle who was seven pounds, 13 ounces, and Garth who weighed in at seven pounds, five ounces. "The good news was that the babies were big and healthy. The bad news was that we all went home five days later to manage as best we could."

Mary's mother, who had just retired from her job, moved in for a month. "Thank goodness she was still alive then," says Steve. "She was terrific, a wonderful old lady." Jessie Gray would take the babies out for long walks, which gave Mary time to get the laundry done, prepare the bottles, the pabulum and all the rest. Steve had to help out, too. Remembers Mary, "I would get up in the middle of the night to change the babies and get their bottles ready. I would wake Steve and he would feed one while he sat on the edge of the bed watching television."

The twins were born March 2, 1975, and Mary remembers the first time they slept through until morning—it was the night of the Academy Awards, April 13. The birth of Garth and Kyle changed Mary's life profoundly. It wasn't simply the work and attention two rough-and-tumble boys required. They attracted so much attention it was a little like being part of a carnival.

Mary had hoped the twins would be a girl and a boy, because she worried about them becoming too close, too reliant on each other. She had encountered same-sex twins in her classroom, and one always seemed to dominate, often to the detriment of the other. Mary knew of twins who were inseparable—went to the same university, roomed together afterwards, even married sisters—but she wanted her sons to be independent.

Garth and Kyle were born in separate sacks, so it was assumed they were not identical. Yet their physical resemblance is astonishing; both have unusually constructed cleft palates, and one eye of each is slightly recessed. They looked so much alike that, when they were young, Their father couldn't tell them apart. Mary, though, noticed differences in their personalities, even as infants. The boys did everything together and found in each other's company what their sister calls a security blanket. And yet there was fierce rivalry between them.

Mary did everything she could to make sure her daughter didn't feel left out. "I remember very clearly when Garth and Kyle came home from the hospital," says Melissa. "I opened the door to my parents' bedroom and they were lying on the bed. My mom said, 'Go and introduce yourself to your brothers, they have a gift for you.' Each boy had brought me a gold bracelet attached to a locket with their pictures inside. I thought, 'These guys bring nice presents, so, hey, they can stay.'"

Meanwhile, Steve was zig-zagging through one career move after another. After he had obtained his New York Stock Exchange certificate, he joined Bache & Co., but he hated the job. In 1971, he left the business and took a job at Maclean Hunter, the huge Toronto-based publishing company. Steve sold advertising for publications like *Bus and Truck* and *Set Sail*. He was good at it, but the problem was his commission was capped. When a similar organization, Wadham Publications, offered him a job as an advertising sales rep, Steve decided he'd better make the move, although it was a lateral one.

Wadham owned not only *Trucking Magazine* but the Canadian International Automotive Show. Steve could see the potential right away. After the postal strikes of 1976–77 showed how vulnerable periodical publishing could be, he pushed Wadham even harder to get more involved in the trade–show industry. When Wadham evinced little enthusiasm, Steve was ready to jump ship once again.

One night he was engaged in his habitual poker game with the guys, complaining all the while about what he saw as Wadham's lack of enterprise, when an old friend piped up, "Why don't you come and join my outfit?" Steve had worked with Gord Hunter at Maclean Hunter (no connection between the names). Over the next few years, the company of Hunter-Nichols boomed, with offices on Toronto's fashionable Esplanade and a staff of 30. In a few years, it owned nine consumer and two trade shows across Canada and three monthly magazines, including the successful *Computer News*.

The Nicholses' lifestyle reflected this new-found prosperity. In 1976, they bought a larger house in the same neighbourhood on Glen Stewart for what was considered then the steep price of $118,000. Perched at the top of a ravine, in the winter it provided a fabulous view of Toronto and in the summer it nestled in its own green park. It needed extensive refurbishing, which Mary supervised, the first of a number of similar renovation jobs she would take on over the years.

Her primary concern, however, was her children. In public school, Melissa was diagnosed with having an unusual learning disability; she has great difficulty absorbing facts by listening. Mary found a private school, Vista Academy, which specialized in helping kids with such disorders, and Melissa was enrolled there. It was expensive, $10,000 a year, but by the time she graduated five years later, she was ready to go to university.

The boys were quite different. Their fierce competitiveness drove them to do well academically and they always finished near the top of their class. They took music lessons and performed in school plays. Their great passion, though, was sports. Both were in track and field and both made the rep (all-star) team in soccer. There was also summer sailing camp, ski vacations and each year, a delicious month at Camp Kandalore.

In their last year of primary school, a friend used to visit frequently. Every Friday evening, he'd arrive on the Nicholses' doorstep right off the bus, bubbling over with enthusiasm for the private boarding school he was attending, Trinity College School in Port Hope, 50 kilometres east of Toronto. Mary recalls, "I said to Steve, 'I wouldn't mind getting the boys over that Grade 9 hump.' We went down and looked around at the school and we

were still undecided—it was very expensive—but the school said they would
be delighted to have them. We thought, 'Okay, we'll try it for a year or so.'"
The boys ended up taking their entire five years of high school there.

One day in 1984, not long after the renovations on their Glen Stewart
home were complete, Steve told Mary he wanted to move—he had at last
found the perfect house. Perched on the Scarborough Bluffs, it had been
designed for a wealthy executive and his wife, empty-nesters who liked to
entertain a great deal. It had a huge living room with a fabulous view of Lake
Ontario, and there was easy access to the beach. The Nicholses knew they
would have to make major renovations—two bedrooms would have to be
added—but Steve had always longed to live close to a large body of water.

It was an expensive mistake. The Bluffs were constantly being eroded, and
costly measures had to be taken to ensure more and more property did not
disappear into the lake. Fortunately, the guitarist Liona Boyd also fell in love
with the place and bought it from them.

By that time, Mary and Steve couldn't afford to maintain such a grand
place anyway. The two-year sojourn in the house on the lake was symbolic,
both financially and emotionally, of a rocky period in Steve's life. He had
always liked his partner Gord Hunter, thought him "a great guy. We blended
together beautifully," he says. But ironically, as their business became more
profitable, the friendship began to unravel. It began by Gord suggesting
Steve's friends weren't important enough—they weren't beneficial to the
business—and the Beaches neighbourhood wasn't ritzy enough; the
Nicholses should move to a more upper-class area such as Forest Hill or
Rosedale. And Steve was upset at Gord's gambling addiction.

Their relationship became more and more acrimonious. Finally, by 1984, it
was over. Gord Hunter told Steve he wanted him out of the business. Messy
legal problems and lawsuits went on for several years but, since Hunter owned
51 percent of the business and Nichols 49, it was Steve who was forced out.
It was not only a financial blow but a devastating emotional experience.

Yet Steve hardly missed a beat. He was asked to oversee the vast, new
Metro East Trade Centre in Pickering, which he did for a couple of years,
while at the same time thinking up and establishing new trade shows. Eventually he decided the two activities were creating a conflict of interest, and in
1986, started his own trade-show business, S. W. Nichols and Associates.

In the process of setting up an office Steve asked Mary to help his assistant
in decisions involving the leasing of equipment. Mary agreed, and started

going into the office half a day a week. Before she realized it, she had taken on a whole new career.

She now works full time "and much more" for S. W. Nichols and Associates. Steve says Mary is very good at her job and has helped his fledgling company immensely. He also admits her involvement has put a strain on their relationship, more so even than having twins. "We've had our ups and downs," he says. Nevertheless, Steve and Mary have built a happy marriage. "I come from a family," says Melissa, "where my Dad kisses my Mom in the kitchen in front of everybody."

In 1989, the recession hit Canada, and S. W. Nichols suffered accordingly. "We watched one retailer after another going out of business," says Mary. "They were our clients, so we lost a lot of shows."

The Nicholses decided they could no longer afford the fees at Trinity College School. Mary remembers, "I said, 'Guys, I don't think we can do this again' and they were absolutely devastated." But she went ahead and she explained their situation to the headmaster, who fortunately was sympathetic and awarded the boys bursaries.

Both Steve and Mary love golf—in 1986, they joined the posh Toronto Hunt Club which despite its name is dedicated to that sport—and they were amazed there was as yet no consumer golf show in Toronto. The hub of their business now consists of shows devoted entirely to golf, in Toronto and Montreal, although they are also involved in other smaller exhibits such as a motivational-marketing show.

Interestingly it's Steve's daughter not his sons who has followed in his footsteps. Garth and Kyle are far more like their mother than their father; the idea of selling gives them no kick at all. Both are big, handsome young men, good students and superb athletes. Kyle attends the University of Victoria, majoring in biology, although he's interested in English literature as well. He hopes to eventually become a lawyer specializing in environmental law. Rugby is his passion and he is currently on Canada's national team.

Garth has always wanted to be a teacher, like his mother, but at the high-school level. He is studying at Queens University in Kingston, Ontario, majoring in English literature, though he also loves history. He is one of Canada's top varsity rowers. In 1996–97, as part of an exchange program, he spent a year at the University of Edinburgh. His parents visited him there and for Mary, it was a chance to reacquaint herself with her relatives and re-establish her Scottish roots.

A poised and elegantly dressed woman, a feminist and a professional, Mary must have pondered how far she has come from her school days when, as an awkward immigrant, she was deemed an outsider. Her greatest achievement, she believes, is her children, and her sons' praise is her great testimonial. Garth says, "There's never been a time when my mother has treated me unjustly or unfairly. Kyle and I, we owe her everything."

Sons

Which do you think is the harder to bear: a wild beast's brutality, or a mother's?!
I should say a mother's if she's like mine.

Xenophon, *Memorabilia*: 2.2.7, c.385 BC

BECAUSE WE CAN'T TAKE ANY MORE! BECAUSE
YOU FUCKING JEWISH MOTHERS ARE JUST TOO
FUCKING MUCH TO BEAR!

Philip Roth, *Portnoy's Complaint*, 1969

Sometimes I feel that my mother alone really knows who I am—the furtive boy, the trespasser, the secret wanker in my room.

Writer and editor James Atlas, 1993

James Dean killed himself in a car accident on September 30, 1955. I was only 13 at the time, so the tragedy didn't mean much to me. I remember vaguely a front-page newspaper photo of the twisted wreck of his new Porsche 550 Spyder and my grandfather saying it was a pretty high-class car for a punk like Dean.

By the time I got to high school the following year, the cult had taken hold. There was hardly anybody who would admit to *not* having bedroom walls covered with giant posters of the brooding waif, a cigarette hanging out of his scowl. Line-ups to see *East of Eden* and *Rebel Without a Cause* snaked around the block.

The Eternal Rebel supposedly mirrored our frustration at our own fenced-in, ordinary lives, our boredom at school, our contempt for our mothers and fathers. Unlike us, brave and big-hearted youth, our parents were thought to have no soul. Mr. and Mrs. Stark in *Rebel* personified everything that was wrong with 1950s society. The father wore frilly aprons and served his wife dinner in bed when she was not feeling well; in Dean's universe, this symbolized unforgivable weakness, a blow to universal manhood. His mother was a motor-mouth, a nag, beyond contempt—typical, it was understood, of mothers everywhere.

Although I would never admit it to anyone, I didn't worship James Dean at all, although in *Rebel Without a Cause*, he gave off a kind of nobility, a sweetness of soul. What I sensed, I realize now, was his cockiness, his self-assurance, his presuming a place for himself in the sun merely because of his God-given maleness. I sensed he represented not the eternal rebel but the eternal male-child, the son and brother, worshipped over the millennia. Thrice daily, the orthodox Jew intones, "Blessed be God for making me a man," and I somehow felt James Dean, as he gunned his Porsche to unbelievable speed, must have uttered the same words.

There was something else that disturbed me about the cult he had engendered. There was a vulnerability about Dean. His audience knew he could be saved from himself; all it would take was the unselfish, unquestioning love of a girl. But the females in Dean's rebellious world were offered up as a sacrifice. You could mother a wild boy like Dean until the cows came home, but he would eventually desert and humiliate you.

Years later, I came across something James Dean had said that cast a different light on his defiance. The actor Dennis Hopper, who played Buzz in *Rebel*, had asked Dean how he managed such magic in his acting. Dean replied, "I'll tell you what made me want to become an actor, what gave me the drive to want to be the best. My mother died [of breast cancer] when I was almost nine. I used to sneak out of my uncle's house and go to her grave, and I used to cry and cry on her grave, 'Mother, why did you leave me? I need you—I want you.'" The civilizing force in his life was gone, and she herself was being blamed for it. His mother, by dying, was held responsible for his anti-social behaviour. Mother as nurturer, protector—and deceiver and tormentor. It's a drumbeat that has sounded loudly through history.

I

Five days after a baby was born in ancient Greece, he was placed in the ashes of the family's hearth and held upright by the father, symbolizing both the flame that dances vertically and upstanding mankind. The infant's name was formally announced, which gave it its legitimate place in its family and society, proclaiming to the world it was freeborn and not a slave. The ceremony meant the father had made an important decision—the infant would not be placed in a standard clay pot and allowed to die on a hillside of starvation or exposure. The chances of a healthy boy suffering such a fate were much slimmer than if he had been born female; a male child was considered not only more important than his sister but also his mother.

Until the age of seven, a freeborn baby boy spent almost all his time in the company of women: his mother, grandmother, aunts, sisters, servants. On vase paintings, we catch a glimpse of these privileged sons. In one such scene, a young boy is held by a female figure, likely his nurse, while his arms are extended towards his mother. Another youngster stands between them, in a similar pose. The boys are naked and their genitals are fully exposed, front and centre. Like all depictions of male children, it's the penis that is all-important.[112]

The education of an upper-class boy consisted of learning how to sing, play the lyre and the flute, and recite Homer and other poets. Reading and writing were required, but the skill that was emphasized was oratory. Everywhere the schoolboy went, he would be escorted by a *paidagogos* (a teacher/bodyguard) armed with a big stick to keep the sodomites at bay.[113]

At about 16, the boy cut his hair, symbolically becoming a man. It must have been a pleasant time, for he was free to lust after any of the beauteous household slaves, who were required to serve his pleasure. He worked out daily in the gymnasium to build up his physique—as important as his intellectual education—and to ready himself for military training. During this period he might become involved with an older man who had fallen in love with him. (The youth would expect lavish gifts in return, and often resorted to blackmail if they weren't forthcoming.) Once these various apprenticeships were over as his teen years ended, he could take his place in society.

The writers who emerged from these privileged backgrounds created remarkable female characters, some of them outright monsters. Clytemnestra, for instance, seems hardly to blink an eye when she kills off her sons. For centuries, scholars have pondered the dilemma of how such aggressive, forceful and often evil women could emerge in literature when the average Greek wife and mother was seen as submissive, uneducated and thoroughly uninteresting. Philip Slater in his 1968 book *The Glory of Hera* claims to have uncovered the answer:

Rejection and derogation of women mean rejection and derogation of domesticity—of home and family life, and hence of the process of rearing young children. The Athenian adult male fled the home, but this meant that the Athenian male child grew up in a female-dominated environment. As an adult he may have learned that women were of no account, but in the most important years of his psychological development he knew that the reverse was true. Men were at that time trivial to him—all of the most important things in his life were decided, as far as he could see, by women.[114]

Women indeed ruled the roost at home but, claims Slater, because they were constantly denigrated, they developed an unhealthy dose of penis envy. Castrating bitches is what they basically became, taking their vengeance out on their male children while at the same time doting on them, as though they were little emperors. No wonder, says Slater, the Greek male was so neurotic, full of narcissism and even madness. It's not surprising that from such men's imaginations sprang the female fiends: Medea, Clytemnestra, Hecuba.

Feminist writers have recently pointed to what they consider are errors in Slater's arguments.[115] Greek men were not absent from home as much as he suggests and probably had a fair amount of influence on their children. A not atypical vase painting shows a mother handing over her infant—his pronounced little penis insuring we know what sex he is—to a nurse while a doting and obviously caring husband hovers in the background.[116] Several of the comedies depict a warm and joyful relationship between father and son. And, of course, most ordinary, non-fiction women of antiquity were not monsters but devoted, loving mothers.

The life of a teenage boy in ancient Rome was coloured by contradictions. On the one hand, he enjoyed remarkable freedom.[117] When he was 17 or 18, he was permitted to live in his own apartment or house, and, if his parents were wealthy, given a substantial allowance to live on. He was free to take up a serious career, perhaps working on the staff of a governor or consul or attaching himself to a famous orator in preparation for a political career. He might work as a law clerk in the provincial assizes or train in the tactics of warfare, all jobs that required dedication and responsibility.

On the other hand, the young man was totally at the mercy of his parents. If he were a student radical, say, his father had the authority to yank him off the rostrum right in the middle of a speech. If the son proved totally incorrigible, his father could have him put to death without fear of legal consequences.[118] But his mother, too, was an all-pervasive influence in his life. Indeed, the strong and durable bond between mother and son during Roman times has perplexed historians for centuries. Since the female was supposedly of such little significance in Roman society, how could she have had such influence over a male, even if he were her son?

Roman literature typically depicts the relationship as loving and jolly. In his diary, Emperor Marcus Aurelius (AD 121–180) paints a charming picture of a visit to his beloved mother at her country estate. It's cocktail hour, and he's kibitzing with her as they gossip and laugh, she perched on a couch near his chair.[119] It is an image of affection and playfulness coupled with genuine respect for the older woman's wisdom.

A mother oversaw her son's early training and directed his education. If she were a widow—and in a war-obsessed society such as ancient Rome, this was often the case—she had absolute control. She spent much time and energy finding an appropriate bride for her son and then persuading him to accept her choice. She was the guardian of his morals, and was expected to censor inappropriate philosophic and political materials he came across. If the lad were strapped for cash, she could help him out by dipping into her dowry. (If her husband were alive, she would have to persuade him of the young man's needs, since her husband was the administrator of her wealth.) Terrified her son might perish in battle, a mother might convince a commander that he was unsuitable for military duty because of his health or other reasons. She wouldn't hesitate to confront powerful men whom she or her relatives knew in order to win a promotion or appointment for her boy. If her son obtained a position of influence, she would act as a go-between for various suppliants in important political and financial matters. The aged mother of the legendary hero Coriolanus, for example, led a delegation of women to her son's camp to urge him not to attack Rome. He was persuaded, and the city was saved from sacking.

The 1st century BC is often called the Age of the Political Matron, so influential were the mothers. As the historian Richard A. Bauman points out, "Where previous ages had thrown up a few women whose status and abilities had enabled them to influence public affairs, the last century of the Republic saw the emergence of the influential woman almost as an institution. In the private law sector she was as emancipated as she ever would be, with manus-free marriage [lack of male authority] the general rule and guardianship little more than nominal."[120] Nevertheless, she was not allowed by law to directly take part in politics. It's no wonder, then, that to an ambitious, energetic woman, a son was often more important than her husband. Her male child became the one and only vehicle for her frustrated but mighty ambition. This tradition carried on for centuries.

Roman history is studded with intrigue between Roman emperors and their mothers, but no story is so full of darkness and complexity—the Freudian overtones are hard to ignore—than that of Agrippina the Younger (c. AD 15–59) and her son Nero (AD 37–68). Agrippina was born in a remote Roman outpost, the daughter of the Roman general Germanicus Caesar and the famously strong-willed Agrippina the Elder. Mother and daughter would have more than their names in common. Both developed into expert political schemers, both felt free to use their important connections among the nobility in the never-ending palace intrigue and both were superb fund-raisers for political and military campaigns.[121]

The daughter was the more ruthless of the two. As the historian Tacitus put it: "She held honour, modesty, her body, everything cheaper than sovereignty." She had one over-arching ambition: to put her son Nero on the throne.

Agrippina the Younger was a woman of great charm. She was an extraordinary conversationalist with a literary bent and striking good looks. She married three times, first to her cousin Domitius Ahenobarbus, who died three years after the birth of a son Lucius (later Nero). She stole her second husband, the wealthy Passienus Crispus, from her sister-in-law, and when he proved an obstacle to her ambition, she got rid of him by poisoning him. Finally in AD 49, she managed her great coup: she married her uncle, Emperor Claudius I. Immediately she put in motion her carefully devised scheme to elevate Nero to the emperor's chair.

The first step was to marry Nero to Octavia, Claudius's daughter from a previous marriage. There was one problem—the girl was already engaged. Agrippina overcame that bothersome obstacle by having the fiancé publicly accused of incest with his sister. He promptly killed himself and Octavia and Nero were wed.

In AD 50, Claudius agreed to adopt Nero, even though it meant his own son, who was three years younger, would be passed over as emperor. The adoption brought enormous honours, not only to the emperor-in-waiting but also to his mother. As Richard Bauman writes: "Agrippina received the title of Augusta, the first living consort of a living emperor to be so honoured. She was given the right to use the *carpentum* [special chariot] at festivals. She attended a mock battle on the Fucine Lake wearing a military cloak, but one made of cloth of gold, in contrast to Claudius and Nero who wore regular military uniforms."[122] As an added inspiration, the colony where she was born was named "Colonia Agrippinensis" (modern-day Cologne) after her.

Agrippina began to meddle more and more in the affairs of state, which naturally won her many enemies. Even the besotted Claudius began to wonder if he had done the right thing in marrying her. Agrippina responded to his disaffection by having him poisoned. Nero became emperor, but there was always a menacing shadow at his side—his mother.

At first, Agrippina felt quite secure. Seventeen-year-old Nero had her publicly proclaimed *Optima Mater*—the Best of Mothers—and issued coins imprinted with her profile to honour her. However, her situation quickly deteriorated. Roman mothers may traditionally have had moral sway over their sons, but unlike fathers, their authority had no legal basis; in any serious contest before a court, a son could easily defeat a mother. It didn't help that this particular mother had always been so unrelentingly critical, so insufferably arrogant. When Nero grew tired of Agrippina's interfering in matters of state, when she sided with his wife against him, when she criticized him for wanting to marry his mistress, when she plotted and schemed against him, he struck back. He harried her with lawsuits, forced her to move out of the palace, humiliated her in public. All this did nothing to halt her intrigues.

One night in AD 59, two assassins burst into Agrippina's chambers and crowded around her bed. Immediately she tore her clothes off and, as Tacitus describes it, she cried, "Strike here!" pointing to her abdomen. Blow after blow fell, and she died.[123] Many years before, astrologers had warned her that Nero would become emperor, but he would also end up killing his mother. Her reply was in character: "Let him kill me—provided he becomes the emperor."[124]

Not all Romans agreed with Agrippina's fate. The historian Dio records that shortly after her death, a baby boy was exposed in the forum at Rome. A sign read, "I will not raise you, for fear you might kill your mother."[125]

II

The Frankish King Chilperic (d. 584), a cruel and vengeful monarch whom the historian Gregory of Tours has called "the Nero and Herod" of his time,[126] faced a dilemma. He loved the Visigoth princess Galswinth "very dearly, for she had brought a large dowry with her." However, there was also Fredegund, whom he had married before Galswinth and whom he truly loved. Naturally, there was rivalry between the two women, and their complaining and arguing got on his nerves. He found a simple solution. He had Galswinth garrotted and then seized her dowry. Still, the monarch was not totally without heart. "King Chilperic wept for the death of Galswinth but within a few days he had asked Fredegund to sleep with him again."[127]

King Chilperic and Queen Fredegund paid for their black deed. When an epidemic of dysentery swept through the Rhine area, the royal couple's two sons perished. In her grief, Fredegund "beat her breasts with her fists" and cried that as punishment for their greed, they had lost "the most beautiful of our possessions." With broken hearts, they buried the children.

That was not the entire nemesis. A third son died of dysentery at age two. Queen Fredegund was convinced witchcraft was involved. She rounded up a slew of housewives, tortured them into confessing, then had them put to death by the most hideous means. The grieving queen, writes Gregory of Tours, "gathered all [her dead son's] clothes, some of them silk and others of fur," and all his other possessions and burned them, melting down the gold and silver objects "so that nothing whatsoever remained intact to remind her of how she had mourned for her boy."

Such grief of a mother and father, even if their hands were dripping blood, wouldn't seem remarkable if it were not for an academic debate that has raged for decades. Philippe Ariès ignited the furor when he wrote in his 1962 book *Centuries of Childhood: A Social History of Family Life*, "In medieval society childhood did not exist." He insisted parents did not welcome infants into their hearts or their homes, basing his opinion on the lack of vivid or sentimental images of children in the iconography or literature of the Middle Ages. He writes:

No one thought of keeping a picture of a child if that child had either lived to grow to manhood or had died in infancy. In the first case, childhood was simply an unimportant phase of which there was no need to keep any record; in the second case, that of the dead child, it was thought that the little thing which had disappeared so soon in life was not worthy of remembrance: there were far too many children whose survival was problematical. The general feeling was, and for a long time remained, that one had several children in order to keep just a few.[128]

Certainly there is little sense that children were a source of comfort and joy. As historian Shulamith Shahar points out, since sexual intercourse was thought to be sinful—the old Adam and Eve equation at work—children were therefore a reflection of a parent's guilt, the product of wrong-doing. What God permitted, God, with a blink of an eye, could take away. The incredibly high infant-mortality rate—in the Italian city of Pistoia during some years of the Middle Ages, 32.4 percent of the children died before the age of 14[129]—was proof that a mastermind vengeance was at work. For their own mental health, parents had to shield themselves from repeated emotional battering, and they supposedly did so by remaining aloof from their offspring.

Even if they survived, many children spent hardly any time in their parents' home. Aristocratic and middle-class babies were handed over to wet nurses, who often cared for them in their homes, sometimes until the late age of ten or 12. (Peasant mothers, on the other hand, suckled their own infants, and as a result there may have been a closer bond between children and parents among the lower classes.)

Sons of the nobility were often sent to other aristocratic households, often of a distant relative, to train as knights. If there were too many sons for an upper-class family to support, they would suffer a fate similar to that of their sisters. They would be shuttled off to a monastery, there to spend the rest of their lives serving God. According to the historian Georges Duby, who studied the records of Cluny monastery in Burgundy, only one of four or five sons was allowed to marry; the rest entered the service of the church or remained restless bachelors forever.[130]

By the late Middle Ages, the system of primogeniture was firmly in place whereby the eldest son inherited everything. It was left to the mercy of the father or eldest brother to leave the younger children enough with which to scrape by. The historian Lawrence Stone described the results of such a system.

... both the elder and the younger children suffered. The latter normally inherited neither title or estate, unless one of them happened to be heir to his mother's property, and they were therefore inevitably downwardly mobile, until they had made their own fortunes in some profession or occupation. Some were kept hanging around on or near the estate, as a kind of walking sperm-bank in case the elder son died childless and had to be replaced. As for the elder sons, their entrepreneurial drive was sapped by the certainty of the inheritance to come ...[131]

At age six or seven, middle-class boys were sent away to schools attached to monasteries, colleges or in their tutor's homes.[132] Once they had mastered their letters, they often were dispatched to some business establishment, there to learn the ropes. In 1248, a Marseilles lawyer sent his son William to live with a money-changer. While William served his two-year apprenticeship, his father paid a hefty sum in money and grain for the lad's "bread and wine and meat." If he caused the money-changer any trouble, he could be disciplined—a whip was always handy—and his father promised to reimburse the money-lender for any financial losses incurred by the boy's stupidity or laziness.[133]

Peasant children were expected to do chores almost as soon as they could walk. Boys guarded the sheep, watered or pastured the oxen and horses, and, during harvest, gathered the grain left behind by the reapers. As soon as the child reached adolescence, he began working full time in the fields.

A 13th-century poem portraying the plight of a peasant named Helmbrecht provides an interesting sketch of a father's and mother's response when their son strayed from the straight and narrow. The worst sin of the young man in question was his refusal to accept his position in life as a peasant. As a teenager, Helmbrecht joined a band of robber-knights. Eventually, he was caught and, on the order of the lord's bailiff, horribly punished—his eyes were gouged out and one each of his arms and legs hacked off. Blind and crippled, he made his way to his parents' home. His father could only think of getting rid of him. "Betake yourself you faithless boor in greatest haste forth from my door; your suffering is nothing to me." "But the mother," writes the poet, "who was not as hard as he passed out as to a child a crust."[134]

This incident is sometimes cited as an illustration of how good-hearted mothers could be in the Middle Ages. To contemporary eyes, it might not seem like compassionate mother love, but it does illustrate one important point. The few examples of devotion between parent and child most often involved a mother and son, often with the son showing far more affection for the mother than the other way around.

One example of a mother who appeared none too fond of her son is found in the biography of Saint Peter Damian (1007–1072). In the pathetic household into which he was born, there were so many children that when the mother became pregnant with Peter, her older son chastised her for adding yet another heir to the already dwindling family holdings. The mother reacted to this with utter despair, declaring she was wretched and unworthy to live. She then "wholly rejected the baby," refusing to even touch him. Poor, abandoned Peter became so weak, "only the barest whisper came from his scarcely palpitating little chest." Finally a woman who had been a servant in the family stepped in and reprimanded the mother. How could a Christian woman reject a child formed in the image of God and shaped in her own womb? Overcome with guilt, the mother took the infant to nurse, but Saint Damian never did feel much loved by his family.[135]

Probably families in the Middle Ages loved and dedicated themselves to their children far more than historians like Philippe Ariès give them credit for. Small but colourful scenes that attest to this are found throughout the literature. Cosimo de' Medici (1389–1464), for example, the powerful Italian banker and statesman, interrupted a meeting with an important foreign delegation because his grandson arrived and demanded his *nonno* carve him a toy whistle. Taking up his whittling knife, the magnate told his visitors, "My lords, know you not the love of children and grandchildren? It is as well that he didn't ask me to play it, because I would have done that too!"[136]

Yet what seems to be missing is a joy, a zest, at even the idea of children. In the Middle Ages, even that most close of relationships—the mother-son bond—often seems to be lacklustre. Centuries would have to pass before it would heat up to its fiery and neurotic potential.

III

Hamlet's mother Gertrude is an odd character. She seems befuddled, shallow, even prissy, but there she was, caught in the grip of a lust so overpowering that only two months after the death of her husband, the King of Denmark, she married his brother Claudius. An outrageous transgression, since in her society, such a marriage was considered incestuous.

Hamlet was clearly overwhelmed by the event. Even before the ghost appeared with the startling news that his uncle had poisoned his father to seize the crown, the young man's tortured soul had become enveloped in "an inky cloak." So conflicted were his emotions, so tormented was he, that he contemplated suicide. His mother's sexual passion offended Hamlet more, it seems, than the murder of his father. "Maternal malevolence, maternal spoiling,"[137] a symbol of original sin, sits at the heart of Shakespeare's most enigmatic play.

What happens in Hamlet's fertile mind is that Gertrude's sin of remarriage—and, really, is it any of his business?—swells into a dark fantasy, representing the tremendous fear of sex, the terror of the female body, that young men in Hamlet's day grappled with as they came of age. The scholar Janet Adelman points out that *Hamlet* and many of the Shakespearean tragedies that follow "thrust the son into the domain of maternal dread inhabited by all the avatars of strumpet fortune—the wicked wives, lovers, daughters, mothers and stepmothers, the witches and engulfing storms—that have the power to shake [the male character's] manhood."[138]

That a young man should fight back against such malevolent, potentially consuming female power, using any weapon he could muster, has always been considered perfectly normal. Writes Adelman, "Gertrude's appetite is always inherently frightening, always potentially out of control; as the image of the unweeded garden itself implies, it always required a weeder to manage its over-luxuriant growth."[139] If the father is not available as gardener, then the son must step in.

Hamlet takes on the job, confronting his mother in his belligerent and arrogant way. In the end, Gertrude makes the ultimate sacrifice, as all good mothers should, by drinking Hamlet's wine cup of poison.[140] Neither the nonentity so often depicted by the critics, nor evil, Gertrude is perhaps confused, indecisive, but surely that was a result of having to cope with all the overbearing and arrogant men in her life.

The mother-son relationship in *Hamlet* is interesting in itself, but it also reveals a great deal about the status of women generally. From the 15th century on, the literature—advice manuals for the family, courtesy books, even medical treatises—insisted women, the descendants of Eve, were weak creatures, easily given over to their emotions and appetites. It was imperative they be tutored and disciplined, gently but firmly, by men: fathers, uncles, husbands and sons. By the laws of the country, a young adult male, no matter how irresponsible and profligate, was considered a superior being by virtue of his sex, no matter how intelligent or capable his mother.

Just the same, the lives of young men could hardly be considered easy. Before the 1660s, corporal punishment, which was sometimes very brutal, was all too common. School discipline was particularly harsh; laying a child over the back of a bench and flogging his naked buttocks with a bundle of birches until the blood flowed was a common practice. Since, by the 1500s, more and more boys were being sent away to be educated, more were being abused.

The mother's hand could be just as heavy as the father's. Joseph Lister, born in 1632, remembered being regularly strapped by his mother. The Spanish writer and humanist Ludovicus Vives wrote that "there was nobody I did more flee, or was more loathe to come nigh, than my mother when I was a child."[141]

Historian Lawrence Stone believes harsh corporal punishment was a way of breaking a child's spirit so he would accept "with passive resignation" his parents' decisions on the two most important aspects of his life: his marriage and his career. (Girls were beaten just as much, if not more, but theirs is a different story.)

Right up until the Age of Enlightenment, the parents' authority to chose a marriage partner for their son was the source of bitter and often heartbreaking conflict. The mother was often intricately involved in these arrangements. After the Protestant Reformation took hold, she was promoted as the overseer of the family honour, which involved finding a young bride suitable in terms of both morals and money. Stone describes the wedding in 1719 of the son and heir of the Duke of Richmond and the 12-year-old daughter of Lord Cadogan:

The marriage was made to cancel a gambling debt; the young people's consent having been the last thing thought of: the Earl of March was sent for from school, and the young lady from the nursery; a clergyman was in attendance and they were told that they were immediately to become man and wife. The young lady is not reported to have uttered a word: the gentleman exclaimed, 'They are surely not going to marry me to that dowdy.'[142]

Against all odds, the union turned out to be a happy one. Many, if not most, did not.

Even more important than marriage was the choice of a young man's career. Would he be a country gentleman, a trader, train for a business career or apprentice as a craftsmen? By the 17th century, formal education was necessary for many careers, and that age-old parental tradition of nagging children about their grades began. In 1685, Edmund Verney wrote the following furious letter to his 19-year-old son, who had suggested he might like to quit school. "I hear you hate learning and your mind hankers after travelling. I will not be taught by my cradle how to breed it up; it is insolence and impudence in any child to presume so much as to offer it." When the young man died some months later of fever, his father could see the hand of God in the tragedy; the terrible nemesis was a result of his son's mild act of insubordination.[143]

By the 18th century, according to Lawrence Stone, there was a remarkable change in the way parents, at least those of the middle and upper classes, began treating their sons, and for that matter, their daughters. Suddenly, children were considered little dolls; they were "dearest little creatures," "little bumpkins," "little pets." It became fashionable to indulge offspring at the feast of St. Nicholas, bestowing toy pipes and drums, rocking horses, gingerbread men and spinning tops. Excessive corporal punishment was suddenly frowned on; as Jonathan Swift wrote, it was now accepted wisdom "that whipping breaks the spirits of lads well-born."[144] Whether they became clerics or clerks was left up to the young men to decide. And with a new emphasis on romance, they could insist on marrying only the loves of their lives.

This was a result of the times—the period was called the Age of Enlightenment for a reason—and a fundamental change in the power structure of the family, which undermined the patriarch's absolute authority. To a degree, this benefited women, too. It became acceptable for a husband to leave instructions in his will that his wife would have control over the children, including any sons, even if she remarried. In 1775, Hester Thrale was granted the power in her dead husband's will to settle her portion of the inherited estate (not his property, though) on the children as she saw fit.

This did not mean, however, that mothers were suddenly free from the tyranny of their sons. The male child maintained his privileged position, both legally and morally. Maidservants who were about to marry were advised to buy a shop with their savings, in the likely case they should be widowed and their sons mismanage their inheritance. As the historian Olwen Hufton put it, "The shop was always there, a buttress against the plight of the widow who sent her son to market with their remaining cow and saw him return with a bean which was allegedly magic."[145]

IV

As the Victorian age progressed, with the father's domain firmly established in the outside world and the mother's at home, the nurturing of children became an obsession.

At the beginning of the 19th century, upper-class European boys were sent away to school at the early age of seven. Once the mother's care was perceived as beneficial, though, it was thought wise to keep the very young at home. By the end of the century, boys were usually 12 or 13 before they were shuttled off to boarding school.[146] With the master away conquering the world, the maternal influence became all-powerful. A mother worried about her son's health and kept a close watch on his studies. If she disapproved of some chum or other, she wouldn't hesitate to suggest, "Well, dear, you know he's not really our type." But the mother's most important job was to oversee her son's religious life and his ethical development. In the

Victorian era, this meant his sexuality; "purity in thought and deed" became the motto mothers espoused. Members of the Female Moral Reform Society in New York went so far as to take a vow to guard their sons' innocence even if it meant marching into a brothel and yanking the young wretch out of a hussy's bed.

George Sand, in her novel *Indiana*, paints a deliciously ironic portrait of mother as moral guardian. The son is Raymon de Ramière, "a brilliant young man, intelligent, talented and with many virtues, used to social success and fashionable love-affairs."[147] He also has the ethics of a crayfish, preying on young women by seducing them with stories of true love, getting them pregnant and then breaking every promise he made. For the women, the result is humiliation and broken hearts. As for Raymon, he always manages to wiggle out of "embarrassing situations" because of his handsome looks, his incredible charm and the influence of his mother.

When one of his dalliances finally results in the suicide of his lover, he feels some remorse, if only for a minute.

At first he detested himself and loaded his pistols with the very serious intention of blowing his brains out, but a praiseworthy feeling held him back. What would become of his mother ... his elderly mother, in poor health ... that poor woman whose whole life had been so troubled and so full of sorrow, who lived only for him, her only asset, her only hope? Must he break her heart, shorten her few remaining days? Definitely not. The best way to atone for his crime was to devote himself henceforth entirely to his mother, and it was with this in mind that he went back to her in Paris and put all his efforts into making her forget the kind of neglect in which he had left her for a great part of the winter.[148]

So back into gay Parisian society Raymon whirls. Mothers could be most useful.

It was all very well if the custodian of moral values was virtuous herself, but what if the mother violated the standards society, and her son, had set for her? Hamlet had had his nervous breakdown and 300 years later, many a young man suffered a similar fate. Charles Baudelaire's mother Caroline was 28 and his father 61 when the poet was born in 1821. The father, a former priest and teacher turned bureaucrat with a taste for the arts, died seven years later. The marriage had been one of convenience. Caroline had been a school teacher determined not to become an old maid; M. Baudelaire was a lonely widower. Much to everyone's astonishment, within a year of her husband's death

Caroline fell head over heels in love and flung herself into a passionate love affair. She was already seven months pregnant (the child was stillborn) when she married Major Jacques Aupick on November 8, 1828.

Baudelaire had been extremely close to his mother. "There was in my childhood a period of passionate love for you," he once wrote. According to him, her affair with Aupick, "her betrayal," scarred him for life. He never forgave her. His biographer Joanna Richardson writes:

Illegal pregnancy and stillbirth would have been hard to explain to a child of seven, a child who had been conventionally brought up; but Baudelaire was aware of events. They had inspired him with revulsion for the sexual act, for the animality of love, with contempt for the generality of women. In later life he was to dream of his mother as the madam in a brothel. Not only had Mme Baudelaire become Mme Aupick, she had prostituted herself in her widowhood; not only had she betrayed her first husband, she had betrayed her son, and she had replaced him with a stillborn child. He had lost his mother, his childhood and a great part of himself.[149]

That his mother's marriage was an extremely happy one, that the couple remained utterly devoted to each other until Major Aupick died 29 years later, mattered not at all to Baudelaire. He would continuously write of his "anger, bitterness and grief" at his mother's second marriage. "When you have a son [like me]," he was to say, "you do not remarry."

The deference with which male children were treated had other dire results: the emotional and sometimes physical undermining of the girls in the family. Flora Thompson and her sisters, daughters of a farm labourer in Oxfordshire, had been sent to work as domestics in the 1880s so their wages could help support the family. Flora later commented:

Strange to say, although they [her parents] were grateful to and fond of their daughters, their boys, who were always at home and whose money barely paid for their keep, seemed always to come first with them. If there was any inconvenience, it must not fall on the boys; if there was a limited quantity of anything, the boys must still have their full share; the boys' best clothes must be brushed and put away for them; their shirts must be specially well-ironed, and tit-bits must always be saved for their luncheon afield.[150]

For a girl with intellectual or artistic talent, the favouritism displayed towards her brothers could be devastating. The situation of Emily Dickinson

(1830–1886), perhaps the most original of all American poets, is a particularly startling case in point.

Dickinson was born into a straight-laced, Puritanical family whose ancestors could count eight generations of New Englanders. Her father Edward was a lawyer, a politician who served a term in the House of Representatives in Washington and one of the leading citizens of Amherst, Massachusetts. Emily was well-educated for her time: she attended Amherst Academy for seven years, where she was a brilliant student, and then studied at Mount Holyoke Female Seminary for a year. As her biographer Cynthia Griffin Wolff puts it, "When she reached maturity, however, and it was time to take her place in society, Father expected her to put aside all the energies and talents that had been awakened and nourished by her schooling and become domesticated."[151]

The apple of Edward Dickinson's eye was his only son Austin; it was he who was expected to make brilliant the reputation of the House of Dickinson. While Edward belittled Emily's ambition, he relished the idea of a literary son. He considered Austin's letters from college "altogether before Shakespeare," and he promised "to have them published to put in our library." As Griffin Wolff writes, "Father had never taken the least notice of his *daughter's* precocity or literary genius."[152]

Austin Dickinson was an intelligent enough man—he went on to become a lawyer and a partner with his father—but he showed little original literary talent. The real brilliance in the family was not only ignored but ridiculed. Such undermining was probably one reason Emily lacked the confidence to subject her work to the public eye—less than 20 of her verses were published during her lifetime. A huge cache, 1,775 poems, was found in a locked box after her death by her sister. What if it had been thrown out as the debris of a mere woman, an old maid at that? Edward Dickinson's cold indifference, his ridiculous preference for his son, would have meant a gift to humanity was lost forever.

V

It was Freud and his infamous Oedipus complex that sullied the mother-son relationship. An affectionate kiss at bedtime suddenly turned into a potent signal of sexual longing. A mother's caresses became smothering and debilitating, her devotion a force against which to struggle.

The baby, said Freud, unconditionally wallows in his mother's love, but at what he termed the "phallic phase," between three and five, the little boy begins to pay attention to his sexual apparatus. First, he notices he possesses a penis, which neither his sisters nor his mother do, a fact that astonishes and delights him—already he has one up on the females in his family. Then he experiences a delicious tingle of pleasure when he or someone else touches his little organ. This piques his interest even more and he begins asking questions, specifically, where do babies come from? Finally, he happens upon his mother and father making love, "the primal scene," as Freud called it. The child believes this towering masculine figure, who has always been rather distant to him, has forcibly taken his mother. He also understands that it is the adult, with his mighty penis, who has automatic access to her.

All of this—the violent sexual act and the fact that some have penises and some do not—awakens in the boy a profound castration complex. With the jealous, omnipotent patriarch always looming in the background, the boy feels guilty about his great love for his mother and terrified his genitalia will somehow shrivel up. The only way he can rid himself of his great fear and anxiety is to renounce his mother's love and identify with the person of authority and strength: his father.

Freud's theory has had a profound influence on society. As Adrienne Rich has concluded:

The fundamental assumption here is that the two-person mother-child relationship is by nature regressive, circular, unproductive, and that culture depends on the son-father relationship. All that the mother can do for the child is perpetuate a dependency which prevents further development. Through the resolution of the Oedipus complex, the boy makes his way into the male world, the world of patriarchal law and order. Civilization—meaning of course, patriarchal civilization—requires the introduction of the father (whose presence has so far not been essential since nine months before birth) as a third figure in the interrelationship of mother and child. The Oedipus complex thus becomes, in Juliet Mitchell's phrase, 'the entry into human culture.' But it is distinctively the father who represents not just authority but culture itself, the super-ego which controls the blind thrashings of the 'id.' Civilization means identification, not with the mother, but with the father.[153]

Where does this leave the mother? She can acquiesce in her inferior position in the family or she can fight the dominance of her husband and raise what has long been called a Mama's boy. Either way she will then be blamed for anything that goes wrong, not only in her son's life but in society as a whole.

It is D. H. Lawrence's autobiographical novel *Sons and Lovers*, first published in 1913, which has etched the concept of the Oedipus complex into the 20th-century mind. The story revolves around Gertrude Morel, the daughter of a poor but respectable family of dissenters, people who have long held rigid standards of honesty and propriety. She herself is sensitive, proud and clever. Her tragedy is in falling for the charming Walter Morel, "with his rich, ringing laugh," a man who "is feckless, idle and unprincipled," a heavy drinker who is prone to violence. He is also a hard-working miner who cares for his family, but that does not prevent an irreparable gap widening between husband and wife. They disagree on just about everything, but particularly about the raising of their children.

In the years that follow, husband and wife battle for the minds and hearts of their four offspring. Because Mrs. Morel spends so much time with them, and because she is so much more articulate and high-minded, she wins hands down. Morel becomes isolated in the family, treated by all as a fool and a boor.

The first son William dies from pneumonia but Paul, the second son, quickly fills the breach. He is utterly devoted to his mother. "He kissed her forehead that he knew so well: the deep marks between the brows, the rising of the fine hair, graying now, and the proud setting of the temples. His hand lingered on her shoulder after his kiss."[154]

Gertrude Morel will do anything to prevent the bonds with her son from being severed. She knows Paul must marry one day, but she is determined that while his bride might have his body, she will not possess his spirit. Just such a threat is represented by the first young woman about whom he becomes serious. Miriam Leivers is the shy but intelligent daughter of a local farmer and something of a soul mate for the artistic Paul. Mrs. Morel fights her with all her strength. In one of the novel's many emotionally devastating scenes, Paul suggests that because of his mother's age—she is in her early fifties—she might not have as much in common with him as Miriam does.

'Yes, I know it well—I am old. And therefore I may stand aside; I have nothing more to do with you. You only want me to wait on you—the rest is for Miriam.'

He could not bear it. Instinctively he realized that he was life to her. And, after all, she was the chief thing to him, the only supreme thing.

'You know it isn't, mother, you know it isn't!'[155]

Only Mrs. Morel's death by cancer frees Paul to pursue a life of his own. It seems like an open and shut case of a young man who loved his mother too much, an overheated Oedipus complex, but there is something dark and ignoble stirring in this book. For all his expressions of love and devotion, as the critic Margaret Storch points out, deep down, Paul hates this suffocating tyrant of a mother. The novel depicts several sadistic fantasies in which Paul destroys, sometimes mutilates, the female form, which, according to Storch, represents the mother. And, in fact, he ends Mrs. Morel's life by lacing her milk with a fatal dose of morphia. Her pain had become unbearable, and therefore Paul is supposedly justified in the murder, but there is something cold about the way he goes about it.

> That evening he got all the morphia pills there were, and took them downstairs. Carefully he crushed them to powder.
> 'What are you doing?' said Annie [his sister].
> 'Is'll put 'em in her night milk.'
> Then they both laughed together like two conspiring children. On top of all their horror flickered this little sanity.[156]

Storch writes that D. H. Lawrence believed the male "must assert his independence from female domination and must live in harmony with the dark centres of his being, a harmony threatened by female-induced idealization and abstraction." His subsequent writings "continued to pour scorn and invective upon overdominant women, specifically mothers."[157] He wasn't the only one. The entire Western world began to enthusiastically dump on mothers.

During World War II, the Canadian military brass called mothers "a menace" because they had raised "sissified young men" who "were punk" as soldiers. They wet their beds, collapsed during strenuous workouts, had nervous breakdowns in the trenches, all because their mommies had "babied" them too much.

During the 1950s, the grown-up male who was not a success—who hadn't taken the world by storm—was almost certainly labelled that most pathetic of creatures, a mamma's boy. To a female Canadian journalist writing in 1952, it was straightforward:

> Are you a mother? Have you a son? Will your son be a man? Or will he be in any degree at all that crippled, misdirected person who will be called a 'mamma's boy?'

A mamma's boy is a man who refuses to grow up. If my little son refuses to grow up, it will be *my* fault.[158]

Society of the 1950s was obsessed with the idea of homosexuality and how young men caught such a "disease." It was all the mother's fault, of course. Betty Friedan, in her influential *The Feminine Mystique*, unquestioningly accepts Freudian theory and doesn't hesitate to place the blame firmly on the mother's shoulders.

The role of the mother in homosexuality was pinpointed by Freud and the psychoanalysts. But the mother whose son becomes homosexual is usually not the 'emancipated' woman who competes with men in the world, but the very paradigm of the feminine mystique—a woman who lives through her son, whose femininity is used in virtual seduction of her son, who attaches her son to her with such dependence that he can never mature to love a woman, nor can he, often, cope as an adult with life on his own. The love of men masks his forbidden excessive love for his mother; his hatred and revulsion for all women is a reaction to the one woman who kept him from becoming a man.[159]

The ultimate insult to motherhood was presented in Philip Roth's *Portnoy's Complaint*. On its publication in 1969, a roar of laughter, mostly from young males, washed across North America; the *New York Times* called the novel "wildly funny." These days, it seems nothing more than a collection of the worst kind of pornography, with ethnic Jews bearing the brunt of the ridicule, but since Roth himself was Jewish, none of this was to be considered anti-Semitic. It may have been the archetypal Jewish mother Portnoy was barking at, but every mother felt something of the sting of humiliation.

It was no wonder that by the time the women's liberation movement blew into full gale in the 1970s, young women were sick of the stereotypical image of the mother and wanted desperately to escape it. Still, the painful question of what to do about sons had to be grappled with. Some women argued that no time or energy should be spent on male children, no matter how young, because woman-hating society would dictate they grow into macho young men. (What they were going to do with these little boys was never resolved.) Others argued that boys raised by politically conscious mothers would become "New Men" in tune with the feminist cause.

As their sisters have become emancipated, young men are losing ground. Statistics are mounting that indicate many are failing at school, at work and in the family.[160] They need support, which may be why the wisecracking, affectionate and sympathetic mother-son relationship is once again considered important. One of the many contemporary testaments to this is a book of portraits by American photographer Mariana Cook called *Mothers [and] Sons In Their Own Words*, a collection of the famous—Bill Clinton and his mother Virginia Clinton Kelley—and not so famous. It is an outpouring of sentiment with an undercurrent of playful derision. The Parisian fashion designer Sonia Rykiel gives this cryptic insight into her relationship with her musician son Jean-Philippe Rykiel. It has a decidedly modern ring to it.

Mother-son, a funny relationship
Difficult contacts, mutual respect.
He is a musician. I, a maker—on that level it works.
Endless conversations about invention, pain, beauty,
creativity. More complicated conversations about life.
How to live, but a real complicity of hearts.[161]

2. The Married State

Elizabeth

In our bouffant skirts, we looked like a group of bluebells or buttercups. The desired effect was produced through two devices: the elastic cinched belts— I had two, one in cherry red and one in lime green—that tightly squeezed our already puny middles, and crinolines, those petticoats of stiff, net–like material we wore underneath. We didn't realize it, but these fashions represented the last gasp of the 18th and 19th century's encumbering of females, when the hoop skirt, those parrot cages of metal strips, had reigned supreme. The Victorian version was more extreme than our tame drip-dries, but the effect was the same: by accentuating little waists and larger bosoms (if we had any at all), and offering titillating glimpses of leg, the outfit signified the 1950s love of daintiness, prettiness and ladylike behaviour.

In our class, no one could match Elizabeth Mastin in the crinoline-skirt department. She could boast the largest number, the bounciest, the most intricate, all made by her mother. Watching Elizabeth sway along the hallway in yet another extravagant creation always struck me as a little incongruous, for she hardly seemed the epitome of femininity. A chunky girl with a round, cheery face, she liked to horse around. "Don't be saucy," she'd yell as she jabbed her elbow into the ribs of some fellow who had been teasing her.

Elizabeth, unlike the rest of us, was always comfortable around the boys. Her house was full of them. She had two brothers: Paul, a year older, and Bruce, 18 months younger, both of whom we considered gorgeous hunks. Paul was a star of the school football team, and the line-up of girls with a crush on him was legendary. For those of us who didn't have a hope of attracting such a prize, there were always Paul's and Bruce's friends.

Elizabeth's Midland Avenue home had a large family room and there the gang gathered. The Saturday night parties were famous. A little petting went on, the dancing was sometimes hot and heavy and now and then, one of the older guys would produce a beer from under his jacket, but mostly these gatherings were remarkably innocent. The girls in my class seldom managed even a kiss, much to their disappointment. Still, the crowd was lively, the music loud, the amount of Coke and potato chips consumed was enormous. We sometimes wondered how Elizabeth's parents put up with it.

Jim and Edna Mastin didn't seem the kind to preside over teenage boister-ousness. They were older (Edna was in her mid-thirties when her children were born), they were very English, very proper and they themselves never socialized. Says Elizabeth, "I don't remember a friend of my parents ever coming to our house. There were no friends, none at all." The family was everything. That was why the rec room was daily turned into a clubhouse. Edna Mastin knew where her kids were, downstairs, not smoking cigarettes in a hang-out like the Bo Peep restaurant.

Elizabeth's grandfather Benjamin Mastin had emigrated from the county of Kent in England in 1910, the year after Jim was born. Then war intervened. The rest of the family remained in England while Benjamin worked to estab-lish his tool-and-die business in Toronto. It took 13 years before it was prof-itable enough to support his family. Jim had already finished school in England by the time the Mastins were reunited in Toronto. A job was wait-ing from him in his father's factory.

Edna Mastin was born in Toronto in 1911, but it might as well have been London. Her parents' thinking was completely rooted in 19th-century England. Says Elizabeth, "My mother was brought up in a very prudish atmosphere, and I would say my home was Victorian, with traditional values."

Tool-and-die making was considered essential to the war effort, so Jim was exempted from military duty during World War II. War contracts helped build up the company, though, so that by the time Jim took over after his father's death in 1945, the business was prospering and the family was comfortably off. "My mother was the one who doled out the money and she was an extremely capable manager," recalls Elizabeth. "We kids were never deprived. One year we were all bought bikes, good ones that cost $35 each, a lot of money in those days, and when we went to college, we each got our own car."

When the Mastins were first married they lived with Jim's recently widowed father in his house in working-class east end Toronto. Her mother was something of a snob, says Elizabeth, and she didn't approve of the neigh-bourhood. It took the Mastins almost five years of constant searching to find the home they wanted. It was a brand-new, two-storey house on Midland Avenue in Scarborough, with a huge backyard that backed onto a ravine. It also had a family room where Edna could keep track of her kids.

Despite what the rest of us saw as an enviable social life, Elizabeth's adolescence was not a happy time. "I hated our high-school years. With a passion, I hated them. My friends were all as immature, unworldly, uninteresting as I was. We were totally focused on studies, spent all our time competing for marks. I would get up at five or six in the morning to study for exams. We were dull and boring, we really were."

Elizabeth seldom dated—a strict curfew was in force—and the extracurricular activities she engaged in were of the egg-head variety: the Classics club, the library club, the orchestra in which she played the cello. What she really wanted to do after school was to go home to a house full of her brothers' friends and the cheery company of her mom and dad.

The Mastins insisted all their children complete Grade 13. Paul, the eldest, went into the family business immediately on graduation, and Bruce took science at the University of Toronto. Elizabeth managed to get high enough marks to be admitted there, too, but she had no intention of going. She was exhausted from her five years of competitive academics. "I thought, 'I can't do this any more. I don't like it now, I don't want to do it for another three years.'" She'd always wanted to be an elementary-school teacher anyway, and along with many of her classmates, she enrolled in teacher's college.

By that time she had met her future husband. He lived around the corner, a buddy of her brother Paul, one of the guys who used to hang out in the Mastins' rec room. Ellery Hollingsworth was shy, soft-spoken, very serious. Elizabeth says she was his first and only date.

Ellery's father was an Irish immigrant who was the foreman of the picture-framing department of Eaton's department store. His mother was born in Canada, but her parents, too, were of Irish-English descent. It was important to Elizabeth that Ellery's background be similar to hers. That, she believes, is the basis of a sound relationship.

Elizabeth says theirs was not a head-over-heels love affair. She and Ellery simply started going out and somehow the idea of spending the rest of their lives together naturally evolved. He was an old-fashioned kind of guy who believed in preparing for marriage. It would take six years, but by 1967, they had scrimped and saved the $10,000 needed for the down payment on a house on Shirley Crescent, not far from where both had been brought up. To this day, they live in the same home.

In 1961–62, Elizabeth attended teacher's college, a year she remembers with no pleasure at all. She was still living with her family, still abiding by a midnight curfew. "I think I was far too young, only 18. I had lived in this close little family and now I was expected to go to work, meet people, stand up in front of a class, and I didn't do that very well."

However, she had no trouble finding a job. She was hired as a Grade 3 teacher at Cliffside Public, the school she herself had attended from Grades 4 to 8. Many of her former teachers were still there, so it was like being welcomed back into a family. She realized, though, that teaching would be a short-lived career. Just like her mother, as soon as she married she would become a full-time housewife.

Academics had never been Ellery's strong suit, and at the end of Grade 12, he left high school to enroll in the private Radio College of Canada. After graduation, he was hired at the Canadian Broadcasting Corporation in the lowliest of jobs, dragging cables, although he was soon promoted to an audio-video technician.

Most weekends were spent at the Mastins' house, watching television and yakking with Elizabeth, her brothers and their myriad of friends. Through the long years of their engagement, sexual intercourse was not even considered a possibility by either. An unwanted pregnancy would have been a catastrophe; both sets of parents would have disowned them. Their wedding date was finally set for August 12, 1967, but the year before proved one of the most unsettling in Elizabeth's life. She still gets teary-eyed when she thinks about it.

Jim and Edna had been brought up as Anglicans and were married in the Church of the Resurrection, but when they moved to Scarborough, they lost interest in the establishment faith. That didn't mean religion wasn't an important part of the household. Old Testament morality hung in the air. Elizabeth was raised on Bible sayings; she remembers hearing often from the book of Proverbs: "A diligent woman is a crown to her husband." Unconventional sects fascinated Jim Mastin, especially those that concentrated on Biblical interpretation. For a time, he became a Christadelphian. But it was the Mastins' youngest son Bruce, then a student at the University of Toronto and searching for inner peace and confidence, who persuaded the family to embrace the Worldwide Church of God.

Originally called the Radio Church of God, it was founded in January 1934 by Herbert W. Armstrong of Des Moines, Iowa. A Grade 10 drop-out, Armstrong sold radio advertising for 16 years before his wife Loma discovered the Church of God-Seventh Day Adventists. Armstrong was ordained a minister in that faith in 1933, and set up his headquarters in Salem, Oregon. The following year, he began broadcasting his Good News message.

Some of Armstrong's beliefs were eccentric, to say the least. His doctrine rested on the belief that the true Israelites were not Jews but Anglo-Saxons. They were directly descended from the lost tribe of Israel, he insisted, and therefore the rightful heirs to the land and riches God had promised to the offspring of Abraham. For this reason, Armstrong emphasized the Old Testament; his adherents maintained a kosher diet and celebrated Hebrew, rather than Christian feast days. Many of his teachings were heresy for the Seventh Day Adventists, and in 1933, Armstrong was ousted from his pulpit. He responded by setting up his own congregation, carrying on his ever-more-popular radio ministry and publishing his magazine, *The Plain Truth*.

During World War II, Armstrong made several prophecies about the imminent coming of Armageddon, all of which turned out to be false. That didn't seem to deter his followers. The church grew an average of 30 percent a year. In 1946, the ministry was relocated to Pasadena, California, where Ambassador College was established to train ministers to spread the gospel of Armstrongism. By 1968, there were about 200 congregations and the name was changed to the Worldwide Church of God.

Since Jim Mastin had long been attracted to Adventist concepts—tithing (in the Worldwide Church of God, it ran as high as 30 percent of one's annual income), immersion baptism and the belief that unrepentant sinners, those not of the faith, are doomed to eternal damnation—his son Bruce had little trouble convincing him that Armstrong really was Christ's ambassador on earth. Edna, who believed it was a wife's duty to follow her husband no matter what, also joined the church, as did their eldest son Paul. Suddenly all the family rituals Elizabeth had enjoyed for so long were skewed: the Sabbath was now observed on Saturday, not Sunday, and Christmas and Easter were no longer celebrated, though Passover was. "It changed our whole way of doing things as a family," she says. "I still get choked up thinking about that." Worse for Elizabeth, she was torn between her family and her husband-to-be.

The Worldwide Church of God was not interested in having only half of a married couple join its ranks, and Ellery made it clear he was not interested in the teachings of the church. Elizabeth says there were long discussions with her brothers, tears, enticement: "You're part of this family. You believe the same things we do. Why would you marry a heathen?" Elizabeth says she had always been taught by her mother to obey the Biblical instruction that a wife should cleave unto the husband, and so she did.

In the end, Elizabeth's family did not want to be alienated from her and respected her decision. She was married to Ellery on August 12, 1967, in the same Anglican church as her parents had been.

Although Elizabeth had not joined the Worldwide Church of God, her thinking was coloured by its dogma. Birth control was forbidden—her brother Bruce eventually had eight children—and Elizabeth would not even consider "unnatural" methods such as the birth-control pill. Her first child Chris was born ten months after her wedding, her daughter Rebecca on her second wedding anniversary. She miscarried a few months later, and then the third child Jeremy was born, 18 months later. By that time, Elizabeth was desperate. She was simply not willing to face pregnancy every year for the next 20 years. Although she was fearful of what her family would think, she underwent a tubal ligation.

Elizabeth had quit teaching by this time so she could centre her life entirely around her children. "My mother was a little disgusted with me, because when she used to come over, there'd be diapers all over the place and I'd be sitting on the floor reading to the kids. 'What if your husband comes home and finds this mess?' she'd ask. I'd say, 'My children come before a spotless house.'"

When Ellery was young, his father had been so heavily involved with his Masonic order and other community organizations, he was almost never home during the evenings. Ellery decided this was not the life for him: he would put parenting first. He worked shifts at the CBC so he was often home during the day, and he'd take the kids on trips, coach the basketball teams, talk to them about their schoolwork. It was all part of Elizabeth's dream to create the kind of sheltering, comfortable family life she had enjoyed so much as a child. She admits she was a protective, worrisome mother. "I babied my children, and probably still do." When Rebecca, at age 22, moved to Buffalo, New York, to attend teacher's college for a year, she phoned her mother every day.

Yet by the time her youngest child was 13, Elizabeth realized she was utterly bored staying at home all day. "I do not join clubs, I don't enjoy shopping. I don't like visiting girlfriends, and I'm not house-proud." She decided to return to teaching. Ellery supported her, but her mother was horrified. "She said, 'Why are you doing this? Your kids need you.'" Elizabeth compromised by working only half time so she could be home to make lunch.

In 1987, however, she took on a full load as a Grade 8 teacher and librarian at the Bliss Carman Senior School, located around the corner from where she lives. It was not an easy time for the family. "My kids were spoiled dreadfully when I stayed at home. I did not expect them to make their beds or do the dishes. That was my job, my role. It was a big mistake. When I started back to work, I still had to do their beds, their washing, ironing, and I resented it. I was already 40 years old, and a little bit more selfish I guess."

Despite this bit of friction, the 1980s were a prosperous and happy time for Elizabeth. She discovered her maturity was a real help in her teaching. Her students represented a rainbow of colours from different ethnic backgrounds, and many were living near the poverty line. And their age, 12 or 13, was considered an exceedingly difficult time. Nonetheless, Elizabeth loved her job, and still does. She is so good at it, she is assigned an unusually large number of children—over a third of her class—who don't speak English or who have special needs. "I think I have an ability *not* to turn them off. I love them. I mean, they tick me off at times, but I love them." Her classroom, she says, is like a family with all the respect, affection and discipline that entails.

Ellery, meanwhile, was also succeeding in his profession. He methodically worked his way up the corporate ladder until he was named manager for on-air broadcasting for the CBC. In 1996, he retired from the corporation and set up his own business making videotapes.

The Mastins, the family of her childhood, continued to play a central and dramatic role in Elizabeth's life. Years earlier, her father had bought a 15-acre farm north of Toronto as a holiday retreat. Elizabeth fondly remembered the fun-filled summers of her youth, and she and Ellery and the kids often spent their vacations there. So did Paul and his two children, as well as Bruce, his wife and their brood of eight. For Jim and Edna, it was a precious time of renewal. But in the 1990s, the farm, the symbol of clan unity, was sold and the Mastin family shaken to its very core. It had everything to do with their religion.

By 1970, the television and radio broadcasts of the Worldwide Church of God were more popular than ever, circulation of *The Plain Truth* had soared to two million and over $50-million a year was collected through tithes. Herbert Armstrong had long predicted the apocalypse would descend in January 1972; every human would suffer a fiery death except, of course, the members of his church. That Armageddon did not arrive on time was only the first in a series of setbacks for the Worldwide Church of God. Rumours began flying that Armstrong's son and heir apparent, handsome Garner Ted, was a fornicator. Evidence of his adultery, in the form of the testimony of young students, was popping up everywhere. In 1978, he was excommunicated, whereupon he promptly established his own cult, the Church of God, International, and continued with his popular radio shows.

Garner Ted wasn't the only one accused of indulging in a lavish lifestyle. Herbert Armstrong himself and his chief aide, a converted Jew named Stanley R. Rader, were charged by dissident members with pilfering church assets valued at $60-million for their personal use. In 1979, a California judge placed the church in temporary receivership. Only after years of lengthy and expensive court battles was the court order finally removed.

Despite the scandals, the church managed to maintain its membership levels, in 1987 estimated at 68,000 world-wide. The Mastins were among those who remained faithful. Elizabeth's youngest brother Bruce had been so enamored of Armstrong's doctrine that for two years, he had attended the Worldwide Church of God's Ambassador College in Pasadena. In the end, he decided the ministry wasn't for him, and he became a high-school science teacher in Brighton, Ontario. He, his wife and eight children, however, remained devoted to their religion.

Paul, too, strengthened his connection to the church by marrying within it. Elizabeth says her mother picked out his bride for him. Sally and Paul were married in 1970, and had two children four years apart. They were relatively happy, at least until Paul decided he, too, wanted to serve the church. Says Elizabeth, "My two brothers have always had sibling rivalry. And when Bruce chose not to be a minister, Paul, who had always suffered from an inferiority complex, decided he would. It was not good for his wife." A minister has enormous prestige and authority, but he and his family live in a fishbowl, where any transgression of the moral code is keenly observed. Elizabeth says it was all too much for Sally. "She was a lovely girl and I loved her dearly, but she was very intimidated by social status. She was out of her depth."

In a 1952 booklet *Does God Heal Today?*, Herbert W. Armstrong had condemned medical science as "sorcery," "witchcraft" and "idolatry." The belief brought enormous suffering and even death to legions of his followers. By the 1980s, the church's stance on this doctrine was softening, but many of the more enthusiastic followers, especially ministers like Paul Mastin, refused to believe Armstrong's initial pronouncement was false.

In 1986, Sally Mastin was suffering from severe back pain. Unwilling to trust a medical doctor, she consulted an iridologist (someone who believes illnesses can be diagnosed by examining the eye), who determined Sally not only had gallstones but also dangerously high blood pressure. A holistic regime of natural herbs and medicines was prescribed, and in fact, Sally's gall-bladder problem eased, but her high blood pressure did not. Still no medication was sought; after all, Armstrong had written, "Don't pay any attention to how you feel, or what you see, after you have called on God for healing." In 1989, during a meeting at the church, Sally suffered a cerebral hemorrhage and died instantly. She was 42.

The family was devastated, but they were further disturbed when, within a year, Paul married again. His bride was a follower of the church, a widow with two young children. Elizabeth says the marriage was not a happy one. Paul pined over Sally; he said he felt as though he had a limb missing, and his children, now 14 and 18 years old, did not like their stepmother. Paul's answer was to draw even closer to his parents.

Ever since he had left school, Paul had worked for James Mastin & Company, his father's tool-and-die-making company, and it had provided a nice living for both families. Jim Mastin was now in his eighties, and it was naturally left to Paul to make many of the financial decisions. Elizabeth says they were not wise or "family-oriented." The business began to lose money, and Elizabeth and Bruce blamed it on Paul.

Relations were even more strained when it was discovered the family vacation spot, the old farm, would have to be sold to pay off business debts. Elizabeth had always been told it was *her* inheritance, and it held great significance for her—a symbol of family unity and happiness. She asked her father and brother to hold off until she and Ellery could raise a mortgage on their house to buy the property themselves. Paul went ahead with the deal anyway, and the precious cottage was gone. "I phoned my brother and said, 'You are going to pay for this one!' I still feel the guilt for that."

It was soon discovered that Paul was mortally ill with cancer of the liver. He was nursed at home. His mother and father went to see him every day, his brother and sister often. On September 12, 1992, he died at age 50.

Paul's children, as it turned out, had been bitterly resented by his widow. Elizabeth says Sarah and James walked out of the house the day he died and never returned, except to pick up their clothes. The father had left them not a cent. The Mastins were even forced to take Paul's widow to court to retrieve Sally's few jewels and other personal possessions, the only mementos the children had of their mother.

The Mastin family has survived this tragedy, regrouped and become close once again. Elizabeth's father died in 1996, and her mother now lives with her and Ellery. She talks to her brother Bruce and his family frequently. Her own family, meanwhile, has settled into the solid unit she always wanted, a relationship based on mutual interests and admiration.

Elizabeth's daughter Rebecca was married last year and is pregnant with her first child. It is she who best exemplifies both the seductiveness and rootedness of a closely knit family. She says she doesn't like films much and she doesn't read books at all. What she really likes to do is clean. "I love washing the floor, tidying up drawers and closets, making my house spotless." It's torture for her to be away from home; she doesn't like travelling, even on vacation. Most important, she can't imagine living a long-distance phone call away from her mom. Elizabeth, after all, is the heart of the family.

The Family

The extent of wives' subjection doth stretch itself very far, even unto all things....
William Gouge, *Of Domestical Duties*, 1622

The notion that a man's wife is his PROPERTY is the fatal root of incalculable evil and misery.
Frances Power Cobbe, *Fraser's Magazine*, 1878

Oh God
That men and women
having undertaken to vanquish one another
should be allowed
to shut themselves up in hot boxes and breed

Mina Loy, 1916

Most Friday nights, I plopped myself down in front of the television for a delicious, and I thought exotic, half-hour of *The Plouffe Family*. That they had such strange names and spoke with such funny accents only added to their charm. The one I liked best was Ovide, the eldest brother and family intellectual. A sensitive young man who liked to read poetry, he worked cutting out shoe patterns in a Quebec factory. Rita Toulouse worked there, too, and although Ovide was utterly smitten with her, she loved lots of men and didn't hesitate to tell him so.

Cecile was the only daughter, a 38-year-old spinster, a little sour but also independent-minded. She had a boyfriend called Onesime, a bus driver, whom she insisted must save $10,000 before she'd marry him. Poor, frustrated Onesime was perpetually $1,000 short.

I thought Napoleon, the second brother, a goof. Like so many boring males I knew, he cared not a jot about anything but sports. Though he wasn't much good on the ice himself, he was an amateur hockey coach, always dreaming of making the big time. The Montreal Canadiens were his gods. Guillaume was the baby of the family, adored by all, at 19 a budding and talented athlete. Promoting Guillaume's career was Napoleon's life ambition.

The head of this brood was Papa Plouffe, a plumber, who seemed to spend most of his time drinking beer with his cronies. Papa was rather pathetic, tired all the time, always leaning on his wife for support.

It was Mama Plouffe who was the heart of the family. Indeed, she wore her own heart on her sleeve, constantly snuffling over the tragedies she encountered in the cheap, paperback novels she read by the dozens. A warm-hearted, sweetly idealistic character, she was the symbol of family unity, the major theme of the television series. The Plouffes never failed to rally: when Papa lost his pay envelope, when Rita once again rejected Ovide, when a cyst was found on Napoleon's lungs. It was the warmth, the concern, the sympathy shown by each family member that attracted me and the many thousands of other viewers.

These days, the characters would probably be labelled stereotypes, the plots considered not politically correct, the drama slow-moving, but at the time, the Plouffes hinted at something intriguing and foreign in my totally WASP world, and I was a devotee for as long as they were on English-language television. But Ovide, Cecile, Guillaume represented far more than just a warm-hearted clan who got themselves into hilarious scrapes. It was the only taste of Québécois culture I ever remember experiencing during my school years: the two solitudes of French and English were rigidly in place. Later, I understood a nation could develop into a dysfunctional family, addicted to constant arguing and recriminations. Back then, though, I simply enjoyed the big-hearted, bickering Plouffes and all trials they underwent together.

I

Hammurabi, the king of Babylonia from about 1792–1750 BC, is remembered by history for his system of rules and regulations, the first such body of law discovered in its entirety. The Code of Hammurabi makes it very clear the patriarchal family had already been firmly established 2,000 years before the birth of Christ. As the historian Gerda Lerner puts it, "Having established patriarchy as the foundation of the family and the state, it appeared immutable and became the very definition of social order. To challenge it was both ludicrous and profoundly threatening."[162] This would prove to be a leitmotif of family life for centuries to come.

Under the Hammurabic Code, the male head of the house held absolute authority over his children; they were regarded as his private property. He could have them put to death; he arranged their marriages; if they were female, he could consecrate them to a life of virginity in some temple. The wife maintained some legal and property rights that could be enforced by her kin, but how limited these were is illustrated by one remarkable section of the code: the head of the household could use his wife and his children as collateral for his debts. If payment was not forthcoming, they would be enslaved to the debtor for a period of three years.[163]

What is important about the Hammurabic Code, as Lerner points out, is not only that the family was a reflection of the authoritarian, paternalistic state but that the state was equally dependent on the family for its stability and ability to govern. Lerner writes, "The metaphor of the patriarchal family as the cell, the basic building block, of the healthy organism of the public community was first expressed in Mesopotamian law. It has been constantly reinforced both in ideology and practice over three millennia."[164]

The family in Ancient Greece was of no less central social importance. Witness the picture on an ancient Greek vase of one contented group. The lovely mother Ariadne watches with pleasure while her little son Oenopion is being bounced on his father's knee. A pert nurse, holding a bouquet of flowers, smiles at the tomfoolery going on. The adoring father is none other than Dionysus, Greek mythology's ultimate party boy. The son of Zeus, Dionysus (also known as Bacchus) was the god of wine and good cheer, of carousing, dancing and singing. His followers, particularly the women, were given to wild, orgiastic worship. That it was deemed necessary the god of sensual pleasure be depicted in a harmonious and respectable household indicates how essential the family was to the ancient Greeks.

In Classical society, the all-consuming preoccupation was how to keep the money in the family. An Athenian girl usually married at the time of menarche, about age 14, and was probably wed to a close relative, an uncle or first cousin, for this was a way of consolidating the family resources. He would be twice her age, partly because he had already spent ten years in military service and partly because there were so few females (many girl babies having been put to death by their fathers). Because her husband was so much older, if she survived childbirth, a woman could expect to become a widow several times over. Again to insure the wealth stayed in the family, her dying husband often dictated whom she would next marry.[165] Simone de Beauvoir saw this passing-down of property as more significant than the mere transfer of material possessions, and interpreted it as a clinging to immortality, no less.

Whether these marriages would be happy or not depended on luck. There did exist an ideal of marriage in ancient Greek society that, as historian Christopher Lasch puts it, "could combine sexual desire and mutual respect. Rather than act as a disruptive force, passion could civilize and democratize social relations."[166] How many women were treated to that ideal is unknown, but they were certainly in the minority. The married state was more likely to be as Plutarch described it: the husband as the sun, a king, a knight, the master; the wife, a mirror reflecting the glory of her husband, his servant, his student, his horse.[167]

Even if a father died leaving no heirs but his daughter, a woman could not escape her role as conveyor of family assets. A woman without a husband was labelled an *epikleros* and required to marry the closest male relative available. This was a rich source of material for Greek comedies, Menander's *The Shield* among them. A household slave returns home from the battlefield with the sad news that his master has been slain. Happily, there also arrives a huge amount of booty, which the dead man had acquired during various battles. His only surviving close relative is his sister, who thus becomes an heiress, but under the laws pertaining to the *epikleroi*, an ugly old uncle can claim her as his bride. Fortunately, the slave is as cunning as he is good-hearted. He dangles the prospect of an even richer *epikleros* in front of the greedy old man, who falls for the trick and renounces his first claim. The sister is saved, at least for the time being.[168]

Interestingly, marriage among the Greek gods, when there was marriage, was not full of the *Sturm und Drang* of earthly unions. Since the family of gods lived in one community on Mount Olympus, the divine bride did not have to leave her childhood home. (Persephone is the exception, which is why her story is of such significance.) Nor did the goddesses, once married, become doormats; Aphrodite, for instance, paid almost no attention to the fact that she had a husband.

The one divinity who was closely linked with marriage was extremely powerful but also a shrew: Hera, who was described as "by far the most beautiful of the immortal goddesses, the glorious daughter of subtle Kronos and of Rhea the Mother, the venerated divinity whom Zeus with his immortal designs made his accomplished and respected wife."[169] Despite these accolades, she was a pretty miserable example of a helpmate and mother. She seldom showed any affection for her children. Most of her time was spent trying to punish the philandering Zeus, as well as anybody involved in his extramarital affairs and intrigues. Burning people alive, turning them into cats, tormenting them with gadflies, delaying a woman's labour in childbirth as long as possible were only a few of the tortures used by Hera to get even. Was it symbolic, perhaps, of how mortal women felt about marriage? Were they lamenting the depressing institution that had been created to subjugate them?

Euripides, in his tragedy *Medea*, sums up the Greek woman's place in the family:

> Surely, of all creatures that have life and will, we women
> Are the most wretched. When for an extravagant sum,
> We have bought a husband, we must then accept him as
> Possessor of our body. This is to aggravate
> Wrong with worse wrong. Then the great question:
> will the man
> We get be bad or good? For women, divorce is not
> Respectable; to repel the man, not possible.
> ... And if in this exacting toil
> We are successful and our husband does not struggle
> Under the marriage yoke, our life is enviable.
> Otherwise death is better....[170]

This is not to say that women always took abuse without a whimper. In mythology, at least, their revenge could be awesome. Take the 50 daughters of Danaus, King of Argos. When the Danaides were forced to marry their cousins against their will, they waited until the husbands were snug in their conjugal beds before they stabbed them to death and cut off their heads.

The ancient Romans paid lip service to the value of the family. Nevertheless, life styles often intervened. Augustus, emperor of Rome from 27 BC–AD 14, for example, faced a dilemma. Decadence was eating away his empire. Sexual promiscuity, lavish dress and jewels, extravagant entertaining were indulged in by the upper class. Not many young people wanted to marry, and those who did, produced few children. Divorce was rampant and the birth rate falling. The family, the very foundation of the Roman state, was crumbling. What was an emperor to do?

Well, he and his clan could set an example. Since Augustus wanted to give the appearance of being the ultimate sober and responsible family man, he took to wearing only plain togas spun by the women in his household. He was always solicitous of his wife Livia, who herself seemed to be the model of wifely obedience. (Never mind that Augustus had been so anxious to marry Livia that he had her obtain a divorce while she was still pregnant by her first husband.) Livia saw to it that the females of the family behaved with decorum; they never, for example, attended a rowdy gladiator match.

Augustus also wanted his subjects to know how much he cared for his offspring. When his youngest grandson died in childhood, both he and Livia made a great show of grief and dedicated a temple statue to him. The emperor could also be brutal if relatives didn't adhere to his family values. His daughter and granddaughter, both named Julia, were exiled when it was revealed each had committed adultery. Augustus even had the younger Julia's baby put to death.

But Augustus had to do more than mount a propaganda campaign if his empire were to be saved. In 18 BC, he convinced the Senate to pass a whole basketful of laws intended to regulate the private lives of his subjects, especially women. Under the new legislation, adultery (by women, of course) was severely punished, often by death or banishment. A neighbour was required to report adulterous activity or else take the risk of being jailed himself. Young people who refused to marry or remained childless were penalized through restrictive inheritance laws. There were also rewards and incentives. A man who married and had three legitimate children (both sexes counted) received political favouritism and his career was suddenly enhanced.

Ironically, given Augustus's old-fashioned ideas, it was the freeborn wife who gained the most. Until that time, a woman had no independence under law whatsoever. In the early years of the Republic, the power (*manus* or hand) of her husband over her was unlimited. He could, for example, murder her without fear of legal reprisal if he caught her in an act of adultery. By the 3rd century BC, a new kind of marriage had been introduced that brought some relief to women. It was known as *sine manu* (without power transferred). A woman's guardianship was retained by her father or his family, not given over to her husband. This meant she kept her inheritance rights as a daughter and therefore could enjoy some independence from her husband. Still, as the historian Ross Shepard Kraemer points out, the system was hardly without conflict. For one thing, a father could force his daughter to divorce and marry someone of his choosing, often for political expediency.[171]

Under Augustus's new rules, if a woman produced the required three healthy babies, she became completely autonomous, free of the guardianship of husband and male relatives. A son or uncle or brother-in-law could no longer dictate how her dowry should be spent, choose her new husband if she were a widow or decide to whom she would leave her inheritance.

Like most family-values campaigns throughout history, Augustus's laws did almost nothing to raise the birth rate, and it's questionable whether the morals of his subjects got any better. But the status of women improved, which probably did more to stabilize the family than any moralizing by an emperor.

II

The family in the Middle Ages wore two distinct and contradictory faces. In the secular world, it was the entity, the household as a whole, that was important; individuals and their silly emotions mattered hardly at all. Marriage was used as an instrument to shore up and enrich family prospects. As historian Lawrence Stone puts it, "... romantic love and lust were strongly condemned as ephemeral and irrational grounds of marriage."[172] From aristocrat to peasant, all marriages were arranged.

At the same time, a religious ideal of the family was evolving. The Church wanted a union of "hearts as well as hearths."[173] While the idea that an engaged couple should be in love was quite foreign to the clerics—love would come after years of struggling to make a life together—both bride and groom should at least give their consent to the union. That in reality, the Church often turned a blind eye to its own teachings, allowing betrothals arranged at five years old, for example, did not mean the sentiment was not preached.

Over centuries, the Church gradually managed to impose the Christian model of marriage as a sacrament, a lifelong, indissoluble merger; the fleshly union came to represent the union of Christ and the Church. Exchanging vows at a wedding was the Church's attempt to impose its control through public ceremony, thereby undermining clandestine, "unblessed" marriages based on promises given in the heat of passion or marriages arranged by the family head entirely for the benefit of the clan's prosperity. However, it was a fierce struggle. It was not until 1563, for example, that the service of a priest in the wedding ceremony was an essential element of a Catholic marriage.[174]

While the ideal of marital consent was a humane step forward, there was still darkness at the heart of Church doctrine. It was entirely centred on the belief that the husband ruled and the wife obeyed. Ephesians 5:22–23 admonished, "Wives, submit yourselves unto your own husbands, as unto the Lord.

For the husband is the head of the wife, even as Christ is the head of the church." A wife's duty, according to the all-male clergy, philosophers and literary moralizers, was "to conform her will perfectly to her husband's."

Of course, this philosophy extended beyond the Church into secular life. The 18th-century legal authority William Blackstone described the status of women under English common law during the Middle Ages thus:

By marriage, the husband and wife are one person in law; that is, the very being or legal existence of the woman is suspended during the marriage, or at least is incorporated and consolidated into that of the husband; under whose wing, protection, and *cover* she performs every thing....[175]

To insure this male-dominated idea of the family prevailed, the legal authorities, both secular and ecclesiastical, encouraged wife-beating. "A good woman and a bad one equally require the stick!" ran an adage at the time, which might have been humourous except it was the basis of most European legal systems. In the 13th century, a French law decreed: "In a number of cases men may be excused for the injuries on their wives, nor should the law intervene. Provided he neither kills nor maims her, it is legal for a man to beat his wife when she wrongs him." The English were no better. Laws of the 14th century allowed a husband "lawful and reasonable correction."[176] No wonder the courts record cases of wives seeking revenge; poisoning or casting wicked spells were not uncommon.

That the absolute legal and doctrinal power of the male householder was a sure-fire recipe for the making of a dysfunctional family is obvious from the literature of the day, particularly the lustful and often hilarious satires. Chaucer, Boccaccio, Rabelais celebrate the refusal of wives to demurely accept their lot in life. A husband's jealousy and ineptitude are the unsavoury grist for these writers' mills. The female characters scold, nag and even beat their husbands. They spend the household funds on expensive, fancy dresses. They encourage young lovers. Indeed, the cuckolded husband, wearing absurd and faintly obscene horns on his head, could be considered the ridiculous mascot of the High Middle Ages.

Nowhere is the contradictory attitude towards marriage exposed so deliciously than in "The Wife of Bath," one of Chaucer's *Canterbury Tales*. She is anything but the ideal wife—modest, faithful, long-suffering—pictured by the moral arbiters of the time. She is lustful, manipulative, witty, bossy, clever, an opinionated woman who doesn't hesitate to interpret Church doctrine for herself, especially as it applies to virginity and marriage.

In her youth, she was, she says, "stubborn and strong and jolly as a bird," with a taste for sweet wine and a love of dance. Her career as wife to five husbands, now all dead, has had its ups and downs. For the Wife of Bath, marriage has been one long, often ferocious war, but there's no question she loves the battle, indeed wallows in it. Her first three husbands were older than she—she married them for their money—and she had no trouble keeping them in line.

> Poor dears! I tortured them without remorse,
> For I could bite and whinny like a horse....

The fourth husband was something of a rotter, a party boy who kept a "paramour." The Wife didn't hesitate to fight back. "And God and he alone can say how grim/How many were the ways I tortured him." He was carried off to his maker pretty quickly.

It was the fifth husband—"The one I took for love and not for wealth"—with whom she struggled almost to the death. Despite her infatuation with handsome Johnny, the Wife refused to curb her carousing; she admits she loved a good time. "I went off gadding as I had before/From house to house, however much he swore." Johnny's answer was to pile up volume upon volume of the great misogynist writers of the ages and then read aloud their platitudes of female wickedness. This almost drove the Wife of Bath mad.

> The torture in my heart? It reached the top.
> And when I saw that he would never stop
> Reading this cursed book, all night no doubt,
> I suddenly grabbed and tore three pages out
> Where he was reading, at the very place,
> And fisted such a buffet in his face
> That backwards down into the fire he fell.

Johnny, perhaps understandably, responded by hitting the Wife on the head with such a blow she became partially deaf. Yet the battle seems to have cleared the air; the couple makes up, the Wife of Bath mended her partying ways and became as "kind as any wife." It's clear, though, she emerges as the winner, at least in her mind.

He gave the bridle over to my hand,
Gave me the government of house and land,
Of tongue and fist, indeed of all he'd got.
I made him burn that book upon the spot.
And when I'd mastered him, and out of deadlock
Secured myself the sovereignty of wedlock
And when he said, 'My own and truest wife,
Do as you please for all the rest of life,
But guard your honour and my good estate,'
From that day forward there was no debate.[177]

There was another justice of sorts. Even though her handsome Johnny was 20 years younger, the Wife of Bath outlived him, probably, judging from her sprightliness, by many years.

III

The 16th-century manor house was usually overflowing. Mother, father, children, cousins, friends, boarders, travellers, indentured apprentices, servants, farm hands were all considered part of the family.[178] The mortality rate among young adults was so high—mothers died in childbirth, fathers from an unimaginable number of diseases, accidents and battles—that marriages seldom lasted longer than two decades; nine to 12 years was more the norm. Finding a substitute mate for widows and widowers as quickly as possible became the pressing business of every family member. The result was that households, at every level of society, were often a crazy quilt of stepfathers and stepmothers, never mind a whole slew of stepchildren. Since there was so little privacy in houses, great or small, this horde lived mostly on top of one another.

This overflowing vessel was commanded with absolute authority by the patriarchal captain, his wife serving as a kind of first officer, subordinate to no one except him. Involuntarily thrown together, they may or may not have been fond of each other. It didn't matter much as long as the two of them kept the ship afloat.

The work of two famous Renaissance artists, the Belgian Frans Hals and the Flemish painter Peter Paul Rubens, signals the two quite contrary ideas of love and marriage that sat at the centre of three centuries of debate in the early-modern era.

Between 1650–1652, Hals painted two companion portraits, one of

Stephanus Geraerdts and the other of his bride Isabella Coymans. They are probably wearing their marriage finery, perhaps just back from the wedding feast. He is oozing with self-satisfaction; he has just landed himself the golden goose, the daughter of a wealthy family. Only one hand is ungloved, and it is extended greedily towards his young wife, who holds out a rose to him, a symbol of her dowry. There is little passion in his eyes. He hasn't even taken off his cloak; perhaps he's off to his paramour before he inaugurates his conjugal bed. She has a coy, mocking look, as though she already knows her new master will be anything but faithful to her. Maybe she will collect her own lovers. It's a beautifully rendered illustration of loveless marriage forged entirely for reasons of property.

The Rubens masterpiece, painted about 1633, is entitled *Rubens, his wife Helena Fourment and her first-born*. The artist gazes on his wife with an erotic devotion so intense it seems excessive. For her part, Helena looks with amazing tenderness at her first-born, who obviously adores his mother. She is holding a string attached to the toddler, and Rubens gently touches her hand, as though he hesitates to interfere in the mother-son communion but is slightly resentful he is being excluded. It is a moving portrait of great family love.

Marriage was a state most people aspired to, "a highly privileged status," as historian John R. Gillis puts it. His research indicates that in 16th-century England, married couples made up no more than 30 percent of the population. A good ten percent, both peasants and aristocrats, were never able to collect enough wealth to set up a household appropriate to their status and therefore remained single forever.[179]

In the towns, young people were held hostage to the brutal cycles of an emerging industrial economy; pauperism, even starvation, constantly lurked at the door. "Such a prospect must have been," as historian Olwen Hufton writes, "a powerful deterrent to and perhaps the ultimate corrosive of a lasting human relationship."[180] In his diary written in the mid-18th century, the rector of Bletchley described the fate of peasants in his parish:

Will Wood junior, wants to be married to Henry Travel's Daughter, the prettiest Girl in the Parish, being uneasy with his grandmother [who can't afford to settle him].... The Times are so hard, small farms so difficult to be met with, the spirit of inclosing and accumulating Farms together, making it very difficult for young people to marry, as was used [to be]....[181]

When young people did settle down, they were required to adjust their behaviour to suit their new status and responsibility. According to the Church, an aura of holiness permeated the Renaissance household. For Catholics, the model was the Holy Family: Joseph, Mary and Jesus. After the Counter-Reformation, the Church abandoned the insidious comparisons between the celibate and married states. While virginity, both for men and women, was still esteemed, family life was now considered as holy. The fat, healthy baby, his young, charming mother and his saintly grandmother became the predominant family motif. For centuries, Saint Joseph, the elderly, asexual father, had played a minor role, but from the 15th century onwards, a cult evolved around him. He became the "virtuous carpenter and earthly father who taught Christ his craft and saved the Virgin Mary from earthly infamy."[182] The family was established as a comfortable nest of "solace and succor" for each of its members.

In Protestant countries the Holy Family took the form of an artisan's establishment, with the master craftsman in charge, his sons as apprentices and his wife and daughters making sure food was on the table and the living area was clean and comfortable, as well as managing the finances of both household and business.[183]

Always lurking over all Christian households, however, was the example of the first family and the Garden of Eden. Everyone knew what happened when the "natural" power structure was bent askew, when the husband was not vigilant or strong enough: frivolous Eve teamed up with the Devil to tempt Adam with the fatal apple. Robert Abbot, one of the moralizers of the time, emphasized the importance of the first family:

You know that the first government that ever was in this world was in a family; and in the first disorder that ever was in the world was in a family; and all the disorders that ever fell out since, sprung from families. If families had been better, Churches and Common-Wealths all along had prospered.[184]

Given that the dominant idea that emerged during the Reformation was that matrimony was man's normal state and celibacy abnormal, one might have assumed a woman's status in marriage would have improved. She no longer had to compete with the Virgin Mary as society's ideal; she was no longer "second-best."[185] And yet historian Lawrence Stone maintains that, in the 16th and 17th centuries, the power of the male head of the household over his wife and children became even greater than during the Middle Ages.[186] One reason for this was the gloomy, cockamamie views of womankind held by Reformation philosophers—Martin Luther, for example: "Men have broad shoulders and narrow hips, and accordingly they possess intelligence. Women have narrow shoulders and broad hips. Women ought to stay at home; the way they were created indicates this, for they have broad hips and a wide fundament to sit upon, keep house and bear and raise children."[186a] But it took a poet to pithily sum up the reformed churches' emphasis on patriarchy. In the mid-17th century, John Milton wrote, "He for God only, she for God in him."[187]

The husband, therefore, remained firmly on his throne, although he was now portrayed as an enlightened despot. He was to watch over the behaviour of his flighty, irresponsible wife, lecture her, reprimand her, but always with kindness. The popular advice manual *A Godly Form of Householde Government*, reprinted five times between 1598 and 1630, succinctly outlined this new approach:

A wise husband and one that seeketh to live in quiet with his wife, must observe these three rules. Often to admonish: seldome to reprove and never to smite her. The husband is also to understand, that as God created the woman, not of the head and so equal in authority with her husband: so also he created her not of Adam's foot, that she might walk jointly with him, under the conduct and government of her head.[188]

What was considered the ideal and what was reality were, as usual, two quite distinct animals. Restoration comedy, for example, was not only a reaction to sexual Puritanism but to the patriarchal family as well. The swaggering, sneering gallant of the period hated the very idea of marriage. As the playwright William Wycherley (1640–1716) wrote, "A spouse I do hate for either's she's false or she's jealous." Men of the time seemed to live in terror of either being cuckolded themselves or having their own affairs discovered by a jealous wife. The main theme of these misogynist comedies, however, was the hypocrisy and unhappiness that came with arranged marriages.

In fact, as the 17th century progressed and the concept of individualism developed, young people were given far more freedom to choose their mate. Affection and fidelity in marriage became more common, and sexual gratification something not unheard of. The family itself changed, especially among the upper classes, becoming smaller, more insular, more inward-looking, more nuclear. As political philosophers such as John Locke and Thomas Hobbes came to define civil society as a social contract between a sovereign and subjects, so, too, was marriage to be considered a contractual relationship based on "common interest and property." Both mother and father were to share parental authority over the children, and the authority of both the husband and wife over each other was also to be acknowledged. Neverthe-less, when there was disagreement between them, the old rules held. John Locke wrote that when "the last determination—i.e., the rule—should be placed somewhere, it naturally falls to the man's share, as the abler and the stronger."[189]

The idea that the female was inferior to the male was so deeply embedded in Western Europe's collective psyche that partnership in marriage was simply outside rational discussion. Eighteenth-century philosophers did not stop to consider the great paradox staring them in the face. Marriage, they said, must be a voluntary contract between two individuals, yet at its heart lay the submission of the wife. This, they said, was the natural order of things. In Rousseau's *La Nouvelle Héloïse*, a tutor offers Sophie the following advice: "In becoming your husband, Emile became your master. Your place is to obey, as nature intended. When a woman is like Sophie, however, it is good for the man to be guided by her. This, too, is a law of nature."

If you were not deemed "a woman like Sophie," you were left at the mercy of what was often a selfish, domineering and irrational husband. From the court and other records in the archives of the diocese of Cambrai in North-ern France comes an 18th-century cry of abuse and unhappiness. Out of these documents emerges a composite profile of the worst kind of husband. He was "an army officer with expensive tastes, a disinclination for work or business, with a pistol in his drawer and expensive horse in the stable."[190] With one complaint uttered by his long-suffering wife, he was ready to flee, either to the arms of his mistress or to the wine cellars and his companions at the cabaret. The notion of equality in marriage was a long way off.

IV

Three women novelists tell everything about the state of marriage in the early part of the 19th century. Mme de Staël in her 1802 book *Delphine*: "A woman's fate has run out when she fails to marry the man she loves. Society allows women only one hope when the lots are drawn and when one has lost, that is the end of it." Jane Austen in *Pride and Prejudice,* published in

1813: "Without thinking highly either of men or of matrimony, marriage had always been her object; it was the only honourable provision for well-educated young women of small fortune, and however uncertain of giving happiness, must be their pleasantest preservation from want." George Sand in her 1832 book *Indiana*: "In marrying Delmare she had only changed masters; in coming to live at Lagny she had only changed prisons and places of solitude. She did not love her husband, perhaps only because she was told it was her duty to love him...."

In the Victorian era, that roll of the dice called marriage became even more crucial to a woman's well-being and survival; the home and the family were her only *raisons d'être*. "Being married gives one one's position, which nothing else can," wrote Queen Victoria to her daughter in 1858, by which she meant that any husband was better than none.[191]

It all had to do with economics. As the Industrial Revolution took hold and cottage industries were swallowed by huge factories, the home as a separate economic unit was no more. As prosperity came to the bourgeoisie, lifestyles changed. Garden suburbs flourished, homes were built that were more palatial and servants were hired by the half-dozen. The middle-class father went off to earn his pay cheque in the new dog-eat-dog world while the mother (with the help of the cook and washing woman) created a private nest of comfort and peace, a bulwark against hostility and competitiveness. As the century progressed, the distance between these two worlds, the separate spheres, yawned into a gaping abyss.

In 1854, Coventry Patmore wrote a popular poem sentimentalizing a wife as "The Angel in the House," a selfless creature who devoted herself to pleasing her husband and caring for her children. A few lines give the flavour:

> But, ten times more than ten times all,
>   She loves him for his love of her.
> How happy 'tis he seems to see
>   In her that utter loveliness
> Which she, for his sake, longs to be![192]

A near-saint she may have been, but she certainly wasn't the boss. In 1880, Pope Leo XIII reaffirmed the doctrine of paternal dominance in the encyclical *Arcanum*: "The man is the head of the woman. As Christ is the head of the Church." Lord Tennyson put a more flowery spin on it:

Man for the field and woman for the hearth:
Man for the sword and for the needle she:
Man with the head and woman with the heart:
Man to command and woman to obey;
All else confusion.[193]

In most European countries and in North America, a woman continued to be a legal nonentity, in the same category as children or imbeciles. She was barred from making a legal contract, serving as a witness in court or initiating lawsuits. All her property, her inheritance, her jewels, even her pay cheque if there were one, was considered her husband's property. The husband could dictate where the family lived, even if he decided on moving to darkest Africa. He could forbid his wife from working for wages if he felt like it. Canada's first female lawyer Clara Brett Martin described Victorian marriage as a "suspension of the independent existence of the wife, and an absorption by the husband of the woman's person and all her belonging...."[194] She had almost no legal recourse against a cruel and abusive husband.

At the same time women were becoming home-centred, they were receiving more formal education. They had, after all, to raise sons equipped to take their proper place in society. This created a paradox—at the moment when they were supposed to be utterly devoted to the family unit, women began to see themselves more as individuals with their own intrinsic worth.[195] They began to fight back against marital tyranny, even if only in their own domestic domain. In many households, they controlled the family budget, often in an iron-fisted, mean-spirited way. British working-class men in particular got into the habit of giving their pay envelopes, often unopened, to their wives, who handed back their pocket money. By using their seductive charm or through sheer force of personality, the angels of the hearth manipulated or bullied their men. They used sex as weapon against errant husbands, sometimes denying their husbands pleasure for their entire married life. Some women were labelled hysterics and turned themselves into invalids, languishing in bed or on the chaise lounge in a lie-down strike that could go on for years.[196]

In Britain, housewives lined up at Mudie's Select Circulating Library to borrow bestsellers, many of which featured heroines chopping up their husbands. As historian Joan Perkin points out, in potboilers such as *Lady Audley's Secret* or *Cometh Up as a Flower,* both written by women in the 1860s, the female protagonists "went off the rails, [and] invariably came to a bad end, but sinners got a good run for their money and were rarely wholly unattractive characters."[197]

That women were beginning to deeply resent not the family itself but the power imbalance contained within it is reflected in an 1838 editorial in *The Advocate,* the voice of the American Female Moral Reform Society:

A portion of the inhabitants of this favored land are groaning under a despotism, which seems to be modeled precisely after that of the Autocrat of Russia.... We allude to the tyranny exercised in the HOME department, where lordly man 'clothed with a little brief authority,' rules his trembling subjects with a rod of iron, conscious of entire impunity, and exalting in his fancied superiority....

Instead of regarding his wife as a help-mate for him, an equal sharer in his joys and sorrows, he looks upon her as a useful article of furniture, which is valuable only for the benefit derived from it, but which may be thrown aside at pleasure.[198]

During the 19th century, a head of steam was being built up over the obviously inequitable position of the "adored mother" in the family. As a result, married women's legal status dramatically improved. In the United States between 1869 and 1887, some 33 states granted married women control over their own wages and savings. In some progressive places, New York State, for example, women became joint guardians with their husbands of the children.[199] In England, after a long struggle, the 1882 Married Women's Property Act was passed, which gave the wife legal title to "all real and personal property which belonged to her at the time of marriage or was acquired later." In Canada, Ontario passed a similar law in 1884, and other provinces followed suit. France and other countries using the Napoleonic Code were more backward, but by 1881, French women were at least able to deposit money in a bank, even though they were forbidden to withdraw it without their husbands' consent.[200]

It was primarily the New Women who pressured and bullied and finally convinced the politicians, all men, to make these legislative changes. Though far from solving all problems, these reforms remain among the greatest achievements of the First Wave feminist movement. But it was a man who dramatically laid bare the discontent festering at "that sacred place, that vestal temple," the family hearth.

When the Norwegian playwright Henrik Ibsen's *A Doll's House* was first performed in 1879, it "exploded like a bomb into contemporary life."[201] The debate that it fuelled raged across Europe and North America for decades. Its basic idea—that a husband was not preordained to be the king of the castle—was the passionate stuff of books and magazine articles, sermons from the pulpit, public meetings and, most dangerous, according to critics, family arguments. "It is a miracle," said one Norwegian feminist.

A Doll's House is the story of upwardly mobile lawyer Torvald Helmer and his charming, childlike wife Nora. He is ridiculously patronizing towards her, forever referring to her as his twittering skylark, his little squirrel, his squander-bird. "My little songbird mustn't droop her wings," he says.

Some years before, Nora, without telling her husband, had borrowed a rather large sum so that Torvald, then seriously ill, could recuperate in the sunnier clime of Italy. Now Nora is being blackmailed by the money-lender, who finally exposes her. Her husband is predictably horrified. "Oh, what a dreadful awakening! For eight whole years—she who was my joy and pride—a hypocrite, a liar—worse, worse, a criminal! Oh, the hideousness of it! Shame on you, shame!"

These dramatic events awaken Nora in a most astonishing way. She arrives at the conclusion that she is a complete nonentity, her marriage a lie. She tells Torvald, "You've always been very kind to me. But our home has never been anything but a playroom. I've been your doll-wife, just as I used to be papa's doll-child. And the children have been my dolls." A transformed Nora not only takes a courageous moral stand but follows through with definite action, something Torvald would never have been brave or perhaps foolhardy enough to do. She is determined to leave her husband and three children and, without resources, face a world she knows is hostile and difficult. She tosses her husband the words that will ring down through the next century: "I believe that I am first and foremost a human being, like you—or anyway, that I must try to become one."[201a]

V

From time immemorial, the family was regarded as an immutable institution based on the Biblical truth of Adam and Eve, husband as the head, wife as helpmate, children as subordinates. The Victorians were therefore startled when, in mid-century, this supposedly self-evident truth began to be seriously challenged. Over time, the philosophers hypothesized, the family took on different configurations, had different purposes, in other words possessed a unique history all its own.

J. J. Bachofen started the controversy with the publication of *Das Mutterrecht*

(*Mother Right*) in 1861. Influenced by Charles Darwin, he saw society as evolving from barbarism to a modern civilization. Early on, the matriarchy had dominated—"At the lowest, darkest stage of human existence [mother-child love was] the only light in the moral darkness"[202]—but it was overwhelmed by patriarchy, which he equated with superior religious and political thought.

In his *Origins of the Family, Private Property and the State* (1884), Friedrich Engels advanced these ideas further. He wrote, "One of the most absurd of the ideas that the Enlightenment has left us is that woman, at the inception of society, was man's slave. Among all the savage tribes and all barbarian peoples of the inferior or middling stage and even among some of the higher stage, women are not only free but highly respected."[203]

But it had been Karl Marx, writing 40 years earlier, who had hit the nail directly on the head. Allow a woman her rightful place in the labour market, pay her a decent wage, provide her with equitable working conditions and she would surely become emancipated. That is exactly what has been happening, slowly but surely, as the 20th century evolves. In the process, as Marx predicted, the traditional family has taken an awful beating.

By the turn of the 19th century, marriage had already lost favour with at least a small segment of society. Many a well-educated, career-oriented New Woman wanted nothing to do with it. For the British suffragette Christabel Pankhurst, female celibacy was the only way of combating "sexual slavery"; to her, marriage meant venereal disease, disgrace, forced sex and unwanted pregnancies.

Political revolutionaries such as Emma Goldman were even more outspoken. For her, "the family, the home, even at best they crush the individual, the man, the woman and above all, the child."[204] Yet she had always wanted a "nest" of her own. How was she to express her great love for Ben Reitman if not by setting up house for him? She would create a new, modern type of family, entirely free of conjugal strife, by establishing a communal household. In June 1913, she and five other people, including her lover Ben, moved into 74 West 119th Street, New York City. The noble experiment ended pretty quickly, though, when only months later, Reitman's mother moved in with them. Wrote Goldman:

Ben had started again the old plaint about his mother. I listened in silence for a while, and then something snapped in me.... In blind fury I picked up a chair and hurled it at him. It whirled though space and came crashing down at his feet.

He made a step towards me, then stopped and stared at me in wonder and fright.

'Enough!' I cried, beside myself with pain and anger. 'I've had enough of you and your mother. Go, take her away—today, this very hour!'

He walked out without a word.[205]

During World War I, many women found themselves living without men for the first time in their lives. Armed with government cheques paid to soldiers' dependents, most found they could manage quite well, thank you, and this gave them a real sense of self-worth. Yet the end of the war saw an astonishing regrouping, a strengthening of family life. The conflagration had been so appalling, soldiers had faced such unmentionable horror to protect their loved ones, that quiet domesticity centred around a devoted and loving wife seemed the only fitting reward.

Throughout the Western world, propaganda campaigns were launched to convince women that marriage and career mixed as well as oil and water. Magazine articles and short stories, newspaper reports all set out to convince the female that she would find her bliss only in the kitchen. Government initiatives such as Britain's National Baby Week were designed to make the working mom feel as guilty as possible, never mind that she might be the sole breadwinner.[206]

Perhaps not surprisingly, women who had made gains in the workplace immediately retrenched. A female executive expressed the accepted wisdom in the Canadian Bankers Association's journal: "When the opportunity offers, the most successful banking women amongst us will cheerfully retire to her own hearthstone, preferring the love of a husband and little children to thousands a year and a seat in the council of the mighty!"[207] And given that most women in the Western world, especially in the working class, were paid such abysmally low salaries, getting married did often mean a step up in the world.

But the post-war family in the Western world was far different than the Victorian model. For one thing, it was much smaller. Births had been declining for 100 years; by 1900, the birth rate was half that of 1800.[208] In the 1920s and '30s, it dropped even further. The household itself shrank dramatically. Gone were the numerous servants, the second cousins, the visiting friends that had dominated Victorian, middle-class domesticity. Mother, father and three children at the most—that was it.

Couples came to expect a great deal out of marriage. Sexual enjoyment, camaraderie, spiritual union and simple good fun were now part of the conjugal landscape. As historian Nancy F. Cott put it, family life was touted as "becoming a specialized site for emotional intimacy, personal and sexual expression, and nurture among husband, wife and a small number of children."[209] However, marriage might be deeply rooted in love, but at the core remained the same old patriarchal structure. Equality had not yet reared its ugly head. "Men are God's trees; women are his flowers" was the motto of a 1920s American women's club, by which was meant that men were encouraged to seek power and achievement, ladies to cultivate charm and improve themselves.

In 1929, Diana Rubin, Radcliffe-educated, ambitious and pretty, married the intellectual Lionel Trilling. Although both were somewhat neurotic with deep psychological problems, the union proved a fairly successful one. He became a renowned literary critic and she a reviewer of books for *Nation* and *The Partisan Review*. Yet theirs was far from an equal partnership. In her 1993 autobiography *The Beginning of the Journey*, Diana writes perceptively of women of her generation:

Whatever their pretense of emancipation the women of our acquaintance exercised only such control of their lives as their husbands granted them. They were ingenious indeed in contriving new ways to indulge the men to whom they were married, accommodate their eccentricities, subordinate themselves to them. They went nowhere that their husbands did not want them to go and did nothing that their husbands did not want them to do. Had their husbands not wanted them to work, they would not have worked—this was true of me and of all my married women friends.[210]

Women certainly did their part in the struggle, particularly as munitions workers during World War II. Yet just as in the previous war, once the soldiers came home, women returned *en masse* to domesticity. In November 1949, an article appeared in Canada's *Saturday Night* magazine with the blunt headline "Careers and Marriage Don't Mix." The anonymous author begins her article, "A 'FOR RENT' sign hangs on my office door. It is the symbol of a decision. I would like to shout from the roof tops that the married woman cannot have both a career and a happy husband."

Nobody raised an eyebrow when Mamie Eisenhower, the wife of the president of the United States, explained in an interview that her recipe for a happy marriage was to recognize the husband as "the head of the house." "I never told him anything," she explained. "He told me."[211]

The problem was that being stuck out in the suburbs with a bunch of kids and a humdrum routine was not exactly the paradise many women envisioned. The headlines in the all-powerful ladies magazines gave an indication all was not well in Suburbia: "Why You Should Never Quarrel with Your Husband," "Why You Bore Your Husband," "How 'Victim' Wives Spoil Their Marriages," "Are You Jealous of Your Husband's Job?" Whatever the problems facing matrimony and the family, it was unquestionably entirely the woman's fault. Dr. Marion Hilliard, a regular advice-giver in the Canadian magazine *Chatelaine*, lectured her readers:

The burden of creating a happy marriage falls mainly on the wife. A man's life is much more difficult than a woman's, full of the groaning strain of responsibility and the lonely and often fruitless search for pride in himself. A cheerful and contented woman at home, even one who must often pretend gaiety, gives a man enough confidence to believe he can lick the universe. I'm certain that the woman who enriches her husband with her admiration and her ready response gets her reward on earth, from her husband.[212]

When the sexual revolution finally exploded in the mid-1960s, marriage came under startling attack. In the 1970s, *Playboy* magazine called it a "financial trap." Better to spend one's hard-earned wages on fancy sports cars or golf vacations rather than become one of the "sorry, regimented husbands trudging down every woman-dominated street in this woman-dominated land."[213] In her bestselling *Sex and the Single Girl*, Helen Gurley Brown also slammed matrimony. "Marriage," she wrote, "is insurance for the *worst* years of your life. During the best years you don't need a husband."[214]

To some degree, this propaganda worked. In 1960, the marital index—the probability that a person would marry before age 50—was 90 percent in all Western countries. By the mid-1980s, it ranged between 48 and 66 percent, and was falling sharply.[215]

Part of the reason for this phenomenon was that women were working in record numbers outside the home. As American demographer Paul Glick put it, "Women who enter the marketplace gain greater confidence, expand their social circles independent of their husbands, taste independence and are less easy to satisfy and more likely to divorce."[216]

Nowhere is the new economic, demographic and technological reality reflected most dramatically than in the family. It is undergoing a profound metamorphosis. In 1981, the traditional formation—mother, father and kids—made up 55 percent of the population in Canada. By 1995, that figure had dropped an amazing 11 points to 44.5 percent. Similar astonishing figures have been reported in countries throughout the Western world. Family formations are now a grab bag of married without children, single mothers and fathers, common-law couples with or without children. In 1981, living-together arrangements made up six percent of the population; by 1995, such relationships had jumped to 12 percent.[217]

Within marriage itself, the relationship between spouses is also experiencing a remarkable transformation. While women still do most of the housework and child care, there's hope these burdens are lightening. Michael Ulmer, a Canadian newspaper columnist, reflects the status of marriage, circa 1995: "I possess some basic housekeeping skills. While our children invariably cry out for their mother's and not my touch in the middle of night, I bring as much to the family table as she does. The kicker is, I have made myself self-sufficient but I remain dependent. I don't need my wife to live, I need her to make living worthwhile."[218]

Ursula

We thought of Princess Grace or Deborah Kerr, she was so poised, so elegant. Her drawl was exotically Southern, like Vivien Leigh's in *Gone With The Wind*. Her wardrobe was so sophisticated as to be entirely out of our league. There was talk that she was already engaged to a man much older than herself who wore dark sunglasses. She was even seen driving a BMW to school.

Ursula Koehnke *was* more worldly than we were. She had spent her early teenage years in Nashville, Tennessee, immersed in the cliquish sorority life that dominated the high-school scene there. But her maturity, expressed as a calmness, a fatalism unusual for someone so young, sprang from a darker source.

Ursula is not sure where her mother Margarethe and her father, Hans Koehnke, met, but there were stories of how they made love on a park bench. It must have been quite a sight, since both were so extraordinarily beautiful. Says Ursula, "When the two of them walked around together, they practically took your breath away because they were so stunning." Her mother had lovely, dark brown hair, pronounced classical features and the striking green eyes that Ursula inherited. Her father was tall, over six feet, with a masculine build, altogether movie-star handsome.

Margarethe and Hans were married in 1933, though not without opposition from his family. The Koehnkes didn't feel Margarethe's family was good enough for their son. They were a family of wealthy business people; Margarethe's father, on the other hand, was a weaver from Goerlitz. Hans's father, who had been an executive in a railroad-manufacturing business and made a lot of money, suffered a heart attack and died when he was only in his forties. Hans's mother was an elegant woman, a fashion plate, who wore her hair piled on top of her head, but Ursula also remembers her grandmother as being cold and stern, the type who gave you handkerchiefs for Christmas and expected you to be grateful. Her husband had left enough of an inheritance that she didn't have to go out to work, but the family had to be careful with their money. Hans had badly wanted to become a doctor, but his mother insisted she could support him for only a couple of years at business school. For his entire life, Hans regretted he hadn't gone to university; as successful as he would become, he always felt it had held him back.

He was hired by Siemens & Halske, the huge German electrical concern, and shortly after his marriage, he was assigned to the company's branch in Ireland and then in Kanpur, India, where Ursula's sister Eva was born. But it was the booming automobile industry that fascinated the ambitious Hans Koehnke. The family settled in Steyr, where Hans became an up-and-coming executive in a car factory there and where the Koehnkes' second child Peter was born.

When the war began, Hans was 39 years old, and had been diagnosed with a tubercular spot on his lungs. Instead of serving in active duty, he was sent to Poland to manage a munitions factory. Margarethe, along with Eva and Peter, joined him there. In 1942, Margarethe returned to Germany, to her hometown of Goerlitz, to give birth to her last child, Ursula.

It was a distressing time for the family. Hans was not a Nazi, and yet the plant he managed depended on the forced labour of Jews, who were brought each morning from a nearby concentration camp. They would arrive half frozen, and one of the first things Hans did was to install hot baths. It was both a humanitarian and practical gesture: the workers' hands were so numb, they couldn't operate the factory machinery.

During this time, Margarethe first suffered from the heart and circulation problems that would plague her for the rest of her life. "I don't remember my mother being well during all the time I was growing up," says Ursula. "There was always something wrong with her, and she was often quite seriously ill."

As the war drew to its ghastly close, the Koehnkes fled to East Germany. Ursula has memories of the family crammed in cattle cars, being deloused in the ugly Quonset huts that served as immigration depots, of herself as a four-year-old breaking out in a rash, having all her hair shaved off, the kids calling her a boy. The entire family suffered from malnutrition; Hans weighed 123 pounds. Peter came down with typhoid fever and Margarethe was terribly ill, almost unable to go on.

In 1949, the Koehnkes settled in Frankfurt. These are Ursula's happiest childhood memories. They found a house in a pleasant suburb, Ursula began school, which she loved, and although, like most Germans immediately after the war, the Koehnkes had very little money, life took on some normalcy. "I know we were extremely poor because one day my shoes were taken to the cobbler's and I had to go to school without them. That was probably the worst school day of my life. But my mother had a wonderful way of making the best of what she had. There was always linen on the table, and flowers and some good silver." There was also a cleaning lady who came in twice a week, and a seamstress to make the family's clothes. No matter the deprivations, it was evident the Koehnkes were used to being part of the upper class.

There was also a dark side to the family. Hans travelled a great deal in his job. "My mother was very unhappy," says Ursula. "And she was often ill.... And my father had a very bad temper, so that side of him was not much fun."

Hans eventually ended up as a manager for a car manufacturer, but eventually the company went bankrupt. By that time, though, Margarethe was looking for something more. For one thing, the Koehnkes' marriage was in bad shape. She had discovered Hans had been having an affair with his secretary. "It had gone on for some time," says Ursula. "She was not an attractive woman, so I don't know what the appeal was.... There were a lot of tears, a lot of arguing, but for some reason, they never divorced." Instead, although both were close to 50, they decided to emigrate.

Margarethe had always had a philosophic, religious side to her—she liked to read and write poetry—and in the 1940s, she had been attracted to the evangelist and reformist Church of Christ. The Koehnkes joined the church in Frankfurt and, through that connection, they hosted a young couple from Tennessee who were touring Germany. The Americans promised the Koehnkes that the Nashville Church of Christ would sponsor them if they decided to emigrate to Tennessee.

The idea was appealing for several reasons. Eva, the Koehnkes' eldest daughter, had been working as a secretary at the U.S. army base and had fallen in love with an American GI. He was from Indianapolis, but after they were married, they settled in Nashville. Hans and Margarethe liked the idea of being close to Eva, whom they felt had been neglected during the war. In addition, the Koehnkes never stopped worrying about the aggressive intent of the Soviet Union. They were convinced another war in Europe was a real possibility. In January 1954, with only a small sum of money and a few precious heirlooms, they set sail for New York. Ursula was 12, her brother Peter, 14.

The United States was not what they had expected. "The train ride into the South was shocking," recalls Ursula. "Even though, after the war in Germany, we had seen bombed-out buildings and pretty sad living conditions, we saw nothing like the kind of poverty we saw from the train window."

The family felt even more dejected when they arrived in Nashville. The accommodation provided for them by the church was in a run-down part of the city, the top floor—two small bedrooms and a living room—of a two-storey house owned by teetotalling Seventh Day Adventists.

The Koehnkes also found it difficult to deal with the bigotry deeply embedded in their adopted society. Black Americans, still confined to the back of the bus, were the most obvious victims, but German immigrants also came in for their share of racial taunts. Recalls Ursula, "My mother said she knew every time a Nazi movie was on TV, because the next day at the grocery-store checkout counter, she'd experience some sort of hostility, discrimination." Life was hard for Margarethe in other ways. For the first time in her life, she had to work, first as a seamstress and then as a lab assistant at Vanderbilt University.

One of the reasons Hans had agreed to move to Tennessee was he had been promised a job with a scrap-dealer—even then, he could see a fortune could be made in recycling—but when he arrived, the company was laying off employees. A newly arrived German immigrant was certainly not going to be hired in their place. Hans worked as a gardener, then as a mechanic repairing gasoline pumps. Finally, in 1959, he landed an administrative position with Kerrigan Ironworks, an outfit that manufactured ornamental iron gates. The family's standard of living shot up dramatically. They moved to a classier part of town, into an apartment in one of the grand, old houses on Kensington Place near Vanderbilt University.

Meanwhile, Ursula had been making her own way in the hostile, new environment. "I think I was very depressed at first, not only living in that run-down part of town that was so foreign to me but also not having the language. I would come home from school and cry because I didn't understand what the homework was. I had to sink or swim, and ultimately, I learned how to swim, but it was very, very hard for me."

The move to a better part of town, however, did wonders for her morale. She quickly became a classic Tennessee belle. Even at the junior high-school level, Grades 7 to 9, sororities were the centre of social life. The young girls were called sub debs; Ursula, tall and elegant for her age, and charming—"I quickly learned to become Miss Personality," she says—was obviously meant to be one of them.

At West End High, attended mostly by upper-middle-class kids, the sorority sisters spent much of their free time washing cars, selling doughnuts, putting on musical comedies, all in aid of raising money for the all-important proms. "It taught these young women a great deal about the kind of organization and volunteer work that they would do in the future," Ursula says. The strain never showed. "We were expected to be pleasant all the time. You had to have a smile on your face no matter what the pain in your heart." It was training for their future roles as society matrons.

When Ursula met her future husband Whayne Quin, a tall, lanky student at Vanderbilt University, she thought he was good-looking enough, but when he asked her out, she flatly turned him down. He was five years older, far too mature and sophisticated for a 16-year-old. A year later, once again out selling sorority doughnuts, Ursula thought of one customer she could count on and she stopped at Whayne's fraternity house. They began dating that day. Says Whayne, "I was fascinated by her European background and her European beauty." The romance would have blossomed right then if Hans Koehnke hadn't made a startling announcement. He had been offered a good job with BMW Canada. The family was moving to Toronto.

It was a great opportunity for Hans, offering far more money and in his area of expertise. Margarethe had never liked the humid Tennessee climate and she was happy to return to a more northerly clime. As well, both Koehnkes enjoyed big, cosmopolitan cities with good restaurants and, as an added bonus, Toronto had a large German émigré population. Ursula, however, fought the move "tooth and nail." By this time, she was 17, just beginning her last year of high school. "You have all sorts of privileges in your senior year. I had great hopes of being a star in the firmament and they were just dashed." She begged her parents to allow her to stay with friends, but they wouldn't hear of it.

The family moved into a brand-new home on Nuffield Drive in Guildwood Village, which was considered one of the most affluent enclaves in Scarborough. In Nashville, Margarethe had finally found a job she liked a great deal, as a translator, German to English and English to French, for a Methodist publication, *The Upper Room*. In Toronto, she continued to edit and translate textbooks. Hans revelled in the social position his new job afforded him. For Ursula, though, the move into a higher class of society didn't matter much. It was a disjointed, disquieting period of her life.

Ontario's school system was quite different from Tennessee's; for one thing, there was a fifth year of high school, the dreaded Grade 13. "I was always playing catch-up in every way. It was very hard," she says.

There were compensations: she made friends readily. Ursula's father sometimes allowed her to drive one of the classy BMWs to school, the clothes she so ably sewed made her a fashion plate compared to the rest of the students and she found a very sophisticated, sexy and, by our terms, wealthy boyfriend. Gunter Aswald[219] was eight years older than Ursula, also a German immigrant and a graduate student of sociology at the University of Toronto who ran his own real-estate agency on the side. Only months after they met, they became engaged. Ursula's parents didn't say much, but they weren't happy about the situation. They thought that at 18, she was still too much of a child to think of marriage.

She, too, wanted to continue her education. "I felt I wanted to marry somebody who had a university education, that was very important to me, and I think for that reason I also wanted to go to university." She chose sociology and philosophy. Social work was perceived as a woman's profession, and Ursula thought vaguely about going into that. As it turned out, she would be the only member of the R. H. King Collegiate graduating class who would have no career outside the home.

Ursula had kept in touch with her old Nashville flame Whayne Quin. When, at Christmas of 1963, she visited her sister, then living on Staten Island, she knew Whayne was visiting *his* sister in New Jersey. Still, she was surprised when he showed up, suitcase in hand, on Eva's doorstep. His nephew had come down with mumps, and Whayne had been ordered out of the house. He claimed he had nowhere else to go.

By this time, Ursula's love affair with Gunter was languishing, and Whayne set out to put an end to it once and for all. During the next few months, he frantically drove back and forth between Charlottesville, where he was studying at the University of Virginia, and Toronto, where Ursula was also at university. At the end of one such visit, as Whayne got ready to again head south, Ursula's mother offered to fix him a snack. Pausing for a road break, he found a note in one of his sandwiches pleading with him to come back as soon as possible. "We love you," wrote Margarethe.

As it turned out, so did Ursula. "There was a gentleness and a kindness about him. I always knew in my heart of hearts that we were right for one another." By the summer of 1964, she had decided not to return for her final

year at university. She and Whayne were married that September in a small
Anglican church in Scarborough. Ursula wore a plain, white dress to empha-
size the beautiful veil of Belgian lace that Whayne's sister and several cousins
had worn on their wedding days. The Tennessee relatives arrived for the
reception at the Guild Inn, and Ursula's school chums were amazed at the
strange mixture of German accents and Southern drawls. Ursula and Whayne
spent their honeymoon touring Europe by car.

Whayne's father had died from leukemia when Whayne was eight years
old. His mother was a strong-willed, determined person who, as a young
widow, had decided to take over the family farm, and she made a financial
success of it. However, after a childhood of never-ending chores, Whayne
decided the last thing he wanted to be was a farmer. There were a number
of lawyers and judges in his family, so Whayne naturally thought of law. He
had graduated by the time he and Ursula married, and, since the job market
was very tight at the time, he had signed on as a law clerk for a United States
district court judge in Washington, DC.

The Quins lived in a downtown apartment for several months, but when
a friend offered them an attractive house in the country, about 25 kilometres
southeast of Washington, they gladly moved there. It satisfied a deep and
constant need of Ursula's: her own space, time to herself. "It was isolated, but
that didn't bother me at all. I loved it out there. It was peaceful and quiet and
beautiful." She had toyed with the idea of returning to university, but soon
she found the duties of a young housewife—the cleaning, washing, gardening—took all her time. "I love ironing beautiful things, because I like the
way they look when they are done. It is such a pleasure to see it. Here is this
wrinkled mess and out comes this beautiful piece of linen or embroidery or
whatever."

The couple's sojourn in the country set a pattern that would weave
through the Quins' married lives: deep involvement in their community.
Ursula began a lifetime of volunteer work at a well-baby clinic for mothers
who couldn't afford medical care. The couple also found their place in the
upper echelons of their society. Their social lives centred around the Hunt
Club in Upper Marlborough. "We didn't join the hunting activities," says
Ursula, "but there were parties and dances and picnics."

Both Ursula and Whayne had hoped to start a family right away, but
months and then years went by and nothing happened except for one ectopic
pregnancy. "We went to fertility specialists, went through all the tests and

examinations, but they couldn't figure out why." The Quins finally chose adoption. "It didn't matter where the children came from—they didn't have to be part of our bodies. And there was no problem with Whayne's ego as there would have been for many men." The adoption was arranged privately through high-placed connections. Gretchen was only three days old when she arrived in the Quin household on a lovely September day in 1972. "She was a very easy baby, a wonderful baby," recalls Ursula. "She was sunshine from the word go, always happy, always smiling. I really spent a lot of time with her as a little person. I just couldn't wait for her to wake up."

By the end of the '60s, the daily commute was becoming increasingly hard on Whayne, and the Quins decided to move into the city. They were driving around one weekend and spotted a house for sale on a cul de sac in the quiet, affluent neighbourhood of Kent in the northwest part of Washington. It had a lovely bay window overlooking a huge yard, and Ursula fell in love with it. There was one problem—nothing had been done to it since it was first built in the 1940s; there were even pegs for curtains separating the rooms, rather than doors.

Over the 22 years they lived there, the Quins gradually renovated and enlarged it. "I loved that house," says Ursula. "It was part of me." Then in 1990, Whayne decided he wanted something grander, something that better suited the Quins' social position. They found a place not far away on northwest Lowell Street, and they live there still. It's a magnificent, Georgian-style home with a circular driveway, large garden and pool, five bedrooms, airy sitting rooms, decorated in Ursula's exquisite taste—an appropriate reflection of upper-class Washington society.

It was Whayne, of course, who was responsible for the family's growing affluence. In 1966, the judge for whom he clerked invited him to join his old law partners. Wilkes, Artis, Hedrick and Lane, a large firm established in 1926, which practised general law but concentrated on real estate, in particular land use and zoning by-laws. Whayne decided to specialize in this field. He couldn't have done a smarter thing.

By the early 1970s, the U.S. capital was booming, its skyline transformed, but it was a struggle of epic proportions. New environmental laws, including height restrictions, were designed not only to cut down on pollution but to ensure city dwellers saw some sunshine peeping through between skyscrapers; powerful citizens groups were determined to preserve the heritage of their city; transportation had to be coped with before the city turned into one giant traffic jam. Whayne's clients were developers, some-times huge corporations, wanting to build office towers and shopping malls; often institutions—all five universities in the District of Columbia, for example; the foreign governments of Italy and Japan; and banks and life-insurance companies.

There's no question in Whayne's mind that he was able to accomplish so much because of Ursula. "Without her, I couldn't have practised law with the devotion I do. I couldn't have had a family. I wouldn't have had time to read, keep up on what's going on in the world." Ursula herself has no doubt about her contribution. It is more than supportive, she says; it is a partnership.

Her role has been to establish the Quins as pillars of the society in which they live with as much graciousness, elegance and unaffectedness as she can muster. There are the all-important social events: cocktail parties and banquets for important clients or other professionals, elaborate fund-raising dinners or tea parties, neighbourhood block parties, school-sponsored events.

More significant has been her volunteer work, specifically the never-ending fund-raising, squeezing ever more money out of the Washington elite for this or that worthy cause. This has involved running hospital gift shops, supervising antique shows, organizing huge raffles for cars, cameras, vaca-tions. She has sat on any number of boards, from the Washington Animal Rescue Aid shelter to the ladies' auxiliary of the Children's Hospital, an insti-tution to which she has given years of service. For Ursula, it's a matter of giving back to a community that has given so much to her. "I would say I've had a privileged life from the time I married. And I'm very grateful for all the things I have, because it's just a matter of luck where people end up. This isn't something I did, something I created myself. But then, who knows where luck comes from?"

The Quins' affluence and their place in society have brought many bene-fits: membership in the posh Chevy Chase Golf and Country Club, a share of a fishing lodge in Montana, frequent travel to Europe and elsewhere, large and expensive cars, and private schools for Gretchen and David, the second child they adopted in 1978.

Now in her mid-fifties, Ursula feels free to use her time as she pleases. She jogs an hour every morning with several women friends with whom she is close. She attends lectures at the National Gallery of Art, belongs to a garden club, a book club, which she loves, and an investment club, golfs whenever she feels like it, has lunch or dinner in the best restaurants with friends. She belongs to that class of people who seem to have everything, and yet when she is asked if there is anything in her life she regrets, her reply is surprising. "I should have had a career," she says. "I would have been more focused. I would have accomplished more."

Class

For my 13th birthday, a friend of my mother's gave me a subscription to *Mademoiselle* magazine. It was a rather inappropriate gift, since it was aimed at fashionable college students or young career women, and I was a particularly unfashionable teenager. Mother's friend probably thought the pert, well-groomed creatures who floated through its pages would provide a good role model for a klutz like me. Each month, I would put it on my bedside table, vowing I'd read every word and study every illustration of the interminable how-to-be-beautiful articles. I seldom got past page eight: the frilly, lace ball dresses, eight tiers deep, "accessorized" with Kay Fuchs gloves and I. Miller shoes and strands of Richelieu pearls, stopped me in my tracks.

Mademoiselle was first published in 1921, and by the mid-1950s, it was one of the four American heavies, along with *The Ladies' Home Journal*, *Redbook*, *McCall's*, as well as, in Canada, *Chatelaine*, which supposedly had a profound influence on the lives of middle-class, suburban women. My mother had a visceral reaction to what she referred to as "the ladies' Bibles" and they were not found in our house, although *Saturday Evening Post*, *Life* and *Maclean's* certainly were. *Mademoiselle* was tolerated because it was a gift, but she found it distasteful.

In some ways, though, it was not as bad as some of the others. "Naturally we believe in marriage and babies," exclaimed an editorial in January 1956, "but we don't go along with the thinking that considers these the exclusive aim for education for women nor do we find marriage and careers mutually exclusive." However, despite these stirring words, every page of the magazine was designed to offer up young females as sacrifices to the consumer society. Every advertisement, from Living Bra magic girdles to Maybelline eyelash-curlers, yelled, "Catch a husband. That's your job!"

The lesson that *Mademoiselle* taught me was that I was not of the right class. The lifestyle of the debutantes to whom it was dedicated was so far beyond my means that I couldn't even dream their dreams. I never longed for the right kind of marriage or an upwardly mobile future in the suburbs. I knew I would have to make my own way financially. And although by the time I reached my twenties, I had found out you didn't need a collection of Oneida silver to snare a doctor or engineer—they could be had easily enough, if that's what you wanted—I had already tasted independence and found it delicious.

I

It was the American historian Gerda Lerner who so effectively pointed out the link between the subjugation of women and the development of slavery. A mind-set had to be created among human society that made acceptable the idea that some people are fundamentally inferior to others before slavery could be institutionalized. As Lerner says, "At the very beginning of state formation and the establishment of hierarchies and classes, men must have observed the greater vulnerability in women and learned from it that differences can be used to separate and divide one group of humans from another."[220]

In early warring societies, male prisoners of war were considered more trouble than they were worth. They might rebel at any time and therefore required constant—and expensive—guarding. Slaughtering them on the spot was a lot more convenient. Women, on the other hand, often pregnant and therefore more passive and vulnerable, could be brought into the household as much-needed domestic servants, and then used as sex objects. The *Iliad,* written in the eighth century BC, frequently brags about how the mighty warriors distributed their bounty—which is to say, enslaved women.

As the system of slavery became an integral part of society, a man's riches—

his property, livestock, slaves, concubines—determined his position in society. For a woman, status had everything to do with her sexual identity. Writes Lerner, "At the bottom stood the slave woman, whose sexuality was disposed of by powerful men as though it were a marketable commodity; in the middle the slave-concubine, whose sexual performance might result in her upward mobility, the bestowal of some privileges and the winning of inheritance rights for her children; the top the wife, whose sexual services to one man entitled her to property and legal rights."[221]

A wealthy Roman family might own as many as 400 slaves scattered over many estates, performing all kinds of work. By that time, the value of strong males was understood, and three-quarters of them would be men.[222] Male slaves, especially among the captured Greeks, were sometimes highly educated and included scholars, historians, poets, artists. This elite found a secure place in aristocratic Roman households as administrators, legal advisors, stewards. Those not so fortunate—the majority—were used as manual labourers.

The female slaves of Roman households could have once been wives, mothers or daughters captured during the never-ending wars that established Rome's empire, or they may have been born to a slave mother and therefore became a chattel of the master at birth. Among those captured were a lucky few who possessed skills or talents—midwives, actresses, translators—that were considered of value and who would be treated accordingly. Most likely, though, captured slaves would join their house-born sisters as spinners, weavers, menders, wet nurses, kitchen help and performers of general domestic duties. (Since Roman engineers had invented mechanical means of transporting water, theirs wasn't such a heavy load as that of Greek slaves, who spent much of their time carrying huge jugs.) A particularly bright girl might catch the eye of the matron and be trained as a secretary, reader, masseuse, beauty technician, lady's maid, nurse or governess.[223]

Almost every female slave had an important parallel duty: to satisfy the sexual urges of her master or any freeborn male living in the *familia* compound. This by no means upset the mistress of the house. Once a Roman matron gave birth to three children, by law her sexual obligations ended. She was happy to hand over a libidinous husband to a voluptuous slave girl, thereby ending interminable and dangerous pregnancies.

Satisfying the urges of her masters was only a small part of the slave's job; she was also a slave-breeder. Under her master's guidance, and when she was as young as 15, she was required to co-habit with a male slave and produce slave babies. The children of these marriages were owned by the master to do with as he saw fit: incorporate them into his household or, often at a very young age, sell them for profit.

To lose a child wasn't the only calamity that befell slave unions. One of the partners could be abruptly sold or transferred to another estate owned by the same master. And the mortality rate, both among slave children and hardworking adults, was very high. Interestingly, marriage among slaves, for all its insecurity and disruption, was just as stable and affectionate as that of Roman citizens.[224]

There was one thing a slave could look forward to: the chance of being freed and even becoming a Roman citizen. A lady's maid or hairdresser or masseuse sometimes became intimate with the free women of the house, who would often hand over large tips. She was allowed to save these and eventually buy her freedom. A drudge who spent her days spinning or washing the clothes had not much hope of accumulating a nest egg but she, too, could hope for freedom. Once she had given birth to four children, thereby replenishing the household's stockpile of slaves, it was deemed appropriate that she be given her liberty.

Sometimes a slave's freedom was an outright gift. It became fashionable for a master to dictate, as part of the terms of his will, that his favourite slaves be manumitted on his death; in fact, this became so popular that Augustus, alarmed by what he saw as the disruption of his society, passed laws in the first century AD limiting the number of manumissions at any one time. Still, it was not uncommon for 100 slaves to gain Roman citizenship overnight.

Slaves had no acknowledged bloodlines, so it was customary for them to take their master's family name. Julia, freed slave of Petronia Themis, for example, became Petronia Julia. Her mistress then became her patron. Freed slaves were required to perform duties gratis for the *familia*, but not to spend so much time serving the family that they were prevented from making their living. Some ex-slaves, especially women, preferred to remain with the family with whom they had often lived their entire lives. Petronia Julia, for example, was a superb hairdresser and was happy to remain in the protective employ of her former mistress.

A few freedwomen, usually the concubines of emperors or heroes, were extraordinarily rich and powerful. Marcus Aurelius (AD 121–180), a philanthropic emperor and Stoic philosopher, chose to live with his favourite concubine after the death of his wife, partly because he loved her and partly to avoid squabbles that were sure to follow if heirs were produced from a legitimate wife. She, meanwhile, amassed a fortune, which she passed on to her children, and, of course, she had her own collection of slaves.

Most freedwomen, however, were not so privileged. They went out into the world to earn their living. Along with the lowest ranks of the freeborn, the Plebeians, they formed a large part of the working class. What is amazing is the number of different jobs they did. They laboured in small, industrial enterprises as weavers, in laundries as washerwomen and in mills where grain was ground. They were found among the butchers, bakers and brick-makers. They were merchants of all kinds: those who had been captured in the East often specialized in perfumes or exotic foods. They were dealers in beans and "sellers of snails," or fisherwomen who caught their haul and hawked it in the streets.[225] They were landladies, money-lenders and even ship-owners.[226]

At the bottom end of the social scale were the prostitutes. A Greek statue, not Roman, of the third century BC, tells everything about those unfortunate women of antiquity who, through necessity, had to sell their bodies. The woman is old, her wrinkled face turned upwards as if in supplication, and it expresses horrible anguish. Sitting on the ground, she clutches a huge wine jug. This is her last lover. In a society where a woman's sexual legitimacy is everything, she dwells on the lowest possible ring of the hierarchical ladder. She is a pariah.

II

In the Middle Ages, there was no question that God dictated one's position in society, so there was little use railing against fate. Medieval society was sharply delineated by social class, with little upward mobility, especially for women. Yet every station had its advantages and disadvantages; it all depended on how much freedom an individual was allowed in her daily life.

Those born in the lap of luxury were not always the luckiest. Aristocratic marriages were entirely business affairs, high-level alliances, forged through intricate contracts concerning land, money and financial affiliations. Marital intimacy, writes historian Claudia Opitz, "consisted in large part of sharing a bedroom, and even that did not always occur on a regular basis."[227] The master of the castle was seldom at home. Crusades, wars, business affairs, duties at court often kept him travelling for many months or even years.

Noblemen were not only on the road a lot but they got themselves killed in many diverse ways and at a young age. In the 14th and 15th centuries, 46 percent of English dukes died violently: in jousting contests, fighting in civil wars or being ambushed by highwaymen. Their life expectancy was only 24.[228] Their wives, even with the ever-present danger of childbirth, lived on average until age 32.

The end result was that noblewomen were often forced to take on enormous responsibilities. By the high Middle Ages, a woman could own fiefs through inheritance (if she had no brothers) and, if she were a widow, through the one-third of her husband's property that was her dower right. Whatever her personal stake, she ran the domicile and, when her husband was dead or absent, the vast estates and properties.

The wealthy household was huge and complex, as can be seen from the 1473 account books of Anne Neville, the widow of Richard Neville, Earl of Warwick (true to his class he had died in 1471 at age 43 in the Battle of Barnet). According to her recording, in that year she managed over 60 servants including knights, ladies, clerks, squires, sergeants-in-arms, lesser clerks, women of the chambers, yeomen, grooms and pages, all carefully ranked and paid accordingly.[229]

The manor house was, in fact, a small industrial enterprise: bread was baked, beer brewed, butter churned, meat smoked, cloth woven, candles and soap made. The lady of the house was required to oversee it all. For the agricultural enterprise of the estates, she usually relied on a trusted steward, but she was also required to keep a sharp eye on the finances.

Entertaining in a lavish manner was one of the most important of the highborn woman's roles. Writes historian Jennifer C. Ward, "It was the occasion when she displayed the power and status of herself and her family to the locality through the food and drink she offered, the entertainment she provided, and the splendour and magnificence of her setting." This was provided not only for visiting royalty, clergymen or friends but to her servants and the neighbourhood as a whole. Her hospitality "was as significant in its way as the wages, fees and liveries."[230]

By the end of the Middle Ages, castle life became increasingly luxurious, elaborate and comfortable. Elegant and colourful furnishings, elaborate gold or silver plate, expensive, flamboyant clothing and jewellery all became fashionable, an indicator of a family's status in society. The moralizers of the time were always preaching that aristocratic ladies, because of their "God-given position" in society, should serve as role models for the underclass and obey moral strictures more closely than anyone. Louis IX's daughters were told to "be perfect in every way, so that whoever hears about you or sees you can follow your example."[231]

Serving as a paragon of virtue was not the only disadvantage to life in a drafty castle. In smaller, isolated areas, upper-class women, forbidden to communicate with the lower orders and with their husband constantly absent, often lived lives of unbearable loneliness. Women of noble birth managing alone could also face grave danger, particularly when they were called upon to defend their estates against enemy attack. In 1341, in a ferocious battle against Charles of Blois, the countess of Brittany organized women and children to dig up paving stones, which her male servants hurled at the enemy. She routed Charles but, still not satisfied, proceeded to launch an offensive, leading an army as far as Brest. She was said to have "the bravery of a lion."[232]

More often, however, such attacks ended tragically. When Edward I finally broke down the defenses of Berwick Castle in the wars between the Scots and English at the end of the 13th century, he imprisoned the Countess of Buchan in a cage that he hung above the castle walls in order to humiliate her.[233]

A noblewoman was expected to be able to ride a horse well enough to hunt, breed falcons and release them during the hunt, play chess and backgammon, dance, sing, embroider, recite poetry. She attended jousting tournaments, where some knight infatuated with her might wear her colours and flirt with her. But she didn't have much to do with her husband. By the end of the Middle Ages, many of the high aristocracy associated with the great courts of Europe maintained completely separate households. Depending on whether you loved or loathed your husband, this could be a tragedy or a blessing.

For a girl of the merchant class, the size of her dowry also determined her place in society. If it were fairly hefty and/or she had a father with pull in an important guild, she might marry a master craftsman, a large-scale merchant or a professional such as a lawyer. Then she would spend her days as a housewife, a constant round of shopping and, with the help of one or two servants, emptying the chamber pots, doing the kitchen work, making the beds, washing the clothes, beating the fur and woollen clothes to get rid of moths and, of course, looking after the children. Well-to-do, middle-class families often had as many as 24 children.

If the dowry was of a skimpier size, a girl would have to marry someone further down the totem pole: a craftsman just starting out (her dowry would be used to buy him raw materials and a membership in a guild), a small merchant or perhaps a tavern-owner. In order to feed and clothe the family properly, she, too, would work. As historian Shulamith Shahar points out, "One could scarcely envisage production in the medieval town or its internal commerce without the activities of women."[234]

Some women found places in the guilds of artisans or petty merchants, having either been trained by their fathers or apprenticed to craftswomen. Many worked in the spinning and weaving industries, and would often do their labour at home. But in various towns of Europe at various times, women performed many tasks. They made ribbons, bindings, wigs, hats, scarves, furs. They worked as goldsmiths, coffin-makers and even metal-workers. They processed leather and made belts, straps, gloves and shoes. They were talented silk-weavers and wonderful embroiderers. A few were renowned as illuminators of books, and others as actresses and musicians in the guild of singers and players.

In Paris of the 13th century, six of the 100 listed guilds were open to women only; those specializing in decorated purses or elegant headdresses, for example.[235] Eighty more listed women as active participants. Guild restrictions usually came about when the work being done involved large amounts of money, and some of the largest and most important guilds—the great retail-merchants' guilds, for example—closed their doors to women altogether. In 13th-century Paris, 14 guilds did not allow female membership.

Many women, of course, were unskilled, with no way of obtaining membership in a guild. They still worked to help feed their families as tavern-keepers, landladies, bathhouse attendants, domestic servants. Wives of petty merchants hawked their goods at the local fairs and markets, selling chickens, fish, spices, butter, used clothes.

Towns were dirty, smelly places, but women still enjoyed the lively and colourful social life of the streets. They went to church, took part in festivals and religious pageants, flocked to hear renegade preachers, gossiped and fought, participated in protests, drank in taverns, partook of the bathhouses, enjoyed live theatrics and musical performances (although they often weren't allowed to act in the plays).

All of these women, though, had a second full-time job—the care of their families. It must have been hard on most of them. Health was a constant, nagging worry, especially in the towns. The infant mortality rate was enormously high; couples who had as many as 14 children could be left years later without an heir. When the great epidemics of the Middle Ages, including the Black Plague, swooped down, it was the towns they devastated. Brown rats scurrying among the street garbage carried in their fur the fleas that sparked the deadly contagion.

Against this background, it's tempting to romanticize life in the open air of the countryside. For one thing, peasant marriages, whether happy or otherwise, seemed somehow more vital, more passionate than those of the other classes. Young people usually married in their twenties or older, and, while families often arranged the matches for financial gain, the couple at least usually knew each other before betrothal.

Men did the outside work—the ploughing, sowing, reaping, haying, winnowing and threshing—while women performed the so-called inside jobs, although, in fact, they were outdoors a lot. Their work included cooking, milking, making butter and cheese, spinning and weaving, maintaining the hearth, feeding the poultry, weeding the vegetable patch, foraging in the woods for berries and nuts, fetching firewood and water.[236] At harvest time, they joined the men labouring in the fields.

Gathering together at communal wash-houses, grain mills or bread ovens, as well as frequent trips to a well or spring, provided women with plenty of opportunity to visit and gossip. Practical jokes, tomfoolery and superstition—fortune-telling of all kinds—coloured village life.

Yet this idyllic portrait is hardly accurate. There was a dark side. Houses, even for the prosperous, were crowded, one- or two-room affairs, dark—windows were shuttered, not glazed—drafty and, when the fire was going, smoky. In such close quarters, tempers were often frayed. Wife- and child-beating were all too frequent.

For the vast majority of peasants who were serfs bound to the land, life could be extremely hard. A serf had to give the lord of the manor a significant amount of his labour, as well as paying various fees. When a serf's daughter wanted to marry, for example, a hefty sum had to be handed over to the lord, which meant she might end up with no dowry at all.

Some villagers, whether serfs or free, were so poor they could scarcely keep alive. Among this group of unfortunates was often found the widow. Chaucer gives a poignant glimpse of her sitting in her humble village cottage in "The Nun's Priest's Tale."

Sooty her hall, her kitchen melancholy
And there she ate full many a slender meal;
There was no *sauce piquante* to spice her veal,
No dainty morsel ever passed her throat,
According to her cloth she cut her coat....
She drank no wine, nor white nor red had got.
Her board was mostly served with white and black
Milk and brown bread, in which she found no lack;
Broiled bacon or an egg or two were common
She was in fact a sort of dairy-woman.[237]

III

If there were a barometer in the early modern age that registered the distinction among the classes, the haves and have-nots of society, it was the fate of
the widow. Among the privileged, no female enjoyed more autonomy; the
wealthy widow presaged the liberated woman of 300 years later. Among the
lower classes, though, no individual was poorer or subject to more humiliation and discrimination.

For an aristocrat who controlled her jointure (the income guaranteed to
her from the dowry she brought to the marriage) and was also left part of her
husband's estate, widowhood could be the great liberating event of her life.
The incomparable Mme de Sévigné, after she was widowed at 25, fought off
suitors for years and never did remarry. She always insisted she preferred to
date her beginnings not from the day of her birth but the day of her widowhood. This was, she wrote, "quite a nice and quite fortunate thing."[238]

Lady Anne Clifford (1590–1676) was another example of a woman who
relished life a lot more after the death of her two abusive husbands. She
fought with her first, Richard Sackville, Earl of Dorset, a philanderer of the
first order, about her own inheritance. She was determined to retain the lands
of her vast estates in northern England; he wanted to sell them to get his
hands on the cash. At one point, the argument grew so bitter that Lady
Anne's son was removed from her care. Fortunately for her, Lord Dorset died
in 1624, but unfortunately for her, her second marriage to Philip, Earl of
Pembroke and Montgomery was also a disaster. "The marble pillars of Knole
in Kent and Wilton in Wiltshire [the family homes of her two husbands]
were to me oftentimes but the gay arbours of anguish," she wrote.[239]
Happily, Lord Pembroke passed away in 1649.

Lady Anne lived another 30 years, and if her autobiography is any indication, she enjoyed every moment of it, indulging herself in her many interests and philanthropies. She had a passion for literature, and in her old age, she kept at her side two well-educated female companions who read out loud, not only from the Bible but also from bawdy Chaucer. The poet John Donne said she was a woman who "knew well how to discourse of all things, from predestination to flea-silk [a plant], a wonderful housekeeper who could still open her mouth with wisdom."[240]

Such a powerful woman, under the thumb of no man, was considered a dangerous loose cannon by the male moralizers of the time. The lifestyles of Mme de Sévigné or Lady Anne were not at all what they advocated. The ideal widow was not supposed to flit about but dedicate her life to the memory of her long-dead husband. Moreover, marrying a widow was considered a kind of bigamy. The physician William Harvey, who discovered the body's circulatory system, was of the view that "he that marries a widow makes himself cuckold [by the dead husband]."[241]

Widows were supposed to live quiet, cloistered lives—grey mourning doves, as historian Antonia Fraser puts it—devoting their time to the salvation of their souls. As the English writer Richard Brathwaite put it in *The English Gentlewoman*, "For a widow to love society … gives speedy wings to spreading infamy … for in such meeting she exposeth her honour to danger, which above all others she ought incomparably to tender."[242] Implied in this advice is something that every male believed: widows had uncontrollable sexual appetites and constantly preyed on men in the hope of satisfaction.

The most scandalous thing a high-born widow could do was to marry beneath her. Hester Thrale shocked the world and lost many friends when she married the Italian who tutored her children. Likewise, the Duchess of Leinster, who had fallen in love with her son's teacher, waited for only a month after her husband's death to marry him.[243]

That this was the nightmare patriarchs most feared is revealed in John Webster's grim tragedy *The Duchess of Malfi*, first performed in 1614. The Duchess of Malfi is a young widow who falls deeply in love with her steward Antonio, marries him in secret, though legally, and bears him three children. The revenge of her two brothers—one, her twin, a megalomaniac duke and one a corrupt cardinal—is truly bloodthirsty and pitiless. It's not clear why they oppose the marriage—Antonio is an admirable fellow, even if he is of lower rank—except that a mere female had the nerve to disobey their wishes. The Duchess's suffering is on a par with Job's. She is made to believe her three children are dead; she is pronounced a slut in public; finally she is imprisoned and murdered. What is interesting about the play is that the Duchess, a woman, a widow, has many times the courage, strength, integrity and wit of any of the male characters. She is truly a martyr to her gender and class.

The fate of a widow of the lower orders, be she merry or in distress, depended entirely on her financial circumstances. Her husband could have left her a prospering business that would yield her a good income or a debt load that would tumble her and her children into abject poverty.

Common law did protect the widow to some degree. Typically, on the death of her husband, she had a right to the dowry she brought to the marriage or the income derived thereof, as well as her jewels, clothing and furnishings. Beyond that, she was allowed a third of the wealth accumulated during the marriage (or more, if her husband specified it in his will). A widow's dower rights were also secure from her late husband's creditors (although the rest of his estate was not; indeed, the widow could be held responsible for those debts).

If her husband had been a master craftsman, her future was dicey. Many guilds would allow her to continue her husband's business, but some would not. She could run an undertaker's as long as she hired hefty men to carry the coffins. She could manage a stationer's company as long as a male journey-men pulled the presses.[244] Many guilds placed damaging restrictions on a widow; for example, she was often not allowed to hire new apprentices, the cheapest form of labour, which meant it was difficult to keep prices compet-itive. The most effective solution, if she could abide the man, was to marry a journeyman of the same guild as her late husband. He could then buy his way into a mastership.

The best way to keep a town family afloat was to own a small business not controlled by a guild: a café, a tavern, a pie or muffin shop, a grocery store. London's streets were full of widows' children selling hot pies and sweet-meats.

Farm women were in a similar situation. The widow of a solid landowner or a tenant farmer with a long lease might live a prosperous, active life, as Samuel Johnson portrayed so well in *The Rambler*. Lady Bustle pulls on her rubber boots, hitches up her skirts and marches into the fields each morning, barking out instructions to the farm hands, after which she does her "woman's work."[245]

The one-third of a farmer's worth that was earmarked for a widow often took the form of a small cottage and a living allowance. Often she took up residence with her son's family, no matter how much she might detest her daughter-in-law. Her material needs were thus provided for, but she lost the influence and power that a productive economic base provided.

In both town and country, there were widows, most often with children, who had no skills, land or a business to provide them with an income. These women had to scrounge out a living as farm labourers, scrub-women, sellers of beers and bread, hawkers of needles and ribbons. Poor widows would sometimes help each other out. As many as 30 would cluster together in village cottages so they could share the cost of rent, fuel and food. They would grow vegetables in their gardens, distribute hand-outs from relatives, bargain for cheap fish and meat. They often made their living, such as it was, by lace-making. Historian Olwen Hufton estimates that in some French villages in the early modern period, widow communities accounted for between 16 and 20 percent of all households.[246]

At the bottom of the heap was the poor, old widow without children to care for her. She was often reduced to begging in the streets or appealing to church charities, niggardly as they were, for a little food. As Antonia Fraser points out, she had an added disadvantage. In a society obsessed with feminine beauty, her shrunken, gnarled body was thought of as grotesque and her soul as impure: "… physical ugliness (the common woe of the old) signified a base moral nature, if not something worse."[247]

This widespread abhorrence of old women ended in tragedy. They often came to be seen as instruments of the devil, witches to be harassed, tortured and burned at the stake.

IV

Emma Woodhouse in Jane Austen's novel *Emma*, published in 1816, is a snob of the first order. Her preposterous condescension leads to disaster when she decides to take the young Harriet Smith, a gentleman's daughter of dubious birth, under her wing. "*She* [Emma] would notice her; she would improve her; she would detach her from her bad acquaintance and introduce her into society; she would inform her opinion and her manners."[248] The "bad acquaintance" is Robert Martin, a prosperous farmer and an ethical, hard-working man who dearly loves Harriet.

Luckily for Emma, she is witty and beautiful, otherwise her pretentiousness would be intolerable. Had Austen lived 50 years later, she might not have created such a snooty, meddling heroine. By that time, girls as clever as Emma were out saving the world.

As industrialization continued to spread in the 19th century, the middle class grew larger and more prosperous. A mark of upward mobility, not only for a banker or doctor but also a clerk or schoolmaster, was his wife, who no longer worked for wages but kept a comfortable home. Yet this led to a dilemma. Middle- and upper-class households usually included a number of servants to do the cooking and housework and look after the children. What was a middle-class female, better educated than ever, supposed to do with her time? Why, help clean up the societal mess left by the Industrial Revolution.

The ill-treatment of the working class, the poverty and brutality of the lives of the poor, was shocking. It was particularly hard on women. Excluded from learning a craft, a trade or profession, they were made to do drudge work at the lowest wages. The story of Ann Eggley brought tears to the eyes of the middle-class matrons who crowded into a London auditorium to hear testimony at the 1842 Children's Employment Commission. Ann was an 18-year-old mineworker whose job it was to push carriages loaded with ore from the face of the mine to the shaft.

We go at four in the morning, and sometimes at half-past four. We begin to work as soon as we get down. We get out after four, sometimes at five in the evening. We work the whole time except an hour for dinner, and sometimes we haven't time to eat.... The work is far too hard for me; the sweat runs off me all over sometimes. I am very tired at night. Sometimes when we get home at night we have not power to wash us, and then we go to bed. Sometimes we fall asleep in the chair. Father said last night it was both a shame and a disgrace for girls to work as we do, but there was nought else for us to do.[249]

Middle- and upper-class ladies in both Europe and North America rolled up their sleeves—something had to be done about the depravity, the squalor. They threw themselves into the evangelical revivals that provided much of the inspiration for their Good Samaritan work. They joined temperance and abolition movements, fought to reform prisons, campaigned against prostitution, ran soup kitchens, helped out in lying-in shelters where poor women gave birth and worked in asylums for the insane, the blind and the destitute. It wasn't easy for these pampered females to face the slums in the underbelly of the city. The biographer of Octavia Hill, one of the British pioneers of social reform, wrote, "There is no doubt that working in poor areas was rough for the hitherto protected girls, from middle- or upper-class homes. They had to steel themselves to witness horrors of every kind: drunkenness, starvation, the signs of physical abuse on women and children."[250]

As women came face to face with the devastation that capitalism had wrought, some began to question the political system their husbands so admired. Conflict naturally resulted, followed by ridicule. The male establishment might have wanted to jeer at "chatter-box do-gooders," but it was hard to sneer at a woman of the stature and accomplishment of Josephine Butler. As the writer Joanna Trollope points out, she had ties with the ruling Whig aristocracy, she had married an accomplished academic, she was beautiful, exquisitely dressed and articulate.[251] She was also a tiger, who for years fought ferociously to improve the lot of destitute girls, vagrants and prostitutes.

Women swelled the ranks of organizations set up to encourage hygiene in working-class homes or "moral purity" or free education for the poor. From working at so many fund-raising bazaars, they became good at managing money. Reform campaigns made them knowledgeable about infant mortality or slum housing or dealing with municipal, state and federal governments. They began to form intricate networks and collectively demand political and civil rights for women. In the United States, for example, Elizabeth Cady Stanton shifted from fighting for abolition of slavery to campaigning for women's suffrage. In France, Hubertine Auclert fought to reform women's rights under the Civil Code, and then went on to spearhead a campaign to get women the vote.[252]

It was discussions at meetings of this or that society or club or league where the first seeds of a full-blown female consciousness were planted. As historian Carroll Smith-Rosenberg has pointed out, the New Women who emerged at the turn of the century were mostly the daughters of the Victorian matrons who headed the philanthropic and educational crusades.[253] Women who had thrown themselves into the public realm could no longer be satisfied with sitting by the hearth, peacefully, like an angel. The hand that rocked the cradle was growing ever more powerful.

V

Throughout history, a woman's place in society has been determined by her husband's credentials. If he had wealth, a profession, political alliances, it was her job to make sure his footing remained secure on the social ladder. Clarissa Dalloway of Virginia Woolf's *Mrs. Dalloway* (1925) is just such a helpmate.

She is married, rather unhappily, to a pillar of Victorian society, a Conservative member of parliament. Her job, and she has enjoyed it, has been to create the kind of social life where the rough male world of politics and finance could be refined by feminine culture and concern.

She made her drawing-room a sort of meeting-place; she had a genius for it.... Infinite numbers of dull people conglomerated round her, of course. But odd unexpected people turned up; an artist sometimes; sometimes a writer; queer fish in that atmosphere. And behind it all was that network of visiting, leaving cards, being kind to people; running about with bunches of flowers, little presents; So-and-so was going to France—must have an air-cushion; a real drain on her strength: all that interminable traffic that women of her sort keep up; but she did it genuinely, from a natural instinct....

... Nothing else had she of the slightest importance; could not think, write, even play the piano. She muddled Armenians and Turks; loved success; hated discomfort; must be liked; talked oceans of nonsense; and to this day ask her what the Equator was, and she did not know.[254]

Presiding over gala social events was meaningless to women of the lower orders, but their rank, too, was defined by their husbands. Often their contribution was making do with the limited opportunity they had married into. D. H. Lawrence's *Sons and Lovers* centres around a marriage turned tragic when working-class and middle-class mores clash. Gertrude Morel is the daughter of a "good old burgher" family. Her grandfather had gone bankrupt in the lace-making business, which plunged the family into poverty, but that didn't prevent the members from having middle-class pretensions. Walter Morel went down into the mines when he was ten, and his family has no pretensions at all. The union of the two turned into a prolonged and bitter war.

The pity was, she was too much his opposite. She could not be content with the little he might be; she would have him the much that he ought to be. So, in seeking to make him nobler than he could be she destroyed him. She injured and hurt and scarred herself, but she lost none of her worth. She also had the children.[255]

At the turn of the century, First Wave feminists, mostly daughters of the bourgeoisie, had attempted to understand class and what it meant for women. As they became social workers in settlement houses, organizers for unions, nurses visiting slums, hospitals and laying-in shelters, they gained first-hand knowledge of the life of the underprivileged. They read Marx, and began to understand the insidious use of class in a capitalistic society. To a large degree, World War I broke this connection. In 1918, German feminist Christiane Eifert lashed out at those women who, after the war, had so easily sacrificed the lower classes, indeed abandoned feminism altogether, for a life of peace and quiet.[256] It was a refrain to be repeated over and over in the 20th century.

By the 1920s, the flapper—glittering, insouciant, flip—was interested primarily in herself, certainly not in the undeserving poor or the mannish, severe New Woman. Even with her new-found individualism, her success in the gay new society was determined almost entirely by the social position of her husband. Daisy Buchanan in F. Scott Fitzgerald's *The Great Gatsby* remains the most sharply drawn example of the carefree and careless 1920s woman. She is a daughter of a wealthy Mid-Western family; her voice "was full of money—that was the inexhaustible charm that rose and fell in it, the jingle of it, the cymbals' song of it.... High in a white palace the king's daughter, the golden girl...."

She might have married the man she had fallen in love with, Jay Gatsby, but she gets tired of waiting for him to return from the war in Europe. She chooses instead someone not only of her class—Gatsby had lied and told her he was wealthy—but of her class temperament, the wealthy, brutish Tom Buchanan. Fitzgerald gives a remarkable description of the man. "Not even the effeminate swank of his riding clothes could hide the enormous power of that body—he seemed to fill those glistening boots until he strained the top lacing, and you could see a great pack of muscle shifting when his shoulder moved under his thin coat. It was a body capable of enormous leverage—a cruel body." He is an insensitive, stupid bigot whose extramarital affairs create scandals, but when Daisy is given a chance to run away with the still-adoring Gatsby, she reneges. His fabulous new wealth has come through bootlegging and other sleazy activities. He is not of the right pedigree, and Daisy knows her status in society will be diminished. She doesn't even send flowers to his funeral.

The Great Depression brought the distinction between privileged and underprivileged sharply and painfully into focus. Hollywood responded with a series of class-conscious films, many to do with women and their families.[257] None was as emotionally wrenching as the 1937 weepie *Stella Dallas*. When we first meet Stella, played by Barbara Stanwyck, she is in the front yard of her shabby, working-class house, watching out for what she considers is the one eligible bachelor in the New England mill town where she lives—the upper-class, Harvard-educated Steven Dallas. Through her good looks and vitality, she manages to snare him. They marry and have a daughter, Laurel, but it soon becomes apparent he is appalled by Stella's low-class manners. Her dresses are too tight, she wears fake jewellery asparkle on her neck and ears, she talks too loudly and with the wrong accent, and she loves a good time. Steven is promoted to a job in New York, but she refuses to go with him— she is tired of being lectured on decorum every moment she's awake. He takes the job anyway, and they never again live together.

Stella loves her child dearly, but as the years go by, she is made to realize, through a whole series of humiliating and zany incidents, that her mode of thought, her friends, her manners prevent her from bringing up a proper young lady. She devises an elaborate scheme to have Laurel placed in the upper-class home of her former husband and his new wife. The film ends with Stella standing on the lawn outside the Dallas house in the pouring rain, watching with joy as her lovely daughter marries into the bourgeoisie.

Film critic E. Ann Kaplan points out that Stella is doubly penalized: "The film punishes her first by turning Stella into a 'spectacle' produced by the upper-class, disapproving gaze (a gaze that the audience is made to share through camera work and editing), but secondly, and most devastatingly, by bringing Stella to the recognition that she is an unfit mother for her daughter."[258] The movie's one happy conclusion is that the love between mother and daughter remains firmly anchored, even though lower-class Stella is in many ways an embarrassment to Laurel. What is truly sad about the film is none of the characters, neither Stella nor Laurel nor Steven's sympathetic new wife, questions the basic assumption—an upper-class male is born to lord it over a lower-class female.

Following World War II came the exodus to the suburbs; the back-to-the-kitchen movement kicked into gear. It took only a few years, though, before it dawned on at least some North American women how humiliating it was to be judged entirely by the accomplishments of one's husband. A housewife was always just a housewife, no matter how delicious her jam or how shiny her floors. She could be an excellent mother, but it would not get her a promotion or a raise or any kind of recognition from society at all.

Interestingly when the women's liberation movement finally shook society's cage, class was not a priority topic of debate. All the energy and anger went into railing against gender domination; the special case of the working-class housewife or the black mother or the Asian immigrant was of little concern. American feminist Audre Lorde wrote, "By and large within the women's movement ... white women focus upon their oppression as women and ignore difference of race, sexual preference, class and age. There is a pretense to a homogeneity of experience covered by the word sisterhood that does not in fact exist.... Unacknowledged class differences rob women of each other's energy and creative insight."[259]

It seems an unfair assessment today, when the bugaboos of race, class and sexual preference dominate women's literature from *Chatelaine* to *Ms.* magazine to scholarly journals. Surely a consensus has been reached that, if cutbacks in social programs for poor women, discrimination against lesbians, equal opportunity for visible minorities are not an important part of the feminist agenda, the movement will wither and die. As women have begun to occupy important positions in society, they've gained status through their own efforts, not their husbands', and that is a great achievement of Second Wave feminism. Nonetheless, class remains a powerful, sneaky and insidious current in Western society.

Ellen Pall, in her novel *Among the Ginzburgs*, presents a contemporary view of racism and snobbery: it's there, but it's not supposed to be. Mimi is pregnant, and her sister Sunny wonders why she and the baby's father Jesse don't marry. Sunny asks:

'It isn't that he [Jesse] doesn't believe in monogamy?'

'No, nothing like that.'

'Or are you worried because of his background? Because he's kind of a different ... class than we are?'

'A different "class"?' Mimi was suddenly furious. 'Is that what you think about him? This family is unbelievable! *Class*.' Mimi breathed the word so dramatically that for a moment Sunny imagined she was about to break into a musical number. But Mimi merely shook her head and went on. 'So Jesse earns his living with his hands. So what do you think I do? I'm a waitress, Sunny. Or do you really mean that he isn't Jewish? Man, for a bunch of supposed-to-be liberals, this family is so prej—so bigoted.'

'Sorry,' Sunny said.[259a]

Sandra

She skittered about the periphery of our group, not really part of it, but not an outsider either. At five-foot-six, skinny, with an upturned nose and black, curly hair, Sandy Amos was considered something of a card. Though we didn't much like her taste in fashion—she favoured the poodle skirt, made of felt and decorated with a rhinestone-collared dog—we thought she was pretty, vivacious and funny. We particularly appreciated her wisecracking, so quick and sometimes deadly.

We would have been shocked had we known Sandra's picture of herself was so entirely different. She was convinced she was a geek, a world-class klutz. In Grade 10, when the good-looking paper boy turned down her invitation to the Sadie Hawkins dance, she asked herself what could she expect? She was so funny-looking, shy, unpopular.

High school was a misery for her. She made few close friends because she believed no one liked her. She didn't participate in after-school activities because she felt she had nothing to offer the basketball team or the poster club. Sandra Amos had an overwhelming sense of inferiority, not an uncommon feeling for girls her age but a tormenting one just the same.

She believes now that her family background had a lot to do with her lack of self-esteem, although it wasn't much out of the ordinary. Sandy's father Bob married Margaret Boyd in 1942, just before he was shipped off to war. He was part of the signal corps, and spent two and a half years driving a truck in a convoy wending its way through Europe. He was injured in Normandy and sent home, but by that time, the war was winding down anyway.

The first time Bob saw his daughter Sandy, she was two years old, and they bonded immediately. Even though her mother was always home and her father worked long hours, grabbing any overtime he could, Sandra has vivid memories of her dad and would always feel closer to him than her mother. He was a quiet, private person, but he liked being with his children.

Bob Amos worked as a welder for Supreme Aluminum, a large factory situated only a block away from his home. He made pots and pans for the same company for his entire working life. His parents owned a house on a large piece of land on Eastwood Avenue in the southwestern part of Scarborough, where Bob had been able to purchase half the lot. With the help of his two brothers and other family members, he built the three-bedroom bungalow by hand. Since one set of grandparents lived next door and the other not far away, Sandra's childhood was enriched by a large extended family who enjoyed getting together a lot.

Except for the odd part-time job, her mother stayed home and looked after the kids; two sons were born after the war. Margaret was the dominant one in the household, the organizer and the disciplinarian, and she held strict, traditional views about child-rearing.

The relative whom Sandra most admired was her father's sister, her aunt Betty Amos. Betty had been better educated than her brothers; she finished high school and continued taking night courses until finally, 40 years later, she received a degree from the University of British Columbia. She was a career woman who never married, strong, independent and opinionated. She doted on Sandra, treating her to concerts and the theatre and each summer, the Stratford Festival. The unfortunate decisions about Sandra's future were always made during Betty's absences from Toronto.

It would have been a secure and happy childhood except for an accident that occurred when Sandra was four and a half years old. She was severely scalded with boiling water. There were months of hospitalization and years of skin grafts and other treatment. Her left arm was left badly scarred, but even more unfortunate, her psyche was equally damaged. She was a quiet, introverted kid anyway, but after the accident, she became terribly fearful of everything. Her family gave her a great deal of sympathy, but it was of the wrong sort. It was poor Sandra this and poor Sandra that. She came to feel different than other kids—like damaged goods. The result was the low self-esteem that plagued her throughout childhood and adolescence.

Despite her unhappiness at high school, she managed pretty good grades especially in sciences and math. In Grade 12, her class went for a tour of the University of Toronto and Sandra fell in love with the science labs. Her future, she decided, would be in scientific research of some kind. It was a dream that was quickly and cruelly punctured.

Her parents sat her down and said, "We're sorry, but we can't do anything to help you financially. We have two sons to educate." Sandra applied for the few scholarships available, but to no avail—the competition at the time was horrendous. She thought of working and going to school at the same time, but it wasn't done much in those days; the work load was too heavy. Anyway, she had had trouble balancing her part-time jobs with her high-school studies, never mind university-level courses. Her Aunt Betty might have offered some emotional and financial support, but she wasn't in Toronto at the time. Sandra finally said, "Piss on it. I won't do it then."

She had a Grade 13 diploma, which was considered a big deal in those days, but, since she had no practical skills, it wasn't that easy finding work. Bell Canada finally took her on as a receptionist in their engineering department. It wasn't exactly a prestigious job, but Sandra enjoyed it. She had some money in her pocket at last, and met lots of new friends. "We'd get all doodled up and boot around, looking for guys.... We were always on the prowl." It was while she was prowling at the Balmy Beach Nightclub one Saturday in 1962 that she met her future husband.

There had already been a few boyfriends, older guys who lived in the neighbourhood but weren't part of the R. H. King scene. In her last year of high school, she had started going out with a boy studying engineering at the University of Toronto. He was nice enough, but a little dull. Robert[260] was something else altogether.

"He was taller than me, and this was a bonus—I could wear my high heels. He was four years older, a real man of the world, or so I thought." He had a nifty car and took her to bars where his wisecracking friends hung out. He was an ambitious, driven person who was going to set the world on fire. She thought, "I'll hook up with him and have a whole different life, get out of this family, this neighbourhood."

Sandra's parents disliked her new boyfriend intensely. Her mother was keen on her marrying the engineer student, not this slick fast-talker. Robert's mother had committed suicide when he was 15 years old. Sandra says he never recovered from the tragedy and was as psychologically scarred as she was, but he quickly realized one thing: he could talk anyone into buying anything. He was working as a salesman in a camera shop when he met Sandra, and he had great ambitions.

She was only 19 when she and Robert eloped in October 1963. The ceremony took place at Toronto's City Hall, and only the groom's father and Sandra's Aunt Betty were there. Sandra had quarreled bitterly with her parents over Robert, and she had moved out of the family home just months before the wedding. It was the beginning of a rift, an alienation from her mother in particular, which would go on for years.

Robert and Sandra were typical young marrieds with a downtown apartment, new furniture, lots of friends. Two incomes meant plenty of money to spend, and since Sandra was on the Pill, there was no worry about unwanted pregnancies. As she would her entire life, she began taking night courses, accounting and bookkeeping, skills that would stand her in good stead. She found a job for a large plumbing-supply company and quickly became the manager's assistant.

Keen on setting up his own business, Robert thought the Niagara Peninsula might just be the kind of up-and-coming place he was looking for. He and Sandra moved to St. Catharines in 1968, and Sandra began working for a convenience-store chain as a bookkeeper. Meanwhile, Robert found what he considered was the perfect business opportunity in Welland, a town 20 kilometres south. Right on Main Street he came across what he was looking for: Manor's Cameras, owned by an elderly man who was anxious to retire. Robert agreed to buy it on a contingency basis. It was a sweet deal, says Sandra, and one that would prove auspicious.

Before Robert took over, the store had barely provided a living. The displays were old-fashioned, the merchandise not up to date. Robert arrived with plenty of fresh ideas about stock, promotion, selling. In 1968, the big chains—Blacks or Japan Camera—did not yet dominate the business. Customers liked the independents because the sales staff possessed some know-how, and Robert was always charming and patient with his customers. The renamed Camera Barn became a depot for photo-finishing as well as a supplier to big corporations who ran their own labs. It began to make money—lots of it.

Within a year, Sandra quit her job at the convenience chain and became a full-time employee at the camera shop. She looked after the financial end of the business, but she also helped out in the store, too, becoming quite knowledgeable about the equipment. There was a drawback, however, and it would become more pronounced as time went by. Sandra puts it this way, "If you're the type of woman that I was, you tend to lose your identity. Your husband's the boss, and you just become part of the business unit."

Robert and Sandra opened another camera-equipment outlet in the nearby village of Fonthill. Although Sandra says it was a poky little store, it turned into a money-maker, too. They bought a house in the same area for $17,000, fixed it up and within a year, sold it for $30,000. They then found a farm house on an acre of land with big, old barn. They paid $28,000 for it, and poured money into renovations. Within five years, it sold for $130,000. They bought the building downtown where the camera store was located, along with several other residential and business properties. For a long time, everything they touched turned to gold.

Sandra enjoyed her new-found affluence. She always loved shopping for clothes, and Robert never made much of a fuss about her spending money on them. The way she looked, after all, was a measure of *his* affluence and success. The couple entertained a lot, lavish dinners and cocktail parties for people in the business—photographers, suppliers and important customers. Sandra did much of the preparation. She was not only helping in the business but she was the perfect homemaker.

In 1973, Sandra's doctor advised her to go off the Pill and shortly after, she became pregnant. Neither she nor Bob were overjoyed at the timing; a second store at Fonthill had just been opened. But Sandra, who was 31 at the time, knows that if she hadn't had a baby then, she never would have. Matthew was born on January 31, 1974, and within a month, Sandra was back working. She carted Matthew into the shop every day, breast-fed and changed him there, and became an utterly devoted mother. "I loved that baby, enjoyed everything about him. He became a very large part of my life."

With an adored child, a lovely house that she had decorated herself and a thriving business, Sandra's life would seem ideal. Yet it had an ominous undercurrent. Robert had begun to drink a lot, and when he was drunk, he was, as Sandra puts it, "horrible." To make matters worse, she had come to despise the very characteristics that had first attracted her to her husband: the super salesman, the artist at cutting a deal. She felt as if she were married to Donald Trump. "I came to hate the wheeling and the dealing and the lack of ethics and the shaving of corners and the manipulating. It wasn't me."

Worst of all was the incessant undermining of her self-esteem. She thinks now that Robert was insecure himself, and he handled this by trying to keep her in a submissive role. There were always put-downs and mind games going on. He would push her so far, and then they'd have a screaming match. Sandra would get her own way for a while, but then Robert would be back manipulating and belittling. Sandra says he made important business decisions without consulting her, pretending she only had a small role in the running of the shop when in fact, she was working just as hard as he.

By the early 1980s, Robert's touch of gold was turning to brass. The big chains were opening stores in new shopping centres and their lower prices made for fierce competition. As the recession tightened, interest rates soared, which hurt the overall business because Robert and Sandra had mortgages on several of their properties. After the smaller of the stores was closed, Robert decided to get out of cameras altogether. The business was sold and then, says Sandra, "he lay on the couch in between drinking bouts for the better part of a year."

By this time, their marriage had disintegrated into a never-ending battle. It was the child who suffered, of course. Matt was nine at the time, and Sandra believed her husband was starting to do to her son what he had done to her. The boy would come home with an A and a couple of Bs on his report card. According to Sandra, Robert would yell, "Why aren't they all As?" Says Sandra, "I had to get this kid out of there. It wasn't for me that I finally got up the courage." On her 40th birthday, she finally steeled herself to tell Robert the marriage was over.

It was difficult convincing him a divorce was best for everybody. Even though there was nothing left of their relationship, says Sandra, he didn't want out of it. He was comfortable the way he was. Finally, reluctantly, he agreed to move out of the house. Then he promptly disappeared for six months, leaving her to cope with the financial mess.

Over the years, their lives had become intricately intertwined. For tax reasons, the business was a partnership, and they jointly owned the cars, houses, properties, investments, pension plans. Trying to extricate themselves from such a tightly woven knot was a horrendous job. "The worm turned, believe me," says Sandra. "Far from being the submissive little wife, I got really nasty. I had a lawyer on my side and he negotiated a tough deal. Everything was split 50–50."

When the new owner went bankrupt, the camera shop ended back in Sandra's lap, and for two years, she struggled to keep it alive, managing to make a bare living. Finally, in 1984, she packed it in and put the building up for sale. Although there was little left of their once-considerable wealth, she still had about $7,000 in the bank and a few investments, enough to give her a break before she started job-hunting. She thought, "Okay, I've been through this marriage breakdown, the trauma of this dying business. I'm going to take a few months off and regroup." What followed instead were two years of abject misery, because by that time, Sandra was an alcoholic.

Right from the time she first dated Robert, she had enjoyed drinking at a bar or with a group of friends. She had a tremendous capacity for alcohol, never seeming to suffer from hangovers. "That was an early warning sign," she says. "Given the type of person I was—shy and without a lot of self-confidence—I found alcohol a magic thing. It allowed me to relate to people, to cope." Throughout their marriage, both Sandra and Robert drank a lot. It became an integral part of their lifestyle, the glue that held their marriage together. Once Sandra no longer went out to work every day, she became even more addicted.

She isolated herself in her Welland house; it became her skid row. She started to see various men who were mostly younger and who loved to booze as much as she. She was soon consuming more than 40 ounces of vodka a day. She stopped eating and dropped 45 pounds in a year. The only thing that kept her going was her morning routine of washing down a half-dozen different vitamin pills with her orange juice, even if it was laced with a hefty slug of vodka. She became yellow and bloated; she didn't have a line on her face because it was so swollen.

She knew she was in trouble. Nightmares of ending up permanently brain-damaged, in jail or a mental institution, or killing herself in a car crash haunted her. Even this terror wasn't enough to stop her drinking, though; the addiction held her entirely in its terrible grip.

There was no one to whom she could turn for help. After she was married, Sandra had patched things up with her mother and would chat now and then, even about her deteriorating relationship with Robert. Mrs. Amos bit her tongue, didn't say, "I told you so," but there was never an offer of help either. In fact, Margaret Amos had no idea her daughter was wrestling with a severe drinking problem. By 1986, Sandra had cut herself off from everybody; mother and daughter had all but lost contact.

That fall, Sandra was shaken by several traumatic events. A man whom she had been dating, and whom she quite liked, dumped her. A nephew whom she was fond of was killed in a motorcycle accident in Texas. And problems were developing with Matt, who had just turned 13. There were brushes with the law over petty theft and other misdemeanors.

One morning she woke up to find her mind was crystal clear. She said to herself, "I'm screwed up. What I need is a shrink." She tried to call around but it was impossible to get hold of a psychiatrist on a Sunday morning. What she did instead was leave a message on the Alcoholics Anonymous answering service.

It took only a couple of hours before two AA members, a mother and daughter team, arrived at her house. They talked for four hours straight, finally persuading her to attend an AA meeting that night. The meeting didn't start until nine, and by seven, Sandra was in bad shape. Still, she kept her promise not to drink. She was hauled off to a dank church basement and there experienced her first AA session while suffering a hangover of nightmarish proportions.

After attending a couple of meetings, Sandra managed to remain sober for a week and a half, but then she started drinking again. A number of AA members, all former alcoholics themselves, conspired to help her. They would check in periodically; sometimes she would be sober and sometimes drunk. They ignored these binges and continued to take her to meetings anyway. Finally, it all came together for her on Christmas 1986. Since that auspicious day, she has not touched another drop.

Once Sandra got over a week of shakes and withdrawal, she had, surprisingly, no desire to drink. Not only did she quickly regain her mental and physical health but the AA members whom she had initially found uninviting in effect became her family. This led to a discovery of faith. It was nothing to do with religion, she says. It was getting in touch with the spiritual side of your nature, a side that, she discovered, she had long abandoned.

Among the most supportive in the AA group was a gravel-voiced, rumpled man, a long-time recovering alcoholic by the name of Rick,[261] who became her lover and then her live-in partner. He is 15 years older than Sandra, not nearly as well-educated, articulate or healthy as she is, and yet she remains devoted to him. "What I love about the man is not his age or the way he looks. It's the emotional connection we have that's important. He's the most empathetic, caring person I've known. He's the only man I've had a relationship with who accepts me absolutely for what I am, warts and all." And she does the same for him.

An essential part of the AA philosophy is that those who benefit from the program should help others. Sandra volunteered at the Niagara Treatment Centre for Women, a ten-bed facility in an old house located in downtown Welland that dealt with addictions of all kinds: alcohol, drugs, particularly cocaine and heroine, eating disorders and combinations thereof. When the woman who ran the office went on maternity leave, Sandra took over her job part time, and also started taking courses in psychology and addiction research at Niagara College. A year later, she was offered a full-time position as a front-line counsellor.

The next six years of her life were both chaotic and deeply satisfying. She dealt daily with troubled women, women who supported their $800-a-day cocaine habit by prostitution or dealing drugs; women who had such low self-esteem they could barely talk; women who had been horribly abused by their parents and husbands and went on to abuse their own children. In fact, it was rare to encounter somebody who hadn't been abused.

Sandra worked 14 hours a day, often on the midnight shift, and still continued to take college courses relating to her work. Because the burn-out rate was so high, the most important lesson to learn was not to get too attached or involved with the clients. By the time Sandra had worked there for six years, she was emotionally and physically exhausted.

The program was funded by the Ontario Ministry of Health, and in the early 1990s, government officials began to question the professional qualifications of the front-line workers. Counsellors with masters degrees and Ph.D.s became the vogue, even though they might not have any real-life experience. As the facility came under scrutiny, the political bickering, the in-fighting, the budget cuts and the demands of the board of directors became intolerable. Finally, in 1993, the Niagara Treatment Centre closed and the funds were transferred to other programs. Sandra was devastated—she felt she and her colleagues had helped so many desperately needy women. At the same time, she also felt relief that such an incredibly draining job was ending.

At 51 years old, Sandra had to start all over again, and the jobless rate in Welland was soaring. She handed out applications to every business she could think of, whether they had advertised for help or not. She had a good résumé by this time, lots of training and business skills, but there was simply no work. She was finally rescued by, of all people, her son Matthew.

Sandra had taken out an insurance policy with the intention of cashing it to help Matt through university, but when he finished high school, he decided not to continue his education. "I think there were so many traumas in my life that I just wanted to be on my own, with my own money," he says. Ironically, he chose the business his parents had carried on for so many years: camera-retailing. He was managing a Sooter Studio when the treatment centre closed and was able to hire his mother, if only on a temporary basis.

In the fall of 1995, Sandra found a full-time job as an accounting clerk for a company in St. Catharines that manufactures circuit boards. Dealing with "ordinary, sane" people is a relief, she says, and by five o'clock every day, the work is finished. She can, for the first time in years, do what she wants: take yoga lessons, read a book, relax.

She is deeply appreciative of her present life. She has a relationship with her son based on trust and good humour. She continues to enjoy the warmth and security offered by her partnership with Rick. She is even reconciled with her mother. The one person she can't forgive is her former husband—and not because of her drinking problem; as she puts it, "For many years I blamed him for my alcoholism, but now I know it was my own doing. I chose to pick the glass up and put it down, not him." What haunts her is his attempt to mold her into a submissive personality, someone artificial, tainted by his ethical standards. That, she believes, was at the heart of their marriage break-up and her descent into an alcoholic abyss.

Breakdown

They are no longer two but one flesh. What therefore God hath joined together, let no man put asunder.

Matthew 19:6

They said they would prefer death in prison to living together. They claimed they were living in daily fear of their lives as it was.

A judge commenting on the request by John
and Margaret Colwell for a legal separation, 1442

As her husband, he has a right to all that is hers: as his wife, she has no right to anything that is his. As her husband, he may divorce her...: as his wife, the utmost 'divorce' she could obtain, is permission to reside alone,—married to his name.

Caroline Sheridan Norton, 1855

It was passed surreptitiously from one school locker to another, carefully hidden not just from the beady eyes of teachers or, God forbid, the vice-principal but the hungry glances of the boys. That any of us should be caught reading the bestselling potboiler *Peyton Place* by the young Grace Metalious was an embarrassment too terrible to contemplate.

Yet we all became hooked. It is, after all, the story of a young girl, Allison MacKenzie, who gradually and painfully makes an independent life for herself by becoming a writer. As the narration tracks her progress, it cracks open the hard shell of respectability encasing Peyton Place, which supposedly represents not only a village in New Hampshire but all of small-town America. Out pour greed, dishonesty, lust, rape, adultery, incest, sexual intrigues of all kinds, and an obsession for malicious gossip. These truths, crudely but honestly put, are what made the book so notorious.

By 1958, *Peyton Place* had sold six million copies and had been made into a movie starring Lana Turner. Its devotees, it turned out, were primarily women. Critics would later claim it had touched a sensitive nerve, the first small glimmer of deep-down discontent that would lead, ten years later, to the women's movement. *Peyton Place* offered up one basic lesson: women who depended on men lost out on life; those who stood on their own two feet were the winners.

Sadly, though, there was another painful undercurrent in the novel, one that, in the end, would destroy Metalious's reputation as a writer. Women, even the independent ones, were portrayed as aggressive sexual predators. The opening lines of the book signal the message: "Indian summer is like a woman. Ripe, hotly passionate, but fickle, she comes and goes as she pleases...." In her fourth and last novel, *No Adam in Eden*, it became clear the author had always loathed her own gender, individually and collectively. It was they, flouting their licentiousness, who were responsible for societal breakdown. Metalious had joined a large crowd. For centuries, male commentators and moralizers have put the blame for the disintegration of marriage and the family firmly on female shoulders.

I

Since Athenian women were sequestered so securely in their homes, it's hard to imagine how they could engage in adulterous love affairs. The Greek orator Lysias (c. 459–c. 380 BC) provides a hint in a story found in one of his orations. Suspecting his wife of hanky-panky, Euphiletos, an Athenian citizen, gathered together a group of his friends and, torches ablaze, they marched into his house. There they discovered Eratosthenes of Oe, lying stark naked beside Euphiletos's wife, and they beat him to death. Although, under Greek law, killing one's wife's lovers was justifiable homicide, the dead man's relatives persecuted Euphiletos for murder, claiming he had plotted to entrap Eratosthenes. In pleading his case, Euphiletos painted this portrait of his domestic life:

It is true that in the early days, Athenians, she was the most excellent of wives; she was a clever, frugal housekeeper, and kept everything in the nicest order. But as soon as I lost my mother, her death became the cause of all my troubles. For it was in attending her funeral that my wife was seen by this man, who in time corrupted her. He looked out for the servant girl who went to market, and so paid addresses to her mistress by which he wrought her ruin.[262]

Eratosthenes, apparently, was something of a rake, with a penchant for seducing other people's wives. In the past, when caught *in flagrante delicto*, he had always been able to buy his way out of the mess. In fact, the exchange of money was a more common penalty for adultery than death; on the one hand, ancient Greeks treated infidelity with dead seriousness and on the other, as something of a joke. A philanderer would sometimes be punished by having his hair pulled out or his face tattooed, humiliations with which Greek comedy had a great deal of fun.[263]

A cuckolded husband had two choices. He could bring a charge of rape if the intruder had forced his wife into sexual intercourse, or, if she had happily complied, he could accuse the adulterer of seduction. The penalties for these crimes tells a great deal about how antiquity viewed women. If the accused was found guilty of rape, he simply had to cough up some money; if seduction, he was put to death. Euphiletos himself explained the rationale: "Those who achieve their end by force are hated by the persons forced: while those who used persuasion corrupted thereby their victims' souls....[264]

What about the corrupted soul of Euphiletos's wife? It would be interesting to know what the "best of wives" saw in her seducer and with what enticements he lured her to bed. But since this was Euphiletos's oration, he was not the least interested in telling her side of the story. Nor do we know what happened to her.

Typically, she would have been divorced by her husband, deprived of caring for her children and ostracized by society. Ex-wives guilty of adultery were barred from all public rituals; they basically lost their citizenship. If they were caught worshipping, say, at Aphrodite's shrine, they became fair game for abuse. They could be stripped of their clothes and jewellery, beaten and kicked, although they were not to be killed or maimed. It was all meant, as the law-maker Solon pointed out, "to disgrace such a woman and make her life not worth living."[265] Even if the husband of an adulterous woman wanted to forgive her, he couldn't. It was unlawful for him to stay married to her.[266]

Adultery was by no means the only cause for marriage breakup in ancient Greece. There was no stigma attached to divorce at all. A husband could simply send his wife back to her natal home whenever he felt like it. There was a big catch, however, one which likely prevented many a disenchanted husband from even thinking of repudiating his spouse. By Greek law, he had to pay back every cent of his wife's dowry to her family. In affluent circles, the marriage contract went so far as to stipulate that the husband must guarantee his wife's allotment through mortgages on his own property in the event the marriage collapsed. If his wife's money was tied up in their estates or businesses and not easily returnable, he had to pay a hefty 18 percent interest per annum to cover her living expenses.

A wife could demand a divorce, too, but it was a lot more difficult. To begin with, she had to elicit the sympathy of a male guardian—her father, brother, uncle—in whose home she would subsequently reside. Her relatives were often loath to take her back; marrying her off a second time was too much bother. It was traditional that a male delegate publicly request a divorce for a female relative before a magistrate, and indeed, there is only one recorded case in the Classical period of a female taking the matter into her own hands.[267] This was Hipparete, who suffered the singularly unfortunate fate of being married to Alcibiades.

Alcibiades was the most famous playboy of fifth-century Athens. He was so extraordinarily handsome as a youth that, as Plutarch put it in his *Lives,* "It was not long before many men of high birth clustered about him and paid him their attentions. Most of them were plainly smitten with his brilliant youthful beauty and fondly courted him."[268] Among them was Socrates, who was totally besotted with the young man. Pampered Alcibiades developed into an arrogant bully, a con man and a terrible debaucher who, during his lifetime, worked his way through an unbelievable number of lovers, male and female.

Why Hipparete's father arranged a marriage to such a reprobate remains a mystery. The first time they met, Alcibiades punched the old man in the face, on a bet from a friend. The father soon regretted his decision. The marriage agreement stipulated Hipparete's dowry would be ten silver talents, but as soon as the first child was born, Alcibiades confronted Hipparete's brother Callias, demanding an equal amount of money. Alcibiades insisted a similar payment should be made every time a baby was produced. Callias was too frightened of him to refuse.

Plutarch writes that Hipparete was "a decorous and affectionate wife," but that didn't stop her husband from consorting with most of the city's courtesans. She finally fled to her brother's house, and, since Callias could see bankruptcy looming as each of her children was born, he welcomed her return.

Alcibiades' behaviour became ever more scandalous until finally, Hipparete demanded a divorce. Plutarch doesn't tell us why she, instead of her brother, approached the magistrate. Perhaps Callias was intimidated by his bully of a brother-in-law. He does tell us what happened when Hipparete demanded her divorce.

On her appearing publicly to do this, as the law required, Alcibiades came up and seized her and carried her off home with him through the market place, no man [including her brother] daring to oppose him or take her from him.[269]

Hipparete would have remained a virtual prisoner in her home but she died shortly afterwards—one way of escaping a rotten marriage.

II

The legal codes of the Greeks and Romans permitted easy divorce if both partners wanted it. The Germanic group of tribes in the early Middle Ages went further. A man could rid himself of his wife because the marriage was barren (the female has always been blamed for childless marriages) or if she had committed a crime—adultery, for example. Even if she had been the "best of wives," he could dump her if he were prepared to pay back double the amount of the bride price.

Divorce initiated by women was forbidden. According to Germanic laws, the punishment for attempting such a brazen act was for the hussy to be covered in slimy mud. As historian Suzanne Fonay Wemple points out, "A wife had to remain faithful and obedient to her husband, even if he were a drunkard, a gambler, mistreated her or was adulterous."[270] Visigothic law was fractionally more liberal towards women. If a man was a pederast or forced his wife to have sexual relations with someone other than himself, she could demand a divorce.

Partly as a reaction to the disregard for women found in such laws and the growing notion that the family was sacrosanct, the early Christian church formulated the ideology that marriage was a religious sacrament and therefore binding for life. Divorce became a mortal sin. However, it would take centuries of sometimes furious debate before the doctrine of marital indissolubility would finally be set in canon law.[271]

First of all, the Church fathers had to contend with conflicting messages in the Bible. Mark was unequivocal in quoting Christ: "Whosoever shall put away his wife, and marry another, committeth adultery against her. And if a woman should put away her husband, and be married to another, she committeth adultery" (Mark 10:11–12). Luke preached pretty well the same thing. But then there was Matthew. He insisted that Christ taught marriage was indissoluble *unless* one of the parties—in some interpretations, only the woman—committed adultery. Then presumably divorce would be permitted.

Other Biblical texts resulted in different interpretations of marital problems. Slowly, however, through the influence of the early Church fathers, the Church's position on divorce solidified: marriage was a commitment for life, even if both parties wanted it dissolved, even if adultery was involved.

Secular law slowly followed suit. The Roman emperor Constantine (c. 274–337) and the Byzantine emperor Justinian I (483–565) both restricted divorce, although the laws were not as strict as the credo put forward by the Church fathers. However, in 789, that old warrior Charlemagne (742–814), king of the Franks and emperor of the Romans, prohibited remarriage after divorce, a law applied by the civil courts throughout the empire. Eight years later, at Charlemagne's request, the bishops assembled at Friuli to confirm this edict. (Despite the fact that Charlemagne's own two marriages ended in divorce, his daughters lived common-law and he kept many concubines.)[272]

Meanwhile, the Church was still having a hard time making up its mind. Various popes, canonists and synods kept reversing Church doctrine on whether adultery could be justification for marriage breakdown, and remarriage allowed. The debate continued until the principle of indissolubility was finally made canon law in 1563.

Over the centuries, common folk often either ignored or rebelled against Church doctrine that sentenced them to lifetime unions of discord and misery. The Church fathers had to come up with an indisputable rationale for their ideas of no divorce and no remarriage. Marriage, they said, was based on the first union of Adam and Eve, and, despite their troubles, that couple certainly never resorted to a divorce. Christian marriage was a union of the flesh represented by the union of Christ with the Church. How could it possibly be torn asunder? Most insidious was the idea of fidelity linked with chastity, the ultimate womanly virtue. If a woman's body was a sacred vessel for the singular use of procreation, how could it be violated by anyone except the man who had originally relieved her of her virginity? Feminine chastity became everything.

Both the ecclesiastical and secular courts meted out harsh punishments for adultery. Under the legal code of the Holy Roman Emperor Frederick II (1194–1250), a wayward wife was not only thrown out of her home but had her nose cut off. Her lover was merely fined. In towns of southern France, an unmarried couple caught in the act were stripped naked, tied together and forced to run through the streets, all the while being whipped by onlookers. The laws of London stipulated a loud, raucous band would lead the adulterers, their heads shaven, from one jail to another. Historians aren't sure how often these harsh penalties were actually imposed. Most likely, the payment of a hefty fine was enough to satisfy the authorities.[273]

All the same, the Church came to understand that some husbands and wives simply could not live together. While divorce remained forbidden, legal separation became a possibility.[274] Three grounds were allowed: adultery, cruelty and heresy (including the abandonment of one's faith). It was the judges' decision whether complaints of this sort were serious enough to warrant separations. A 1974 study of the English court system in the Middle Ages found a separation was granted only if extreme cruelty was involved; ordinary wife-beating was not considered sufficient cause. Even if a separation were approved, neither partner could marry again. It simply meant they no longer had a duty to have sexual intercourse with one another.[275]

There was one other recourse to ending a horrendous marriage—through annulment. This was granted if it could be proved Church rules had been infringed at the time of the marriage. Consanguinity was the principle most often violated. By the 12th century, matrimony was forbidden as far as the seventh degree; one historian estimates there were 2,731 relatives that a young man was forbidden to marry. In a small town, that didn't allow much leeway for finding a bride. "... Whether he were a great lord marrying into his own class, or a peasant bound to the soil, he would be unable to marry all the marriageable girls he could possibly know and a great many more besides."[276] On the other hand, it wasn't too difficult for a unhappy couple to suddenly discover they had fifth cousins in common and demand an annulment.

However, these cases remained rare. It was a long and expensive procedure, with no guarantee the Church judges would believe the evidence; indeed, they were rather loath to do so. It was the great lords and monarchs of Europe whose marriages remained chess games of money and power and who attempted to use the ecclesiastical courts to their own ends. The most striking example of this is the manoeuvring of King Henry VIII.

Catherine of Aragon was first wed to Henry's sickly brother Arthur, although the marriage was never consummated. When Arthur died of consumption, Catherine was handed over to Henry. Since marrying one's brother's widow was forbidden by the Church, a special dispensation had to be obtained from Pope Julius II. After 20 years of marriage, only one child, Mary, lived to adulthood. Desperate for a son and heir and embroiled in international politics, Henry decided it was time to get rid of Catherine. Using Leviticus as his ammunition—"If a man shall take his brother's wife, it is an impurity: he hath uncovered his brother's nakedness; they shall be childless"—Henry argued his marriage was invalid. Never mind what Julius II had said; it was God, not a pope, who could decide such royal matters.

The new pope, Clement VII, refused his request. What ensued was monumental: the Anglican break with the Roman Catholic Church. There was a great irony in this: of all the Reformation countries, it was only England that did not break with the Roman Catholic doctrine of marriage indissolubility.[277]

III

From a modern perspective, the Othello of William Shakespeare's tragedy has all the attributes of a wife-beater. He has an attitude, having suffered years of discrimination and humiliation because of his dark complexion; he is a North African ex-slave and an alien in the snobby world in which he operates. In winning the lovely Desdemona, the only child of a wealthy senator, Othello worms his way into the Venetian society that had so often demeaned him.

Even though he has achieved the lofty rank of warrior general, his manhood and machismo remain an obsession. Once the hint is presented to him that his young wife may be unfaithful, Othello's jealousy quickly swells.

Othello considers himself an honest man, a blunt man, and yet he is incredibly stubborn and close-minded, the kind of person who, once he gets a bee in his bonnet, won't listen to anyone. He takes the word of a fast-talking, duplicitous male like Iago rather than believe a sincere and honest female like Desdemona. He therefore becomes putty in the evil hands of Iago who, full of resentment because he has not been promoted, sets out to destroy Othello by undermining his love for Desdemona. Othello turns into a murdering brute, and an arrogant, stupid one at that.

What about "the divine Desdemona"? She is the 16th century's ideal female victim. Despite Othello's emotional abuse and his battering—at one point, he strikes her, later he suffocates her—she remains loving and faithful. Finding Desdemona near death, her lady-in-waiting demands to know who has committed the wicked deed. Desdemona, in her last breath, protects Othello: "Nobody—I myself. Farewell./Commend me to my kind lord. O, farewell!"

In the early modern period, domestic strife with its accompanying emotional abuse and terrible violence, was a blood-red thread running through society's tapestry. Many factors combined to make life an unrelenting hell for many married couples. Despite the Protestant Reformation, divorce was still a rarity. Although most reformers had rejected the Roman Catholic idea of marriage indissolubility, divorce was thought not to be a remedy for marriage breakdown but a punishment for matrimonial misdeeds and a relief for the injured spouse.[278] Release from marriage vows remained a solution of last resort, and divorces remained few and far between.

Even if dissolution had been possible, most women could not have walked away from their marriages. They had no way of making a living, they had no control over their property and they would have lost custody of their children. All of this meant that, as historian Olwen Hufton puts it, "a high tolerance level of marital violence and sexual infidelity was demanded of the pious Christian wife."[279]

The one thing a battered wife could do was demand a separation from the ecclesiastical authorities, and by so doing, obtain some of the family's assets. The records of these requests, as well as civil- and criminal-court proceedings, paint a dreary picture of marital abuse in the 16th to 18th centuries.

Violence was cited by 80 percent of the women who came before the authorities asking for a separation—extreme violence, for if it were not life-threatening, she might as well not have bothered. In almost every judicial system in the Western world, it was considered a man's right to physically punish his wife if he felt she deserved it. When, in 17th century New England, one Daniel Ela was hauled into court for brutally beating his wife, he argued she was "his servant and his slave" to do with as he would.[280] It would take a long time before this insidious notion would disappear.

Punching, slapping, hitting with a club, restraining with a rope or chain were all considered acceptable, as long as the woman was deemed by the judge (always, of course, male) to have deserved her punishment. In Maine in the 17th century, a husband kicked his wife and hit her with a club because she wouldn't feed the pig. The judge ruled the health of the porker was of utmost importance to the well-being of the family and sided with the husband.[281]

The records of the divorce courts during the French Revolution portray many a sad case of wife abuse. In May 1793, for example, Marie Vasse's husband

without reason or excuse … seized the fire shovel which was by the chimney, and dealt his said wife three blows with it, hurled himself upon her like a madman, dealt her various blows to the head and to the body, threw her to the ground, and tore at her hair while she was on the ground, while threatening to break her arm or leg if she should have the misfortune to cry out.[282]

In this case, the judges sided with the woman, but whether Marie was in any shape to enjoy her new-found freedom was not revealed in the records.

There were, of course, more subtle forms of domestic ill-treatment than outright violence. Historian Roderick Phillips cites the following examples: forbidding a wife to make contact with her family, locking her in her home and evicting her from her house to seek refuge with neighbours, friends or families. "Men displayed their domestic superiority by destroying their wives' property or by selling it to finance gambling or drinking."[283] Women who were kicked out of their homes had to make a public display of not taking any household property. One divorce petition in Rouen recorded that "When leaving the house she [the expelled wife] turned out her pockets to show that she was taking nothing from her husband's house." To retrieve the most essential items—her clothes, including her undergarments, her bedding or even her mirror—she was forced to petition the courts. There was so much heartache that a cult sprang up around Rita of Cascia, the patron saint of suffering and battered wives, who, even into the 20th century was more popular among many women than the Virgin Mary.[284]

With so much unhappiness, it naturally followed that the philosophy of indissoluble marriages began to be debated and contested. If, as the Enlightenment would have it, marriages should be "affectional unions," it seemed reasonable that loss of affection would justify ending it. By the end of the early modern period, divorce in Protestant Germany was becoming increasing common. One star-studded list of female writers published late in the 18th century included 19 divorcees.[285] Marriage in Germany, especially Prussia, wrote one English commentator, was considered a simple contract that could be revoked by mutual agreement, leaving both partners free again to remarry with the same ease as if they had been left widowed.

Finally, in 1792, during the French Revolution, divorce was legalized in France for the first time. The law was remarkable because it recognized absolute equality between the husband and wife. Terminating a marriage by mutual agreement with incompatibility as the grounds was considered the ideal, although contested divorces were also allowed after attempts at a rapprochement had broken down. Over a period of 11 years, almost 20,000 divorces were granted, an amazing figure at the time.[286] What really astounded observers, however, was that almost 75 percent of them were initiated by women. It was men who were supposed to hate marriage and, given any chance to fly the coop, would do so. The laws were repealed in 1816, and divorce all but eliminated, not because women were suffering under them but because they were said to be abusing them.

IV

I found her [my wife's] nature wholly alien to mine, her tastes obnoxious to me, her cast of mind common, low, narrow, and singularly incapable of being led to anything higher, expanded to anything larger.... I found that I could not pass a single evening, or even a single hour of the day with her in comfort; that kindly conversation could not be sustained between us, because whatever topic I started, I immediately received from her a turn at once coarse and trite, perverse and imbecile....[287]

Poor Rochester. He had been duped into marrying a lunatic and now, when he has found his heart's desire, the crazy wife in the belfry has been discovered. Rochester had hoped Jane Eyre would live with him anyway, but she knew what her Victorian society would make of that. Her reputation would be so damaged that even Rochester would come to despise her. Fortunately, the creator of these passionate characters was able to whip up a fantastic fire that killed the insane wife and maimed and blinded Rochester (presumably for his sin of even considering a life with a woman other than his wife).

What Charlotte Brontë depicts so well in *Jane Eyre* is the hopelessness, the anguish, of a husband or wife caught forever in a hellish marriage. The prudish 19th century was stern about divorce. Between 1816 and 1884, France had no divorce law; nor was divorce permitted in Italy after 1815. Britain's much-debated Divorce Bill of 1857 did nothing to liberalize the law; it just moved the distasteful problem from the Parliamentary and ecclesiastical authorities to civil court. By Confederation, most of the Canadian provinces had divorce laws, but the double standard so firmly embedded in them rendered them useless, at least for women. Only in certain areas of the United States was it possible to dissolve an unhappy marriage without humiliation and huge expense.

As educated women began to analyze the patriarchal foundation of marriage and divorce legislation, they became more and more incensed. The injustices were outrageous. Article 213 of the French Civil Code stated bluntly: "A husband owes protection to his wife, a wife, obedience to her husband." Napoleon insisted the article should be read aloud at every wedding for, at a time when women "forget their sense of inferiority," it was important "to remind them frankly of the submission they owe to the man who is to become the arbiter of their fate."[288]

This philosophy was deeply ingrained in the French laws that dealt with marital crimes. A woman who infected her husband with syphilis was automatically guilty of adultery; a man who did the same thing was considered blameless, even though he knowingly inflicted the disease on his wife. (When divorce became legal in England, one-fifth of all the petitions filed by women between 1858–1901 cited their husbands' deliberate transmission of venereal disease as the cause.[289]) A husband who was attempting to prove a wife was unfaithful could use private correspondence—from her lover, her sister, her priest—that he had purloined. The wife was allowed no such recourse.

The grievances were so painful that women throughout Europe began to take matters in their own hands, demanding reform of the divorce laws. The tortured tale of Caroline Sheridan Norton (1808–1877) is an astonishing example. Caroline was a beauty from a distinguished, cultured family—her grandfather was Richard Brinsley Sheridan, the playwright and politician— but she unfortunately had no fortune of her own. At age 19, she married George Bentley Norton, brother to Lord Grantley. George turned out to be a cross between Othello and Iago, a jealous man, arrogant and vindictive, and a bully to boot.[290] Caroline described her life with Norton:

We had been married about two months, when, one evening we had all withdrawn to our apartments, we were discussing some opinion Mr. Norton had expressed: I said (very uncivilly) that 'I thought I had never heard so silly or ridiculous a conclusion.' This remark was punished by a sudden and violent kick; the blow reached my side; it cause great pain for many days, and being afraid to remain with him, I sat up the whole night in another apartment.[291]

Caroline had three sons by Norton, and it was they who kept her in a marriage that grew ever more violent. She knew that, under law, her husband would automatically obtain custody of the children. (George Norton was a lawyer and well aware of his legal rights.) Meanwhile, Caroline had become something of a literary light in London. She wrote poetry, plays, novels and edited a fashionable women's magazine, all of which yielded her a pretty good income. George, who had a habit of making bad investments, was constantly short of money and simply confiscated Caroline's earnings. Finally, in 1835, while Caroline was away visiting relatives, she and George had a horrible argument. He sent the children off to relatives and forbade Caroline to see them. Meanwhile, he filed a law suit claiming the then prime minister, Lord Melbourne, was having an affair with his wife. The case was considered something of a joke and thrown out of court, but it did irreparable harm to Caroline's reputation. (It rather boosted Lord Melbourne's.)

After nine years, the Nortons finally separated. Caroline had managed to get a court order allowing her access to her children, but George simply took them off to Scotland, where English law did not apply. It was at that point, in 1837, that Caroline Norton first took direct aim at the patriarchal society by writing a stinging pamphlet, *The Natural Claim of a Mother in the Custody of her Child as affected by the Common Law Right of the Father*. It was a powerful piece of writing. In it, she described not only her own experience but cases far more tragic. A member of parliament, Serjeant Talfourd, who had been deeply affected by the examples he had come across in court of mothers losing their children to horribly abusive husbands, took up the cause. Although his bill failed, another pamphlet by Caroline, this time signed with a male pseudonym, did bring results. In 1839, the Infant Custody Act was passed. It was very limited. A court could give a mother custody of her infant children and those under seven, but even those few rights could be forfeited if adultery had been proved against the woman. Still, it was the first in a number of bills that, over the century, would chisel away at male supremacy in domestic affairs.

Meanwhile, Caroline's and George's marital war was heating up even more. Since he had a legal right to all her wealth, he initiated a court action, successfully as it turned out, to get his hands on an inheritance left to Caroline by her father. He next subpoenaed Caroline's publishers, forcing them to hand over her earnings, which he then used for his own purposes. He even obtained a lien on copyright of all her works, so her future royalties would be his. Finally, when he discovered a legacy left to Caroline by her mother was legally secure, he simply cut off her maintenance allowance. By 1855, she had not received a penny from him in three years and had run up enormous bills for her food, lodging and clothing.

Caroline continued to rail publicly against these outrageous injustices perpetrated by the court system on her husband's behalf. In 1853, she published a rigorous and effective polemic, *English Law for Women in the Nineteenth Century*, followed two years later by *A Letter to the Queen on Lord Chancellor Cranworth's Marriage and Divorce Bill*, which was an outraged attack on the male-dominated English legal system. She wrote:

An English wife has no legal right even to her clothes or ornaments; her husband may take them and sell them if he pleases, even though they be the gifts of relatives or friends, or bought before marriage.

An English wife cannot make a will....

An English wife cannot legally claim her own earnings. Whether wages for manual labour, or payment for intellectual exertion, whether she weed potatoes, or keep a school, her salary is *the husband's*....

An English wife may not leave her husband's house. Not only can he sue her for 'restitution of conjugal rights,' but he has a right to enter the house of any friend or relation with whom she may take refuge ... and carry her away by force, with or without the aid of the police.[292]

Caroline Norton's case was taken up by feminists and other reformers, and their outrage eventually led to the 1857 Matrimonial Causes Act. Ironically, although this legislation became a *cause célèbre* and was bitterly debated in the House of Commons, it did not change grounds for divorce one iota.

Since the 1670s, there had been one method of obtaining a divorce in England: through a special act of Parliament. It was a costly and complicated affair. A wife's adultery had to be proved in a common-law court and her lover fined before a husband could even apply for the Parliamentary disposition. A woman who wanted to petition Parliament not only had to determine her husband had committed adultery but that he was guilty of a far more serious offence: bigamy, incest or cruelty. In the 187-year history of British Parliamentary divorce, only 325 petitions were granted, of which four were obtained by women.

The 1857 Act did not broaden the grounds for divorce. It simply transferred the jurisdiction from ecclesiastical courts and Parliament to a special divorce court. It was thought this would make legal proceedings less expensive and therefore available to people other than the aristocracy. More significantly, the Act changed the rules with regard to property. A divorced or separated woman finally had control over her own assets. Divorce did increase, but not by much; between 1859 and 1909, 17,952 petitions were granted, 7,525 to women.[293] The simple fact was most females could not endure the insidious social stigma and economic hardship that came with being a divorcee. The angel by the hearth was supposed to be the instrument that knit the family together, not a pickax smashing it asunder.

There were those, however, who survived society's censure and, in the end, benefited from getting out of a marriage. When Emily Landry was divorced by her husband Leonard in 1882, on a trumped-up charge of having an affair with his friend, her mother wrote from Peterborough, Ontario: "Don't think of coming home. Neither your father or myself could stand it. The gossips have had their knives sharpened. Already I've heard you called a pariah, a witch, a harlot." Emily opened a clothing shop in Toronto on the proceeds from the divorce settlement. The store grew into a chain, and soon Emily was richer than her husband, her parents and the gossips all put together.[294]

V

Divorce underwent a profound metamorphosis during the 20th century. From an evil to be shunned at all costs, it came to be perceived not only as an individual right but, at times, as beneficial to society.

It began with World War I, that soul-destroying conflagration that skewed all of Western society's ideals. With death in the shadows, romantic love in its most bittersweet rendition was enthusiastically embraced. A couple who had little in common, and whose interest in each other would have faded after a few dates, didn't hesitate to march to the altar. Once he returned from the war—if he did—they quickly discovered how ill-suited they were. Marriage breakdown followed.

Even some long-time marriages that had seemed stable before the war fell apart afterwards. The couple's experiences had diverged so much—he, having faced bloody hell, and she, tasting independence either in the household or by working outside of it—that they were no longer compatible and certainly not soul mates.

What really struck at the heart of marriage, though, was that old spoiler, adultery. Temptation was everywhere: the lonely war widows packing the canteens and nightclubs, prostitutes prowling the streets in every city and, of course, the age-old disgrace that gnaws at the heart of any war—the rape of female enemy. By 1917, almost one-fifth of the British fighting forces had contacted syphilis; that year, the authorities finally faced reality and issued condoms.[295]

Of course, it wasn't just the husbands who were unfaithful. "Who can resist a man in uniform?" went the old refrain. Sometimes soldiers came home to find either an unexpected child in the house or their wife pregnant.

The divorce rate soared in European countries and North America. In England, in each year between 1910 and 1913, the average number of divorces was 701. In 1921, the number had spiralled to 3,956. Even in the United States, which had not entered the war until March 1917, the rate increased by a phenomenal 40 percent.[296]

It was in the Roaring Twenties that divorce became more prominent and even fashionable. Frederick Lewis Allen, the associate editor of *Harper's* magazine, had this observation about the "decline in the amount of disgrace accompanying divorce":

... there was often about the divorced person just enough of an air of unconventionality, just enough of a touch of scarlet, to be considered rather dashing and desirable. Many young women probably felt as did the young New York girl who said, toward the end of the decade, that she was thinking of marrying Henry, although she didn't care very much for him, because even if they didn't get along she could get a divorce and 'it would be much more exciting to be a divorcee than to be an old maid.'[297]

The 1917 Russian Revolution and the ensuing rethinking of the family also had a profound influence in Western Europe and North America. The Soviet Union's Family Code of November 1926 allowed so-called postcard divorce. A simple written request by either party mailed to the authorities would automatically dissolve a marriage. It was heartily praised by critics in the West as a liberating step forward. After a tour of Russia, George Bernard Shaw wrote, "At present [in England] a deserted wife or husband, by simply refusing to sue for divorce, can in mere revenge or jealousy or on Church grounds, prevent the deserter from marrying again. We should have to follow the good example of Russia in refusing to tolerate such situations."[298]

However, in a few years, it was obvious the new policy led to cynical abuse. Husbands abandoned their families in record numbers, leaving their wives to fend for themselves and their children. There were even reports of peasants tapping marriage as a valuable source of unpaid labour. A man would marry a healthy young woman in the spring. She would help with the planting and harvesting, but in the winter, when she began to complain a little or demand a new dress or when her relatives showed up, he would file for a divorce— just in time to find a new slave labourer for the next season.

Soviet laws governing alimony were vague, and often the husband either couldn't or wouldn't pay up. During the 1930s, financial penalties were imposed that made walking away from a marriage less attractive. Then, in 1944, new codes authored by Stalin made divorce all but impossible.

The same phenomenon occurred under fascism. Spain in the 1930s had passed one of the most liberal divorce laws in Europe. Under General Franco, the legislation was repealed, and in 1938, divorce was made illegal. The trend in France during the 1930s was towards simpler divorce procedures but, under Vichy government laws of 1942, supporting one's family became "a moral obligation" and desertion a crime. Divorce all but disappeared.

In Germany, grounds for divorce actually widened, but only as an integral part of the Nazi campaign to increase population and insure racial purity. In 1938, for example, a new law permitted divorce if one of the partners had a "hereditary illness" such as insanity, a physical handicap or was infertile or had been sterilized. Divorces were even granted if one of the spouses complained the other made a habit of shopping at stores owned by Jews.[299]

Meanwhile, divorce laws in Great Britain, Commonwealth countries and many American states were slowly being liberalized. In 1923, a bill was passed in the British Parliament that at last permitted a wife to sue her husband for divorce on the grounds of *his* adultery. Canada followed suit in 1925. Not surprisingly, the number of women seeking to end their marriages soared. By the end of the 1930s, divorce petitions by British wives represented 60 percent of the total. In 1937, British laws were further liberalized. As well as adultery, grounds included a separation of three years, cruelty and prolonged and incurable insanity. A woman could also dissolve a marriage if her husband had been convicted of rape, sodomy or bestiality.

Just as marriage breakdown was shaking off its sinful hue, the biggest scandal to hit the British monarchy in centuries erupted, centering, on the surface at least, around divorce. King Edward VIII (1894–1972) was dapper, blond, handsome and incredibly popular. Ordinary people thought he actually cared about them. He was crowned with great pomp and ceremony in January 1936. Eleven months later, in a quiet, sad voice, he told the nation he was abdicating.

The wrongdoing he had committed was to fall in love with a stylish American, Mrs. Wallis Warfield Simpson. It wasn't so much that she was a commoner (and many people remarked that she was, indeed, common) or worse, an American, but that she had committed the greatest of all sins not once but twice: she was divorced. The couple lived out their long lives in exile, mostly in France, remaining favourite targets for satirists and novelists.

(Almost 60 years later, another royal couple, the Prince and Princess of Wales, would again shock the world. This time they themselves divorced, but attitudes had changed—somewhat. It wasn't so much the divorce that created the scandal but the licentious and sometimes outrageous details of both their extramarital affairs, blatantly laid out in the media, that offended the British public.)

World War II was another world-shattering event that precipitated a soaring divorce rate. In the United States, more than three million divorces were granted between 1942 and 1948, compared with 1.75 million in the previous seven years.[300] For one thing, many a war bride was deserted by her war groom. In New Zealand, quickie marriage between locals and American GIs was so common that in 1947, special legislation had to be passed to make divorce faster and easier.

For the most part, though, as was the case during the World War I, it was often just a matter of one or both of the spouses changing profoundly from their war-time experiences. To their wives' horror, husbands came home hopeless alcoholics; sometimes these marriages lasted less than a month. Other men were thought either too ambitious or not ambitious enough for wives who had spent the war dreaming of a prosperous new life. Some women had worked for the first time, found independence and refused to knuckle down to a domineering husband. These conflicts usually meant severe emotional upheaval. Doris Lessing describes just such marriage breakdown in her novel *A Proper Marriage:*

When a woman left her husband, or threatened to leave him—that is, a woman of her type, who insisted on her rights to behave as a man would—then the husband went through certain actions like an automaton, beginning with the confiscating the contraceptives, threatening to make her forcibly pregnant, accusing her of multifarious infidelities, and ending in self-abusing weeping appeals that she should change her mind and stay.[300a]

Not surprisingly, in the conservative 1950s, the divorce rate abruptly flattened. A longing for calm family life after the chaos of World War II, economic prosperity in most of the Western world and a restoration of the traditional hierarchy where men went to work and women stayed home all combined to halt the climb in the number of divorces. (The divorce rate didn't go down; it simply remained stable at a figure higher than in the 1930s.) Politicians felt it appropriate to leave well enough alone; almost no new legislation was passed anywhere in the West during this time. Yet underneath the calm surface seethed real frustration.

"During the past year no social problem has been the subject of a greater— or more futile—public furor in this country than Canada's outmoded divorce laws," wrote journalist Christina McCall Newman in *Chatelaine* of April 1961. The problem was that adultery remained the only grounds for divorce, and there was to be no "collusion, condonance or connivance" involved in obtaining proof. It was a big joke, of course. The usual *modus operandi* went something like this: a couple would agree that one of them would rent a room in a sleazy hotel. At an appointed time, a woman, whom the husband had never seen before and would never dream of having sex with, would show up. Shortly after, a detective would burst in, ignoring the fact that nothing was going on. With a co-respondent—who was in the pay of the detective—now in the bag, the wife could then sue for divorce.

But that was only the beginning. Humiliating and costly divorce proceedings followed. McCall Newman quotes a Toronto divorcee, "a sensitive and accomplished woman with a *summa cum laude* university degree": "All through those terrible years when I was involved in the circus of the divorce courts, I felt cut off from people leading normal lives. It was a little like being the Scarlet Woman in a Victorian melodrama and it took me a couple of years to recover the belief that I was still a first-class citizen."

Between 1960 and 1986, divorce policy in virtually every Western country was substantially reformed or, more commonly, completely revised.[301] No-fault divorce, in which neither of the spouses are blamed for the marriage breakdown, became the norm. It was a reflection of the new, social-sciences approach to society's problems. An individual was not entirely responsible for his or her actions but was deeply influence by the environment.

As this principle worked its way into the collective psyche, the predictable happened: divorce rates soared—but beyond anyone's expectations. In Canada, the divorce rate has shot up from two percent of all marriages in 1951 to 42 percent in 1985, levelling off in the 1990s at around 33 percent. In the United States, 50 percent of 1990s marriages end in divorce. In most European countries, statistics tell a similar story. Countries that had outlawed divorce—Ireland, Spain, Italy, for example—brought in more liberal legislation.

There have been serious repercussions. Circumstances vary from country to country, depending on how generous is the social-welfare system and how equitable the courts are in distributing assets, but studies have found that generally, mothers left to look after children are considerably poorer after a divorce. One researcher found most wives "experience rapid downward social mobility after divorce, while most husbands' economic status is substantially improved."[302]

Even more serious is the argument by some social scientists (certainly not all) that children of divorced parents fare less well than children who are raised in unhappy marriages. Canadian journalist Margaret Philip wrote in July 1995, "The harsh fact remains that divorce levels are a strike against children, and parents who dump their marriage embark on a lifelong struggle to compensate for the disadvantage that their decision bestows on their kids."[303]

The religious Right in the United States, Canada and elsewhere insists that single-parent families are breeding grounds for drug addiction, crime, depression and suicide. Said one television commentator, "Every night on the bus, I see this mother with two little kids, dragging them home to some squalid high-rise. I doubt she'd have enough strength to feed and bathe them properly. Is she better off than putting up with an unhappy marriage?"

Yes, if divorce statistics are to be believed. Generally, more women initiate divorce procedures than men, not for frivolous reasons but most often because of physical and emotional abuse, drug or alcohol addiction, and desertion. Stricter divorce laws would not protect the most vulnerable in society; tough regulations regarding child-support payments might.

The 1997 comedy *First Wives Club* is the usual Hollywood fantasy full of nonsense and fun. It tells the story of four best friends, graduates of Middlebury College, class of '69, who, 25 years later, have all been dumped by their husbands for much younger women. Cynthia, the wealthy socialite, commits suicide, and this spurs the other three friends to get together and talk over their troubles. "Why did Cynthia do it?" asks Annie (Diane Keaton). Elyse (Goldie Hawn) replies, "She probably gave Gil [her husband] the best years of her life, sacrificed her youth, always put herself last, would have bolstered his ego, his drive, his ambition, and just as her dignity was hanging on by a thread, he lopped it off by running off with a preschooler."

In no time, the First Wives Club is formed, and the fierce threesome are ready to wreak revenge on their husbands. They're wonderfully successful, even managing to get the men to cough up large sums for a centre for abused women named after their dead friend. At the opening reception, the three divorcees show up in similar, all-white, designer outfits, looking much like Arthurian knights in shining armor. They go out into the night—one supposes to defend womankind—belting out the theme song: "And don't tell me what to do/And don't tell me what to say/Don't try to change me in any way/Just let me be myself/To live my life the way that I want./I'm free and I love to be free...."

Dale

They made an odd couple, these two best friends. Little Mary, dressed so primly she looked liked a child, hunched over by the weight of her bulging book bag, and big-boned Dale, her outfits mismatched and slightly shabby, her slim binder casually carried under her arm. Mary Beattie was the great brain; Dale Bartlett always stood near the bottom of the class. Yet these two were inseparable, a comfort to each other, one supposes, in their quaintness, their eccentricity. Neither fluttered in the social circles. Mary, we knew, was studying at home, up to her ears in trigonometry so that another 98 percent would grace her report card. But what about Dale, with that great, beaming smile? Why did she never have a boyfriend, never show up at a dance? Her nonchalance regarding the social whirl irritated us. Who was she not to care that she didn't have a date for the Indigo Ball? Typically insensitive teenagers, we had no idea of the responsibility Dale bore every single day.

Dale has always hung on to a golden memory of her childhood—she and her mom Norma, skipping around a big tree that grew in the middle of the sidewalk while they sang together, "Bread and butter, apples and oranges"— a silly game that always sent Dale into howls of laughter.

There was a down-to-earth quality, a strength of character about Norma Bartlett that appealed to everyone who met her. Nonetheless, she was a lady through and through. No one ever heard a swear word issuing from her mouth and she wouldn't dream of smoking.

Norma's father Fred Legge died of cancer when she was only six years old, and her mother Annie was left to support Norma and her sister Isabelle or Bel, as everyone called her. Annie eventually got a job at the nearby Honey-dew food-processing plant, but money was very scarce. After Grade 8, Norma decided it was time she pulled her weight, and she went to work on the assembly line of Flash Fasteners, a zipper factory.

Bel, who was quite a few years older than Norma, led quite the social life. She liked to dance and flirt, and many beaux came and went. Norma, on the other hand, was attached to one guy. A friend at work introduced her to her brother Walter Bartlett, a serious young man, and he and Norma became sweethearts. They planned to marry, but in 1941, Norma met Terry Whiting, a handsome young naval officer, who swept her off her feet. It was an exciting, whirlwind romance—the couple ended up marrying only a few months after they met. Their daughter Dale was born in 1943. When her husband was shipped overseas, Norma moved in with her sister Bel, who agreed to look after the baby while Norma continued to work in the zipper factory.

After the war, Terry returned home, but it quickly became obvious he and Norma were not compatible. Dale still has photographs of her father holding her as a baby and looking quite jubilant. Beside them stands Norma, appearing not nearly as happy. The couple was divorced in 1947, and thereafter, Terry Whiting entirely disappeared from Dale's life. Years later she tracked him down. He, too, was still living in Toronto. He agreed to meet with her, but at the last moment called and cancelled.

Norma wasn't too upset by her failed marriage because Walter Bartlett had never really disappeared from her life. He was still very much smitten and willing to forget her unfortunate digression. They married in 1949. They had just enough savings for a down payment on a small, two-bedroom bungalow on Hollis Avenue in Scarborough. Dale lives in that same house to this day; she finally paid off the mortgage in 1977.

Walter could do anything with his hands—repair cars, do plumbing and electrical work, fix broken toys. By trade he was a carpenter, hired at various construction sites around the city. It was seasonal work, though, and, probably for that reason, Norma took an assembly-line job at the Ely Lilly Pharmaceuticals plant not too far from their house. Then the babies started to arrive. In 1951, Lynn was born, and two years later, Jill. Dale's sisters were playmates for her, and Walter always treated her exactly the same as he did his own daughters.

The family's happiness came to an end when in 1954, Norma was diagnosed as having cancer. One breast was removed, and she underwent intensive and painful radiation treatment. She never let on to her children how ill she was, not for one moment. She refused to be admitted to hospital, refused to be away from her young family. Every day, during the long process of radiation treatment, she travelled downtown by bus and streetcar to Toronto General Hospital and back again. She never complained. Dale, who was 11 when her mother first became ill, remembers feeling put out when she was asked to hang up the washing. Only later did she realize how painful and exhausting that job must have been for Norma, who was then in the middle of radiation. The cancer spread, and finally a full mastectomy was undertaken, but to no avail. Norma died on October 17, 1959. She was only 37 years old.

All along, Dale had been told her mother would get better, so her death came as a horrible shock. For six months she could hardly get out of bed. Then one morning, she woke up and said to herself, "I have to go on with my life." She developed an unflinching, almost irritating determination to see the bright side of everything that persists to this day. She wore such a sunny, almost silly smile, few of her classmates had an inkling of what she was going through.

She had just started Grade 9 at R. H. King Collegiate and she kept thinking about her mother, who, since she herself had had to quit school after Grade 8, had been looking forward to vicariously living Dale's high-school years. That summer before her death, one of the things Norma most liked to do was to study Dale's timetable, talk about which courses her daughter should take, what the teachers would be like.

Walter Bartlett never flinched in his duties as a single father. He came home to his children every day after work, and insisted they have dinner together and talk about what they did at school that day. They'd watch television together, although Walter would pretty well choose the programs. He liked films about war, gun-blazing westerns and action-packed adventure stories. It rubbed off on Dale; to this day, she adores Sylvester Stallone movies.

Each spring, Walter sent for the holiday-guide booklets supplied free by the big oil companies. An itinerary was carefully mapped out, and each daughter was allowed to pick the spots she wanted to visit along the way. Then, with the dog in tow and a tent trailer attached to the car, they would set out on their long, carefully planned vacation. They travelled to British Columbia and Nova Scotia, California and Mexico. Dale remembers these trips as the loveliest of times. They were very much part of Walter's plan to bring the family closer together. For all his devotion, though, he was a traditional male; housework was not part of his landscape. It was left to 14-year-old Dale to look after her sisters, age five and three, and manage the household.

It was hard on her. She prepared the supper every evening, peeling potatoes, baking cookies, figuring out how to cook yet another version of hamburger. She did the dishes, the washing, the ironing and the cleaning. A great-aunt pitched in to help with the serious cleaning that got done once or twice a year, a family friend gave Dale easy recipes and useful cooking hints—she still roasts the turkey in a paper bag—and a neighbour helped looked after the children. Despite this assistance, the main housekeeping burden fell on Dale's shoulders. Child care was particularly onerous to a young high-school student. She had to rush home every day to collect her sisters from babysitters or school, which ruled out any extra-curricular activities, and she was so exhausted by the end of the day, her homework suffered.

The family was badly hurt by Norma's death in another way. In 1956, Canada had not yet established a universal, government-supported health plan. For some insane reason, the Bartletts' private health insurance paid for the mastectomy operation on one of Norma's breasts but not on the other. Nor were the costs of radiation treatments covered. If Norma had agreed to stay in the hospital, the insurance company would have coughed up the money, but she insisted on being home to care for her young family, and out-patient care was not part of the insurance package. On her death, Walter Bartlett was handed a bill for over $3,000, about what he earned in a year.

It left the family financially strapped. There was no spare money, certainly none for fancy dresses. Dale's clothes were hand-me-downs or things she sewed herself, none very expertly. In the summer months, when her school-mates were all working to pay for their wardrobes, she was at home, babysitting her sisters. Her unfashionable dress was one reason Dale never dated, not once during the entire five years of her high-school career. Nor did she feel she could bring friends home. She never had time to keep the house properly clean and tidy, and the furniture became ever more shabby. Dale decided she was shy anyway, didn't want to be part of the crowd.

For all his financial difficulties, Walter Bartlett insisted each of his daughters complete high school. University, however, was out of the question. There simply wasn't enough money. It didn't matter much to Dale. Since she was eight years old, she had longed to be a teacher. No tuition was required at the Toronto Teacher's College, and her Aunt Bel gave her the money for books.

Dale was still taking care of the household when she started college, so it was a demanding year, but she loved it, and knew at once she had made the right choice. Students were paid for the two-week practice teaching that concluded the course. With her first cheque, she paid an outstanding dentist bill, bought a couple of dresses and, with her friend Mary Beattie, went to the Stratford Shakespearean Festival.

Dale managed an A average at teacher's college, so she had no difficulty finding a job. The Scarborough Board of Education hired her to teach Grade

3 at their newly constructed Bendale Junior School in the north part of the suburb.

Once she was working, Dale began taking university courses during the summers. It was a pleasant time for her. She'd sit through two hours of lectures a day at the University of Toronto, have lunch with some classmates, then take a swim before heading home—her first taste, really, of a full-fledged social life. Nine years later, she finally earned her B.A., majoring in English.

During all this time she was still living at home and contributing financially, slowly helping to pay off the bills related to her mother's illness. As her sisters got older, they were able to take care of themselves, but Dale was still doing all the housework, still going on vacation with the family in the summers, still watching the television programs her father chose. The house had become even more ramshackle. When her sister Lynn was about to marry, Dale wanted to have a shower for her, but rather than face the embarrassment of the unsightly Bartlett furnishings, she persuaded a neighbour to hold it at her place.

In the early 1970s, Walter Bartlett developed emphysema, brought on by his smoking and the wood dust he inhaled every day. He became increasingly ill until finally, in 1973, he died of liver failure. He was only in his early fifties, and his daughters deeply mourned his death.

Despite her stepfather's untimely death, the '70s turned out to be a time of liberation for Dale. The family house had been left to all three children, but by that time, Lynn and Jill had married or were pursuing careers of their own. Dale bought them out, and had the bungalow refurbished as a charming bachelor-girl's abode. With her degree came a hefty raise in pay, and for the first time, she had money in her pocket. In 1971, she bought her first new car. She had a circle of friends, many of whom were single or divorced, and they felt free to call Dale up on the spur of the moment to watch a movie or go for dinner. She took all sorts of courses: macramé, yoga, swimming. In the winter, she went cross-country skiing. What she liked the most was volleyball. She played with the teachers every Friday afternoon, and also with a group at a recreational centre. She still plays the sport. It was as though she was finally catching up on the games she had missed during high school.

Dale had always felt herself to be naïve and awkward around members of the opposite sex. She'd never gone out with boys at high school, never had a date even at teacher's college, but in 1974, a man came into her life. He was the disc jockey at her sister's wedding reception although, as it turned out, that job was only a sideline. He worked as a sound engineer for the Canadian Broadcasting Corporation, primarily recording classical music. He and Dale liked each other at once and started dating steadily. They'd go to concerts and the theatre together; they both had a passion for cross-country skiing, liked picnicking and canoeing. It was one of the happiest times in her life, yet when he got serious, started talking about marriage, she refused even to discuss the matter. She says, "I had done all that—looking after children, the house—and I didn't want to do it again." The relationship gradually ended and she has not had a steady male friend since.

In 1980, Dale was transferred to Corvette Public School, located in an inner-city neighbourhood full of newly arrived immigrants, most of whom were living on very low incomes. Many of the children didn't speak English. That first year was something of a shock for Dale, but having to deal with so many backgrounds and cultures, she believes forced her to change her attitudes and techniques, and in the end, made her a better teacher.

During the 1980s, there were so many teachers and so little chance for promotions that the Scarborough School Board realized it had to somehow compensate for this lack of upward mobility. A scheme for paid leave of absences was devised. Eighty percent of a teacher's annual salary would be paid each year for four years, so that the fifth year could be offered as a sabbatical, no money lost, no strings attached. Dale jumped at the opportunity. With her family's rather dismal longevity record, she didn't want, as she says, to put all her eggs in the retirement basket. She used her year-long holidays to indulge in what had become her great passion: travel.

She has travelled around the world. The Middle East—Egypt, Israel, Jordan—and Europe—Germany, Greece, Italy, France, the Scandinavian countries, England many times—as well as the South Pacific, Australia, New Zealand, Hong Kong, Mexico, Kenya. She has crisscrossed Canada and the United States, island-hopped in the Caribbean, walked the Cotswolds, cruised down the western South American coast, taking in the Galapagos Islands. Often she goes with a friend or a tour group, but sometimes she is entirely on her own. The only thing she loathes is having to eat by herself in the evenings, but this rarely happens. She doesn't hesitate to approach a table of diners and ask, "May I join you?"

Perhaps because so many of her relatives died young or disappeared from her life, Dale has thrown herself into another hobby: tracing her family roots. She is a serious genealogist, combing through various archives and libraries for birth, marriage and death records, visiting obscure British hamlets where some ancestor or other might have been born and using a computer program to keep track of it all. She found out her great-grandfather mounted guard outside Buckingham Palace, discovered he and her great-grandmother were married in the Tower of London, knows her grandfather was born in Windsor Castle barracks. This pursuit of her past has allowed her to fix her family vividly in her imagination, and in fact, keep them alive.

Years ago, Dale realized she would probably be single her entire life. Most of the men she met were already married; those few who weren't, she seldom found acceptable. In a universe dictated by couples, she has learned to be content. She sees her sisters often, has two nephews to whom she is close and many female friends, almost all of whom live alone.

Her mother is often in her thoughts. When Dale had her kitchen renovated, she imagined how the new dishwasher and microwave oven would have amazed Norma. She knows her mother would have been pleased she had become a teacher, and would have admired her for her independence, would have thought she was fortunate. Says Dale, "I don't feel good about all the deaths in my family, I never win the lottery, but I'm happy. It's a mind-set. You have to believe you're lucky and then you will be."

Frances

I remember having only one conversation with Frances Holmes during the entire time we were at high school together. I met her walking a dog, a mangy-looking beast, part terrier, part German shepherd, called Mickey. Given what the future held for Frances, my associating her with dogs was prescient, to say the least.

Frances Holmes was Mary Gray's best friend, part of the satellite clique that buzzed around the periphery but that never really took part in the school's social life. That gang always went to Frances's house after class, gathering around her kitchen table where her mother's homemade strawberry shortcake would be waiting for them. Etta Holmes was so amiable, so glad to see her daughter's friends she'd even go out and play volleyball with them in the driveway. We were always a little envious at the thought of such a warm and comforting homecoming.

What we considered odd about Frances was that she never had a boyfriend. She'd go to parties and horse around with the guys—she loved to have a good time, and was kind of loud and mouthy. But during her entire five years at R. H. King Collegiate, she dated not one single guy. In her mind, boys could not possibly be attracted to her because she was so plain. She wasn't, of course. She had a pretty, round face, smallish features, lovely, reddish-brown hair, a nice figure. By using her sense of inferiority as a shield, she could protect herself from hurtful or embarrassing encounters, a characteristic that has, to some extent, molded her adult life. It may have had something to do with being an only child in a family of stiff-upper-lip British stock.

Her father Bert was employed by the Canadian Bank of Commerce (later the Canadian Imperial Bank of Commerce) for his whole working life. It was through a neighbour that Bert met his future bride Henrietta Moon, or as everyone called her, Etta. Both were outgoing, gregarious and had a good sense of humour. Just the same, some people thought it an odd match. She was tall and thin; he was short and stocky. She had a short fuse; he was, as his friends said, cool as a cucumber. Etta had attended Scarborough Collegiate, later known as R. H. King, the same high school her daughter would graduate from, and then started working at Eaton's department store, selling piece goods: materials, ribbons, thread.

There was a strict rule at the bank: employees were not allowed to marry until their salary reached a certain level. Bert and Etta had to wait eight long years. They finally wed in 1940, and Frances was born two years later, but it remained a struggle for them financially. Etta quit her job immediately on marrying, and Bert's salary as a bank teller was still very skimpy. They didn't own a car until well into the 1950s. They lived in a small, one-bedroom apartment on Kingston Road until Frances was 12 years old. Every night, she would fall asleep in her parents' bed. When it was time for them to retire, the rollaway would be folded out and a sleepy Frances deposited on it.

All the same, Frances considers her childhood ideal. The Holmeses had hoped for another baby, but when it didn't arrive, Etta made up her mind that her daughter wouldn't suffer from being an only child. Neighbourhood kids—and there were plenty of them living in the same apartment building— were encouraged to drop in whenever they wanted. Etta would organize games for them and take them on picnics. Frances was urged to join clubs such as Girl Guides, and there was camp in the summer. She was good at sports and, although she never got up enough nerve to try out for the school teams, she played baseball and basketball for the church and other leagues.

In 1954, the Holmeses finally managed to save the down payment for a house, a three-bedroom bungalow on Kidbrooke Crescent in south Scarborough. Frances finally had a bedroom to herself. There was also a basement, and while the Holmeses couldn't afford to turn it into a fancy rec room, it was painted and clean. Parties and sleepovers were held there.

The same year the house was bought, Bert also purchased a car. As soon as Frances was 16, she was allowed to drive it whenever her parents weren't using it. It was indicative of the Holmes idea of child-raising. She was given a great deal of leeway—there were no curfews when she went out at night, for example—but she was expected to shoulder the responsibility that went along with such freedom. She believes she developed a profound sense of independence, but it also was an unemotional, rather distant way to rear a child. Frances says hers was not a "touchy-feely" kind of family at all.

Sometime during her first years of high school, Frances stopped reading the children's books she loved so much and started doing math problems instead. She got good grades in algebra, trigonometry and geometry, and she began to dream of becoming an engineer—until everybody, her teachers, her parents, her friends, told her it was an impossibility; this was a field exclusively for men. Maths, physics and chemistry was another prestigious course at the University of Toronto in which a few women were enrolled, but it was very competitive, and high marks were required to get in. Frances applied and, after writing the difficult Grade 13 papers, was overjoyed when she was accepted.

At that point, her parents sat her down and told her that, even though she was their only child, they had no money to send her to university. Frances understands now that the family lived from one pay cheque to another, and that, in fact, they really didn't have the cash at hand, but it was a bitter blow. To this day she keeps the University of Toronto acceptance letter in her desk drawer.

Frances had also applied to the Toronto Teacher's College, and so, with university out of the question, decided to head there. It was a miserable year for her. For one thing, she kept dreaming of the university math classes she was missing. More important, she had no interest in teaching young children and was never comfortable with them. In the middle of the winter, she and Mary Gray were sent to practice-teach in farm country near Stayner, Ontario. It was a one-room school, Grades 1 to 8, and the two young novices were expected to do everything in the classroom. Mary enjoyed every moment of it; Frances hated it, and her grades showed it. It happened to be one of the few times during the 1960s in Ontario when there was an over-supply of new teachers, and by the end of the summer, Frances still hadn't found a position. She admits it was something of a relief.

By a stroke of luck, a job came along that was far more suitable. In October 1962, Frances was hired by Bell Canada. She was trained to read engineering plans that detailed additions to the telephone company's cables and equipment. Her task was to ensure these changes were made in the working drawings and maps. It was a job that, with her mathematical mind, she thoroughly enjoyed, and she was good at it. A month after she began at Bell, the East York School Board offered her a position teaching math at a junior high. It was the one field she was interested in, and she thought about it long and hard, but finally declined. It was the right decision, she feels, and she's still thankful she made it.

Frances had one overwhelming ambition: to earn a university degree. If she couldn't be a day student, she'd do it in her spare time. In the summer of 1962, she took her first university course, and did the same thing for seven years. During the fall and winter, she would sign on for two, sometimes three full semester courses, which meant four nights a week were devoted to classes and the weekends to studying and preparing essays. She took philosophy, English, economics, a variety of sciences and, of course, her favourite: mathematics. In 1969, she received an Honours B.A. with a major in math.

By this time, Frances had her sights set on a better-paying, more challenging job. If she couldn't find it at Bell Canada, she was prepared to look elsewhere, but Frances's boss was a woman, a friend and a supporter. She happened to notice among the materials coming across her desk a competition for a intriguing position involving computers. Surely such an up-and-coming field, she thought, would be perfect for Frances. She put her name forward.

By the early 1970s, it was generally understood the vitally important role computers would play, so the competition for the job was extremely stiff. Finally, three people were informed they had made it, Frances among them.

One of the most attractive things about the job was that it meant "male" money. In those days, Bell's management positions were streamed by gender, the women, of course, making less than the men. One of the other successful applicants accepted a demotion in rank to take the new job, yet she ended up making more money.

The work involved Bell Canada's first computerized network messaging system. Frances was sent for intensive training to Univac Computer Systems, manufacturers of the mainframes that marked the beginning of the modern computer era.

During all this time, Frances continued to live at home. A bedsitting room and a bathroom were installed in the basement of her parents' bungalow. (Not a kitchen, though. She continued to enjoy her mother's cooking.) This allowed her to come and go as she wanted. She owned a Volkswagen brightly painted with flowers. She had a full wardrobe of tailored but fashionable clothes. She travelled a lot on business. She loved to bowl and did so in Bell Canada's league. She took art classes and went on skiing trips to Mont-Tremblant. Although her parents weren't religious, Frances had always attended the Anglican Church and she started teaching Sunday school at St. George's, eventually becoming the superintendent—a kind of vindication of her unhappy experience at teacher's college. She played tennis and golf with girl-friends every weekend and she went out on lots of casual dates. It was a busy life, but also a comfortable, predictable routine. She was dismayed, therefore, when in 1976, Bell Canada informed her she was being transferred to Ottawa.

One reason Frances wasn't overjoyed with the idea was that she knew there was a surplus of single women in the capital city. Her chances of finding a husband would be greatly diminished, and, indeed, this has proved to be the case. During the late '60s, she was involved in one serious relationship with a banker, just like her father. They were engaged, but the relationship fell apart soon after. The only comment Frances will make about the breakup is it was the best thing that could have happened. But by 1976, she was again dating steadily, this time with a buyer of housewares and toys for a large department-store chain. He was a man with whom she had lots of fun and high hopes for the future. She was afraid, though, it would not survive as a long-distance relationship, and she was proved right.

But Frances had no choice in the matter of her transfer. Bell Canada had decided to establish their software computer group in Ottawa, so she either went or she lost her job. In retrospect, she thinks it was fortuitous. "If I hadn't moved, I probably would still be rotting in my mother's basement."

At first, she didn't much like Ottawa. She missed her friends and was constantly worried about her parents. When he was only 50, Bert Holmes had developed a serious heart condition, and although he held on until 1988, he led an invalid's life. He was prescribed so many drugs, his personality changed for the worst. Gone was the man who was as "cool as a cucumber." By the time of his death, says Frances, he was miserable. She was naturally worried about the effect this was having on her mother, and tried to get home whenever possible.

The travelling and worry became ever more of a strain and Frances finally decided she would move back to Toronto, whether she had to give up her job or not. Again, she changed her mind. Another major promotion came her way that she says she would have been out of her mind to turn down. She became the first woman to hold such a senior management position in engineering at Bell Canada's Ottawa offices. She not only supervised programmers but also engineers. It was another kind of vindication—she had finally realized her vanquished dream of being part of that male-dominated profession.

By this time, Frances was thoroughly enjoying herself. She was making good money. She played a lot of tennis and golf, and gradually "floated" into a wide circle of friends. Finally, she bought her own house in the suburb of Kanata, which, she thought, was a lot like the Scarborough neighbourhood where she had grown up. It was an upwardly mobile, satisfying life until, in the mid-1980s, she hit the proverbial glass ceiling.

Frances had always boasted that she had suffered no gender discrimination in her workplace—quite the opposite. She was always breaking barriers that had previously fenced women off from certain jobs. Perhaps for that reason, she lacks sympathy for the women's movement and flatly denies she is a feminist. There are some goals she agrees with: equal pay for work of equal value, for example, but she disapproves of such things as subsidized daycare. To have a baby is a personal choice, she thinks, and the rest of world shouldn't have to pay for it. As she neared 50, though, she began to have a better appreciation of what feminists were talking about.

In 1983, Frances was promoted again, but this time it was a temporary arrangement until a permanent employee was named. Someone else was given the job, a woman as it turned out—Frances says she might have hit the roof if it hadn't been—but when the position came open again, and then again, Francis was always passed over. Finally a colleague with a great deal less experience was selected. He was not only of the right gender but ten years younger. Frances never felt the same about the company again. She didn't complain too loudly, that wasn't her style, but the snub rankles to this day.

As a result, Frances decided to join a new company called Stentor, an alliance of Canada's telecommunications companies. She was in on the launch of the enterprise, setting up the program-management department, organizing the staff, money and other resources, but it eventually became clear she wouldn't be asked to run the department. She was female, 49 years old and therefore, she says, "toast."

In the fall of 1993, a retirement package was offered to Bell and some Stentor employees, including an inviting lump sum of cash. Frances decided to take it. Her pension would bring in only 50 percent of her salary, but there was that cash to play around with. "When I told my boss, he almost fell off his chair. I guess he thought I would be furniture forever," she says. Frances didn't miss a beat. Retirement simply meant she could leave behind the daily grind and indulge a full-time passion: her dogs.

Dogs had always been part of her family. All her cousins had dogs, an aunt bred chihuahuas and Frances's father had one as a child. When her parents bought their house in Scarborough in 1954, Mickey, the mixed German shepherd-terrier of my acquaintance, arrived in the Holmes household. Frances and her father developed a keen interest in canine events—purebred shows and retriever trials—and their weekends were often spent in this arcane world. The Sportsmen's Show at the Canadian National Exhibition was a favourite time of year.

In 1979, when she moved into her Ottawa townhouse, she yearned for a pet, but it couldn't be just any dog. Benji of Walt Disney movie fame was her ideal. During a visit to friends in Montreal, she came across a litter of Tibetan terriers and there she found the dog of her dreams. Twelve-week-old Nici arrived at Christmas 1979 and, according to Frances, was an exceptional animal. Other pets followed, including Sabrina and Puppet, both Tibetan terriers, and Rush, a golden retriever. But dogs have become more than mere pets for Frances; they are a business, an added source of income.

When Frances first bought Nici, she was advised to have her professionally trained. Tibetan terriers are not complacent animals, like, for example, golden retrievers, and obedience school is considered necessary to turn them into good house pets. Frances found a trainer in Ottawa and soon was so enthused with the project that, when the woman became pregnant, Frances took over her classes. She has been teaching obedience training ever since.

She makes it very clear that what she is involved with is a sport, very different from a spectacle like a dog show, where purebreds, poodles or English springer spaniels are judged according to the standards of their breed. Obedience trials are competitions that test the dog's talent to obey commands. Precision heeling, both on the leash and off, standing perfectly still for examination, sitting and laying down for what seems like interminably long periods of time and coming, practically at the flick of the trainer's eyebrow, are essentials of the sport.

There is an offshoot of obedience trials that is even more thrilling to watch. Agility competitions require a dog to navigate obstacle courses that include tunnels, hoops, poles, seesaws and walks, all accomplished within a period of time. It is the fastest-growing dog sport in Europe and North America. Frances doesn't yet teach it, but her dogs are competitors.

Frances's world is devoted to dogs. Her large, shiny van is labelled DOG-MOBILE. She wears sweaters patterned with golden retrievers; brooches and other jewellery feature dog profiles. Her house is a virtual shrine: one room is devoted to paintings, ribbons, plates, trophies, all memorials of past and present dogs. The basement has been turned into a training track. There is doggy wallpaper, and a stuffed toy dog standing at the fireplace. Photographs of vacations spent with dogs are displayed; every other year, Frances travels to Bermuda to attend obedience trials, and at other times enters her dogs in "trialings" in the United States and Canada. Various canine books and the magazine *Dogs in Canada* lie about her living room, and a large collection of dog leashes hangs each in its proper place. Frances's computer is full of dog business; she is involved with some half-dozen different clubs and often takes on executive positions such as president of the Ottawa Retriever Club.

Then there is the dogs' volunteer work. Rush and Sabrina have been certified by St. John's Ambulance to visit hospitalized sick and elderly, who sometimes find great joy in their company. Most important, Frances operates a company called Paws4Thought: Canine Education, which is thriving. She teaches as many as four classes a day to owners and their dogs who compete in obedience trials.

Frances insists she is not obsessive. She has some life outside the canine world: she golfs and plays tennis with non-doggy people, likes to go the theatre and still keeps in contact with her friends from Bell Canada. Although her mother died in 1998, she remains very close to an elderly aunt.

She's never had a serious romantic relationship since moving to Ottawa, partly, she says, because the canine circle she frequents attracts few eligible men. She's still hopeful, though, although any potential partner would have to fit himself into her dream for the future: to buy a country place with a professional dog-training hall and a large agility field. One of her closest friends, another teacher of dog obedience, says the problem with Frances is she enjoys her independence too much. She bristles if a man even hints at telling her what to do, but she could never be attracted to a milquetoast. It is easier and safer, says a friend, to forge emotional ties with the likes of Sabrina, Rush and Puppet.

The Single Life

[The article I wrote] was about old maids. 'Happy women' was the title, and I put in my list all the busy, useful, independent spinsters I know, for liberty is a better husband than love to many of us.

Diary of Louisa May Alcott, February 14, 1868

... in remaining single, Louisa [May Alcott] had aligned herself with a group of women who were ridiculed and condescended to. She was tolerated as eccentric, regarded as pitiful and incomplete, probably disagreeable, and as a faded woman, incompetent to attract a man, fit only for the fringes of family and social life.

Martha Saxton, *Louisa May: A Modern Biography of Louisa May Alcott*, 1977

As final exams neared, the weather sunnier, the students more restless, the English teacher Miss Hoffman wisely organized a three-day festival of films. They were old chestnuts, things that she herself loved, I suppose: *Meet Me in St. Louis* with Judy Garland or *All the King's Men* with Broderick Crawford. The one that stuck with me—in fact, given my later career, likely imprinted itself on my subconscious—was the 1940 comedy *His Girl Friday*. The film's title was a misnomer; the so-called Girl Friday was not some office clerk but a superb reporter, expert at out-scooping every one of her seedy colleagues, all of whom were male.

The film begins with Hildy Johnson, played by the wonderful Rosalind Russell, announcing she is giving up the life of a reporter to take on a new career: wife and mother. She wants, she says, to become respectable and live a "half-way normal life." Her husband-to-be is a wimpy insurance salesman who doesn't smoke or drink (Hildy does both), but who is anxious to "look after her." The plot revolves around the intricate and devious schemes concocted by managing editor Walter Burns (Cary Grant at his best) to lure his ace reporter back to the job. "No one else on the paper can write like you,

Hildy," he says, and means it. Everyone in my circle gave a rousing cheer when Hildy Johnson sat down and began banging out her sensational story.

Hildy was not a spinster. She had already married and divorced Burns, and would probably marry him again. That wasn't the point, as far as we were concerned. She was a wisecracking, smart career girl. Even mired deep in the reactionary '50s, some of us longed for such a life. Whether to marry or not, whether to give up one's independence, whether to face a life of aloneness in a couple-oriented world would remain, for many of us, our most perplexing, difficult and frightening dilemma.

I

After poor, blind Oedipus died, his daughter Antigone, who had spent all that time caring for him, returned to her birthplace, the city-state of Thebes in Egypt. In her absence, her brothers Polyneices and Eteocles had assumed the throne, each taking his turn to rule, but inevitably they had quarrelled, and civil war erupted. During the terrible battle that ensued, Polyneices and Eteocles killed each other. Creon, the nearest surviving male relative of the two brothers, emerged as the supreme ruler. He immediately passed a law prohibiting burial of the body of Polyneices, whom he considered a detestable traitor.

Antigone understood it was her womanly duty to sanctify her brother's body, even if it meant sacrificing her own life. Creon's guards caught her performing sacred burial rites—covering Polyneices' corpse with sand—and she was arrested.

In her defence, Antigone maintained the laws of the gods were superior to those decreed by man. Creon was outraged at the impudence of his niece, a mere female after all. "Now she would be the man, not I, if she/Defeated me and did not pay for it." He sentenced her to death by starvation, entombed in a cave. She promptly hung herself instead. Her last words before she was taken away were not an exultation of her accomplishments: her brave, independent action, her selflessness, the courageous defence of her ideals. Instead, what issues forth is a deep-felt lament: death was facing her and she had never married. She was still a virgin.

> No chanted wedding-hymn, no bridal-joy,
> No tender care of children can be mine;
> But like an outcast, and without a friend,
> They take me to the cavernous home of death.[304]

Antigone is one of the most courageous and admirable women in the literature of antiquity. She also dramatically illustrates that a female whose family was dead and who had no husband was considered so perverse, she might as well have three heads. Wife and mother, under the tutelage of father and husband, were supposedly the only roles that were possible for a Greek woman other than a priestess.

Antigone is not the only unmarried heroine of great stature in Greek myth. Like everything else in antiquity, entirely different ideas about single women percolated in the collective subconscious. Three of the six Olympian goddesses were virgins. Immune to Aphrodite's love darts, they maintained their independence, each in a quite different way. Artemis was the freedom-loving hunter. Often pictured clad in a short tunic of leather, her bow at her side, she roamed the mountains and forests of Arcadia. As Homer's *Hymn to Aphrodite* describes her: "She loves archery and the slaying of wild beasts in the mountains, as well as the lyre and dancing and thrilling cries and shady woods and the cities of upright men."[305] Freedom–loving Artemis was not going to be tied down in marriage.

Athena was the intellectual, the promoter of necessary war and certain peace, the sponsor of literature, art and crafts. The *Hymn to Aphrodite* says of her that she "delights in wars and the work of Ares [god of war], in strifes and battles and in preparing famous crafts. She first taught earthly craftsmen to make chariots of war ... and she also teaches tender maidens in the house and puts knowledge of the homely arts in each one's mind."[306] Athena, it seems, was too busy to look after a husband.

Then there was Hestia, goddess of the hearth, the only one of the virgins pictured as a traditional old maid. It was not that she was unattractive—both her brother Poseidon and her nephew Apollo wanted to marry her, or at least make love to her. However, the very idea repulsed her, and she swore by the head of Zeus to remain forever a virgin. Thereafter she eschewed the emotional entanglements that the other Olympians thrived on. Hestia didn't enjoy rowdiness, partying and the banquets so beloved by most of the gods; she preferred to sit at home, guarding the hearth fires. Despite her devotion, or perhaps because of it, she emerges as a not very interesting or romantic figure. The literature of antiquity seldom mentions her, and her image is almost never found in the art of the time.

It's not farfetched to see in these three goddesses, and Antigone as well, archetypes of the independent woman, the career girl, the old maid, the spinster, the sacrificing maiden aunt, the swinging single that have echoed down through the centuries and are with us still.

II

To be a single woman in the Middle Ages was not only unpleasant but downright dangerous. An aristocratic girl, if she were an heiress and had somehow managed not to be married off at age eight or younger, was always in danger of being kidnapped. Ralph Stafford, for example, was intent on furthering the fortunes of his family. He served in the Hundred Years War, which helped him in his upward mobility, but more successfully, after his first wife died, he abducted and married Margaret Audley, heiress to one-third of the inheritance of the Clare Earls of Gloucester. With his new wife's vast lands and wealth, Stafford gained the status necessary to nudge Edward III into naming him an earl. There's no record of what Margaret thought of her aggressive, ambitious husband.[307]

It wasn't just the upper classes that were in danger. Records of the episcopal courts in the north of France in the 14th and 15th centuries dramatically show how women living alone were considered fair game for any kind of intimidation. The young men of the villages felt free to break into the homes of independent women and rape and manhandle them. The point being made was that a single woman was in such need of protection, marriage to a thug was better than no marriage at all. In court, it was the women who appeared as the defendants on charges of immorality.

The biggest threat by far to women on their own, however, was poverty. There were few ways single females could make enough money to even put bread on the table. The textile trade, spinning and weaving, was where most work was found (from this derives the term "spinster"), but the wages were notoriously low. A worker would barely earn enough to feed herself, never mind buy clothes or pay rent, so that many of the desperate or ambitious switched to more lucrative occupations: thieving, or buying and selling stolen goods. Court records of the era are full of women being charged with these offences, but their poverty was so severe, judges often either turned a blind eye or gave them light sentences.[308]

Many women were forced (or preferred) to turn to the oldest of professions, prostitution. By the late Middle Ages, it was a thriving trade in the cities. The "official" prostitutes were connected to bawdy houses, there to service the many unmarried journeyman at loose ends. Other freelancers simply went on the streets whenever they were desperate for money.

The life of a prostitute was anything but easy. The enormous fees paid to the brothel-owners, along with the high cost of clothes and jewellery that made the lady of the night attractive to their customers, meant many slipped further and further into debt until they became virtual slaves of the house to which they were attached.[309] Those who were freelancers, without protection of a madam or pimp, lay completely at the mercy of violent or dishonourable clients. The discovery of the badly beaten body of a murdered prostitute would elicit almost no response from the authorities. Indeed, many Church moralizers of the time blamed the women themselves for their gullibility and unworthiness. As a 13th-century preacher put it, "The sin of the prostitute is one of those sins which do not cause harm to the sinner herself alone but to others; not only to the property or the body of others but to their souls."[310] It goes without saying that few of these Church fathers ever talked about the reasons—abject poverty, for the most part—which led the women into a life of sin in the first place.

There were, of course, unmarried women in the Middle Ages who led satisfactory and accomplished lives. Upper-class women could insist their dowry be handed over to a convent where they would spend their entire lives in peace and contemplation. These were the non-conformists: the religious who had genuine vocations, the intellectuals and artists who yearned for peace and space to work, and the independent and the lesbian, to whom the idea of sexual intercourse was abhorrent and who refused to be bullied by men.

In the towns, there were a few unmarried women who were allowed to join high-paying craft guilds, became masters and made a good living. These could be guilds exclusively for women or guilds for both sexes. Cecilie Wollerin, the unmarried daughter of a wool-weaver in Regensburg, carried on her father's business after his death. When she died in 1341, her will revealed she had left a fortune.[311]

In the countryside, an unmarried woman was allowed to manage her own holdings, although, of course, she was also responsible for providing the required taxes and services to the lord of the manor. In fact, single females generally had more rights than married women did. In most medieval jurisdictions they could sue or be sued, and they could give testimony in court. They could draw up contracts and borrow money, and in their wills, they could leave their wealth to whomever they wanted.

What is remarkable about the Middle Ages, at least the latter part of it, was the number of people who remained single, especially since marriage was considered a holy state. In the early 14th century, the percentage of the population that remained unmarried in Basel was 67.2, in Ypres, 65.4 percent, in Freiberg, 61.3 percent and 50 percent in Dresden.[312] It had to do partly with economics: the ever-increasing size of dowries, the punitive inheritance laws for younger sons, the financial devastation wrought by the incredible decrease in population as a result of the plague. The increasing number of old maids was considered a troublesome problem by everyone, except possibly those women who had the resources to carry on a decent life and who were only too happy to remain unwed.

III

Elizabeth I of England, the Virgin Queen, to this day remains the most stubborn example of an old maid. Her determination to resist the pressure of royal relatives, stately advisors and her own beloved people, all of whom kept telling her it was her duty to marry and produce an heir to the throne, was unrelenting.

When Elizabeth first came to the throne in 1558, the outrage expressed at the very idea of a woman ruling England was virulent. John Knox thundered away in his pamphlet *The First Blast of the Trumpet against the monstrous regiment of Women*: "For to promote a woman to bear rule, superiority, dominion ordinance or empire above any realm, nation or city, is repugnant to nature, continuously to God, a thing most contrarious to his revealed will and approved ordinance and finally it is the subversion of good order, of all equity and justice."[313] Despite the obnoxious prattling of Knox and others, Elizabeth turned out to be a glorious queen.

Through all the years of her rule, she refused to marry and have children. Certainly, she was wooed; potential suitors were constantly showing up on her doorstep. She would toy with them, pretend to listen to hysterical petitions from Parliament demanding she wed, but in the end, she always rejected these would-be husbands.

It was not only that she realized marriage would undoubtedly mean loss of power and prestige—a king would certainly bring masculine control—but she also knew her virginity was a symbol of goodness and light for the cantankerous citizens of her country. Like the Virgin Mary, in remaining unwed she would be mistress, wife and mother to her people. The image is still vivid today. Sitting rigidly correct on her huge, white stallion, she is dressed in a stiff, white velvet dress, encrusted with pearls, silver armour over top. Behind her a page carries her helmet, replete with silver plumage. Purity of body, purity of spirit, purity of reign—all without the help of a husband. "I know I have the body of a weak and feeble woman, but I have the heart and stomach of a King,"[314] she said, as yet again she rejected a panting suitor.

Elizabeth's refusal to marry might have seemed to be perverse, but as queen, she was generally immune to the snickering and insults that were the lot of ordinary spinsters. In the early modern era, a "natural" woman gladly took her place at the heart of the family as daughter, wife and mother. Deviating from this norm was considered an affront to God himself. As one historian put it, "Any woman left without a husband in either this world or the next relinquished all hope of achieving a prestigious position in society."[315] "Thornbacks"—stingrays with ugly spines lining their backs—was a favourite epithet for old maids. Chagrin, peevishness, meddling were sure to "infect their tempers." With such denigration permeating society, it's a wonder any independent woman could hold up her head, but in fact, the period is sprinkled with the names of spinsters who made their mark in history.

Marie le Jars de Gournay (1565–1645) was the daughter of a French nobleman who served at the court of Charles IX. When her father died in 1580, the family's circumstances were reduced, and they were forced to move to their country estate. The isolation suited Marie just fine. She taught herself Latin and Greek, and any other subject she could find in books. Her mother strongly disapproved of such scholarly pursuits and was determined to present the young girl at court. Back they went to Paris. There, Marie met Michel de Montaigne, the 54-year-old statesman and theorist who became her mentor and lifelong friend. After his death in 1592, de Gournay became the editor of his works.

Marie de Gournay devoted her life to study. She translated *The Aeneid* into French, and published many books of poems and essays. Her most famous work consisted of her two feminist treatises, *The Equality of Men and Women* (1622) and *Grief des Dames* (1626). Both were radical documents, extraordinary for their time in stating the unconditional belief that men and women were equal. "The human animal is neither man nor woman.... Man and woman are so completely one that, if man is more than woman, then woman is more than man."[316]

Throughout her life she was ridiculed and belittled: for her relationship with Montaigne, for her attempt at serious scholarship, for her feminism. She purposely never married, probably realizing she could not dare to express such provocative and outrageous opinions if she had the reputation of a husband and children to worry about.

Probably the most famous spinster of the 17th century, because, without inherited wealth, she had to make her way completely independently, was the British writer Mary Astell (1666–1731). Her father had been a coal merchant in Newcastle, but he died when Mary was 12, and by the time she was of marriageable age, the family fortune had dwindled. Not enough was left for a sufficient dowry to attract a suitor of the right class, and social standing was vitally important to her. Throughout her life and at all costs, Mary maintained the trappings of her gentry background; she might live in poverty, but it would be genteel poverty.

She managed to get a good education, although she couldn't read Greek, which she always felt was a hindrance to her scholarly activities. When she was not yet 20, she came to London to make her name as a writer, primarily of political tracts, and was remarkably successful. She was a Tory to her very roots. A society not based on a strong class system—the king and his subjects in descending order—was, to her, a society enmeshed in chaos. The great contradiction in Mary Astell's life was that the hierarchy she felt so necessary must, of course, apply to the family—the husband as the head of the household, the wife subordinate. Since she could not abide any man telling her what to do, a husband would have been a problem. Her answer, described in *A Serious Proposal to the Ladies*, published in 1694, was to insist that by far the best prospect for a woman was to remain single. In fact, Astell could never understand how, if she had the choice, a woman would even consider choosing the married state over the unmarried.

How, then, would these independent women live? In co-operative communities, something like the Catholic convents but without the veil, the vow of obedience or the dictates of male clergy. This is how she described it in *A Serious Proposal*:

Happy Retreat! Which will be introducing you into such a *Paradise* as your Mother *Eve* forfeited, where you shall feast on Pleasures, that do not, like those of the World, disappoint your expectations, pall your Appetites, and by the disgust they give you, put you on the fruitless search after new Delights.... Here are no Serpents to deceive you, whilst you entertain yourselves in these delicious Gardens....[317]

We can assume the serpent in Mary Astell's universe was male.

She lived an austere life: her clothing prim but plain, the food on her table simple, her cottage in Chelsea neat but small. She had little or no private income, and her polemical writings brought in almost nothing, but she managed to survive and even be part of the social scene. This was accomplished entirely through the monthly stipends allotted to her by her wealthy female friends. They were an amazing circle of women. Most of them never married, all were known for their old-fashioned piety, all were highly literate; one, Lady Ann, countess of Coventry, had one of the best libraries found anywhere.[318] They shunned the fashionable London court scene, preferring instead a life of philanthropy and cheerful do-gooding. They adored Mary Astell, and gave her the financial support and companionship that made her later years comfortable and secure.

In the middle of the 18th century, the number of spinsters suddenly increased all over Europe and North America. In England and Scotland, for example, single women accounted for 25 percent of the female population. There was a explanation behind this phenomenon. Aristocratic families, hoping to preserve their estates intact, willed everything to the eldest male. Younger sons were left without a means to support a wife, and therefore couldn't marry. Many emigrated to the colonies. Men also seemed more susceptible to the plague than women. There was also the violence of revolutions and wars, in which many men were killed. As Moll Flanders complained in Daniel Defoe's novel of the same name, "The market is against our sex just now."

A letter published in 1798 in *The Lady's Monthly Museum* nicely illustrates how desperate the situation was for young women:

My pappa and mamma have been trying for the last three years to match me, and have for that purpose carried me from our country seat to London, from London to Brighton, from Brighton to Bath, and from Bath to Cheltenham, where I now am, backwards and forwards, till the family carriage is almost worn out, and one of the horses is become blind, and another lame, without my having more than a nibble, for I have never yet been able to hook my fish. I begin to be afraid that there is something wrong in their manner of baiting for a husband or in mine of laying in the line to catch him.[319]

However, it wasn't just economics or demographics that dictated the large number of spinsters. Some chose independence. Historian Lee Virginia

Chambers-Schiller, describing American women of the period, writes, "... the decision not to marry followed from a rigorous assessment of the marital institution that found it wanting and in conflict with female autonomy, self-development, and achievement."[320]

Jane Austen's irrepressible, strong-minded heroine Emma, of the book of the same name, apparently has no fear of being an old maid. She says:

I have none of the usual inducements of women to marry. Were I to fall in love, indeed, it would be a different thing! But I never have been in love; it is not my way, or my nature; and I do not think I ever shall. And, without love, I am sure I should be a fool to change such a situation as mine. Fortune I do not want; employment I do not want; consequence I do not want: I believe few married women are half as much mistress of their husband's house, as I am of Hartfield [the family home]....[321]

Beautiful, headstrong Emma does fall in love and does marry. All of Jane Austen's characters do; any other happy ending would have been inconceivable in her day. It's always assumed Austen is being satirical or ironic in the words she puts in Emma's mouth, but was she really laughing at this ode to singleness? The young women in Austen's work are intelligent, witty and full of fun; it is, after all, the one time in their lives they have real power, if only to withhold their favours from desirous men.

Austen herself remained a spinster, probably intentionally, since it's known she received at least one serious proposal. Having witnessed first-hand what the demands of marriage and the ordeal of childbirth had done to her sisters-in-law, she probably realized that, once married, she would never write another word.

IV

No other age spent so much time talking about, debating, worrying about, praying for single women than the 19th century. Partly it was because there were so many of them. In France in 1851, women over the age of 50 living without men made up 46 percent of the female population. The census taken that same year in Britain indicated there were a half a million more women than men. In the United States, 11 percent of females born between 1865 and 1875 were destined to remain single for life. An 1850 edition of *Punch* magazine satirizes the alarmist foghorn—mostly bellows from overwrought men— that was being constantly sounded at the time:

If the surplus female population with which we are overrun increases much more, we shall be eaten up with women. What used to be our better self will become our worst nine-tenths; a numerical majority which it will be vain to contend with and which will reduce our free and glorious constitution to that most degrading of all despotisms, a petticoat government.[322]

The Victorian male's shirt was in a knot, not so much because of the numbers of single females but because they represented the antithesis of what was considered the ideal of womanhood: the angel by the hearth, the mother and wife happily carrying out her God-given duties.

If a woman had the misfortune, or worse the audacity, to remain single, the least she could do was to fit in with the spirit of the times. Utter devotion to others, physical and emotional self-abnegation, an absorption into other people's lives to the point where she became almost invisible—that was what was expected of the exemplary spinster.

In the short story "Old Maids," published in 1835 in *Tales and Sketches*, American writer Catharine Maria Sedgwick paints a portrait of a single woman so adept at self-denial, so selfless, that she might have been called Saint Sarah.

Had Sarah been married she would have been a thrifty wife, and painstaking mother, but she wore away her youth in devotion to the sick and old—and now her kindness ... always imparting and never diminishing, is enjoyed by all within her little sphere.... She not only has *comfortables* for shivering old women, and well-patched clothes for neglected children, but she has always some pretty favour for a bride—some kind token for a new-born baby. And then what a refuge is her apartment for the slip-shod members of the family who are in distress for scissors, penknife, thimble, needle, hook and eye, buttons, a needle-full of silk or worsted of any particular colour. How many broken hearts she has restored with her inexhaustible pot—mending tops, doll's broken legs, and all the luckless furniture of the baby-house.... Sarah Lee's labours are not always in so humble a sphere—"He who makes two blades of grass grow where one grew before," says a political economist, "is a benefactor to his race." If so, Sarah Lee takes high rank.[323]

This kind of busy-work lifestyle with no privacy, no time to oneself, was the fate of many 19th-century single women, who had to rely on the charity of this relative or that for even a roof over their heads. The emotional and physical toll such self-denial took must have been terrible.

A poignant echo of the hopelessness many unmarried women faced is
found in the life of Charlotte Brontë. In an 1852 letter to her friend Ellen
Nussey, she writes, "The evils that now and then wring a groan from my
heart—lie in position—not that I am a <u>single</u> woman and likely to remain a
<u>single woman</u>—but because I am a <u>lonely</u> woman and likely to be <u>lonely</u>. But
it cannot be helped and therefore <u>imperatively must be borne</u>—and borne
too with as few words about it as may be."[324]

The jobs available to single women reflected society's belief that altruism
should entirely colour the spinster's personality; it was work dedicated to
helping others and the pay was horribly low. Young, lower-class women
were hired as maids—in Britain in 1851, there were 750,000 female domestics in employ[325]—or shop girls, cooks, seamstresses or waitresses. Most of
them were required to quit their jobs the moment they married. Educated,
middle-class spinsters earned their way, barely, by being companions to
wealthy widows or housekeepers in large families or nurses to the elderly.

But if there is a symbol of the 19th-century spinster that predominates, it is
the unfortunate governess. Her uncomfortable, isolated role in the Victorian
family is wonderfully illustrated in an 1854 painting by the British artist
Rebecca Solomon. A young, seemingly well-to-do couple are utterly absorbed
in one another. She is either just finished playing or about to play a piece on
the piano, and his tender, adoring gaze indicates he thoroughly appreciates her
talents. Obviously, because there is much flirtation going on, they are sweethearts, or engaged or perhaps even young marrieds. They are bathed in intense
sunlight, which renders lush her coral-pink dress and his burgundy jacket. On
that side of the painting, passion flares. The other side represents passion
denied. The governess sits straight-backed and decorous, one arm around a
child who is reading a book open on her knee. Dressed in dark, sombre clothing, the governess stares forlornly into space as if acknowledging she will never
partake of the gaiety and warmth that is going on nearby.

Governesses usually hailed from modest, middle-class families: the daughters of clergymen, government officials, orphans or the youngest in a
merchant family of many girls. They were considered genteel and therefore,
despite being employees, were allowed to join in a family's daily routine. In
reality, they were in an awkward and difficult position, always uncertain as to
how far the intimacy could go.

Not only was the life difficult but the pay was miserable. The most capable governess—who, since Victorians had huge numbers of children and

often took in orphaned relatives, would, in effect, be managing a small school—would make at the most £100 a year; the majority earned between £30 or £40. They were to be role models to those in their charge, which meant strict adherence to Victorian values. Any hint of a love affair, illicit or not, meant instant dismissal. It made for a dreary, penny-pinching life.

Such an oppressive existence was sure to end in defiance. After 1870, as post-secondary education became available to young women, a new species of single woman emerged. She was usually from a well-to-do, urban family. She was educated, and had access to the professions such as social work, settlement-house employment, union organizing, high-school and college teaching. She belonged to a wide circle of like-minded friends, groups that often had real political clout and that advocated radical economic and social reform. Most astonishing of all, she vowed never to marry. In the United States, single blessedness, as it was called, became a virtual cult. Between 1889 and 1905, 53 percent of Bryn Mawr graduates remained single; of the 3,000 women who attended Cambridge before 1909, only 22 percent married.[326] Canada experienced the same phenomenon: half the 392 women who studied at Dalhousie University between 1885 and 1900 remained single.[327] As one historian put it, "To remain celibate rather than lose one's soul in the marriage lottery: this principle was inherent in the individualist ethic that steadily invaded Western culture in the nineteenth century."[328]

It didn't mean the struggle was over. The male establishment simply lumped the New Woman with the Old Maid, all the better to belittle, deride and humiliate her. "Unlike a man, being single for a woman flies in the face of all that is natural, proper, and civilized," wrote Canadian journalist Edward Hogan in 1895. Society's dictum—remaining unmarried was an unfortunate deviation from the biological determinism that defined woman as mother and wife and nothing else—was still firmly in place. It was waiting, however, to be challenged.

V

The worse thing the unmarried woman had to face in the 20th century was the stereotyping. It was as pervasive and powerful, if slightly more subtle, as the image of the slothful nigger conjured up by bigoted white people in the American South. Virginia Woolf, in her 1937 novel *The Years*, gives a glimpse of how this pigeon-holing permeated society. "The man on whose toe she [Eleanor Pargiter] had trodden sized her up; a well-known type; with a bag; philanthropic; well nourished; a spinster; a virgin; like all the women of her class, cold; her passions had never been touched...."[329]

Probably the most famous of Woolf's old maids is the artist Lily Briscoe in *To The Lighthouse*. The thoroughly married and magical Mrs. Ramsay describes Lily thus: "With her little Chinese eyes and her puckered-up face she would never marry; one could not take her painting very seriously; but she was an independent little creature, Mrs. Ramsay liked her for it...."[330]

Lily is indeed her own self, somehow realizing that her artistic talent, whatever its worth, is more satisfactory than being a wifely servant to a selfish man. In one of the most remarkable scenes in Woolf's work, meek little Lily rejects the advances of the distinguished, self-important Mr. Ramsay, who is in great need after his wife's untimely death.

Instantly, with the force of some primeval gust (for really he [Mr. Ramsay] could not restrain himself any longer), there issued from him such a groan that any other woman in the whole world would have done something, said something— all except myself, thought Lily, girding at herself bitterly, who am not a woman, but a peevish, ill-tempered, dried-up old maid presumably....
All Lily wished was that this enormous flood of grief, this insatiable hunger for sympathy, this demand that she should surrender herself up to him entirely, and even so he had sorrows enough to keep her supplied for ever, should leave her, should be diverted (she kept looking at the house, hoping for an interruption) before it swept her down in its flow.[331]

It took an incredibly brave and strong woman not to succumb to the temptations of marriage and the respect that state brought. Such an eccentric, supposedly wrong-headed idea as remaining single was considered the ultimate in selfishness, when, in fact, there were all sorts of reasons for such a decision.

The bloody conflagration of World War I resulted in a huge shortage of eligible men and a large number of spinsters. There were women who rejected their fiancés—veterans returning without arms or legs, badly scarred, blind, mentally ill, perhaps impotent—who insisted they couldn't face life with a mangled wreck. Many young women who had been engaged to those who perished decided to remain faithful to their true loves, dead or not. Others used the excuse of virgin widowhood to keep hold of their independence.

When Alice Whitemoon, half Cree, half White, living on the Sintuluta Indian Reserve in Saskatchewan, became engaged in 1912 to William

Stamphorse, a full-blooded Sioux of Cheyenne Indian Reservation in South Dakota, everyone thought it was a perfect match. She was the most beautiful of her four sisters, he was already well established on his own ranch. Nobody understood why they didn't marry before he went off to war, except that Alice seemed reluctant. When she received notice of his death, she swore her undying love, and throughout her long life, refused to even consider marriage offers, although there were plenty. On her death at age 90, her great-granddaughter found a packet of letters in an attic cupboard that had been returned with William's body. In the last of these, Alice had broken off their engagement. She was too independent-minded, she said, and wanted to lead her own life. She asked for his forgiveness.[332]

The 1920s saw the birth of that dazzling, liberated creature addicted to independence and a wild life: the bachelor girl. Actually, she was the creation of the French writer Victor Margueritte. The heroine of his novel *La Garçonne* is determined to be financially independent by having a career of her own. With her bobbed hair, she has a masculine aura about her. She is also talented, logical and can handle her own financial affairs. "I belong to no one but myself," she declares.

What upset the establishment even more than her fierce independence was the character's perceived promiscuity. She experimented with bisexual love affairs before finally settling down, not with a husband but with a male partner. The debate that raged over the novel was amazing. A million copies were sold in 121 languages; almost a quarter of the French public read it. In 1923, the British government, although it never formally banned the book, seized copies shipped by mail.[333] In the end, however, few people, men or women, were prepared to defend *La Garçonne*. She was simply too liberated, too unconventional. As the dismal 1930s approached, the scandal over the book disappeared from newspaper headlines. Pretty soon the bachelor girl had gone the way of the passenger pigeon.

The Depression was a miserable time for women living alone. Even though they had no means of support except their own earnings, single women found themselves being laid off and their jobs turned over to male heads of households. In most countries, Canada included, single women were not eligible for government relief. Nor were they welcome on any of the government-financed make-work projects. It was expected that their families or a charitable organization, often connected with the Church, would take care of them. If they had no relatives willing to provide, and if they didn't want to beg, they could perish. In a small town in Alberta, in February 1937, the emaciated body of Lillian Crombie, a laid-off school teacher and an eccentric, was found in her bathroom six days after she died. She had starved to death; not a scrap of food was found in the house. Her neighbours said it wasn't that they didn't care. It was just that she was so "snooty" when anyone tried to help her. She was only 50 years old.

Even when women could qualify for some government help, it was often a humiliating experience. Male relief inspectors felt free to size a woman up and then sneer that, "with a figure like hers," she shouldn't need relief.[334]

In some countries during World War II, single women who joined the Armed Forces were presented with career opportunities far more interesting than those to which they normally would have had access. A member of Canada's Women's Naval Service remarked at the time, "When you passed your exams and you received your flags, it was like getting your degree."[335] That was indeed the case for the few single women who stayed on in the navy or army or air force.

But the war also brought more denigration, more misery for single women, especially those living in fascist countries or the Soviet Union. A woman of child-bearing age was supposed to be producing soldiers, or as some people cynically remarked, "cannon fodder" for the country, not leading a life of "pampered independence." If, by choice or otherwise, women remained single, they would be punished for it. In July 1944, for example, Stalin abolished common-law marriages in the Soviet Union and heavily taxed single people, male or female, while at the same time increasing family allowances and establishing the Order of Maternal Glory and other honours for women with huge numbers of children.[336] The dregs of society—that was the label applied to women alone.

Most people in the 1950s were so completely enamored of the suburban family—mom, dad, kids and the dog—that they seemed to resent the independent woman. There was an impatience with her situation, a kind of "shape up or ship out" attitude. This was particularly reflected in the powerful women's magazines. Dr. Marion Hilliard, writing in Canada's *Chatelaine*, gave this obnoxious advice to single women who complained that they were unhappy:

The first move is to stop being selfish and self-centered. A woman who feels unwanted is bound to get into trouble: she's looking for it. The unmarried woman has to face up to herself and her life. She's got to stop expecting life to be fair. Life isn't meant to be fair. Life isn't meant to be that way at all. Life doesn't owe her a handsome adoring husband and two beautiful children full of bright sayings—life owes her nothing....

This is the bitter, desperate adjustment that the single woman has to make. Nothing will again be as painful as the moment she realized that she will live all her life alone; no moment will ever hurt so much.[337]

Apparently Dr. Hilliard had never encountered women who chose not to marry because the freedom of a single life appealed to them. But then, it seems, neither had Betty Friedan. In her ground-breaking *Feminine Mystique,* she hardly mentions the single woman, as though she didn't exist at all.

The sexual revolution and the feminist movement blew apart the old clichés about unmarried women. These days, the label is losing its meaning as so-called single-unit families increase dramatically. Just after the war, one-person households accounted for six percent of the total in Canada and 19 percent in France. By 1980, that figure had jumped to between a quarter and a third in both countries.[338] In Canada between 1991 and 1995, the number of adults with no partners had jumped an amazing 11 percent.[339] Although these numbers included widowed and divorced people, a large proportion were never married. What is interesting is that many of these singles are involved in stable love relationships. In other words, they have their cake and eat it too; they maintain their independence, living alone, and still enjoy a serious sexual relationship. The modern-day old maid is represented by someone like the dazzling feminist Gloria Steinem, who has had many lovers and no husbands.

That is not to say the question of whether to stay single or not is an easy one. It remains a witches' brew of heartache. No one has more poignantly dramatized this than the British novelist Anita Brookner. Her books are full of women (and men) who have atrophied in passionless marriages or who, emotionally frigid, are unable to make a commitment. Her most interesting characters are those who must chose between marrying someone unsuitable or not marrying at all.

In her 1984 novel *Hotel du Lac,* her heroine Edith Hope, a writer of romantic novels, has long been involved with a married man. Finally, she decides the sporadic love affair is unsatisfactory and decides to accept an offer of marriage from Geoffrey Long, "a sturdy man." At the last moment, as she

is being chauffeured to the church, she peers through the car window at the
neighbourhood she loves and is about to leave. She begins to get cold feet.
"And then she saw the church. And then she saw, in a flash, but for all time,
the totality of his [Geoffrey's] mouse-like seemliness." She tells the chauffeur
to drive right past.

Her embarrassed friends decide to send her on a vacation to the Swiss
Hôtel du Lac. There she meets the wealthy, uptight Philip Neville and almost
commits an even more dreadful mistake. This time, her would-be husband is
a horror, a man who doesn't love her but wants to use her as a front for his
respectability. Popping the question, he says:

'I am not a romantic youth. I am in fact extremely discriminating. I have a small
estate and a very fine house, Regency Gothic, a really beautiful example. And I
have a rather well-known collection of *famille rose* dishes. I am sure you love
beautiful things.'

'You are wrong,' she [Edith] said, her voice cold. 'I do not love *things* at all.'

Edith finally accepts this ludicrous proposal for two important reasons.
Neville assures her that, with financial security and a social standing, she will
be in a position to write something more than the romantic novels she is so
good at. She also takes to heart the man's cruel assessment of her. "You are
a lady, Edith," Neville says. "They are rather out of fashion these days, as you
may have noticed. As my wife, you will do very well. Unmarried, I'm afraid
you will soon look a bit of a fool."

Fortunately for Edith, she discovers the pompous ass sneaking out of the
bedroom of another female guest. "'And if I were to marry him,' she said to
herself, knowing this, knowing too that he could so easily and so quickly
look elsewhere, 'I should turn to stone, paste: I should become part of his
collection.'" With that she quickly books her flight, anxious to return to her
London neighbourhood, to her own small house, and to her married, unre-
liable lover.

3. The Body

Gail

Since we were all obsessed with our bodies—too thin, too fat, too pimply, the laments never stopped—Gail Towner's metamorphosis became a matter of endless theorizing and gossip. We watched in awe as she mutated from an overweight "bug," shy and retiring, to a svelte size 12, as outgoing and self-confident as any of us. What we didn't know—it would never have entered our heads—was that she was using Biphetamine, a stimulant that dampens the appetite. The drug was prescribed by her doctor, who apparently had no idea how psychologically addictive it could be. Gail went through Grade 12 blissed out, believing she could do anything. A trigonometry exam was no problem at all; she just had to pop a pill. The mood swings were fierce, though—exhilaration one moment, depression the next. When she finally lost the weight and the doctor refused to give her any more pills, Gail crashed.

She recovered with no lasting side effects, as far as she can ascertain, but when she looks back at that time, she's amazed she would have done such a thing, because even then she was health-conscious. It perhaps had to do with her mother and father. Although they cared deeply about their daughter, they were such conventional people that a doctor's prescription would never be questioned.

Both Laurence and Georgina (Dodo) Towner's sets of parents had emigrated from England. Both families were solidly working class: Larry's father laboured in the car barns for the Toronto Transit Commission; Dodo's dad was a bricklayer.

Dodo attended business college after high school and became a secretary to a Toronto lawyer, a job she held for years until she became pregnant with Gail. She could have had a career in singing. She had studied voice for years, and won many medals in the competitions she entered at the Canadian National Exhibition. When she was 20, she was offered a slot singing solo on the radio, but by that time, Larry had come along. Luckily for her, Larry shared her passion for music. He had a beautiful tenor and sang in the same church choir as Dodo. As for Larry, he worshipped the ground Dodo walked on, and always would.

After Larry graduated from Malvern Collegiate in 1929, he headed straight for a job in a bank. Larry and Dodo were faced with the absurd regulation that prohibited them from marriage until Larry's salary had reached $2,000 a year. They solved the dilemma by marrying in secret one weekend in 1933.

It was Larry Towner's great regret that, although he donned a uniform during World War II and was ready to fight for his country, he never left Canada. Instead, he was stuck at Camp Borden in the paymaster's office, working on the air force and army's vast payroll. In the end, though, it wasn't a waste of time. When the war was over, his experience landed him a job with Imperial Oil as an accountant in the dividends department. He would spend the rest of his working life at that company.

During his pre-war days at the bank, it had been necessary to keep his marriage hidden from the bank's prying eyes, and he and Dodo needed two incomes to survive during the Depression. For these reasons the Towners waited nine years to have the babies they wanted. When Gail finally came along in 1942, her mother quit work for good. A son was born three years later.

The Towners lived for years in east-end Toronto, but in 1950, they joined the march to the suburbs. The house they bought on Fenwood Heights, not far from Cathedral Bluffs Park, was relatively large, three bedrooms with an unfinished rec room (that remains unfinished to this day), with picture windows and a lovely back yard. When they moved in, telephone lines had not yet been installed in the area, there were no libraries or community centres and the landscape was treeless and barren.

Gail was bused every day to the Scarborough Village School, many blocks away. She was a shy, quiet, straight-laced child and, with the combination of being one of the new kids and having to endure the raucous bus rides, she resorted to what became her emotional comfort throughout her life—eating. She became the fat kid in the class, which brought even more ridicule than being the new kid. On top of that, the school was obsessed with sports— gymnastics, track and field, baseball—and Gail wasn't the least bit interested in physical activity. What saved her from a miserable childhood was her music. The entire family loved to sing. Christmas day was spent around an aunt's piano, with an uncle playing the violin and the rest of the relatives belting out carols. Music remained Larry's and Dodo's great passion.

Soon after they moved to Scarborough, St. George's Anglican Church, a serviceable, not very elegant building—cement block and white pine trim— was constructed on St. Clair Avenue East. Dodo directed the choir there for

22 years. As soon as she was old enough, Gail joined the junior section, and when she reached her teenage years, it was R. H. King's Glee Club that made high school bearable. Still overweight and self-conscious about it, Gail realized no matter how much she wanted it, she would never be selected as a cheerleader. Thanks to her size, she felt she couldn't do sports, and she didn't have many dates. Then two events occurred that changed her life. With the help of amphetamines, she lost 40 pounds, and she met her future husband.

Don Moore attended the same Young People's Group at St. George's as Gail did. She thought he looked a lot like the Fonz, her favourite television character, although he was fairer and chunkier. They were just casual friends until the group went camping on the cottage grounds of Don's grandparents. While roasting marshmallows and singing around the camp fire, something clicked. Suddenly Gail had a date for the skating party at Little Switzerland and the Sadie Hawkins dance, just like everybody else. For her, this was new-found bliss. "What attracted me to him was that he was attracted to me," she says.

She lost weight and her confidence blossomed. She became a prefect, one of the school elite. She was chosen to be the secretary of the Student Administrative Council. The popular clique even began taking a second look at her, despite the fact they considered her boyfriend something of a klutz.

Gail was in Grade 11 when she met Don, and, although he was just six months younger, he was only in Grade 9. Then he failed again, which meant he was three years behind her. But Gail was so enraptured at having a real, live boyfriend, she didn't mind much.

Gail had always been a hard-working student, managing 80s in math, biology, French. After she started dating Don, her grades dipped slightly, but she still had a high enough standing for admission to university. Since the career she had decided on didn't require a university degree, she decided not to go.

Guidance counseling at R. H. King Collegiate consisted of slotting the girl students into one of three pigeon-holes: secretarial, nursing or teaching. Now and then, a flight of fancy might overtake the elderly guidance teacher, and if the student were particularly pretty, he would suggest, his eyebrows raised in alarm, a career as a stewardess. Female lawyers, doctors, journalists, actors, writers, dentists were not part of the guidance office's landscape. Gail chose nursing. She's not sure why; there were no nurses in her family. It had to do, she says, with old-fashioned teenage altruism, a genuine longing to be a Florence Nightingale.

In 1961, the vast number of RNs (registered nurses) took their training at the large teaching hospitals. The first of these schools had been established in St. Catharines, Ontario, in 1874, and the basic philosophy had not changed much since. Student nurses were regarded as a source of cheap labour. In Gail's time, only six weeks of classroom training were provided before the students began working the wards, giving sponge baths, changing beds and bed pans, getting rid of dying flowers, which was the worst job of all because they stank so much. The first two years, the nurses were not paid a cent, although the hours were long and the work often difficult. There was only token tuition, but the books and uniform—three dresses, three stiff collars, six bibs, six aprons, three caps, shoes and stockings—were expensive. Gail says her family couldn't have afforded it if she hadn't got a bursary from her father's employer, Imperial Oil.

The hospital she chose was the relatively small Wellesley Central on Sherbourne Street in downtown Toronto, and it provided her with one of the happiest times of her life. She loved evenings in the common room, where the girls gossiped and stuffed themselves with tea, toast and jam, and sang songs on the hit parade. Every 21st birthday—and there were many of them—was celebrated with champagne. A couple of times, at the never-ending, all-girl, burning-the-blues parties, Gail got hopelessly drunk and learned what a major hangover was all about.

During her three years at Wellesley, Gail studied every kind of nursing, from surgical to psychiatric, but she quickly realized what she was best suited for: obstetrics. It has been her specialty ever since. She has the ability to relax and calm women in labour, knows how to help them deal with their pain. She is deeply sympathetic towards them, never condescending or impatient. To this day, she personally experiences a rush of joy at the miracle of each birth.

All during her years of training, she had continued to date Don Moore, using her once-a-week late-night pass to advantage. Gail was grateful to have a boyfriend, because finding a man, any man, was an obsession with the student nurses. Diamonds were aggressively flashed about. Finally, one evening, while he was wining and dining her, Don popped the question. The morning after, Gail woke up to find her hand being waved about by her two roommates, who were squealing over her engagement ring.

The wedding took place on April 17, 1965. Gail thinks the weather might have been a foreboding of the entire marriage. It was a lovely sunny day when she woke, but by the time she got to the hairdresser's, sloppy, wet flakes of snow were falling. In her wedding pictures, she's entering St. George's Anglican Church under an umbrella, holding her long dress knee high. Still, it was a lovely service, very musical, with her mother happily directing the choir.

After their honeymoon, the couple took up married life in the small city of North Bay, 360 kilometres north of Toronto. Don had quit school after Grade 12 and joined the Ontario Department of Highways as an apprentice draftsman. When part of the unit was transferred to the Gateway to the North, as it was called, he agreed to move.

Gail had no difficulty finding a job, and it was just what she wanted. The North Bay Civic Hospital required a nurse for its 16-bed obstetrical unit. The staff rotated, working several months in labour and delivery and then, for the same period, looking after the new babies in the nursery. Gail was very green, with a lot to learn—she made only $325 a month—but she was utterly engrossed in her job.

Very quickly she experienced her first encounter with infant mortality and its dreadful arbitrariness. A perfectly formed fetus, a girl, had strangled on its own umbilical cord and had been dead for three weeks before it was finally delivered. It was Gail's job to comfort the mother who, like many women in her position, blamed herself for her baby's death.

The Moores' sojourn in North Bay lasted only a year. Don found another job as a draftsman with an engineering firm located in Whitby, a community stretching along Lake Ontario, 48 kilometres east of Toronto. Gail liked the place at once. It had a small-town feel to it and was not too far from where she had been brought up. She has remained in the area ever since.

Gail found a job at a general hospital in nearby Ajax. She had been hired in obstetrics, but when she arrived for work, she found she was assigned to the isolation room. Her first patient, a victim of cancer, had maggots in his ears. It was the beginning of a trying time. The head nurse was a martinet, the hospital was rigid in its rules and old-fashioned in its attitude, and the staff was treated like servants. The evening after her first day on the job, Gail sent out her résumé, and in September 1966, she was offered a position as a general nurse in a doctor's office. It wasn't the perfect job, but it was better than the hospital.

Gail worked there for two years until her Colin, her first child, was born. She stayed home at that point, but the Moores had a hard time living on one income. When construction on the Whitby General Hospital was completed in 1969, Gail took a part-time position there. She quit work again when her second child Kathy came along in 1970, but not long after and against her will, Gail was forced to go back to work full time. It was the beginning of the end of her marriage.

In the first years, Don's and Gail's life together had been relatively happy; they did lots of things together, had fun. Over the years, however, their circles of interests and friends began to spin in different directions. Don joined Whitby's volunteer fire department, and loved the challenge, the physicality so much that, when it became a professional operation, he joined as a full-fledged fire-fighter. The Moores' social world centred on the macho world of firemen and police officers. There were dance parties, picnics with the kids and hockey games. Don loved it all. He took up archery and scuba diving, spending hours at these pursuits. Gail, meanwhile, was totally absorbed in her small children.

Gail was having coffee with a girlfriend one day in January 1973 when Don suddenly arrived home and said he wanted to speak with her in private. He announced that, for the last two weeks, he had been meeting with a real-estate agent and they had found a house in the small Ontario town of Brooklyn. He wanted her to look at it immediately because he had to make a decision that night. Gail was shocked and hurt that he would have done such a thing without consulting her. She was horrified when she saw what he had come up with.

She hated the house on sight. It was small, 800 square feet, a war-time bungalow that had sat empty for eight months. Dirty dishes were piled in the sink, a sump hole in the basement reeked, the nubbly, lime-green carpet was pitted with cigarette burns, mice had taken over and there was excrement everywhere. "Oh my God, you can't possibly ask me to move here!" Gail cried. But the real-estate agent insisted that, at $36,000, it was the only house they could afford.

At Don's urging, Gail signed the offer of purchase, but she was deeply resentful. Just a few years before, lovely homes in a brand-new subdivision had come on the market for $25,000. Gail couldn't convince Don even to look at them. No way would he tie himself to a mortgage, he said. He promised to renovate the Brooklyn bungalow, and he did, eventually, although Gail says there was rot in the walls and the smell never disappeared. She was never reconciled to "the house from hell." She refused to entertain, she was so ashamed of it, and she never forgot that Don had imposed the place on her. His imitation of a dictator never stopped festering.

To meet the monthly mortgage payments, Gail had to go back full time in the obstetrics department at Whitby Hospital. Both she and Don worked shifts, which required complicated strategizing to ensure the children were looked after. Sometimes there was no alternative but to leave the babies alone. This happened late at night, when it was impossible to get a babysitter, and was usually only for a half hour, but it worried Gail immensely. The kids say they hardly recall their mom and dad being together in the same place at the same time. Kathy Moore remembers that every Christmas morning, she woke up to find one parent missing. Gail describes the family's life at that time as "hell on wheels."

Such a hectic routine resulted in tremendous stress for everybody, and in 1976, Gail decided she'd look for less demanding work. She found a job with Durham Region Public Health, giving vision and hearing tests to school-aged children. It meant travelling the by-ways to small-town schools, but she had summers off and there was no shift work. She had been told the job would include post-natal counselling, but since she didn't have a university degree, it was decided she wasn't qualified, never mind that it had been part of her job as an RN for over ten years. She was stuck checking kids' eyes and ears, which she found not in the least challenging.

It did, however, give her more time to herself, and she took advantage of it. She returned to what she loved so much: choral music. In 1976, she joined the County Town Singers, a choir based in Whitby, consisting of some 50 singers, male and female, all ages. At the time of Gail's involvement, they performed in school auditoriums, nursing homes and at charity banquets, and they travelled—to Miami, the Maritimes, Western Canada and Austria (although the European trip was before Gail's time). The County Town Singers became the centre of Gail's life. Don, too, was involved, but only peripherally, helping with the lighting and sound. By that time, they were living distinctly separate lives; their paths seldom crossed. It was one of the reasons Gail was attracted to Hank Verwoerd.

He was the best tenor in the group, and she fell for him primarily because of his beautiful voice. His singing range stretched from bass to tenor and he had perfect pitch. Beyond musical talent, though, he seemed an odd person to engage in a passionate love affair. He was 13 years older than Gail. He had a wife who was totally dependent on him—a quiet, conventional woman who never learned to drive a car—and four children, although they were already adults and on their own. Hank himself was hardly a liberated male. A Dutch immigrant, he had grown up in the European tradition of a rigid family patriarchy. Paradoxically, it was Gail's independence, her own pay cheque, her ability to drive, her strong character that attracted him to her. What attracted her to him was his devotion. For the first time in her life, she says, she was treated as someone special.

For a couple of years, they carried on a clandestine affair until finally, Hank said that was enough of deception—either commit or forget him. After much heart-searching, Gail decided to leave her husband. The result was the shattering of two families; Gail had been married for 15 years and Hank for 27. Gail says it was she, not Hank, who was considered the villain of the piece. "I was the bad guy, really the bad guy," she says. She bore the criticism raining down from all sides, but it was a time of anguish for her.

She knew Colin, who was 12 at the time of the split-up, would want to stay with his dad. They had always spent a lot of time together, and both were into sports. But eight-year-old Kathy, Gail thought, needed her mother. Gail had consulted a lawyer before she moved out of the marital home into a rented townhouse, so it came as a shock when legal documents arrived that accused her of abandoning her children. Don decided he wanted both Colin and Kathy.

What followed was an ugly, three-year custody battle. The children lived with Don but Gail had extensive visiting rights. She went to parent-teacher sessions, had copies of the kids' report cards made, tried to show she cared about them deeply. She believed her ex-husband, either consciously or unconsciously, continuously denigrated her in the minds of her children. She, on the other hand, was accused of spoiling them, trying to garner their favour during their visits to her house. With each passing month, the situation grew messier, until it became evident a settlement could not be reached out of court. Psychiatrists were called in to assess the children. Finally, in 1983, Gail was awarded custody of Kathy and Don of Colin. When Gail went to fetch the child, she found her sitting on the front lawn, sobbing her eyes out, her belongings beside her in a paper bag.

At the same time as the bitter divorce proceedings, other avenues of Gail's life were blossoming. Her relationship with Hank was so full of happiness, she kept thinking the bubble was going to burst. They bought a house together in Oshawa, a large, semi-detached with three bedrooms, two bathrooms and a large family room complete with fireplace. Gail couldn't help but contrast it to the place in Brooklyn she had endured for so many years. They travelled: Barbados for their honeymoon, Florida for winter vacations, motoring trips in Ontario. As well, of course, they had their music in common. When they were married in 1983, the County Town Singers performed at their wedding. Most important to Gail, though, was that they talked; conversation was the meat of their relationship.

Gail's professional life was also more satisfying than it had ever been. In 1983, she joined the small hospital at Port Perry, a pretty tourist town near Uxbridge, as an obstetrics nurse. One of the things she most liked about the job was the head nurse. Rae Robson held a wonderfully progressive philosophy about the whole business of giving birth, ideas that she was able to express concretely when a new obstetrics wing was on the drawing board. It took five years of planning and much battling on Robson's part to see her ideal implemented, and because she listened carefully to her staff, Gail contributed a great deal. She feels the New Life Centre, a five-bed unit that opened at Port Perry Hospital in June 1994, is everything giving birth should be.

When an expecting mother is admitted to the hospital, she is ushered into a large, pastel-coloured room with comfortable chairs and pretty curtains, which is her domain during her entire stay. Here the mother-to-be labours, delivers and looks after her newborn. When she is ready to give birth, a baby-care unit, or infant heater as the nurses call it, is wheeled into the room. Everything is contained there for the doctor's and nurses' use, from a suction pump to clean the newborn to overhead radiant heaters. Any person the mother wishes can remain with her during delivery; the husband often cuts the umbilical cord. The mother, if she is capable and willing, will start nursing the baby immediately after the birth. If she can't breastfeed right away, it doesn't matter; she will have three or four days to be coached in the skill. She will keep the baby in a crib beside her, except for those times when she needs some rest and the infant is then wheeled to another room. Unlike many other hospitals in Ontario, Port Perry is a lot more than a baby factory.

The only disadvantage to working at Port Perry was the long drive from Gail's and Hank's home. In 1985, they bought a spacious, suburban-type house in the small, farming community of Greenbank, near Uxbridge. Although it was a nice house, the move marked the beginning of the end for Gail's bubble of happiness. Her daughter Kathy and her second husband did not get along. Hank expected obedience and respect. Young girls were meant to clean house, help cook the meals and do their homework. His own daughter had rebelled against this regime and run away from home when she was 18. Gail, on the other hand, had always been lenient with her children—Kathy, Gail says, was spoiled rotten—and now, in trying to make up for the trauma of the marriage breakup, she became even more permissive. Not surprisingly, what resulted was an unhappy household. Hank complained he was being ganged up on by two women, Kathy claimed she had no rapport with the man at all and Gail felt like the ham in the middle of the sandwich. Eventually, the tension became so great, Kathy moved back in with her father, although only for a short time. She soon quit school, took a job as a receptionist-secretary in Markham and set up her own apartment. Once Kathy had moved out, Gail and Hank's marriage improved, although it never entirely regained its former rosy glow.

Hank had worked for 33 years at the Oshawa division of Dupont Canada, the manufacturers of nylon and other synthetic fibres, eventually becoming a systems trainer, teaching others how to use new computer software. In 1993, the company, in the spirit of the times, was downsizing, and offered him an early-retirement package. Since he was already 63, he felt obliged to take it.

Not long after Gail and Hank had got together, they had attended a concert of the Dukes of Harmony, a barbershop chorus of 120 men founded in 1954. Hank had been delighted with the sweet, harmonic sound, and Gail's brother, who was a member, had an easy time persuading him to join. After Hank retired, it became all the more important to him. Gail became involved with the female equivalent, a group of Sweet Adelines called the Pineridge Chorus. The Verwoerds' life became centred on their music: practices and preparing for performances, travelling to concerts and competitions, social events. This became even more intense when they bought a piece of Harmony Ranch.

Located on 88 acres near the town of Baldwin, Harmony Ranch is a camp ground owned by barbershoppers and their families. There's swimming, miniature golf, fishing, shuffleboard and just about everything else that is done in Ontario cottage land, the big difference being that every now and again, a group will break into a rendition of "Cruising Down the River On a Sunday Afternoon." Gail and Hank loved the time spent there in their trailer, loved the people, the social life, the barbecues. Gail thought Hank was thriving in his retirement. Yet shortly after he stopped work, she began to notice a marked change in his personality.

Hank had always made Gail laugh with his wisecracks and practical jokes. It was what Gail liked most about him. While he kept up his affable façade in public, in private he was growing more morose and cranky. Gail attributed this change to the drugs he was taking. Shortly after his retirement, he had been diagnosed with polymyalgia rheumatica, a rheumatism in the muscles. It started with a sore neck and then spread to his legs; sometimes he was in such pain, he had to crawl up and down the few stairs between the kitchen and the family room. Doctors prescribed prednisone, a strong and sometimes dangerous drug, but in Hank's case, it eased his condition. Although he was sometimes grouchy and irritable, he never complained about his aches and pains, he ate well and kept fit, so Gail assumed that he was in relatively good health. Still, she thought winters in the sun would do him good. They had vacationed in Florida and Hank had loved it there, so half a year in the south and half a year at Harmony Ranch seemed the perfect solution. Gail could continue to work while they were in Ontario to make some extra money.

In the fall of 1995, the Verwoerds decided to sell their home in Greenbank. Gail wanted to wait until after Christmas to put up the For Sale sign, because her father was coming to visit and she knew it would upset him. It turned out to be a particularly pleasant holiday, and Gail and Hank were looking forward to a big New Year's Eve bash. They would head south in January.

On December 28, Gail was scheduled to work, but she was just getting over the flu, so she decided to call in sick. Hank also wasn't feeling well. He hadn't slept the night before, and he grumbled at her that her puttering about was disturbing him. "I'm just getting my breakfast," Gail retorted. "Then I'll go in the living room. Okay?" She soon regretted having been so short with him.

At noon, Gail heard a snoring noise, odd because it was so loud, and rushed into the family room. Hank was lying slouched on the couch, frantically struggling to catch his breath. Gail phoned 911. While she was performing CPR on him, a fire truck and police cruiser arrived and he was carried to an ambulance. Gail had a terrible premonition, and when she got to Port Perry Hospital, it was confirmed. Hank had died of a massive heart attack.

There was still another shock in store. When Hank retired, both he and Gail had been worried about the shortfall in their income. Hank talked to Dupont, his long-time employer, about the situation and told Gail he had found a way to get his hands on more cash each month. He asked her to sign a document stipulating that, on his death, she would get not his full pension but a portion of it. Gail says she didn't know the details of what she was sign-ing. After Hank's death, Dupont informed her she would not receive a penny of his pension, never mind that he had contributed to it for 33 years. She has taken legal action, but so far has not received a cent.

Although she still has her bad days, Gail somehow manages. She sold the Greenbank home full of memories—it was too big for her anyway—and bought a townhouse in Uxbridge. Her children have become closer to her. Kathy works in Uxbridge as an office manager and her son Colin, a univer-sity graduate in business, runs his own travel agency. Gail still spends part of the summer in her trailer at Harmony Ranch. For a while, she was president of the Pineridge Chorus, and she is also involved in the nurses' union. Each day, she thanks God for her job. Not just for financial reasons. Caring for a pregnant mom, overseeing the birth of a baby have become her *raisons d'être*, now even more than in the past.

Health

thrice would I stand in arms
On the rough edge of battle, e'er once bear
The pangs of childbirth.

Euripides, *Medea*, 431 BC

Suffocation of the uterus is when a woman's heart and lungs are thrust together by the uterus so that the woman seems dead except for her breathing, and some call it a heart attack because it is a malady of the heart.

Medieval Woman's Guide to Health, early 15th century

I feel weaker every morning, and I suppose am beginning to sink; still I can at times take up my pen. I have had my long black hair cut off. Dear papa wears a chain made from it. Mamma will have one too.

May 27, 1839 diary entry of Emily Shore, written two weeks before she succumbed to tuberculosis

When I was 18, a man of the world came into my life. He wasn't that much older, maybe three or four years, but he had already left school and lived on his own. That his job was as a lowly shipping clerk and his bachelor pad one room in a flea-bitten boarding house didn't matter. He possessed all the trappings of that most intriguing of creatures, the intellectual. He wore round, wire glasses, carried around a large volume of Proust and took me to my first opera.

It was Puccini's *La Bohème*. I loved it and, although I thought of it as a gorgeous fairy tale, one aspect of it left a mark. It was the first time I realized someone young—and in this case quite stout and rosy-cheeked—could actually die.

There had been no serious illness in my family. Grandparents had faded away, but always of old age. A friend of my mother's had spent years in a sanitarium with the disease that had killed Mimi, but by my teenage years, tuberculosis was no longer a threat, at least to the middle class. By high school, all of us had been inoculated with the Salk vaccine against that most

feared of plagues, polio. The Cold War and the possibility of nuclear destruction were certainly a threat, but this remained a backdrop in our lives, a catastrophe so irrational, we paid little attention to it.

As to "women's illnesses," they didn't bother me much. Menstruation had
been nicely explained in a film produced by a sanitary-napkin company, in
which audacious little cartoon sperms jig-jagged about until they encountered cute, unsuspecting ova. I never suffered much from monthly cramps,
and if my friends did, they didn't talk about it. We had a grin-and-bear-it
attitude towards our "monthly discomfort." It certainly didn't get in the way
of playing basketball or writing an exam.

The 1950s now seems a golden age as far as physical well-being is
concerned. My daughter's generation daily confronted death. AIDS haunted
their young years, destroyed their naïveté, despoiled the sweetness of teenage
romance. We took good health for granted. For them, illness lurked as a dark,
sinister and unforgiving spectre, but then, that has been the case throughout
most of human history, most calamitously for women.

I

In Euripides' tragedy *Hippolytus*, written in 428 BC, the chorus neatly sums
up the central dilemma of women in antiquity.

> But women are always weak, and their
>   ways are strange;
> Their very being is a blend of terror and helplessness
> At the pains and follies their sex inherits.
> I have felt this fear thrill through my own womb;
> But I cried to the heavenly helper of all women,
>   Artemis of the arrows;
> And always—the gods be praised!—she came to my deep
>   need.[340]

In classical Greece, the womb was the centre of the female being. It
informed everything a woman did in the world (in this case, falling passionately in love). Paradoxically, in a society that was obsessed with producing
male heirs, it was not a badge of honour but a symbol of fundamental weakness. It damaged her health and led to a woman's lowly status in society.

From the moment she was born, a girl's physical well-being was undermined. As an infant, she was breast-fed for a shorter period than her brother,

and her mother was given smaller rations because she had given birth to a female. In Persepolis in 489 BC, a mother received twice as much wine, beer and grain if the newborn was a boy rather than a girl.[341] As the female child grew older, she was more and more confined indoors, away from fresh air and sunshine. She was also fed considerably less than her brother. One of the greatest threats to her health, though, was her early marriage. Girls were married off at the moment of menarche, usually 14 or even younger, and expected to become pregnant at once.

Even though renowned thinkers—Hesiod, Plato, Aristotle—railed against early marriage for girls, their advice was largely ignored for pragmatic reasons. Once a daughter was married, her family could give up the arduous task of guarding her virginity; child brides were easier to train; and most important, the sooner she produced a male heir, the sooner her husband's family could breathe easy. Even today, the closer a young woman is to menarche at the time of giving birth, the greater the risk to both mother and child. In classical Greece, mortality for girls under 16 was as high as ten to 15 percent; from age 14 to 26 was considered the most dangerous time in a woman's life.

Of course, it wasn't just the young who died in childbirth. Having babies was a risk throughout a woman's entire reproductive life. There might have been some compensation if maternal death had been as glorious a sacrifice as being slaughtered in battle, and for centuries historians believed this attitude held sway. Recent scholarship, however, has debunked the theory. From a study of funerary monuments, scholar Nancy Demand writes about women in classical Greece: "... as childbearers, they were passive while men were active; they could display patience and submission, but not an active courage to match that of the warrior. They elicited pity, while warriors inspired admiration and emulation."[342]

That maternity was not a subject of much importance or interest to the male establishment is reflected in Greek art: there are almost no representations of childbirth. The one maternity theme that was sometimes portrayed was odd, to say the least. Hephaestus, with the assistance of the midwife goddess Eileithyiae, brings down his ax and splits open the head of Zeus. Out pops Athena, fully armed, ready for business. Zeus, apparently, suffered only a slight headache. A parable further from true-life, messy childbirth would be hard to imagine.

For the male, it was simply a repugnant, although sometimes momentous event. This is vividly illustrated by the belief the mother and baby were somehow contaminated. Not until purification rituals were performed days after the birth would the husband deign to visit his wife.[343]

While the Greeks seemed not much interested in finding ways to ease a pregnant woman's discomfort, the Romans were slightly more concerned. Roman fathers were expected to absent themselves from their businesses on the occasion of a child's birth (although not to attend at the actual delivery). Seneca, in his book on marriage *De matrimonio* wrote, "If the wife is that *rara avis*, a good and gentle woman, we wail with her in delivery and suffer if she is in danger."[344]

The gynecologist Soranus (c. AD 98–138), the Dr. Spock of his day, recommended ways to relieve labour pains and make the mother more comfortable. Pregnant women, he advised, should "promenade, exercise the voice and read aloud with modulations, take active exercise in the form of dancing, punching the leather bag, playing with a ball, and by means of massage."[345] He advocated breast-feeding and most important, he insisted the welfare of the mother should take precedence over that of the baby.[346] However, he also wrote that death was often inevitable and not too much lamented.

This mixture of sadness and loss combined with a resigned fatalism is found on the grave-marker of one Macria Helike, a Christian, living in Rome some time in the second or third century AD. It was written by her husband.

She had looks like golden Aphrodite, but she also had a simple soul dwelling in her breast. She was good, and abided by all God's laws. She absolutely broke none of them. She has brought joy to her survivors. She began as a slave, but now has won the crown of freedom [in the next world]. She bore three live children, and she was the mother of two sons. After she had seen the third, a female, she left her life painlessly, on the eleventh day. She had an incredible beauty, like an Amazon's, to inspire passion more when she was dead than when she was alive. She lived simply for 20 years. The dark tomb conceals Macria Helike.[347]

II

Floriana was a young Polish noblewoman living in Kraków in the mid-13th century. If the preparations for the delivery of her first child were typical, her laying-in chamber would have been carefully readied. Everything would have been scrubbed and new rushes laid on the floor. The silver and bronze cups, the best bedspreads, the fancy-worked cushions, the enamelware would be put on display. Little dishes of sugared almonds and candied fruit would be placed about. All cupboard drawers and doors would be opened, and all knots—on garlic strings, for example—untied.[348]

Once Floriana went into labour, the guests would start arriving, all female, of course: her mother and mother-in-law, various aunts, cousins and neighbours, and the midwife. With her help, Floriana's hair would be loosened and all the pins removed. Once the pains began in earnest, belly and thighs would be rubbed with pungent oil to ease her labour and hurry it along.

In all likelihood, Floriana would hold in her left hand an amulet made of jasper, a reddish-brown or yellow quartz. Hildegard of Bingen, writing in the 11th century, described the significance of this:

And when the woman bears a child from that hour when she conceived it until she delivers, through all the days of her childbearing, let her have a jasper in her hand, so that the evil spirits of the air can do so much the less harm to the child meanwhile, because the tongue of the ancient serpent extends itself to the sweat of the infant emerging from the mother's womb, and he lies in wait for both mother and infant at that time.[349]

During her labour, Floriana would likely be wearing a birth girdle made of snakeskin accredited with supernatural powers. A precious eaglestone might also be placed in the vestibule of the vagina, because, as one writer put it, the stone "instantly draws away both Child and Afterbirth." Some midwives advocated tying a hoof of a horse or ass, or a piece of red coral to the thigh.

Midwives believed that, by the ninth month, the fetus was running out of food, and by turning itself head down and battering the bag of waters until it broke (thus causing the mother pain), it could crawl through the birth canal to the outside. It needed all the gravitational help it could get, so women gave birth in a squatting or standing position. In the 14th century, birthing chairs—basically a stool with a hole cut in the middle—became popular, at least in cities. A noblewoman such as Floriana probably used one.[350]

Unfortunately, Floriana's pains became more severe without any sign of the baby being born. The midwife applied more balms, rose and damask oil. Finally, she forced her hand up the uterus until she felt the crown of the baby's head. At that point, she began her prayers: "Oh infant, whether living or dead, come forth because Christ calls you to the light!"[351] Unhappily, the head was lodged tight and could be neither pushed back or pulled out. Meanwhile, the mother suffered unrelenting, devastating pain, which continued from three in the afternoon until six at night. At last, the midwife again placed her finger on the infant's head and intoned, "Creature of God, I baptize you in the name of the Father, Son and Holy Ghost." To the mother she said, "I commend you to God's grace." Whereupon Floriana died.[352]

Perhaps because midwives and doctors were so helpless in the face of a difficult birth, or any of the other scores of female ailments, superstition enveloped medicine of the Middle Ages. Every wife had her own weird and wonderful remedies. Headaches were relieved by washing one's head in a wine-based pudding. For indigestion or malaria, drinking a mixture of hot wine and millet was recommended. Downing powdered ivory in vinegar and sugar might ease sciatica.

Professional gynecologists were just as arbitrary in diagnosing and treating illnesses. The *Medieval Woman's Guide to Health*—probably the first gyneco- logical handbook written in English—was published in the early 15th century. It is, interestingly enough, considered "a landmark in women's attempts to seek solace and assistance from other women."[353] One wonders if the cures it recommended weren't worse than the diseases. The following is suggested for menstrual distress:

Mix bay oil (from leaves of the laurel tree) and oil of roses together, both an equal amount, and anoint their arms and hands, legs and feet with it, and have a heated bleeding glass put on the genitals without variation. And let the patient smell stinking things that are exceptionally odorous, such as burnt felt, dog's hair, goat's hair, or a horse's bone set alight and then extinguished, or hartshorn, old shoes, burnt feathers, a wick moistened in oil, ignited and then extinguished, a woollen rag, or a live smoking coal.[354]

Of course, it wasn't just ailing women who were subjected to the misin- formation and superstition of the times; the entire study of medicine was based on it. All the same, gender did play a special role. The misogyny that so permeated the Middle Ages could also colour, in a most detrimental way, a physician's idea of how diseases were transmitted. It was thought women were the carriers of that most dreaded of scourges, leprosy. A woman who slept with a leper would not contract the disease herself but pass it on to the next man who climbed into her bed. Some doctors believed a man who had intercourse with a menstruating woman would contact the dreaded affliction; others argued a child conceived under such conditions would certainly develop the illness.[355]

In the early Middle Ages, a woman's life expectancy was probably only 36.

In the 11th and 12th centuries, a more nutritious diet meant women were healthier, taller and heavier. They lived longer, although this seems to have had more to do with their class and economic position than their gender. But in the later part of the era, a calamity of unimaginable proportions struck that undermined the health of both men and women. The Black Death, at its most vicious in the 14th century, scarred the European psyche for centuries and greatly damaged the populace's soundness of body.

III

In the early modern age, water was deemed the carrier of contagious diseases, especially those two terrors, the plague and syphilis. As one midwife put it, "Women get bathed for the first time when they are born, for the second time after they die."[356] Public baths were shut down, and, in private homes, the bath tub was used only for medicinal purposes. Queen Elizabeth I of England carted her own special tub from one castle to another, but it was to be employed only twice a year on doctor's orders.

By the 17th century, hot water, even it were not contaminated, was regarded as definitely bad for one's health. It opened the pores, allowing the body's "vapours" to escape. This, according to historian Sara F. Matthews Grieco, was thought to provoke "the loss of vital forces, weakness, and even more serious ills such as dropsy, imbecility, and abortion."[357] If one did, for whatever foolish reason, indulge in a hot bath, one could be expected to rest in bed for several days afterwards.

New, dry methods of personal hygiene came into vogue. Giving oneself a rub down with a slightly damp cloth, applying layers of powder to cover the grime and following that with a good dose of strong perfume to mask the stink was the typical toilette of the well-to-do. The lower social orders seemed to have given up the idea of personal cleanliness altogether. They simply wallowed in filth.[358] This naturally resulted in all kinds of ailments, including lifelong infections of the skin, ears, eyes and scalp. Menstrual blood was allowed simply to soak into one's garments. As historian Edward Shorter points out, dried blood that had settled in clothing or in the folds of the thigh or labia was a perfect growth medium for pathogenic organisms. Chronic vaginal infections, often with the resulting discharge of mucus and pus (leukorrhea), abounded.[359] The misery this caused can only be imagined.

There was another, serious repercussion of the European epidemics that resulted in damage particular to women. In the wake of the Black Death came societal breakdown and with it, famine. As was so often the case, in times of food shortages, the most nutritious and largest proportion of the family's rations went first to the men, secondly to the children and lastly to the women of the household. From the 14th to the 18th century, females actually became smaller and lighter. Girls reached menarche—determined by a ratio between age and body weight—at 16, compared to the medieval average of about 13 to 14.

Lack of nourishment brought on a whole variety of ailments: scurvy, skin diseases and, most prevalent of all, rickets. A childhood disease attributable to a lack of calcium and phosphorus, rickets causes bones to grow crooked, bodies to become deformed. While it afflicted both genders, it was the female who suffered the most. Not only would she grow up stunted and bent but her pelvis was often twisted terribly, with the result that childbirth became a horrendous ordeal. The mortality rate among women in the early modern period soared even higher.

Meanwhile, a woman's reproductive organs were blamed for almost everything that afflicted her. The womb was a unrelenting tyrant, and because women, unlike men, were obliged to follow its dictates, they were deemed weaker, and therefore inferior, beings. The womb could be quite irascible, sending up all sorts of venomous vapors and convulsions if it were annoyed. This displeasure could be especially severe if a woman were uppity and refused to obey her biological destiny—staying single when she should have been married, for instance.

In 1674, when Mme de Sévigné was 48 years old, her usual robust health gave way and she fell gravely ill. She recovered, but not until she had badly frightened her family and friends. It's not known what the malady actually was, although her cousin Count de Bussy-Rabutin certainly thought *he* knew. In August, he wrote:

In August, I learned that you had been ill, my dear cousin. That gave me so much concern that I consulted a very able doctor in this region. He told me that hale and hearty women like you, who have been widowed early and who repress their natural instincts, are subject to the vapours. That relieved my fears of a more serious ailment because—with the cure readily available, I cannot believe that you hate life enough not to avail yourself of it, not to take a lover as readily as you would an emetic [to induce vomiting.][360]

Mme de Sévigné replied, "But the same reluctance which prevented my taking the proper preventive measure against the vapours precluded my taking the cure." No lovers, no remarriage, and she lived to the then ripe old age of 70.

IV

It's not surprising that, in an age when women were either treated as cogs in the Industrial Revolution machine or sequestered in the home, women were perpetually sick. In the Victorian age, a female's life was full of physical crises. The onslaught of puberty, childbirth, menopause, the ordinary life-cycle events were all considered disabling, overwhelming mishaps. Menstrual flow, for example, was thought to emanate from a "wound" in the ovaries that threw the female's emotional equilibrium off balance.[361] This "weakness of the feminine nature" ruled out women from ever even aspiring to the accomplishments of the hardy male. Dainty and fragile, her place was beside the hearth.

The fact was that, during the Victorian era, women *were* more unhealthy than their male counterparts. There was an excessively high female mortality rate: at the beginning of the century, the average life expectancy for a British woman was only 44 years. Pulmonary tuberculosis had a lot to do with it; one in ten young women died of the affliction.[362] It was considered the romantic disease. Young women, with their ghostly pallor and pathetic coughs, simply faded away.

A single family could be terribly afflicted by consumption, a fact that is sadly illustrated by the history of the famous Brontës. Of the five sisters, Maria succumbed to the disease in 1825 at age 11, Elizabeth, a month later, age ten, Emily in 1848 at 30 and Anne in 1849 at age 29. (Charlotte died in 1855, not from TB but from the strain of a pregnancy that did not come to term. She was 38 years old.)

It has been assumed the Brontë children suffered under the rule of a stern and puritanical clergyman father in an isolated, culturally deprived place, all of which contributed to their early deaths. What probably killed the younger girls was the poor food and terrible living conditions at the Clergy Daughter's School, while the older ones were affected by the dampness and darkness of the Haworth parsonage. Physicians seldom thought about their patients' physical environment—children working in mines, governesses living in unheated rooms with little to eat. Emotional trauma, the feminine weakness, was supposed to be the cause, perhaps a broken heart like Mimi in *La Bohème*.

There was another idiosyncrasy of the Victorian era that undermined women's physical health: deeply ingrained prudery. Women simply would not subject themselves to vaginal examinations. It was not surprising that family physicians knew little about diseases of the female genital organs. Many believed metritis (inflammation of the uterus) was a condition that almost all women suffered from, so why worry?[363]

The male medical establishment was particularly negligent when it came to venereal disease, which was rampant in the Victorian society. Even if a doctor found a woman were infected, he often wouldn't treat her until he had received permission from her husband. The guilty secret was to be kept just that, even to the detriment of the woman's health. As historian Yvonne Knibiehler puts it, "We will never know how many young wives, married to safeguard their well-being, were sacrificed in this way to male collusion."[364]

The quintessential Victorian disease was that strangest of afflictions, hysteria. In the mid-19th century, women all over Europe and North America suddenly began having fits. They would scream, cough and sneeze, hurl themselves about, shout insults, sometimes even obscenities, laugh or cry hysterically. Some suffered severe palpitations of the heart; others clutched at their throats as if they were suffocating. Sometimes they would try to batter their fathers or husbands. Once exhausted from this frenzy, they would become mute, sometimes descending into a death-like trance.

Hysteria often came on in full force after some sudden shock: a miscarriage, a death of a relative or friend, a financial disaster. Not every hysteric was subjected to fits; other manifestations could be equally disabling: chronic fatigue, headaches, a penchant to burst into tears over nothing. Some women threw themselves on the couch and refused to get up, sometimes for years on end. The reason for this outbreak was not hard to ascertain. To become an invalid was to escape constant pregnancies, the monotony of housework, the burden of endless entertainment and the thwarting of one's desires, that slow death that came with a life of no social status, no recognition.

Doctors were befuddled by this strange phenomenon. Was it a disease, perhaps of the uterus, or was it a behavioural disorder, a mental illness? Certainly, the treatment resembled punishment more than medicine. Under doctors' direction, hysterics were suffocated with pillows until the fit subsided, beaten across the face and body with wet rags, given cold showers, their heads were shaven and they were humiliated and embarrassed in front of their families. The French physician Jean-Baptise Louyer-Villermay

(1776–1837) described in a case book the following treatment prescribed for a 21-year-old, upper-class Parisian. Her parents had insisted she abandon the young man whom she loved.

… In the space of six months she experienced several hysterical attacks with convulsive movements, the sensation of strangulation, hysterical boils, choking, tingling in the uterus, etc. Medical treatment was limited to the prescription of a few leeches to the vulva.

Shortly afterwards, the young person found a letter from her sweetheart in her parents' possession, which they refused to give to her. She was immediately seized by an attack much stronger than the preceding ones, which was accompanied by a lethargic coma, an absolute loss of feeling and movement, and lockjaw and rigidity of the pharynx to the extent that swallowing was nearly impossible. Her regular doctor prescribed copious bleeding by means of six leeches applied to each ear….

… [then Dr. Louyer-Villermay was called in]. It was deemed advisable to apply a new blistering agent to the nape of the neck, and when the sweating had been completed, compresses of salty water and vinegar were applied to the head. In addition, her neck was rubbed with oil, camphor, laudanum, and ether; finally she was given injections and partial injections of camphor and asafetida [vaginal douches of anti-spasmodic drugs].[365]

According to the doctor, his young patient recovered in a week. No more mention was made of her lover.

In rare cases where hysteria brought embarrassing sexual behaviour, nymphomania or obsessive masturbation, surgeons would surgically remove the clitoris.[366]

The injury a hysterical woman did to her family could be extreme. As historian Carroll Smith-Rosenberg writes, "Children were hushed, rooms darkened, entertaining suspended, a devoted nurse recruited. Fortunes might be spent on medical bills or for drugs or operations. Worry and concern bowed the husband's shoulders; his home had suddenly become a hospital and he a nurse."[367]

Hysteria was a massive, if passive, rebellion, a revolt against the often constricted and dependent life that was the Victorian woman's lot. If women were to be treated like children, they would act, even if subconsciously, as children.

V

The 20th century was one of increasingly robust health. One set of statistics tells the story. It could involve any developed nation, but Canada will do. In 1910, the life expectancy of an average woman was 52 years. By 1931, it had risen to 62, by 1971, to 76 and by 1994, it had shot up to 81 years, an astonishing over-all increase of 55 percent. For the first time in history, women lived longer than men, in the 1990s in the United States and Canada, six years longer.

Part of the reason for this fortunate turn of events was childbirth, that savage killer, had been tamed. In 1867, Joseph Lister published a paper in a scientific journal that had enormous repercussions for medical practice. He discovered that if the skin around a wound were washed with phenol (carbolic acid), deaths from infection dropped drastically. In 1874, the Germans and French adopted the Listerian method for obstetrics, and the following year, Lombe Atthill, the master of the Rotunda Hospital in Dublin, laid down a rule that nurses and students must wash their hands with carbolic soap before a birth and then rinse in a solution of carbolic acid afterwards. Soon maternity hospitals throughout the Western world had adopted this practice.[368] Deaths from infections and puerperal fever dropped drastically.

There was another important medical breakthrough that cut the death rate of both mother and infant—the Caesarean section. Before the 19th century, Caesareans had been performed only in desperation. Usually the mother had died or was dying, and the operation was an attempt to save the child. Of the 120 Caesareans performed in the United States between 1852 and 1880, for example, 58 percent resulted in the death of the mother.[369] With the adoption of antiseptic principles in 1867, coupled with the invention of anaesthesia in 1847, abdominal delivery began to be taken more seriously by medical researchers. In the 1880s, German doctors outlined in detail the surgical tech-nique towards which, as historian Edward Shorter writes, "many others had been groping for some time: the surgeon would carefully approximate the edges of the uterine incision and firmly stitch them together."[370] From that time on, Caesareans grew to be an ever more important instrument in childbirth. By 1990, one in seven American women delivered by Caesarean section.[371]

During this century, there were other crucial obstetric developments. The most important were the increase in hospital, rather than home, births and the rise of the specialist—the obstetrician and the surgeon.

These new directions have not been without controversy. Feminists complain about the "medicalization" of the female body, and the tyrannical practices of the male medical establishment. One fact remains clear, however: in the developed world, the risk of dying of pregnancy and childbirth has been dramatically reduced. (The underdeveloped world is another matter. In North America, deaths from pregnancy are 1 in 3,700; in Africa, that figure is 1 in 6.)[372]

While the inauguration of safe childbirth has had an enormous impact on women's health, another earthshaking breakthrough probably has had a greater effect, at least psychologically. In the winter of 1950, two forceful women—Margaret Sanger, the courageous and indomitable fighter for birth control, and Katharine McCormick, a wealthy philanthropist and a supporter of Sanger's—were asked to a meeting of a New England branch of the Planned Parenthood Foundation. There they met a brilliant and charming biologist who had been experimenting with hormones. Sanger asked if it were possible that some sort of drug could be used to prevent contraception. The scientist hedged, but in the end, said, yes, he thought it possible.

Gregory Goodwin (Goody) Pincus, the son of Russian immigrants, was the brains behind the Worcester Foundation for Experimental Biology. (Pincus had been denied tenure at Harvard because he was a Jew.) This conversation with Sanger goaded him into thinking about a birth-control device that would use progesterone to block ovulation. With Sanger's influence and McCormick's wealth, along with the help of distinguished gynecologist Dr. John Rock, Pincus set to work to develop an oral contraceptive. In 1960, the U.S. Food and Drug Administration authorized the marketing of Enovid. By the end of 1961, 408,000 American woman were on the birth-control pill. By the following year, that figure had risen to 2.3 million. In a mere decade, the Pill was taken for granted, a fact of life.

There was angry reaction, particularly from religious authorities. The Roman Catholic Church still forbids the use of contraceptives, although a large percentage of its flock have simply ignored the ban. In 1990 in Catholic France, for example, 48 percent of women of childbearing age who did not want to conceive were on the Pill and another 26 percent were using intrauterine devices; only three percent were using no birth control at all.[373] For many women, especially those who had already had children, surgical sterilization became the birth control of choice. In the mid-1980s, nearly half the married women in Quebec either had had tubal ligations or were married to men who had had vasectomies.[374]

The importance of the new birth-control devices has been so profound that the shock has still not worn off. As historian Nadine Lefaucheur puts it, "When women chose these forms of contraception, men, for the first time in history, could no longer expose them to the risk of pregnancy against their will."[375] Whole generations of young women came to realize they were now in control of their own bodies and reproductive organs. It wasn't much of a stretch to understand they could also direct their own intellectual endeavours, their own careers, their own lives.

In the latter part of this century, new physical terrors have come to haunt women. Stress has taken its toll. In the Western world, heart disease is by far the biggest killer; women of 60 are just as likely to have a heart attack as men. Smoking and exposure to polluted air have made lung disease the leading killer among killing cancers. Breast cancer ranks second and seems to have taken on epidemic proportions.

Yet almost every year, the life expectancy of women in the developed world increases. There is no comparison between the healthy, energetic 70-year-old of today who plays tennis and studies Urdu and one Christina Laflueve, a Parisian mother of five, who, when she died at age 36 in 1689, was so emaciated and worn, her village priest didn't recognize her and wouldn't bury her.

Pat

While she wasn't a particularly close friend, I always felt comfortable around Pat Inglis. She was quick with her mouth: "You're not very smart, are you?" she was fond of declaiming, and answer herself with a loud laugh. She was pretty, in a lissome, coltish sort of way, and a lot of fun, not utterly obsessed with getting good grades like some of us.

One February morning in our third year of high school, we had just settled into Miss Caldwell's history class when the loudspeaker barked that the principal wanted to see Patricia immediately. We were dying of curiosity, although we knew whatever he wanted, it wouldn't be serious. None of the girls in the academic stream ever did anything really wrong. Still, we were concerned, and, as it turned out, for good reason.

When Pat reached the principal's office, her family doctor was waiting to break the news. While shaving that morning, her father had suffered a massive heart attack. He had died almost immediately.

William (Bill) Inglis's death at age 48 would affect his daughter in many profound ways, even the career she would choose, and her mother's sad reaction to the tragedy would reinforce a pattern in Pat's life.

Misfortune was certainly not new to either Bill or Inez Inglis. Both came from working-class, WASP families in which hardship was a fact of life. Bill's father was gassed during World War I and died a few years later, leaving behind a widow and two young sons. Bill's mother packed herself and her two sons off to Canada. In Scotland, Bill had managed a few years of high school along with some business courses. In Toronto, he got a job as a book-keeper for a group of stockbrokers. He was a quiet, reserved young man, very serious about life, so it came as a surprise when he began dating Inez Bevin. "A born rebel," that's what people called her.

Inez's father Edward Bevin had been a professional bell-ringer in the town of Bridgewater, near Bristol, England. Her mother Liz was already pregnant with Inez when, in 1910, the Bevins emigrated to Canada. Edward and Liz eventually bought a nice house on Preston Street in what was then remote Scarborough. When the Depression hit, Edward lost his job and his house, and the family was forced to move into the garage that had been made into a cottage of sorts, although there was no indoor plumbing. Edward barely managed to support his family by doing odd jobs.

After Grade 8, Inez got a job packing biscuits at Weston's Bakery. That wouldn't have been unusual, but she also left home and moved into her own room in a boardinghouse. She played second base in the ladies' softball league at Sunnyside. She dated whomever she wanted, even joined a Young People's group at a "foreign" church. Her three sisters, perhaps with a touch of jealousy, called her wayward.

Bill and Inez met at the Palais Royal. Both liked to dance, and the Palais was the most swinging spot in all of Toronto. (Several of the parents of the Class of '61 met there, including my own mother and father.) What attracted them to each other is hard for Pat to fathom. Bill was quiet, introverted, seemingly unemotional, while Inez was gregarious—a "hellion." They were married in 1938, when Bill was 29 years old and Inez 28. She was pushing 33 when in December, 1942, she gave birth to Patricia, their only child.

Pat's not sure, but she thinks the reason her father was never drafted into the Canadian armed forces was that he had poor eyesight. Remaining a civilian meant he had a chance to get ahead, and by the time the war was over, he was working as a stockbroker for Davidson & Co. It was an odd occupation for a man who was so quiet and reserved. Pat believes that, almost from the beginning, the stress of the instant decision-making, the buying and selling, the excitement and chaos of the game undermined his health.

Her mother worked as a hairdresser and then, so she could be closer to home to keep an eye on Pat, as a salesclerk for a ladies' dress shop in the Beaches area. By 1952, the Inglises had saved enough to buy a brand-new, three-bedroom bungalow on Birchlawn Avenue in Scarborough.

Pat says that as an only child, she was often very lonely. There weren't many kids her age living in the neighbourhood, and she remembers spending one entire summer doing nothing but watching television and eating bread and jam until she got boils all over her bottom. To make matters worse, her father always wanted her to be with him. He wouldn't allow her to attend summer camp. "Oh no, she'll go with us on our vacation," he'd say. He wanted her beside him when he gardened—she had her own climbing rose bush, which was *his* pride and joy. For the most part, though, it was a happy home, even if emotions were seldom overtly expressed. Pat was raised almost entirely with adults; she could always converse much better with her parents' friends than with her own.

Probably because she spent so much time by herself, Pat was overjoyed to go to school. She was a gregarious person and here, at last, were friends she could talk to and play with. She wasn't a bad student, although she had to work at it because she was so easily distracted. By the time she got to high school, she was truly in her element. Since her mother worked in the dress shop, she had lots of nice clothes, good wool skirts and pretty sweater sets, and thanks to Inez's expertise, Pat's hair was always nicely permed and styled. She had a summer job she really liked at Eaton's, selling fabrics, and she enjoyed her classes, even if she was hopeless at math.

Yet she looks back on her teenage years with some sorrow. She was only 12 when her father suffered his first coronary. He promptly had four heart attacks within a month. Although the angina was terrible, once he was released from hospital, he went back to work, hardly missing a day. He was so tired and weak that Inez was always afraid he would collapse in the street before he could get home from work. Nitroglycerin pills were his life line. Inez, a nervous person anyway, worried all the time. "Don't argue with your father," she would say to Pat. "Don't make a noise, don't bother him." Pat's way of helping was by making sure she never did anything foolish or mischievous. No matter what, she mustn't ever let her parents down.

The anxiety at home was relieved somewhat when Pat found herself a boyfriend. Bob Doran had gone to the same elementary school, but in those days, Pat had thought him a real geek. He wore his pants too short, he had a brush cut and he seemed to care about nothing but his bicycles. In high school, though, the two waited for the bus at the same stop every morning. One day, Pat realized with a shock that an amazing metamorphosis had occurred. Suddenly, there was this tall, thin, "really cool-looking" guy. Bob and Pat were both members of the same Young People's group at St. Paul's United and one night, when they were in Grade 10, he phoned and asked her out to a church dance. After that, they started dating pretty steadily.

Bob was as a solid as rock, there for Pat when the massive heart attack finally killed Bill Inglis in February 1959. Pat needed all the support she could get, because her mother collapsed as well. For years, Inez had walked a fine line, every day living with the terror of not knowing if her husband would make it home from work alive. When the worst finally happened, there was no one except her teenage daughter to turn to for support. Her sisters had always been cool to her. Her mother was an invalid by that time, and since Bill's brother had died only six months earlier, also from congenital heart disease, her mother-in-law was too wrapped up in her own sorrow to offer any comfort.

Inez tried to deal with her grief. The house in Scarborough was full of memories, so she sold it and she and Pat moved into a small apartment. She bought a new car; since Pat had passed her driving test, they would at least have some freedom. She got a job at Eaton's department store. Yet a few months after her husband had died, Inez was admitted to the psychiatric wing of Toronto's St. Michael's Hospital suffering from acute depression. Electric-shock treatments followed.

Inez would be ill off and on for the rest of her life. Pat remembers that every time she was scheduled to write exams, her mother was in the hospital. The nature of the relationship between the two was completely reversed: from the age of 16 onwards, Pat was her mother's care-giver.

Visiting the wards of St. Mike's, as she often did during her teenage years—both Bill and Inez were hospitalized there—Pat had been awed by the starched, white uniforms. She read Sherry Ames's *Ministering Angels* and decided she wanted to do something that mattered to society.

Pat could have gone directly to nursing school from Grade 12—many students did—but she decided to get her senior matriculation; her father had made it clear he wanted her to have that much general education. Since she only needed a few subjects to be admitted to nursing, she carried a lighter load, and Grade 13 wasn't as terrible a year for Pat as it was for many of us. She drank a lot of tea at the Bo Peep restaurant, chatting endlessly with other girls who were heading towards the same career, and she dated a lot of different guys because, by that time, she had broken up with Bob Doran.

There were a couple of things about Bob that bothered her. When she first met him, she had happened to mention she didn't like dating men younger than herself. His birthday was five months after hers and he didn't want to blow his chances, so he lied about his age. Eventually, she found out and was put off by the deception, small as it was. Not only that, he was so enamored of her, he would do anything she wanted. That made her squirm. They were too close, they weren't growing, she wanted something more, she said. He thought, "Well, if that's the way she feels, I'm not going to try to sell myself any longer." They split up, but ironically, it would be Pat who would come crawling back—but not until three years had passed and she was a student nurse.

St. Michael's Hospital had been established in downtown Toronto in 1892 by the Sisters of St. Joseph, whose mission was to care for the sick and poor. Even today, the hospital still calls itself "Toronto's urban angel." Pat liked the idea that it was a Catholic institution, reasoning that it would broaden her outlook.

From her first day, she learned how dedicated the nursing sisters were and how much they demanded from their students. Study period was rigorously enforced; silence was to be maintained. The first year, the students worked on the wards for only two hours a day. The rest of the time was spent in class, studying anatomy, physiology, pharmacology, nursing arts. Pat found it hard going, the exams difficult, but she plugged away and did well.

It wasn't all work, of course. Pat went to all the frat parties and dances, although she considered them "meat markets." She kept comparing the men she met on these dates to Bob Doran, and telling everybody what a great guy he was, how nice and how funny. Her exasperated mother finally said, "Why don't you call him? Get him out of your system, one way or another." It took Pat a few days to get up her nerve, but finally she did just that.

His sister answered the phone and recognized Pat's voice at once. She'd tell Bob that Pat had called, she promised. "I'll either hear from him or not," Pat said to herself. What she didn't know was that Bob and a friend had just gone on a holiday to Florida. Three weeks went by, and Pat had just about given up hope when she found a telephone message in her box. She let out a screech and ran straight up six flights of stairs to the telephone. After a long walk along the Scarborough bluffs, their old haunting ground, Pat and Bob agreed to start dating again.

At the end of September, she received her diploma. She and Bob were on the way to his family's for a dinner celebration when suddenly, a car shot through a red light and broadsided them. Pat remained unconscious for a time, and then was placed in traction for several months with severe whiplash. There were two repercussions that flowed from the accident. During her stay in hospital, Pat came to appreciate the nuances of good nursing care. And Bob realized how much he loved her.

Pat had been getting more and more impatient. Their relationship didn't seem to be going anywhere. There was a lot of hot and heavy necking, and Pat was afraid of getting pregnant. She wanted to get on with her life, not hang around in limbo forever. Was he going to marry her or not? Bob always tried to deflect the subject: he was just starting his career, he didn't want to be tied down financially. After the accident, though, there was poor Pat, strung up in ropes and pulleys. On Christmas Eve 1964, Bob finally popped the question. Of course, he'd give her time to think about it, he said. Thirty seconds passed before she let out a resounding "yes!"

Bob and Pat were married on September 24, 1965 in St. Paul's United Church, but it was a very stressful wedding, primarily because Pat's mother had been ill once again. Inez had not only recovered from her depression but had married again. Pat liked Inez's new husband Bill Kearsley, whom she called Pops, and got along well with him. And Pat relished her new-found freedom once her mother was out of her care.

In the spring of 1965, Inez and Pops had gone to England on a search-for-your-roots expedition. Inez even found her father's name inscribed on the church wall where he had been the bell-ringer. However, on their return in May, she had suffered a massive coronary. She recuperated at St. Michael's until the end of June and returned home, only to have another heart attack. This time, she was hospitalized for months. At the same time, Pat's paternal grandmother Effie Inglis was a patient at East General Hospital. Pat spent the summer before her marriage running from one hospital bed to another. Her stepfather suggested postponing the wedding, but it occurred to Pat that she might never get married if she delayed every time there was a family illness.

By the time the newlyweds returned from their Florida honeymoon, Inez had undergone major heart surgery. Once again, Pat was there for her, only this time she was a registered nurse. Inez recovered enough to go home, but health problems would continue to plague her. She died in 1972 at age 60.

After her graduation, Pat had stayed on at Saint Michael's. She hadn't found a specialty that appealed to her, but she enjoyed being a general-duty nurse. "I was very comfortable, and very proud of what I was doing," she says. Within a year, though, she had changed jobs. She had decided that working nights and weekends was no way to lay the foundation of a strong marriage, and she found a nine-to-five job at Eaton's as an occupational-health nurse. Her main duty was to be on hand in case of accidents or illnesses, but serious mishaps were rare. Pat found herself mostly dealing with the off-sick forms of employees and with testing eyes and ears. She found it boring, but the money was good and the hours regular.

By 1967, the Dorans had saved money for a down payment on a house.

They chose a brand-new, three-bedroom back-split in Unionville, a bedroom community a short distance northeast of Toronto. Although she had applied at and been hired by Centenary Hospital, which was then under construction, by the time it was completed, Pat was pregnant. Jeffrey was born in January 1968, and 18 months later, a daughter, Lesley. Pat never did start her job, because by that time she had followed her husband to North Bay.

Bob Doran had never been a very good student. At R. H. King, he had had a wonderful time socially—he had plenty of friends, and played football and basketball—but his grades were not impressive. It was a favourite great-aunt who gave him the right advice. "Oil, Bob. That's the field you want to be in." When he saw a newspaper ad for a job at Sunoco, the distribution arm of Suncor oil and gas company, he applied and was hired. He has never worked anywhere else.

His first position was as a market manager, responsible for 25 retail gas stations in the North Bay area. As there was no Sunoco office in the vicinity, Bob worked out of his home, without help of a secretary or a teletype machine. Once a month, he would spend a week in Timmins, visiting the stations in that area.

It was a lonely time for Pat. Bob was on the road a lot, she had no friends in the community and she was confined at home with three small children—Christina was born in 1972. She didn't like the climate—it rained a lot in the summer—and after Toronto, she felt the shopping was limited. Nonetheless, she regards the time her children were babies as one of the happiest in her life. She breastfed them all, her youngest until she was 18 months, she played with them, cared for them when they were ill. Her nursing background, she believes, is what made her a good mother. She understood how a child developed physically and she was not frightened by sickness. Common sense, she insists, is what care-giving is all about.

During this time, Bob's career was blossoming. In 1974, he was transferred to the real-estate department of Sunoco's head office in Toronto. When the Dorans moved back to the Toronto area, the town of Whitby was just about to mushroom into a good-sized bedroom community, and there they found a house to suit their family.

The next few years were hectic. Pat did all the things connected with raising three kids in the suburbs: driving them to Brownies and swimming practice and hockey games, making the costumes for ballet recitals, getting involved with the home and school committee. She became part of a group of mostly former nurses who did yoga together and exchanged ideas about child-raising, recipes, crafts. As the years passed, they went back to work one by one. When Pat applied for part-time work at a hospital and was told her techniques were not sufficiently up-to-date, she began taking college-level upgrading courses, although Bob made it clear he would prefer it if she stayed home.

He was very busy himself and engrossed in his job. Not only did he put in from ten to 16 hours a day at the office but he had a daily, two-hour commute. He was taking courses at York University in real-estate appraising. As well, since he had always been a man who enjoyed his children, he tried to spend as much time with them as possible. In his late 30s, he was always pushing himself, testing himself. He now understands that the stress was intolerable.

In the summer of 1979, Bob told Pat he had an odd, rather large canker on his tongue. She thought it a result of his eating too many acidic foods, especially tomatoes and peaches, which he particularly liked. When it didn't go away, she urged him to go to the family doctor. Bob was sent to a plastic surgeon, who removed the growth, but a biopsy revealed it was cancerous. Bob was immediately admitted to hospital and the operation was performed again, only this time, the incision was deeper and finer. He was also examined by specialists at Princess Margaret Hospital, a well-known centre for cancer research in Toronto. Radiation or chemotherapy treatment was not recommended at the time, since it was felt the surgery might have done the trick. However, Bob was to be closely watched.

Thirteen months later, at Christmas 1980, Bob came down with a bad sore throat and his lymph glands swelled up. Both the surgeon and cancer specialist told him not to worry; it was the effect of the cold. Two months later, the Dorans were getting ready to travel to Florida for the winter break when Bob suddenly said, "You know, I can't move my neck. I'm afraid I won't be able to drive." He was quickly seen by an ear, nose and throat specialist, who discovered a malignant growth wrapped around one of Bob's carotids, the major artery in the neck that supplies blood to the head.

Bob underwent 96 hours of chemotherapy. Amazingly, he never felt really sick, never missed a day of work. Early in the morning, he would drive downtown to Princess Margaret Hospital, undergo the chemotherapy and then go about his day's business. He says, "Stability is very important for a person going through chemo or radiation therapy. You crave normality."

By the end of May 1981, Bob, Pat and the kids were told they could take their postponed vacation to Florida. Bob was also able to attend Jeffrey's Grade 8 graduation. In June, he underwent radical neck surgery; a tumour wrapped around a carotid artery was unusual, and the surgeon had a hard time removing it. The operation was considered a success, and the Dorans went back to living normally.

One evening a year and half later, Pat and Bob were taking the dog for its nightly walk when Bob said, "I hate to tell you, but I have another canker on my tongue." For the first time, Pat could see real anguish in her husband's eyes.

Bob was immediately admitted to Saint Michael's Hospital and a few days later, was operated on once again. This time, a portion of his tongue and his salivary glands were removed, which proved malignant. Miraculously, though, that was the end of it. The cancer had finally all been cut away. Sixteen years later, there has been no recurrence of the disease.

Not surprisingly, Bob's illness left its mark on the entire Doran family. The kids were always worried. If their dad were unusually quiet, they were afraid he had found some symptom that might mean the cancer had come back. If he were upset, they thought it was because of a new illness. As well as worrying, they also grew closer to him, developing an innate understanding that time was precious to them all. Pat believes that was also the reason none of them was rebellious. Just as Pat had in her teenage years, the Doran kids helped out by not making trouble and doing as well as they could at school.

The professional side of Pat kicked in, not only for Bob's benefit but for her own emotional well-being. It was a form of defence against her husband's stoicism. He never complained, never talked about his illness, which made it hard to gauge how she could help. She tried to read his body language. Was he uncomfortable? Was he feeling ill? Pat felt so frustrated that at one point during Bob's treatment, she did something her family thought was very strange: she agreed to care for a three-month-old baby whose mother was working. Pat's job as a paid babysitter lasted for only six months, but it served its purpose. "It got me over the winter. She was somebody I could love and cuddle and care for."

Naturally, Bob himself was deeply affected. He was told by doctors, and has become convinced, that the pressure of his job brought on the cancer. Avoiding stress has become an obsession, and this, he admits, probably means he's not as effective at work as he once was. He kept his position at Sunoco, but he has not been promoted since his illness. "I said goodbye to a very promising business career," he says. "But that's okay. I'm happy. I have more balance in my life."

The downside of his hobbled career was that his pay cheques did not increase much. With three children to help through university, Bob could no longer object to Pat returning to her profession. After taking upgrading courses in anatomy, physiology and pharmacology, she worked for an agency, looking after wealthy private patients or filling in at hospitals when staff nurses were sick or on holiday. For a while, she took a part-time job in a doctor's office.

Pat's college course included geriatrics, and she was surprised at how much she enjoyed it. In 1987, when a job as a registered nurse at Fairview Lodge, a 196-bed home for the aged, became available, she grabbed it. Most of the patients are very elderly, some over 100 years old; almost all will die there. Many have no teeth and have to be fed, some are incontinent. Some are cognitively aware; others have Alzheimer's and other dementia. Physical problems—arthritis, diabetes, strokes—are normal. Enormous patience and compassion are required to look after such people, yet Pat finds great satisfaction in her work. "They are all individuals, they have all contributed to society." In her previous nursing career, she had never had a patient die in her care. Now it's an everyday occurrence. "I'll say, 'Let go, Mary. It's no use hanging on.' It's not an unhappy event, because they've lived their lives already.... I think because I work with the elderly and because of Bob's illness, I've learned to take each day as it comes. 'Sit and watch the snow fall' is my motto."

All three children remain close to their mother. Christina says of her, "She is very level-headed and can handle any crisis well. I respect that in her. She is very kind and very giving. Above all, she loves to be needed."

Care-givers

They weren't expressly forbidden, but my mother considered magazines such as *True Confessions, Modern Romances* and *Real Story* in such bad taste, I wouldn't have dreamed of bringing one into the house. Yet when I found a stack of them in the corner of a friend's basement during a sleepover, I pigged out, devouring delicious nuggets like "We Traded Husbands! A Woman's Shocking Confession" or "Sex Drive Makes a Difference—18 facts a girl should know." I was soon gagging on the tribulations of the working-class female, but one piece stayed with me.

It was about a nurse who, on a dark and snowy night, comes across a horrible car accident. She immediately sets to work saving the lives of just about everybody. An 85-year-old grandmother is one of the fatal casualties, but, as the writer pointed out, she had already lived her life to the full. The driver of the half-ton is in serious condition, but he pulls through. The nurse later checks on him in hospital and, of course—what else?—they fall madly in love and eventually marry. That she probably gave up her career after that never occurred to me. All I could picture was this courageous angel of mercy, cool as a cucumber, applying her incredible skills. It was images such as this which prompted me and a few of my classmates to gather one night in the dark of a bedroom and secretly swear "to serve mankind through administering to the sick and wounded."

I

Phrastor of Aegilia was in a terrible state. He had married the young and beautiful daughter of Stephanus, a friend and fellow Athenian. But the matchmaking turned out to be an elaborate fraud. His bride was in reality the child of Neaera, who suffered the worst kind of handicap—she was foreign-born and therefore not a citizen. Phrastor promptly kicked both his wife, who was pregnant, and Neaera, his mother-in-law, out of his house.

Phrastor must have been a cantankerous man, for he fought with all his relatives and when he fell deathly ill, there was nobody to look after him. As the orator Demosthenes pointed out, "He got into a dreadful condition and became utterly helpless."[376] Neaera and her daughter moved back into his home, and night and day, the two women ministered to him, preparing special medicines and eventually nursing him back to health. There was a reconciliation of sorts, and Phrastor acknowledged his newborn son. However, when Phrastor's clansmen refused to recognize the child, claiming he was an "alien," Phrastor once again repudiated his little family. His next wife, he made sure, was an Athenian citizen.

At the heart of the ensuing divorce and other legal proceedings was whether Neaera and her daughter, in nursing Phrastor, had coerced him into taking them back. As the jury was told, "... you know of yourselves what value a woman has in the sick-room, when she waits upon a man who is ill." In the end, mother and daughter lost their case only because they were such superb care-givers.

Women in antiquity spent a lot of their time attending the sick. An entire culture dedicated to various treatments and herbal medicines permeated female society. But it was the business of childbirth that required the most skill and knowledge. Midwives, called *maia*, were most often older women who in the past had given birth themselves. These women moved freely through city streets, offering households their wide range of services. They served as matchmakers, and would physically examine a bride-to-be to determine if she were a virgin or not. Midwives gave advice about menstrual problems, fertility and birth control. They provided drugs to induce abortions, and they claimed to be able to forecast the sex of a child. They delivered the baby, and they were the first to judge if the infant should be sold, exposed or accepted by the family. (The father made the final judgement.) At the time of a death, they laid out the corpse.

These women had a profound knowledge of the female anatomy and reproductive system. They may have audited medical lectures, even been able to read and write. The Roman doctor Soranus, in his treatise *Gynecology*, written in the early second century AD, gave this description of a good midwife:

[She] must be literate in order to be able to comprehend the art through theory too: she must have her wits about her so that she may easily follow what is said and what is happening.... She must love work in order to persevere through all vicissitudes (for a woman who wishes to acquire such vast knowledge needs manly patience). She must be respectable since people will have to trust their household and the secrets of their lives to her and because to women of bad character the semblance of medical instruction is a cover for evil scheming.... Long and slim fingers and short nails are necessary to touch a deep-lying inflammation without causing too much pain....[377]

Sometimes a male physician would be called in if complications arose at the time of a birth, although it's hard to imagine what he could do. Since childbirth and gynecological problems were considered beneath a man's dignity, and many midwives didn't exactly go out of their way to share their expertise, the doctor's knowledge of female anatomy must have been very limited. Soranus himself had weird ideas about the reproductive process. Probably all the doctor's intervention did was to increase the stress on the birthing mother, who would be ashamed of being exposed before a strange male, medical man or not. Yet, according to historian Nancy Demand, by the fifth century BC, male physicians were involving themselves more and more in childbirth, although almost always using midwives as assistants.

There were several reasons for this trend. A male physician enjoyed far more prestige than a mere female, no matter how much medical knowledge or skill she had. More important, husbands were deeply suspicious of female medics. Midwives often helped women abort a pregnancy. Who knows? The fetus may have been a male heir. Not only that, midwives were known to sneak substitute babies into the household. A female infant born to the lady of the house might be exchanged for the male offspring of the cook, a physically or mentally handicapped baby replaced by a healthy one. In a society where bloodlines were everything, these suspicions became an obsession.

There were both good and bad repercussions following on the increased interest of male physicians in childbirth and female pathology. The women who assisted these doctors got a toe-hold in the professional club. As Nancy Demand writes, "In a profession without licences or established standards, this foot in the door could—and did—lead to a gradually widening sphere of female activity in the treatment of other women, and to women, who would more and more lay claim to the title 'woman doctor.'"[378]

But there was also a serious and long-term negative consequence arising from the male physician's entry into the female domain. Everything that was known about women's health was written down—gynecology makes up one-eighth of the entire Hippocratic treatises. Most of the material in male-authored books such as *Diseases of Women* are full of remedies and medicines that had, for centuries, been passed down orally from mother to daughter. However, there also developed a decidedly male slant to this material. The specialty of gynecology, under the control of the male medical establishment, had come into being. As Nancy Demand writes, "The doctor, in possession of his written treatises, assumed control over female lore and the reproductive capabilities of women."[379] Thus were planted the seeds of what slowly became the norm—the male domination of the medical profession, including all aspects of women's health.

II

It would take centuries, though, for women to be shoved out completely. In medieval times, they were still important healers of the sick, active in many branches of medicine. In the 15th century, Frankfurt city records listed 16 practising women physicians, many of them specialists in diseases of the eye. The daughter of Frankfurt's leading medical officer apparently took over her father's flourishing practice when he died. The records indicate she received payment for treating mercenary soldiers who had been hired to protect the city.[380] There were female surgeons, though they were few in number. Nuns in particular were known for their ability to wield a scalpel. When Clare of Montefalco died in 1308, the sisters of her own convent skillfully opened her heart, hoping to find material signs of the passion of Christ. (It was said the delicate operation yielded the following: on one side, the cross, three nails, a spear, a sponge and a rod; on the other, a five-tailed whip and the crown of thorns.)[381]

When medical schools in universities were founded in the late Middle Ages, female physicians began to lose ground, for good reason—most of these institutions denied entrance to women. As historian Claudia Opitz writes,

"... academically educated (male) doctors began to guard their status jealously, making efforts to drive traditionally trained women healers out of the profession."[382] In 1421, a petition from Oxford and Cambridge universities declaiming the dangers of allowing "ignorant, unskilled persons" (meaning primarily women) to practise medicine was received by the British parliament. Those who were not university-trained were prohibited from practising; several famous physicians and surgeons lost their licences simply because they were women.

An illustration in *Epitre d'Othéa,* a book authored by Christine de Pisan in the early 15th century, reveals a great deal about the growing professionalism and exclusivity of the medical establishment. The Greek god of medicine Asclepius, dressed up as a medieval physician, stands beside a young woman who is probably his patient. He holds up to the light a flask of what looks like urine, which he earnestly examines, thereby indicating how scientific he was. Meanwhile, an old woman dressed in rags is in the foreground. Circe, in Greek mythology the sorceress who had a bad habit of turning humans into animals, is catching the toads she will use in her magical potions. He is the image of methodical professionalism; she represents the uneducated, unsophisticated female practitioner.

There was one area of medicine, however, into which male physicians of the period could not make much inroad: gynecology and obstetrics. The morality of the times prohibited them from even carrying out vaginal examinations. Midwives still reigned supreme, but from the 14th century onwards, they became subject to more and more control. By the end of the Middle Ages, almost every city had established regulations outlining the training and qualifications required to practise the art. Official oaths became obligatory; the earliest of these that has survived is from the city of Regensburg in 1452. Midwives had to swear they would deliver all women with the same commitment "whether rich or poor," except for Jews.[383]

As they became more and more a part of the establishment, midwives were turned into moral arbiters. They were required to report illegitimate births and infanticide to city officials.[384] The courts insisted they give expert testimony in cases where a wife was alleging impotence on the part of her husband, and the Church demanded the midwife perform emergency baptisms according to a specific formula. It meant she became the first to announce a death of an infant or a mother.

For all of these reasons, midwives were not exactly popular. As historian

Chiara Frugoni concludes, "Given the staggeringly high infant and puerperal mortality rates, it is easy to understand how grief shifted responsibility for death onto the person who had assisted the mother or baby."[385]

In the great witch hunts that swept across Europe from the 15th to 17th centuries, it was often the elderly female healers who were condemned. They were accused of hating newborn babies—it was rumoured they murdered them and drank their blood. It was they who devised the magical potions that were said to restore virginity to a young trollop or sap the potency of a man whose wife had accused him of demanding too much in bed. If the master of the house suddenly became deathly ill, it must have been caused by a spell that a visiting midwife had cast. The women had far too much unhealthy knowledge; they were far too close to the evil forces of nature.

Witch-hunting became an obsession with the moral authorities. Bernardine of Siena (1380–1444), canonized by the Roman Catholic Church in 1450, personally condemned a large number of old, helpless women to fiery deaths. Their only crime had been assisting in the delivery of hundreds of births.

III

Saint Vincent de Paul's life work is mirrored in his words. "The poor are our masters. They are our kings, and they must be obeyed. It is not an exaggeration to speak of them like this, since Our Lord is in the poor."[386] Louise de Marillac was exactly the kind of charitable woman de Paul was looking for to help him carry out his mission. She was wealthy, a widow and an aristocrat. That she was also illegitimate, although an acknowledged daughter of a nobleman, meant she was not entirely part of the establishment, and that appealed to the priest as well. She was devout, of course. As a teenager, she had had a revelation that she would serve God by helping her neighbours; once her rich husband died in 1624, she set out to do just that. She had influential contacts through an aunt who was a cloistered Dominican at Poissy. On top of it all, she was acceptable to *les dévotées*, wealthy women of the French upper class called the Ladies of Charity, who siphoned their money off to good causes.

Through a network of relief societies funded by the Ladies, peasant women had been recruited to visit village homes to administer medicine and other aid. Vincent de Paul wanted to set up something similar in the cities, but he faced a major obstacle. The papacy frowned on female religious who actively worked in society. Only a few years before, in 1629, the Ursulines of Paris were told they must live under a strict rule of closure. The problem was that de Paul simply could not find enough good Catholic matrons to carry out the distasteful work of nursing the ill. His Ladies of Charity would give money, but they wouldn't enter the hovels of the sick and destitute.[387]

Enter Louise de Marillac. Under de Paul's guidance, she founded *Les Filles de la Charité*, the Daughters (later Sisters) of Charity, a corps of strong-willed and strong-muscled young women dedicated to carrying out the work of God. De Paul's plan was to "keep all the appearances of secularity [so as to avoid cloistering] while giving his company the substance of religious life." His instructions to them, accepted in the form of a simple vow, tell everything:

Your convent will be the house of the sick, your cell a hired room, your chapel the parish church, your cloister the city streets or the hospital wards, your enclosure obedience, your grille the fear of God, your veil modesty.[388]

De Marillac began by enlisting "good country girls" to work with the urban poor in cities or villages. Typically, two or three Sisters, usually daughters of farmers or artisans, would live together as a small community. Their main task was to care for the sick, but they also taught children their catechism and even worked manually to support themselves—the Ladies of Charity provided some financial backing, but not enough.

What the Sisters of Charity managed to accomplish over the years was amazing. In 1651, when Paris was decimated with epidemics and shortages of food, the Sisters distributed soup from the kitchen in Louise de Marillac's house. De Paul estimated every day they fed 1,300 Parisians, as well as 800 refugees from the countryside.[389] Among the afflicted they visited were the galley slaves imprisoned in Paris, which gave birth to their reputations as angels of mercy on the battlefield.

The Sisters paid a high price for their devotion. Many succumbed to the diseases of those they nursed. Others suffered physical and emotional collapse from overwork and the hugely difficult conditions under which they laboured. It was amazing that their numbers grew.

Their patrons, the wealthy Ladies of Charity, were aristocrats, very much concerned with preserving the status quo. When the French monarchy in the mid-1660s decided the poor and the sick should be rooted out of society and enclosed in institutions, the Ladies felt they must obey their monarch, although both de Paul and de Marillac did not approve.[390] Those with money prevailed, and the nursing sisters began staffing hospitals.

The Hôtel Dieu as an institution had actually existed since the Middle Ages, but in the 17th century, it was revitalized and reorganized so it could take advantage of the services of religious orders such as the Sisters of Charity. In return for their room, board and clothing, the nursing sisters took on the day-by-day running of the hospitals. They looked after all kinds of sickly poor, from migrant workers suffering from sunstroke to silk-industry workers ill with tuberculosis.[391]

Male doctors and surgeons working in the hospitals were paid cash, of course, and they considered themselves superior, which sometimes led to serious conflict with the nuns. Money was often extremely short, and when a Sister was faced with a choice between drugs or herbs prescribed by a doctor and good beef broth to fatten up an emaciated patient, she sensibly chose the food over the medicine, much to the disgust of the physician.[392]

On the other hand, the nursing sisters disapproved of doctors who wanted to do autopsies and thereby further the knowledge of anatomy and the way the body functioned. The souls of their patients concerned the Sisters as much as their corporal beings; an intact body, they believed, was necessary for an afterlife.[393]

Vincent de Paul envisioned another kind of institution, fuelled by the devotion of the Sisters of Charity. The Hôpital Général was supposed to be a shelter for the orphaned and the disabled. However, the monarchy wanted semi-prisons to store the lunatics and crippled beggars, thereby removing annoying eyesores from the streets of Paris. They were terrible places to work. The young boys, foul-mouthed and wild, had somehow to be contained until they could be apprenticed at 14. The girls, often equally insubordinate, had to be taught sewing or other skills. The blind had to be hand-fed. The crippled were somehow carried about. As historian Olwen Hufton writes, "… the life was one of unremitting toil for the sisters. In addition, they were perpetually under pressure to expand their services in difficult or inflationary conditions."[394]

Despite all this, the Sisters of Charity continued to attract dedicated women. When Louise de Marillac died in 1660, the Order had about 70 institutions under its management. By 1789, it administered over 420 organizations, of which 175 were hospitals.

During the French Revolution, the Sisters and similar nursing groups were labelled enemies of the people. Some were imprisoned, others went into hiding, but they never completely disappeared. During the Napoleonic period, they re-emerged, their spirit of dedication and stamina intact, to again form the backbone of services to the poor.

When French nuns visited other countries, particularly Britain, they were shocked at the terrible conditions in the hospitals and the primitive nursing care they found there. In the next century, Florence Nightingale insisted that if the Sisters of Charity had existed in England, there would have been no need of *her* services.[395]

IV

If you were sick in Victorian times, the last place in England you would want to end up in was a hospital. They were rank, crowded, dirty, poorly lit, with little ventilation. Basically, they were places to catch diseases. There were no anaesthetics—alcohol was the one relief, and it was poured freely—or antiseptics, so that any treatment was bound to be horribly painful. Surgery was an agonizing affair, and most often a failure. Hospitals were a last resort for the poor, the indigent and the troubled, who mostly went there to die.

In the early 19th century, anybody with two cents to rub together stayed home if they were ill. A doctor would visit, prescribe treatments and medicines, and then the lady of the house would take over. Families didn't hesitate to impose the burden of health care on females, who were thought to be naturally altruistic and caring. If they were single, they were at everyone's beck and call. In 1877, when she was only 18, Rachel McMillan, the British social activist and social reformer, was pulled from school so she could nurse her sick grandmother. The old lady obviously wasn't failing rapidly, for Rachel looked after her for 11 long years, putting her own important career in abeyance.[396]

In her novel *Shirley*, Charlotte Brontë paints a marvellous portrait of one of these selfless care-givers. Miss Ainley is an elderly spinster, the village saint.

... She would watch by any sickbed: she seemed to fear no disease; she would nurse the poorest whom none else would nurse: she was serene, humble, kind and equable through everything.

For this goodness she got but little reward in this life. Many of the poor became so accustomed to her services that they hardly thanked her for them: the rich heard them mentioned with wonder, but were silent, from a sense of shame at the difference between her sacrifices and their own.[397]

It followed that if the Miss Ainleys of the time demanded no payment, those women who had to make a living caring for the sick would be looked down upon simply because they demanded compensation. They were uneducated, of the lower classes, treated as servants and paid even less. They were all thought to be drunks. The contempt in which society held them is best illustrated by Charles Dickens's great clown Sarah (Sairey) Gamp, in *Martin Chuzzlewit*. Although in public, Mrs. Gamp expresses heart-felt sympathy for her patients, in the privacy of the sick room, she could care less. She is a tippler of the first order, unhygienic and careless. Above all, she is mercenary. Not only is she a nurse but she makes a pretty penny at a sideline—laying out dead bodies.

In mid-century, two events occurred in Britain that transformed the profession of nursing: a bloody war, and the arrival on the scene of a dedicated, single-minded, irascible bulldog of a woman.

When Florence Nightingale was 16 years old, she recorded in her diary, "On February 7th, 1837, God spoke to me and called me into His service."[398] When she announced she wanted to take up nursing, her mother and sister were utterly appalled, and put every obstacle in her way to prevent this "shame" from falling on their upper-class family. After years of struggle— "The prison which is called a family, will its rules ever be relaxed, its doors ever be opened?" she asked—Nightingale finally received a few weeks' training at the Kaiserswerth Institution in Germany, but almost all her knowledge came from her own readings. She was made supervisor of the Institution for the Care of Sick Gentlewomen in Distressed Circumstance for a short time, but it was the Crimean War that turned her into a household name.

War with Russia was declared in March 1854, and by the following autumn, the London *Times* was reporting staggering death and injury rates among the British soldiers. The conditions were appalling: the soldiers suffered not only from their wounds but from an assortment of diseases: cholera, typhus and dysentery. Death from malnutrition and exposure was common. The government's response to the public outcry that followed was to send Florence Nightingale and 38 nurses to the Barrack Hospitals at Scutari near Istanbul.

Nightingale was outraged at the unsanitary conditions and incompetent management she found there, and immediately set out to do something about it. In the process, she ran roughshod over the army's medical staff. Dr. Andrew Smith huffed, "I was perfectly aware that females can see many things, in which there might be a deficiency or cleanliness and comfort, that men do not see, and even that men have not time to see ... there might be a spot upon a sheet that a medical officer would not notice, and a woman would at once."[399] What the good doctor could not explain was why 16,000 men had died of preventable diseases.

Florence Nightingale returned to England in 1856 as a national heroine, the image of the Lady with the Lamp indelibly imprinted into the collective conscious. What most people didn't know was that a deep antagonism had developed between Nightingale and the 38 women she had taken with her. These nurses were poorly educated, poorly trained and often undisciplined. Nightingale laid down a regime that was so strict, a Sister of Charity would have balked. The nurses were unhappy and sometimes rebelled. The result was that Nightingale came back to England determined to mold a superior type of nurse.

In 1860, she founded the Nightingale School and Home for Nurses, associated with St. Thomas Hospital. For over 100 years it would serve as the model for training nursing personnel in the Commonwealth and elsewhere. As biographer Colleen A. Hobbs puts it, "With the backing of enormous goodwill, Nightingale helped create a new paradigm for nurses, one that transformed the capable, working-class domiciliary nurse and midwife into a modern nurse whose work was defined by selflessness, morality, and training that legitimized the profession for women of status and privilege."[400]

The new nurse might have been more educated and better trained than her predecessors, but she also lost any little independence she might have had. Hospital nurses carried out their duties under the close supervision and authority of male doctors. The same held true for midwives, who, because they had no way of learning how to use forceps or undertake Caesarean sections, were banished from the birthing room. Historian Yvonne Knibiehler comments, "As private midwifery became financially unfeasible, midwives took jobs as salaried employees of hospitals and private clinics. There they found themselves in subordinate positions, taking orders from now all-powerful doctors and no longer free to respond to women's needs. A traditional form of female solidarity thus collapsed, and women forfeited all autonomy in the area of reproduction."[401]

This trend might have been countered if women had been allowed to become physicians, but for many years, they were banned from the profession. Indeed, the battle men waged to keep women out of medical schools during the 19th century remains a dark stain on the history of the entire medical establishment.

Hostility, ridicule, even violence greeted any woman who dared try to gain admittance. Male students took up petitions to have her application rejected, claiming they would be so embarrassed by the presence of a woman in anatomy class, they wouldn't be able to concentrate on their studies. When one young woman, training as a nurse, began sitting in on lectures and showing up in the dissecting room at a hospital in Middlesex, England, her male classmates thought it was something of a joke and tolerated her. When she stood top of her class in an exam, the same classmates madly protested and had her thrown out.[402]

In 1870, male medical students surrounded an examination hall and, as five young women approached who had been admitted to the University of Edinburgh medical school, they slammed shut the gate, all the while cat-calling insults "in the foulest possible language." A sympathetic young man, a classmate, managed to pry open the lock for them.[403] All five passed their exams.

The reasons given for not allowing women admission to medical school were insults in themselves. Medicine was "too intellectual" for women, whose mental capabilities were not strong, too physically demanding for their frail physiques and such studying would be a waste of money because it would impinge on their jobs as wives and mothers. "Can we deny that the general delicacy of females is a serious bar to an occupation which necessitates exposure at all hours and in all weathers?" one doctor asked.[404]

Some determined women managed to crash through the barriers and obtain their medical degrees, but what they had to go through to do so was ridiculous. The first English woman doctor was discovered to be a female only after her death in 1865. For her entire working life, she was forced to disguise herself as Dr. James Berry, rising to the position of Inspector General of Hospitals for the British Army.[405]

Elizabeth Blackwell's (1821–1910) perseverance in becoming the first licensed woman doctor in the United States was equally remarkable. After being rejected by one university after another, she finally gained admittance at Geneva Medical School, a small, chartered institution in New York (now Hobart College). The student body had been given a chance to vote on whether to accept her or not; in an uproarious assembly, all shouted, "Yeah" as a huge joke. They told themselves she would never be able to stand the grind, but in 1849, she was granted her licence. Not only did she fight for women's rights her whole life, especially for admittance to medical school, but she was a strong advocate for female sexuality. Women enjoyed sexual intercourse, she insisted, while several doctors, shaking their heads, pointed out that such an outrageous point of view highlighted exactly why women should *not* be physicians.

At the end of the century, as universities began to admit women to other faculties, they could hardly rule medical school out of bounds. More and more women became physicians, mostly administering to female patients. Many turned their minds to medicine and refused to speak out for women's rights; it was enough merely to cope with the hostility they found in medical school and in the profession. Just the same, they were living proof that a woman could do a man's job, even one as highly skilled as medicine. As historians Leslie Parker Hume and Karen M. Offen conclude, "... they confronted the doctrine of two separate spheres head-on and established a new cultural model for their societies."[406]

V

In May 1918, the German army bombarded Allied encampments near Etable in France. In the melee, two Canadian field hospitals were badly damaged. Four nursing sisters died. Others scrambled to help the injured and dying, and for their efforts, received the Military Medal for Bravery.[407]

The nurse became a genuine hero during World War I, the status of the profession soared and yet, in a way, her good deeds only emphasized all those old bugbears about female stereotyping. This is reflected in Red Cross propaganda of the time. The image is striking, painted in the monochromatic colours of gray and red favoured for posters at the time. A gigantic nurse, all soft benevolence and looking much like the traditional Madonna, cradles in her arms a miniature soldier lying on a stretcher. The banner reads: "The Greatest Mother in the World."[408] Nursing was still considered merely an extension of a woman's duties in the home, an attitude that caused resentment on all sides. Historian Françoise Thébaud puts it succinctly: "While soldiers, many of them of lower-class background, appreciated the quiet of the hospital, they felt humiliated and infantilized by the rather aloof women who cared for them like children, saw all their weaknesses, and in the end sent them back to the front."[409]

Even after the valiant efforts in the war and the horrific influenza epidemic that followed, nurses were still treated like nothing more than helpmates by the medical establishment. "Leave the wounds to the doctors and the wounded to the nurses," wrote one French physician.[410] Devotion, discretion and kindness were the important attributes for women, not scientific knowledge or technical skill.

In the decades after the war, nurses tried hard to gain control of their profession and establish the criteria necessary to upgrade it. They were successful to some degree. In 1919, the first university-degree program in nursing in the British Commonwealth was established at the University of British Columbia. The response of the College of Physicians and Surgeons, the medical establishment in that province, was not atypical. Two years of post-high-school education was more than enough, the doctors proclaimed. "The over-training of nurses is not desirable and results largely in the losing of their usefulness."[411]

The administrators were well aware, of course, of the financial advantages of the hospital nursing schools. Unlike universities or colleges, they provided a wonderful pool of cheap labour. Students put in 12-hour work days, not just nursing the sick but scrubbing and cleaning as well. With such unpaid slaves to draw on, why would a hospital hire a registered nurse? In fact, they didn't, or at least, very few. The majority of RNs could find work only with private clients in their homes. It was expected that in her off moments, when Nurse May wasn't attending the ailing Mrs. Smith, she would prepare lunch for the children, scrub the kitchen floor and sometimes go shopping. It was hard and insecure work.

All nursing was poorly paid. In her autobiography, Doris Lessing writes that her mother, a highly competent nurse in London before and during World War I, was paid so little that "she was often hungry and could not buy herself gloves and handkerchiefs or a nice blouse."[412] In a 1929 Canadian survey, 60 percent of the private-duty nurses queried said their salary was so small, they couldn't possibly save for their retirement. Since most were unmarried, they faced a bleak future.[413]

Female physicians did not fare much better. Virginia Woolf, in one version of her novel *The Years*, gives this succinct description of how society regarded women doctors.

Punch [the magazine] was full of pictures of little delicate women in bonnets and crinolines trying to cut off legs and appealing to strong men in whiskers—'Oh

Surgeon, do help me! My wrist is *so* tired!'—to illustrate what would happen if one trusted one's body to a woman doctor.[414]

In 1910 in the United States, there were 9,015 women physicians, six percent of the total, a healthy number given the fact that only a few decades before, there had been not one. (By contrast, there were only a few hundred female doctors in all of France in 1914.) One reason for the increase was that all-women medical institutions had flourished since the mid-19th century. However, when mainstream universities began admitting women, their *raison d'être* disappeared, and many shut their doors; in 1895, 19 women's medical schools were operating throughout the U.S.: by 1910, only two remained.

Once women lost their own colleges, the male medical establishment descended. Universities slapped quotas on female medical students—usually a mere five percent. Even if female students did gain admittance, they had a hard time becoming fully fledged physicians. Hospitals would simply not give them internships, and after World War I, hospital training became more and more a prerequisite for the granting of licences. This outrageous discrimination persisted for decades. In the United States in the 1930s, 250 women medical graduates each year competed for 185 internships; for males, there were 6,000 openings for 5,000 graduates.[415] By the 1940s, the number of female doctors had dropped to only four percent of the total.

During World War II, with the men away fighting, young women suddenly found it wasn't so difficult to become a doctor. At the University of Toronto, girls as young as 16 or 17 were admitted to medical school. With female MDs waiting in the wings, the Women's Medical Society managed to get the quota for female interns at the city's largest hospital increased—from one to two. Interestingly, though, during the reactionary 1950s, medicine was one of the few professions in which the numbers of females did not decline much.

The onslaught of the women's movement in the 1970s brought a deep and critical questioning of the entire medical profession. In a book published by The Feminist Press in 1973, authors Barbara Ehrenreich and Deirdre English raised hackles when they insisted that the diminishing status of midwives, nurses and other female healers was "an active *takeover* by the male professionals." They further wrote:

Ninety-three percent of the doctors in the US are men; and almost all the top directors and administrators of health institutions. Women are still in the overall majority—70 percent of health workers are women—but we have been incorporated as *workers* into an industry where the bosses are men. We are not longer independent practitioners, known by our own names, for our own work.[416]

What infuriated many nurses was they had been trained to be subservient. A century before, Florence Nightingale had insisted nursing sisters above all must be obedient to higher medical authorities, and that philosophy was still prevalent. Thinking for themselves was something nurses were *not* encouraged to do. In the early 1970s, American nurse Thelma M. Schorr, an outspoken advocate for the profession, wrote: "We in nursing have lived long enough with powerlessness. Our acceptance of it, as a given, has led to our acceptance of sub-standard health care as a norm. Our acceptance of powerlessness has cost us our self-respect and that was too high a price to pay."[417] "Nurses rights" became a rallying cry for the next decades.

The changes that have overtaken the medical profession in the wake of the women's movement have been amazing by any standards. In 1982, females made up 18 percent of all Canadian doctors and dentists; a mere 12 years later, that figured had jumped to 32 percent. In 1998 in Canada, half of the students studying to be doctors were women, and many were planning to become specialists. Other countries in the Western world advanced even more rapidly.

The nursing profession has changed just as profoundly. In the 1960s, hospital nursing schools disappeared, replaced by diploma- or degree-granting colleges or universities. In many countries, nurses organized themselves into powerful unions and their wages shot up accordingly. The average staff nurse in the United States makes more than $35,000 a year, and while this is a far cry from a specialist's salary of $135,755, it's not starvation wages. Doris Lessing's mother would be able to buy her gloves and nice blouses.

The vast majority of nurses today are employed in hospitals. However, in recent years, this has not brought stability or satisfaction. As privately owned hospitals—in the United States for example—cut costs to improve their profit margins and publicly funded institutions in countries such as Canada and Great Britain do likewise to save tax dollars, nursing jobs have been chopped by the thousands. The result is not unexpected: frustration, tension and anger. Heather Henderson, president of the Nova Scotia Nurses Union, puts it this way, "Nursing is in crisis. Workloads are increasing and patients are sicker. Nurses are starting to be very worried that they cannot provide care to all their patients in a safe way."[418]

There is no doubt that society is asking RNs to redefine their jobs and take on heavy new responsibilities. As in the past, they have become not only caregivers but moral arbitrators.

Marilyn Pearson is a nurse in her late fifties who works for Toronto's Children's Aid Society. Her job is to watch over those infants who have been deemed high risk, usually those from low-income families. She and the other nurses she supervises oversee mothers to make sure they're looking after their babies properly. Sometimes she visits the same home once or twice a day. If Pearson decides a child's health is in danger, she will see to it that the infant is placed in foster care. "When the home is so clearly out of control that there's something else going on—like a mental-health problem or drug use—we might bring the child into care," she explains.[419] It's estimated that the lives of hundreds of children have been saved through this program.

Pearson's professionalism, dedication and responsibility are so many light-years away from the ignorance, slovenliness and superstition of Charles Dickens' Sairey Gamp as to be astounding—a signal of the profound change in the overall status of women in Western society.

Judy

Judy Davey was one of my best friends in high school. She wasn't into sports, which I loved, nor was she part of the social whirl. She was one of the great brains—studious, dedicated, one of the few people who always completed Miss Smith's French assignments on time. Judy also had a wonderfully wry sense of humour. "Aren't they the most delicious morsels?" she'd say about cafeteria muffins so burnt they looked like dog turds.

With her reddish hair, fair, freckled skin and elfin, sweet smile, she was pretty in a natural way. Tall, but also small-boned and slender, she seemed permanently stooped over, as though carrying around a pile of text books had already taken their toll, but her delicacy belied a backbone of steel.

In Grade 8, she had given a presentation on Jonas Salk and his development of the vaccine that had checked the dreaded polio. The subject had fascinated her—indeed everything about the way the human body worked fascinated her—and she'd worked hard on it. Afterwards, the teacher—all she can remember is that he was a youngish male, very kind and dedicated—asked what she'd like to do when she grew up. Judy already knew that medicine interested her and so, like all young girls, she automatically answered, "A nurse." "Why not a doctor?" the teacher responded. A genuine epiphany! She, a mere female, could actually be a physician.

After that revelation, she never once veered from her course. From Grade 9 on, all her small earnings from babysitting and summer jobs went not to buy new sweater sets or mascara but into a college savings account. She realized that while her parents would be supportive, there would be no money for medical-school tuition. The Daveys were hard-working and industrious, but they had never been well off.

Annie Laurie McIntyre, Judy's mother, grew up on a not-too-prosperous farm near Peterborough, Ontario. Laurie's father died in his early forties, leaving behind six children. The family was so poor, Laurie's mother did odd jobs just to keep a bit of food on the table. Although Laurie adored school and was good at it, her formal education ended when she was 15. She was sent to a Peterborough business college to learn typing, shorthand and some bookkeeping. Then she left home permanently to take a job in Toronto. It was devastating for her. She was lonely living in a boarding-house. She missed her siblings and worried about them all the time—with good reason. Her younger sister died while she was away, and her mother became ill. Every cent Laurie could save from her small secretary's salary was sent home to help out.

Slowly, though, a social life evolved, primarily around people with whom Laurie worked. Some of these women would prove lifelong friends. It was through this circle that she met a quiet, gentle, but witty young man, Wilfred (Wilf) Davey.

The Daveys had immigrated from England just after the turn of the century. Wilf's father got a job with Eaton's department store as a tailor, and Wilf had gone to Scarborough Collegiate, later called R. H. King, the very school his children would later attend. The Daveys, too, had had a hard time making ends meet, and Wilf was forced to leave school when he was 17. Like many moderately educated young men of the time, Wilf spent his whole working life performing an assortment of low-paying clerical and bookkeeping jobs.

Laurie and Wilf met at the onset of the Depression. With neither making much money, it meant a tiresomely long courtship. They finally married in 1940, when Wilf was already 30 years old and Laurie 28. They waited another three years before having their first child. Judy was born in February 1943, and her brother John 16 months later.

Laurie had already worked for 15 long years, so she had no problem giving up her job to devote herself to her husband and kids. Still, money was in short supply, so much so that after the war, the Daveys ended up living with Wilf's parents. Finally, by 1948, they had managed to save enough to buy an acre of land on Bellamy Road South, just west of Markham Road in Scar-borough. Except for a little help from plumbers and electricians, Wilf built the smallish, three-bedroom, storey-and-a-half house with his own hands.

When the Daveys moved to Scarborough, there were fewer than a half-dozen other homes in the area; a 100-acre farm was still operating next door. Yet the Daveys felt they couldn't afford a car and didn't buy one until 1963.

Judy's early scholastic career was spent in an old, four-room school, although like the rest of Scarborough, it quickly expanded. She was a quiet, determined little girl, and from the beginning, she excelled. She doesn't remember her parents pressuring her to get good grades; it was all self-imposed. For all that, Judy didn't much like elementary school, finding it rather boring. Only in the upper grades of high school would she be intellectually challenged. The best memories she has of her childhood were long walks in the woods with her father, an accomplished naturalist who liked to talk about the various plants and animals.

There was no question she would be selected for the A form at R. H. King and stay there for her entire high-school career. About the only thing she didn't excel in were art lessons and Mr. Graham's vocal music class. Athletics wasn't exactly her forte either, but everything else was a piece of cake. Latin, French, German, English literature, history, physics, chemistry, algebra, geometry and trigonometry, she mastered them all. She knew she had to if she wanted to get into medical school, and that ambition utterly dominated her high-school years.

A few dates with one boy comprised her social life. At school, she belonged to the Scholarship Club and the Classics Club, she was the only female member of the Science Club and she was a library assistant. On weekends, she worked as a volunteer with mentally handicapped children and taught Sunday school. Altogether, it wasn't exactly the sexy, social scene of the popular clique, yet nobody called Judy boring or nondescript. For one thing, she always wore bright red boots.

Studying for the Grade 13 departmental exams was torture, even for Judy, although, unlike most of us, she didn't have much to worry about. She had been preselected for the premedical course at University of Toronto. As everybody expected, she did well in her exams.

In early 1961, just months before Judy's graduation from high school, her father's employer, the Russell Construction Company, went bankrupt. After decades of loyal service, Wilf, at the age of 51, was suddenly unemployed. Judy found herself faced with the same dilemma her mother had had so many years before. Should she give up her education to help support her family? It was a big relief when news came that Wilf had found another job.

Judy enjoyed the two-year premed course; after Grade 13, it didn't even seem difficult. Of the 130 students, about 20 were women, and they became Judy's closest friends. While the men could frequent the elegant, male-only Hart House, with its swimming pool, spacious common rooms and good restaurant, the women were assigned a basement cubbyhole in an old medical building as their gathering place. Judy dated off and on during those years, but there wasn't much time for anything but study.

At that time, the University of Toronto's premed course was under the auspices of the Faculty of Medicine; if a student did reasonably well, he or she would automatically gain admittance to medical school. Judy placed in the upper third of her class.

The first three years of medical school were heavy going. Classes were packed solid from nine to five weekdays and from nine to one on Saturdays, and, of course, there were hours upon hours of studying. Judy could only afford to live with her parents, which meant a twice-daily, two-hour journey back and forth from Scarborough. But Judy found her fascination with the human body, its mechanisms and its mysteries, deepening each day, and that proved compensation enough.

There was drudgery in medical school, certainly, but there was also the exciting clinical work that began towards the end of the second year. Groups of nine or ten students would examine patients at St. Michael's or Toronto Western hospitals under the auspices of a staff doctor. Some of these clinical instructors were women, and Judy appreciated their kindly bedside manners. They provided a nice contrast to certain male professors, who were stereo-typically chauvinistic, uncaring and insensitive. One in particular, an orthopedic surgeon, liked to demean his patients, and Judy was appalled at his rudeness and arrogance. One of the basic tenets of her practice has always been to show respect and sympathy towards those under her care.

At the end of her first year, she was hired as a scrub technician—basically a surgeon's assistant—for the summer, in the operating room at the Scarborough General Hospital. She had never been squeamish about the human body. Once, in anatomy class, she noticed maggots running all over the cadaver she was working on, and that gave her a turn, but she quickly got over it. Her summer in the operating room, full of blood and guts, desensitized her and, at the same time, piqued her interest in human physiology even more.

By the mid-1960s, medical schools were experimenting with what was called clinical clerkships. At the end of her third year, Judy applied for one of these, and was one of the 20 or so chosen. Downtown Toronto's Wellesley Hospital had no interns at the time, so while they were still considered medical students, she and her colleagues did hands-on patient care, rotating through all the departments from emergency to obstetrics, on call during the nights. Every now and then, they would return to the university for specific lectures. On Judy's name tag was boldly printed "Dr. Davey." "It was a thrill," she admits. "I couldn't believe I had actually come this far." She lived in the hospital residences for the year, and it was a big relief not to have to travel back and forth to Scarborough every day.

Judy graduated from medical school in July 1968. Her parents arranged a dinner party to mark not only her huge accomplishment but a milestone in a far-from-wealthy, middle-class family. It was held at the Guild Inn in Scarborough, where so many of Judy's high-school classmates had celebrated their weddings. All her family were there, aunts and uncles and cousins, but she herself did not have a date. During all her years at medical school, as she says, "Men were put on hold."

On the spur of the moment, Judy decided to accept an internship at University Hospital in Edmonton, Alberta. She realizes now that she should have thought more seriously about it, but she wanted to go west. It turned out to be the worst year of her medical career. For one thing, she didn't like Edmonton, which she thought smacked of the Wild West and Klondike days. "There were even wooden sidewalks," she says. She hated the winter, which was particularly severe in 1968–69. The most disappointing aspect, though, was her medical experience.

She had just spent her year before graduation at Wellesley, a smallish hospital dedicated to teaching. In contrast, University Hospital was large, impersonal and in the habit of using interns as a source of cheap labour. They were on call five and a half days a week, and all night every other night. Judy wandered about in a sleepless daze for a lot of the time. More upsetting was the actual work involved. Interns were paid less than technicians and so were used as such. They took blood, started IVs, changed dressings—all routine drudge work. The mysterious intricacies of the body, the enigmatic, sacred aspect of medicine, faded in a haze of exhaustion.

On rare occasions, Judy had two days off in a row. If the weather were nice, she would stuff the tent she had bought half-price at the Army and Navy into her ten-year-old Volkswagen and head off for the mountains. Camping by herself in the most beautiful country she has ever seen saved her sanity.

Judy had done well enough in medical school to think about specializing. For a fleeting moment she considered psychiatry, but the idea was pretty quickly dismissed. Since the age of 14, she had harboured a belief in what medicine was all about: the old-fashioned family doctor, entirely dedicated to his or her patients' well-being. This idealized notion had not diminished during university; indeed the birth-to-grave range of experience found in such a practice appealed to her more than ever. But she felt she needed more specialized knowledge and experience. Formal family-medicine programs were just being established at Canadian universities, and Judy decided to take a residency at St. Joseph's Hospital, which was connected to the University of Western Ontario in London.

Because the program was so new, it was rather disorganized, but still it proved to be a satisfying, and invigorating time. Once again, Judy rotated through the departments, but this time, she was a fully fledged MD, entirely responsible for her patients' care. There were many scary moments, especially in emergency. While it was the casualty officer who decided if a person would be admitted, the patient was then turned over to Judy. "I can remember sitting up many nights worrying that a heart-attack victim might arrest," she says.

At the end of her residency year, Judy had to get a job and, like everybody else, she looked in the newspaper want ads. Finally, she found what she wanted at the Beaches Clinic in Toronto's east end, where the senior physician had recently died. Judy inherited some of his patients, many of them elderly. They had all adored the departed doctor—Judy says he had pretty well given them any prescription they wanted—and here she was, young and, even more suspicious, a female, who refused to hand out any old drugs, some of which were actually on the restricted list.

Nonetheless, Judy enjoyed herself. Finally, at age 28, she had a life outside her work. Although she didn't make much money—about $5,000 a year— she was able to pay off her student loans. She rented an apartment on the ground floor of a lovely old Beaches house and hunted for antiques to furnish it. She bought a snazzy red sports car. She went on a skiing trip to Austria and bought a half interest in a sailboat.

She also found herself a steady boyfriend, an engineer. She had dated during her internship and residency, but only occasionally. Once she was actually making money, as she says, "I found that I became much more desirable." When the question of marriage arose, Judy realized she had to think seriously about the future.

Several senior physicians had left the Beaches Clinic and Judy didn't agree with some of the policy decisions made by those remaining. Not only that, she longed to travel. Her ears perked up when a doctor friend of her neighbour mentioned he had been working for the Canadian military in Europe. It was a great job, he said, a wonderful job. Judy asked where she could get an application form.

Within two months, she was boarding a military aircraft on her way to

Lahr, West Germany, at that time the headquarters of the Canadian NATO forces in Europe. It was a large base of some 10,000 to 15,000 soldiers and their families. Most of the physicians were military personnel, but the clientele was so large, civilians such as Judy were also necessary.

Judy worked as a GP, treating the wide variety of ailments that occurred in such a diverse (although mostly young) population. She had her own office and her own patients, and there was a small hospital where she and other doctors were regularly scheduled 24- or 48-hour shifts. The care was all-encompassing, from delivering babies—and there were a great number— to repairing the victims of car accidents that had occurred on the nearby autobahn.

Many of Judy's regular patients were young wives who suffered from severe stress. They were small-town girls, often speaking only French, who had never been away from home before. Since the base itself was bursting to the seams, many families had to find housing in the outlying villages or towns. There were no phones, and their husbands were away on exercises for six to eight weeks at a time. "We saw some sad things," says Judy, "because the women became so depressed."

It was a wonderful life for Judy, though, being single in a place full of eligible men. She was invited to all the social events, the mess dinners and the dances. Free weekends were spent touring West Germany and other parts of Europe. She had lots of friends, and a pleasant, one-room apartment in the officers' quarters.

There was only one phone in the residence, and it happened to be located outside her door. Sometimes she got tired of answering it, but one night, she thought she had better. The caller asked for one of the young officers living upstairs. She went up and knocked on the door—she could hear a party going. Finally, someone answered and told her that particular soldier wasn't in but his roommate was. Bill Lye remembers the moment clearly: "Judy was standing in the doorway, dressed in her housecoat and with bare feet. Her long, ash-blonde hair shone in the light. I said, 'Who is that?'"

The next morning, Judy left for a weekend holiday in England, but that didn't deter Bill Lye. He bribed the caretaker to open the door to her room, and there he placed a bouquet of flowers with a note asking her out to dinner. Within six months, they were married.

Bill's family was military to its core. His paternal grandfather had served in World War I. His father was a respected career officer; at the time of his retirement, he was Commandant of the Royal Military College. All the time Bill was attending high school in Chilliwack, British Columbia, William Lye Senior was the commander of the military base there. There were good and bad aspects to such a pedigree. After Bill and Judy's son was born, a friend of the family's, a retired general, and his wife came to visit. "I hope you're not as hard on that youngster as your dad was on you," the man said. Bill was shocked. He hadn't thought of his father as being such a disciplinarian. "There were certain standards," he says, "which were black and white, honesty being one of them. And there may have been pressure, but frankly it didn't bug me."

Perhaps this was because Bill was academically gifted and sailed through high school. "I had absolutely no doubt in my mind that I would go to university wherever I wanted to go, in whatever course I wanted to take and, at the end of it, I would get a job in a company or organization that would give a good salary and provide advancement and opportunity for growth." Given his family's background, it was not surprising he chose the Royal Military College in Kingston. Only the smartest were selected to study engineering, and naturally Bill was among them, never mind that his best subject was English literature.

"The combination of the outdoors, the man in training to command and the technical challenge appealed to me," he says. "There was a sense of priesthood among the students. 'Truth, duty, valor' was RMC's motto, and we believed in it." It was a brotherhood, certainly, but of upper-middle-class, mostly Anglican males who firmly believed "they were born to run things."

Bill graduated in the spring of 1969, and immediately left for London, England. He had won the Athlone Fellowship, funded by the British government and awarded to newly graduated, top-ranking engineers for two years of study and career experience anywhere in England. As his scholarship came to an end, he was offered jobs in several large corporations, but he decided instead to stick with what he had always considered his destiny: the military. He was posted to the Canadian NATO brigade in West Germany.

His job involved combat engineering: providing mobility for the Canadian armed forces, building bridges, canals and railroads, and, in time of war, blowing them up. Bill had just returned from six weeks in the field when he met Judy for the first time. He was four years younger than she was, but he had already tasted what he calls the "flesh pots" of London while he was there, had been engaged to an actress and was ready for someone with intelligence, education and ambition.

The only problem was that the idea of becoming a military wife was abhorrent to Judy. "I told Bill, 'I can't do this. I can't become a DW [dependent wife],' as they were called." She had no intention of giving up her medical practice. "I had to be up-front and honest about it. The marriage is not going to work if you're resentful." Fortunately, the days of military wives devoting their lives to their husbands' careers were coming to an end. Bill continued in the armed forces and Judy continued as a professional. She didn't even change her name, something almost unheard of in Bill's milieu.

Judy and Bill were married in Dover, England, in October 1972. Although Judy says she is not a romantic, she had not wanted to say her vows in German because she felt she wouldn't fully understand the nuances of meaning. They returned to Lahr, and Bill was immediately posted to Chilliwack, British Columbia for three months of training. A traditional wife might have gone with him; Judy remained in Lahr, caring for the sick.

The next three years were a golden time for Judy and Bill. Lahr was an old German town, population 25,000, full of charming old homes and with the remains of a medieval fortress in its downtown pedestrian mall. There were plenty of cafés and restaurants. Bill and Judy had money, not a lot of it but certainly sufficient for trips all through Europe.

However, such an idyllic, and rather artificial, life naturally had to come to an end. In December 1974, Bill's three-year tour of duty concluded, and he was posted to Ottawa. By that time, Judy was pregnant with her first child, but that did not prevent her from finding a job, first in the emergency department of the National Defense Medical Centre and then at the Dalhousie Housing Community Service. Located in a poor area of Ottawa with a large immigrant population, Dalhousie was designed to provide a whole range of services, from housing to medical. It suited Judy for a time, because she could work regular, limited hours. She was determined to devote as much time to her children as she could.

Judy went back to work immediately after the birth of her children, but she wasn't very satisfied with her job. As part of a social agency, she was required to attend endless meetings. "I'm not good at this stuff. It's not my game, agonizing who they were going to hire as receptionist." More important, perhaps, the centre did not have hospital privileges and she missed delivering babies.

In 1978, two major events occurred in the Davey-Lye family: Judy decided to go into private practice and Bill decided to leave the armed forces. "It was implicit in my mind that if Judy was going to start her own private practice, I wasn't going to go roaring around in the army. You don't invest that kind of emotional or financial resources and then pick up and move time and again." His choice didn't entirely concern Judy's career. He had been offered a promotion, a senior combat position in Victoria, but it was not the job he had wanted.

In 1979, Judy met a colleague she had worked and socialized with in West Germany, an Irish immigrant who had come to Ottawa to start a practice on his own. The two decided to open up an office together at Riverside and Bank streets in the middle-class Alta Vista area, and eventually a third partner joined them. Judy obtained privileges at Riverside Hospital, which meant she was finally able to build a traditional, all-round family practice.

Judy had just made the decision to go into business for herself when she discovered she was pregnant again. It had not been planned, and she and Bill considered an abortion, but quickly decided against it. What Judy chose for herself, however, had no bearing on how she advises her patients. She is firmly pro-choice, believing the decision to have an abortion should be left entirely to the woman concerned. Interestingly, while she was pregnant with her third child, she sat on a hospital therapeutic-abortion committee. Before the committee system was finally done away with by the Canadian Supreme Court in 1988, three doctors, often all male, decided whether a woman would be permitted to end her pregnancy or not.

On Judy's committee sat an older doctor whose philosophy concerning access to abortion depended on which side of the bed he got up on. "My wife had a baby at 39, so why can't this woman?" he'd say, never mind that his wife was well off and the applicant a poor immigrant. There was also a younger physician who was anti-abortion, and, as Judy says, had no right to be there. "There I was with these two guys, arguing why we should be doing it. I didn't feel we had any right to turn anyone down unless her case didn't fit the requirements—she was too far along, for example." It gave Judy a rather dramatic, first-hand experience of the age-old, all-powerful authority of the male medical establishment and how a woman's physiology rules her life.

Judy and Bill bought a lovely brick home on Range Road in the affluent Rock Glen area of Ottawa. It was renovated and added to as their family grew. Bill was hired by the Bureau of Management Consulting, a Crown agency that did work not only for the federal but for various provincial governments, basically finding ways to improve public-sector programs and make them more efficient. It meant he travelled a great deal, often for weeks at a time, and Judy was often called away for emergencies or the delivery of babies. There was no alternative but to hire live-in nannies. Judy says they were lucky; two were so compatible, they became part of the household. Still, privacy was sacrificed, and everybody breathed a sigh when, after ten years, it was thought the children were old enough to cope on their own.

Although she was sometimes on call in the evenings and weekends, during the years her children were young, Judy restricted the hours of her practice. She would close shop early in the afternoon and then do her hospital rounds, but she was almost always home by the time the kids arrived from school. "I decided I wanted to be a mother," she says. "I was a reasonably involved parent." As she points out, she was not the primary bread-winner, so she could afford the luxury of a small practice.

Bill and Judy enjoy an affluent life. For nine years, Bill worked for the Treasury Board's secretariat, overseeing the vast property owned by the federal government. He took early retirement in 1997, and now teaches part time at Queen's University's School of Urban and Regional Planning. Judy is a one-woman operation now, and her practice has grown and thrived. A long-time patient put it this way: "I have never encountered a doctor who listens as well as she does, who is so sympathetic, who explains things and gives me some say in what my treatment will be."

Through it all, Judy has maintained her fascination with the human body, its mechanisms and chemistry, its cycles, its disintegration and regrowth, the spiritual dimension of medicine. In recent years, she has become involved in palliative care. As well as taking care of the dying in hospital, she will make house calls, making sure those who wish to stay in their homes are as comfortable as possible. "If you are working with a patient and the family long enough, you really feel you have done something quite wonderful and helped everyone in the family. After all, death is inevitable."

An elderly woman had wanted to stay at home rather than in hospital because she loved her garden so much. Judy looked after her for four months, visiting her often, chatting about this flower or that plant. After the woman's death, her daughter and daughter-in-law showed up one day in Judy's office, carrying a carton full of plants. The flax and Liatris and meadow rue grow in Judy's garden to this day.

Physiology

Females are by nature weaker and colder [than males], and their nature must be considered naturally deficient.

Aristotle, *On the Generation of Animals,* c. 332 BC

Any woman who is logical, philosophical, scientific departs from the normal woman in her physical as well as her mental characteristics.

The British medical journal *The Lancet,* 1868

They hold their hand up to their hearts,
They sigh, oh they lie.
They say they only care for us.
We die, oh we die.

A song sang on the way to a protest meeting
at Harvard Medical School, 1975

As a teenager, the most shocking thing that happened to me was not that a man exposed himself in the laundry room of our apartment building, nor that I was, one horrible summer evening, mistaken for a prostitute and almost forced into a car. No, what offended me to my very soul was a painting I came across called *The Rape* by the Belgian surrealist René Magritte. In it, a large female head has been transformed into a naked torso. Breasts are located where the eyes would have been; a belly button displaces the nose; and the vulva, complete with pubic hair, forms the mouth. Later, I would realize the work was supposedly a vivid illustration of the objectification of women—how a rapist views his victim, say. But at 16, it utterly repelled me. Little did I realize that the patriarchy, particularly the medical establishment, has been distorting and falsifying female anatomy for eons—an attempt, say feminists, to denigrate women and thereby gain power over them. Whatever the reason, the ideas conjured up almost entirely by men about female physiology have been, for the most part, utterly ridiculous.

I

The earliest extant medical treatises—two Egyptian papyruses dating from about 2,000 BC—describe what, for thousands of years, would be the commonplace notion of female physiology. The quaintly named "wandering womb syndrome" referred to the supposed fact that the uterus roamed freely throughout the body. If it were in a volatile mood, it could sometimes be quite violent, pressing up against various organs and making women ill.[420] The Kahun Papyrus (c. 2000 BC) claimed that "When [a woman's] eyes ache, it is the fall of the womb in her eyes." If she had a headache, it was the uterus banging on her brain; if her feet were swollen or she felt nauseous or suffered indigestion, same thing: it was the womb's refusal to stay put that was at fault.

The remedy for female maladies, Egyptian and later Greek physicians would claim, was to lure the wayward womb back to its proper place. If the vagina was smoked with sweet-smelling vapors, or if stinking fumes from waxes or hot coals were inhaled through the nostrils, surely the uterus would be enticed to move downward to where it belonged.

The belief in the wandering womb was perpetuated by those Greek physicians whose work, written in the late fifth or early fourth century BC, make up the Hippocratic corpus. They believed the womb was not just a part of a living body but a creature unto itself. Plato, in his *Timaeus*, put it succinctly. The womb, the "matrix of women," was "a living creature within them with a desire for childbearing,"[421] sometimes vicious, always capricious.

Since it was a separate entity, the uterus had to be nourished separately. In fact, it was its search for food and moisture that caused it to propel itself upwards towards the brain. The answer to satisfying its appetites, according to the medical writers—every one a male—was semen. The more it got, the better. "If women have intercourse, they are more healthy; if they don't they are less healthy," the Hippocratic writers concluded. "This is because the womb becomes moist in intercourse and not dry: when a womb is drier than it should be, it often suffers violent dislocation."[422]

The uterus was also supposedly desperate to bear children. As Plato wrote in *Timaeus*, "if it be left long unfruitful ... [it] is vexed and aggrieved, and wandering throughout the body and blocking the channels of the breath, by forbidding respiration brings the sufferer to extreme distress and causes all manner of disorders."[423] If these ideas had been nothing more than fanciful dreams of medical men, they wouldn't have mattered much, but they reflected and reinforced Greek society's belief that a woman was an inferior being, both physically and mentally.

In Aristotle's view, the female was slightly less than human. In his words, she was "as it were, a mutilated male." The male body was the standard model and compared to it, the female version was deficient, weak and incomplete.[424] The male sperm was the dynamic force in life, the actual conveyor of the human soul that, after orgasm, nestled in "cooked" menstrual blood collected in the womb. The mother was merely "a passive incubator for the male seed."[425] If the child were a girl, that was because the father hadn't been his usual strapping and aggressive self during intercourse; the mother had to help out a little with her thinner, weaker secretions. If the father were really feeling his oats, the offspring would certainly be a male. The male adult was the artist; the female provided the workshop.

Aeschylus in his play *Eumenides* puts it crudely by having Apollo say:

> She who is called the child's mother is not
> its begetter but the nurse of the newly sown conception.
> The begetter is the male, and she as a stranger for a stranger
> preserves the offspring, if no god blights its birth[426]

This concept of the female as a deformed, incomplete male spilled everywhere, like sour milk. As Aristotle insisted, "Females are weaker and colder in nature [than males], and we must look upon the female character as being a sort of natural deficiency."[427]

There were medical theorists who challenged the wandering womb theory. The famous Greek physician Galen (c. 130–200) wrote that the notion of a free-floating womb was "preposterous," and the Roman gynecologist Soranus insisted "the uterus does not issue forth like a wild animal from the lair, delighted by fragrant odors or fleeing bad odors...."[428] Unfortunately, the Christian era largely ignored such logic and good sense.

II

During the high Middle Ages, ideas regarding women's physiology were mostly an attempt to shore up the Genesis story of creation. Ironically, since few original ideas on medical matters were forthcoming, it was the pagan Greeks who provided the ammunition: Galen (and through him, the Hippocratic writers), who was translated by Arab scholars in the ninth century, and

Aristotle, who was widely read from the 13th century onwards. The theory was straightforward: since Eve had been created from Adam's rib, it followed that her anatomy must be symmetrical to his, including, of course, her genitals.

Historian Thomas Laqueur calls it "the one sex body," by which he means that the female's reproductive system was considered a distorted mirror image of the male's; the vagina was the penis, the uterus the scrotum, the ovaries the testicles.[429] While the male organs were carried outside the body, the female were inverted and turned inward. The uterus and vagina, supposedly a single organ, looked like a fat bottle with a long neck hanging downwards.

The women's organs were, of course, thought to be inferior to the male's. They were smaller, less potent and, most detrimental, tucked inside. Women's reproductive anatomy was like a plant that never saw sunshine, never blossomed but lay folded up in the cold dark. Any body part that didn't fit this paradigm was rejected; the clitoris, for example, was simply omitted from medieval anatomy.[430]

Did a mother contribute anything to the creation of a child, other than her womb being the incubator and providing nutrition? It was one of the great debates of the era. The defenders of Aristotle thought some form of female sperm might exist—after all, a woman supposedly had testicles—but it definitely didn't play a role in the moment of conception. As one historian put it, "If it existed, it possessed no 'formative virtue' and contributed nothing to the constitution of the embryo."[431]

The revered theologian St. Thomas Aquinas adopted Aristotelian biological ideas with, as Marina Warner, points out "far-reaching consequences on the attitude to women's role in European society."[432] He, too, saw the male as the vital source in creating life, while the woman was the incubator. It was not such a leap to explain the virginity of Mary, the mother of God. The spirit of the Holy Ghost simply entered her body and created Jesus.

The followers of Galen were more inclined to believe that the female had some role to play in reproduction. But what? A common theory was that female seed was emitted only at the time of sexual climax: no orgasm, no pregnancy. Through first-hand experience, ordinary women knew this was a lot of nonsense, but their voices were seldom heard, even when serious matters concerning their well-being were being considered. It was, for example, almost impossible for a pregnant woman to convince authorities that a man had raped her. If she hadn't experienced orgasm during their sexual encounter, she couldn't possibly be with his child.

It went without saying that the male semen or seed was thought to be more virile than any woman's secretion. The semen was the carpenter and the menstrual blood the wood—it was as simple as that. Medieval thinkers seemed to be oblivious to the fact that a child, even a male, might take after his mother both in appearance and personality.

Just as in antiquity, perceptions of female physiology were reflected in the overall status of women in society. As the philosopher Giles of Rome (1243–1316) put it, "The soul matches the constitution of the body; women's bodies are limp and unstable, and so women are unstable and unsteady in desire and will."[433]

III

The Renaissance brought a new spirit of scientific inquiry and a new curiosity about anatomy, the female's in particular. However, even this new empiricism, and the passion for cutting up cadavers, did not dispel the myth that the uterus was a penis in disguise. As Thomas Laqueur puts it, "The more Renaissance anatomists dissected, looked into, and visually represented the female body, the more powerfully and convincingly they saw it to be a version of the male's."[434]

The problem, according to historian Evelyne Berriot-Salvadore's analysis, was that physicians and anatomists were so in awe of the ancients, they refused to come to grips with what they had actually discovered. In *La dissection des parties du corps humain*, published in 1546, Charles Estienne made an effort to accurately describe female genitalia. His aim, he said, was to show "by illustration everything in the female body not found in man." His drawings did so, but in his written observation and analysis, he contradicted his own empirical evidence, reverting back to the woman-as-mirror-image theory of Galen.[435] In 1547, another French physician, Phillipe de Flesselles, published what he called a full description of the human body, yet he included not a word about female anatomy, explaining that "sexual difference is merely accidental."

Paradoxically, these very same scientists didn't hesitate to attribute magical, and often evil, attributes most basic female functions. Menstruation, for example, supposedly nourished the fetus *in utero* and then turned itself into breast milk for the feeding of the newborn. Those same physicians also believed menstrual blood was a poisonous, noxious substance that was fortunately eliminated at the time of birth. Others saw the menstrual flow as having no value at all. As one historian commented, they saw it as "a 'superfluity,' the result of a temperament too moist and cold to convert all the nutriment into useful blood."[436]

Sterility was blamed entirely on the woman, because of her clamminess and the imbalance of her "humours." Her womb was a cold, damp field where the man's seed was apt to rot. Ugly women were more inclined to be barren; their disagreeable personalities upset the all-important "temperament."[437]

Paradoxes and confusion abounded, yet steadily, society's perception of female physiology began to change. Two scientific breakthroughs paved the way. In the early 17th century, the microscope was invented, allowing scientists to see the difference between the male sperm and the female ova. The function of the ovaries and the complicated reproductive cycle became a little clearer.

Finally, in the eyes of medical authorities, the womb gave up its affinity to wander about the body. The renowned English physician Thomas Willis (1621–1675) conducted autopsies on women who had supposedly died of *furor uterinus*, hysteria caused by an angry, hungry womb. He wrote that the uterus "is so strictly tied by neighbouring parts round about, that it cannot of itself be moved, or ascend from its place."[438]

Slowly, as it dawned on mankind that a woman's body was a distinct entity, with a purpose of its own, it became ridiculous to argue that God had somehow made a mistake, that the female was a defective copy of the male. André du Laurens, the regent of the Medical Faculty of Paris, wrote in an article published in 1646, "The sex organ of the female is no less the perfection of her species than that of the male of his, and woman must not be called an accidental animal, as the Barbarians called her, but a necessary creature instituted by Nature firstly and of itself."[439]

Women themselves began to defend the "sacredness and blessedness" of their bodies. In responding to a scurrilous attack against women, including a disgusting description of their anatomy published in 1615 by one Joseph Swetnam (a pseudonym), Rachel Speght, a well-educated daughter of an English clergyman, wrote, "She [Eve] was not produced from Adam's foote, to be his too low inferior, nor from his head to be his superior, but from his side, near his heart to be his equall."[440]

Curiously, as physicians began to appreciate the intricacies of the uterine function, women were caught in another vicious web. The reproductive system was perceived as being so important, so central to the continued existence of the species (and a particular nation) that it became the be-all and end-all for the human female. As Evelyne Berriot-Salvadore puts it, "Hidden and protected in the secret recesses of the body, the womb possessed a potent and mysterious symbolic value as the seat of conception and gestation."[441] She says the uterus was no longer seen as an animal, banging about the body; instead, petulant, enigmatic and fragile, it reigned at the centre of a woman's being. It remained a tyrant, dictating a female's every action and thought. Rousseau's famous dictum, "The male is male only at certain moments. The female is female her whole life.... Everything constantly recalls her sex to her," became a reality.

IV

During the 19th century, the male medical establishment used women's supposedly delicate and unstable physical nature as a weapon to bludgeon any aspirations they might have to participate in the larger world. The prestigious medical journal *The Lancet* would blatantly proclaim in 1868, "Any woman who is logical, philosophical, scientific departs from the normal woman in her physical as well as her mental characteristics."[442]

What was particularly galling was that it was the physicians themselves who defined female physiology as dysfunctional. From puberty to menstruation to menopause, a woman's life, as depicted by the medical profession, was one long series of crises and sicknesses. American physician George J. Englemann, in his lament for the female's afflicted life, might have been writing a soap opera:

Many a young life is battered and forever crippled in the breakers of puberty; if it crosses these unharmed and is not dashed to pieces on the rock of childbirth, it may still ground on the ever-recurring shadows of menstruation and lastly, upon the final bar of the menopause ere protection is found in the unruffled waters of the harbor beyond the reach of sexual storms.[443]

As the century progressed, a new specialization, gynecology and obstetrics, was developed that totally excluded female care-givers. To most of these male physicians, the female was seen merely as a reproductive unit, destined to a life of multiple pregnancies, breast-feeding and child-care. For their own good health, women must accept the protection of their much stronger and more vital husbands and fathers. Any attempt to leave the hearth, to break free from their ordained roles as daughters and mothers, would only lead to terrible illness and even death.

Once again the villain was the uterus. "Woman exists for the sake of her womb," declared a popular American health manual late in the century. American physician Horatio Storer wrote in 1871 that a female is "what she is in health, in character, in her charms, alike of body, mind and soul because of her womb alone."[444]

Actually, it wasn't so much the uterus as the ovaries that were the disabling factor in the female's too-sad destiny. As one doctor explained, "Ovulation fixes woman's place in the animal economy. With the act of menstruation is wound up the whole essential character of her system."[445]

The menstrual flow supposedly emanated from a "wound" in the ovaries, and was thought to cause all manner of dire illnesses: headaches, sore throats, indigestion, kidney, liver and heart disorders, even tuberculosis were blamed on the female's monthly cycle. At the first showing, young girls were told to go to bed and stay there, a monthly ritual that sometimes went on for years. Menstrual pain or heavy flow were not only considered pathological but supposedly the fault of a too-flamboyant lifestyle. If a woman ate too much rich food, danced late into the night, thought "prurient" thoughts or had illicit affairs, her ovaries were apt to "erupt."[446]

While the medical men felt free to pontificate on women's physiology, they had almost no clue as to what to do about "feminine" diseases. At mid-century, they were still injecting tea, milk and water into the uterus, applying leeches to the vulva and cervix, and administering silver nitrate or "white hot irons" to the affected area.[447] They also freely prescribed opium, primarily in the form of morphine, oblivious to the fact, it seems, that it was horribly addictive.

Elizabeth Barrett Browning was only 14 when morphine was first prescribed for her inexplicable illnesses that doctors blamed on "feminine weaknesses." For years, she remained sequestered upstairs in her bedroom, an invalid and a recluse, dipping many times a day into what she called her "elixir." Only the arrival of fellow poet Robert Browning saved her. During their courtship, he convinced her to cut her dosage of opiates, whereby she gained the strength to stand up, walk around, finally marry him and eventually, at age 42, give birth to a son.

Doctors insisted menstruation sapped all a woman's strength. Certainly, the female could not bear the strain of a university education. If she were to engage in such difficult intellectual pursuits, the physicians insisted, she could seriously damage her reproductive organs. To demand higher education was called a selfish act. A woman would endanger her ovarian functions, and thereby deprive both herself and her nation of healthy children.

Pregnancy was supposedly a "natural" function, yet the expectant mother was treated much like a sickly child. She was to avoid all ugly sights and situations; she was not to have angry thoughts or, heaven forbid, erotic daydreams; and she was to avoid sexual intercourse after the fourth month. At their doctors' orders, many a perfectly healthy young woman spent months of her pregnancy inside a darkened room, lounging on plumped-up pillows and eating chocolates.

The part of a woman's life cycle that was viewed with the greatest distrust and distaste was menopause. In a society where childbearing was a female's one mark of prestige, an older woman was considered a useless thing. It was, as one physician put it, "the death of the woman in the woman."[448] Physicians believed that menopause was the cause of any number of diseases: rheumatism, hemorrhoids, diarrhea, constipation and even syphilis.[449] More frightening, though, was the transformation in personality that doctors were absolutely convinced came with the change of life. Peevishness, selfishness and moral decay all supposedly followed menopause. Doctors found the condition so distasteful, they were embarrassed to even discuss it, and, often as not, medical texts depicted the menopausal woman as an ugly, disagreeable crone.

As the century progressed and gynecology as a specialty flourished, physicians and medical scientists gained new knowledge of the female reproduction system, and this gave them more power and influence. Their voices were increasingly heard in the popular press, so much so that critics grumbled the doctors had become more of a nuisance in dictating what went on in the bedroom than clergymen. Most of the medical men were rigidly traditionalist in their attitudes. A few doctors would fit diaphragms and dispense birth-control information, but most were dead set against any "mechanical" means of contraception. Even coitus interruptus was frowned on. It was thought to be a form of masturbation, and that was absolute anathema to the medical profession. Anxious to promote their own respectability in society, physicians promoted the three so-called natural techniques: abstinence, prolonged nursing and rhythm. The first method hardly made for a good marriage, and the other two didn't work. Family size, however, continued to shrink, an indication, perhaps, that the medical men were largely being ignored.

If birth control had merely been a matter between a physician and his patient, that would have been bad enough, but from the 1860s onwards, doctors, particularly in United States, congealed into a powerful force of reaction. Abortion was their *bête noire*.

Traditionally, in the Western world, abortion before quickening had been thought of as a disagreeable but necessary fact of life. Suddenly, the doctors made it out to be a selfish, self-indulgent, disloyal transgression against all that was decent. The AMA's Committee on Criminal Abortion (on which, obviously, no women sat) had, in 1871, this to say about a "lady" who wanted an abortion:

She becomes unmindful of the course marked out for her by Providence, she overlooks the duties imposed on her by the marriage contract. She yields to the pleasures—but shrinks from the pains and responsibility of maternity; and, destitute of all delicacy and refinement, resigns herself, body and soul, into the hands of unscrupulous and wicked men [abortionists]. Let not the husband of such a wife flatter himself that he possesses her affection. Nor can she in turn ever merit even the respect of a virtuous husband. She sinks into old age like a withered tree, stripped of its foliage; with the stain of blood upon her soul, she dies without the hand of affection to smooth her pillow.[450]

With the co-operation of the Roman Catholic Church, Protestant clergy and conservative politicians, the AMA successfully waged intensive and well-funded political campaigns. Between the 1870s and 1890s, the dissemination of birth-control information through the mail was outlawed, brothels were closed and abortion was criminalized. Doctors in France, Canada, Great Britain and Russia might not have been as active as their American counterparts, but collectively, they, too, developed into expert lobbyists. As early as 1803, the British parliament had made it illegal for anyone to assist in abortion, and in 1861, self-abortion became an offence. In Canada, the law was all-embracing; anybody who had anything to do with abortion or birth control could find themselves in jail.

The medical men had decisively won the day, but they seemed oblivious to the harm they would cause: families rendered terribly poor by the Industrial Revolution forced to have more children than they could feed, for example. Nor did it occur to the medical establishment that desperate women will always seek abortion. According to some statistics, even after abortion became illegal, 20 to 25 percent of pregnancies ended that way.[451]

And, of course, doctors never held themselves accountable for the thousands upon thousands of deaths resulting from botched abortions carried out by back-room butchers.

Physicians had become guardians of both the morals and the bodily functions of the "weaker" sex. It would take 70 years and the onslaught of the feminist movement before women would begin to effectively fight back.

V

Physical sickness was one thing, mental illness another. In dealing with an ailing mind, physicians felt free to be even more dictatorial, insensitive and arrogant towards women.

Virginia Woolf suffered from bouts of mental illness for much of her life, leading eventually to her death by suicide in 1941. Her first serious mental breakdown occurred in 1904, when she was only 22 and not yet married. She was placed in the care of Sir George Savage, a prominent member of the medical school that believed the basis of insanity was anti-social and non-conformist behaviour. "Hysterical" female patients were treated by separating them from their families, keeping them in bed and forcing them to drink huge quantities of milk every day. Intellectual activity of any kind was prohibited. A patient must learn that, in the presence of her doctor, "her supplications are useless and that she will revolt in vain against a will that is enlightened and superior to her own."[452]

Virginia Woolf loathed Savage's method of treatment. "I have never spent such a wretched 8 months in my life," she complained after one such forced rest cure. Biographer Hermione Lee believes her encounter with psychiatry affected her life and writing profoundly. "There is no doubt that the development of her political position, her intellectual resistance to tyranny and conventionality, derived to a great extent from her experiences as a woman patient."[453]

In her 1925 novel *Mrs. Dalloway*, Woolf paints a dark, fierce picture of just such a medical tyrant. Septimus Warren Smith has been driven crazy by his remembrances of World War I and the bloody fighting in the trenches, and has committed suicide rather than submit to the mind-obliterating treatment of the psychiatrist Sir William Bradshaw. Mrs. Dalloway is lamenting the death of the young man.

... there were the poets and thinkers. Suppose he had that passion, and had gone to Sir William Bradshaw, a great doctor, yet to her obscurely evil, without sex

or lust, extremely polite to women, but capable of some indescribable outrage—
force your soul, that was it—if this young man had gone to him, and Sir William
had impressed him, like that, with his power, might he not have then said
(indeed she felt it now), Life is made intolerable; they make life intolerable, men
like that?[454]

But it wasn't just psychiatrists who were so powerful and self-righteous. In
the 1920s and '30s, the medical establishment slowly tightened its control
over the most important aspects of a woman's life. Child-rearing, in particular, was subjected to rigid rules dictated by scientific authorities, rules so
unnatural and cruel they made women cry in anguish. Never mind that
babies howled with hunger, they were to be fed only at fixed times. Children
were to sleep when scheduled, not picked up a moment before their nap
time ended. They were to be weaned at nine months, not a month later or a
month earlier. No matter what the pace of their development, they were to
be toilet-trained at a specific time. While parents were supposed to love their
children, hugging and kissing were frowned on. Such affection would
produce spoiled ne'er-do-wells, and it would be all the mother's fault.

Mary McCarthy in her novel *The Group* paints a picture of these rigid
child-rearing methods in action. Priss has just had a baby and is recovering in
hospital. Not only is she at the mercy of the obstetricians but her domineering husband is a physician as well.

At eight o'clock that night, right on the dot, down in the nursery Stephen started
to cry. She [Priss] knew his voice—the whole floor knew it. Sometimes he
would whimper and then go back to sleep for a while, but when he began noisily, as he was doing now, he might cry for two solid hours—a scandal. It was
against the rules for the nurses to pick him up; they were allowed to change him
and give him a drink of water, and that was all. The babies were not supposed to
be 'handled.'[455]

The problem is that Stephen is slowly starving. The doctors, including her
husband, insist Priss must breast-feed the infant, never mind that she is obviously not capable of it. Rather than have the medical men admit defeat, Priss
and the baby are made miserable.

Ironically, it was another scion of the medical establishment, Dr. Benjamin
Spock, who finally succeeded in pointing out how ridiculous this all was. His
The Common Sense Book of Baby and Child Care, published in 1946, finally

broke the oppressive, dangerous and guilt-making regime that had sentenced both mother and baby to such torment.

It was not just the never-ending rules but the arrogant, often blasé attitude of doctors towards their female patients that drove women to distraction. In 1956, a well-known GP in Toronto nonchalantly told my harassed mother, who, in her mid-thirties, had given birth to two boys in two years, that he wouldn't think of fitting her for a diaphragm. He was Roman Catholic and did not approve of birth control. She got what she wanted from another doctor, but she never got over the humiliation of being lectured about what was the most private part of her life.

As many women began to feel frustration with the suburban-housewife role they had embraced during the 1950s, the medical establishment once again played its part in maintaining the status quo. An advertisement in *The American Journal of Psychiatry* of December 1966 tells it all. Sitting on the edge of a bath tub, a seemingly distraught woman looks as though she's about to slap the naked child in front of her. The ad shouts, "Her kind of pressures last all day—shouldn't her tranquilizer?"[456] The over-prescribing of anti-depressants during the 1960s and '70s for "nervous exhaustion" and other "feminine disorders" was an outrageous scandal. Even today, in the Western world, women are prescribed twice as many tranquilizers as men.[457]

When the women's movement finally sprang into being, the medical profession and its insensitive, inept, if not abusive practices became a prime target of female hostility and distrust. So angry were these feminists, their language of reprimand was often white with rage. Poet and feminist Adrienne Rich, for example, wrote in 1974 of childbirth, "The loneliness, the sense of abandonment, of being imprisoned, powerless, and depersonalized is the chief collective memory of women who have given birth in American hospitals."[458]

At conferences, demonstrations and meetings, women began to complain. They talked about their run-ins with arrogant, overly confident doctors, about the dangerous drugs that had been prescribed them for such things as morning sickness, about their experiences with back-room abortionists. Know Your Body courses were organized, and, in the early 1970s, The Boston Women's Health Book Collective published *Our Bodies, Ourselves*, a work that was to have a profound influence throughout North America and Europe. Clinics specifically for women and centres for birth control were set up.

The long and bloody abortion struggle in Europe, Canada and the U.S. was fought and mostly won, and not just in the courts. Despite fierce opposition, there has been a growing acceptance of the procedure; a 1998 poll indicated that 78 percent of Canadians believe abortion is a medical matter between women and their doctors.[459]

If there is a last remaining battle to be fought, it is in the field of health research. The vast majority of drugs prescribed for women have been tested on men only. In an American study that concluded an Aspirin a day reduces the chance of heart attack, over 20,000 volunteers took part, every one of them a man—and this despite the fact that heart attacks are the number-one killer of both sexes. The pro-male bias is obvious not only in the testing of drugs. In Canada, the Medical Research Council discovered that just five percent of health-research spending is directed to work that focuses on women only: hormone replacement therapy, for example, or breast cancer. The figure is better in the United States, but it's still only 15 percent of the total medical research done.[460]

In medical text books, it still common to find illustrations of a male body labelled simply "adult," while the female body is called "female." The male model is the standard, the female still a deviant. It's a throwback to the time when the uterus was considered an upside-down scrotum and wombs roamed the body with abandon.

Gwen

Every term, there was that dreaded moment when the list of those who had made the school sports teams was posted on the bulletin board. My name usually appeared, but right near the bottom as a guard on the basketball team, a sub on the volleyball squad. Never mind, I was in bliss simply donning my blue-and-gold uniform. To be honest, though, I felt envious of Gwen Mode. Her name always appeared first, for she was that most incredible of creatures, a natural-born athlete.

Basketball was her best sport; she was fast, clever and deadly. With decisive and unerringly astute moves, she would skillfully manoeuvre up the court, befuddling the opposition guards, one or two of whom would occasionally break into tears. Springing like some serene, self-assured cat, she would effortlessly—or so it seemed—net the ball. Then she'd let out a whoop of unabashed joy.

For someone perched on so lofty a pedestal, Gwen was remarkably approachable. She had a happy, lopsided grin and a boisterous laugh, a cross between a snort and a whinny. She was certainly boyish looking—angular and thin, with short-cropped hair and plain clothes—yet she considered herself one of the girls, as interested in dating as anyone else. What was truly different about her, I came to realize later, was her single-mindedness. More wimpy girls like me tried hard enough, but our mothers' admonishments—don't tire yourself, be lady-like, don't hurt yourself—prevented us from being truly bloody on the court. Gwen possessed the killer instinct.

Ruth and Bruce Mode must have been astounded at what they had produced in their only child, their beloved little girl. Nothing in their background had prepared them for such a rambunctious, noisy tomboy. Neither one was athletic or aggressive. Ruth was a clever but meek and soft-spoken woman. Bruce was the kindest, most gentle and quietest of men. His father had been a Baptist minister from the Ottawa Valley who made a business out of lecturing about the Holy Land. In the 1920s, he seems to have undergone a crisis of conscience, realizing with some astonishment that there were many faiths equally as valid as his own. He turned to making money instead. He managed both the Peerless Gold Mines and the Sturgeon Bridge Gold Mine, and by the time Bruce was born, the family was quite well off.

All the brothers went to university and became professionals, except Bruce who liked working with his hands and was good at it. He attended Danforth Technical School in Toronto, and then apprenticed as a carpenter. Like all his siblings, Bruce was a member of the youth group of the Calvary Baptist Church in Toronto's east end, and there he met his future bride, the quiet but appealing Ruth Lyons.

Ruth was a mild-mannered, sweet child who grew up utterly terrified of her father. Just before she died in 1995, she told her daughter stories of physical and sexual abuse. She had loved school with a passion and won many academic awards, including a major scholarship to the University of Toronto, but her father wouldn't even entertain the idea. Crying bitter tears, she gave up her dream and went out to work as a secretary in the office of Canada Dry Ginger Ale. For her whole life, she was frightened of men, even the teenagers whom Gwen brought home as dates.

Several of her sisters married men who were as violent and abusive as their father, but Ruth was smart enough to look for something else. She often said that if she hadn't found Bruce Mode, she wouldn't have married at all. In 1930, when she met him at a church social, she was attracted to him at once, not for his good looks or his distinguished family background but because he was as kind and gentle and witty as she was. They fell deeply in love.

Gwen was born in September 1942. By that time, her father was serving in Europe with the Canadian army engineers. He wouldn't meet his daughter until she was three years old.

Like many men, the war changed Bruce. Although Gwen says his daily life mirrored Christian values, he never went to church again. His loss of faith was a result not only of the carnage he had witnessed but also of the sadness that greeted him on his return home. Within three years, his father, mother and younger sister had all died of cancer.

Bruce got a job with the University of Toronto, building display cases for exhibits put on by the different faculties. Ruth had undergone a hysterectomy and, with no more children in her future, she decided to go back to work. When she was in her forties, she passed her certified public-accounting exams and so was able to get a higher-paying job at Scarborough Public Utilities as an accountant.

Ruth managed the household finances, but Bruce did almost everything else. He washed the floors, got up at five on Saturdays to buy fresh meat and produce at the farmers' market, cooked the big Sunday dinner. His biggest responsibility, he felt, was coddling his adored wife. It was a supremely happy marriage. Says Gwen, "They loved each other in a way that, in all my years, I've never seen duplicated. It was truly a match made in heaven."

Even with two incomes, though, they never had much money. When Bruce returned from the war, the family lived in a small flat above a dry-cleaners, and finding a decent home became a priority. In 1946, when one of Ruth's sisters divorced, the Modes were able to take over the mortgage payments on her property. It was a huge lot on McIntosh Street in south Scarborough, but the house itself was tiny, with two bedrooms, a small front room, a larger kitchen and a cramped basement where Bruce spent hours at his work bench. The Modes always planned to renovate their home, make it bigger and more airy, but Bruce could never decide exactly how he wanted it. Finally, they decided to leave it alone, and spent the money on a cottage instead.

Directly behind the Modes' property lived the Moran family. One morning, when Gwen was only four, she wandered over to their house, knocked on the door and was greeted by a pudgy boy of the same age who, as it turned out, was also an only child. Thus began a incredibly close friendship that Gwen says will last a lifetime.

Eddy Moran was a genius, or so his mother thought. There was to be no rough and tumble in the little boy's life; he played the violin, and his hands had to be protected. He wasn't the kind of kid who liked to fight or play football, anyway. Gwen spent her childhood sticking up for him. If bullies were after him, Gwen would hide in the bushes, then jump out and "beat the shit out of them." Eddy didn't like doing anything physical; Gwen couldn't even get him to catch a ball. He used to call Gwen "ass-lete" in retaliation.

All through high school, Eddy and Gwen remained inseparable. In the summers, she'd be invited to his family's country retreat, an old log cabin, and he was a frequent visitor to the Modes' cottage. He never had girlfriends, and sometimes Gwen would fill in as a date to an important prom or other social event, but there was never any romance between them.

Willful might be the kindest word to describe Gwen as a child. She was hot-headed and loud, always slapping her thigh and letting go with her horsy laugh. She loved Westerns, and tried to emulate her hero Roy Rogers. It was slam, bang all over the house. Ruth would say, "Be gentle, Gwen dear, be gentle." Her parents understood what kind of kid they had on their hands and wisely sent her off to camp every summer. Camp Shawanaga was prestigious and expensive—real sacrifices were made by the Modes—but for Gwen, it was paradise. She learned to sail and canoe and swim. She became a hot-shot at tennis and got her first taste of organized sports, playing badminton. Her best memories, though, are of adventures on the overnight camping trips: the violent thunderstorms, being swamped in a canoe.

As she grew older, she became a leader, though she didn't have much compassion for anyone who was not as tough as she was. She remembers one canoe race in particular. It was very hot, and everyone was paddling as hard as they could. When a little, red-headed girl complained she was going to faint, Gwen yelled at her, "Don't you dare if you know what's good for you."

What Camp Shawanaga provided for Gwen was a venue to discover how talented she was in anything to do with physical activity. It gave her a self-confidence that stood her in good stead all through high school.

If there were an important influence on Gwen's life during those years, it was her physical-education teacher. Joyce Woodward was a large-boned, flamboyant but plain woman who was always sweeping in or sweeping out of a room. She loved to entertain—Gwen remembers her making tapes of just the right music to play at her lavish dinner parties—and sports-inclined female students were among her frequent guests. Gwen was often invited to her house, to have tea or dinner or just talk. The two went shopping together, and Joyce visited the Modes' summer cottage. Many of Gwen's classmates thought it odd that a teacher should be so friendly with and so close to a student, but Gwen saw nothing wrong. She thought Joyce Woodward had a warm heart, and it was a shame she was so plain and a spinster. The two remained friends for years.

From Grade 9 on, Gwen had decided athletics were her future. The University of Toronto's physical- and health-education program was a tough course, though. Phys. ed. majors not only took on a heavy load of sciences and arts but also studied subjects relating to the theory of physical activity and the functioning of the body: physiology, genetics, kinetics. There were also the sports: track and field, gymnastics, field hockey, synchronized swimming, basketball, volleyball, badminton. It was more like a military boot camp than a university program of studies. Several of the teachers, all women, were fanatics, seeing to it that the female students endured even more physical rigour than the men. Gwen has memories of herself and her classmates crawling, exhausted, from one gym to another. Many of the intense exercises they did several times a day—the sit-ups, bending and jumping, running 35 laps of the Varsity Arena—are now considered dangerous and not permitted. Gwen believes her body underwent severe distress, even trauma, during her college years, the root cause of the many physical injuries she would suffer in the future.

The course was so intense, it was often after midnight when Gwen limped off the bus home. It left little time for partying. She had always had boyfriends at high school, even one that had been a steady, but few dates had come her way at university. By her third year, she was definitely on the look-out.

Gwen had worked for Scarborough's Department of Parks and Recreation during the summers, organizing sports activities for children, and in 1964, she was assigned to Warden Avenue Public School. It was a tough playground, so Gwen wasn't surprised when one of the kids reported his bicycle had been stolen. She phoned the police, but just as the officer arrived, the bike was found in the bushes. Gwen liked the look of the lanky, red-headed cop, so smart in his uniform, and appreciated his friendly smile and warm ways. She invited him into the staff room for a coffee. As Frank Murphy was leaving, he asked Gwen for her phone number.

Eventually, he asked Gwen out on a date, but when he showed up, she was shocked. Instead of his trim uniform, he was dressed like "a bum" in a grubby T-shirt and socks so full of holes that his toes peeked through his sandals. All was forgotten and forgiven, however, when Gwen got a look at his car: the most beautiful Chevrolet Impala in the world.

Gwen and Frank began dating regularly, which meant her final term at university was chaotic. Frank worked shifts, and Gwen often popped out to see him at one in the morning. Then in February, Bruce Mode became seriously ill.

During her university days, Gwen had grown even closer to her father. He was still working as a carpenter at the University of Toronto, and they'd drive there together every morning, chatting away. He knew all her classmates and would wave at them as he drove around the campus. Sometimes he and Gwen would have lunch together. He seemed to get a vicarious delight from hearing about her studies, her friends, her escapades on the courts and fields. Four years earlier, Bruce had been diagnosed with bowel cancer, but he had undergone surgery and made a remarkable recovery. Now a tumour was found on his lungs. As it turned out, this cancer had nothing to do with the previous one.

When he died in August 1965, Gwen slipped a memorial in his pocket— a ticket to her graduation ceremonies. She is very forthright about the effect his death had on her. "It was the single most devastating thing that ever happened to me. It changed my whole life. It took the heart out of me."

Bruce Mode was 54 when he died. He had received no sick pay, he had no savings and almost no pension. His widow and daughter ended up with very little except the family home, which, thank goodness, was paid for. Fortunately, Gwen had no trouble finding a job; school principals were actually fighting over who would hire her. She finally decided on Agincourt Collegiate in Scarborough, because she'd be reunited with her old friend Joyce Woodward. Joyce had spent three years in Germany working for the Canadian armed forces—Gwen had often written to her—and on her return had become head of Agincourt Collegiate's physical-education and health department.

Joyce made Gwen feel comfortable in the first difficult months, encouraging her and giving her advice. As well as her teaching, Gwen coached team sports, which she loved, and there was a social life that she had never had the opportunity to enjoy at university. Lots of young teachers had been hired, and they'd go out drinking together on Friday nights.

Frank was still in the picture, though. He had come to realize that, with a Grade 10 education, he was hardly worthy of someone with a college degree. It was a struggle, but he finally made it to university, majoring in economics and political science. He had to give up his high-paying policeman's job and that meant, of course, he had little money. Instead of a beautiful Chevrolet Impala, he drove a beat-up Volkswagen.

When Ruth had first met Frank, she had told her daughter, "Watch that guy. With red hair and a name like Murphy, he's bound to be a Roman Catholic." Indeed, he was. Gwen didn't want to convert, but she agreed to take the necessary instructions. It was a battle, because Gwen wanted to argue with the priest about everything from birth control to abortion. Just in time, a truce of sorts was worked out, and in June 1967, Frank and Gwen were married in St. Theresa Shrine of the Little Flower Catholic Church. The reception, however, was held at St. Paul's United Church. Gwen was so thin at the time that her size eight gown was big on her.

She returned to teaching, but she was starting to become disillusioned.

Since, in those days, recreational sports such as golf, curling and tennis were not taught—it was all basketball and gymnastics—only sports buffs truly liked their gym class. As one girl told a thunderstruck Gwen, running around the gym ruined her hair-do. Faced every day with kids who moaned about how much they hated her class, Gwen became discouraged. Nonetheless, when in 1968 she was asked to become head of the girls' physical-education department at Woburn Collegiate Institute in Scarborough, she was ambitious enough to accept, especially when she found out it meant a $4,000-a-year raise. She couldn't have made a bigger mistake.

The Murphys went on their first holiday together that summer, a camping trip out west, and Gwen realized she wasn't feeling well, either emotionally or physically. It didn't help that when school started in September, she was faced with an intolerable situation. The woman she was replacing, who had left because she was pregnant, had been enormously popular with the students. They resented Gwen, and their displeasure grew when the former teacher miscarried and lost her twin babies. "Why couldn't she have her job back?" the students wanted to know. Gwen had to walk into the gym or classroom knowing that the faces looking up at her were frowning a message: she had no right to be there. By Christmas, she couldn't stand any more, and she walked away from the job.

Gwen now realizes it was more than just an unpleasant situation at school that made her leave. In her attempt to bolster her mother and begin married life with some optimism, she had suppressed her grief over her father's death. Suddenly, it overwhelmed her, and she became deeply depressed. This might have eased after she discovered she was pregnant, but in the fourth month, she lost the baby, the first of many miscarriages she would suffer over the next few years.

Meanwhile, the Murphys' sources of income had dried up. Frank graduated from university that spring, but it took him a year to find a job. He and Gwen finally moved in with his parents, who fed them and put a roof over their heads, but it was an embarrassing and uncomfortable situation.

Frank's parents wanted to retire and, to do so, they had to sell their farm. First, they gave each of their children two acres. Though they had only a few hundred dollars in the bank, Frank and Gwen decided to build a house on their portion. It would take years of hard work, but the Murphys eventually ended up with a homey place they loved.

Meanwhile, Gwen began supply teaching at a nearby high school. She found the students astonishingly disrespectful. It wasn't uncommon for a student to tell her to fuck off, and there was little she could do to exert control since she didn't even know their names. She also never knew whether she was going to work until the phone rang early in the morning, so she couldn't sleep properly. She finally said to herself, "You couldn't pay me enough to do this any more."

Over the next few years, she took less challenging jobs, working as an order-desk clerk in the Playtex factory in Malton and as a clerk in Coles bookstore. She began to have pains in her neck that grew worse and then her left arm went numb, so she couldn't even hold a clipboard. The doctors kept telling her there was nothing wrong, but in 1979, they finally operated. A lump the size of a tennis ball was found on her collarbone. Situated at an odd angle, it hadn't been visible on the X-rays. The doctors were fearful it might be malignant, but it turned out to be an old injury, perhaps from her university days, which had been eaten through with arthritis. The orthopedic surgeon was able to repair it to some extent, although Gwen has never regained the full use of her left arm.

There was another health problem that plagued Gwen and that was far more serious, at least psychologically. She kept having miscarriages. In 1975, she was five months pregnant, the longest she had ever kept a fetus. She was so desperate for the baby to survive, she converted to Catholicism. A family should be of the same religious faith, she decided. Unhappily, she miscarried shortly afterwards. This time, the doctors told her not to try again; it would be too damaging to her health.

She and Frank had desperately wanted babies, thinking that only with children would they become a real family. Finally, they realized adoption was the solution. In just six weeks, Gwen received a telephone call from the Catholic Children's Aid announcing that a month-old baby boy was waiting to be picked up at a foster home. Since the day they brought him home, Patrick has been nothing but a joy to Gwen and Frank.

In 1979, the Murphys decided to sell the house they had laboured over for so long. The decision came out of Frank's long-time dream of operating a farm, just as his father had. After Frank had graduated from university, he'd found a management job in the sales office of Continental Can in Brampton, but he didn't like it much. Selling real estate in the booming Brampton area, which was rapidly becoming a bedroom community of Toronto, seemed the answer, but it occurred to Frank that he could not only hold that job but also run a farm. Gwen was dubious at first, but said she'd agree as long as it wasn't located further than 80 kilometres north of Toronto. To Gwen's amazement, they quickly found what they thought was the perfect property, 100 acres near the town of Thornton, 12 kilometres south of Barrie.

The deal included an old-fashioned, red-brick, gabled Ontario farmhouse with two storeys and ornamental brick work. It hadn't been renovated for decades, if ever, but the Murphys thought they could put up with that until they made enough money to fix it up. Sixteen years later, it remains very much the same as when they moved in.

Frank believed that a mixed farm would provide his family with a nice income. He quickly found out how wrong he was. He tried to grow wheat, but didn't have the capital to purchase large enough machinery, tractors and combines, and what he did have kept breaking down. The Murphys also tried raising animals, primarily beef and hogs. (No chickens or turkeys— Frank hates anything with feathers.) Gwen remembers wrapping two or three newborn piglets in an electric blanket and watching over them all night to make sure they survived. In a year or two, though, it became obvious it was costing more to feed the livestock than was being recouped by selling them. The Murphys finally admitted defeat and sold off their entire stock. These days, they rent half of their land to a neighbouring farmer and grow hay, which they sell, on the other half.

The experience has meant hard times for the Murphys. In the early 1980s, with interest rates soaring, the real-estate market collapsed, and Frank had to take a job on the assembly line at General Tire. It was supposed to be temporary, but he ended up working there for 11 years until the plant was shut down. Meanwhile, Gwen had gone off in a completely different direction.

In 1982, she found a position at a Barrie mental-health centre funded by Share Life, the Catholic United Way. She started out as a receptionist, manning the telephones and receiving clients, but gradually, she took on more responsibility until she became an intake counsellor. It was a job she thoroughly enjoyed, and she enrolled in the social-work program at York University. By the end of the '80s, though, qualifications in social work were changing. Gwen realized if she wanted to be a therapist, she would have to get her Masters degree. It all seemed too much.

One day in 1989, she was having lunch with a psychologist friend who said, "The kids these days—they can't write, they can't spell, they can't read." Gwen perked up. "I can do something about that," she said, and decided right then to return to teaching, although she knew it wouldn't be as a physical-education teacher; her age and injuries precluded that. She was taken on at Holy Trinity High School in Bradford as a fill-in for a teacher on maternity leave. When the special-needs teacher quit, the principal, impressed with the social-work courses Gwen had taken, asked her if she would like the job. For the next five years, she instructed handicapped kids and loved it. Unfortunately, one day she was helping a young student off with her coat and somehow twisted herself badly, hurting her back and losing the use of her arm once again. It meant intense physiotherapy and eight months off work. Gwen is back teaching English, but she has to be extremely careful.

Throughout all the years of injuries, illness and financial hardship, Gwen's love of sports has kept her going. Her house is strewn with books on athletics and copies of *Sports Illustrated*. She loves watching golf or skiing or football on television; it's a family activity, the glue that has held them together. Happily, her son Patrick has turned out to be as talented an athlete as she once was. He was a hockey player at school, where Frank and Gwen loved nothing better than cheering encouragement at his games, and is now studying kinetics at York University in Toronto with the hope of becoming a sports psychologist.

Because of her injuries, Gwen hasn't been active in organized sports for years. She swims as much as she can, works out a little in the gym and in recent years, she has fallen in love with horses. She has obtained her grooming certificate and spends a lot of time with standard breeds, preparing them for harness racing. "I know I will never be whole again," she says, "unless I am involved in sports. They represent all the values that are important to me."

Physical Activity

No Spartan girl
could grow up modest, even if she wanted to.
You never find them staying at home; no, they go out
With bare thighs and loose clothes, to wrestle and run races
Along with the young men. I call it intolerable.

Euripides, Andromache, c. 425 BC

No Sweet feminine girl (and, I repeat, what male doesn't want girls to be sweetly feminine, and nice and sweet and frilly?) can be much good at the more robust forms of athletics.

Elmer Ferguson, Maclean's magazine, August 1938

What I remember after she touched the breakwater: the bright red flares lighting up the night sky, the cacophony of horns and whistles, the hysterical spectators, some of them up to their knees in the icy water of Lake Ontario, the ecstasy shared by everyone. She symbolized many wonderful things: she was a Canadian outdoing an American; she was young, only 16, a high-school student; and most important she was female, a healthy, strong, determined girl who, although she was only five-foot-one, had performed a physical feat beyond the capability of any man.

It's hard to believe now that a marathon swim could create such a sensation, but from the time Marilyn Bell pushed off from a log retaining wall at Youngstown, N. Y., at 11:10 p.m. on September 8, 1954 until her fingers touched the slimy breakwater at Toronto's Sunnyside 20 hours and 58 minutes later, the city hungrily ate up every detail the hysterical media could provide. She had five miles to go but she was pleading to be pulled out; now she was sleeping—maybe she'd just vanish into the black, icy waters; no, no, she had revived again, her legs were moving, so were her arms. It went on all day and into the evening.

Two other marathon swimmers, both women and one a well-known American marathoner, had started with Marilyn but were pulled out about half way. No wonder. Huge lamprey eels attached themselves to their stomach and thighs, the water was cold, 15-foot waves meant unbelievably slow going. When Marilyn Bell reached the breakwater, she was the first person to have swum across Lake Ontario.

My mother, like many other people, was glued to the radio that day, but she worried. Surely Marilyn's health would suffer irreparable damage. She must have lost at least 20 pounds. How would she ever gain her strength back? When a doctor examined her shortly after she had been pulled from the water, he found that not only was her heart rate normal and her respiratory system unchanged but she had gained a pound. So much for feminine delicacy.

Interestingly, Marilyn wasn't portrayed as a freak or even chastised for not being feminine. By the 1950s, women had established themselves as remarkable athletes. It was one of the fundamental breakthroughs of the 20th century. Women's feats of athletic prowess finally shattered the most disabling and pernicious of all myths about females: that they were physically weak, fragile creatures who at all times and in all circumstances needed a man's strength and protection.

I

The most vivid image of the sporty woman that has passed down from ancient Greek literature is of Artemis (the Roman Diana), one of the 12 Olympian divinities and the goddess of the hunt. There was another tomboy, though, named Atalanta, whose story may have more appeal because she was mortal, the earthly equivalent of Artemis.

Her father typically wanted only sons, so the infant Atalanta was left on a mountainside to die. She was rescued by a she-bear, who suckled her and raised her as one of her own cubs. Atalanta grew up loving freedom. She could run as swiftly as a deer, she was as strong as her adoptive mother and her hunting ability was legendary.

Eventually, after a series of adventures—she is sometimes named as the only female Argonaut—she was reunited with her father and returned to human society. Despite her muscular body and mannish dress, Atalanta had sex appeal. Young men lined up. She, however, had no interest whatsoever in marriage and devised a interesting means of getting rid of suitors. Each had to take her on, either in a wrestling match or a foot race. If she won, which was always the case, she was allowed to slay her would-be bridegroom. In the sprinting contest, she would wait at the finish line and, as her victim approached, spear him to death with her javelin.

Atalanta, being a mere female, had to be mastered, of course. Aphrodite, the goddess committed to marriage, provided the means in the form of three shiny, gold apples. She talked Atalanta's cousin Meilanion, known as the black hunter, into wooing her, and gave him the apples. Each time Atalanta was about to sprint ahead, he threw an apple into her path. Curious, and perhaps a little greedy, she stopped to pick the treasure up. Meilanion was thus able to beat her, if only by the narrowest of margins, and claim her as his bride. Atalanta seems to have taken to marriage, at least the physical part. One legend has it that she and her new husband committed the sacrilege of making passionate love in a sacred grove of Zeus, who turned them both into lions.

The myth of Atalanta reveals a great deal about antiquity's attitude towards women and their physical prowess, the repercussions of which are still being felt today. Men were attracted to a woman who was quick, strong and agile— she was sexy and intriguing—but on the other hand, a physically powerful female was a terrible threat to the male's mastery of the opposite sex. As historian Allen Guttmann puts it, "The defeat of Atalanta by Me[i]lanion ... reassured Greek men that they had not lost control of their women."[461]

This ambivalent attitude was reflected in the Greek attitude towards the mighty Spartans. In the city state of Sparta, physical fitness for girls was not only permitted but compulsory; they were required to compete in various sports competitions. The Roman Sextus Propertius (born between 54 and 47 BC) was one poet who honoured the sporty females of Sparta:

> O Sparta of outlandish laws, outlandish custom,
> how I envy your virginal gymnasia,
> Where naked girls enjoy the fun,
> the wrestling,
> retrieve stray balls, run
> to the song of hoopstick & hoop.
> Girls stand dust-drifted
> at the race's end goal
> & in Sparta a girl may join the pancration
> giving & receiving her share,
> glove tight on delighted fist.[462]

It was thought a healthy girl was more likely to produce stronger sons, which, in a war-loving society like Sparta, was supremely important. Plutarch (AD 46?-100), writing about the famous law-maker Lycurgus, who lived in the seventh century and who devised the constitution that established Sparta as a military state, described the philosophy towards young girls:

He [Lycurgus] ordered the maidens to exercise themselves with wrestling, running, throwing the discus, and casting the javelin, to the end that the fruit they conceived might, in strong and healthy bodies, take firmer root and find better growth, and withal that they, with this greater vigor, might be the more able to undergo the pains of child-bearing.[463]

Spartan women were considered the most attractive in the Greek world. Indeed, their beauty was legendary; after all, Helen's home town was Sparta. They were also thought to be the healthiest, and were in great demand as wet-nurses. It was possible their mortality rate at childbirth was the lowest. Yet in the Archaic and Classical periods at least, Athenian parents profoundly disapproved of the way Spartan girls were raised. They wanted daughters who were meek and obedient, not aggressive tomboys.

Athletic competition was an integral part of Greek society, tightly inter-woven into the religious and political rituals of the *polis*. Historian Donald G. Kyle writes, "Athletics provided a means whereby men displayed and tested their prowess to the delight of gods and visitors and in veneration of dead friends, leaders and heroes."[464] Women were almost entirely left out of this loop. The gymnasia for physical training or the stadia for competitions were out of bounds to them. At the renowned Olympic Games held in honour of Zeus, they were not even permitted the role of spectator.

Physical activity wasn't entirely forbidden, however. Every four years in the city of Elis, a few miles from Olympia, an athletic festival dedicated to the goddess Hera was held for unmarried girls, perhaps as a kind of pre-marriage fertility rite. These young women let down their hair, wore short tunics to free their legs, bared their right shoulders and raced to beat hell. The victors were given crowns of olive leaves and a share from the cow that was sacri-ficed in Hera's honour. Their names were recorded for posterity. The Heraia may not have been as prestigious as the games at Olympia, but to the girls who participated, it held great significance, a rite of passage that marked the transition from childhood to adulthood. There have always been girls for whom athletics has meant honour and prestige, the very spice of their life, and there have always been men who, while enjoying the spectacle of competing women, have shaken their heads in disapproval.

II

Organized sports were not a passion of the Middle Ages. The memory of the Roman gladiator games, during which Christians were often eaten by lions, was still too uncomfortably vivid, and the idea of women making an athletic display of themselves was even more abhorrent. The early theologians, the story of the expulsion from the Garden of Eden rattling around in their heads, held a disgust for the female body. To make up for Eve's carnality, women were to emulate the saintly Virgin Mary. Passive and docile, her head bowed, her knees bent in prayer, she certainly was not into running races or throwing the discus.

Despite this peaceful picture, playing aggressive games seems as much a part of human nature as making war. At fairs and religious festivals, all sorts of races and contests went on. Huge stones or sacks of grain were heaved remarkable distances. Folk football—a violent game in which everyone participated—was popular. Men dominated, of course, but women were in there, too, pushing, shoving, kicking, yelling—and suffering almost as many broken bones as their husbands or brothers. Single girls loved racing, running barefoot across meadows, cheered on by some gallant who might later ask for their hands in marriage. The prize was a dress (hence the name smock races) or a bolt of cloth.[465]

In the margin of a medieval manuscript in Latin called the *Alexander Romance*, there is an interesting drawing. A nun holds a ball and a monk, a bat. He looks as though he is readying himself for her pitch. Out in the field are a group of religious, waiting, it seems, to catch a line drive.

The origins of modern baseball are based on a Middle Ages game called stoolball played by young women. A milkmaid would stand in front of her milking stool while her opponent tried to knock it down with a ball. If the milkmaid didn't catch the ball, or at least deflect it, and her stool were knocked over, she would change places and become the thrower. According to sports historian William J. Baker, this provided the rudiments of a game called rounders that, centuries later, turned into American baseball.[466]

However, women played no active role in the crossbow contests that sometimes went on for weeks with great fanfare in medieval towns. It was only towards the end of the epoch that there were reports of women's archery contests. Female aristocrats, though, were far more sporty. For one thing, when their husbands were away, it was their responsibility to look after the estate, and riding a horse was essential to getting around in order to carry out the necessary inspections. Medieval manuscripts are full of illustrations of women on horseback surrounded by their hunting dogs; some even sported long bows. Handling falcons was thought to be a particularly female skill. In his treatise *Policraticus*, the English philosopher John of Salisbury (c. 1115–1180) espoused the theory that women were more skillful breeders of these powerful birds of prey than men.[467]

There were other women in the Middle Ages who defied the example of a sedate and passive Mary. There are accounts of female gymnasts, jugglers, dancers and acrobats. Particularly popular was a saltatrix (acrobatic dancer) called Maude Makejoy, who was often called on to perform for English royalty. At the Christmas feast of 1296, she amused young Prince Edward (1312-1377, later King Edward III) with her "vaults," and 15 years later, she was doing the same thing for his half-brothers.

Most interesting is an account by a local burgher in the *Journal d'un Bourgeois de Paris* written in 1427. It reported that 28-year-old Margot Hainault had come to town to challenge the men to their favourite sport: tennis. They laughed at her, whereupon she promptly beat them all.[468]

III

The only sport available to women in the early modern age was hunting, and that was for the aristocracy only. However, leisure time—what there was of it—wasn't spent sitting in chairs. Dancing was a passion shared by the entire society. As historian Jean-Paul Desaive puts it, "A [dance] ball was a unique occasion for women to demonstrate that they too could move gracefully, vigorously, briskly, or with abandon."[469]

Formal balls weren't available to country people, but they certainly enjoyed themselves. Their dancing was full of passion and joy, exaggerated gestures, pantomime, abandonment. Holding onto each other's shoulders or waists, they would face inwards and prance around in a circle, chanting and singing, as though recalling some ancient sacrificial rite. On May Day, a tall pole was bedecked with garlands and greenery like a tree, while around it the dancers wove ribbons—symbolizing the branches—into complex patterns, a vestige of a time when the forest was worshipped.

Folk dancing was not for the faint-hearted. Long lines of people would follow a leader sometimes for miles, straight through one village to another. These chain dances had a lot to do with courtship—it was a good way to see how much spirit a young man or woman really had—and it was this aspect that was incorporated into the more stately and mannered dancing of the upper classes.

Over the years once energetic court balls, however, lost most of the boisterousness of folk dancing. The gallant no longer burst from the line to embrace the object of his desire, throwing her into the air in the process. An aristocrat sedately knelt and took his partner's hand. Energetic strides and jumps and kicks contracted into glides and intricate steps with small poses, bows and curtsies. The galliard, the volta, the English morris, the Spanish morisca and eventually the waltz and polka were devised, the steps becoming more and more complicated. The chief promoter of dance in England during the 16th century was Elizabeth I, who loved performing and was very good at the galliard, with its four springing steps followed by a leap.

Dance schools popped up in every major European city, and the dancing master had remarkable influence in society. Many of these instructors were Jewish, descendants of the Klesmorim, a group of medieval entertainers. Highly educated, if only by themselves, they wrote long treatises on the intricacies of dance and tyrannized high society in the process. Pierre Rameau, for example, in his *Le Maître à danser,* written in 1725, dictated to the women of the court the following on "the Manner of carrying the Head":

... if she holds it [the head] upright, and the Body well disposed, without Affectation, or too much Boldness, they say there goes a stately Lady; if she carries it negligently, they accuse her of carelessness; if she pokes her Head forward, of Indolence; and in short, if she stoops, of Thoughtlessness, or want of Assurance.[470]

At the same time as social dancing, theatre was blossoming in the courts of Europe, lavish spectacles centering around a mythological plot or theme, with elaborate costumes and stylized sets that could be moved about by stage machinery. These productions featured verse set to music, singing and acrobatics, but the most important ingredient was the dance. In 1581, Catherine de Médicis, queen mother of France, celebrated the betrothal of her sister by mounting what is now considered the first ballet for which a complete score has survived. *Ballet comique de la reine* revolved around the complicated story of Ulysses' escape from Circe, and combined music, dance, stage design and an intricate plot woven into a dramatic whole.

It was the flamboyant Louis XIV of France (1638–1715) who did more than anyone during the epoch to encourage professional dancing. He loved to dance, thought himself quite good and often played the starring role of the Greek sun god Apollo in elaborate court extravaganzas (hence his popular name, the Sun King). In 1661, he founded the Académie Royale de Danse to establish scientific principles related to the art. Before long, ballet dancers of great proficiency emerged. In 1739, Barberina Campanini (1721–99) took Paris by storm, executing jumps and turns of such speed and daring, she changed the idea of dance forever. She also made nonsense of the notion that women were physically as fragile as glass. Campanini was only the first in a long line of remarkable ballerinas who would demonstrate at each performance that they were as agile, vigorous and durable as the men they partnered.

IV

In her *Vindication of the Rights of Women* (1792), Mary Wollstonecraft wrote: "I wish to persuade women to endeavor to acquire strength, both of mind and body. Let us then by being allowed to take the same exercise as boys … arrive at perfection of the body, that we may know how far the natural superiority of man extends."

It would be another 100 years or so before her advice would be put into practice. For most of the 19th century, women lived in a kind of detention, "moving from chair to chair, finding comfort in none and tired of every employment."[471] This static state of affairs had to do with the Victorian idea of the nature of women. Whereas men were intrinsically aggressive, competitive and decisive—attributes perfectly suited for the court or playing field— women were emotional, passive and always physically at risk, all of which meant that playing the piano, a brisk walk or perhaps a sedate game of Carpet Croquet was as much physical exercise as their bodies, or minds, could tolerate. An 1890 article in *Blackwoods Magazine* laid out the prevalent, condescending male attitude towards the idea of women engaging in athletic competition. The unnamed author wrote that women's bodies were simply not constructed for physical activity. When they ran, for example, it was with "a kind of precipitate waddle with neither grace, fitness nor dignity."[472]

That women menstruated, bore children and suckled them was all proof of their innate physical weakness. As historian Jennifer Hargreaves puts it, "... although these essential biological differences need not prevent healthy women from exercising (except for short periods during a pregnancy and following the birth of a child), they have provided the major justification for limiting women's participation at all times of their life-cycle."[473]

In fact, though, it was this concern for a woman's biological function that slowly made physical exercise legitimate, the old "healthier mothers make stronger babies" adage coming once again into play. Physicians began prescribing gentle forms of exercise taken for short periods of time. Gymnastics, the mild, Swedish kind, became popular by mid-century, and suddenly, privately owned gymnasia and health spas were popping up everywhere, offering the equivalent of today's aerobics classes and massage therapy. By the 1880s in England and Germany, deportment—the only physical activity taught girls in high schools—had been replaced by Swedish calisthenics. Corsets, of course, had to be cast aside, at least for that particular lesson.

By mid-century, women were beginning to play games. Croquet, for example, became all the rage for middle-class women, although it wasn't exactly strenuous. One writer put it this way:

Nobody could have called it a good game played, as it was, with only one hand in order that womenfolk might be able to hold up their parasols to guard their complexions from the sun ... a game of frills and fancies, of petticoats, giggles and maidenly blushes.[474]

It was the bicycle, introduced late in the century, that finally set women free. Newspapers reported with astonishment the remarkable sight of women actually riding these wheeled contraptions. In 1883, the Canadian Brampton *Conservator* exalted that Miss Lillie Roberts had "the proud distinction of being Brampton's first lady bicyclist.... The graceful appearance she presents while passing through town on her wheel will no doubt lead others to take up the healthy pastime."[475]

The journalist was quite right: if ever there were a craze, cycling was it. For women, it meant previously undreamed-of mobility and independence. There was disapproval, of course. Many men and some women deeply resented this breaking of the patriarchal stranglehold on women's physical movement. In 1895, six of 19 Toronto school trustees—all men, of course— voted for a motion that would have forced school inspectors to report the names of female teachers caught riding bicycles while wearing bloomers.[476]

It was one thing for women to get around on bicycles, but it was quite another for them to compete. This was considered laughable, ridiculous and, worst of all, man-like. In 1897, Grace Denison wrote of her experiences touring United States and Canada on her bicycle. It was an exhilarating experience until she came upon a women's cycling race. Her description of the event was nasty, to say the least:

... the winner, a fat lady, with a moustache and snapping black eyes ... promptly fell off in a faint and was immediately sat upon by a scraggy lady whose hair had gotten loose.... Being revived [she] snapped her eyes at the dishevelled one and said acidly, 'I beat you, anyway, smartie!' It was the most ludicrously feminine way of expressing sport, taking, as woman contests nearly always do, such a pointedly personal turn.[477]

Despite criticism and ridicule, there were women who grew to love competitive sports. Tennis, which had begun as a decorous game of pat-ball sometimes played by both sexes together, gradually turned into a strenuous and sometimes ferocious contest. The women, however, had their tedious clothes to contend with on the court, which didn't help their game or their reputations. As one writer put it, "The ladies tied their long dresses back with an apron with pockets in it for spare tennis balls and ran about with little straw hats firmly pinned on their hair, determined to show off their athletic abilities."[478]

As women gained access to universities, they began competing in varsity leagues. Basketball was introduced at Smith College, Northhampton, Massachusetts, in 1892, and field hockey was a going concern by the turn of the century. In England, students at Cheltenham Ladies' College had 26 tennis courts to choose from, a two-acre playground and facilities for fencing, riding and swimming. They were expected to compete in badminton, netball, lacrosse, cricket and field hockey. Once girls got a taste of inter-varsity competition, they became obsessed. The following is a description of Roedean School, which emphasized sports:

On the whole students were games mad. Entire student bodies turned out for major house and school matches.... Militant school songs ... were sung with religious fervor. A plethora of trophies were objects of grail-like devotion, as were the colours awarded to outstanding athletes who themselves were virtually worshipped. Photographing of teams for posterity was an annual rite, and sporting language conjuring up masculine images was considered smart.[479]

Despite this seeming progress, the idea of women enjoying physical activities and competitive games was a hard lump to swallow for many men. Two cartoons in the British humour magazine *Punch* illustrate how women's sports were ridiculed and how reluctant the male establishment was to accept the fact that the sporty woman was a permanent part of their landscape. The first cartoon depicts a group of young women playing field hockey. In the middle of the melee, the male umpire, in his checked suit, is jumping up and down, a horrified look on his face. He is being thrashed about the ankles by hockey sticks wielded by long-skirted females, who are intent on winning their game and aren't thinking about him. The caption reads, "One of the inferior sex who volunteered to umpire soon discovered his office was no sinecure." The second was published in *Punch's Almanack* for 1897. It shows a group of women, dressed in long skirts and large hats, bicycling along a country road. The two in front are talking to each other. Ethel says, "I hope bicycling will go out of fashion before next season, I *do* hate bicycling so!" Maud replies, "So do I! But one *must*, you know!"

Bicycling didn't go away, and neither did sporting women.

V

In 1900, Benarr MacFadden, the editor of *Physical Culture*, a magazine published out of Boston, scandalized the sporting world with this editorial:

The writer has maintained in this magazine since its inception that there should be but very slight difference between the strength of man and woman—that the proverbial feminine weakness is simply the result of growing into womanhood hampered by the conventional skirt, the bigoted prejudice of parents against play of a romping nature and with the internal organs distorted, bruised and diseased by the terrible corset.[480]

At the turn of the century, the kind of female athlete to whom MacFadden referred was a reflection of that remarkable creature, the New Woman: bold, energetic and breaking free at last of Victorian restraint. World War I reinforced this direction. At times of great national crisis, it was patriotic to be healthy and strong, at the ready to perform strenuous and perhaps dangerous physical feats. By the 1920s, women wearing short tennis skirts or tank suits or even pilot goggles was not an uncommon sight. The decade is considered the Golden Age of Sports and women athletes were an integral part of it.

Their achievements were truly remarkable. In 1926, Gertrude Ederle swam the 20.6 miles across the English Channel, shattering all records, including those of the men. Amelia Earhart flew across the Atlantic with a male pilot and mechanic (she was the log-keeper) in 1928 and instantly became an American heroine. Phyllis Dewar of Moose Jaw, Saskatchewan, won four gold medals for swimming at the 1934 British Empire Games, a record that was held until 1966. In 1924, a 20-year-old American woman broke the world record in the backstroke for men as well as women. The Edmonton Grads dominated women's basketball from 1915 to 1940. Dr. J. Naismith called them "the finest basketball team that ever stepped out on a floor."

The famous track and field champion Mildred "Babe" Didrikson won a silver and two gold medals at the 1932 Olympics, breaking the record in javelin by an amazing two metres. She then became a golf pro, winning 82 golf tournaments, 17 of them in a row. Babe didn't seem to have much fellow feeling for other women competitors, though. Her biographer writes that she "made it very, very hard on a lot of women golfers because she'd walk right up and say, 'What are you girls practising for? You can't win this tournament.' She did it all the time, and there were a lot of them that didn't like it one damn bit."[481]

Suzanne Lenglen was perhaps the most famous female athlete of the 1920s. From 1919 to 1926, she won 269 of her 270 tennis matches.[482] Born to a wealthy French family, Lenglen was arrogant, coquettish and liked being in the limelight. She dressed spectacularly, in short, pleated skirts designed by Jean Patou and "two yards of brightly coloured silk chiffon" wound around her head. She demanded wine be served before her matches and the authorities caved in, changing the rules. She had a fit when in 1926, Queen Mary asked that a match at Wimbledon be rescheduled to suit the royal timetable. Lenglen sulked in her dressing room until, after much pleading, she finally agreed to participate. The British public, shocked that monarchy had been thus insulted, watched in surly silence as Lenglen won for the sixth time.[483]

However, for all the flashy publicity, society's attitude towards female athletes had not fundamentally changed. It was typical of the flapper era's advancement in women's rights: all show and no substance. Moreover, the backlash was, inevitably, denigrating to women. Montreal journalist Elmer Ferguson felt free to write an article in *Maclean's* magazine headlined "I Don't Like Amazon Athletes."[484] Men apparently did not like girls with sweat on their faces, pungent odour or dirty feet. (Marathon swimming, on the other hand, a clean sport in which almost all the world records are held by women, has always been in favour.) Ferguson wrote of one champion sprinter as "a big lanky, flat-chested, muscular girl, with as much sex appeal as grandmother's old sewing machine."[485] Even the previously androgynous Babe Didrikson began adorning herself with lipstick, perfume, nail polish, hats and girdles to counteract the charge that she was not quite female, a "Muscle Moll."

If the backlash had consisted only of diatribes by misogynist sports writers, it wouldn't have mattered much, but the world of female athletes in fact contracted. Nowhere was this more obvious than at the universities. Suddenly, competition among women became unsavoury. The American organization that controlled women's physical education at the college level adopted a philosophy that "the motivation of competitors in athletic activities should be play for play's sake"—not for awards or honours. Intercollegiate and national championships in sports such as basketball and volleyball were all but eliminated for women. As early as 1911, female students at the University of Toronto petitioned for a sports gymnasium, but when the elegant Hart House was built in 1919 as a centre for sports and extra-curricular activities, women were not allowed in the door. When the new Currie gym was built on Montreal's McGill Campus in 1939, women were assigned the lowest priority in space and time in the use of the facilities. They were repeatedly told they were there "on sufferance." A French professor of physical education told his male students that, since women athletes could never be "world-class" in comparison with men, he couldn't understand why they were bothering with sports at all. The age-old idea that a woman's physicality should be dedicated entirely to her reproductive role—not to running around a sports track—reappeared with a vengeance.

Historian Susan K. Cahn has a feminist interpretation of what happened during the 1920s and '30s. "Fearing any erosion of patriarchal privilege and resenting female intrusions into a formerly male terrain, men often viewed women's athletic gains as their own loss of a clearly masculine preserve.... If not in 'manly games' where would men learn masculinity, prove their manhood, and sport their virility?"[486]

In the lucrative world of professional sports, of course. The modern-day addiction to pro sports began in the 1920s and reached its current frenzy after World War II. To be picked up by the National Hockey League, the National Basketball Association or the British soccer league became the ultimate dream of sports-minded boys. Nothing was more important than a talented young baseball player making the big leagues, and all the financial support and public attention that had previously gone to amateur sport was siphoned off to the training of professionals. Women's athletics were completely overshadowed, and there were few chances for women to make money. In 1991, American golfer Pat Bradley finally topped the $4-million mark, but it took her 18 years as a professional, far longer than any male of equal calibre. Even those that did perform in the professional circuit were paid little attention by the media. It all perpetuated the idea that women's sports were a pale imitation of men's.

Like everything else, the women's movement began to change all that. In 1970, one of the greatest tennis players of all time, Billie Jean King, organized a boycott of the Pacific Southwest tournament because the prize money for the men was eight times higher than for the women. King was one of the first outspoken feminists on the court, and when Bobby Riggs challenged her to a match to prove male athletes were naturally superior to women, she accepted. Although he was 25 years older than her, women around the world cheered when she beat him. Within King's competitive lifetime, women's and men's winnings became almost equal.

Title IX of the Education Amendments Act adopted by the U.S. Congress in 1972 made discrimination against female athletes illegal. Even though it wouldn't be enforced for six years, many schools began revamping their physical-education programs, allocating more money to girls' sports. The result was both immediate and phenomenal. In 1972, only four percent of female high-school students played sports; by 1987, that number had jumped to 26 percent, and in the 1990s, to 33 percent. (However, the battle over sports funding continues in North America and Europe. In May 1998, the British Columbia Human Rights Commission deliberated over a test case that calls into question the unequal way money is spent on boys' and girls' sports in municipalities across Canada. At this writing, it remains unresolved.)

Even pro sports, that universe of male exclusivity, is slowly accepting female participants. In the United States, the top women's basketball teams are playing to sold-out houses. Spectators, it seems, enjoy the finesse, skill and speed that women athletes demonstrate. For many, the professional men's game has become too fast and complex to follow. The same thing is happening on the tennis courts. The men, especially playing on fast surfaces, have turned the game into, as one columnist put it, "a boring exchange of unanswerable serves." The result: long lineups to watch the women. And specialty sports channels have discovered they can actually sell advertising time for women's tennis tournaments.

In Canada, after years of fighting for ice time and being ridiculed for playing a man's game—"Want your teeth jammed down your throat?" was a common male response—women's hockey has taken off. Approved for the first time as an Olympic event in 1998, it was such a favourite, there's talk of a professional league. Companies such as the footwear giant Nike are handing out lucrative endorsement contracts to women athletes; a basketball shoe called Air Swoopes was named after the Houston Comets star Sheryl Swoopes.

The next step, of course, is competition between men and women. Ninety years ago, British figure skater Madge Syers insisted on competing with men at the world championships since there were no rules forbidding her from doing so. Much to everyone's amazement, she finished second to Ulrich Salchow, ten times a world champion, and many who saw her performance said she should have won. The reaction of the male establishment was immediate: women were barred from ever competing with men, and the ban still holds good in all Olympic sports except equestrian show-jumping, dressage and three-day events. Says Susan Nattrass, Canada's six-time world trap-shooting champion, "If one's going to play amateur psychologist, I'd say men in sport need to be secure within themselves before they accept women. Otherwise, there's a sense that they want to isolate you or alienate you. They try to be hurtful, like they're trying to break you."[487]

The male establishment still finds the idea laughable of women competing with men in Olympic events such as swimming and track field. It will simply never happen, they insist, and point to statistics that show women's times as consistently slower than men's; the world record in the women's 100-metre race is 10.49 seconds, for example, compared to 9.84 seconds held by men. But there is another set of statistics that, given the barriers thrown in women's way throughout history, reveals far more. The performance of female athletes is improving much more rapidly than that of males. One of many examples: in 15 swimming events, the difference between men's and women's records was 12.41 percent in 1936, 11.36 percent in 1956, 9.27 percent in 1976 and in 1980, in the 400-metre crawl, 5.2 percent.[488]

Baron Pierre de Coubertin, the founder of the modern Olympics, fought for 30 years to exclude women from the Games. Athletic women, he said, were against the laws of nature and "the most unaesthetic sight human eyes could contemplate." The Olympic Games must remain the exclusive preserve of men, for "solemn and periodic exaltation of male athleticism." The reward for these superior male athletes, he said, would be female applause.[489] One feels he would have been disgusted by the sight of Geraldine Heaney at the 1998 Winter Olympics, dressed in pads, gloves and helmet, skating down centre ice, out-manoeuvring an opponent and then, with a bullet-fast shot, scoring a winning goal.

Lynne

We were attracted to her like grey moths to a golden flame. She was the Queen of the Mood Indigo Ball, the biggest money-maker at the Slave Girl Auction, the epicentre of the most popular clique in the school. Tall, slender, a brunette with violet-blue eyes and perfectly symmetrical, Anglo-Saxon features, she reminded us all of the movie star Leslie Caron. Yet she was not what, in later years, would be disparagingly called a Barbie Doll.

There was a charming insouciance about Lynne Campbell, an unaffectedness, a sense of fun. One of her front teeth was darker than the others, a yellowish-brown colour, the result of being hit in the face with a puck while she was playing hockey. This defect drove her admirers wild, and they would suggest this or that dentist, but she flatly refused to have the tooth repaired, as though she realized it marked her with a certain individuality. At any particular moment, Lynne was, and remains, entirely happy with herself, where she is, what she is doing, the people she is with—the result, she believes, of a near-utopian childhood.

Not much is known about the Campbell side of the family. When Lynne's father Leslie was only nine, his mother died of a brain tumour and his father disappeared. Leslie and his brother Graham, two years younger, were brought up mostly by their grandparents, who lived in a grand house on Glen Manor Drive in Toronto's Beaches area. Only a few blocks away, on Elmer Avenue, sat the semi-detached, somewhat ramshackle home of the Macklems. Mr. Macklem was in the shoe business, and drove around his large territory from one Dack outlet to another. It provided an income, although only a modest one, for his family of eight boisterous children. Their house was small—various sons slept in the back sunroom/porch— but the kitchen was huge and there was always a crowd around the dining-room table. The middle girl, Bernice, was pretty, although rather shy and retiring compared to her fun-loving sisters. The first time Leslie Campbell, who was used to his grandparents' well-organized, sedate household, came to court Bernice, he was confronted by pandemonium and the family's pet squirrel sitting beside him on couch. Leslie and Bernice were married in

1938, and four years later, their first child Marjorie Lynne was born.

Leslie Campbell joined the Royal Canadian Air Force and was sent to Brandon, Manitoba, to be trained as a navigator for bombers, although he never did see active service; the war ended just as he was about to be shipped overseas. Bernice's closeness to her family helped her endure the loneliness of the war. At that point, Lynne was the only grandchild, and the Macklem family sang to her and cooed at her. When her Aunt Joan, only 11 years older, taught her how to ride a bike, the relatives rushed out to buy Lynne her own bicycle. She was the apple of her paternal grandfather's eye, as well, and he also lived nearby. Her world, she admits, was her oyster from a very young age.

After Leslie returned from the war, he got a job as a lithographer and photo-engraver for the Sears department store catalogue. In 1948, he and Bernice found a strange, old house called Robin Woods, built by an eccentric chemist as a replica of his family home in England. It had black-timber beams, leaded windows and hammered-copper chandeliers. The Campbells transformed it into a charming family home, all the while retaining its quirky character.

It was located on Chine Drive, which snaked along the edge of the wooded St. Augustine Seminary until it reached Scarborough Bluffs Park. The south end of the street was a tightly-knit neighbourhood with an amazing number of artists and intellectuals. There were communal barbecues in the summer and potlucks in the winter, fireworks displays, New Year's parties and athletic competitions. Lynne spent her childhood summers playing badminton and croquet, and in the winter, skating rinks were created. Best of all was tobogganing, often with the monks and priests of the nearby seminary joining in. The seminary was still a working farm, and summers were spent playing in the wheat fields and occasionally patting the horses. It was altogether, says Lynne, a childhood Valhalla.

Her home life was just as blissful. A friend of Lynne's brother once said you could die of terminal kindness in the hands of her parents. They were the type of people who would quietly help you out and never expect anything in return. Lynne thinks that perhaps her mother and father were too good-hearted.

She and her two younger brothers were coddled. Their parents were always solicitous, always worried about whether the children were hungry or thirsty or comfortable. Nothing much was required of them, maybe a few dishes washed now and then or some yard work. Lynne floated along, quite happy to be adored by one and all. At school, she was bright enough, but was never challenged, never truly exerted herself. At the Campbell house, it was always, "You've been studying too hard. Come down and have some cocoa."

By the time she got to R. H. King Collegiate, she was already an integral part of the social scene. Of course, she became a cheerleader. She was so popular and good-looking that her cousin went into business selling her telephone number to infatuated classmates.

Even though she did almost no homework, Lynne managed to get by, never achieving great grades but not failing either. She floated along, often faking it, the teachers smitten by the smile and the happy-go-lucky charm. However, as the Grade 13 final exams approached, Lynne realized she was in serious trouble. Her best friend Louise Zurosky tried to rescue her. The two girls got up at seven in the morning, did their exercises and started working. A strict schedule was maintained: study blocks of two hours, followed by quizzes. Lynne loved it, loved the discipline and the sense of achievement, but it was too little, too late.

The five subjects she studied under Louise's strict regime she passed with flying colours, the other four she flunked. It meant another year at high school but, in reality, it didn't bother her too much. The consequences were never very dire for a golden girl like that. In fact, it was in trigonometry class during her repeat year that she met her future husband.

She had always felt comfortable around guys. There were so many in the Chine Drive neighbourhood and so few girls. She was always throwing footballs around with them, climbing trees, racing up the bluffs. She also realized very early the power she had over boys—she was always the first up to bat—but she became adept at warding off any advances. "Just forget it—back off," she'd say.

At first glance, Roger Bywater didn't seem to be her type. He was good-looking enough—tall, lanky, blond—but also very serious and hard-working, a super-brainer. While Lynne was taking six years to complete the regular five, he was doing it all in four. Lynne took one look at him and, even though he was two years younger than she and not that sophisticated, decided he might be interesting. She phoned to ask him to the Sadie Hawkins dance that year. He already had a date and refused, but when he put the telephone down, he thought, "What's going on here?" The most beautiful girl in the school at the centre of the most popular clique was after him, a social dud. He quickly phoned her back.

Roger and Lynne were immediately smitten with one another; the chemistry was powerful. "We were pretty hot and heavy right from the first day," says Roger. "We spent a lot of time melted together in the driveway." Lynne made it clear, though, that she was not ready to settle down. She had worked in the summers and on weekends supervising children's sports and gym activities for Scarborough's Parks and Recreation Department. She was very good at it—one year, her volleyball group won the Scarborough championship—so she naturally thought of teaching as a career.

Her year at teacher's college was enjoyable. She made good friends and, although she wasn't named the queen of the ball, she was the first runner-up. She also worked hard, standing near the top of her class, and at graduation, she had three job offers.

In the fall of 1963, she began teaching Grade 2 at the newly built Bendale Public School, located in one of the mushrooming, new Scarborough subdivisions. There were 42 children in classrooms designed for 30. She says what she and her colleagues did was simply try to survive. It helped that the young teachers were full of enthusiasm, and they tried out all sorts of original ideas. Lynne evolved two principles that have remained at the heart of her teaching philosophy: troubled or naughty kids can be turned around if they are reached before age eight, and the only way to achieve this is by having fun in the class.

Meanwhile, and not surprisingly, her social life was booming. She started dating the scion of a wealthy Montreal family that owned cement and heavy-construction companies. She was taken to the best restaurants, flown around in private planes, vacationed at the family's summer place at Shediac, New Brunswick. In 1964, Lynne became engaged and, to the delight of her parents, her future in high society seemed assured. Sometimes, though, she would run into Roger, and both were surprised to find the chemistry still bubbling away.

Roger had, in fact, devised an amazingly calculated plan for so young a man. He knew three weeks after he had first dated Lynne that he wanted to marry her, but he realized he couldn't compete with the wealthy guy she was dating. Roger had no money and no immediate prospects. "I knew I had to get my ticket. I couldn't get distracted from that." Roger's ticket was a degree in electrical engineering. A year before he graduated from the University of Toronto—when real prospects were in sight—he cleaned out his bank account and, on the first day of spring, he sent Lynne 13 yellow roses. Roger said, "It's time we got together," and Lynne, even though she had been engaged for two years, agreed.

She had a terrible time extricating herself—her fiancé and his family were hurt and angry—but once that was accomplished, she and Roger couldn't wait to be married. Lynne says it was the only time in her life her mild-mannered parents rebelled. They were shocked when suddenly, Roger was back on the scene, and they persuaded their daughter to hold off for a year. It did nothing to dampen either Lynne's or Roger's ardour.

In June 1967, they were married in a lovely ceremony at St. Paul's United Church, with the reception at the Cedarbrae Golf and Country Club. Everything about the ceremony expressed Lynne's appreciation of beauty: flowers from her parents' garden, a cake she had designed herself, an exquisite wedding dress she had made herself.

The early days of marriage, though, were a rude awakening. Roger had a year left at university, so they had to live on her salary of $3,800 a year. It was the first time in her life she had wanted for anything. Hamburgers were the big meal, with fried onions. Roger did nothing but study. Once he graduated, he readily found a job with Imperial Oil, the company where he spent the rest of his professional life. By 1971, he and Lynne had their first house, an old and charming cottage in the Beaches area. They renovated most of it themselves. When it was sold four years later, they made a handsome profit. Like others of their generation, it was their first major step up the financial ladder.

In December 1971, their daughter Alicia was born. Until that time, Lynne had enjoyed great success as a teacher. She had been selected chairman of the primary division of her school and earmarked for major promotion. Once her child was born, however, she didn't hesitate to become a full-time mother. So sure was she that she'd never go back to work, she cashed in her pension and insurance plans, using the money to buy a washer and dryer. The change was not nearly as easy as she had anticipated. She had always earned more than Roger. Now, after nine years, there was no monthly pay cheque of her own. "I had to learn to be dependent," she says. "I had to force myself to get used to it."

In May 1974, she gave birth to their son Christopher. He was a breech delivery and moreover, he weighed a hefty ten pounds. The doctors noticed something wrong right away—the infant's body was shaped like a kind of V—and diagnosed dysplasia (abnormal development) of the hips, an uncommon and dangerous condition. Eventually, both of Lynne's daughters, Alicia and Sarah, who was born in 1977, developed scoliosis (curvature of the spine), Alicia more seriously than Sarah. Lynne now believes her womb is structurally small for babies of such a large size, and the fetuses weren't able to move properly. Jammed in one position, they developed abnormally.

The prognosis for Christopher was unclear. Years of hospital stays, dangerous medication and painful treatments lay ahead, the one cloud that had darkened Lynne's otherwise golden life. She was determined to cope, though, and was just getting used to the routine of caring for the baby when another bombshell fell. Roger announced he was being transferred to Imperial Oil's office in Calgary.

When she boarded the plane on Halloween 1974, Lynne was in tears. For the first time, she was leaving her family and the beloved childhood neighbourhood that was still part of her life. The house on which she had worked so hard had been sold. In her arms was a six-month-old encased in a body cast from his armpits to his ankles. She herself had pneumonia. On top of all that, Lynne didn't much like Calgary or the West. Toronto was French restaurants, Asian boutiques, East Indian food stores. Calgary was a WASP stronghold that closed down after work and where the social highlight was dining at Hy's Steak House. Lynne felt isolated on the prairies, and was shocked by her first "monochromatic Fall."

To make matters even bleaker, Christopher was a constant worry. When, at a year old, his cast was removed, he had to endure a body brace for six months, as well as painful sessions in traction. Finally, though, he was declared free of any handicap. By the time he was six, he was skiing down Whistler Mountain.

Once Christopher was out of danger, life in Calgary seemed far more pleasant. Lynne grew to love skiing, understood what a Rocky Mountain high is about, came to appreciate the incredible, indomitable landscape. This aesthetic sense was developed when she took classes and workshops in pottery, stained glass and weaving. She began to create beautiful and practical handicrafts. It was difficult to lug Chris about when he was in his body cast, so Lynne created a sling made out of canvas and snaps. She believes it was the forerunner of the baby carriers that became so popular; her husband thinks if she had only patented the idea, they'd be truly wealthy. She also made hand puppets and a line of plush, pastel cushions called Pillow Pals, decorated with huge eyes. At first, she gave them away to friends as gifts, but later, she began to sell them on consignment at a Calgary co-op and a

Toronto boutique. They were very popular. "Fisher Price finally figured out what I was doing and mass-produced them," she laughs.

Roger would say to her, "You've got so many great ideas. Why don't you market them better?" But being entrepreneurial and taking risks was not part of her makeup. She says she only has what she calls a "sparkle brain." It's an attitude that frustrates her husband. "If I was home and had this platform to work from—time, a car and a phone in the car—I would be creating a real business," he says. However, Lynne's artistic expression and her amazing energy have gone into raising her children, and Roger concedes she is a super mother. Her youngest says she can't remember the television ever being on when she was a child. There was drawing and making up stories and painting pictures to go with them, and playing make-believe with the toys Lynne had made.

Lynne was sympathetic to the women's movement as it developed during the 1970s and admired what it was trying to accomplish, but she also resented the idea that became predominant at the time: women working in the home were somehow second-class citizens. "You had to be a really strong person to resist the pressure *not* to go back to work," she says.

In 1980, Roger was transferred back to Toronto. He and Lynne spent a week with real-estate agents, searching for exactly the right home. They finally settled for a two-storey back-split, nestled in a densely wooded area and with a view of Lake Ontario, not far from, and not unlike, the Cline Drive neighbourhood in which Lynne had grown up. She and Roger immediately set to work renovating and decorating, creating a haven of beauty. Gardening has become a passion for her, another expression of her artistic sensitivity.

Eventually, though, Lynne found staying home lonely, and in 1983, she began supply teaching, filling in when a teacher was absent. By 1988, she was working full time. She teaches Grades 2 or 3, the age group she likes the most, at Knob Hill Public School. The children are mostly from immigrant, low-income families, and are sometimes very deprived. One of her biggest challenges is fighting against the all-pervasive influence of television, which, in some of her students' homes, is never turned off. She is always steering her students towards the play trunk, hoping some toy will tweak their imaginations and their ability to visualize for themselves will come back. She says, "I tell them that whatever line they put on paper is beautiful, that they can write beautiful things, that they are beautiful in themselves." It's the motif that has threaded its way through her life.

Her own children have grown up good-looking and accomplished, and adore their mother. In her mid-fifties, Lynne remains physically attractive, her unique aesthetic sense evident in her jewellery and clothes, but there is still that whimsical, live-for-the-moment quality about her. "I look at things just for the beauty in them, whether it's a rock or a gorgeous model with superb bone structure or a baby's fat face," she says. In this sentiment are heard echoes of a childhood full of sunlight and loveliness, and the golden girl who lived a charmed existence.

Beauty

Physical beauty is only skin deep. If men could see beneath the skin, the sight of women would make them nauseous.

Odo, abbot of Cluny, tenth century

I desired to be tall, stately, and finely developed in figure; I felt it a misfortune that I was so little, so pale, and had features so irregular.

Jane Eyre in Charlotte Brontë's *Jane Eyre*, 1847

[A woman] is never quite satisfied, and never secure, for desperate, unending absorption in the drive for a perfect appearance—call it feminine vanity—is the ultimate restriction on freedom of mind.

Susan Brownmiller, *Femininity*, 1984

My mother, who rarely went to movies, was taken by a friend to see *The Prince and the Showgirl*. All she could talk about afterwards was how Marilyn Monroe had *not* worn a girdle: you could actually see her stomach bulging a little in her skin-tight dress. This, my mother thought, showed how natural, how unaffected she was. In fact, the pre-eminent 1950s sex goddess was as wholesome as a triple martini.

During my teenage years, the ideal of feminine beauty was manifested in a movie star who wore dresses so tight, you could see the slit in her behind, whose lips were always puckering like a baby's and who talked in a silly, little-girl voice. Her nose and chin had been chiselled to perfection by the plastic surgeon's knife, her teeth straightened, her hair bleached until it looked like candy floss, her skin heavily painted with foundation makeup until it achieved the golden glow everyone raved about. Her lips were made ruby red with layers of lipstick and her so-called mesmerizing eyes were heavy with eyebrow pencil, eyeliner, eye shadow and great dollops of mascara. When, in Grade 11, I was taken by a date to see *Some Like It Hot*, my cheeks burned with embarrassment. An empty-headed blonde who talked like a prattling infant was not my idea of a role model, even if she were supposed to be every male's ultimate sex fantasy.

When, in 1962, Monroe committed suicide, I couldn't bring myself to even feel sorry for her. With what amazement, then, did I greet the unsavoury phenomenon of my teenage daughter worshipping the blonde bombshell 30 years after her death. By then Marilyn had metamorphosed into something other than a sexy movie star. She had become a mythical figure on a par with Helen or Aphrodite. Her films had little to do with this transformation; girls my daughter's age watched few of them, and those they did see, they considered satirical—Marilyn mocking the uncontrollable male libido. To them, she was an underprivileged, sexually abused orphan who had fought her way to fame and glory. Her tragic end? She was lucky to have died so young—she would remain forever beautiful. She was not a victim of the patriarchy—that would have demeaned her—just a girl who had used her God-given assets to get whatever she could. What could be more natural?

I

The power, the danger and the seductiveness of female beauty is nowhere more wonderfully expressed than in the story of Helen, whose face "launched a thousand ships." The most beautiful woman in the world was supposedly human, yet her father was said to be none other than the mighty Zeus, who one night formed himself into a giant swan and raped Helen's mother Leda. (Helen also had an earthly stepfather, Tyndareus, Leda's husband.) Just as she reached puberty, the lovely young girl was kidnapped by Theseus, the king of Athens. He was a randy old goat. His one remaining desire was to mate with a daughter of Zeus, and gorgeous Helen nicely fit the bill. That she was only 12 years old didn't bother him; he raped her.

Eventually, Helen was rescued by her brothers and returned to Sparta. An army of suitors, most from distinguished, rich families, some of them famous war heroes, immediately began swarming about her. Helen's stepfather Tyndareus finally insisted the young men must swear on oath: once the choice was made, they were not to fight among themselves or with him. Further, they were to pledge to defend the security of the marriage in the future.

Once these oaths were taken, Tyndareus promptly chose the powerful and wealthy Menelaus, who would soon become king of Sparta. Despite his stellar credentials, he was more prosaic than he was handsome or exciting, but

Helen had a daughter by him and their union seemed happy enough, if not exactly passionate.

A few years after the royal marriage, Sparta was ravaged by a plague. An oracle advised Menelaus to travel to the city state of Troy and perform sacrificial rites. There he met an old friend Paris, son of the king of Troy.

Considered among the most beautiful of ancient Greece's beautiful boys, Paris had led a pretty eventful life. At the time of his birth, an oracle had predicted—accurately as it turned out—that he would be the ruin of Troy. His worried father ordered that he be left to die on a hillside, but he was found by a king's shepherd, who brought him up as one of his own. While Paris was tending his flock one day, the mighty goddesses Hera, Athena and Aphrodite approached him and demanded he judge whom among them was the most beautiful. Each tried to bribe him: Hera promised him Europe and Asia, Athena said he could lead Troy in victory against the Greeks, and Aphrodite, who knew men better than anyone, offered to deliver up to him the most beautiful woman in the world, Helen. Naturally, being the lustful young man he was, he accepted Aphrodite's offer.

At the time he met Menelaus in Troy, Paris was in trouble, having killed a friend in an athletic contest, and the Spartan king kindly invited him to seek refuge in his household until the scandal blew over. The two arrived together, but almost immediately, Menelaus left to attend a funeral in Crete. Gorgeous Helen was left alone to entertain Paris, who was not only handsome but, having been tutored by Aphrodite, charming and possessed elegant manners. Thanks to the goddess who was pulling the strings, the two fell madly in love. They ran away together—according to some reports, not before Paris had plundered Sparta's treasury.

The couple finally arrived in Troy, where they were greeted by an excited citizenry who thought Helen even more beautiful than they had imagined and immediately adopted her as one of their own. Back in Greece, all those suitors who had taken an oath to defend Helen's marriage to Menelaus were marshalling their troops. What followed was the Greeks' famous ten-year siege of Troy.

By the ninth year of the war, both sides were sick at heart at the devastation to their ranks. Paris finally challenged Menelaus to a duel; as Homer puts it in his *Iliad*, "for Helen and the Spartan gold./Whoever gets the upper hand in this/shall take the treasure and the woman home;/let the rest part as friends."[490] The Trojan elders, watching Helen climb up the ramparts to observe the battle, lament:

> 'We cannot rage at her, it is no wonder
> that Trojans and Akhaians [Greeks] under arms
> should for so long have borne the pains of war
> for one like this.'
> 'Unearthliness. A goddess
> the woman is to look at.'[491]

This, in a nutshell, expresses the age-old male dilemma. Beauty such as Helen's is an omnipotent force, an uncontrollable law unto itself. Neither she nor anyone else can be blamed for the catastrophe that has overtaken them.

The duel between Paris and Menelaus is inconclusive; the Greek is the superior fighter, but Aphrodite, seeing her beloved boy in trouble, sweeps Paris to safety enveloped in a cloud. Not long afterwards, the city gates are swung open by gullible Trojans to admit a huge wooden horse. The Greeks win, but only by deceit. Troy is sacked and Paris is killed.

In the burning wreckage of the city, victorious Menelaus frantically searches for his ex-wife, wanting to kill her in revenge for her adultery, but when he finally finds Helen, her breasts are bare (purposely we're told) and, after 20 years, when even a daughter of Zeus might well have developed a wrinkle or two, her beauty is utterly divine. Faced with this spectacle, Menelaus's anger evaporates and the two are reconciled.

After eight years and many misadventures, Helen and Menelaus arrive safely home in Sparta, where they happily take up married life. Herein lies the central irony. Helen was neither slaughtered nor enslaved, as many of the Trojan women were. The individual who had caused so much suffering for so many people lived happily ever after. Her beauty is her protector and her fortune.

Over the centuries, Helen has been blamed for the defeat of Troy, and portrayed variously as cold and unrepentant, a woman above the suffering of ordinary people. Homer's *Iliad* paints quite a different picture. To Priam, her father-in-law, whom she loves dearly, she says:

> Painful death
> would have been sweeter for me, on that day
> I joined your son, and left my bridal chamber,

my brothers, my grown child, my childhood friends!
But no death came, though I have pined and wept.[492]

These are hardly the words of an unfeeling, insensitive woman. Helen comes to understand why Zeus has inflicted such an "evil fate" on herself and Paris, "our portion, all of misery, given by Zeus/that we may live in song for men to come." In other words, the consequence of great and seductive beauty will be argued forever throughout history, a prophecy that has proved true.

The heroic poems attributed to Homer, such as *The Iliad* and *The Odyssey*, were probably composed in the eighth century BC, but the events they depict occurred four centuries before. By the Classical period (c. 500–300 BC), attitudes towards women were more negative, and this is reflected in the interpretations of Helen and the siege of Troy. Historians found it unbelievable—and unacceptable—that a long war should have been fought over a mere female, even if she were the most beautiful woman in the world. That a marriage could have such political and economic repercussions was ridiculous. Herodotus, writing in the fifth century BC, suggested Helen wasn't even in Troy at the time of the war but had fled to Egypt. Thucydides, in the same period, dismissed the importance of Helen and her beauty altogether. The Greeks fought the Trojans, he said, to extend their military might over all of the eastern Mediterranean world.[493] As well as the historical writings, almost all the literature written in the Classical period denigrates Helen whenever she is mentioned, which is often.

The status of women was lower during this period than centuries before. Women in classical Greece were sequestered, not permitted a role in civil society and often cast aside in favour of the sexual enjoyment of either young boys or prostitutes. It was as though the male establishment had grown more leery of the seductiveness of female beauty. By denigrating women, they could control the power their beauty held over them—or so they thought.

II

From the early Middle Ages on, feminine beauty was the bane of male theologians. Many of them were deeply misogynist and they were terrified of the power a woman's charm had to undermine their ideal of celibacy. Beauty was the deadliest of traps to those who were determined to renounce the flesh. In his *On the Apparel of Women*, Tertullian wrote in the second century, "No one of you at all, best beloved sisters ... [should desire] too ostentatious a style of dress; rather, you [should] go about in humble garb and affect meanness of appearance, walking about as Eve mourning and repentant.... Do you not know that you are Eve?"[494]

Like most medieval philosophies involving women, the period's concept of beauty had its roots in the story of Adam and Eve. Once the original couple was thrown out of the Garden of Eden, their sinfulness was forever signified by the fact that they now had to wear clothing. They who had been created in the image of God must cover their shame with the skins of beasts. The complex connection between dress and sin was explained thus by an English preacher:

At first a tunic of skins was fashioned for the naked body, in token that through his sin man was become like the beasts which by nature are clad in raiment of skins alone. But later, as their pride grew, men used garments made of wool. Third, through much more ample nourishing of carnal delight, they used garments made from plants of the earth, namely of linen, and fourth silken garments which are fashioned from the entrails of worms—all of which kinds of raiment are now rather for vainglory and worldly pomp than for the necessity of nature ... and assuredly most of all to excite lust.[495]

Eve and her daughters were most at fault, since it was they who were the temptresses of Adam and his sons. Even the old snake was portrayed as a beauteous young woman with blonde hair, blue eyes and curling eyelashes. Eve's beauty, concluded the rhetoricians, was the most powerful weapon of temptation the devil hoarded in his arsenal.

The descendants of Eve were by nature flighty and insincere, preoccupied with their looks rather than their souls. As historian Carla Casagrande writes, as far as the social critics of the time were concerned,

A sumptuously dressed and ornamented woman subverted God's will by privileging the cheap exterior of her body over and above her precious inner spirit. The enjoyment of an item of clothing, a color, or a hairstyle betrayed too much interest in external features, and too little for the loving cultivation of her virtues.... To contest the looks endowed by God—worse to try to improve them [especially by makeup and wigs]—was sheer pride, an unforgivable attempt to defy the God-given laws of the world."[496]

James of Vitry, after watching a young girl primp before a mirror, frothed, "Her body is still home, but in God's eyes she is already in a brothel, trussed up like a whore preparing to ensnare the souls of men.[497]

Paradoxically, the more the sermonizers preached against ephemeral beauty, the more elaborate clothing became, especially as the wealth of the Renaissance grew. When visiting outside their homes, upper-class women of the High Middle Ages dressed in exquisite gowns layered with gold and silver thread, pearls or lace. They wore jewellery and furs, makeup and wigs.

By the 15th century, the farthingale had become all the rage. These were hoop-like frames worn underneath the skirt that kept the yards and yards of material swooping and swaying. (The clerics hated these garments because improper pregnancies could be hidden under them.) The effect was accentuated by chopines, unbelievably high platform shoes made of leather, wood or cork on which fashion plates hobbled about, barely able to walk.

It wasn't just women who were caught up in the fashion craze. Men were even more elaborately decked out, with large, billowing sleeves, flowing cloaks, velvets, satins and silks, furs and chunky jewellery. Their robes became increasingly short to show off muscular legs, and the infamous codpiece was invented; it would become ever more fancy and prominent. Indeed, the sumptuary laws designed to curb the worst excesses of extravagant fashion were aimed as much at men as women. However, by the end of the period, the concept of women as slaves to fashion's dictates, as creatures who thought of nothing but the clothes on their backs—an idea that lives with us still—had become embodied in the collective psyche. A fashion writer in France during the reign of Louis XIII (1601–1643) put it succinctly: "Fashion is a Disease of women, whereas it is merely a passion of men. We esteem ways that are in vogue, but they idolize them."[498]

The clerics, meanwhile, had never stopped hammering away at that deadly sin, female vanity. It was the irrepressible Wife of Bath who put the never-ending sermons, castigation and ridicule aimed at women by neurotic Medieval males in perspective. One would hope a lot of her sex felt as she did:

> And when a woman tries a mild display
> In dress or costly ornament, you say
> It is a danger to her chastity,
> And then, bad luck to you, start making free
> With Bible tags in the Apostle's name;
> 'And in like manner, chastely and with shame,
> You women should adorn yourselves,' said he,
> 'And not with braided hair or jewellery

With pearl or golden ornament.' What next!
I'll pay as much attention to your text
And rubric in such things as would a gnat.[499]

III

In an official portrait of Elizabeth I by an unknown artist, painted around
1590 or 1600, the queen is already in late middle age, but she looks as majestic and divine as ever. Her clothing is sumptuous: a gown of plush, cardinal-
red velvet with great, puffy sleeves, a cloak lined with ermine, a ruffed collar
of the most delicate lace, an exquisite gold crown encased with jewels. Pearls,
the symbol of her majesty's virginity and virtue, are dotted everywhere on
her costume: a double strand of the chunky variety around her neck; her hair
is decorated with these ethereal studs; the collar that encircles her shoulders
is heavily encased with pearls, as well as with rubies and emeralds. Although
her expression is rather pensive and worried, her profile has all the attributes
of the epoch's ideal of comeliness: the small, cupid-bow mouth, the long,
slender nose, the severely plucked eyebrows, the high, domed forehead, the
golden-red, curly hair. She is the ultimate thoroughbred.

In the early-modern age, a woman's appearance was more than a form of
self-expression; it was a strict and precise code signalling everything about her
identity and destiny. Most of all, it revealed her position in society: The
costumes of aristocrats like Queen Elizabeth resembled a peasant's as much as
a peacock did a grub.

By the end of the 16th century, perfumed powders of various tints had
become an important ingredient of the daily toilette of every patrician, male
or female. It partly had to do with the period's disdain for bathing. Water was
considered life-threatening, the carrier of such diseases as syphilis and the
terrifying plague. The soap-and-water bath all but disappeared, at least among
the upper classes, replaced by ghostly white powder that, it was thought,
could mask the most obnoxious of body odours. By the 18th century, young
and old alike sported bouffant, silver-white locks, either their own powdered
variety or dusted wigs. Historian Sara F. Matthews Grieco comments: "An
absence of powder came to signal not only a dual impropriety (hygienic and
social) but also social inferiority: it was the bourgeois and their inferiors who
had 'black and greasy hair.'"[500]

Perfumes were thought not only to aid powder in concealing the smells of
an unwashed body but also to ward off infectious vapours and contagious mias-

mata. One's scent was also a sign of one's social standing. In 1709, a French chemist working on behalf of the king devised three categories of perfumes: *parfum royal, parfum pour les bourgeois* and *parfum des pauvres*. This last was hardly a come-on; made of oil and soot, its one purpose was to disinfect the air.[501]

Another sign of good breeding was linen, which, as the period progressed, began to appear everywhere: elaborate ruffs around the neck, fancy collars, cuffs and eventually, shawls that covered necks and shoulders. Since it represented the purity (although perhaps not the cleanliness) of the skin underneath, it had to be immaculately white. As Matthews Grieco points out, the craving for pristine body linen increased in direct proportion to the disdain for soap and water. By the 17th century, a daily change of shirt or chemise was considered de rigueur by the upper classes. They were the only ones who could afford such luxury. Students, artisans and workers wore shirts made out of hemp, housewives put on skirts of grey or beige burlap. A hemp doublet cost about a quarter of a linen garment, but was still the equivalent of three or four days' wages for an ordinary labourer.[502]

Dress of the early modern period codified a person's identity in another essential aspect: gender. This was an epoch when sexual dichotomies were rigidly fixed. Baldassare Castiglione in *The Book of the Courtier* (1528) expressed a common view: "I hold that woman should in no way resemble a man in her ways, manners, words, gestures and bearing. Thus just as it is very fitting that a man should display a certain robust and sturdy manliness, so it is well for a woman to have a certain soft and delicate tenderness, with an air of feminine sweetness in her every movement."[503]

Fashion served this sentiment well. Gone was the preference for unsweetened, acid or sour sauces that had resulted in the slim-hipped, small-breasted elegance of the Middle Ages. Women from the 16th to 18th centuries developed a taste for butter, cream and sweets. Plumpness became fashionable; thinness was regarded as ugly, a sign of ill-health and poverty. The neck and hands had to be long and slender, though, the feet small and the breasts, "the two beautiful globes," round and firm. Busks—stiffening material made of wood, metal or whalebone—were sewn under gowns to make skirts appear even more voluminous and waists smaller. By the 18th century, constricting corsets with whalebone stays had become all the rage. Breasts were almost or entirely exposed, the nipples made rosy with the help of rouge. Skin had to be luminously pale, white being associated with chastity, purity and femininity (helped, of course, by powder).

A woman's true glory, however, was her hair, thick, wavy and above all, blonde. The period's passion for blondes was extraordinary. Dark hair, it was thought, meant a taciturn disposition; by contrast, light hair signalled a sunny, happy nature. Italian women spent hour upon hour attempting to bleach their brown-black hair. The juice of lemons and rhubarb, along with concoctions of sulphur or saffron, was also thought to produce golden locks. "In all the peninsula cannot be found one brunette" was a common saying.[504]

But what marked the era's fashion more than anything else was the use of makeup, partly a result of having to hide the scarring of smallpox. Foundation paint, powder, rouge, creams and mascara became all the rage. A 16th-century Italian preacher complained that all his female parishioners painted themselves, "even the dishwashers."[505] Women of all classes spent hours concocting formulas for various tinctures; recipes were passed around among friends like hotcakes. Ground-up pearls, silver and precious stones, earthworms, nettles and blood were some of the ingredients.[506] Strong and often dangerous chemicals such as the sublimate of mercury were used. A 16th-century tract insisted some of these concoctions were corrosive, "so that simple women thinking to grow more beautiful, become disfigured, hastening olde age before the time, and giving occasion to their husbandes to seeke strangers insteede of their wives, with divers other inconveniences."[507]

Most women, of course, were not born beautiful, but it was up to them to repair or hide those defects that so offended the male sensibility. In *Epicene* (1609), Ben Jonson gave the following now-infamous and idiotic advice:

If she be short, let her sit much, lest, when she stands, she be thought to sit. If she have an ill foot, let her wear her gown the longer, and her shoe the thinner. If a fat hand, and scald nails, let her carve the less, and act in gloves. If a sour breath, let her never discourse fasting, and always talk at her distance. If she had lack and rugged teeth, let her offer the less at laughter, especially if she laugh wide and open.[508]

By the 17th century, beauty was no longer considered evil or dangerous, as it had been in the Middle Ages. In fact, quite the opposite philosophy had emerged. A woman handsomely endowed must possess a virtuous soul, an amiable character, a natural grace. To be ugly was not only to hold an inferior place in society but to be full of vice. British playwright John Ford put it succinctly in his 1633 play *'Tis Pity She's a Whore*. "So, where the body's furniture is beauty/The mind's must needs be virtue." If you had straight, dark hair, a hooked nose or a sallow complexion, if you were too thin, too tall or, worst of all, poor, you might as well not exist.

There was another face to the beauty coin. Women became accomplished at using their looks as a tool to get what they wanted, either in the home or society at large. Coquetry reigned supreme. As historian Véronique Nahoum-Grappe puts it, "When a woman succeeded in captivating a man's attention, she could propose her own views and assert her own way of being in and thinking about the world."[509]

Suddenly, in the middle of the 18th century, fashion changed. Partly as a reaction to the extremes to which the use of makeup had been put—masks of paint were applied so thickly, the wearer was prevented from smiling, talking or even turning her head—the craze for artifice suddenly disappeared, replaced by a taste for the natural look. Grace, simplicity and wholesomeness became all the rage. Soap and water made a comeback as part of the daily toilette, which meant a new appreciation of freshness. Smallpox had, to some extent, been checked, so disfigured complexions were not as common, but most important, with the Enlightenment came the idea that beauty was indeed only skin deep. There might be something more to a woman than the way she looked.

This new attitude is nicely reflected in the 1796 novel *Camilla* by British writer Fanny Burney. It is the story of a poor but honest Anglican minister and his comely daughters. Rev. Tyrold's older brother, a baronet and heir to the family's fortune, moves to an estate nearby. Sir Hugh is guardian to his niece Indiana, who lives with him, but it is Camilla, Rev. Tyrold's eldest daughter, with her happy and vibrant personality, whom he comes to truly adore. The plot weaves around three young women: the insipid Indiana, Camilla and Camilla's sister Eugenia, who is by far the most interesting and intelligent of the characters.

There is much talk in the book about which of the three girls is the most beautiful. They are all lovely in their own way, although Eugenia is judged by many as the prettiest. That changes when Sir Hugh, in his good-hearted but stupid way, begins to meddle. On an outing, Sir Hugh ignores Mrs. Tyrold's warning and allows Eugenia to wander off. She soon calls out the dreaded words, "Little boy, what's the matter with your face, little boy?" Eugenia comes down with smallpox, and while she survives, her face is horribly disfigured. To make matters worse, during that same outing, Sir Hugh carelessly allows her to fall off a plank, with the result that she becomes partially crippled as well. The old uncle is so horrified at what he has wrought, he tries to make amends by changing his will and leaving his fortune to Eugenia.

A strict covenant is undertaken by the Tyrold family: the young girl's physical disfigurement must never be mentioned. She grows up not knowing that the outside world considers her repulsive. Reality intrudes in two heartbreaking incidents. In a rather ridiculous twist of the plot, she and Camilla, along with an ineffectual escort Mr. Dubster, are stranded on the top floor of a cottage under renovation and are forced to call out for help. Eugenia looks out the window and a boy yells out, "What are you up there for, Miss? To frighten the crows?" The farm women then hurl insults at her. "Miss may go to market with her beauty; she'll not want for nothing if she'll shew her pretty face!" Realizing for the first time how truly ugly she is considered, Eugenia faints.

The second sad incident involves Sir Hugh's nephew Clermont Lynmere, Indiana's brother, who has been studying abroad. Sir Hugh has selected him as Eugenia's future husband and, wanting the marriage to take place before he dies, summons the young man to his estate. On his arrival, Clermont unexpectedly encounters Eugenia in the garden, and, having never met her before, assumes that since she is so plain, she must be a servant. His meanspirited sister Indiana confirms his opinion of the once-beautiful Eugenia: "I'm sure I think she's the ugliest little fright, poor thing! I never saw in the world, poor thing! Such a little, short dumpty, hump backed, crooked, limping figure of a fright ... poor thing!"

Not surprisingly, Clermont rejects Eugenia as a wife. Since he is so loathsome—a fop, vain and arrogant—it is a great relief to all, but nevertheless, the young woman has endured yet another deep humiliation. She tells her father, who is trying to comfort her, "Can you, indeed when once her eyes are opened, can you expect to reconcile to existence a poor young creature who sees herself an object of derision and disgust? Who, without committing any crime, without offending any human being, finds she cannot appear but to be pointed at, scoffed and insulted!"

Eugenia's travails are not over. She is kidnapped by Bellamy, the most vile character in the novel who is after her money. He forces her to marry him, and, because vows, never mind virginity, have been taken, the straight-laced Eugenia will not allow her parents to seek legal recourse. She resigns herself to life with this monster, but, fortunately for her, he accidentally shoots himself and dies. Eugenia returns again to the family home, and, with her books and her intellect, she is meant to be happy in her widowhood. In the late 18th century, it was out of the question that some man might fall in love with her and marry her, despite her appearance. Such a happy ending would have to wait for another 50 years to become even remotely possible.

IV

As the Industrial Revolution progressed, men dressed up for the sooty, fast-paced new world it created. Gone completely was the foppishness and ostentatious display of the previous centuries. The wardrobe of the Victorian gentleman expressed the new pragmatism with dark colours, well-tailored suits of good cloth, accessories that bespoke power and authority.

At the same time, female fashion spun in the opposite direction. Bustles, corsets, crinolines, trains, bodices, long, voluminous frocks—anything that restricted movement—became an essential part of a woman's dress. Flounces, piping, tassels, bows, lace, beads—all symbols of the "frivolous sex"—became mandatory decorations. Writer Susan Brownmiller put it this way: "... the woman of fashion remained a perishable confection, a wedding-cake vision of conspicuous consumption whose impractical clothes reflected the aristocratic values of centuries past."[510] Indeed, if there were ever a historical period that dramatically demonstrated the direct link between fashions that restrained a woman's movement and her restrictive role in society, it was the 19th century.

This is well illustrated by what was considered that most essential of items: the corset. Out of style by the end of the 18th century, the undergarment made a comeback in 1810. Made of heavy cotton, with ribs of whalebone and a bust of whalebone or wood laced up at the back, it functioned as a brassiere and girdle in one. The desired effect was to make the waist look tiny—tight lacing could contract the waistline to 20 inches, or even less— while pushing out the backside and uplifting the bosom. The image of the high-born matron floating along like a battleship was the stuff of many a hilarious cartoon.

Girls were forced into these cramping devices at an early age. British scientist Mary Somerville remembered having to wear stays at school at the turn of the century; educator Jane Ellen Harrison underwent similar torture in the 1850s.[511] Doctors complained the tight lacing resulted in sometimes permanent damage to the body: stomach ulcers, gallstones, rib dislocation, dizziness, headaches and curvature of the spine were common.

The corset had another important purpose. It permitted so-called proper women to mold their shape, to be in control of their "private attributes;" unrestrained busts and derrières jiggled and shook far too much for the prudish Victorians' liking. In fact, as historian Yvonne Knibiehler points out, there was an almost neurotic urge "to cover up, wrap up, and hide" women's private parts. The proliferation of undergarments—bloomers, pantaloons, petticoats, camisoles, bodices, tuckers—was amazing.

By mid-century, voluptuousness had become the vogue. Rounded shoulders, ample hips, chubby cheeks, full bosoms and fat ringlets called English curls that flopped over each ear all contributed to the much-vaunted image of delicacy, sensibility and softness that spelled out the ideal beauty. Rosy cheeks, though, were not in fashion; that would indicate robust activity out of doors. The angel sitting by the hearth was plump and pale and passive in her controlled, uncomfortable dress.

Not surprisingly, as well-educated women began to seek a larger role for themselves, they rebelled against the dictates of such punishing fashion. Bohemians such as the French writer George Sand flaunted their independence simply by donning trousers. They were savagely ridiculed. In the public's eye, to wear trousers was to claim the rights and privileges of the patriarchy.

In the 1850s, American feminists attempted to adopt a rational style of dress in the form of the bloomer. This originally consisted of ankle-length pantaloons with an overskirt that came to the knees, much like a Turkish sultan might wear. It was a rather elaborate affair, but at least there wasn't a floor-length skirt that caught underfoot all the time. The press howled its mockery; indeed, the ridicule was so great that within two years, even the staunchest of women's-rights advocates, Susan B. Anthony and Lizzie Stanton, were back in long petticoats. If it were any compensation, a few decades later the bloomer, in the form of knickerbockers, would return with a vengeance.

There was also another kind of defiance going on, an underground rebellion of sorts that wasn't connected with fashion so much as with beauty as a symbol of the repression of women. The all-too-pervasive premise that the only worthwhile woman was a pretty one—her beauty defined by the male establishment—was finally being questioned. "You can't tell a book by its cover" became the rallying cry for writers and others attempting to redefine society's often cruel judgements about a woman's desirability.

But women who didn't fit male society's ideas of beauty continued to be dismissed, however intelligent they might be. One such woman was Charlotte Brontë. How plain she was depends, of course, on the beholder. Some people found the intelligence so obvious in her facial expression quite appealing. However, not the novelist William Makepeace Thackeray. Writing about her novel *Villette*, he offers up the usual condescension aimed at talented women:

The poor little woman of genius! The fiery little eager brave tremulous homely-faced creature! I can read a great deal of her life as I fancy in her book, and see that rather than have fame, rather than any other earthly good or mayhap heavenly one she wants some Tomkins or another to love her and be in love with. But you see she is a little bit of a creature without a penny worth of good looks, thirty years old I should think, buried in the country, and eating up her own heart there, and no Tomkins will come.[512]

Fortunately for generations of Brontë readers, Thackeray didn't know the "creature" had such backbone and such insight into male vanity and ego. In Brontë's novel *Jane Eyre,* Jane escapes her wretched boarding school and takes a position as a governess in the establishment of Edward Rochester. Jane knows she is not a beauty, but she also understands that whatever physical attraction she does possess is a product of her personality. Rochester, too, finally gets the point that it is not Jane the adorned princess he loves, but Jane the ethical, strong-willed person. It's a hard lesson, though. At one point, when they are about to be married, Rochester says, "I will attire my Jane in satin and lace, and she shall have roses in her hair; and I will cover the head I love best with a priceless veil." Jane's response seems startling, even ungracious:

And then you won't know me, sir; and I shall not be your Jane Eyre any longer, but an ape in a harlequin's jacket—a jay in borrowed plumes. I would as soon see you, Mr. Rochester, tricked out in stage-trappings, as myself clad in a court-lady's robe; and I don't call you handsome, sir, though I love you most dearly; far too dearly to flatter you. Don't flatter me.[513]

Jane obviously has remarkable strength of character, as Rochester finds out to his chagrin when she refuses to live with him once the mad wife in the attic is discovered. In the end, he is blinded by a fire at his estate. Jane returns to him but entirely on her own terms. It's tempting to think that, through Rochester, Brontë is punishing the entire male establishment for all those centuries of denigrating and dismissing the "so little, so pale," plain woman of character.

V

In 1914, London was in the grip of guerrilla warfare. During the previous half-dozen years, the suffragettes had become increasingly militant, their tactics more and more desperate. Bombings, cutting telegraph wires, mass window-smashing and, for some males worst of all, the destruction of golf greens were all part of their arsenal. So was martyrdom. In 1913, on Derby Day, Emily Wilding Davison hurled herself under the hooves of the King's horse as it raced at Epsom Downs. Her funeral prompted an outpouring of grief.

When, a few months later, Emmeline Pankhurst was manhandled by police, arrested for the 13th time and thrown into Holloway Prison, the anger of her devotees reached boiling point. One of these women, Mary Richardson, decided on a dramatic way to express her outrage. On the morning of March 11, 1914, she walked into the National Gallery and, using a small ax she had concealed up her sleeve, she slashed the famous Velázquez masterpiece, the *Rokeby Venus*. She later said she wanted to disfigure the most beautiful woman in mythological history because the British government was destroying the woman with "the most beautiful character," namely Emmeline Pankhurst. The British press seemed more concerned about how much the painting had cost—£45,000—than the destruction of a piece of art. They applauded when Richardson was sentenced to six months in prison for her act of vandalism.

What was remarkable about Richardson's attack was that she had made the link between the patriarchal worship of ideal feminine beauty and the confinement of women to second-class status in society. It was a slippery connection that feminists would struggle with throughout the 20th century.

Ironically, by the time of Mary Richardson's infamous act, the inhibiting fashions of the Victorian period were already being modified. The passion for bicycle-riding that developed in the 1890s meant slit skirts and even knicker-bockers became permissible in society's eyes. By the turn of the century, Americans were busy inventing wonderful, ready-to-wear fashions—shirt-waists, tailored skirts, good-looking jersey blouses—that working girls could feel comfortable in and that required little effort to keep smart.

The model female form changed dramatically as well. A slender, athletic body replaced plump shoulders and ample bosoms. In 1905, one famous Parisian couturier had the audacity to shelve the corset altogether and design elegant evening gowns that flowed and shimmered over a slim silhouette. The dancer Isadora Duncan burst on the scene, dressed in diaphanous silk tunics in a style she imagined the Greeks had worn, her arms and legs bare, her long hair flowing. She was a sensation. Men adored her, and women even more so.

For an artist such as Mina Loy, the manner in which she dressed was a statement of her membership in the avant-garde, and her clothes an expression of her creativity. Her one-time husband Stephen Haweis wrote of the Paris they lived in at the turn of the century: "The move towards simple clothes began in the Quarter, and began chiefly because good corsets were very expensive and the fashionable clothes of the time were not adapted to the life our girls led in the studios."[514]

The male establishment disapproved, of course. French author Émile Zola groaned, "The idea of beauty is changing. You are vesting it in sterility, in long, slender figures with shrunken flanks."[515] It didn't matter how much the patriarchy complained. World War I dramatically brought home the idea that women could live independent lives, and by the 1920s, this new freedom was flamboyantly expressed in fashion. The boyish look became the craze: bobbed hair, no waists, chests flattened with suppressers, short skirts. For a feminine touch, the flapper added long strings of beads, splotches of rouge and bright lipstick pertly painted into the Clara Bow.

It was during this decade that advertising came into its own, and the connection between the sexual come-on and selling a product was cemented for good. As an ad for perfume insisted, "The first duty of a woman is to attract a man."

During the depressing 1930s, women's dress patterns sobered, hem lines dropped, necklines rose, fitted sleeves coyly covered arms, hats veiled the face. The constricted body made a comeback. The corset was gone,[516] replaced by a two-part gadget: a rubberized girdle and a brassiere. Depression-era fashion had a severe, no-nonsense look to it; sex wasn't used to sell anything.

During World War II, many women donned smartly tailored military uniforms and the civilian population followed suit. At the end of her shift, Rosie the Riveter changed her work clothes for a dress or a suit with large, padded shoulders, low-heeled shoes and smart hats, fashions that signalled a new self-confidence.

What was not being talked about, or even thought about, not since Mary Richardson had attacked the *Rokeby Venus*, was the extent to which that unyielding dictator—fashion—controlled women's lives. Two world wars and a world-wide depression had diverted everyone's attention "from such frivolous nonsense," as a judge in a suffragette case had put it. By her very nature, a female was a clotheshorse—that's all there was to it. In her 1952 novel *Martha Quest*, Doris Lessing imparts a sense of how powerful a force fashion remained. "The dress had the power to destroy ... false images, and she [Martha Quest] examined it with love, almost with physical pain.... She knew that the moment this dress clothed her body she would be revealed to herself, and to others, as something quite new, but deeply herself."[515a]

During the 1950s, naturalness as an ideal of feminine beauty all but vanished. Not only was it a decade when women languished in their suburban homes but also a throwback to the dark days of the painted, trussed-up artifact. Marilyn Monroe's baby-voiced cooing was indeed the sound of the times.

Margaret Drabble's first novel, *A Summer Bird-Cage*, intriguingly describes how appearance utterly dominated the lives of young women, even of the brightest and the best. The story takes place in 1958, and involves the two Bennett sisters, Louise, who is arrestingly beautiful, and Sarah, who, while not as stunning, is still very attractive. Both are bright and Oxford-educated, yet neither has career ambitions. They both work at insignificant jobs, killing time until the right man comes along and marries them. "She [Louise] was far too intelligent to do nothing, and yet too beautiful and sexy to do all the first-class things like politics or law or social sciences—and she was naturally afraid of subsiding into nothingness." Louise finally ends up marrying a wealthy, neurotic writer who intrigues her but whom she doesn't love. When her shocked sister asks her why she would marry for money, Louise responds, "Partly it's looking the way I do. I must have clothes. I'm only young once, as they say, and I'm already twenty-four, and if I don't have the clothes now I'd feel I wasn't paying a debt to nature."[515b]

Tiptoeing through the novel is the sisters' cousin Daphne, a hard-working, honest history teacher who has the great misfortune of being born plain. She is treated as a pariah by Louise and Sarah; they will do anything to avoid her. Sarah says, "Daphne is slack and dull, muscles in her legs instead of in her belly, no curves, no shine, no shape, and one can't shut one's eyes and pretend it isn't so, that it doesn't matter. It does matter." Louise responds, "… the Daphnes of this world aren't worth a moment's worry. By worrying about them you get like them and that makes two disasters instead of one."

Jackie Kennedy would have understood. In the first two years she was First Lady, she spent the then huge amount of $100,000 on her wardrobe. When her husband complained, she was quoted as saying, "The president seems more concerned these days with my budget than with the budget of the United States."

The obscene fixation with physical appearance had to end, of course. How could a woman take her rightful place in society if she relied entirely on her morning makeup and very little on her brains? As the women's movement heated up, the attack on what feminist writer Naomi Wolf was to dub "the beauty myth" became increasingly more ferocious

Early feminists such as Simone de Beauvoir and Betty Friedan blamed women themselves for their obsession with their looks. "For a woman to hold some 'man's position' and be desirable at the same time has long been a subject for more or less ribald joking," wrote de Beauvoir. "… it is very difficult for women to accept … their status as autonomous individuals and their womanly destiny; this is the source of blundering and restlessness which sometimes cause them to be considered a 'lost sex.'"[517]

During the 1960s, the blame shifted as feminists began to analyze the major role society played in the beauty fixation, particularly by the advertising industry and its never-ending variations of sex for sale. Blondes had more fun, teeth brushed with a certain toothpaste made a kiss "irresistible," a Playtex bra would give a girl the shape she needed to catch a man. It was not surprising that the women's liberation movement announced itself to an astonished world by rudely disrupting the 1968 Miss America Contest in Atlanta City. "Women in our society are forced daily to compete for male approval, enslaved by ludicrous beauty standards that we ourselves are conditioned to take seriously and to accept," said one protester. Beauty, or as the feminists more dramatically put it, the sexual objectification of women, sat at the core of debate over the next few decade reaching its apotheosis with the publication in 1991 of Wolf's *The Beauty Myth*.

The book's basic premise is an astonishing one: the Western world's economic structure, controlled by men, is involved in a massive conspiracy to weaken, through starvation, the brightest and best of today's young womanhood. This is accomplished through the unceasing brainwashing of advertising, which insists that thinner is better, thereby promoting eating disorders such as bulimia and anorexia. The male establishment does this because they want to continue to control women, and they certainly don't want to have to compete with their talent and brains in the marketplace.

What is astonishing about this strident, angry polemic is not so much its exaggerated message as its success. It became an instant bestseller, a companion for millions of young women, many of them college students. Certainly it illustrates the dilemma that tortures many of that age group: "If I'm independent-minded, my own person, why then do I find myself spending my money on Anaïs Anaïs perfume and Max Factor's Cherry Blossom lipstick?" It's a contradiction that causes so much anger and pain that Wolf's call to arms must seem a healing salve. She writes, "Let's be shameless. Be greedy. Pursue pleasure. Avoid pain. Wear and touch and eat and drink what we feel like.... And once we break through and change the rules so our sense of our own beauty cannot be shaken, sing that beauty and dress it up and flaunt it and revel in it."[518] Helen of Troy would surely have applauded, but Tertullian must be rolling over in his grave.

4. The Mind

Danielle

There was something disconcerting about Danielle Martin. There was the French factor: her given names—Danielle Jacqueline, her amazing, rapid-fire ability with languages, the smart, European-looking blazers she wore. But there was something else more ordinary: a hee-haw laugh, a rather large face with big rosy cheeks—a profile Dickens would have loved—and her plain, Anglo-Saxon last name: Martin.

In fact, Danielle was a product both of stiff-upper-lip British and flamboyant French stock. She was born in southwest France in the village of Vic-Fezensac, population 3,000, just north of Auch, a steep and hilly town with a lavish Gothic cathedral perched on its top-most point. Encrusted in history, the region is famous for the Three Musketeers and Armagnac brandy. Danielle's grandfather Jean-Marie Baylac made wooden shoes with pointed toes, just like the Dutch variety, which peasants wore over felt slippers while working in the fields. Her grandmother Augustine sold the shoes in the family's shop and also travelled with her wares to the neighbouring markets.

Danielle's mother Yvonne, the eldest of the three Baylac children, was a bit of a cut-up. She liked to poke fun at authority, and she had too much fun at school to get really good grades. As a result, she wasn't accepted at teacher's college, something she regretted her entire life. Yvonne went to Paris instead to train at the Ville-Neuve St. Georges Hospital. Eventually she became an operating-room nurse. There were plenty of young interns and other single guys who would have liked to court the attractive Yvonne Baylac, but she fell for a serious-minded Englishman 11 years her senior.

Henri Martin's background was both interesting and tragic. His father had been a landscape gardener, and the Martin family had won many prizes, some international, for their horticultural talents. Martin Senior happened to be in Germany designing gardens for the aristocracy when World War I broke out. He, his wife and their two children, Henri and his sister, were interned. Although the men and women lived separately, and the food was pretty poor, the internees tried to lead as normal a life as possible. Henri and his sister went to school, and both became fluent in German. Unfortunately, their father fell ill with dysentery and died in 1917.

After the war, Mrs. Martin and her two children were reunited and returned to England. In their absence, the business had been destroyed, and Henri, at age 14, was forced to go to work. Danielle says this lack of formal education never hindered her father. He was entirely self-taught, an intellectual who loved learning simply for its own sake.

Henri found a job with a large typesetting outfit and set out to learn the business. In the 1930s, Henri married a woman who was an author of some note, a poet and writer of science fiction. Since, for her, Paris was the centre of the universe, the couple moved there, and Henri established his own foundry and typesetting enterprise. Unhappily, in 1933, Henri's wife died while giving birth. The baby girl was sent back to England to be cared for by her mother's sister, but since Henri's business was just getting off the ground, he remained in Paris.

Henri socialized with a group of young entrepreneurs who, among other things, owned a barge on the Seine where they liked to hold parties. Nurses were particularly welcome. It was at one of these gatherings that Yvonne Baylac caught Henri Martin's eye. He was far more sophisticated and debonair than the men she was used to dating. He took her to nice restaurants and treated her in his proper English manner. Her attraction for him? She was a great lover of life who was a dedicated nurse to boot. Soon they were going out regularly.

When the Germans invaded France in 1940, Henri, Yvonne and her aunt and uncle fled south to Yvonne's home village of Vic-Fezensac. They didn't exactly receive a warm welcome, at least not after Yvonne's parents realized how involved their daughter was with the Englishman. The Baylacs were old-stock French; they didn't mix with the Brits. They even refused to attend their daughter's wedding, but when Danielle was born in 1943 (an embarrassing few months after the wedding), Augustine, at least, came around.

During the war, the people in the south of France did not suffer as much as those in the north. Although food was rationed, it was not in dangerously short supply. The Vichy regime, though, could be heavy-handed. One day, a notice arrived at the Baylac house demanding that Henri Martin report to the Auch police station. Other so-called aliens who had obeyed a similar order had simply vanished. The crucial question facing him, and the Baylac family, was whether, if he fled, the authorities would come after his wife. It was decided that Yvonne was so well known in the village, she would be protected. Augustine finally found a peasant family in a nearby district who was willing to hide him, and there he remained for the duration of the war.

After the war, the family regrouped in Vic-Fezensac. Henri started a factory labelling, bottling and corking Armagnac brandy, but so many people had left the little town for Paris or other cities, it was almost impossible to find workers. He set up a similar operation in Auch, but it, too, wasn't much of a success. A son, Bernard, was born in 1945, and another daughter, Rosemary, a year later. The Vic-Fezensac school went only to Grade 5, and Henri and Yvonne began to worry about where their children would be educated after that.

Henri finally contacted the London typesetting company he had worked for in London, and they told him a position was available—in Montreal. The Martins decided to emigrate to Canada.

Henri went ahead to get established, and it was almost three years before Yvonne and the three children followed him. They flew to Montreal on December 26, 1954. It was a shock: cold, snowy, with the houses and their strange balconies all looking identical. On one street lived the French Canadians, on the adjoining street, the Jews. Since the Martins could barely understand the Québécois patois and they spoke no English, they were literally without a language.

Henri tried to make his family as comfortable as possible. Even though there wasn't much money, he had bought Christmas presents for the children and an apartment full of furniture for Yvonne. Unfortunately, it was not what she would have picked out, which furthered her sense of alienation. Finally though, they all settled in, and English lessons, led by Henri, began around the dining room table. "My name is ...," "I live at ...," the children and Yvonne would intone.

St. Malachy was an old Catholic school with large windows and high ceilings. Both English and French kids attended it, but there was no mixing between the two, except for the odd snowball fight. The teaching philosophy at St. Malachy was simple: if you don't understand, you must be stupid. Danielle was placed at the back of the class, and would have been totally ignored if it hadn't been for two bad habits that drove the teacher wild. Her handwriting ran straight up and down rather than slanted, and she had learned decimals rather than fractions. Lunch hours were spent under the watchful gaze of the vice-principal, who made sure her As and Bs angled from right to left. Meanwhile, she learned almost no English.

In the summer of 1955, Henri was told he was being transferred to Toronto, where the company's Canadian head office was located. By that time, the Martins had saved enough money for a down payment on a house in Scarborough. It was a storey-and-a-half with a long back yard overlooking Scarborough Bluffs and a great view of Lake Ontario.

Danielle's English rapidly improved because she so desperately wanted to be like everybody else. It was all that mattered. "It was important to wear two pairs of socks with your moccasins and a skirt that was just the right fullness," she says. Whatever she did, though, there was no getting around the fact that her family was different. Danielle switched to French as soon as she walked in the door; this was especially true when her grandmother Augustine Baylac came to visit. The Martins didn't eat dinner until after 7:30, after a leisurely glass of sherry, which meant Danielle and her siblings were trapped inside when everybody else in the neighbourhood was out playing baseball. Danielle didn't have curfews like the other kids, but her parents were very strict about how to behave. Asking to be excused from the table, using an appropriate tone of voice, eating everything on your plate, showing respect to one's elders were important.

When Danielle was in Grade 8, the guidance counsellor told her she was not capable of finishing high school and she might as well accept the fact. Danielle feels now that language might still have been a problem—she wasn't speaking up in class, and her test scores weren't high—or perhaps, since both her brother and sister were told the same thing, it was simply a prejudice against children whose first language was not English. Not surprisingly, Danielle didn't much like Grade 9 at R. H. King and didn't do very well, but after that, once she had become totally fluent in English, she excelled.

As it turned out, English literature became one of her favourite subjects, though she also liked math, physics and art classes. Languages, of course, were a piece of cake, and she took Latin, German and French.

There was something a little daring, a little rebellious about Danielle. She went out on a couple of dates with a guy who rode a motorcycle, a real hood. All they did was sip cherry Coke at the club hangout, but when she arrived home on the back of his Harley, her parents went crazy. She had a recklessness on the basketball and volleyball courts that was unnerving, although she was always chosen for the inter-varsity teams. "I've always like to move around, throw myself into physical activity, lose myself in it," she says. Living a little dangerously is still a pleasure for her.

At high school, she was thought to have a terrific personality and she was very popular, part of the elite group and with plenty of boyfriends. Yet there was something that always distinguished her in the crowd: a certain *savoir-faire*, an independence. She had taken part-time jobs, first as a dishwasher and then as a waitress at the Rouge Hill Golf and Country Club, and there she met an older crowd. Many of them were in university and they had a lot more finesse than your average crew-cut male at R. H. King. More intriguing still, she spent the summer after Grade 12 in what we considered was the most romantic place in the world: France.

Danielle and her sister stayed with their grandparents, and Danielle loved everything about Vic-Fezensac. She enjoyed walking down the street and having everyone smile at her because they remembered her sprightly mother. She loved taking bicycle rides into the countryside, visiting the market overflowing with flowers, arguing with the large extended family about weighty subjects at meal times and even, since there was no shower in her grandmother's house, enjoying the talk and laughter at the communal bath house. To cap it off, towards the end of the summer, she was permitted to tour Italy by bus with a group of young people.

Back at R. H. King, Danielle was considered the most exotic of creatures. Perhaps because of that, she had trouble adjusting to her last year of high school. She was desperate to do well and, like many of us, probably put too much pressure on herself. "I remember closeting myself in the basement, wrapped in a blanket, trying to memorize all those facts." Marks in the 80s had been her goal, but when the Grade 13 grades were released, hers were much lower. It was a humiliation she never forgot, even though her average was still high enough for admission to the University of Toronto.

Although money was still pretty tight, the Martin family assumed that the children would go to college. Danielle took a three-year Bachelor of Arts, specializing in English, French and Spanish. She chose University College because it was non-denominational—by this time she had had enough of religion—and she also thought it more cosmopolitan. The building was old and creaky, exactly what Danielle thought a university should be.

Her parents didn't have the funds to provide much more than free room and board, but Danielle found the trip back and forth to Scarborough gruelling, and for that reason, her first year was difficult. In her second year, she found part-time jobs proofreading for *Who's Who* and bookkeeping for an elevator company, which provided her with enough money to rent a large room with plenty of big windows in a boarding house close to the university.

Danielle was no longer stressed about her studies. She enjoyed philosophy and French literature—she read the French-Canadian writer Gabrielle Roy with particular pleasure—did the extra recommended reading, got good grades in her term papers. Most exciting of all, the Big Romance happened.

John lived in a fraternity house around the corner from Danielle's place, but she actually met him at the Rouge Hills Golf Course where he was head lifeguard. He was very good-looking and, as a physical-education student at U. of T., sports-minded. He was also, says Danielle, very creative and poetic. She fell head over heels for him. "It was a wonderful relationship for me at first. Very physical. All love and lust."

Then a certain instability became obvious. John came from a profoundly dysfunctional family, with some mental illness, and had run away from home when he was 17. In his last year of university, he suffered a breakdown and had to be admitted to a psychiatric hospital. Danielle began to wonder if this was what she wanted in a life partner. John recovered and graduated, but by that time, the relationship was shaky. While he was away teaching elsewhere in the province, Danielle met someone who was solid as a rock, who "knew who he was and where he wanted to go." He wore a tweed coat, smoked a pipe and was something of an intellectual, just like her father. His steadfastness was such a relief after the emotional turmoil of the big romance that Danielle ended up marrying him.

Angus D. K. (Don) MacKenzie was the eldest child in a family that proudly traced its Scottish origins back generations. His father was the manager of catalogue advertising for Eaton's department store. Like the Martins, the MacKenzies stressed education; Don and his two sisters all obtained degrees and have professional careers.

Don had enrolled at the University of Toronto, specializing in history, political science and Eastern European studies. He and Danielle were in the same French class, but it was two guys from R. H. King whom they both happened to know who introduced them over coffee at the JCR room. They started to chat, and eventually went out on the odd date, but Danielle was still deeply involved with John. It would take her some time to realize she preferred stability to an emotional—albeit romantic—roller-coaster ride.

As her graduation approached, Danielle had still not decided on a career. A job as a translator at the United Nations or some similar agency appealed to her, but she didn't know how to go about it. Following her third and last year at university, she had another wonderful summer in Europe. This time, she travelled throughout Spain with an uncle who was a bull-fight aficionado. She had a brief fling with the son of a man whom her mother had gone out with; the son turned out to be just as sexy as the father. In Lausanne, she was hired as a tutor for the child of a famous actor, but she still had plenty of time to herself. She loved the city, just walking about, idling away the hours in outdoor cafés. She was hoping she might find a job as a translator, but she didn't really try very hard. For one thing, Don was lurking in the background in Canada.

At the end of the summer, she returned to her parents' house, but it was a miserable time for her. Suburban living in Scarborough was a let-down after her travels in Europe. In her dreams, she constantly relived her experiences. Finally, after several dull jobs, she decided to become a teacher.

She isn't sure why she resisted this career decision for so long, for almost immediately, she knew she was a natural and this was her true vocation. "I liked it right away. I didn't have any qualms. I knew I wasn't a good teacher because I hadn't any practice, but that I would be in the future." By the fall of 1965, she had a job at Toronto's Humberside Collegiate, teaching French and physical education.

Meanwhile, her relationship with Don MacKenzie had slowly been evolving. After university, he ended up in a management course with Manufacturers Life Insurance Company, but he soon realized he needed something more challenging. In 1964, he enrolled at Osgoode Hall law school. However, with Danielle making reasonably good money as a high-school teacher, they could get married.

The wedding ceremony took place at Thomas Aquinas Anglican Church, and the reception was held at the Guild Inn in Scarborough in late August of 1965. Life wasn't easy at first. Danielle was making about $5,000 a year, and their rent alone, in an apartment where cockroaches reigned supreme, was $85 a month. They got pretty sick of hamburger and lived in the hope that one of the sets of parents might invite them home for a good meal. On the other hand, they saved enough money for a two-month trip to Europe in the summer. It was important to Danielle that Don experience first-hand the French side of her.

In 1969, Danielle gave birth to her first child, Monique. By that time, Don had graduated from law school and was working for the prestigious Toronto law firm Lang Mitchner. Since he now had a salary, small as it was, Danielle quit teaching. "I found it really difficult. It was one of the worst times for me. Don was a new lawyer in a big firm. There was a lot of stimulation there, and he would come home and tell me about the things he was doing. I was really jealous and very unhappy being at home. But not for a moment did it occur to me to change it. That was my job."

Don had met Philip Upshall at a bar-admission course. Like Don, Phil was spending his first year as a lawyer working in a well-established Toronto firm. The two liked each other, and Phil invited the MacKenzies to his house for dinner. Danielle was surprised to learn she knew his wife. Wilma Upshall had attended R. H. King; she and Danielle had been active in the girls' Hi-Y club. The couples got along so well together that Phil and Don decided to set up a law practice together.

Toronto was definitely not the place to locate. Competition was stiff, and they didn't have the money to support themselves for very long. They decided on the smallish city of Brampton, the political and judicial seat of Peel County, 32 kilometres northwest of Toronto. The two young lawyers studied the economic indicators and correctly predicted the area was about to boom. In 1970, when Don and Phil opened up their law firm, the population was about 50,000; by 1998, it had mushroomed to 283,000. Such a real-estate boom generated a lot of legal business, but it wasn't easy simply to hang up a shingle. "It was very difficult the first two or three years. We essentially lived on the bank's money," says Don. They took any case, criminal or civil, that came over the transom.

One of the major drawbacks Upshall & MacKenzie (a third partner, Eric Kelday, joined the firm in 1973) faced was that they were the new kids on the block. Although a small city, Brampton had a rock-solid elite. It was, for example, the family seat of long-time Ontario Premier William Davis. The only way to break in was to become totally immersed in the community. Don joined all the service clubs, became involved with municipal politics, was elected the youngest president in the history of the Brampton Chamber of Commerce. Don was Phil's campaign chairman when he won a seat on the Brampton Town Council. Phil was the local president of the Progressive Conservative association for several years. Don worked for various Liberal candidates. Their dedication paid off. In ten years, their practice grew from two to seven lawyers—but it also meant the two men were rarely home.

Danielle says she and the other young wives, including Wilma Upshall, who eventually had four children, just accepted it. "Our role was to make sure the family ran smoothly." To this day, Danielle says Don does not know how to run the washing machine or the dishwasher, nor does he have any idea how the vacuum works.

In 1971, the MacKenzies' second child, Martine, came along, and two years later, their third and last, Robert Bruce Alexander. Danielle was tired after the third baby. "By that time I wanted to do other things, but with three small children, I was really tied down." In the little time off she did have, Danielle became involved in the university women's club, with its bridge and book clubs and guest speakers. "That was my saving grace," she says. She and the other young mothers swam at the Y and played tennis in the summer. They would make sure all the chores and shopping were done during the week so the weekend would be stress-free for their husbands. The social life was compensation too. "We played hard," says Danielle. They partied a lot, accompanied their husbands when clients were taken to dinner, looked forward to formal balls—long dresses were worn even to the opening of the Brampton Flower Festival. "As the wives of young lawyers, we were fêted by the community," says Danielle.

As the law firm flourished, the MacKenzies' lifestyle also blossomed. "My perception is we got caught up in this lifestyle," says Danielle. "It was expected that you would go away for a winter vacation to Nassau or Guadeloupe, whether you could afford it or not." The MacKenzies, starting to slide into debt, realized they needed two incomes to maintain their standard of living. In 1983, Danielle went back to teaching.

Money wasn't the only reason, of course. "I was really having a hard time. It was bizarre. I lost my sense of balance. I'd be sitting and the room would start to spin. I don't know what it was—stress, tension—I was really getting a little concerned." Danielle ended up going to a psychologist who specialized in relaxation techniques. It was at that point she realized that, for a person as energetic as she was, she had too much free time on her hands.

Danielle started out part-time as a supply teacher but soon got heavily involved in school activities. Pretty quickly, she was hired full-time teaching two classes of Grade 7 and 8 French immersion and one of core French. In her immersion classes, she doesn't just teach French but teaches many subjects *in* French. She soon became one of the most popular teachers in the system.

Danielle was pleasantly surprised when, 1989, she was made a consultant to the Peel Board of Education. Her job was to act as liaison between the board's head office and the resource teachers in the schools. Implementing new reading programs for children in French immersion kindergarten and Grade 1 was her first task, but she also advised on curriculum and new technology. Since she was involved in hiring teachers, she made frequent trips to Ottawa and Montreal. It was one of the most satisfying periods of her life. "It was an amazing job. I loved it." Unfortunately, it was a non-renewable appointment; at the end of three years, she was required to return to the classroom. A new junior high, Hazel McCallion School, had just been constructed and was equipped with all the latest computer and video technology. Danielle decided to go there.

She has remained enthusiastic about teaching and utterly dedicated to her students. "There's a certain feeling you get when kids are turned on. It's amazing to watch them. I love it when they come back and talk to you about whatever they're thinking about. I try to keep open to new ideas, to allow my students to take risks. To become a dinosaur in the classroom—that would be awful." The balance for a superb teacher like Danielle is fostering creativity among her students and yet implanting self-discipline so they can learn the necessary basics.

As the '90s have progressed, government cutbacks have made the life of a public-school teacher miserable. Danielle now teaches significantly more classes—she has 115 students and sometimes can't even remember their names. When she was a consultant, her administrative abilities shone, and she thought she might try for a principalship. Now she says she is too old; the climb up the ladder should have started many years before.

The early 1990s was not a happy time for Danielle in other ways. Her mother became so ill, she had to move in with the MacKenzies, and she died in 1990. Yvonne Martin had adjusted amazingly well to life in Canada. She became fluent in English, took courses on how to make hats, learned to drive. When her children were grown, she retrained as a nurse and worked for close to 20 years at Princess Margaret Hospital. Henri had died in 1968, but Yvonne managed to maintain her love of life. She was such an enthusiastic spectator of news and current affairs that her children bought her foam bricks so she could toss them at the television screen. Her death left Danielle with a large hole in her life.

Something else occurred during those years that rattled the MacKenzie family to its core. In November 1991, Don's partner Philip Upshall, by then a Q.C., was charged with defrauding clients of more than $2-million in investment funds. Half the money had been lost on the stock markets, and there had been shady deals involving Brampton's hot real-estate market. Upshall attempted suicide, and was incarcerated for a time in a psychiatric unit, where he was diagnosed as a manic depressive. In October 1992, he pleaded guilty and was sentenced to two years less a day in a provincial reformatory. Later, he lost his licence to practise law. Since it's expected that senior partners keep an eye on each other's dealings, the scandal cast a dark and long shadow. The law firm that had been so prominent simply crumbled away. However, unlike some of the other lawyers who lost their jobs, Don MacKenzie was very fortunate. In May 1992, he was appointed a judge to the Ontario court's general division.

As for Danielle, one of the great passions in her life has always been skiing. When her kids were small, she was careful, worried she might break something and not be able to look after them. These days, prudence is thrown to the wind. "I go faster, down steeper hills, don't avoid jumps and bumps and stuff like that. I like to push it, love the thrill of it." It could be a metaphor for Danielle's entire life. Cautious when need be, but open to experiences of every kind. Education for her has not been confined to the classroom but has embraced many different worlds. It is the knowledge gained from exuberant living that she brings to her students, and which makes her a superb teacher.

Education

It if were customary to send little girls to school and to teach them the same subjects as are taught to boys, they would learn just as fully and would understand the subtleties of all arts and sciences. Indeed it may be they would understand them better....

Christine de Pisan, *The Book of the City of Ladies*, 1405

We are educated in the grossest ignorance, and no art omitted to stifle our natural reason.

Lady Mary Wortley Montagu, 1753

Resolved, That the education of woman should be in accordance with responsibility in life, that she may acquire that self-reliance and true dignity so essential to the proper fulfillment of the important duties devolving on her.

Resolution of the Ohio Women's Rights convention, 1850

"A bombshell" is what everyone called Miss M. E. Lane. With her curly blonde hair swept up, her open, heart-shaped face, her dazzling smile, she was considered the most glamorous of teachers. She had even been a stand-in for Marilyn Monroe in *The Prince and the Showgirl*. At least that was the rumour that percolated through the school during all our years at R. H. King. We never found out if it were true. None of us was bold enough to confront Miss Lane directly, and anyway, we didn't want to know the truth. It was all too delicious, a juicy morsel we could gnaw away on over lunch in the drab, smelly cafeteria. You could bet the Bombshell was at some elegant café, drinking red wine by candlelight and whispering in the ear of a handsome man. (We always assumed he would be in business, a lawyer perhaps, because the male teachers we knew were not nearly debonair or rich enough.)

A few years later when I read Muriel Spark's *The Prime of Miss Jean Brodie* and then saw the movie in which the eccentric Scottish teacher is superbly played by Maggie Smith, I thought of Miss Lane. She didn't exactly have a hand-picked coterie of girls to influence and confide in, as Miss Brodie did, but there was a gaggle of devoted followers who would pick up the books she dropped as she rushed to class or who stood in the doorway in the hope that La Belle Lane's coat sleeve might brush against them. Miss Lane probably had a secret love affair as Miss Brodie had but, 20 years later in a different society, she was not forced into early retirement because of it, thereby shortening her prime. The two teachers had one thing in common, though: both deeply influenced their female students, not through what they taught or even the knowledge they imparted but simply by being who they were. Miss Lane and Miss Brodie both understood that education was everything for their girls. Without it, they would be at the mercy of each and every man who stepped into their lives.

I

Education in Classical Greece emphasized rhetoric, music and physical education, and had one objective: to create good citizens by preparing them to hold public office, to vote, to serve as jurors, to fight as soldiers. Since women were not allowed to do any of these things, why bother with them? As classicist Eva C. Keuls puts it, "The aim was to keep women frozen in their development, so that they would become, as it were, perpetual children, and this attempt may have been successful."[519]

A girl's mother would teach her how to weave, manage the household and look after the children. That was all the formal education she needed. As far as character development, a father could see to that. Daughters were to be submissive, silent and subservient. At the age their brothers were being sent off for advanced education, girls were already married and bearing heirs. Since their husbands would not only be older but much better-educated than they, the marriage seldom developed into one of mutual respect or friendship. For one thing, wives were so secluded in the home, they could hardly share in their husbands' far worldlier experience.

For all that, women, at least in the upper classes, did get a smattering of learning, if only reading and writing. Sometimes they were taught by the males in the family; overhearing the lessons given by a brother's tutors was a common way of grabbing bits of knowledge. In their own neighbourhoods, there was often an underground of learned women who would act as mentors.

There were also men who realized how ridiculous it was to promote ignorance in those who had such a profound influence on the sons of the family. Plato was the chief among these. In the Fifth Book of his *Republic*, he advocated equal education for the "guardians," the upper class. "They [women] must have the same two branches of training for mind and body and also be taught the art of war, and they must receive the same treatment."[520] Even before Plato, the famous philosopher Pythagoras (c. 582–c. 507 BC) could boast of women disciples who had been admitted to his circle on equal terms with men. This meant rigid discipline: cutting back on superfluous spending and often abstaining from sex, for example.[521] Epicurus (341–270 BC) also admitted women to the school conducted in his lovely garden, and he, too, expected as much of them as the men.

Women themselves realized ignorance and illiteracy hardly enhanced them in the eyes of their children. The following epitaph was written for the mother of Philip of Macedon (238–179 BC):

Eurydice of Hierapolis set up this tablet, when she had satisfied her desire to become learned; for she worked hard to learn letters, the repository of speech, because she was a mother of growing sons. [522]

During the Hellenistic period (approx. 323–30 BC), schools for girls became more common. The curriculum was much like that of their brothers': physical education, oratory, music and reading. One can picture generations of little girls scribbling away on their wax tablets while reading aloud the poems of Sappho.

The Romans approved of at least a rudimentary education for girls, either in schools—some even admitted daughters of lowly plebeians—or with a tutor at home. It became fashionable for the daughters of upper-class families to be intelligent and cultivated. Senator and author Pliny the Younger (AD 62?–c. 113) painted this picture of a 13-year-old who died just before her marriage:

How she loved her nurses, her preceptors, and her teachers, each for the service given her. She studied her books with diligence and understanding.[523]

Stoic philosopher Musonius Rufus (c. AD 30–101) was one of the chief advocates of educating females. His beliefs were more rational and more humane than many of the misogynist views expressed by early Christians, including St. Paul. Rufus wrote:

Female Dogs are trained to hunt just like male dogs, and if you expect female

horses to do a horse's job effectively, you must see that they have the same training as the male horses....

It is reasonable, then for me to think that women ought to be educated similarly to men in respect to virtue....[524]

Among the elite, it became trendy for well-educated husbands to instruct
their wives. Pliny the Younger and his friend Pompeius Saturninus made a
hobby of encouraging their spouses' talents. Pompeius's wife wrote letters
that were admired for their purity of Latin. Pliny's wife nicely set his writings
to music.[525]

Pliny and Pompeius were sophisticated and progressive, but represented
only a narrow stratum of their society. The vast majority of Roman men
believed small doses of learning were good enough. If a woman's head was
full of philosophy, she would neglect her duties as mother and housewife.
The satirical poet Juvenal (c. AD 65–c. 128) had a heyday attacking intellectually inclined women.

Still most intolerable of all is the woman who as soon as she has sat down to
dinner commends Virgil, pardons the dying Dido, and pits the poets against each
other, putting Virgil in the one scale and Homer in the other. The grammarians
make way before her; the rhetoricians give in; the whole crowd is silenced: no
lawyer, no auctioneer will get a word in, no, nor any other woman; so torren-
tial is her speech that you would think that all the pots and bells were being
clashed together.[526]

What is illustrated in this diatribe is not so much Juvenal's contempt for the
educated female but what a large number of well-versed and intellectually
sharp Roman women there must have been.

II

In the early Middle Ages (fifth to tenth centuries), women in the nobility
were often better educated than the men. In the never-ending warfare of the
period, the most important training for sons was in martial arts; the study of
literature or philosophy was left to their sisters. Amalasuntha, the daughter of
Theodoric the Great (c. 454–526), the king of the Ostrogoths and conqueror
of Italy, was a prime example. Like her father, Amalasuntha had studied and
admired Roman culture, laws and literature. Three of her letters have been
preserved, and these show such a fluency in Latin that she must have been

well-educated indeed. After her father's death, she was regent for her son. When he died, she and her husband were joint rulers of Italy, until he became power-hungry and had her strangled to death.

In the sixth century, the ancient Germanic tribe of Thuringia was conquered by the Franks. Many of the Thuringian ruling class were killed, others were captured and treated as booty. Radegund, a female child of the Thuringian nobility, was chosen to be the bride of Chlotar, the Frankish King Clovis's youngest son. She was sent to a French convent to be educated, where she learned to read and write both in French and Latin and emerged something of a scholar.[527]

Chlotar turned out to be a brute (as well as having four other wives) and deeply resented both Radegund's learning and her piety. When he finally murdered her brother, Radegund sought the protection of the frightened Bishop Medard, who reluctantly made her a deaconess. In 550, she founded Sainte-Croix of Poitiers, a cloister of 200 nuns that became an important cultural and educational institution—as well as a refuge for high-born women fleeing tyrannical husbands.

It was religious communities such as Radegund's that offered peace, safety, access to libraries and time to think and pray to those who chose to dedicate their life to God. Almost all nuns had to learn to read and write so as to be able to recite their prayers. As well, they studied selections from the scriptures, lives of the saints, writings of the early Church fathers and the rules of their orders.[528] Although it was customary to read Latin texts aloud at meals, few understood what was being said. Only the more intellectually inclined learned the classical languages, the key that opened the door to science, literature and philosophy. These women became librarians, scribes (copyists), illuminists and teachers. Some were truly remarkable in their dedication. Leoba, the founder of the famous Bischofsheim Convent, is just one example.

Leoba's aristocratic, Anglo-Saxon family promised her to the religious life at birth. She was educated at the nunnery on the Isle of Thanet, off Kent, and later at Wimborne Abbey, where she took her final vows. She was a studious child, devoting herself to her books, spurning jokes of all kinds and "girlish romance."[529] She corresponded often with her cousin, the missionary bishop Boniface, and it was he, impressed with her intellect, who suggested she be sent to Germany to set up the Bischofsheim Convent. It became famous throughout the European world for the help it gave to the poor—Leoba herself washed the feet of all guests, no matter how humble—and the advice it gave to the powerful. Its library, scriptorium and herb gardens (for medicines) were praised everywhere. Eventually, Bischofsheim became the training ground for future abbesses, a network that spread throughout the Christian world. Leoba supposedly committed to memory everything she read and, so as not to waste a moment, asked her nuns to read to her while she was sleeping.[530]

It was not just the religious themselves who benefited from a world within walls. Daughters of noble families and later, those of wealthy burghers were sent to convents to receive instruction in religion, reading, writing and simple arithmetic, all considered proper preparations for marriage, the only secular career available. Equally important, though, were the domestic skills taught: needlework, spinning, weaving and, at some nunneries, fine embroidery work.[531]

As the Middle Ages progressed, elementary schools were established in the cities and towns. These were for the children of prosperous merchants and minor nobility. Those without money—most of the population—remained illiterate. In Paris in the late 13th century, 21 women were listed as mistresses of authorized schools.[532] According to historian Giovanni Villani, in 1338 in Florence, some 8,000 to 10,000 boys and girls were attending such schools, and one of the teachers who taught Latin was a woman. In Germanic countries, public schools slowly evolved as German became accepted as a language. Sometimes Beguines, lay sisters, were employed as teachers by the municipalities, but often a husband and wife team would run a particular school.

For over a century, boys and girls were taught together, but by the end of the 14th century, in most countries co-education had come to an end, primarily on the Church's orders. From that point on, the girls' curriculum leaned less towards academics and more to the domestic.

The Church fathers had always been nervous about women going to school. They believed that while the rational male was capable of coping with new knowledge, the daughters of Eve, still being punished for the transgression in Eden, had to be protected from outside influences for their own good. Innocence meant ignorance. Education for the female had one purpose: to install piety, modesty and subservience. A woman should be able to read her prayers, but, said many church theorists, there was no need at all to teach her to write. Philip of Novara in *Les Quatre Ages de l'Homme* revealed what men were really worried about in literate women:

Women should not learn to read or write unless they are going to be nuns, as much harm has come from such knowledge. For some men will dare to send or give or drop letters near them, containing indecent requests in the form of songs or rhymes or tales, which they would never dare convey by message or word of mouth. And even if the woman had no desire to err, the devil is so crafty and skillful in tempting that he would soon lead her on to read the letters and answer them....[533]

The gap between male and female learning turned into a yawning abyss. Women were not admitted to universities, schools of law or mathematics, theological institutions or to the preparatory schools that readied students for such higher learning. As historian Gerda Lerner explains, "In general, education becomes institutionalized when elites—military, religious or political—need to assure their position in power by means of training a group to serve and perpetuate their interests. Whenever that has happened, historically, women were discriminated against and excluded from the very inception of each system."[534] This discrimination was to last for centuries and to have profound and tragic results. Paulette L'Hermite-Leclercq writes, "Women remained confined to traditional roles, serving humanity or God, while men enthusiastically discovered the world, and all that it held in the way of instruction, adventure and experience."[535]

III

A 17th-century French engraving, perhaps a frontispiece for a book, tells the whole story. In the middle of the picture, larger than life, sits the mistress of the school, looking like Mother Goose. She wears a benevolent expression, as though she's mighty proud of her students. Both her arms are extended, as if she is introducing them to the viewer. These are little boys, busily reading (probably the Classics), doing geometry, writing and studying the art of war. In the foreground sits a gaggle of pretty girls, dressed to the nines, ignored by the mistress. They're practising sewing of one kind or another, all the while chatting and gossiping.[536]

During the early modern age, more and more girls (and boys) learned how to read and write, but the quality of girls' education did not improve. As one historian put it, no matter what school a girl went to, there was little chance she would emerge a scholar.[537] The reason was straightforward: almost no time was spent on academic subjects. Girls were instructed to become good household managers, dedicated mothers and perhaps most important, deeply committed Christians. As the period progressed, gender differentiation in education became ever more deeply ingrained. Lady Chudleigh expressed what was going on when she wrote in 1645: "As if we were for nothing else designed/But made, like puppets, to divert mankind."[538]

The major historical events of the period would, on the surface at least, seem to promote the education of women. The invention of the printing press in the middle of the 15th century and the publishing industry that grew in its wake increased literacy all round. The Reformation did the same thing. It was Martin Luther's desire that each man and woman would look directly to the Bible for their own inspiration; everyone, therefore, should be able to read the word of God themselves. Moreover, it was up to mothers to teach their young children their ABCs.

But even as Luther fought for new schools for boys and girls, he made it clear a woman's role was definitely not as an intellectual; a preacher or philosopher was a masculine being. As well, the Bible had been translated into the vernacular. In that age, not knowing classical languages was an insurmountable barrier to gaining knowledge of any academic subject from medicine to literature; as one historian wrote: "Not to be able to read Latin was to go in blinkers."[539] With the Bible available in English, though, the major reason for teaching women Latin had disappeared.

The Counter-Reformation also brought more schooling to a larger number of females. The reformers had figured out that pious little girls would eventually turn into pious mothers, who, if literate, could better insure their children's allegiance to the Catholic Church. Convent-run boarding schools in the cities of Catholic countries proliferated; by the end of the 18th century there were 43 in Paris alone. These were very expensive. In 1750, tuition fees were typically 400 to 500 *livres* a year, which could double when combined with personal expenses and private music or dancing lessons. The total was two-thirds of the annual income of a skilled workman.[540]

For all the money, the education such blue-blooded girls received was often dismal, not so much because the teaching sisters were incompetent but because the wealthy parents dictated the timetable. While their brothers were sent to preparatory school for as long as eight years, most girls attended boarding schools for a year or two at the most. Girls would enter or leave school at any time, depending on the demands of the social whirl, so it was impossible for a real course of study to be followed. (Only the Ursulines insisted their students adhere to a curriculum.) What was important was obedience to convent rules and religious piety, not academic learning. Throughout the day, bells never stopped pealing, calling the young students to prayers, constantly interrupting their concentration. Most were there only to prepare for their confirmation, anyway. After that, formal education was cut off.

In England, the educational opportunities for high-born girls were not so much inadequate as nonexistent. Once King Henry VIII had closed the monasteries and disbanded the religious orders and their schools, intellectual training for daughters of the upper class ceased for over a century—except for those few households wealthy and wise enough to hire tutors. It shows in the correspondence of the 16th and 17th century female. Women's letters gradually exhibit appalling spelling and grammatical errors. The satirist Jonathan Swift lamented that "Not one gentleman's daughter in a thousand can read or understand her own language or be the judge of the easiest books that are written in it.... They are not so much as taught to spell in their childhood, nor can ever attain to it in their whole lives."[540a]

Eventually private boarding schools were set up—the first opened its doors in London in 1617—but, since the profit motive was usually foremost, most were truly awful. The biographer of the early feminist Mary Astell describes the situation by the end of the 17th century thus:

In Astell's neighbourhood in Chelsea, where once had lived Sir Thomas More's enlightened household, in which daughters and sons were educated equally, there was Josiah Priests's school satirized ... as an establishment where young female boarders spent their time flirting with lecherous teachers and consuming large quantities of bread and butter. Where once Margaret Roper strolled in the courtyard with Erasmus, discussing Quintilian, the girls in Josiah Priest's Chelsea school imitated the gestures of their dancing master; where once the great Holbein had sketched the remarkable More family, these boarding school girls now japanned boxes.[541]

While girls from affluent homes "tripped along in dainty slippers down the ornamental path of their education," as one critic puts it, those from the lower classes actually benefited from the spread of education. In Paris, a network of elementary schools was set up, usually overseen by religious organizations such as Notre-Dame Cathedral. These *petites écoles* charged fees, but they were low enough that merchants or artisans could afford to send their daughters. Girls commonly spent three or four years between the ages of six and ten in class, studying catechism as well as spinning, sewing and lace-making. While *petites écoles* served the middle class, convents used the boarding schools' high tuition fees to set up adjutant free schools for the poor. Girls were lucky, though, if they were given a year or two in these institutions.

Almost a century later, the Society for the Propagation of Christian Learning established charity schools throughout England, Ireland and Wales. One such was endowed at Great Marlow in Buckinghamshire to teach 24 girls to knit, spin and make bean-lace. Twenty-four boys, however, were taught to read.[542] It quickly became fashionable for the upper crust to donate to these institutions, sometimes quite large sums. A dose of religious studies and the learning of ABCs or lace-making were thought to be ways to impose discipline on the unruly, smelly kids running loose in the streets of cities such as London or Birmingham.

These new schools hired female teachers. Finally, a woman had a way of leading an independent life, even if salaries were often pitifully low. Some even founded schools themselves. Mary Ward was born in Yorkshire in 1585 of a prominent Catholic family, all recusants (those who refused to worship in the Anglican Church). Mary eventually joined the Poor Clares at St.-Omer in northern France. She founded a community of sisters that specialized in teaching English girls who were Roman Catholics, either refugees or those sent abroad to be educated. Eventually, almost a dozen boarding schools were set up in places as far apart as Liège, Cologne, Vienna, Prague, Rome. With each was established a day school for the poor. The curriculum, modelled on the Jesuit schools for boys, set much higher standards than similar institutions.

Mary Ward had many run-ins with the Pope, who frowned on female religious teaching ragamuffins in the city's slums. Once, she was branded a heretic for refusing to be cloistered, and on another occasion, she was imprisoned in a tiny cell in a German prison on the orders of the Church. Eventually, in 1639, she returned to England and, despite persecution there, was director of a girls' school in her native Yorkshire until her death in 1645.

Bathsua Pell Makin was Mary Ward's near contemporary. Born in 1612, she was the daughter of the rector of Southwick in Sussex and sister of the renowned scholar John Pell. Orphaned at an early age, married and quickly widowed, she was reputed to be the most learned woman in all of England. She was tutor and governess to the children of Charles I, and ran a school for girls where she set out to dispel the notion that a young woman's prime occupation was "merely to polish their Hands and Feet, to curl their Locks, to dress and trim their Bodies." Her specialty was foreign languages, and her most celebrated student, Princess Elizabeth, daughter of King Charles, could supposedly read and write Greek, Latin, Hebrew, French and Italian by age nine. Makin could be bitter about her society's deeply ingrained prejudice against female intellectuals. "A learned woman," she wrote, "is thought to be a comet that bodes mischief whenever it appears."[542a]

However, it was that formidable, brainy spinster Mary Astell who made the biggest breakthrough in the philosophy of education. She flatly stated women should be educated not to make good wives and mothers but as an end in itself—a notion viewed as so ridiculous, it would not take root for 200 years. She wrote with some bitterness:

Boys have much Time and Pains, Care and Cost bestow'd on their Education, Girls have little or none. The former are early initiated in the Sciences, are made acquainted with ancient and modern Discoveries, they study Books and Men have all imaginable Encouragement; not only Fame, a dry Reward nowadays, but also Title, Authority, Power and Riches themselves, which Purchase All Things, are the Reward of their Improvement. The latter are restrain'd, frown'd upon, and beat, not *for* but *from* the Muses; Laughter and Ridicule, that never-failing Scare-Crow, is set up to drive them from the Tree of Knowledge. But if, in spite of all Difficulties Nature prevails, and they can't be kept so ignorant as their Masters would have them, they are star'd upon as Monsters, censur'd, envied and every way discouraged.[543]

She envisioned female colleges as quiet and peaceful refuges, where women could engage in strenuous intellectual pursuits free from the harassment of males. What really annoyed Astell, though, was that she saw, as her biographer writes, "men of lower class than herself succeeding as writers, preachers and scholars, while she had difficulty simply finding a way to feed herself or to buy paper to write on."[544] In 1709, Mary Astell opened a charity school for girls in Chelsea, financed by her wealthy female friends. It evidently provided much better education than most of its ilk. The Bible was studied and so was sewing, but the girls' main purpose was to become literate, and by and large they did.

The Enlightenment brought exciting and addictive new ideas about the power of learning to transform. With the proper education, a new social being would come into being, devoid, at last, of all the old superstitions and full of marvellous reasoning. Unfortunately, this superior creation was male. Females were, of course, the mothers and first teachers of the New Man, and therefore had to receive an education of sorts, but it was designed only to make her more interesting and appealing to males. Rousseau, in *Emile*, his influential manual on education published in 1762, put it succinctly:

Thus women's entire education should be planned in relation to men. To please men, to be useful to them, to win their love and respect, to raise them as children, care for them as adults, counsel and console them, make their lives sweet and pleasant; there are women's duties in all ages and these are what they should be taught from childhood on.[545]

At least now there was criticism. Hannah More, Maria Edgeworth and Catherine Macaulay wrote strong rebuttals. Mary Wollstonecraft, in particular, was outraged. She responded to Rousseau's contention that the worst thing about educating women was they would lose their influence over men by writing, "I do not wish them to have power over men; but over themselves."[546]

But it would fall to a character in the 1818 Jane Austen novel *Persuasion* to express most poignantly what the tragedy of a disadvantaged education meant to a woman. Anne Elliot is about to be reconciled with the love of her life, Captain Harville. To provoke her, he puts forth the argument that all women are fickle.

'... I do not think I ever opened a book in my life which had not something to say upon woman's inconstancy. Songs and proverbs all talk of woman's fickleness. But, perhaps, you will say, these were all written by men.'

Anne replies:

'Perhaps I shall. Yes, yes, if you please, no reference to examples in books. Men have had every advantage of us in telling their own story. Education has been theirs in so much higher a degree; the pen has been in their hands. I will not allow books to prove anything.'[547]

IV

Education in the Victorian period was often pragmatic. A young man was trained for his role in life, whether he were a minister, a trader in slaves or a shoemaker. Since no jobs were open to any middle-class female except that of the dreaded governess, there was no point in educating her beyond the most rudimentary learning. As one writer put it, "Men who enjoyed the utmost rigours of education wished to preserve the tender home bloom of maidenly innocence, sweetness, chastity, which might suffer if women were allowed to read Latin and Greek."[548]

It remained very much in fashion to ridicule learned women. Even Sophie von La Roche, the literate grandmother of the German writer Bettina Brentano and the person who had taught Bettina from babyhood, wrote articles in which she repeatedly warned that "knowing too much" would lead to a girl being neurotic or, worse still, a spinster.[549]

In Europe, it was the fashion among upper-class families to tutor young women at home, and then perhaps to send them off for a year or two to a fashionable convent or finishing school. This sometimes produced exceptional women; Virginia Woolf's education, for instance, took place entirely in her father's library. If a household didn't have a highly educated father willing to teach, or money for governesses and tutors, private boarding schools were the alternative. The product of these schools were often silly, naïve and shallowly educated girls, as Charlotte Brontë so wonderfully describes in her novel *Villette*. The young woman in question is Miss Ginevra Fanshawe, who proudly boasts of her ignorance:

'Oh the number of foreign schools I have been at in my life! And yet I am quite an ignoramus. I know nothing—nothing in the world—I assure you; except that I play and dance beautifully—and French and German of course I know, to speak; but I can't read or write them very well. Do you know they wanted me to translate a page of an easy German book into English the other day, and I couldn't do it. Papa was mortified: he says it looks as if M. de Bassompierre—my god-papa, who pays all my school-bills—has thrown away all his money. And then, in matter of information—in history, geography, arithmetic, and so on, I am quite a baby; and I write English so badly—such spelling and grammar, they tell me. In the bargain I have quite forgotten my religion....'[550]

Miss Fanshawe can afford to be flippant about her stupidity; she's very pretty, and therefore will have no trouble finding a husband.

Yet by mid-century, strong undercurrents of reform welled up that would change the nature of women's education forever. There were several reasons for this. To survive in the cut-throat world of the Industrial Revolution, boys needed an early start in life, and that meant an educated mother, who could teach him a thing or two. As well, women involved in the budding first-wave feminist movement came to understand that access to education was as much a woman's right as equality under the law or access to housing or medicine.

Finally, brainy young women themselves began demanding a better quality of education. In her valedictory speech at the Young Ladies' Academy in Philadelphia, Priscilla Mason shocked her audience with sentiments that would have pleased feminists 200 years later:

'Our high and mighty Lords (thanks to their arbitrary constitution) have denied us the means of knowledge, and then reproached us for the want of it. Being the stronger party, they early seized the sceptre and the sword ... they denied women the advantage of a liberal education, forbid them to exercise their talents ... Happily a more liberal way of thinking begins to prevail.'[551]

In Catholic countries, the secularization of women's education began. Curricula that had been composed of 60 percent religious studies and 40 percent academics—mathematics, literature or science—flipped their priorities around entirely. In France, legislation was passed in 1882 requiring all schools to teach certain secular subjects, and a second law in 1886 made the hiring of lay teachers mandatory. The new state *lycées* for girls included a wide range of subjects, including science and mathematics, but not the classical languages that were required for entrance to university. Such reform did not occur without a huge struggle. The Roman Catholic Church fought state-sponsored secondary schools tooth and nail. Bishop Dupanloup, for example, threatened to excommunicate any Catholic in his diocese who allowed a daughter to attend one.[552]

Another major step forward was the setting up of public schools in countries throughout the Western world; by 1880, every major European and North American nation had established such a system. In 1867, the French government instituted a requirement that every commune of more than 500 residents must maintain a primary school for girls, and a law in 1879 created

67 Normal Schools for women who would serve as teachers in these new schools. The United States, which throughout the century led the reform of women's education, had set up public elementary schools in the early 1880s, in which boys and girls were actually taught together. By 1893 in Great Britain, school attendance for both sexes was made mandatory. In Canada by 1905, all provinces except Quebec had passed laws requiring young children of both sexes between the ages of five and 12 to attend elementary school.

Public secondary schools for females were another matter. Even if they had been established by the state, most such institutions charged fees and often did not teach the subjects required for entrance to university. When, in 1870 in Berlin, the Victoria High School was dedicated to the future empress of Germany, the writer Fanny Lewald said it was a fine institution—for the rich. "What we lack is not the top of the tower but a solid foundation," she said. "We need schools, secondary schools for women as well as men."[553] Two years later, the first Berlin public high school was opened. In the United States by 1890, twice as many girls graduated from high school as boys.[554]

Yet it was the private institutions for girls that led the way to true academic excellence. Early in the century, there was a great flourishing of female academies in the United States, Canada and Europe. From 1840 to 1846, the poet Emily Dickinson attended one of these, the Amherst Academy in her home town of Amherst, Massachusetts. To a friend, Emily wrote, "There are Mental Philosophy, Geology, Latin and Botany. How large they sound, don't they? I don't believe you have such big studies."[555]

With girls performing so well in the academies, it was almost a given that post-secondary education would at last become available to them. It started first with women's colleges, which popped up all over the place: Elizabeth Jesse Reid's pioneering Bedford Ladies College in London, Emma Willard's Troy Female Seminary in Troy, New York, the Durham Ladies College in Quebec. The big three American liberal-arts colleges for women were established during this period: Vassar in 1861, Smith in 1871 and Bryn Mawr in 1885. Wellesley College, opened in 1875 in Wellesley, Massachusetts, promised to furnish "to young women a collegiate education, opportunities fully equivalent to those usually provided for young men." It was, said the founders, to become an "Adamless Eden."

Finally, the all-male universities were forced to open their doors to females. In 1875, Mount Allison University in New Brunswick granted a B.Sc. degree to Grace Annie Lockart, the first university in the British empire to graduate a woman. London University admitted women three years later, and McGill University in Montreal and the University of Toronto granted admission to women in 1884.

But it was often a struggle. Girton, a college founded in 1869 for women and connected to Cambridge, is a case in point. It was first located miles from the main campus so as not to cause even a hint of scandal. Moved to the outskirts of Cambridge in 1873, the women were only allowed to take exams unofficially; permission from each professor had to be obtained. It came as a shock when, in 1887, Agnata Ramsay, a Girton student, scored top marks and got a first-class degree. No male that year achieved higher than a second. Over the next few years, Cambridge struggled with the question of whether women should receive degrees. The old boys argued the quality of students would decline, there would be a shortage of rowers for the varsity blues and finally, there was the question of the future: the professions were already overcrowded. In May 1897, a referendum was conducted among the university population; women lost by 1,713 to 662 votes.[556] Until well into the 20th century, female graduates of Oxford and Cambridge were not awarded full degrees but were given something called certificates of degrees to distinguish them from the piece of paper the males carried away. Fortunately, everyone realized how ridiculous this was, and it didn't much hamper female graduates in their job-hunting.

Many male students openly resented their female colleagues and made life miserable for them. M. Carey Thomas, the future president of Bryn Mawr, was a member of the first class that admitted women to Cornell University. She came to understand the difficulty facing women trying to break into male-dominated privilege. At the end of her senior year, she wrote:

There is much that is very hard for a *lady* in a mixed university and I should not subject any girl to it unless she were determined to have it. The educational problem is a terrible one—girls' colleges are inferior and it seems impossible to get the most illustrious men to fill their chairs, and on the other hand it is a fiery ordeal to educate a lady by coeducation—it is impossible to make one who has not felt it understand the living on a volcano or a house top ... yet it is the only way and learning *is worth it*.[557]

Many women felt it was indeed worth it. In the United States, women flocked to the colleges and universities. By 1880, they made up 32 percent of all undergraduates; by 1910 it was almost 40 percent.[558] In Canada in 1900, it was 11 percent, but growing. Just give them the chance at higher education, at intense and difficult study, at knowledge of a world beyond the home, and women would seize it.

V

The revolution in women's education continued after the turn of the century. In France, women were finally allowed to sit for their baccalaureates, which gained them entrance into universities, business and commerce schools. In 1918, the prestigious engineering institute École Central accepted its first female student. When Austrian institutes of higher learning opened their doors to women in 1901, Lise Meitner was delighted. On the eve of her 23rd birthday, she enrolled at the University of Vienna and had the good fortune to study under the pre-eminent physicist Ludwig Boltzman. Five years later, Meitner received her Ph.D., and went on to become one of the greats of the golden age of physics, a co-discoverer of nuclear fission.

By the 1920s in Canada, about 16 percent of the undergraduates at universities were women. In the United States at the same time, almost half the students were female and 15 percent of the Ph.D.s went to women. During the first decade of the century, the number of women faculty members rose sharply, until they made up a third of the whole. There were so many women involved in the scholarly life, male academics began to get nervous. Gustave Cohen, a professor at the faculty of letters in Paris, wrote in *Les Nouvelles littéraires* in 1930, "If someone were to ask me what was the greatest revolution we have seen since the war, I would answer that it was the invasion of the university by women. As scarce as hen's teeth in my youth 32 years ago, their numbers increased until they accounted first for one-third, then for half, then for two-thirds of the student body, to the point where one has to ask, with some anxiety, whether, having once been our mistresses, they will soon become our masters."[559]

Professor Cohen and the many others who thought like him need not have worried. The heady ascent of female scholars came to a dead stop during the 1930s. The reactionary forces against women's progress lined up once again, and the furious backpedalling would not halt until the 1970s.

The weak spots were obvious. While there were a record number of women undergraduates, very few were enrolled in the professional schools: medicine, dentistry, law, sciences of all kinds. Engineering in particular remained an exclusively male preserve. Legions of female scholars might have been hired, but very few got beyond the bottom rung on the academic ladder, no matter how talented they were or how experienced. In the United States in 1920, only four percent of the full professors were women. This meant not only low pay but being left out of the all-important mentor loop. The Great Man who could pull strings for research grants and promotions almost always took male students under his wing, not female. The restrictions on female academics were so severe that one study in the 1920s concluded it simply wasn't worth a woman's time or money to obtain a Ph.D.[560] One of the respondents, a college professor of French, said, "Unless a woman wants to meet with untold discouragement, I certainly would not advise her working for a Ph.D. She cannot hold a very good position in the teaching profession without one, but I feel that women as a whole are treated so unfairly, that I would advise a woman to seek another field of labour....."[561]

Most revealing of all were two surveys, also taken in the 1920s, which indicated only 12 to 13 percent of wives with degrees had paying jobs. This was the dilemma in a nutshell. Women were still being educated not to take their place as economically important members of society but rather as unpaid wives and mothers. "The great woman question of today" and "the very essence of feminism," wrote the lawyer and political radical Crystal Eastman in 1927, "is how to reconcile a woman's natural desire for love and home and children with her equally natural desire for work of her own for which she is paid."[562] There was to be no reconciliation in Eastman's time. When the enormous financial crunch of the Depression hit, women's education was once again called a frill.

In the aftermath of World War II, there was much talk in Europe and North America of not only equality in education between the sexes but also among classes and ethnic groups. Secondary school did become available to almost everyone, and the time allotted to gender-specific subjects such as domestic science (hated by legions of girls) was reduced so both sexes pretty well studied the same academic subjects. Still, there was something holding women back. In 1950, the number of female undergraduates in American colleges had fallen to 31 percent of the total, the lowest number in decades. The same held true in most Western world countries (except the USSR), including Canada. Probably Dick and Jane had something to do with it.

He was a cute, tow-headed boy who played with his boats, flew his kite, jumped and ran around. She was all blonde dimples and played with her dolls, although now and then she was seen riding her tricycle. Handsome Dad arrived home in his shiny, new car to be greeted by smiling Mom in her apron. The *Fun with Dick and Jane* books were how many North American kids learned to read well into the 1960s. By age ten, Dick and Jane thoroughly understood their respective roles in society.

How deeply ingrained the stereotypes were in the Age of Suburbia is illustrated by the commencement address that the poet Sylvia Plath listened to when she graduated from Smith in 1955. The speaker was Adlai Stevenson, who maintained the highest vocation a woman could have was to manage a creative marriage, to be, as Nancy Hunter Steiner remembered it,

thoughtful, discriminating wives and mothers who would use what we had learned in government and history and sociology courses to influence our husbands and children in the direction of rationality. Men, he claimed, are under tremendous pressure to adopt the narrow view: we would help them resist it and we would raise children who were reasonable, independent, and courageous.[563]

Rousseau would have liked the sound of that.

The feminists of the 1970s set out to dig much deeper into their society's soul than their counterparts had in the last century. They would expose the educational system for what it was: an aggravator of gender inequality, a strategy for legitimately passing power down the male line, a propaganda tool to instill in a young woman the belief she and only she was responsible for home and children. A protest sign put it succinctly: "FUCK DICK AND JANE!"

In the last three decades of the 20th century, there has been remarkable progress in the education of women, at least in the Western world. Canadian statistics tell the general story. In 1981, about 11 percent of all those in their 20s, both men and women, obtained degrees; by 1996, that figure had jumped to 20.7 percent for women and only to 16.2 percent for men.[564] In other words, in Canada, at least, very soon many more women than men will have completed university. They are also entering professional schools in record numbers; at many universities, they make up 50 percent or more of law, medicine and journalism. Female MBAs are a dime a dozen. Even those male bastions of architecture and engineering are luring female students to their doors. Girls are doing better in high school, too. A 1996 study in the province of Saskatchewan found the average girl's grades were higher than a boy's in geometry, trigonometry, chemistry, English and French.[565] "It's a trend that's showing everywhere," said the author of the report, "and it dispels the myth that girls 'can't do' science or math." Socrates was only partly right. Not only are girls capable of being trained in exactly the same things as boys, they are often brighter and more diligent.

Mary B.

She was so small, so primly dressed, so naïvely wide-eyed that we used to laugh and say she reminded us of Little Bo-Peep, yet she had the most formidable intellect in the class. No matter what the subject—French, German, trigonometry, physics—Mary Beattie scored in the 90s. You might have thought those ambitious, brilliant boys headed for engineering or medicine or law would have been incensed that this pretty little girl always placed ahead of them. Behind her back they did call her Mary the Super Brainer, but to her face, there was never a disparaging word—they had that much respect for her. Not that it would have mattered much. Mary Beattie was pretty well oblivious to the world around her; her studies were everything.

Not surprisingly, her family was academically oriented. Both her parents had university degrees and rather artistic backgrounds. After graduating from high school, Mary's mother Elinore Lindabury studied for a year at the University of British Columbia, hoping to get into medical school. It would have meant years of study, though, and would also have been very expensive. Even though her father was contributing financially to her education, Elinore knew she couldn't afford it and in the end, decided to take home economics at Macdonald College, a part of Montreal's McGill University.

She graduated in 1939, and found a job at Upper Canada College, the exclusive high school for the sons of the Anglo-Saxon elite. It was at UCC that Elinore met her future husband. Norman Beattie was born in Gapview, a small village near the small town of Forget in the southeastern corner of Saskatchewan. While he was still a child, the family moved further west to Nelson, British Columbia. Nobody knows who encouraged him, but he applied to Upper Canada College and was accepted as a full-scholarship student. Only 13 years old, he travelled the many miles across Canada by train by himself. Mary says he never talked about it much, but she feels it must have been hard for a small-town boy like him to board with the scions of Canada's wealthiest families. He seems not to have made lifelong friends or become part of the UCC alumni network as so many boys did.

After graduation, Norman worked in a bank in Nelson until he saved enough money to attend the University of British Columbia to study Canadian history. He obtained his B.A. in 1939 and later, his M.A. from the University of Toronto. Says Mary, "My father was a very good organizer, not only in terms of the mechanics of everyday life but in intellectual terms. He could see and construct patterns in events and ideas, which very much pertains to history. It was definitely a matter of love."

In 1939, Norman Beattie returned to Upper Canada College, but as a master, not a student. This time he did develop a network of friends among his fellow teachers, as well as making the acquaintance of witty, attractive Elinore Lindabury. She was as intellectually curious as he, and the two fell in love.

They were married in 1942, just after Norman had enlisted in the Royal Canadian Air Force. He was trained as a navigator, and served with the RCAF squadrons flying missions to Burma and India. Elinore went to live with her mother and grandparents in Winnipeg, and when Norman visited her there on furlough, he told her there was a good chance he might not return alive. A child would be a nice memorial. Mary was born there in September 1944.

Fortunately, Norman returned safe and sound. His old position at Upper Canada College was not available, so he took a teaching job at Crescent School, another private boys' establishment in Toronto. Mary's first memories are of running around the wooded grounds of an elitist educational institute.

At UCC, Norman's students had been at the high-school level; at Crescent, he taught Grade 8. He didn't enjoy that as much, and the pay wasn't great. In 1950, he decided to take a job with Ontario Hydro as records manager, looking after the archives and other historical documents. He would gradually take on more responsibility until he became manager of office services for the huge public utility.

By this time, the Beatties had two other children, David and Rod, and needed larger accommodation. Scarborough, booming not too far away, seemed the logical choice. The Beatties' first house was near St. Clair and Pharmacy, part of a new subdivision that Mary remembers as being bleak and rather ugly. When the third son and last child was born in 1954, the family moved to a larger, nicer home, a storey and a half on Brooklawn Avenue, further east in Scarborough. On one side was a vacant lot that edged a lovely, green ravine and on the other side were Scarborough Bluffs.

Mary spent most of her childhood with her nose in a book. "The first time

I read a book, it was very difficult, the second time easier and so on." She was four years old.

Mary had started school when the family was still living in East York. She had had her tonsils out, and when, two weeks later, she finally arrived for kindergarten, the class was full. Her mother insisted that she was ready for school, and the principal agreed to give her a reading test. She was immediately placed in Grade 1 and a few years later, skipped again.

Since she had been accelerated two grades, Mary was only 12 when she started high school, and she looked even younger than her years. She certainly didn't hang out with the in-crowd at the Bo Peep restaurant. She played oboe in the orchestra. She taught Sunday school at the local Anglican church. She was a library assistant and helped with *The Bluff*. But she seldom attended any of the social events, not the dances nor the Classics Club banquets. When everyone else was mooning over Elvis Presley and James Dean, she admired the classical actor Christopher Plummer. When she finally went out with a few guys at the end of her last year in high school, she found dating a terrible ordeal. It was partly her comparatively young age, but it was also her personality. "I would have had a difficult time socially no matter what. I guess I was shy, but I was also not fully sensitive to what was going on and how people felt about things.... I felt I was outside the popular circle but as far as dealing with it, I didn't care. I really didn't care." Her studies were everything.

Right from the beginning, she stood at the top of the class, and she was good in just about every subject. French, Latin and German were particular favourites. It wasn't the literature that appealed to her so much as the intricate structure of the languages. When she looks back, though, she doesn't believe high school provided a very creative environment. It was education by rote; discipline and memory work were everything. "I don't think we were really encouraged to take risks," she says.

The classroom wasn't the only source of intellectual stimulation for Mary, not by a long shot. Her own living room was full of the right kinds of books and magazines. Each evening, around the dining room table, the family would discuss and debate any number of topics. If a particular fact were not known, the meal would simply halt. While the soup got cold, one of the children would run and fetch an encyclopedia. "I thought this was normal, what went on in everybody's house," says Mary. There were strict rules about proper behaviour, though, and Mary's mother had strong opinions about what kind of people made suitable companions for her children.

Unlike the rest of us, Mary did not work during the summers. Her parents thought she needed a rest. "Mother was in no hurry to push me out into the world of work." Nor was she required to do many household chores. Mary watched the soaps on television, sewed some of her own clothes and, of course, devoured books. After the Shakespeare Festival began to flourish in the 1950s in Stratford, Ontario, a couple of summers were spent on a lake near the town. Two of Mary's brothers would eventually have distinguished careers in Canadian theatre, Doug as a producer and Rod as an actor.

As the last year of high school approached, Mary had to narrow her interests. There were two teachers who deeply influenced her in this. Her language teacher, the formidable Miss Smith who brought terror to the hearts of most students, was so much liked by Mary that she became a close, life-long friend. Mary appreciated the older woman's scholarly, intellectual approach to things. "If the times had been right, she was somebody who could have had an academic career at a high level."

There was also Jack McKnight, everybody's favourite math teacher— Robin Williams would have played him well. Soft-spoken, with a grey crew-cut and a sense of humour, he had patience for everybody, even those who were utterly hopeless in math. Says Mary, "He had a wonderful enthusiasm for ideas and a feel for the elegance and the rightness of the way to put things. And the best mathematics has exactly that." It was Mr. McKnight who one day wrote on Mary's report card that she could pursue a career in his subject. She had always assumed she would major in languages at university, but now there was something else to think about. "I was alone in my room one day thinking about it. I realized that I was going to have to decide soon and it suddenly just came to me: I should take math." It was a surprise to everyone, particularly Miss Smith, who was upset she had lost her prize protégé.

Grade 13 was as horrible a year for Mary as it was for the rest of us, and probably for better reasons. Once she had decided on math, she had to take them all: trigonometry, algebra and geometry. She also joined an early-morning problems class that introduced advanced topics such as calculus. Chemistry and physics were needed for the course Mary wanted to take at university, but she wasn't going to drop the languages she still loved. She took both English and German literature and composition, and since there wasn't room in her bulging timetable, she studied French under Miss Smith's tutelage after school. It was the most gruelling schedule she would ever experience. "I remember there was one Friday in February [1961] that I came home and I just started to cry. I couldn't stop, so I went to bed and I didn't get up till Sunday. That's never happened to me before or since."

When the final examination marks were released a few months later, Mary's average was in the 90s. She had topped her class once again, and had achieved some of the highest marks in the province. A classmate remembers her at the high-school graduation. Her mother had made her a gorgeous dress that even allowed for a little décolletage. "She looked like a beautiful china doll, but even at that event, you could see she wasn't really present. She was off in some other place."

Mary decided to take mathematics, physics and chemistry, reputed to be among the most difficult courses offered at the University of Toronto. She was only 16 when she attended her first class. Only about 30 of the 250 students were female, and she was scared—for good reason. It was difficult and intimidating. Among the maths, it was geometry that was the challenge. "I found spatial visualization very difficult, as many women are supposed to do, so it was a really hard year for me. But I persevered, and by the end, I began to have a few small successes here and there."

By her third year, she was handling two physics courses but all the others were math-oriented: geometry, abstract algebra, real and complex analysis, and statistics. She was still getting very good marks, ranking third or fourth among the group who specialized in mathematics. "By the end of the third year, we started to get a really inspirational picture and then the joy of it could be felt more than the hard work. So I was lucky that my instinct had been right. That's what I really enjoyed and wanted to be doing for the rest of time."

Mary was happy to live at home with her parents while she went to university. She dated a little, and would go to concerts and poetry readings, finishing the evening at a local coffee house. She was active in the Math and Physics Society. Almost all the friends she hung out with were classmates, mostly male, who were as dedicated to studying as she was.

During the summers, Mary's father got her a job at Ontario Hydro as a statistics clerk and computer programmer. It was good experience for her, and not just because she was putting her mathematics to practical use. "It was interesting going into the office in your white shoes and white handbag, but I never really got into the spirit of office life." After Mary's third year, she and her mother spent the three summer months travelling around Europe. "We had *Europe on Five Dollars a Day* and by the time we were finished, it was really well thumbed. We had rail passes and went to the cheap hotels and got rush seats to the theatre. It was a good experience for both of us."

For Mary and most of her classmates, continuing on to graduate school was a given. By the end of the third year, there was much talk about what university to go to, what professor to study with and, of course, what area to study. One day, quite suddenly, Mary decided that probability was the specialty for her. Simply put, in mathematics, probability is the assignment of numbers as a measure of the chance that a given event will occur. "I found randomness fascinating and wanted to understand it better," she says.

Mary sent applications to Stanford, Princeton and Berkeley, where she knew there were exceptional scholars among the faculty specializing in the theory of probability. The one that not only accepted her but offered financial support was the University of Illinois at Urbana-Champaign. Mary, who was almost 21, was ready to leave home, and a new residence for women graduate students had just been built, consisting of two-room suites with a bathroom in between. There was privacy and yet there were also people to talk to. Mary felt comfortable at once.

By this time, studying mathematics was no longer difficult, although there were always rough patches. The Canadians among the graduate math students were ahead of their American counterparts. Their undergraduate work had been more specialized and intense. None of them had much trouble passing the Ph.D. qualifying exam because it was based on undergraduate material. After the completion of eight courses, an M.Sc. degree was awarded, which Mary obtained in 1966, but her main goal right from the beginning had been to obtain her doctorate.

The university provided a rich cultural life: museums and art galleries on campus, including the exquisite Krannert Center for the Performing Arts; lectures and lots of performances offered by the excellent music faculty and shows of art films organized by students. It was at one of the free concerts, not long after Mary had arrived at U. of Illinois, where she met a round-faced, pleasant-looking Canadian, a civil-engineering student who was also working on his doctorate.

Carl Thompson had a similar background to Mary's; in fact, they would eventually discover they were fourth cousins. His father was an insurance underwriter and his mother, after her kids had grown up, a secretary. Carl had also attended a suburban high school, Bathurst Heights Collegiate, and then the University of Toronto. Mary's and Carl's political and social outlooks were similar, and because his thesis on solid mechanics theory had a lot of mathematics involved in it, they had that to talk about, too. They began dating steadily, and in February 1968, Mary Beattie and Carl Thompson were married.

The wedding took place in Toronto at Trinity College chapel, with an afternoon champagne reception at the Granite Club. Several of Mary's friends from R. H. King Collegiate were in attendance, including the high-school French teacher Miss Smith. There was no honeymoon for Carl and Mary. They hurried back to their "rather nice apartment" in Urbana to prepare for their last year and a half at university.

It would be a stressful time, since both were intent on completing their doctorates. Carl had already taken a job, so he had to defend his thesis in the summer of 1969. Mary completed hers—it bore the weighty title "Continuous time optimal stopping theory and the structure of some particular cases"—the following July. Mary Thompson, as she was now called, was awarded her doctorate in mathematics in September 1969.

By that time, Mary and Carl had moved to Waterloo, Ontario, where the university was quickly gaining a reputation as Canada's academic centre for computer science and mathematics. The University of Waterloo began in 1959 as an engineering and science faculty associated with the University of Western Ontario in London, Ontario, but two years later, it was chartered as a separate university. Canada's first co-operative program was set up there, in which students spent four months on campus studying academics and four months working in industry for practical experience. It seemed a perfect place for both the Thompsons to work.

When Carl had received word that Waterloo had offered him a position as a research-assistant professor, Mary asked her thesis advisor to write a recommendation for her, a customary way to apply for a job. "When he got the reply, he came to me and he told me, 'They say to hell with you.' He handed me the letter. I went away and burst into tears." Actually, it wasn't quite as bad as the professor had made out. Waterloo had written that they didn't think they were interested in hiring Mary, but since she was moving there, she should come in and have a chat. She did just that, and, as it turned out, there happened to be a real shortage of instructors. She was given one subject to teach, then assigned an office, and during the next year, given a couple more courses. It took a few years, but she eventually became a fully fledged member of the department.

The problem was not so much that Mary was a woman, although in 1969 that certainly didn't help. There were very few female academics in the math faculty, only one in the department and some sessional lecturers who were wives of faculty. The more important reason for not hiring her, though, was her field of research. Waterloo specialized in statistics, following in the tradition of the statistician and geneticist R. A. Fisher; probability theory, Mary's specialty, was considered esoteric. "The feeling was that there was no point in doing theory unless you could see the scientific application for it." Mary solved the problem by learning to teach statistics, which fortunately she found intriguing.

Another difficulty in Mary's career advancement was her teaching. She admits she was poor at it. "My first course was frankly a disaster," she says "I had to work very hard at it, and I gradually improved." In explaining complicated mathematics, the goal is to be as clear as possible; Mary sometimes assumed the students knew more than they did. "Like many people fresh from graduate school, I had no memory of how it was to be an undergraduate. You assume that everybody must understand what you are saying, even if they are just off the street." Mary was finally given tenure in late 1975 as an associate professor, and her career has blossomed since. She has received all the appropriate appointments and salary increases but, as she says, "it did take longer for me at the start than perhaps it should have."

Not only was she teaching, doing essential research and writing papers but she was also having babies. Simon was born in 1973, Andrew in 1975 and Alan in 1980. Mary was lucky in being able to arrange her teaching timetable to take a couple of months off at each birth. She says Carl has always contributed more than his share to housekeeping and child care. In 1971, the Thompsons bought a large, old house in downtown Waterloo and, after the arrival of their second child, they hired an older woman who came in every day to look after the kids. There was also daycare, good but expensive, at the nearby United Church. "My approach was to muddle through from day to day," says Mary. "I enjoyed motherhood very much and I enjoyed working very much, and I was glad to have the two to complement each other. Certainly there was a struggle all the way through, when the children were small, to keep doing everything you were supposed to, but I never was really in serious trouble." If Mary had one regret it was that she and Carl got in the habit of spelling each other off from household duties rather than doing things together.

Only five years after she was granted tenure, Mary was made a full professor, a remarkable accomplishment. She wrote influential research papers, and her public lectures were generally well attended. However, as her 40th birthday neared, she experienced a rough patch. Her children were still very young—Alan was only four years old—and she seemed to be fatigued all the time. She developed chronic insomnia. "I remember taking stock at the time and feeling that although I was functioning very acceptably, there wasn't anything really right in any particular area." Her father died in 1985, which profoundly affected her. She took a sabbatical in 1987, during which she wrote a couple of chapters of a book and worked with graduate students, but domestic chores kept intervening, and the year turned out not to have been as satisfying as she had hoped. Nonetheless, by the time the year was over, she was feeling better. "I became more focused. I got a real sense of who I was and what I wanted."

Mary discovered she had a real knack for administrative work. From 1988 to 1991, she was associate dean of graduate studies and research in the Faculty of Mathematics. In 1996, she was named chair of the Department of Statistics and Actuarial Science, the first woman to hold the position. It is a big responsibility. In 1994–95, there were 3,622 mathematics students at Waterloo, the largest such enrollment in the world, and Statistics and Actuarial Science was the second largest of five departments in the faculty, with a teaching staff of 40.

Mary continues to do research, co-authoring scholarly articles with such esoteric titles as "Cumulant generating function and tail probability approximations for Kendall's score with tied rankings." In 1997, after ten years of hard work, her book, *Theories of Sample Surveys*, was published, and it has been well received by her colleagues.

Mary is almost neurotically modest about her achievements. It's what you do with your God-given talents, she says, and if you happen to be born with your nose in a book, then it's up to you to work harder than anyone else— even if, as she admits, the world is so much readier to excuse the singleness of purpose in a talented man than it is in a talented woman.

Intellectualism

Let a woman not develop her reason, for that would be a terrible thing.
Democritus, c. 460–370 BC

A woman especially, if she has the misfortune of knowing anything, should conceal it as well as she can.
Jane Austen, *Northanger Abbey*, 1818

Let woman live as she should.... Let her know that her spirit is fitted for as high a spheres as man's, and that her soul requires food as pure and exalted as his.
Elizabeth Cady Stanton, *The Revolution*, 1870

I loved to help out in the school library at lunch time. It was peaceful and quiet and often not very busy, so you could browse, which was how I came across a biography of Marie Curie. It was written specifically for young people and I devoured it in a couple of hours.

A child of the '50s, I had assumed that, since she was married to a physicist, Marie Curie would have been merely the helpmate. It was wonderful to learn she was a brilliant scientist in her own right. It was her husband Pierre Curie who had joined *her* in her work on radioactivity. She was as much responsible for discovering the two new elements, radium and polonium, as he was. Both shared (along with Antoine Henri Becquerel) the 1903 Nobel Prize in physics for the discovery of radioactive elements. In 1911, after her husband's death, she was again honoured, this time for chemistry. The first female to receive the Nobel Prize, the first person to be awarded it twice. What an incredibly remarkable woman, I remember thinking. I experienced an extra *frisson* when I read she was a martyr to her science, having died from overexposure to radiation.

I had always understood women could be as brainy as men—that was obvious in the classroom—but only in reading the story of Marie Curie did it dawn on me that, if given a chance, female intellectualism could be a powerful and pragmatic instrument in the transformation of society. For me, Marie Curie's story was truly an epiphany.

I

Plato has long been admired for his enlightened attitude towards women. In *The Republic*, men and women of the upper classes would share equally in the running of the state. They would receive the same education, and a woman's talents were to be nurtured, not quelled simply because she was female. However, a closer examination of the text brings disappointment. "There is no occupation concerned with the management of social affairs which belongs either to woman or to man, as such. Natural gifts are to be found here and there in both creatures alike; and every occupation is open to both, so far as their natures are concerned, *though woman is for all purposes the weaker*."[566] (my emphasis) In other words, the best woman could never be equal to the best man.

Everything is relative, though. Given the misogyny of the time, the idea that a woman of greater talent could be superior to a man with lesser gifts was considered radical—and dangerous—to the male establishment. Another Greek philosopher, Democritus (c. 460–c. 370 BC), presented the more common attitude: "Let a woman not develop her reason, for that would be a terrible thing."[567] Historian Gerda Lerner understands what such sentiments have done to the evolution of female intellectualism. She writes, "... women have for millennia been forced to prove to themselves and to others their capacity ... for abstract thought. This has skewed the intellectual development of women as a group, since their major intellectual endeavor had to be to counteract the pervasive patriarchal assumptions of their inferiority and incompleteness as human beings."[568]

Contradiction lay at the heart of Greek culture; its misogynist views of women and their "feeble minds" smacked right up against the idealized symbol of knowledge as female. For it was the goddess Athena who represented wisdom and intelligence among the heavenly pantheon, and while she may have worn a warrior's outfit—shields, spears, helmet—and remained a virgin spinster, she *was* female. Her Roman counterpart, the powerful Minerva, was considered the personification of thinking and calculating, inventing, among other things, mathematics and musical instruments. As one writer put it, she "exercised a charm over the imagination of women in particular who ... felt that they must live by the light of their minds and foster their native skills of hand and eye."[569] Furthermore, in the Latin language, not only was the soul—*anima*—feminine but so was reason, *ratio*. *Virtus* (virtue), *charitas* (charity), *scientia Die* (God's knowledge) and *sapientia* (wisdom) were all female gendered.

In addition, as cultural critic Marina Warner points out, certain writings of the Old Testament—that embodiment of stern and unbending Hebrew patriarchy—often depict wisdom as female. In the Wisdom of Solomon, a book included in early Greek and Latin translations but not in the Hebrew Bible, wisdom is called Hokhmah (or Sophia) and is described thus:

> She is the breath of the power of God,
> and a pure influence flowing from the glory of the Almighty:
> therefore can no defiled thing fall into her.
> For she is the brightness of the everlasting light,
> the unspotted mirror of the power of God,
> and the image of his goodness.[570]

In Ecclesiasticus, another book of the Apocrypha, wisdom is God's nurse and His representative of the moral life. She speaks in her own voice.

> Whoever listens to me will never have to blush,
> whoever acts as I dictate will never sin.
> All this is no other than the book of the covenant of the Most High God,
> the Law that Moses enjoined on us. (Eccles. 24:22–23)

Why, then, were mortal women perceived as being incapable of intellectual endeavour? It was the great lie at the heart of misogyny in command, for there were, of course, women intellectuals, despite the disabling handicap of circumscribed education and the widespread denigration of all bright females. ("There ought to be some things women never understand," mocked Juvenal.) There was the fourth-century Hipparchia, for example, a flamboyant aristocrat from Maroneia in northeastern Greece who insisted she much preferred spending her time educating herself than sitting at a loom. She fell madly in love with and married the philosopher Crates, and the two lived the unorthodox, libertine life of the Cynics, who rejected conventional proprieties and material possessions, lived as beggars and believed in sexual freedom. It was one of the few philosophies that believed in the equality of the sexes.

The most famous female philosopher in Greek antiquity, however, was

Hypatia of Alexandria. She was born c. AD 355, the daughter of a famous astronomer. By 390, she was well-known throughout northern Africa as a teacher and thinker, so much so that male students flocked to her Alexandria academy. Hypatia was a brilliant mathematician and astronomer, but it wasn't simply the mechanics that interested her. As one scholar put it, "Hypatia sought for greater meaning, so the truths of mathematics and astronomy needed to fit into a greater cosmological and ethical framework. This was consistent with the ancient traditions in philosophy from Pythagorean times when philosophy implied a way of life."[571] According to an early biography, "She threw a rough cloak about herself and went forth through the centre of town and gave lectures in public to those who wanted to listen about Plato or Aristotle or the works of some other philosophers."[572]

By the end of the fourth century, Christianity had become the established faith in the Roman world. After centuries of martyrdom, it was now the Christians who brutally persecuted the pagans. Someone like Hypatia, an attractive woman (she had many suitors whom she rejected in favour of remaining single and a virgin), a non-believer, an independent thinker and a teacher with an enormous following, was bound to excite the wrath of the Christian elite. The patriarch Cyril was particularly incensed. The biographer explains:

When he passed by Hypatia's house, he saw that there was a large crowd in front of the door, made up of both men and horses, some approaching, some going away, and some waiting there. He asked what the gathering was and why there was commotion in front of the house, and learned from his followers that the philosopher Hypatia was now giving a lecture and that this was her house. And when he learned this he was very upset, and soon planned her murder, the most unholy of all murders.[573]

The most dramatic description of what happened next remains that written by the famous British historian Edward Gibbon:

On a fatal day in the holy season of Lent, Hypatia was torn from her chariot, stripped naked, dragged to the church, and inhumanly butchered by the hands of Peter the reader and a troop of savage and merciless fanatics; her flesh was scraped from her bones with sharp oyster-shells, and her quivering limbs were delivered to the flames. The just progress of inquiry and punishment was stopped by seasonable gifts [bribes]; but the murder of Hypatia has imprinted an indelible stain on the character and religion of Cyril of Alexandria.[574]

Gibbon might have added that a woman uppity enough to hone her intellect into a powerful tool must certainly be taught a lesson. Moreover, the patriarch Cyril, who not only had Hypatia murdered but drove all the Jews from Alexandria, was consecrated a saint.

II

There was a basic contradiction in the Middle Ages. The misogynist writings of the early Church fathers had emphasized that the daughters of Eve *naturally* did not have the intellectual or creative ability of Adam's sons, and therefore were doomed to ignorance and intellectual dependency. Yet it was in the monasteries and convents, in a life of dedication to that same patriarchal God, where the intellectual flourishing among women occurred. One of early Church scholars, Jerome (c. 347–c. 420), explained the phenomenon of brainy nuns this way. "As long as woman is for birth and children, she is different from man as body is from soul. But when she wishes to serve Christ more than the world, then she will cease to be a woman and will be called man."[575]

The Dominican nuns of the 14th and 15th centuries were particularly industrious in giving themselves a voice at a time when no one in the male establishment wanted to hear it. They created Sister books, histories of their orders or individual nuns. In 1318, Anna von Münziger, the prioress of Adelshausen, wrote not only the epic of her convent but about the lives and mystical experiences of 34 nuns.[576]

However, any kind of intellectual activity for women religious (or for that matter, any woman) was a struggle. They had to overcome their own individual sense of inadequacy, as well as the deep-rooted perception that their entire sex was inferior. Nowhere is this more obvious than in the letters of Héloïse, who was Peter Abélard's brilliant student. After Abélard had seduced her, she had borne his child, they had married and his testicles had been pinched by order of her uncle, both retired to the religious life. Eventually, she became one of the great abbesses of her time; Paraclete Convent became a centre of learning and scholarship for nuns.

Nine years after the traumatic events, Héloïse read Abélard's confessional *The Story of My Misfortunes*. She was upset by it, feeling he had offered a distorted version of what had happened, and began corresponding with him. Three of her letters and his replies, all in Latin, have survived. What emerges are not only contrary ideals of goodness and love but also different concepts of the nature of thought itself.[577]

When she was his student, Abélard had attacked Héloïse for her feminine way of putting things, her "woman's tongue":

The more subtle [the tongue] is in you, and the more flexible because of the softness of your body, the more mobile and prone to words it is, and exhibits itself as the seedbed of all evil. This defect in you is noted by the Apostle when he forbids women to speak in church; not even on matters pertaining to God does he permit them to speak unless they question their husbands at home.[578]

Héloïse did not challenge the accepted wisdom that women were of the weaker sex, but by the time their correspondence resumed, she was prepared to argue with Abélard on matters that she considered fundamental to the human species. She defended the pleasure of sexual relations, promoted the ideal of love. Even if Abélard is not capable of sexual acts, she insists, he still owes her love based on mutual responsibility and respect. Her letters to him are impassioned: "Nothing have I ever (God wot) required of thee save thyself, desiring thee purely, not what was thine. Not for the pledge of matrimony, nor for any dowry did I look, nor my own passions or wishes but thine (as thou thyself knowest) was I zealous to gratify."[579]

This embarrassing show of feminine emotion was the chief reason that for centuries, male scholars refused to recognize Héloïse as a thinker of value (especially compared to the seemingly logical Abélard). But her insights went to the dark heart of medieval society. She believed, for instance, marriage should be constructed on love and respect, not a dynasty's financial gain. Abélard's response was to write cool polemics sprinkled with erudite scholarly references. All sexuality, he insisted, is nothing but ugly and degrading lust. Through his castration, God "cleansed him rather than deprived him" in eliminating what is only "sordid and worthless."

Héloïse has been ridiculed by scholars for refusing to swallow the dualistic metaphysics of the day. She believed a person was a complete organism, not a polluted body joined to a rational soul. She may have sensed that in a universe where dualism prevailed, women would always be associated with the physical rather than the spiritual, and therefore would be eternally inferior beings. From this vantage point, and as far as humanity is concerned, her passion wins hands down over Abélard's rationalism.

III

Nobody knows exactly how Anne Viscountess Conway (1631–1679) was able to write *The Principles of the Most Ancient and Modern Philosophy*. She was always so ill with excruciating headaches. She slept on pillows only of the softest down, since even a feather could touch off her migraines.

The headaches had begun when she was a child, playing about the grounds of Kensington House. Her family blamed her malady on her addiction to reading, which was considered unsuitable for delicate little girls. As historian Laurinda S. Dixon put it, "The inherent feebleness of the female mind, the result of natural coldness, was often cited as justification for barring the entire sex from serious intellectual activities."[580] Anne's nose remained in her books anyway. Before she was 20, she had read Plato in Latin and Greek, Plotinus in Latin, and she immersed herself in the writings of contemporary philosophers, particularly Spinoza and Descartes.

Perhaps because her father had died before she was born, she had a strong attachment to her stepbrother John Finch, who returned her affection. He introduced her to his tutor, the philosopher Henry More, who took her under his wing, guiding her in her studies and introducing her to the *Kabbala*, an esoteric, Jewish interpretation of the Scriptures that deeply influenced her writings. He dedicated an important work to her, calling her his "Heroine Pupil."

In 1651, Anne married the aristocrat Edward Conway, and thereby became chatelaine of Ragley Castle, Herefordshire. Despite all her privileges, though, her life was one of unrelenting suffering. Her headaches had never ceased; indeed, the older she got, the worse they became. Every remedy was tried: doctors and quacks came and went; medicines of all kinds, "red powders," "blue powders," many opium-based, were prescribed. Anne even travelled to France to undergo trepanning, a horrendous operation in which a hole is drilled into the skull to relieve the pressure. Her condition was further exacerbated when her only son died at age two and a half from smallpox.

During Anne's years of illness, a well-known physician and man of letters F. M. van Helmont arrived at Ragley Castle to treat her. He was so taken by her, so perplexed by her illness, that he stayed nine years. It was probably van Helmont who, after her death in 1679, collected her papers, had them translated into Latin (perhaps by Henry More) and then published in book form as *The Principles of the Most Ancient and Modern Philosophy*.

There are two motifs colouring her philosophy: first, her Christian heritage, which was rather unorthodox because of her references to the *Kabbala* (she probably read some Hebrew), and second, the tradition of rationalism put forward by philosophers such as Descartes. (She did not agree with many of his specific ideas and used *The Principles* to refute them.) Her goal was to try to reconcile these two philosophical legacies, and she went some way to achieving this.

For years, Anne Conway's writings were ignored by academics. Recently, however, feminist scholars have taken another look at a work that tackles difficult and profound questions in the tradition of rationalism, not the least of which was the essence of time and God's creation. Conway was, as the scholar Jane Duran puts it, "an original and incisive philosopher of her time, whose work influenced Henry More, and anticipated [and influenced] Leibniz...."[581]

Conway was not, by any means, the only woman of great intellectual stature in the early-modern period. In 1699, 21-year old Dorothea Maria Graff boarded a ship in Amsterdam with her mother and set sail for Surinam, the Dutch colony in South America. It was unusual, to say the least, for two women to be travelling alone, never mind that they were doing so for professional reasons. Dorothea's mother was Maria Sibylla Merian, an accomplished artist and naturalist. Two years later, the two women returned to Europe, laden with plant and insect specimens, the foundation of Maria Sibylla's great work, *Metamorphosis of the Insects of Suriname*, which established her as one of the foremost botanists of her day.[582]

But it was Anna Maria von Schurman (1607–1678) who was perhaps the most famous woman intellectual of the 17th century. Born in Cologne, von Schurman lived most of her life in Utrecht in the Netherlands. A precocious, vivacious child, she was not only talented in the activities at which little girls were supposed to excel—music for example—but she became proficient in mathematics, geography and astronomy, and fluent in all the modern European languages, as well as Latin, Greek, Hebrew, Syrian, Chaldean and Arabic.[583] Her father knew what a prodigy he had on his hands, and encouraged her studies. He arranged for her to attend the lectures held at the newly founded University of Utrecht, although she was always hidden discreetly behind a curtain, and urged her not to waste herself by marrying, advice she heeded until she was 60 years old.

Von Schurman's influence derived from her correspondence with such people as French philosopher Descartes and scientist Pierre Gassendi, Dutch humanist and poet Constantijn Huygens, Cardinal Richelieu and various theologians connected with the University of Leyden. What was interesting was the number of women she counted among her pen pals. These included Queen Christina of Sweden, Bathsua Makin and Dorothea Christiane Leporin (both outstanding advocates for women's education) and the intellectuals Marie le Jars de Gournay and Lucretia Marinella. Princess Elizabeth of Bohemia, herself an important thinker and a confidante of Descartes, was a particularly close friend.

It was not just her letters that established Anna Maria von Schurman's fame and influence. Her Utrecht home became a gathering place for the powerful and famous. In 1642, she published a book in Latin called *The Learned Maid, or Whether a Maid may be a Scholar*, in which she argued syllogistically the case for giving women higher education. Although she advocated schooling only for those girls from well-to-do families who were single, she vigorously defended a woman's right to an intellectual life. As she put it:

No one can properly judge our ability for study until he has first with the best of motives and every possible support encouraged us to undertake serious study so that we may acquire a taste for the joys of it.[584]

As historian Gerda Lerner points out, the sexes reacted quite differently to her intellectual prowess. "... for men she became the prototype of the woman of genius, the grand exception to the generally accepted image of the intellectually inferior woman; to women she became a heroine and an example to be emulated."[585] This perceptual contradiction would fester through the next several centuries, with unfortunate consequences for women.

The parade of female intellectuals that marched through the latter half of the 17th and through the 18th centuries was astounding. In London, the bluestockings, a lively and infamous group of women that included Hannah More, Elizabeth Montagu, Hester Thrale and Elizabeth Carter, would meet at evening soirées to discuss and debate the literature of the time. Parisian salons were full of waggish and clever women who could match wits with the Enlightenment *philosophes*. The wonderfully independent-minded Madame de Staël, for example, was a product of her mother's brilliant salon.

Paradoxically, and depressingly, this exhibition of female erudition seems not to have made an impression on the male philosophers of the Enlightenment. Almost to a man, they believed women either lacked reason altogether or their ability to think was innately inferior to men's. Females, they decided, were creatures of passion and imagination, but incapable of forming concepts or providing explanations. Scientific invention or artistic genius was simply beyond them. As Rousseau explains in *Emile*, "The search for abstract and speculative truths, principle axioms in the sciences, and everything that tends to generalize ideas is not within the compass of women: all their studies must deal with the practical. Their job is to apply the principles that men discover and to make the observations that lead men to establish principles."[586]

The next centuries would gradually see a repudiation of this insidious and debilitating idea of female intellectualism, but it would be a long and hurtful struggle. Women who developed intellectual lives would constantly have to shore themselves up against the insults and injuries heaped on them by the male establishment. In Jane Austen's 1818 novel *Northanger Abbey*, the narrator puts the dilemma succinctly: "A woman especially, if she have the misfortune of knowing any thing, should conceal it as well as she can."

IV

Francinet, first published in 1869, was a popular reader for girls and boys ages eight to 11 in French elementary schools. The author was listed as G. Bruno, a pseudonym, as it turned out, for Augustine Fouillée, the timid wife of a Sorbonne professor of psychology. In this excerpt, Aimée is a bright, enthusiastic student. M. Edmond is her pompous teacher.

M. Edmond—'Well, Aimée. Prove to us once again how quickly you understand and tell us why women are so rarely found among inventors.'

Aimée, very embarrassed—'Goodness! It seems to me, sir, that in order to invent something, you have to be involved in it. I don't know whether women could have invented the locomotive, like Stephenson; but I know that they never had the opportunity; for they have never been assigned to tend machines, and people would find it very funny to see them learning mechanics or mathematics.'

M. Edmond—'Very well reasoned, dear Aimée. Woman's role in society is not at all the same as man's. A woman's life is entirely interior, and her influence on society occurs in a nearly invisible manner. This not to say, however, that her role is any less important or her influence smaller; it is only more hidden, that's all.'[587]

The exchange, silly as it is, between M. Edmond and Aimée nicely lays out the equal-but-different philosophy that dominated the Victorian period. The consensus slowly built that women, while certainly a different species than men, were not biologically or intellectually inferior to them. Indeed, they may very well be superior. As historian Nancy F. Cott puts it, women were said to be "moral, nurturant, pacific and philosophically disinterested, where males were competitive, aggrandizing, belligerent and self interested." The suffragette Jane Frohock wrote in the American reform journal *Lily*, "It is woman's womanhood, her instinctive femininity, her highest morality that society now needs to counter-act the excesses of masculinity that is every-where to be found in our unjust and unequal laws."[588]

Unfortunately, such sentiments further locked the two spheres solidly in place. How would the angel by the hearth, if she were all altruism and appeasement, ever thrive in the competitive universe of the Industrial Revo-lution? How could she escape into the outside world? It was the major dilemma facing those feminists who, during the Victorian period, tried so hard to formulate a philosophy of women's rights. No one illustrates more dramatically how painful could be the strictures of domesticity in conflict with a desire to soar in the outside world than the American suffragette Eliz-abeth Cady Stanton (1815–1902).

Elizabeth was born into a socially prominent and wealthy family. Her father had been elected to the United States Congress and subsequently was named a New York Supreme Court judge. All five of Elizabeth's brothers died, leaving her parents, Daniel and Margaret Cady, bereft. There's a story in Stanton's memoirs of tiptoeing into the parlour where lay the open coffin of the last of these boys. Her father sat ashen-faced and grief-stricken. She climbed on to his knee. "At length he heaved a deep sigh and said, 'Oh, my daughter, I wish you were a boy!' Throwing my arms about his neck, I replied, 'I will try to be all my brother was.'"[589]

Elizabeth kept her promise by learning to ride horses and play chess, study-ing Greek and Latin, and placing first in her graduating class at Johnstown Academy. She wanted to continue her studies at Union College in Schenec-tady, but girls were not allowed and, anyway, that same blinkered father forbade any further formal education for her. She lamented, "To think that all in me of which my father would have felt a proper pride had I been a man is deeply mortifying to him because I am a woman."[590] The most he would grant her was two years at Emma Willard's Female Seminary in Troy, New York, where she learned how to sew, dance and speak French.

In 1840, she married Henry Stanton, a lawyer ten years her senior and an outspoken abolitionist. Elizabeth and Henry spent their honeymoon in London at the World's Anti-Slavery Convention. Much to Elizabeth's disgust, women delegates were excluded from the floor of the convention. The Quaker Lucretia Mott, who, with her husband, had helped organize the American Antislavery Society, was just as angry as Elizabeth. This snub left such an imprint on the two that they would spend most of their lives fighting for the rights of women.

Luckily for Elizabeth, she had indomitable energy. Almost immediately, the babies started arriving; she gave birth to all seven children attended by a midwife rather than a doctor. The morning after her fourth son was born, by her own account, "I got up, bathed myself in cold water and have sat by the table writing several letters."[591] Her husband Henry suffered from congestion of the lungs, and to improve his health, he moved his family to a supposedly more humid climate on the outskirts of Seneca Falls. Whether he felt better or not is not known, but three children contracted malaria and Elizabeth had to spend many months nursing them. Henry wasn't at home very much anyway; he was away pursuing his political and journalistic career. Elizabeth felt isolated and totally consumed by her mothering and household duties. "The novelty of housekeeping had passed away, and much that was once attractive in domestic life is now irksome."[592]

In the summer of 1848, Elizabeth went to visit her old friend Lucretia Mott, who was staying nearby. "I poured out ... the torrent of my long-accumulating discontent with such vehemence and indignation that I stirred myself, as the rest of the party, to do and dare anything."[593] What they dared was to call the first women's-rights convention. It was held at the Wesleyan Chapel in Seneca Falls and attended by about 300 women and a few men. The Declaration of Sentiments, modelled after the U.S. Declaration of Independence, was written by Elizabeth Cady Stanton, and is a remarkably radical statement for the time. In part, it complains:

He has made her, if married, in the eye of the law, civilly dead.

He has taken from her all right in property, even to the wages she earns.

He has made her, morally, an irresponsible being, as she can commit many crimes with impunity, provided they be done in the presence of her husband. In the covenant of marriage, she is compelled to promise obedience to her husband, he become to all intents and purposes, her master—the law giving him power to deprive her of her liberty, and to administer chastisement.[594]

From this convention emerged a powerful movement that would fundamentally change women's status in society, but it would be a long and difficult struggle.

In 1851, Elizabeth Cady Stanton met Susan B. Anthony, a teacher five years her junior. The two women formed a solid friendship, a partnership, really, which protected both of them from the slings and arrows of ridicule. Susan Anthony had purposely rejected marriage so she would not be burdened with children and housework, and she often despaired when Elizabeth announced she was once again pregnant. But she didn't hesitate to rush to her friend's side if she were needed, as Stanton writes, "to make the puddings and carry the baby while I ply the pen." While Elizabeth stayed home and looked after her family, Susan travelled the lecture circuit, proselytizing. Both were tireless political campaigners.

As they grew older, Elizabeth Stanton became more radical than the liberal Quaker Susan Anthony. "The male element," Elizabeth wrote in 1869, "is a destructive force, stern, selfish, aggrandizing, loving war, violence, conquest, acquisition, breeding in the material and moral world alike discord, disorder, disease and death."[595] Such passionate language, and her blunt way of presenting her case, lost her plenty of friends and supporters, but it probably made her feel better. Stanton advocated liberal divorce laws, and by doing so, outraged the comfortable society to which her upper-class family had long been connected. More shocking still, she came to believe religion was a great oppressor of women. The sacred origin of the Bible and the authority of the Church were repudiated.

All these ideas were put down on paper. From 1869–70, Stanton and Anthony published a newspaper they called *Revolution*. The very name offended sensibilities. Elizabeth also carried on a massive correspondence, and she wrote many speeches, papers and books: *The Woman's Bible*, outlining her "blasphemous" ideas on religion, and her historically valuable memoir *Eighty Years and More* are two. As well, she, along with Susan Anthony and Matilda Joslyn Gage, edited the immense *History of Woman Suffrage*.

Missing almost altogether from her writings is Henry, her husband of 46 years. One letter to Susan Anthony does give a glimpse into her domestic life. She wrote: "The pressure on me now is just too great. Henry sides with my friends, who oppose me in all that is dearest to my heart. They are not willing that I should write even on the woman question. But I will both write and speak. I wish you to consider this letter strictly confidential." She concludes, "Sometimes, Susan, I struggle in deep waters."[596]

Struggling in deep waters could have been the theme song of so many daring women who, during the 19th century, fought to establish the fundamental principle that women were independent and individual thinkers.

V

The challenge for 20th-century intellectuals was to undermine a cornerstone of philosophy that had dominated since time immemorial: the metaphysics of the sexes, the doctrine that maintains "there is an essential, indeed a natural, difference between men and women, that has locked them into very distinct societal roles."[597] The problem in this arrangement of the universe was that the male was considered the human template and the female only a shadowy version of the original. German philosopher and sociologist George Simmel put it this way. "The male sex judges itself to be superior to the female, not simply in a relative sense but as the representative of the universal human being that established the general laws which govern the manifestations of the particular male and the particular female. That it can do this depends, through a series of mediations, on the *position of power* that men occupy."[598]

At the turn of the century, this view was reinforced by the blossoming of psychoanalysis, the science of the unconscious. At its heart was the theory that father, mother, son and daughter were hierarchically fixed in the family. Girls grew up understanding they were lesser than boys. They envied their brothers, who had penises, and knew the clitoris was a poor substitute. Once again, the female was defined negatively in relation to the male. As scholar Françoise Collin writes, psychoanalysis "examines the long process by which the male child learns to inhabit his gendered reality and the female child learns to resign herself to hers."[599]

The young women pouring out of the universities at the turn of the century considered both philosophy and psychoanalysis as arbitrary and subjective. What they wanted were neutral scientific standards, based on knowledge, rationality and objectivity, disciplines in which they could show off their professional expertise. This was exactly what the newly emerging social sciences—sociology, psychology and ethnology—were offering. The female scholars who entered these fields were not much interested in women's issues, and for decades, sexual differentiation was not an important theme in their research. Even those women who made philosophy their life's work made little attempt to replace "the metaphysics of the sexes" with another serious corpus addressing the thorny question of gender. All the prefeminist philosophers—Jeanne Hersch, Suzanne Langer, Gisèle Brelet, Jeanne Delhomme, Simone Weil and even Hannah Arendt, who was concerned with her Jewishness—hardly touched the issue of sexual differentiation.

An exception was Edith Stein (1891–1942), a prominent German-Jewish philosopher, educator, lecturer and feminist. At the universities of Breslau, Göttingen and Freiburg-im-Breisgau, she studied phenomenology, a philosophical movement that has at its core the idea of "transcendental subjectivity," intuition in analysing phenomena. In 1917, Stein achieved her Ph.D. *summa cum laude*, and, eventually, published ten volumes unveiling her theories of phenomenology.

For several years, she was also the assistant to Edmund Husserl, the founder of the phenomenology movement. As it turned out, Husserl was not interested in collaborating with her. She was to transcribe his lectures and edit his writings, not bother him with her own ideas. If she had been male, the next step would have been a professorship of her own, but the University of Freiburg refused to even consider her, because the appointment would have been a major break with tradition. It would be another 30 years before a woman actually took up teaching duties in philosophy at a German university.

Edith Stein took teaching jobs at minor academies, including St. Magdalena's school for girls in Speyer. It was there that she began probing into the nature and destiny of women. She came to believe men and women were distinct species. Each had a different essence or nature, neither of more importance than the other, which could be used in tandem to advance human endeavour. Stein also believed a woman's way of knowing is characterized by intuition, an intuitive grasp of the abstract. As one historian put it, Stein believed that women "want the ideological, the conceptual, to be related to the world of persons and things. They want psychology, for example, to have something to do with human beings, sociology to have something to do with the concrete human situation, and physics to be related to the real world of experience."[600] Above all, education was essential for a rich and satisfying life. "The intellect," Stein wrote, "is the key to the kingdom of the spirit.... The intellect must be pressed into activity. It cannot become bright and sharp enough."[601]

The feminism that emerges from the writings of Edith Stein was not a call to arms, a waging of sexual war. Hers was a non-combative philosophy, which is what separates her from the feminists of the latter half of the century. Women were to make full use of their special intuitive nature, but they were also to appreciate the uniqueness of male attributes. Together, they would further the cause of all humanity. It was a humanitarian, even utopian, feminism, made especially poignant by the fact that Stein died in Hitler's death camp at Auschwitz in August 1942. She had converted to Catholicism in 1921 and entered the Carmelite sisterhood, but it proved to be no shield. (In 1987, she was beatified by Pope John Paul II, causing an uproar in the Jewish community; in 1998, she was canonized.)

By mid-century, there was a dramatic shift in the perception of sexual differences. The seals that had locked the categories of male and female into place for so long were broken. It had to do in part with a general loss of faith in the omnipotence of calculating reason; two world wars and a world-wide economic depression had seen to that. Suddenly, there was a new way of relating to the world, a new way of thinking that would have profound implications for women's roles in society.

In 1949, Simone de Beauvoir published *The Second Sex*. In it, she famously pronounced, "A child is not born a woman but becomes one." In other words, the roles that a female is obliged to play are imposed not by her nature but by society. Paradoxically, a large portion of this huge work is taken up with describing the problems of female physiology, from menarche to motherhood to menopause. De Beauvoir also seems to have an inherent dislike for women. She is unsympathetic to them and often denigrates them.

Nevertheless, her work hugely influenced the feminists who emerged in the late 1970s. Her ideas were quickly radicalized, however. Not only the social construction of sex or gender but also the reality of sexual differentiation itself was challenged. Martine Rothblatt, an American lawyer and authority on bioethics, for example, believes the division of humanity into two sexes is the most long-standing and rigidly enforced of all social stereotypes, and has done unimaginable harm to the countless individuals who have not fitted sexual molds. She writes:

Manhood and womanhood can be lifestyle choices open to anyone, regardless of genitalia. It is law and custom, not biology, that makes birth order, birth parents, skin tone, or genitals relevant to one's ability to choose a culture, perform a job, or adopt a lifestyle. Liberated from legal constraints and archaic stereotypes, our social identity can flow from our soul and our experiences, not from our anatomy and our birth status.[602]

Egalitarian feminism, as it came to be called, emphasized legal rights and the attainment of a gender-neutral world in which men and women were thought to be equally capable of raising children and waging war. That these ideas were not accepted by everyone is an understatement. There has been a profound split in the feminist community.

Many other women believe, like the Victorians (hence the name New Victorianism), that women's talents, especially in the nurturing of children and strengthening personal relations, are superior to men's. These qualities should be celebrated; they might even save the world. This philosophy, often called difference feminism, promotes legislation that favours and protects women: maternity leave, for example. As one writer puts it, "Different-voice ideology locates female sexuality in maternity, as did Victorian visions of the angel in the house. In its simplest form, the idealization of motherhood reduces popular feminism to the notion that women are nicer than men."[603] Who can blame women for embracing theories that honour them for the sacrifices they have made on behalf of domesticity and children? It must give comfort to believe they are somehow more noble than their husbands or career women who send their kids to daycare.

In a 1992 essay, American feminist Katha Pollitt effectively signals the danger of such thinking:

Although it is couched in the language of praise, difference feminism is demeaning to women. It asks that women be admitted into public life and public discourse not because they have a right to be there but because they will improve them. Even if this were true, and not the wishful thinking I believe it to be, why should the task of moral and social transformation be laid on women's doorstep and not on everyone's—or, for that matter, on men's, by the you-broke-it-you-fix-it principle? Peace, the environment, a more humane workplace, economic justice, social support for children—these are issues that affect us all and are everyone's responsibility. By promising to assume that responsibility, difference feminists lay the ground-work for excluding women again, as soon as it becomes clear that the promise cannot be kept.[604]

In some women's eyes, the equality-versus-difference debate has meant a choice between masculinization (and thus alienation) or accepting a so-called feminine role that is anachronistic and worn out. At the heart of both these philosophies, though, is the realization that the power struggle between men and women continues, if not necessarily on an individual basis, certainly throughout a society that remains essentially a patriarchy. The crucial philosophical question still facing women is how to break the stranglehold of that dreary, unjust universe perpetuated by the androcentric metaphysics of the sexes, no matter in what new language or interpretation it is couched.

5. The Soul

Mary L.

Mary Lomas would be first up to compliment you on your cherished new pair of saddle shoes and she'd do it sincerely, without a hint of malice. She did everything right: sent a get-well note when the English teacher, Miss Crooke, was ill; passed the ketchup for your french fries without squirting it on you first; and, if she slipped during square-dancing in the gym, said nothing more profane than "Oh rot!"

Tall and slender, an Audrey Hepburn type, Mary wasn't prissy—you could hear her musical laugh echoing through the corridors. She was so courteous, caring and conforming—so ladylike, the trait our mothers had tried hard to impose on us. It was especially astonishing, then, that of all the Class of '61, Mary Lomas would be the one to break the mold so completely.

Perhaps good behaviour and decorum were stressed in the Lomas family because its members were struggling to keep a foothold in the middle class. Mary's grandfather John Lomas worked in the fabric department of Simpson's department store, although that belied his true character. He had been an athlete in his youth, a rugby player. His son Jack was not athletic—his great love was music—and this deeply disappointed his father, a bully who never failed to criticize and belittle his only child.

Jack's difficult early years didn't suppress his natural gregariousness. He loved big-band music, loved to dance, and it was at a party that his eye fastened on a demure, ladylike young woman. "I'm going to marry that girl," he told his best friend. "You haven't a hope in hell," responded his friend. What the friend didn't realize was that Joyce Sweetman was so shy and socially inhibited, she was quite happy to be swept off her feet by someone as extroverted and friendly as Jack Lomas.

Joyce's childhood had also been troubled. Her father had died when she was nine, and, since her mother had to go out to work, Joyce ended up as housekeeper and babysitter for her younger brother. Mary always felt her mother never really had a childhood. By age ten, she was already an overly efficient, take-charge kind of person. Joyce was a clever, efficient young woman—she became a crackerjack legal secretary—and it was those attributes, among others, that appealed so much to Jack Lomas. He thought she had a lot of class.

Joyce Sweetman and Jack Lomas were married in 1939. The early years of their marriage were happy, but, as Mary says, it was almost inevitable that a fun-loving guy like her father and an introverted woman like her mother would end up having problems. "Once the romantic part was over," says Mary, "they didn't have enough in common." By the time Mary was in school, the two were leading quite distinct lives, and in the late 1970s, Joyce and Jack finally divorced.

Once she was married, though, Joyce quit her job to look after her kids. She had already learned a lot about organization and money-management. It was she who set the budget, and Mary says she did a lot with a little. Her passion was home renovating. She'd buy a down-at-the-heels house, fix it up, sell it at a profit and move into another. Mary thinks she never made a killing, but the family was able to move up in the world. Even though theirs was the smallest house on the block, they lived on the prestigious Glen Manor Drive. It also meant Mary changed schools many times in her childhood.

Jack got a job as a meter-reader for Ontario Hydro, but he was also no slouch in providing extra income for the family. Mary says he was something of a hustler, in the good sense of the word, always taking odd jobs on the side. In the late 1950s, he hit upon a sideline that suited him perfectly. He assembled a first-rate sound system with state-of-the-art amplifiers and began making the rounds of weddings and parties, playing records from his huge collection, all before the term disc jockey was part of the jargon.

In the Lomas family, Mary was treated quite differently than her brother. "He was allowed to steer the car when Dad was driving. That looked like fun and I wanted my turn. Oh, no way. I was a girl." Mary realizes now that, from a young age, her life was being carefully scripted by her parents, her mother in particular, and as a child, she was always auditioning for her assigned role of marriage and motherhood.

Mary's refuge from the unhappiness of the strained relations at home was school. She relished every moment in the classroom, loved her friends and the school-yard games. She did well, although she would become upset if she made a mistake or didn't get as high a mark as the student next to her. "I remember one time, it was in Grade 2, I think, I brought home my report card, which had all As. I was thinking, 'This is really going to do it,' because I wasn't getting the kind of praise and reinforcement at home that I was at school. My mother looked at the report card and smugly said, 'That's good, but don't forget, you can always do better.' I pleaded, 'But you can't do any better than all As.'" Mary believes her mother had good intentions. For her own good, a child was to be prevented from becoming vain or overly confident. "But I paid dearly for that puritanical attitude," she says.

There was not much encouragement to do well at high school. Mary says the script read that she would marry, so why prepare for a career? Her mother urged her daughter to take the less-demanding commercial courses, but Mary chose academic subjects and did well at them. She particularly enjoyed Latin, and was part of a group of closely knit students who took it right through Grade 13. In later life, the Greek and Roman myths Mary studied at high school would become ever more valuable to her as she searched for a meaning to her life.

Although she loved high school and had a wide circle of friends, there wasn't much time for after-school activities. Mary was assigned a myriad of household tasks that took up much of her free time. There was also a part-time job as a salesclerk downtown, Saturdays and one evening a week, and as an elevator operator all summer. She remembers being tired a lot of the time, and having painful migraine headaches. When she wasn't performing her many duties, she spent the time alone in her bedroom, reading or thinking. She developed a propensity for solitude and silence that has lasted her entire life. In some ways, it laid the foundation of what would become Mary's intense spiritual quest.

Even though she got pretty good grades, there was no talk of university around the Lomases' dining-room table. It was out of the question. Mary decided to become a teacher, which was uppity enough, but that, at least, would likely lead to a woman's real career as a wife and mother.

After graduating from teacher's college, Mary was hired to teach Grade 1 at Kimberly Public, the school her father had attended. She was happy from the start. "As soon as the door closed and I was alone with my own students, I knew I was in my element. It was my bedroom revisited, only with a bunch of kids in it."

Mary had always been one of those girls who relished having a boyfriend around. In Grade 9, she dated a happy-go-lucky fellow, three years older than she, who took her to the dances she loved so much. After that, there were always guys in the picture, including Ron Macleod. He owned a '52 Ford and taught Mary to drive. Together they would careen all over the countryside. He left school after Grade 13 to go into the financial and

mortgage-brokerage business, but the two continued to date, if only occasionally. Mary suffered a couple of heartbreaks, but Ron was always there
in the background, attentive and loyal, expressing his everlasting love. In
1965, he asked her to marry him and she agreed. "Ron looked stable, with
a lot going for him, and all my girlfriends were getting engaged, so I figured
it was time I did, too." Even then, though, Mary was uneasy about the relationship, especially at what she saw as their incompatibility. "I let myself
believe in the script, the transforming power of love and marriage."

Her parents were delighted though. Money was a mark of success in the
family, and a young man employed by a finance company was considered a
catch. Not only that, he was handsome, charming, clean-cut and, perhaps
most important, he always appeared on the doorstep with flowers in his
hands. However, concealed behind this charm, Mary says, was "ruthless
ambition and a passion to dominate, to win."

Mary says it was her mother who planned the wedding, which was, of
course, in perfect taste. The marriage vows were said in pretty little St.
Nicholas' Church, and the exquisite reception was held at the Guild Inn.
Ron's parents were there. They doted on their son, and, while not snubbing
Mary, did not embrace her either. To her, this was another family that
offered neither warmth nor comfort.

During her first three years of teaching, Mary had lived at home, carefully
accumulating a nest egg. When Ron took charge, it was used as a down
payment on a lovely house on fashionable Crescentwood Road overlooking
Lake Ontario in an older part of Scarborough. "We had the right neighbourhood and the right-size house and I was swept away by it all. When I
suddenly woke up and realized I didn't want this kind of responsibility, it was
too late."

Mary continued to teach school and Ron was doing well in the money-
lending business so they enjoyed an affluent lifestyle. Mary loved shopping
for furniture and things to make her home beautiful. Ron drove fast cars and
boats. There was a swimming pool, a cleaning lady, a lovely garden. Yet
Mary was lonely and unhappy. There was so much responsibility and debt,
so much work around the property. She admits, "I despaired that, in spite of
appearances, the script I'd auditioned for all my life was not fulfilling.
Though I felt trapped and powerless, I worked on improving my performance. Like my parents', Ron's standards for me were high."

Mary gave birth to her son Christopher in 1970. Her pregnancy was a "magical" time for her. "I was never healthier, and I felt so rewarded just being pregnant. All society smiled upon me.... Those were the happiest months of my marriage." Nevertheless, not long after Chris's arrival, Mary knew she and her marriage were in serious trouble. She became depressed and lost weight she could ill afford to lose. "I got so thin and so lifeless that I actually thought I was disappearing, that I would die."

Two and half years after Chris's birth, she went back to teaching. "My friends who were also at home with their children knew little about my problems and were aghast. It was just not done, it was not in the script. I was breaking with tradition, and then on top of it I was not ready to have another child."

Ron had not wanted Mary to return to work, but once it was a *fait accompli*, he accepted it and talked his parents into looking after Chris. Soon, however, even deeper cracks appeared in the relationship. Mary says the lack of shared interests and values finally took its toll. After eight years of marriage, the couple separated permanently in 1974.

Even though it was Mary who had instigated the split, she suffered terribly in the aftermath. "I hadn't realized that it was going to leave me feeling so bereft. It was more than a loss of my marriage, it was the loss of a dream, of innocence and of illusion." She also lost her status as a married woman. For months, she was emotionally paralyzed. "I would sit up all night on the couch, just scared to death at what I had done." It didn't help that her friends and family all believed she was completely wrong. She had removed the mask she was preordained to wear and had become a pariah in the process.

Finally, after six months of anxiety and fearfulness, she began to feel better. One of her teacher friends and her husband loved Dixieland jazz, and they'd go to the clubs two or three times a week. Mary joined them. Many in the crowd she hung around with were recent immigrants of British descent: English, Irish and Australians. She dated a Welshman who was fun to be with, but it was a peripatetic New Zealander with whom she fell in love.

She met Bill Hales in the spring of 1976 at a huge bash thrown by four lads in the group. Bill was easy-going, friendly and—what appealed to her most because it was so unlike her husband—he was a guileless person who scorned any pretentious show. Bill and Mary had a wonderful time together. There were plenty of parties, pubbing at the Black Swan, where the gang of Aussies and Kiwis hung out. Just days before Bill was to leave for England, he asked Mary to marry him. It came as a bolt from the blue. "I never dreamed this wandering Kiwi guy, so carefree and footloose, would want to settle down. I said 'yes' in a heartbeat." It didn't matter to Mary that it meant pulling up her roots and settling half way around the world.

The next few months were stressful and chaotic. Since she would not have been permitted to leave the country with Christopher without his father's consent, Mary had to finalize her divorce. The lawyers hammered out an agreement. Ron, naturally upset that his son would be living so far away, warned, "You'd better leave quickly, before I change my mind." A month later, in February 1977, once all Mary's personal possessions were sold, the threesome were on their way to New Zealand.

Mary loved the place at once, even though it was very different than Canada. The sunny, mild climate, the mangrove swamps, the thick bush full of evergreens, mosses, ferns, the indigenous fauna, the incredible birds and the rich culture of the native Maori people all seduced Mary from the start. This isn't to say she didn't see a dark side, too. The North Island, where she lived, had been almost denuded of trees so sheep by the millions could graze. Where once there had been a dense bush, the landscape was barren and brown, and, Mary thought, very sad.

Bill and Mary soon found a place in what Mary considered was "a small paradise." Titirangi was a village outside Auckland. It consisted of one main street boasting a petrol station, a grocery store, a craft shop, a restaurant and a dentist. It wasn't unusual, says Mary, for people to ride into town on horseback.

Mary says nobody in the family was intent on clawing their way to the top, which was refreshing for her. Bill had trained in the New Zealand military to be a communications technician, and he found a job in Auckland repairing the electronic equipment, radar or depth-finders, of ships that visited the port. He did, however, go through a difficult period of adjustment. He had left New Zealand a carefree guy, and all of a sudden, he had a family to look after. Mary says he took his responsibilities seriously, perhaps too seriously. However, the three of them jelled into a closely knit family. One memory stands out for Mary from that time. Since the winters were mild, the houses had no furnaces, and rainy winter evenings could be chilly. She, Bill and Christopher would wrap themselves in one big afghan and spend the evening watching sports or nature programs on TV.

Mary never considered returning to teaching. Her years of looking after Christopher and working at the same time had exhausted her. She also knew their life was new and strange for a seven-year-old, and she wanted to be there when her son came home from school. Besides, there was still no lack of status in New Zealand in being a housewife and mother. Mary connected with a group of other at-home moms, and together they attended keep-fit and yoga classes.

Nevertheless, at times she was lonely and missed having close friends to talk to. This eventually compelled her to take a step that led to one of the happiest times in her life. She volunteered for a non-profit organization called Lifeline, which provided counselling, both face to face and over the telephone, for people who were in emotional or material need. Among the volunteers, she met a group of like-minded people with whom she became very close. "I found myself in exactly the right place. I was good at it because it wasn't different from teaching." The training that came with the job would serve her well in the future.

Christopher flourished in his new environment. He also got along with Bill who, Mary says, was a good enough dad to him, easy-going and not given to criticizing. She also knew, though, that Chris missed his real father. In the divorce agreement, provisions had been worked out for child support and access—Chris was supposed to visit Canada every summer. Mary says Ron simply ignored these commitments.

In the fall of 1980, Chris was distraught because the families of his three best friends were going to emigrate in December. Mary decided a visit with his father would do him good, and she arranged for him to spend the Christmas holidays with the Macleods in Canada. When she broke the news, Christopher was thrilled.

Bill and Mary happily waved the ten-year-old off at the airport—they were glad to have a little time to themselves over the festive season—but only days after Christmas, Mary received a phone call from her former husband, who told her in no uncertain terms that Christopher would not be returning to New Zealand. It was the beginning of Mary's long nightmare.

The question was whether she should return to Canada or not. Mary realized that, although she had legal custody of Chris, trying to get him back to New Zealand would be impossible. On top of that, Chris, who had been denied access to his father for so long, had been given a princely welcome and had decided he wanted to stay with his Canadian family. Mary also knew that in his heart and soul, Bill was a New Zealander and he would not flourish in Canada. For six long months, she agonized over what she should do.

"Unfortunately, in a situation like this, two people often react differently. Bill and I went into our own shells, and my place was very different from his. We couldn't reach each other any more." The marriage began to crack, and pretty soon it would shatter.

One night, Mary came home from a part-time job she had in a shop and picked up the local paper. It was an odd thing for her to do, because she wasn't a newspaper-reader and she was particularly fatigued that evening. She glanced at the front page. In the margin, as clear as day, was her son's signature. Mary had no doubt it was Christopher's handwriting. She thought immediately that something horrible had happened and it was a message from the dead. As soon as the time difference allowed, she phoned Toronto, only to find he was just fine. She understood immediately that it was something else: her son was calling her to him. She knew at that moment she would return to Canada.

Extricating herself from her marriage and her life in New Zealand was anything but easy. "We had to sell the house. I was staying the last few nights there alone, sleeping on a mattress. I was literally sick to my stomach every night, but I took comfort in some understanding which came to me, that if there was more for Bill and I, it would be shown to us. That enabled me to walk that plank out to the plane." She left the place she considered paradise on the day of her fourth wedding anniversary.

When Mary phoned her family in Toronto to say she was coming for a visit, she insisted her mother not allow Ron to collect her from the airport. She knew she would have to recover her energy after her long flight before she could confront her former husband. "I came out of customs and there was my son's face, beaming, his father by his side. That was typical of my family's disregard for my needs and feeling, and their lack of support and empathy."

Mary realized at once that Ron would not let Chris go without an expensive and demoralizing court battle, and that, as expected, her son wanted to remain with his father. She decided just being near him, being available to him when he needed her, would have to be enough.

Mary stayed with her mother for the first few months, but it was an agonizing time for her. "It was terrible. Despite the severity of the situation, I was supposed to carry on and act like nothing had happened. I don't think there was more grief I could have had at any one time, but that was ignored. I started to cry once and everyone just looked away."

She arrived in Toronto in October 1981, and by the next February, she had rented her own apartment in the Beaches area. By this time, she was suffering from chronic fatigue and full-fledged insomnia. She says, "This horrible grieving was going on and I couldn't sleep at night." Fortunately for her, she found a job that accommodated her condition. Thanks to the tele-phone-counselling skills she had acquired at Lifeline in New Zealand, she was hired by the Community Information Centre, a 24-hour, social-services reference agency located in downtown Toronto. Since her hours of duty were from six in the evening to eight in the morning, the calls were forwarded to her apartment. She could catnap in between.

While Mary still had friends from her high-school and teaching days in Toronto, she spent much of her time alone. She purposely turned away from the world, because by that time, she no longer hoped for, or expected, support and comfort from others. She had begun what would be her life's work, a quest during which she would discover her unique, unscripted self.

It began in New Zealand after she had discovered Chris's signature on the newspaper. Mary came to believe it was indeed her son's spirit calling to her. From that point, countless times, inexplicable things happened to her. "I was thrust by this event into what I see now was the beginning of a spiritual jour-ney, where I had to rely on the most mystical of markers to guide me."

Mary had always been interested in psychology and philosophy, but now her reading intensified. She was inspired by Joseph Campbell (1904–1987), the American writer, editor and teacher. Campbell believed myths were manifes-tations of the need of the human psyche to make sense out of the universe, and in every culture, there are specific, archetypal stories that tell of heroic journeys, pilgrimages that can be made by all. One Campbell aphorism in particular seemed especially relevant to Mary's situation: "We must let go of the life we have planned, so as to accept the one that is waiting for us."

Mary was also immersing herself in the study of world religions. Gnosti-cism—a cult that flourished during the second and third centuries and chal-lenged Christianity with its secret knowledge of the divine within— particularly interested her, especially the belief that an individual was respon-sible for his or her own spiritual growth. She says, "I'm not comfortable with the word God, because I think it has come to be too limiting. I was looking for something far more."

When she first returned to Canada, she had not ruled out the established churches and she did the rounds. She attended an Anglican service with her mother, but quickly discovered "my needs had become so removed from the patriarchal mainstream that I couldn't accept what it had to offer." The Quakers seemed promising, but their meetings didn't work for her either. One night, however, in a Quaker house, she picked up a pamphlet that described the group's various volunteer programs, including regular visits to penal institutions.

She joined a group of half a dozen volunteers who visited Toronto's notorious Don Jail (now called Toronto Jail). They would sit in a circle and talk with the inmates about ordinary things, their families, their ambitions, politics, anything they wanted. The Don is a holding facility for those awaiting trial, so the prisoners had a wide assortment of backgrounds and criminal records. Mary enjoyed the involvement, and soon her week revolved around her Monday-night jail visits. "I related to these people because I, too, was displaced, devalued, no longer in the patriarchal mainstream. I needed to explore the forbidden, dark places that reflected my own psyche's shadows."

One night, during her first year in the program, a striking individual joined the group. He was Ojibwa with long, ink-black hair and searing, dark eyes. Mary's attraction to him was so powerful, she felt as if a magnet had walked into the room, but she had no sense he felt any pull towards her. The next week, she was surprised to see John was the first of the inmates to arrive at the meeting. He sat down beside her and they began to talk.

Just before John Aishinabe (Lawson) was to be released in January 1984, Mary slipped him her name and the phone number of the Community Information Centre where she worked. This was strictly against the rules, but she felt she was already an outlaw, so she could do anything she felt was right for her. He called her, they met, and thus began what Mary calls "the most unconventional and indescribable" relationship. "Ours was a soul connection—at once beautiful and frightening, so profound that it defied our reality, and overpowered our will. It was not based on my meeting his needs or his mine in a patriarchal arrangement. Living together, getting married, having children—this was not ever going to happen."

In fact, they lived in two quite distinct worlds. Hers was a lovely apartment, with the material accoutrements of the white world. His was the underbelly of the city, the bars and alleys where he spent a lot of his time when he was out of jail. He was a drug addict and an alcoholic, with all the problems of a people who have been for so long oppressed.

John's visits were frowned upon, particularly by Mary's mother and brother, especially the few nights he spent at her apartment. His friends disapproved of having a relationship with any white woman, and she was never comfortable in his domain. He was always in and out of jail, serving three or four months, usually for minor offences such as drunkenness or fighting. Sometimes Mary would visit him in prison, but these encounters were often awkward and unsatisfactory. Usually, she would meet him the first day he got out of jail, and he'd visit and telephone her sporadically afterwards. Then he would slowly drift into his world, until he ended up in jail once more.

For all that, she still regards him as the man with whom she experienced the "truest love." "I remember just weeks before meeting John, praying for a mentor. I felt I had done as much as I could on my own, I wasn't finding a church and I wasn't making connections, and then this wonderful teacher comes in disguise. You need to look beyond disguises, as Mother Teresa said."

Their bond was their frequent letters to each other, along with John's poignant drawings and poems. He was an artist who intently explored his Native spirituality, and this was what appealed so strongly to Mary. "He was the most deeply spiritual person I have ever known. And, while he couldn't often articulate it, he managed to infuse in me this invaluable knowledge and wisdom. He saw right through my disguise, too. His was the only voice who said, 'Mary, you have so many gifts. Why aren't you using them? Why don't you know who you really are?'" She began to write poetry, and it remains an important part of her creative life. And what did she give him? "Love and laughter. He learned his heart could open, he could love and be loved, even though I was not Native and therefore in the enemy camp."

In March 1987, John Aishinabe was stabbed to death in a drunken brawl. Mary knew he had long wanted to leave his body and return "home," and in death, he confirmed her belief that the spirit lives on. "I still feel John's presence and our enduring love." He has remained her constant companion on her spiritual quest.

Mary is thankful she was not working when John died, for it allowed her time to recuperate. The Community Information Centre had amalgamated with Metro Community services, and the nature of Mary's job had changed. "Our clients now included people who were calling welfare for emergency assistance. This redefined my role from being a support person, a counsellor, to having to assess, judge and sometimes refuse requests. The patriarchal buck was put right into my hand, and I chose not to accept it."

She took a year off to renew her spiritual quest, once again reading deeply and often simply sitting for hours meditating. She immersed herself in Buddhism, which reinforced her belief in reincarnation. She's sure that, in her past life, she was a tribal person, probably a North American Native. "I came to understand that everything in the universe is connected, it is all one. That is now my clear concept of God. Many people telescope Him into one man, but for me, God is every part of everything."

No matter what spiritual heights she reaches, Mary, too, has to eat and pay her rent. When eventually her savings were depleted, she went back to work. This time, she was hired by the Scarborough Board of Education to teach basic literacy to adults. It was a part-time job, 18 hours a week—fortunately, for she was still suffering from chronic fatigue and insomnia. She worked one-on-one with the inmates in the East Toronto Detention Centre, all under lock and key, talking with them, teaching them, building up their self-esteem and trust. With Mary's help, they wrote their personal stories, which she collected into a small book. It is among her most precious possessions.

Eventually, though, she decided to move back into the classroom to teach adult literacy. Unhappily, because many of the students could not motivate themselves to attend regularly, in June 1995, the class was cancelled. Mary felt it was time to go into hibernation again, to meditate, to read.

A recent spiritual guide is Deepak Chopra, an East Indian physician who dispenses a blend of Eastern mysticism and traditional Ayurvedic medicine. When he says, "I want to be independent of people ... and circumstances. I want my reality to be orchestrated from within me," it could be Mary Hales speaking. Over the years, she has developed friendships with young people who are on their own voyages of discovery. In some ways, they look to her as a wise woman, which Mary regards as a matriarchal term of respect for age and experience, a woman seeking wholeness, not perfection.

Mary and her son Chris still struggle to make peace with the past and with each other. "Though I grieved for the child I'd lost, I honour his journey and the man he has become." In fact, his values and interests are similar to hers. He graduated from the University of Western Ontario, took a masters degree in education and, following in his mother's footsteps, teaches kindergarten for the Windsor Board of Education.

Mary has retired from teaching. Adding the years of her early career to those teaching literacy, she qualified for a partial pension. She lives so frugally and is so removed from the consumer society that it's adequate. She does volunteer work, tutors and, most important, continues her soul-searching.

On a shelf in Mary's sunny apartment sits a dark-brown porcelain statue of a tall, slender woman, dressed in a greatcoat and a bonnet and carrying a muff. All of the figure is glazed except for the face, which has not been sculpted and remains a complete blank. Mary keeps it as a symbol of what would have happened if she had stuck to the script, if she had not had the courage to set sail on her long, difficult but exhilarating spiritual adventure.

Spirituality

For when Adam saw Eve for the first time, he was entirely filled with wisdom, for he recognized in her the mother of his children. But when Eve saw Adam, she looked upon him as though she were looking into heaven....

Hildegard of Bingen, 1158

Ever since I was ten years old I have been a student and a sort of church mother, much given to attending sermons. I have loved and frequented the company of learned men, and I conversed much with them, not about dancing, masquerades, and worldly pleasures but about the kingdom of God....

Catherine Zell, in a letter to a Lutheran clergyman, 1557

Mother and God, to you we sing
wide is your womb, warm is your wing

Catholic theologian Miriam Therese Winter, 1987

When you come from a family dominated by atheists—not casual or careless non-believers, but philosophic heretics who staunchly believed organized religion was the root of all evil—a spiritual experience was hard to come by. When I was 16, I started going out with a Roman Catholic boy, and, because of him, began attending mass at the Church of St. Theresa of the Little Flower on Kingston Road. Although I was fascinated by the ritual, the incense, the Latin chants, the solemn fingering of rosary beads, my foray into the religious life came to an abrupt end about a year later. I had my first meeting with the elderly priest who was to instruct me in the faith. He was so utterly condescending, so convinced I had not a brain in my head, I swore never to go back.

Then I saw the movie *The Nun's Story*, starring Audrey Hepburn. I recall being deeply moved, but in a defiant, desperate way. I couldn't remember why until I watched it again, 35 years later. Filmed in Belgium and the Congo, it's the story of one young woman's agonizing struggle to turn herself into a chaste, virtuous and, above all, obedient nun. After more than a dozen years as a nursing sister, she finally decides she cannot tolerate the Church's neutrality during World War II. I cheered every step she took as she walked out the convent doors. Somehow the spirit of this brilliant, humanitarian young woman had not been broken. As she said, it was now between her and her God; she would express her spirituality in her own way. She began by treating the wounded in the Belgian underground. Despite the constraints imposed by a church steeped in patriarchy, women have always struggled to mold their faith to their own needs and desires.

I

In the summer, several months before the event, litters of piglets were thrown into deep trenches on a hill near the Acropolis in Athens. With them were tossed doughy cakes sculpted into phallic symbols, as well as pine cones the shape of penises. When the Thesmophoria, a festival dedicated to Demeter, goddess of agriculture, occurred in late autumn, Athenian women—scholars debate whether it was only for wives of citizens or for all non-slave females—congregated in a makeshift camp near the Palace of Assembly, the core of male power. The business of the mighty city ground to a halt as a village of huts sprang up, decorated with all manner of greenery.

On the first day, a huge procession of singing and dancing celebrants wound their way up the hill. Certain chosen women, who had refrained from sexual intercourse for at least three days, would descend into the pits in order to retrieve the carcasses of the piglets—not much was left since most of the flesh had been eaten by snakes—the cakes and the pine cones. These were mixed with seed grain and placed on a special altar where Demeter was worshipped.

The second day was a more sober occasion. The women fasted and abstained from even thinking about sex—they sat on mattresses supposedly stuffed with anti-aphrodisiacs. Their purpose was to dramatically relive Demeter's anguish over the loss of her daughter Persephone.[605] They would weep and moan, and every now and then tell a dirty joke in mimicry of the old woman Iambe, who had attempted to cheer up Demeter by whispering obscenities in her ear.

The third day, the Day of Beautiful Birth, was full of celebration and lavish banquets hosted by the wealthy women—and paid for by their husbands. Afterwards, the pig remains and seeds were scattered on the fields to insure a bountiful harvest.

The Thesmophoria hinted at rebellion. It was one of the few occasions women could escape the confines of home. It occupied the symbolic heart of the city and disrupted the business of the *polis*, and it assumed some political significance: the women elected their own magistrates, and decisions regarding the rituals were made by majority vote. However, the Thesmophoria was also a confirmation of women's domestic place in society. It was full of sexual significance. In ancient Greek society, pigs represented female genitalia, snakes the male member, and then there were the phallic-shaped dough cakes and pine cones. It all reminded women that their sexual being as daughters, wives and mothers, their role as bearers and nurturers, were all-important. As one historian put it, "The festival honoured not the women themselves but the 'city of men' it was their function to reproduce."[606]

There was another religious celebration—an expression of deep-rooted, albeit peculiar, spirituality—that, in contrast to the Thesmophoria, was not a recognition but a mockery of the male-dominated society. This was the great collective mourning of Adonis, the beautiful youth whom Aphrodite adored and who was gored to death by a wild boar. In July, at the hottest time of summer, the women of Athens would gather on their rooftops, something they were normally not permitted to do. There, in broken terra-cotta pots with ragged edges, they would plant lettuce, fennel and other seeds. These gardens of Adonis would be watered until the seedlings sprouted, but then the tender, green shoots were left to fry in the savage sun. On the day of the festival, the women would hold a mock funeral, ululating from the tops of the roofs until the whole city vibrated with the eerie noise. With their clothes askew and their hair released from bonds, they danced, made outrageous gestures before the withered garden and chanted dirges: "Woe! Woe, Adonis!"

Eventually, the terra-cotta pots were gathered up, as were masks and pictures of Adonis and, after a sombre mock-funeral march, they were thrown into the sea or river.

The occasion was a genuine mourning for this beautiful, effeminate young man, who was gentle and affectionate, and smelled nice—in contrast to their brawny, aggressive husbands, who were often double the age of their wives and not much interested in their happiness. This religious rite—for that's what it was—was famous for the raucous, uncontrollable laughter of its celebrants. What was so funny? The wilting sprouts reminded the women of another thing that so often wilted in the marriage bed. A great mockery of the male misconception of his importance in fertility and in the production of the world's human and agricultural crops.

As for the Romans, their obsession with categorizing, organizing and apportioning was directly reflected in their religion. Women in particular were ranked according to class distinction: plebeians or patricians, marital status, virgin, married or widowed, moral standards, respectable or prostitute, and by the legal category of slave or free. As is evident in the many cults of Fortuna (Lady Luck), the gods and goddesses were also addicted to arranging women's lives.[607]

A young girl looked to Fortuna Virgo (virgin) for help and protection. After her marriage, that same young woman would likely switch her allegiance to Fortuna Primigenia of Praeneste, the patroness of young mothers. As she matured, she might turn to Fortuna Muliebris, the goddess who honoured the good wife and mother. This cult had a remarkable beginning. In 491 BC, the traitor Coriolanus threatened to lead the savage Volsci against Rome. His mother and wife arrived, leading a delegation of women who first pleaded and then harangued him until he gave up his dastardly plan. The cult originated on the spot, four miles from Rome, where the confrontation between the warrior and his women occurred.[608]

Depending on how bold she was, our young woman may or may not have worshipped Fortuna Virilis, the goddess who worried about the sexual gratification of women. Every April 1, female crowds would congregate at the male bath houses. It's not clear whether the men were present or not; apparently the attraction was simply that those were places where male genitalia were regularly exposed.

From the third century BC, Roman women gradually obtained some degree of control over their economic and sexual lives, and the male power structure didn't like it one bit. Cults were devised and promoted to reinforce the behaviour males deemed appropriate for Roman matrons, particularly sexual purity and marital faithfulness. The Emperor Domitian (reigned AD 81–96) blamed all of Rome's ills on female promiscuousness. He ordered a shrine of Plebeian Chastity be restored, where he expected all women to worship. They did so, but halfheartedly. This was not a goddess who offered much comfort or joy.

No wonder so many women (and lower-class men) embraced with enthusiasm the foreign religious sects that started popping up everywhere in Rome. At least these deities had some idea of warmth, sympathy and human dignity.

Among them was a revolutionary cult, the Jesus Movement, "a deadly super-stition," as the Roman historian Tacitus put it, that challenged the founda-tion of Roman society.

II

An exquisitely carved altar of the Rochuskapelle, in the town of Bingen in southwest Germany, depicts a fascinating scene from the Middle Ages. An angelic-looking little girl of eight years old is being presented to three Bene-dictine nuns. The child seems eager enough, and both the father and the mother, who is nudging her forward, seem content. In the background, though, lurk two servants who look despondent, and for good reason. The little girl was not simply entering a convent to be brought up as a nun—that was common enough. Her parents had made the more radical decision of dedicating their daughter to a life enclosed within the cell of an anchoress. As the monk Godfrey wrote, "When she was about eight years she was enclosed at Disibodenberg—buried with Christ that she might arise with him to immortal glory."[609] This little girl would become known as Hilde-gard of Bingen (1098–1179), the most famous visionary and mystic of the Middle Ages.

Hildegard was born in the Rhineland village of Böckelheim, the tenth child of prosperous landed gentry. She was a sickly and devout little girl, which may have been one reason the parents decided on a religious life for her. The woman who would be her mentor in seclusion was Jutta of Spon-heim, the young and beautiful daughter of a local count. On the day Jutta became an anchoress, the bishop celebrated a mass for the dead in her honour. He then administered extreme unction, locked her in her cell and sealed the door. From that moment on, her only communication with the world was supposedly through a tiny window in her cell, but it didn't quite work out that way. Jutta was of such intense and exceptional spirituality that she attracted many dedicated followers. Daughters of local nobility such as Hildegard were sent to her by the dozens, along with their dowries. Very soon, the simple cell became a small Benedictine convent, attached to and dependent on the monastery at Disibodenberg.

Jutta seems to have tutored her disciples well. Hildegard could read and write Latin effortlessly. She had a knowledge of natural science and astrology that was quite extensive for her day. She knew the works of St. Augustine, Boethius, Isidore of Seville and Constantine the African, the 11th-century translator of Greek medical works. The influence of all of these could be found in Hildegard's own extraordinarily vast and original body of work, which was accomplished at a time when women, if not completely forbidden, were actively discouraged from pursuing intellectual activities. How did she manage it? She became, as she put it, "God's little trumpet."

Hildegard wrote that she began having visions when she was five years old, but she told no one about them except a few sympathetic nuns. Finally, after an illness that nearly killed her, she realized the divine spirit was spurring her on to reveal her inner voices:

In the year of our Lord 1141 when I was forty-two years and seven months old, the heaven opened and a fiery light throwing off great streams of sparks utterly permeated my brain and ignited my heart and breast like a flame which does not burn but gives off heat the way the sun warms an object which it touches with its rays. And suddenly the meaning of the Scriptures, the Psalter, the Evangelium and the other catholic books of the Old and New Testament was revealed to me....[610]

As a mouthpiece of the Lord, she began writing in Latin her rich, detailed, unique visions. The breadth of Hildegard's work is amazing; it encompasses cosmology, theology, ethics, poetry and mystical revelations. As her biographer says, *The Book of Divine Works* "can be seen as a triumph of synthesis in which Hildegard brings together her theological beliefs, her physiological understanding, her speculations of the working of the human mind, and the structure of the universe, into a unified whole."[611]

On the surface, Hildegard seems to accept the Church's orthodoxy concerning the superiority of the male sex; her use of the masculine designations for God—Father, Redeemer, King—is traditional. However, as historian Gerda Lerner so ably points out, rippling under the surface of Hildegard's work is something quite unorthodox. Her interpretation of Genesis directly contradicts the Church fathers' idea of the fall in the Garden of Eden and the perpetual damnation of weak woman:

When God created Adam, Adam experienced great love in the sleep which God sent over him. And God gave form to the love of man and so the woman is the love of man. For when Adam saw Eve for the first time, he was entirely filled with wisdom, for he recognized in her the mother of his children. But when Eve saw Adam, she looked upon him as though she were looking into heaven....[612]

The prevalence of female images, both in the illustrations and literary descriptions of Hildegard's visions, is extraordinary. The Church itself is seen by Hildegard as the "the virginal Mother of all Christians. She conceives and gives birth to her children through the secret strength of the Holy Ghost and offers them to God, so that they are called children of God." Lerner sees great significance in this:

Hildegard's repeated envisioning of the Church as Mother and her descriptions of the creative, life-giving aspects of the Church, which she likens to 'green-ness,' her holistic symbol of the vitality of earth, nature, human life and spirituality, all express her insistence on the unity of male and female principles in the universe, on earth and in heaven. Her theology breaks sharply with the dichotomized categories of the scholastics and with the patriarchal hierarchies embedded in their thought. Hildegard's visions fuse male and female elements, the physical and the spiritual, the rational-practical and the mystical aspects of existence.[613]

Two hundred years after Hildegard of Bingen's death, another female mystic would reveal an even more androgynous God. Julian of Norwich (1342-1416?) was an English recluse who underwent 16 ecstatic visions of the Virgin and of Christ's passion, which she recorded in *Revelations of Divine Love*. Hers is a God with male and female attributes:

And thus in our Creation God almighty is our kindly Father, and God Who is all wisdom is our kindly Mother, with the love and the goodness of the Holy Ghost— all of Whom are one God and one Lord.... Thus in our Father God we have our being, and in our Mother of mercy we have our reform and our restoration....[614]

Hildegard and Julian of Norwich were the first in a long line of female visionaries and prophets who, believing they were authorized by God, broke free of the Church's restrictions that tried so hard to mute women—as St. Paul said, "Let your women keep silence in the churches: for it is not permitted unto them to speak"—and profoundly stirred the soul of humankind.

It wasn't just women religious who were caught up in the spiritual ferment of the times, though. It's remarkable how readily noblewomen abandoned their children for religious callings. Juette of Huy, for example, left behind two toddlers because she wanted to do penance among the lepers. The mother of Guibert of Nogent said farewell to her family to live by the gates of monasteries, begging food in exchange for prayers. Mme de Sévigné's grandmother, the Baroness Jeanne de Chantal, didn't hesitate to desert her three children when her religious calling sounded. Her 15-year-old son "flung himself, in tears and hysteria, across the threshold of the door by which his mother was about to depart the château. If she loved her only son, as she would steadfastly claim she did, she loved God's work ... even more."[615]

Testimony given at the Inquisition sketches an equally poignant scene. A French noblewoman is about to abandon her family to join the Cathars, a popular religious cult of the time.

She had an infant in the cradle and she wanted to see him before she left home. When she beheld him she kissed him and the babe began to smile. She moved away from the cradle in order to leave the room, but retraced her footsteps and again approached the babe. He again smiled, and this happened several times more. She could not leave him. In the end she said to her maid-servant: 'Take him out of the room.'[616]

In this case, the mother paid dearly for her spiritual quest. She was burned at the stake shortly afterwards.

III

In the early modern age—the period of the Protestant Reformation, the Catholic Counter-Reformation and the bursting forth of unorthodox sects—religious life changed dramatically. A cornucopia of new beliefs and rituals was offered up to both sexes. For women, though, it was pretty much the same old story: the daughters of Eve, eternally punished for their transgressions, were not to be priests, rabbis or Protestant pastors. The reformer John Calvin (1509–64) loathed the very idea that women might have an authoritative presence in the Church. In his *Institutes*, he wrote:

The custom of the church, before St. Augustine was born, may be elicited first of all from Tertullian, who held that no woman in church is allowed to speak, teach, baptize, or make offerings: this in order that she may not usurp the functions of men, let alone those of priests.[617]

The Calvinist John Knox's ideas were even more odious: "The holy ghost doth manifestly [say] I suffer not that women usurp authority over men: ... taking from her all power and authority, to speak, to reason, to interpret or to teach, but principally to rule or to judge in the assembly of men."[618] For his part, Luther's view on womanhood was, as historian Olwen Hufton writes, "both gloomy and conservative. He saw women as specific reproductive vessels with inferior reasoning powers and a proclivity to succumb to temptation."[619]

The Catholic reformers were so fearful of the consecrated woman's ability to attract the faithful simply through offering care, advice and sympathy that they were determined to restrict her role. The enforced cloistering of nuns for example. Against the opposition of those who appreciated the valuable charitable work these women performed, the Council of Trent (1545–63) insisted on the closure of convents. These institutions were moved to the outskirts of cities and, as one writer put it, "high walls, heavy gates, innumerable locks and iron bars left no doubt that Christ's brides had bidden the world a final farewell."[620] Convents that had once been cosy and comfortable places to receive visitors, both the mighty and lowly, were now austere, dark fortresses. Nuns could no longer share intimate quarters but must sleep alone or in dormitories.

The Church's grip on women extended to the family. "Honour thy father and thy mother" came to mean something more than simply being considerate of one's parents. Strict adherence to the hierarchical order was expected, either through Scripture or Church tradition; this extended, of course, to patriarchal control of the family. The wife was as much subject to her husband's authority as she was to the Church's and to God's.

For all that, as the 18th century Enlightenment approached, it was men who turned their back on religion; women remained as loyal to their faith as ever. Historians have long pondered on the reason for this, but it boils down to one basic axiom: the Church offered women more than the secular world. It provided a meeting place where women could enjoy each other's company and talk about things that mattered to them—the harvests, childbirth, their husbands—all with the understanding that they shared a common belief system. The few leisure moments they were able to enjoy were connected to church: Sunday services, the great festivals, the important rituals involving birth, marriage and death.

For Catholic women, the Church could be a source of great solace and relief for pent-up emotions. Individual confessions, in a private place, provided the opportunity for women to express their innermost thoughts to someone who must listen: the parish priest. As historian John Martin points out, for many women the confession box was the direct opposite of the household. "There, it was her husband who ruled; here, kneeling before the priest, the woman often found a man who would listen and provide her with a source of authority that could even override the rule of her husband."[621]

The Protestant belief that every soul had equal access to God meant women were encouraged to read and interpret the Scriptures themselves. This became a source of great satisfaction. Writing down one's thoughts about Biblical passages or having discussions with clergy became popular. Women began thinking for themselves, developing a consciousness of who they were as individuals.

The secular world might exclude women from intellectual and professional endeavours, but they could not be denied the never-ending quest for moral perfection, something they were often better at than men. Finally, what appealed to women most about their religion was not only that they could be saved from eternal damnation but that they could hope life after death might offer equality of sexes.

IV

The feminization of conventional religion is one of the 19th century's most intriguing peculiarities. While, in the wake of the French Revolution and the Enlightenment, men abandoned their faith in droves, women remained devout. Eventually, through sheer numbers, they began to have a profound influence on doctrine, rituals and the conduct of the clergy.

"God has changed sex," French historian Jules Michelet proclaimed at mid-century.[622] He was referring primarily to Roman Catholicism; in France, it was estimated that three-quarters of practising Catholics were female. Women also tended to be much more fervent in their beliefs than men, so much so that the symbols and rituals took on a decidedly sentimental cast and were often excessive and artificial.

Whether the husbands liked it or not, bedrooms were crowded with evidence of religious devotion: crucifixes, statues of the Madonna, brightly coloured paintings in which faces of the mother and child were often encircled in fine paper lace.[623] Little girls dressed in frilly white were made to pose for photographers and artists with their eyes devotedly raised to heaven and their hands crossed on their hearts. Young women revelled in their emotions. As one clergymen noted, "Girls love tears so much that I have seen them cry before a mirror to double their enjoyment of that state."[624]

The tenor of prayer changed. Gone was the fear of God's wrath and

vengeance, replaced by sugary pleas that surely one's goodness was all that
should be necessary for the happiness, health and prosperity of the believer
and her entire family. As well as the Virgin Mary, a whole myriad of female
saints were enlisted in this cause. Little books on the meditations of holy
women such as the Spanish mystic Teresa of Avila (1515–82) were carried
around in pockets, so that in spare moments, her maxims—"Accustom yourself continually to make many acts of love, for they enkindle and melt the
soul"—could be savoured.

It wasn't only Catholicism that took on a feminine cast. In Victorian
Britain, more than 65 percent of active Anglicans were women. Performing
good deeds in the name of Christ became an obsession with middle-class
women. There was a great resurgence of celibate sisterhoods; by 1850, there
were 15 Anglican convents in London alone. The mandate of these devoted
women was to care for the poor and sick among God's flock.

In Canada, female religious orders—a few Anglican, but primarily
Catholic—grew at a phenomenal rate; from mid-century onwards, 30 new
orders were founded.[625] In France, the number of women entering new and
old religious congregations rose in 80 years from less than 13,000 to 130,000;
three women chose the religious life for every two men.[626] These sisters
played important educational and health roles; often they had very real power
in their communities.

In some Protestant sects such as Methodism, church services served as a
vital release for repressed emotions, especially for the hard-working women
of the working class. As historian Joan Perkin writes: "Salvation was especially high drama, climaxing in the moment of redemption—the sinner
saved, the taking of the true path of righteousness, the coming of Christ and
the acclamation of the congregation. To be counted among the saved
brought many women happiness, a cheerful conviction that in God's providence there was a place for everyone, however humble, and that each individual was part of God's plan for the universe."[627]

Throughout Europe and North America, the passion and commitment
women felt towards their particular faith formed a direct parallel with the way
in which they viewed their position in the family and society. The ideal
Catholic woman was a devoted wife and mother. Images of a submissive and
self-denying Mary proliferated throughout the 19th century. In Protestant
countries, the angel by the hearth was expected to be religiously devout, to
educate her children in Christian ethics and to make up for the part their

husbands played in putting profits far ahead of humanity during the Industrial Revolution.

However, stirring underneath was a current of rebellion. Women began to question male interpretations of Biblical stories. A sense of this is present in Charlotte Brontë's novel *Shirley*. Caroline is urging her strong-willed friend Shirley to go to church. Shirley responds:

Caroline, I will not: I will stay here with my mother Eve, in these days called Nature. I love her—undying, mighty being! Heaven may have faded from her brow when she fell in paradise; but all that is glorious on earth shines there still. She is taking me to her bosom, and showing me her heart. Hush, Caroline! You will see her and feel as I do, if we are both silent.[628]

For all the adherence to the patriarchal values inherent in their faith, 19th-century women were finally able to use the church to leapfrog from their home to the outside world. Nowhere is this more obvious than the revival movements that bubbled up during the first half of the century. Held in forest clearings, city parks, even shabby theatres, they always involved a charismatic, often fiery preacher who could whip his believers into a frenzy of emotion. As the writer Barbara Goldsmith puts it, "First came the proclamation of sin—the filth and evil clinging to the human soul. Then the mounting fear and terror—the look into the abyss. Then the casting of oneself upon God's mercy—the throwing off of all personality in abject surrender of self. Finally in heightened consciousness and new understanding, the cleansed soul emerged."[629] Hundreds, even thousands, were brought into the fold in a single night.

While the leaders were always male, it was women who thronged to the revivals, seizing what one historian calls "their sacred space." Once the Holy spirit possessed them, they interrupted church services to pray for their loved ones, they cried, they spoke in tongues. They also preached, thereby breaking the silence imposed by St. Paul. And they organized: Bible classes, social gatherings and most important, the huge revival meetings that could not have been held without their labour. Often to their husband's dismay, they left their homes before breakfast for early-morning planning sessions, they pinned up posters all over town, they browbeat the butcher and baker into closing their shops on the day of the meeting. At the appointed hour, they herded their family and friends into the hot, crowded revival tent in the hope that one or the other might finally shriek those vital words: "I am born again in the lamb's blood!"

Even after the preacher left town, female devotees continued their missions, holding prayer meetings in their homes that went on for hours, organizing themselves into moral reform movements, descending on politicians "to clean up the city"—a euphemism for getting rid of brothels. They were heavily involved in the American anti-slavery movement and they were fiendishly dedicated prohibitionists. They became missionaries, carrying God's words into the streets of the city slums. As historian Carroll Smith-Rosenberg writes, "These women for the most part were married, respected members of respectable communities. Yet, transformed by millennial zeal, they disregarded every restraint upon women's behaviour.... They threatened to revolutionize women's secular as well as sacred roles."[630]

What was called the Second Great Awakening eventually petered out, and the once-rebellious preachers embraced the respectability of the traditional Church. Women were encouraged to let go of their spiritual ecstasy, their roles as prophets and teachers, and return to their sedate lives as mothers and homemakers. Many did so, but a powerful, indelible residue was left. Their organizational skills, their ability to influence the outside world, their taste for spiritual self-expression and moral reform did not subside. All this was passed down to the next generation. It was the daughters of these devotees who would emerge in the last decades of the Victorian era as the New Women, ferociously engaged in the first round of feminism. It was they who began hurling embarrassing questions at the Church patriarchs.

V

Bitter and burning, Miss Kilman had turned into a church two years three months ago. She had heard the Rev. Edward Whittaker preach; the boys sing; had seen the solemn lights descend, and whether it was the music, or the voices (she herself when alone in the evening found comfort in a violin; but the sound was excruciating; she had no ear), the hot and turbulent feelings which boiled and surged in her had been assuaged as she sat there, and she had wept copiously, and gone to call on Mr. Whittaker at his private house in Kensington. It was the hand of God, he said. The Lord had shown her the way. So now, whenever the hot and painful feelings boiled within her, this hatred of Mrs. Dalloway, this grudge against the world, she thought of God. She thought of Mr. Whittaker. Rage was succeeded by calm. A sweet savour filled her veins, her lips parted, and, standing formidable upon the landing in her mackintosh, she looked with steady and sinister serenity at Mrs. Dalloway....[631]

Miss Kilman, with her condescending, holier-than-thou attitude, her homeliness, her dreary, lonely life, her stark envy of anyone who has more than she (which is just about everyone), is one of the most offensive of all Virginia Woolf's characters. The novel *Mrs. Dalloway* was published in 1925, at a time when religious belief had been painfully shaken by the horrors of the Great War, but the treatment of the religious zealot in *Mrs. Dalloway* depicts something more than a general loss of faith. Miss Kilman, in all her odiousness, can be seen to represent the contempt with which many women would come to view conventional religion in the 20th century.

After being staunch defenders of their faith, women began to leave the Church, first in a trickle, then in droves. It was more than merely following their menfolk into secularism. Women began forging their own brands of spirituality, a trend that some observers believe is as significant in the history of organized religion as Luther's Protestant Reformation. That God is slowly becoming androgynous is surely the most astonishing development in contemporary religion.

The onslaught flared up in the 1940s with that harshest of critics, Simone de Beauvoir. Her mother had been a devoted Catholic, Simone a pious little girl. This background meant that her wholehearted rejection of the Church and her adoption of atheistic existentialism held great significance for her. De Beauvoir believed women were nothing but silly dupes in the clutches of male-dominated religion, and, as usual, she blamed this oppression primarily on the weak female character itself. As she wrote in *The Second Sex*:

Religion sanctions woman's self-love; it gives her the guide, father, lover, divine guardian she longs for nostalgically; it feeds her daydreams; it fills her empty hours. But, above all, it confirms the social order, it justifies her resignation, by giving her the hope of a better future in a sexless heaven....[632]

The Second Sex sounded a clarion call to intellectuals just beginning to probe the role of the Church in the oppression of women. By the 1960s, the calm halls of academia were being disrupted by feminist theologians, and none was more furious than Mary Daly.

Since women were still not allowed to pursue a doctorate in sacred (in other words, Roman Catholic) theology in the United States, Daly attended the University of Fribourg, Switzerland, where, over seven years of study, she earned two Ph.D.s, one in theology, the other in philosophy. She began writing *The Church and the Second Sex* in 1965, while she was still living in Fribourg. Two years later, she returned to America as a teacher of theology at Boston College, a Jesuit institution. When her book was published in 1969, she was promptly fired.

What followed was a student protest hot-headed even for the late '60s. Daly's dismissal became a *cause célèbre*; petitions, demonstrations and sit-ins followed one after another. Several "witches" hexed Boston college. Finally, the Jesuits relented and Daly was hired back as a tenured university professor. She became an instant celebrity, a star on the lecture circuit, a guru for feminists in the process of questioning their own faiths.

From today's vantage point, it's hard to image what the college officials were so riled up about. *The Church and the Second Sex* discussed the historical oppression of women, but at that point, Daly still had hopes the Church could rectify the inequalities. Thirty years later, she has not only completely rejected Christianity in all its forms but is engaged in a vehement, vitriolic campaign to bring the Church fathers to account. A foreword (or, as she puts it, "Archaic Afterwords") in the 1985 edition of *The Church and the Second Sex* gives a flavour of the kind of renegade language and sentiment she now relishes. "This Event [the death of God] is the Self-Realizing of women who have broken free from the stranglehold of patriarchal religion, with its deadly symbols, its ill logic, its gynocidal laws and other poisonous paraphernalia."[633] To put it mildly, she has become a thorn in the side of the Church patriarchs.

Many of those feminists who, along with Daly, fled from mainstream religion, set out to mold a faith of their own. Devotees of the Great Goddess, for example, believe that long before the male Hebrew God came to dominate, there were goddesses who presided over peaceful and prosperous societies where women, not men, were in charge. Goddess worship allowed women to conceive of a historical identity of their own, and it provided a relief for the rage many felt towards conventional religions. If recently it has become self-centred, childish and disdainful of any critical thought or cultural diversity, perhaps it has served its purpose.

Other brands of feminist religion have evolved, many of them with a benevolent, nature-oriented flavour. The cult of the Greek goddess Gaia, Mother Earth, for example, exalts our planet as a single, living organism.

Others have a distinct New Age self-help cast. Clarissa Pinkola Estes' *Women Who Run with the Wolves: Myths and Stories of the Wild Woman Archetype* is an example. Her message is complicated: within every woman there is a wild and natural creature, a powerful force, filled with good instincts, passionate creativity and ageless knowing. That broad generalizations like these about the female character have held women in a societal corset for centuries seems not to have mattered. The book has sold well over a million copies.

Obviously traditional religion has lost its relevance, even for those who were not harshly critical of it. In Canada, as in most other countries of the Western world, only half the number of women go to church as did 40 years ago; 21 percent of the female population attends services regularly, and that number drops each year. In the United States, that figure has dropped from 49 percent in 1991 to 36 percent in 1996. In Australia, England and much of the rest of Europe, it has fallen to ten percent. Another telling figure: between 1968 and 1986, nearly 4,000 nuns in Quebec broke their vows and left their religious communities, a trend throughout North America and Europe. Stories abound of personal struggles and of the agony that came with the realization that faith in a male Christian god is no longer possible.

Mary Malone is one example. She is a well-known and admired teacher of religious history at St. Jerome's College in Kitchener, Ontario. In 1995, she felt compelled to publicly announce her abandonment of Christianity because, for more than 30 years, she had influenced young Catholic women. She says, "It wasn't that I felt angry—I have absolutely no hostility, or need to attack it [the Church], or any of those things.... In fact it was a very peaceful decision and a liberating decision.... The bottom line for me is that I can't pray and I can't worship. I find I cannot worship a male god. And after working on it for 30 years, I have come to the conclusion that the maleness of God is intrinsic to Christianity."[634]

Many women, however, have remained loyal to their religion, hopeful they could create change from within. To some degree, they've been successful. There has been, for example, a rewriting of the language of religion. A recently published United Church hymnal not only mentions God the Father but also God the All-Holy, Maker and Mother. Bible stories are being retold with a female face. In 1979, when *Crucified Woman*, a nude statue of a female Christ, was installed in front of a United Church in Toronto, there was such outrage from the congregation that she was mothballed. Seven years later, the seven feet of bronze, her slim arms outstretched as if on a crucifix, her small breasts and long hair adding pathos, stands proudly in front of the University of Toronto's Emmanuel College. Young women offer whispered prayers in front of her; bouquets of flowers are left at her feet. A delicate and inspiring figure, she stands as a challenge to 2,000 years of patriarchal tradition.

Betty

Moan about your trig problems and Betty Kirk would fire at you, "Chuck the damn things then." She called a spade a spade, that was for sure. We were on R. H. King's sports teams together, and I liked her a lot because she was funny and irreverent. "Shit!" she'd yell, as the other team scored once again, at a time when saying shit was still shocking. Becoming an Anglican priest was the last thing we would have imagined for Betty. A fighter for the underdog, a scourge of bureaucracy, yes, but someone who wore a black shirt and white collar and gave grave sermons—never. But then, we didn't know about Betty's family circumstances. Merely trying to survive in such emotional hardship would either destroy a child or make her strong. In Betty's case, it built character.

When Betty was three weeks old, her mother brought her from Montreal to Toronto where, in a lawyer's office, she was handed over to her adoptive parents Maurice and Eva Kirk. Betty always knew her birth-mother's name; it was on the back of her birth certificate. Her father was listed as "unnamed."

Her childhood was far from being ideal. There was a lot of conflict and unhappiness in the family, beginning with Betty's adoptive grandparents. Her adoptive maternal grandmother Mary Hamilton had run away from home in Parry Sound at age 18 to marry a man 22 years older than she. The couple settled in Toronto and had two daughters, but Mary's husband developed dementia and had to be institutionalized. Mary ended up having to support the family. Her daughter Eva received very little education; she probably only got as far as Grade 4. Betty says her mother's IQ was marginal, and reading and writing were hard for her. Eva was simple, but also rather sweet. She helped out in her mother's boarding house until finally, at age 35, she fell in love with one of the paying guests.

Maurice Kirk was a couple of years younger than Eva and from a higher-class family. His father had been a fire chief in Toronto, and his sister was university-educated. Maurice's mother was a domineering, high-powered person who ruled her household with a firm hand; her husband, for example, was allowed to smoke only in the garage. She was determined her only son would attend an academic-oriented school and become a professional of some sort. He wanted to go to a technical school and learn a trade. The consequences of the fierce struggle were threefold: Maurice dropped out of high school, he developed a lifelong loathing for authority and he became an alcoholic. His heavy drinking was the reason he had finally been asked to leave the family home and ended up in Mary's boarding house, engaged to Eva.

After two years of marriage, Eva and Maurice realized they couldn't have children and adopted Betty. She grew up as an only child in what she believes was a fundamentally dysfunctional family. Eva relied on her husband for her identity, her very being. As a young woman, she had joined the Salvation Army and had loved the uniform, the singing, the sense of belonging. Maurice didn't like church, however, so Eva stopped attending. Her subservience made it hard to counter Maurice's alcoholism. "I can remember them screaming at each other about this damn drinking stuff," recalls Betty. "He was quite emotionally abusive, and after I moved out of the house, physically abusive. He would slam my mother across the house and all sorts of crap that was pretty horrible. So there was always that tension, and not a lot of affirmation as to who or what I was."

There was one loving presence in Betty's life: her maternal grandmother, who moved with the Kirks when they purchased their nice new Scarborough bungalow in 1954. Mary Hamilton taught Betty how to sew on a treadle machine, fed her brown-sugar sandwiches and provided comfort when she got in trouble with her parents. School provided another refuge. "I was incredibly happy at school. It saved my sanity," says Betty.

So did the Church. Maurice and Eva never attended, but they made sure their daughter went to Sunday school at the nearby Anglican church. Betty had never been baptized, so at 12, she organized the ceremony herself and invited her parents.

Religion has always been important to Betty, but that was particularly true when she was a lonely teenager. It was more home than home. She was a Sunday-school teacher, a Girl Guide leader and active in the Young Peoples group. "Church has always been good for me," she says. "It was a place I could get questions answered. I could be inquisitive and even outrageous."

Intellectual curiosity was certainly not encouraged in the Kirk household. Betty's father urged her to take an office job immediately after high school. She was only going to work for a while before she'd quit to raise her family, so why waste time on things like Latin or geometry? By that time, though, Betty was showing signs of the strong-minded, independent person she would become. She ignored him and selected all academic subjects. Although she never made it to the A class, she did fairly well, particularly at math. She was selected for the intramural sports teams, was named a prefect and was elected to the Girls' Athletic Association. Her social life was another matter. While she had plenty of female friends, Betty claims she was never once asked out on a date. The only time she went out with a guy was to the Sadie Hawkins dance, when she had to ask him. She was attractive enough but, she says, "I didn't have male friends and part of that was my own sense of inadequacy, my lack of social manoeuvring."

It didn't help that she felt desperately poor. Maurice Kirk changed jobs every couple of years, a result of his heavy drinking and his distaste for authority. He was a mail carrier, a janitor in a church, a car man for the railroad, a cleaner of heavy equipment and finally a maintenance worker with VIA Rail. He always managed to provide for his family, but they had a perpetual sense of insecurity. No one quite knew where the next dollar was coming from. As well, the Kirks' attitude towards money was odd. Betty says her parents were consumer-mad. They liked to buy shiny kitchen appliances, the latest gadgets, a new car every three years, a state-of-the-art stereo system. It meant the family was always heavily in debt, and there was little left over for Betty.

This financial situation was one of the reasons she was urged to quit school after Grade 13 and get a job, but she dug in her heels. For a long time, she had nurtured a dream, and despite her parents' indifference, if not outright opposition, she was determined, "come hell or high water," to become a nurse.

Betty chose to train at Toronto's Women's College Hospital, not because it was the progressive, female-oriented place it is but because of its modern, new residences that had been built five years before. Each student had a room of her own, which was unheard of in those days. The hospital was founded in 1883 as a medical college, one of the few places Canadian women could train as doctors. When, in 1905, the major universities finally admitted females to their schools of medicine, Women's College changed directions and became affiliated with the University of Toronto, committed to all aspects of women's health.

Betty loved everything about training. "I got out of the house and had 'sisters' for the first time in my life. Even though I had no rules at home, the unsaid ones were very restrictive, whereas in residence, I was able to call the shots." She knew right away she not only enjoyed nursing but would be very good at it.

There was a bonus: at Women's College there were plenty of female gynecologists who were willing to hand out birth-control pills or even terminate pregnancies at a time when abortion was not legal. Betty said it gave the young women in her class a sense of security.

Betty herself was still painfully shy and awkward with the opposite sex. Everyone—her girlfriends, her mother—was always trying to fix her up with blind dates. On one such occasion, she ended up at a bowling banquet. Betty thought her date was a creep, but she had a good time because she spent the night dancing with another man. Ken Jordan was tall and darkly good-looking. He was three years older than Betty and was smitten by her immediately. That night, he asked her out for the next day and then kept on asking. "I was enamored of being wooed more than anything else. It probably wouldn't have mattered who it was." Within a month, Ken had proposed and Betty had accepted.

Ken and Betty were married on September 12, 1964, in Christ Church, Scarborough, the place where she had found so much comfort during her young years. About 15 people attended the ceremony and the reception at the Kirks' home afterwards. Ken Jordan was a postman. The relatively low status of his job didn't bother Betty, but his crooked front teeth did. "I remember thinking to myself, 'I must do something about those teeth,'" and she did. It was indicative of the entire relationship. Betty was by far the dominant partner; as she puts it, "I ruled the roost." Ken's passivity was fine at first—it allowed her the freedom to do whatever she wanted—but eventually it would undermine her love of and faith in him.

Betty had graduated from nursing on a Tuesday, got married on the Saturday and a week later, began her first job at Queensway General Hospital. She started out as a nurse in female surgery. One year later, she was promoted to assistant head nurse in gynecology, a unit of 22 beds, and in 1969, to head nurse of the recovery room. A rift had developed among the nurses in recovery that had resulted in emotional turmoil. It didn't take Betty long to sort things out, to the relief of the hospital administration. By 1973, she was a supervisor, overseeing the nurses of obstetrics, gynecology and psychiatry.

There were important reasons why she climbed the management ladder so quickly. "I think I'm incredibly caring," she says. "I don't particularly care for myself well, but I know how to care for others." She was also bright, conscientious and had good organizational skills. There was another important quality that would mark Betty's entire career: she stuck up for the ordinary worker against the bosses. "I've always thought that the bureaucracy has enough power so I advocated for the staff. They were very loyal to me, incredibly loyal."

There was a real benefit for Betty in sliding into administrative work. She did not have to endure the chaotic shift work experienced by floor nurses, and she worked days and got most weekends off, which meant she could spend time with Ken. With two salaries, they lived very well. They had a lovely apartment, bought a 1967 red Mustang, went on a three-month trek around Europe in 1969—and spent a lot of time in bars. Ken drank heavily; in fact, he was drunk a great deal of the time. "I knew that I would either drink with him or lose him, so I followed him around to these sleazy places. I got to know a lot of awful washrooms." In 1968, Ken came down with hepatitis, his liver dangerously enflamed and enlarged. He was told that if he continued to consume alcohol, he would soon be dead. He stopped drinking altogether in 1971, but Betty says certain personality syndromes connected to alcoholism persisted.

Betty and Ken had badly wanted a family, and when, after two years, nothing had happened, they consulted a fertility specialist, who discovered Betty was basically allergic to Ken's sperm. She was informed that becoming pregnant would be impossible. There followed a period of real grieving for Betty. She cried and raged, but finally told herself nothing could be done. She would compensate through her career.

Betty had realized that, without a Bachelor of Nursing degree, the glass ceiling for women administrators was very low. She began taking night courses, and eventually realized she would have to attend university full time if she were ever to complete her studies. Ken, too, was tired of his dead-end postman's job. He struggled to complete high school through night courses, and then decided to study engineering. The Jordans diligently saved money, not only for a couple of years' sabbatical but also for an elaborate trip the following summer, travelling on the trans-Siberian express and ending up in Hong Kong.

In July 1971, Betty wasn't feeling well and there was something odd about her menstrual periods. She finally consulted her doctor, who told her with a laugh that she was pregnant. "I wasn't a particularly happy camper. I had come to terms with being childless, I was going to have this career as a clinical-nurse specialist and go on this wonderful trip." The vacation never happened, but she soon got over her misgivings.

Her daughter Tanya was born on March 23, 1972. Betty was back in class eight days later, and wrote her final examinations on April 8. Her obstetrician told her she'd never pass, so she was pleased to inform him that her grade average was B-plus. Another year of study to complete her degree followed, after which she returned to her job as a nursing supervisor at Queensway Hospital. By that time, Ken had found a job, so that with some savings, the Jordans were able to buy a four-bedroom home in the affluent suburb of Mississauga.

In 1974, a son Kirk came along, and Betty realized the combination of looking after two babies and holding down a position with so much responsibility was simply too much. She quit her job at Queensway, but, since the Jordans had a hefty mortgage and two cars, they still needed a second income. Betty not only took a part-time position as a weekend supervisor at York Central Hospital in Richmond Hill but, during the week, provided daycare for the children of a nursing friend. It meant she had four kids to look after, ages one to four.

During this time, she was also busy working on another university degree. It wasn't necessarily meant to advance her career. While she was studying for her nursing degree, she had spotted dozens of liberal-arts courses in the university calendar that appealed to her. She began to take one a semester, three semesters a year, majoring in sociology. It was one of the building blocks that would lead to a second career.

By 1976, the Jordans decided they were tired of the expense and inconvenience of suburban living. They sold their house and bought another in Toronto's fashionable Beaches area. Betty took a part-time job in a doctor's office and, to her great satisfaction, became involved once again in her religious faith.

After her marriage Betty had given up going to church. Ken didn't want the bother and she was occupied with working and looking after the house. Eventually, she and a fellow nurse started attending Sunday morning services at an Anglican church in Etobicoke, but after the friend moved away, Betty's religious involvement again petered out. She was determined her children would have a religious education, however, and once she moved to the Beaches, she began taking them to Sunday school at St. John's Norway Anglican Church. There she found a new appreciation of her faith. "I think you almost have to go away from the church, if you've gone as a child, in order to realize what it is and what it is not for you." Her faith in the Lord, she says, is not an overwhelmingly passionate one. God is simply part of her, like her right arm or left leg. Betty became deeply involved with the St. John's congregation, teaching Sunday school, participating in stewardship teams, acting as deputy warden.

Beginning in 1964, Ken had suffered a series of nervous breakdowns, sinking into deep depressions that left him almost immobile. By 1978, he was too ill to work. It was the beginning of one of the most desperate periods in Betty's life. The family could not manage on what she made working part-time in the doctor's office, and it happened to be a time when there was an oversupply of nurses. Finally, Toronto East General Hospital offered her a job in orthopedics, a field of medicine in which she had never worked before.

The job was physically hard on Betty. She hadn't worked as an ordinary floor nurse for years, and suddenly, there were all these patients in traction and casts who had to be moved. Fortunately, within six months, Betty was asked to apply for a position at Baycrest, a long-term-care facility and home for elderly Jewish people in North Toronto. The job was senior nursing supervisor of the cognitively impaired. It was more money, no shift work, no physical slugging and, as Betty quickly discovered, it was a wonderful place to work. She knew nothing about the Jewish faith when she started the job but, she says, "I would think that Judaism kept me there so long. It really adds a very different ethos to the place. It's more caring, more client-centred."

By 1981, the Jordans were back on their feet. Ken had returned to work and Betty continued at Baycrest. The family needed a break, and they decided to spend the summer in France. To that end, a furnished trailer was rented at the town of Maisons-Laffitte, an hour's drive from Paris.

On the flight over, Betty noticed six-year-old Kirk seemed not to feel well. He was drinking a great deal of water and going to the bathroom a lot, but she put it down to his excitement over the trip. The family settled into the rented accommodation and Betty set off to attend an international congress on gerontology in Hamburg, West Germany. When she returned, she realized Kirk had lost weight. She took him to a doctor, who ordered some blood tests. When the results were known, the Jordans were told to return to Canada immediately. In Toronto, the diagnosis was confirmed. Kirk had diabetes.

The illness became the pivot of the family. "We ate by the clock. Eight, twelve, six we were sitting at the table," says Betty. Although Kirk has had serious reactions to insulin only rarely, it was a constant worry. Equally distressing for Betty, particularly at the beginning, was her husband's reaction. "Emotionally he wasn't good at all. He kept slamming the steering wheel, saying, 'Why wasn't it me? Why did it have to be him? He's only six years old.'"

The discovery of Kirk's diabetes was the beginning of a series of difficult emotional events in Betty's life. Her father died suddenly in 1983, and her mother became increasingly mentally impaired, phoning her 50 times a day for no particular reason. Ken had grown ever more passive. He used to say forlornly, "You are 80 percent of this marriage, and I'm 20 percent." Betty realized it was true and began to bitterly resent it.

By this time, she was assistant director of nursing at Baycrest, a particularly demanding job because her boss, like everyone else, relied on her for emotional support. One day, she decided there was simply too much on her plate. As she had in other times of stress, she bailed out of her responsibilities by heading back to university for a year.

She was working towards a Bachelor of Arts in sociology and it was a comfort to immerse herself in her courses. However, as the school term was ending, she realized she was about to go back into the same old zoo. One of her professors gave her a name of a therapist, probably the best thing that could have happened to her, for it would radically change her life. That fall, she had her mother admitted, against her will, to a nursing home. Eight days later, she sent her husband a letter asking for a separation. "He sat in front of me and read it and said, 'I see. Twenty years wasted.' But he agreed to go." Ken and Betty were divorced in 1994.

For some time, Betty had been interested in pursuing graduate work. She had applied to the Ontario Institute for Studies in Education and McMaster University's Health Sciences and had been turned down by both. She had a close high-school friend who was studying to become an Anglican priest, and that piqued her curiosity. "I remember opening the calendar [for Trinity College, Master of Divinity] and looking over the pastoral stuff and saying, 'Oh, this is quite wonderful.' They talked about different ways of bringing out spirituality, and stuff around the marginalized. I thought, 'This is for me.'" Betty could see herself combining theological training with her nursing experience, perhaps as a director of a palliative-care unit. What she could not envision was actually becoming an Anglican priest. "Somebody asked me if I was going to be ordained. I answered, 'Oh, God no, that's the furthest thing from my mind.'"

Since she was now the sole support for her two children, she had to keep her part-time job at Baycrest while working towards her Master of Divinity degree. An important part of her academic work was a practice placement in the field. Betty wasn't so much interested in traditional church-chaplaincy work as she was in social justice, and she fortunately found the ideal position working at Street Health, a clinic for the homeless connected to All Saints Church in downtown Toronto.

Betty had never worked on the streets before, and it was an eye-opener. She dealt with every imaginable ailment—cuts in the feet, stab wounds, burns, frostbite, fleas, lice—and since she was both a nurse and theology student, these people's state of mind and their spirituality were also very much her concern.

Betty realized some of the Church hierarchy did not approve of a field placement that dealt with the down-and-out; they were used to students working in ordinary Church positions. However, the clinic received so much publicity on television and in newspapers, they could hardly voice their objection publicly. Betty continued to volunteer at the clinic well after her field-placement work was completed.

As she became immersed in her theological studies, Betty began to question her own decision not to seek ordination. She recalled what a thrill she had felt listening to a sermon by Elizabeth Kilbourn, one of the first female Anglican priests in Canada. She remembered a premonition that she was being called to something bigger. The question grew ever more torturous: did God want her as his priest or not? One day she went to visit her bishop. "Arthur Brown is a very large man—a presence that fills the room. That day he was wearing his purple shirt. Sitting in front of his very large desk, I felt like I was three years old. He asked, 'Have you thought about Holy Orders?' Given the history that I've had, the bishop is asking me if I want to do Holy Orders? This is all backwards. I said, 'No, I haven't, but I'll be finished school in a year or two, so I'll think about it then.' He replied, 'I would like you to think about it now.'"

The next six months were torture for Betty. She felt as though she were carrying a huge rock on her back. She simply could not make up her mind whether to seek ordination or not. "I kept thinking, 'It doesn't make sense. I would work longer hours, make less money. I have two children, a house to keep afloat, I'm a great nurse. It doesn't make sense.'"

In 1988, a friend of Betty's was being ordained, and she attended the ceremonies at St. James Cathedral. "It was May, and talk about Hollywood! It was the cathedral and the sun was shining in through the stained-glass windows and the organ was playing. I started bargaining with God. 'Okay God, is this what you really want? I think it's really stupid, it doesn't make any sense to me. But I'll tell you what I'll do. I'll apply, and if you want me ordained, you'll make it happen.' Instantly, the stone was gone. I was free, totally free."

In late 1989, Betty was officially proclaimed a candidate for the Anglican priesthood, but she needed a ministry, usually a church, to which to be ordained, and there was none available. In January, she went to India for three months under the auspices of the Anglican National Church's Volunteers in Mission program. She worked as a nursing consultant, both in the hospital and the nursing school in Ludhina in the Punjab. "I learned more than I taught," she says. When she returned to Canada, she did three months of parish training at St. Bede's in Toronto. There was still no church position open. By this time, she was scrambling for some income, and ended up with three part-time jobs: working for the Victorian Order of Nurses, at the Toronto East Detention Centre clinic and at Baycrest. Finally, in January 1991, she signed on as a liaison between Street Health, the health clinic for the homeless where she had spent so much time, and Wellesley Hospital. It turned out to be one of the most satisfying years of her life.

Here was her big chance to slug it out with the bureaucracy on behalf of the underdog. If a homeless person complained of being weak or dizzy, Betty made sure the medicos asked if he or she had eaten in the last three days. If a prostitute with pneumonia was chucked out onto the street in the middle of the night with a paper prescription in her hand and no money to fill it, Betty would be there, asking why she hadn't been simply given the antibiotics. Betty attended boardroom meetings dressed in a denim skirt, sandals and a T-shirt with slogans that demanded "Stop Violence Against Women." "They [the bureaucracy] needed to get used to someone who looked different but could be articulate about the needs of the community. I was outrageous. It was wonderful."

In the fall of 1991, Betty finally became a deacon. It came as a surprise to her, because she was ordained not to a church but to Street Health, hardly the standard ministry. Over 200 people—from Street Health, from Baycrest, her St. John's Norway Parish, her family and her friends, both Christian and Jews—attended the ordination ceremony. "Everybody was thrilled to be there. It just felt like so much love. Everybody gave a damn."

In January 1992, the Reverend Betty Jordan became an assistant curate at the Church of St. Stephen on Jane Street in Downsview. Later that year, she was ordained a priest.

In 1996, Betty took on an even more challenging position: a store-front ministry in a very needy part of Toronto. Flemingdon Park consists of one square mile in the suburb of Don Mills. Its population of 25,000 lives in high rises or government-subsidized townhouses. Ninety different first languages are spoken, representing 130 different ethnic groups. The problems of poverty, unemployment and crime are as prevalent there as in any similar concrete jungle. The ministry—"about the size of a double-car garage," as Betty puts it—consists primarily of a large room with comfortable sofas, chairs, television, VCR, a kiddies corner, a fridge and microwave, and three small offices. Basically, it's a drop-in centre, "an oasis of peace in lives of chaos."

Cutting through the bureaucracy and finding ways to ease people's pain are what Betty's ministry is mostly about. Daily, she draws on her knowledge and experience, including her nursing skills. "A woman came in saying she had been told she needed a hysterectomy. I made diagrams on the back of Kleenex boxes to teach her what it was. She was bleeding like a stuck pig, and I said, 'You don't need this shit for the next ten years.'" Betty adds, "If you meet the basic needs, the spiritual will follow." There is no Anglican church in Flemingdon Park, so once a month she celebrates the Eucharist in the ministry's shabby drop-in room. Scores of people attend.

To show she had made a total commitment to her parishioners, Betty bought a condominium in Flemingdon Park. The building has cockroaches, only three percent of the residents are white and drug-dealing is a feature of the neighbourhood, but people see her doing her shopping, driving her bicycle, walking with friends, and they know she is with them.

She works 70 hours a week sometimes. On weekends in the summer, she escapes to the quiet of a cottage she owns. She deals with the pressures of her job in the manner she always has—by going to school. She is working on a Doctorate of Ministry at McMaster University in Hamilton, writing a thesis on "concrete-jungle" ministries. When you ask her if she's happy, she says, "That's a funny word. This is where I'm supposed to be."

Consecrated Women

Let your women keep silence in the churches: for it is not permitted unto them to speak; but they are commanded to be under obedience, as also saith the law. And if they will learn any thing, let them ask their husbands at home; for it is a shame for women to speak in the church.... Let all things be done decently and in order.

1 Corinthians 14:34–35, 40

There is neither Jew nor Greek, there is neither bond nor free, there is neither male nor female for ye are all in Christ Jesus.

Galatians 3:28

As long as we believe that God is male, then the male will think he is God.

Feminist theologian Mary Daly, 1974

The only person in my family who was religious was my maternal grandmother, and hers could hardly be called a conventional faith. She was a Christian Scientist. I remember being fascinated by a photograph she had hung up of Mary Baker Eddy, the founder of the religion, because my grandmother looked so much like her. My mother said it was more than just Irish noses in common. Both were smart, headstrong women, and both worried constantly about their health. That was what Christian Science was all about—mind over matter, the ability to heal oneself of physical, financial or emotional ills. My grandmother regarded ordinary physicians as so many African witch doctors.

I didn't know Mary Baker Eddy would turn out to be something of a charlatan. She abandoned her only child when he was a baby, had several rather questionable marriages and suffered from hysteria that manifested itself in disabling diseases—she would often take to her bed for months. What I was taught about Eddy was that she was the only woman who had founded a religion in our part of the world, and she was to be admired and respected. I had no idea the vast majority of faiths took St. Paul's advice to heart: "It is a shame for women to speak in the church." In Mary Baker Eddy's eyes, and in my grandmother's, the Scriptures taught that women and men were equal before God. Only later did I discover that this, to me obvious, truism was anything but, at least in the eyes of patriarchal religion.

I

It remains a paradox. In ancient Greece, one of the most androcentric of societies and most oppressive towards females, women were allowed to hold the highest religious offices, attend at the sacred rituals and share in the honours, privileges and prestige of priestly office, which included the money that came with the job. This is in stark contrast to the suppression and muzzling of religious women that eventually became a feature of Christianity. True, important priestesses had to come from the right families: ancient, wealthy and upper class, but then, so did priests.

Athena Polias was the patron goddess of Athens; her sacred temple, the majestic Parthenon, dominated the Acropolis. Her priestess, always a member of the noble family of Eteoboutadae, was a person of importance in the life of the city state; inscriptions and dedications honouring her abound. Her status meant she also had political influence. In 508 BC, King Cleomenes of Sparta meddled in Athenian politics by opposing a reformer who was popular with ordinary citizens. He attempted to abolish the Athenian Council so he could funnel power to his followers. It was necessary, however, for him to occupy the Acropolis. As the historian Herodotus records: "… he was just going into Athena's temple to say a prayer when the Priestess, before he could get through the door, rose from her chair and cried: 'Spartan stranger, go back. Do not enter the holy place.'"[635] No worshipping at Athena's temple, no influence. Cleomenes was forced to return to Sparta.

The more ordinary kind of priestess was often an assistant to the priests, although she still played important ritual roles. During blood sacrifices, the priestess often carried the sacrificial basket containing seeds to be thrown onto the fire and the knife used to slit the animals' throats.[636] Whether the actual slaughter was performed by women is doubtful.

Not all religious jobs were sought after, though. At Comana in Asia Minor, women who were called *hierodoulai* (sacred slaves) lived in servitude to the temple, performing all the most menial tasks for almost no reward.[637] Others were forced into prostitution in the name of some male god or other.

In the state religions of Rome, women, along with slaves and freedmen, were excluded from the priesthood, with two important exceptions: the priestesses who served Ceres (Demeter), the all-important agricultural goddess, and the famous Vestal Virgins.

Vesta, the Roman version of the Greek Hestia, was the keeper of the hearth. The fire burning there symbolized the fortune and continuity not only of the family but also of the state. In Rome, the sacred flame was perpetually kept alight in the public hearth of the Temple of Vesta, situated in the north-west corner of the Forum. On those very rare occasions when it was extinguished, the city ground to a halt, its identity lost, its prestige diminished.

Traditionally, it was the solemn job of daughters of the household to insure the family's fireplace was always lit, and it was the daughters of the early kings of Rome who tended to the royal hearth. Eventually, the state cult of Vesta evolved, and with it, the office of the virgin priestesses whose sacred duty it was to insure the national flame was never snuffed out.

There were six Vestal Virgins serving at any one time. Usually children of patricians, they were selected by the grand pontiff, who was sometimes the emperor himself. Wearing red headdresses, their hair braided into six plaits like a bride's, these young girls from six to ten years old were delivered by their fathers into the hands of the grand pontiff. A Vestal Virgin's term lasted 30 years: ten as an apprentice, ten in service and ten as a teacher. During that time, the Vestal was required to remain chaste—this represented the purity of Vesta and the eternal flame of the hearth—although afterwards, she was allowed to marry. Few chose to do so, and those who did, often made unfortunate matches.

The rituals of the April 15 festival of Fordicidia, in which the Vestals participated in a complex ritual of butchering a pregnant cow, is typical of the kinds of duties they performed. The sacrifice was meant to insure a bountiful growing season. As Ovid describes it, "After the officiants removed the calves from [the cow's entrails] and placed the butchered pluck in smoking vessels, the eldest of the Vestal virgins burned the calves, the ashes from which were used to purify the people on the day of Pales [April 21]."[638]

Although the Vestals' lives were strictly regulated, in many ways, they were the most liberated of all Roman women. Freed from the legal guardianship of the *pater familias*, they could make wills, and therefore dispose of their estates as they wished, and act as witnesses in court. They were the only women who were allowed to ride in a *carpentum*, a two-wheeled chariot usually reserved for influential males such as magistrates and priests. They were always accompanied in the streets by a *lictor*, an attendant who cleared the way before them. While other women were relegated to the topmost tiers (the worst seats at the games or theatrical performances), Vestals occupied a proud position on the podium, at least in Augustus's time.[639]

The office yielded enormous authority and prestige. If a criminal happened to run into a Vestal Virgin on the way to his execution, he was freed. On the other hand, if a person inadvertently passed under the litter carrying a Vestal, he was killed on the spot.

However, these privileges came with a price. Any Vestal who was found to engage in sexual intercourse was severely penalized. Scourging to death was one punishment, but sometimes the offender was walled up in a room with only a small plate of food and a couch, and left to suffer a long, lingering death by starvation.[640] The worst danger that could befall a Vestal was to become embroiled in politics. When the Roman military force was defeated at Cannae in 216 BC, the Vestals Opimia and Floronia were made the scapegoats for the disaster. After being convicted of not being chaste, one was buried alive and the other committed suicide

In fact, though, such punishment was rare. In its thousand-year history, only ten Vestal virgins are known to have been executed. Mostly they were revered. It's ironic, as historian John Scheid points out, that although the Vestals were subject to men and mostly confined to marginal roles, it was they who performed the religious tasks considered essential for the survival of Rome.[641] As the great poet Horace wrote, his glory and that of Rome's would endure as long as "the pontiff and the silent Vestal climb to the capital."[642]

II

In early Christianity, women played an active and important role. They had been part of Jesus of Nazareth's inner circle. Martyrs such as Perpetua and Felicity faced the lions with such courage and resolution, theirs could hardly be considered a weak or inferior sex. So many wealthy Roman matrons became patrons of the new religion that the emperor attempted to squelch this flow of money to the "deadly superstition," but without much success. Female missionaries joined their male colleagues in spreading Christianity to the heathen tribes of Europe, and they preached and converted members of their own families. As the Church took shape, women became deaconesses, presbyters—a function that came close to the priesthood—and teachers. Some women even baptized others.

Yet by the fourth century, when Christians were no longer being perse-

cuted and the Church had become the official state religion, female leadership had become anathema. St. Paul wrote in Corinthians: "For a man indeed
ought not to cover his head, forasmuch as he is the image and glory of God:
but the woman is the glory of the man. For the man is not of the woman;
but the woman of the man. Neither was the man created for the woman; but
the woman for the man."[642a] The early Church fathers used such passages to
justify women's subjugation to men, as well as to prohibit their right to offici-
ate, preach or celebrate the sacraments. To this day, St. Paul's words are used
regularly to denigrate and restrict the female sex, not only in the Church but
in society as whole.

In his study of religions, the famous German sociologist Max Weber theorized that women are almost always welcomed in the early, prophetic stage
of a religion, when it is considered an unseemly act of rebellion to join the
movement. As missionaries and proselytizers, they excel. Once the religion
becomes part of the establishment—when, as Weber says, "routinization and
regimentation" take hold—women are excluded and penalized.[643] This
phenomenon occurred not only in the Church during the early Christian
period but in the monastic movement as it evolved in the Middle Ages.

The ideal of sexual purity and abstinence that became so prominent
during the third century appealed to many women, who saw the denial of
marriage and childbearing as a way to expand their own roles in society. As
historian Jo Ann Kay McNamara puts it, "Some consecrated women apparently felt that, having transcended their physiological differences from men,
they could break down all gender barriers."[644] At the beginning of the third
century, unmarried women and virgins, known as canonesses, lived together
in communities presided over by deaconesses. This early sisterhood devoted
itself to a life of prayer, preparing other women for Christian baptism and
helping the poor and ill. Thus began a tradition that, during the Middle
Ages, became part of the formalized monastic system. By the seventh
century, women were flocking to the monasteries and living rigorous lives
of dedication.

Despite this, a nun was treated by the Church hierarchy like any other
female. In the early Middle Ages, a whole series of Church decrees restricted
and prohibited her role in the sacramental aspect of the Church. She was not
permitted to carry out holy office, nor serve as a priest. She was prohibited
by canon law from touching the chalice, burning incense or approaching the
altar during Mass. As historian Shulamith Shahar puts it, "The nun, bride of

Christ, could not assist the priest in the holy ceremonies. Like other women, she too was the target of pollution fears, subjected to a code of prohibitions and taboos."[645] Much of this was based on the Judaic idea that menstruation condemned women to a state of impurity during certain times, which made them generally unfit to approach the altar of the male God.

Attempts were also made to control the power of the abbesses. These women in authority could not give benediction to the opposite sex, nor could they consecrate members of their own communities, a right reserved for the bishop. The mother superior could not hear the confession of her own nuns. By an edict of the Council of Verneuil in 755, abbesses were prohibited from even leaving their communities unless a monarch summoned them. As the power of the bishops and abbots grew, women were obliged to submit silently to their dictates.

Despite all these restrictions, many abbesses became powerful and important leaders of their communities. When Gerberga became abbess of Gandersheim in 947, she became head of a small kingdom with an army, courts of her own, a mint and representation to the imperial assembly.[646] In the 11th century, the abbess of Maubeuge controlled not only her monastery but the city and farmland it owned. The abbesses of Regensberg were considered princesses of the Holy Roman Empire, and allowed to send deputies to national assemblies. The abbesses of Herford and Quedlinburg in Germany provided military troops to the Emperor, and were represented in the Diets of the empire.[647]

In many instances, the power of these women religious derived from the great wealth of their monasteries. In other cases, a dynamic or forceful personality would enable an abbess to mold a position of influence and freedom. Hildegard of Bingen is a prime example. Hildegard's prophetic writings were authenticated by Pope Eugenius III in 1148, which brought her enormous fame and influence. In that same year, she had a vision that she and other nuns should move from the monastery at Disibodenberg and establish their own convent at Rupertsberg, 30 miles away. Since the nuns' dowries provided great wealth to the monastery, there was naturally strong opposition from the monks, and Abbot Kuno flatly turned down her request. As she would many times in her life when her will was thwarted, Hildegard took to her bed with an illness so serious, she almost died. The nervous abbot caved in and agreed to let the nuns go.

The move was accomplished. Although the primitive conditions caused great hardship at first, the sisters set about making money: copying books, sewing liturgical garments, fashioning other exquisite handicrafts. Eventually their community became so well-off that even indoor plumbing was installed, a great luxury in those times.

Once Hildegard had broken the restrictive control of Abbot Kuno, she became her own boss, recognizing the authority only of the Archbishop of Mainz, who pretty much left her alone. She became incredibly famous. Emperors and popes, queens and archbishops wrote to her for advice. King Conrad, Frederick Barbarossa, the Holy Roman Emperor and Count Philip of Flanders were frequent correspondents. Monks and priests flocked to visit her. She also broke all the rules by travelling widely throughout the Rhineland, visiting monasteries, preaching to huge crowds in big cities such as Cologne, Seigburg and Liège in Flanders, and distributing her published sermons.

Hildegard thrived as a woman religious because she operated strictly within the confines of Church dogma. She had received her authority from a Pope who believed her visions were the direct voice of God. For those prophets who operated outside the Church's sanction, however, the story was often one of brutal repression.

Marguerite Porète was a Beguine, a lay sister, born in the Belgian province of Hainaut around 1270. She became so renowned for her extensive theological and literary knowledge, she was given the title Beguine Clergeresse. Her famous book of verse and commentary, *Mirror of the Simple Soul*, written between 1296 and 1306, takes the intriguing form of a dialogue between love and reason in which it is revealed that the soul passes through seven stages of divine grace, leading finally to a spiritual union with God. Porète believed this was a journey accomplished by direct communion with the divine, without help from tedious sermons or even the sacraments of the Church.

Naturally, the Church authorities considered this outrageous heresy. In 1306, her book was condemned by an ecclesiastical court at Valenciennes and copies were burned in her presence. She was forbidden to speak or preach from it, an order she promptly ignored. In 1308, she was jailed for a year and a half and then tried before the Inquisitor in Paris. He seems not to have read the entire volume but only a sentence here and there. On this slim evidence, he condemned Porète to death. Throughout her trial, she remained silent and unrepentant, as much a hero of free speech and thought as outspoken men like Galileo.[648]

In 1311, at the Place de Grève in Paris, Marguerite Porète was burned at the stake. Witnesses marvelled at "her unusual dignity and courage" and at her last words: "I am not wrong." After Porète's death, her work continued to be read and cherished. Her books were translated into many languages by monks and preserved in monastery libraries. Historians have concluded, quite rightly, she was persecuted not for her actual beliefs but because, as an uncloistered Beguine, she was perceived as a free spirit and a leader in the community of women.

III

At the beginning of the 15th century, European society settled into a superstitious mind-set that continued for three centuries. People everywhere came to believe that covens of witches and sects of sorcerers dwelt in their midst. These devils incarnate, who were in league with Satan himself, were blamed for the never-ending disasters that descended on a particular village. Storms or plagues of insects that ruined crops, ailing livestock, the sudden death of a baby, a wife who couldn't conceive, a husband who was impotent—every misfortune was the fault of the witches. Between 1560–1660 in Germany, France, Switzerland, England, Scotland and the Netherlands, about 100,000 people were condemned as witches; 30,000 to 40,000 of them lost their lives, either on the gallows, or at the stake. Eighty percent were female.

In any particular village, there was often one old woman, almost always a spinster or widow, who had to make her own way in life by going "from house to house and from door to door for a potfull of milk, yeast, drink, pottage or some such relief without which they could hardly live."[649] They could be a terrible nuisance—illegally pasturing a goat or stealing firewood or yelling at the village kids. Just to keep alive, these old women sometimes resorted to blackmail. "Give me some apples (or potatoes or coins) or I'll cast a hex against you and your family," they would demand, thereby provoking real fear. When a haystack burst into flames or a baby died in its sleep or hail destroyed the tomatoes, who better to scapegoat than the poor, old, eccentric crone? Thomas Dekker's famous *The Witch of Edmonton* (1621) nicely expresses how a woman could herself come to believe she was possessed:

> Some call me witch,
> And being ignorant of myself, they go
> About to teach me how to be one; urging
> That my bad tongue (by their bad language made so)

Forespeaks their cattle, doth bewitch their corn,
Themselves, their servants, and their babes at nurse.
This they enforce upon me; and in part
Make me to credit it.[650]

It's not difficult to understand why the superstitious peasant, knowing hunger or even starvation came with a single crop failure, would embrace the idea of sorcery, but why did the educated elite follow suit? It was, after all, the clerks, judges and clergy—Martin Luther himself insisted all witches should be put to death—who formally condemned these women. The reason is a combination of two events. With the rediscovery of Greek and Roman philosophers came the unveiling of deep-down misogynist ideas about women. More important, perhaps, the Protestant emphasis on the Bible churned up the same old bugbear: Eve succumbing to the lure of the snake, tempting that poor blockhead Adam and the couple being cast out from the Garden of Eden, all of which led to a life of woe and all of which was clearly Eve's fault. Women were morally inferior and therefore were subject to the charms of the Devil.

One of the most famous book of the time, *Malleus Maleficarum* (*The Witch Hammer*), written by two German Dominicans and published in Strasbourg in 1486, became a kind of Bible for witch-hunters. Other similar "Devil tracts" rolled off the early printing presses, especially in Germany. Within a short time, the image of the evil witch permeated European society. These frightening creatures were said to gather in great assemblies in the middle of the night, whereupon they renounced their Christian faith and pledged their loyalty to Satan. At a huge banquet, little children were served up as the main course—the potion rendered from boiling their bones, said to have supernatural powers, was handed out as gifts to each guest—and, in the orgy that followed, the witches copulated with grotesque winged and hoofed creatures called demon incubi.

In Hans Baldung Grien's famous painting *The Weather Witches* (1523), two well-developed nudes are invoking a fierce storm that will likely destroy the about-to-be harvested crops. One stands with her back to the viewer, her legs crossed in a sexy, provocative pose. The other sits, her private parts exposed, lifting up a glass jar in which stands a tiny, devilish-looking imp. A fat child, or perhaps dwarf, clings to her from behind. He holds a huge flame that is obviously the source of the havoc in the heavens. A goat lies between the two women, both of whom wear saucy, malevolent smiles.

Of course, images like this had nothing much to do with the real people who were labelled witches. They were not sexy, powerful harlots but instead were society's poorest: the oldest, the ugliest; often crippled, toothless, deaf, sometimes nearly blind or with only one eye. Their condemnation as witches and the ghastly torture they underwent was an obvious extension of an interpretation of Genesis that labelled women as morally feeble and thus easily seduced by the Devil. As one clergyman pointed out, Eve was made from Adam's crooked rib. Therefore the female mind is twisted and perverse. Sorcery naturally follows.

IV

If women's status in the church were ever to be enhanced, the interpretations of those Scriptures that silenced and denigrated them had to be challenged, and in the 19th century, that was exactly what happened.

It began with an article by Sarah Grimké in the American journal *The Advocate of Social Reform*. The Grimkés were a powerful South Carolina family who had made most of their fortune off the backs of their slaves. Yet both Sarah and her sister Angelina were dedicated abolitionists, travelling the lecture circuit, preaching the evils of slavery. The Grimké sisters were also strong feminists and devoted Quakers, so subscribers to *The Advocate* weren't surprised when Sarah published her long article on women and the Scriptures. There was nothing wrong with the Bible, she asserted, just that it had been translated by men, and mistakes might have been made. As well, it was male theologians who had interpreted it, often skewing the true meaning in the process. Take the infamous Genesis 3:16 passage, for example: "I will greatly multiply thy sorrow and thy conception; in sorrow thou shalt bring forth children; and thy desire shall be to thy husband, and he shall rule over thee." This, Sarah said, was God's prediction of what would happen as a result of original sin, not a blanket endorsement of male superiority. It was time, she insisted, for women to pronounce their own take on the Bible. She wrote:

Men have endeavored to entice, or to drive women from almost every sphere of moral action. 'Go home and spin' is … the advice of the domestic tyrant.… The first duty, I believe, which devolves on our sex is to think for themselves.… Until we take our stand side by side with our brother; until we read all the precepts of the Bible as addressed to woman as well as to man, and lose … the consciousness of sex, we shall never fulfill the end of our existence.[651]

In fact, during the 19th century, a number of feminists in England and the United States became theologians. Some of their pronouncements shocked the religious establishment to its core, particularly their preposterous assertion of male and female equality. The French Protestant Eugénie Niboyet went one better. She maintained that passages such as Genesis 2:18—"It is not good that the man should be alone; I will make him an help meet for him"— proved women were not equal but superior to men. Eve was created from Adam's rib, true, but this was a more worthy material than the clay and dust out of which Adam sprang. What about Eve coming into existence only *after* Adam was created? According to Genesis, God worked backwards: first he made the sea monsters, then the animals, then man and finally the highest creature of them all: woman. This was such an achievement that he was able to rest on the seventh day.

The 19th-century feminist who had the most effect on rethinking the Scriptures was the indomitable Elizabeth Cady Stanton. With a gutsiness unparalleled in her time, she wrote: "When women understand that governments and religions are human inventions; that Bibles, prayer books, catechisms and encyclical letters are all emanations from the brain of man, they will not longer be oppressed by the injunctions delivered so readily by *men* in the guise of divinely ordained authority."[652] The publication of *The Woman's Bible* in two volumes, the first in 1895, the second in 1898, was Stanton's (and seven collaborators') attempt to rectify the distortions in Biblical interpretation. As she wrote in the introduction to Volume One:

The Bible teaches that woman brought sin and death into the world, that she precipitated the fall of the race, that she was arraigned before the judgment seat of Heaven, tried, condemned and sentenced. Marriage for her was to be a condition of bondage, maternity a period of suffering and anguish, and in silence and subjection, she was to play the role of a dependent on man's bounty for all her material wants, and for all the information she might desire on the vital questions of the hour, she was commanded to ask her husband at home.[653]

The publication of *The Woman's Bible* erupted into a fierce scandal. Interestingly, some of Stanton's most outraged critics were suffragists. Rachel Foster Avery, a member of the National American Woman Suffrage Association, under the auspices of which *The Woman's Bible* had been published, had this to say: "We have been held responsible for the action of an individual (an action which many of our members, far from sympathizing with, feel to be unwise) in issuing a volume with a pretentious title, covering a jumble of comment ... without either scholarship or literary value, set forth in a spirit which is neither reverent nor inquiring."[654]

Stanton's punishment was to be sidelined by the women's movement. Nonetheless, she had the last word. *The Woman's Bible* was an instant best-seller, going through seven printings in six months. It had a profound effect on the way Scriptures were perceived in the 20th century, and is still read with some astonishment by feminists. Stanton herself had an understanding of what her work had accomplished. Only a few months before her death, she wrote, "Everything points to a purer and more rational religion in the future, in which woman, as mother of the race, will be recognized as an equal in both Church and State."[655]

V

During the 20th century, when gender discrimination became as abhorrent as racism, the paradox for the Church became ever more acute. How do you keep the moral high ground if you are accused of deep-rooted sexism? It was a controversy that would cause many theologians and others to turn themselves into knots. At times the debate would be vicious, divisive and insulting to women, but in the end, not only was women's aptitude for preaching recognized but female ministers became firmly ensconced in the pulpit.

The first cracks in the Church's male hegemony came in the United States towards the end of the 19th century. The Quakers had always promoted equality for women, and it was a Quaker, Sarah Smiley, who was such a powerful preacher, she was invited to speak in several Presbyterian churches in Brooklyn. Anna Howard Shaw, a graduate of Boston School of Theology and a suffragette, was allowed to lecture at several Methodist churches. These trailblazers were given a chance, as long as they displayed the authority and common sense of a man as well as the modesty and gentleness of a woman.[656]

World War I caused another rent in the Church's patriarchal fabric, especially in Europe. As pastors went off to war, their wives took over. As well as their usual duties, some began to preach, first, perhaps, just reading their husbands' old sermons, but then finding it necessary "to speak more directly to [parishioners'] souls."[657] When there was no one else available, they had to perform marriages and funeral services. In some instances, they even administered the sacraments: baptism and communion. "I was very upset when I performed sacred duties," said a French pastor's wife. "I was shocked, and very thrilled." Some clergy returned home to find a quite different church than the one they had left, and a wife who had proved her spiritual leadership.[658] It hardly made for domestic peace.

Despite women's obvious abilities to preach and minister, there was still a long struggle ahead to accept female clergy. The frustrating tale of Canadian Lydia Emelie Gruchy is an example. Born in Anaif, near Paris in 1894, Lydia Gruchy came to Saskatchewan with her family while she was in her teens. She graduated in 1920 at the top of her class from the University of Saskatchewan, and in 1923, from the Presbyterian Theological College. Gruchy began work as a lay minister, visiting rural schools in Saskatchewan on horseback, leading Bible study and preaching in villages and schoolhouses. In her service to various congregations, she crisscrossed the Prairies every week. Never mind if there were a blizzard, she was almost always at the pulpit on Sundays.

A year after the founding of the United Church of Canada in 1925, Lydia Gruchy requested ordination. Her record as a lay minister was impressive and the congregations of all three parishes backed her. Indeed, they were desperate for her services, since no man would take on such a heavy load. The Church's General Council turned her down. Would she mind serving as a deaconess instead, they asked? Neither Gruchy nor her congregations were interested in such a compromise. At that point, the indefatigable activist and suffragette Nellie McClung joined the cause, and, over the next half-dozen years, she and a small group of supporters fought for Gruchy's ordination.

Lydia Gruchy was finally ordained in Moose Jaw in 1936, the first woman in Canada to become a United Church minister. Seventeen years later, she was the first Canadian woman to receive the honorary degree of Doctor of Divinity.

Despite small victories such as this, the movement to ordain women chugged along very slowly. In Canada in 1941, the number of female clergy made up only 0.21 percent of the total. In the United States, it was about two and a half percent. There were some breakthroughs over the next few decades, though. In the United States, the African Methodist Episcopal Church began ordaining women in 1948—it still has more female clergy than any other denomination—and the Methodists and Presbyterians followed suit in 1956. Even with these advances, the number of female clergy remained pathetically low. It would take the women's movement in the late 1960s and early '70s to fuel what would prove to be an explosion in the number of women entering Protestant ministries.

Recent progress has been remarkable. In the United States, the number of female clergy increased from 16,408 in 1983 to 43,542 in 1996. In Canada in the same period, there has been close to a 300 percent increase in women in the ministry. In 1994, Victoria Matthews was named the first female Anglican bishop in Canada and the fifth in the world. In some of North America's and Europe's most prestigious colleges of theology, female seminarians are now in the majority. However, this success has often not been without a vicious struggle. As one female cleric put it, "Nearly all [of us] can tell tales of painful marginalization, even, in a few cases, of being spat upon, shouted at, verbally abused...."[659]

In 1976, both the Episcopal Church in the United States and the Anglican Church of Canada ordained their first female priests, but it would take the Church of England, the mother of the worldwide Anglican communion, another 16 years to come to terms with the horrifying idea of women as spiritual leaders. A year after the battle was finally won at the annual synod—by only two votes—one male vicar was still snarling to the media, "I'd like to burn the bloody bitches." Rev. Anthony Kennedy offered this opinion as to why he remained adamantly opposed to women administering sacraments: "A woman can't represent Christ. Men and women are totally different— that's not my fault—and Jesus chose men for his disciples."[660] Three years later, the director of Britain's York Mystery Play, a tradition that goes back six centuries, announced that God would be played by a woman, a local antique dealer named Ruth Ford. The Archdeacon of York, George Austin, promptly denounced the decision as "paganism.... We are made in God's image and not the other way around," he declared.

Presently, over half of the 160 Protestant denominations ordain women. Those that don't are mostly fundamentalist, evangelical sects that not only forbid women in positions of church authority but also continue to believe the husband holds the primary power in the household.

To the patriarchs of the Orthodox churches, women's ordination is simply not an issue. Wrote a former dean of St. Vladimir's Orthodox Theological Seminary in Crestweed, New York, "The ordination of women to priesthood is tantamount for us to a radical and irreparable mutilation of the entire faith, the rejection of the whole Scripture, and, needless to say, the end of all 'dialogues'.... This priesthood is Christ's not ours.... And if the bearer, the icon and the fulfiller of that unique priesthood, is man and not woman, it is because Christ is man and not woman." Shortly after his letter was made public, a bumper sticker was pinned on the seminary's bulletin board that read, "Ordain Women or Don't Baptize Them."

It is the Roman Catholic Church that has been the most disappointing in its attitude towards women. In May 1994, Pope John Paul II issued his now infamous *Ordinatio Sacerdotalis*, "... in order that all doubt may be removed regarding a matter of great importance, a matter which pertains to the Church's divine constitution itself ... I declare that the Church has no authority whatsoever to confer priestly ordination on women and that this judgement is to be definitively held by all the Church's faithful." If the Pope thought that would be an end to the controversy, he was sorely mistaken. A few months later, a petition signed by more than a million German Catholics demanded the Vatican reconsider its stand on celibate, all-male priesthood.

In fact, the Roman Catholic Church has since faced one embarrassing situation after another. The persecution of Sister Carmel McEnroy is just one example. Sister McEnroy earned her doctorate in theology from the University of Toronto in 1984. For 14 years, she taught at St. Meinrad's, a seminary in Indiana run by the Benedictines and attended mostly by candidates for the diocesan priesthood.

In the fall of 1995, she and hundreds of others signed an open letter urging the Pope and the United States Conference of Bishops "to open the windows of the church to the fresh air of dialogue on the ordination of women as priests, bishops and cardinals." The following March, Dr. McEnroy was dismissed from her job. What followed was an avalanche of protest, including a newspaper ad in the *National Catholic Register* signed by scores of high-ranking theologians and others. Sister McEnroy herself refused to be silenced. "Any of my colleagues will tell you that I'm a very moderate scholar, and that I'm considered an excellent teacher. It's true that I'm a feminist theologian, but I'm not out to torture men, you know. We're all human beings together. I want a balanced approach, a responsible one."[661] She has since consulted her lawyer.

What the Church expected to accomplish from such intimidation is hard to imagine. Its actions have created bitter resentment among Catholic women and many men. Canadian feminist, teacher and activist Joanna Manning puts it this way:

Come the 20th century, and not even the Vatican can argue a ban on women priests based on women's defective humanity. This new teaching is predicated on women's spiritual inferiority. Women are now equal to men on Earth, but this is a purely secular phenomenon. Christ's maleness makes women eternally defective in heaven. This is a dangerous about-face, which negates the full effects of Christ's resurrection....

Surely this pope must have learned from history that it is impossible to enforce bad theology by browbeating the faithful into submission.[662]

Apparently the lesson has not been learned in the Catholic Church at least, but most women agree. Sometime in the near future, it most certainly will be.

Gay

If among us there was an all-Canadian, 1950s girl, it was Gay Twiner. She sewed all her own clothes, she had lots of dates—always, of course, with the right sort of boys—she was good at archery. She was the student whom teachers loved: diligent at her studies but not impertinent, curious but not obnoxious, fun-loving but never misbehaving. She was, as her friends liked to tease, as wholesome as the cafeteria's gooey apple pie.

Gay considers her childhood idyllic. The Twiners believed in protecting their four kids from the world's miseries. They never argued in front of them, never talked about their financial worries, didn't allow them to attend funerals or visit the really ill. Hot milk was brought to a child who was writing exams. The first sneeze and it was bed and a mustard plaster. Their children's comfort and well-being were what mattered. Later, Gay would wonder if her childhood hadn't been too sheltered. Confrontation with reality in early adulthood almost destroyed her.

Gay's mother Esmé was the heart of the family. She was gregarious, outgoing and athletic. She loved organizing volleyball tournaments; the whistle would shrill, and everybody in the neighbourhood would come running. All the women on that side of the family were fun-loving. Gay's grandmother May Warhurst made costumes for the neighbourhood kids, and while they danced, she'd bang away at the piano.

The Warhursts had immigrated to England when Esmé was three years old and settled in Toronto's east end, buying a house not far from the racetrack. Esmé's father Bill was a railway conductor, and, when he retired from that job, he worked for another ten years sorting mail for the Blue Cross. While the family was never in need, there wasn't a lot of money either. Esmé got as far in school as Grade 12 and then she went off to work in an office.

It wasn't surprising that someone as gregarious as Esmé would be attracted to a guy with as great a sense of humour as Jim Twiner. In later years, Gay often wondered how her father turned out to be such an easy-going, amiable man. His mother was such a difficult, self-obsessed, overbearing person. For some reason, she took offence to Esmé Warhurst; friends said that probably nobody would have been good enough for her son. "It's either me or her," she insisted. Not only did Jim choose to marry Esmé but for years, he would have nothing to do with his mother.

After the war, Jim found work as a cost accountant at Sangamo Electric Co., a job he would hold until he retired. He used his veteran's land grant to purchase a half acre of land right behind R. H. King Collegiate, and there built the one-and-half-storey family home. Over the years, as the four children arrived, it was added onto, but all the same, Gay always shared a room with her sister.

Like everybody else on their street, the Twiners went to the local United Church. Jim became an elder, Esmé was involved with the women's auxiliary and the kids went to Sunday school. However, it was not the United Church services that Gay remembers with enthusiasm. Every Sunday for about a year when she was four years old, a babysitter took her to a Pentecostal church. She says, "I'm convinced that I probably heard the gospel there and probably invited the Lord into my heart at that time, but I don't remember. I've always had a spiritual hunger."

There wasn't much money in the Twiner family. Gay's parents didn't purchase a car until she was well into her teens; the family groceries were carried home on the bus. Now and then, Jim would bring home fish and chips wrapped in newspaper, which was considered a big treat. Television didn't arrive in their household until well into the mid-'50s. Despite having to watch the pennies, though, Gay remembers her childhood as almost conflict-free. The children were expected to keep to a curfew, but apart from that, they were rarely disciplined.

Gay's high-school years were a golden time. She played the violin in the school orchestra, was good at basketball, went to all the sleepovers. Summers were spent babysitting wealthy people's children at gorgeous cottages in Ontario's northland. Gay was pretty and had plenty of boyfriends, but, she says, they were all platonic relationships.

One spring, R. H. King's orchestra was invited to play at another Ontario high school. On the way back, it was decided the bus would make a detour so the students could tour the University of Guelph. Gay was immediately intrigued by the old-Ontario atmosphere of the place. She had always loved home economics and had wanted to continue it through school, but it wasn't available after Grade 8. When she saw Guelph, she says, "I just loved it, and when I heard there was a home-ec. program, something inside said, 'This is what you want to do.'" Gay now believes it was God who was orchestrating her future.

Gay's parents could not support her financially, but enough money was cobbled together—donations from her aunt and a doctor friend of the family, from her summer jobs and bursaries—to pay her tuition for four of what she feels were the most wonderful years of her life.

Gay's major was clothing and textiles, which involved designing and making patterns, sewing—she even sewed her own formals—and studying fabrics. There were other domestic-science classes, nutrition and food preparation, for example, as well as a good dose of liberal arts and science. Gay believes she received a superb, all-round education; she graduated tenth in a class of 60.

While she worked hard at her studies, she also enjoyed a whirlwind social life. She lived in Macdonald Hall, a lovely, old, ivy-covered building that served as the women's dormitory. Since there were ten guys for every girl at Guelph, there was hardly a female there who didn't have a date whenever she wanted. Gay loved to dance, and she had plenty of opportunity to do so. She dated lots, and by the end of her first year, she had already suffered heart-break. The fellow she was smitten with wanted to study medicine, and he told her he wasn't ready for a long-term relationship. She was devastated until, in her second year, she met Gerhard Wiebe.

Gerhard's wooing of Gay was carefully planned. Kept handy in the men's dorms were the yearbooks with pictures of all the co-eds on campus. Gerhard got a pencil and paper, "just like I was going shopping," picked six who appealed to him and then found their names and phone numbers. Gay was at the top of the list. The two met for coffee. Although they had a good long talk and she thought him good-looking, Gay didn't flip over him. As for Gerhard, Gay embarrassed him pretty badly. On one of their first dates, he took her to a Chinese restaurant. Gay mistakenly thought she could take the chopsticks home so she put them in her purse. The waitress loudly demanded she return them. "I guess Gerhard thought I was a thief, because he didn't invite me out any more."

Gay didn't think much of it, but at Christmas, she sent him and his room-mate Christmas cards. That nudged Gerhard into asking her out again and, after that, the more he saw her, the more he liked her—and vice versa. Gerhard graduated that spring, but he kept coming back on weekends to see Gay. That summer, while she was working at a lodge at French River, he sent her his pin. Within two years, they were married.

Only later did Gay learn of the struggles Gerhard had had with his family because of her. The Wiebes had immigrated from Russia at the time of the Bolshevik Revolution. Like many other Mennonites, they headed first for Kitchener, Ontario, working as farm hands until they saved enough to buy some cheap land. It was located on Pelee Island, 20 miles off Point Pelee in Lake Erie, the southernmost part of Canada. Eventually, the Mennonite community there began to fade away, and Gerhard's father realized that, if his three sons were to receive an education, he, too, would have to leave. Since Gerhard had done well at the Mennonite high school he attended, it was he who was earmarked for university. He chose Guelph because it had one of the lowest tuitions in Ontario. He took general science—physics, statistics, mathematics—with the idea that he would eventually teach high school.

The Wiebes were a religious family, very much part of the tightly knit Mennonite community. When Gay appeared on the scene, Gerhard's father was so upset, he asked his brother, a pastor, for help. "Gerhard, what are you doing?" the uncle asked. "Haven't we got enough good Mennonite girls?" "I didn't want to hurt them," Gerhard recalls, "but I couldn't satisfy them and at the same time pursue the person I loved. So I was torn twice." Gerhard's mother soon came to accept Gay and grew to love her, and eventually his father relented, too, but for Gay, it remained a hurtful slight.

Gerhard and Gay were married in June 1965 at Gay's childhood church, Cliffcrest United. It was an elegant affair. Gay sewed her own wedding gown and her mother made the dresses for the four bridesmaids. The Wiebe family showed up, looking glum and disappointed. "They came to the wedding, anyway, and I really appreciated that," says Gay. After a honeymoon motoring around northern Ontario in Gerhard's big Pontiac, the newlyweds settled down to married life.

By this time, Gerhard had found a position teaching physics at Essex District High School, and he and Gay had moved into an apartment in nearby Windsor. Gay had graduated the previous May and decided she, too, would teach. During the summer, she took courses in education, and that fall, began work as a home-economics and mathematics teacher at Essex District High.

She found it heavy going. Before her arrival, only a few home-economics classes had been offered, but now it was being built into the five-year stream as a major component, with new sewing and food laboratories. "I had ten classes with seven different preparations," Gay recalls. "I was the acting head, so I had to attend all the staff teas and the meetings. It was double the load of any of my friends teaching in Toronto." On top of that, she was paid less.

She also found her household duties onerous. Gerhard was no help at all. "I was brought up in the old-country, Mennonite tradition," he says. "I would have a shower. The dirty clothes, I would take them off and drop them wherever they fell, and that's where they stayed until my mother came along. I don't remember ever having made a bed in my life." This tradition carried over into his married life. Gay would ask him to peel some potatoes and, from behind his newspaper, he'd reply that he was sorry, but he was a little tired. He now understands how difficult it was for Gay. "I almost destroyed that lady—I almost killed her."

Less than two years after her marriage, Gay suffered a tragedy that did almost destroy her. Within six months, the three women who were closest to her—her grandmother, her mother-in-law and her mother—were dead, all from breast cancer. Gerhard's mother died in October 1967, Gay's grandmother, who had had the disease 25 years before, passed away two weeks later, and the following April, her beloved mother succumbed. She was only 45 years old. Gay says that even after all these years, she still misses her.

All the related stress simply became too much. Gay suffered a severe emotional breakdown and slid into a deep depression. She was never hospitalized, but it was a close call. Says Gerhard, "She just broke, she snapped. Anyone would have, under those conditions. I thought I had lost her there for a while." She had to give up teaching mid-way through her term, something she has always regretted.

She probably would have quit anyway, since by that time, she was pregnant with her first child. Natasha was born on November 15, 1968. Gay still wasn't well. "I really didn't accept being a mother as a job. I detested every diaper I changed. I remember my husband saying to me, 'If you were getting paid for this job, do you think you'd deserve your salary?' And I had to say no." Gay's second child, Marina, arrived 17 months later. By that time, Gay had developed a severe case of ulcerative colitis, inflammation of the colon that caused bleeding, diarrhea and abdominal pains. She lost 35 pounds in six weeks, and in February 1971, she was hospitalized for three weeks. It's a disease often related to stress, and Gay believes her resentment towards her husband and his judgemental relatives welled up in her. And of course, she was also still grieving for all those women who had died of breast cancer.

One day while she was feeling at her worst, she sat at her dining-room table thinking that maybe she really was dying. Suddenly, as she puts it, "The Lord reminded me that He was there." During her university years, she had attended a meeting at First Baptist Church in Guelph. The preacher was a professor at the university who was born again in Christ. "If you know you are a Christian, I want you to come and talk to me," he had said. Gay remembers, "I was totally convinced in my heart that I was called." While she didn't do much about it at the time, she remembered the encounter with the Almighty and thought, "There is some hope for me."

While she was in hospital with colitis, a friend, a former Mennonite, wrote describing her own conversion experience and inviting Gay to join a Bible study group in her home. "I loved it. It gave me direction and meaning in my life. Several of my friends found the Lord as well." Says her daughter Natasha, "Mom needed support and strength, and she found it in the Church."

The doctors had told Gay her colitis was a chronic disease and would be with her for life. She suffered for five and a half years, hardly able to eat more than a handful of food at any one time. She weighed less than 120 pounds, and she is a tall person. "I thought, 'If God could heal other people, why wouldn't He heal me?' I just started to ask the Lord, 'Is there anything in my life that's preventing me from receiving a healing, because I believe You can heal me?' And He did." She proudly points to the fact that she hasn't taken medication for colitis since April 1976, and there's been no recurrence of the disease.

It would take Gerhard two years before he made the same leap. He tended to mock Gay's religious beliefs and was off on an atheistic quest of his own, reading philosophers like Nietzsche, Hegel and Aristotle. Finally, one evening in February 1973, sitting in the corner of his living room, he suddenly "became part of the family of God." "I said, 'Jesus, I give you authority to come into my life and do with me what you want, to make me the father you want me to be, the husband you want me to be, the teacher and friend you want me to be.'" Gay was relieved. "The marriage would not have lasted if we weren't on the same spiritual wavelength," she says.

Gay and Gerhard started to attend the Essex Gospel Tabernacle, a Pentecostal church, and it quickly became the centre of their world. Gerhard became an elder, and because he was articulate and knowledgeable about the Scriptures, he had great influence. Gay headed the Sunday school, was in charge of the women's coffee hour, organized banquets and pot-luck suppers. She taught Christian Education after hours in the public-school system. "My husband and I had a ministry together," she says, "where we prayed with people who had been abused and were in healing." Eventually, she worked as a volunteer at Windsor's interdenominational Pregnancy Crisis Centre, a pro-life agency; her job was to mend, wash and organize donated clothing for young mothers and their babies. With her own two daughters growing, it was a satisfying and fulfilling time for her. But in April 1980, Gay discovered a fair-sized lump in her breast.

Given her genetic history—her grandmother and mother died of breast cancer, and sister has had the disease—it shouldn't have been a surprise, but it was. Says Gay, "I figured, well, I'm a Christian now. I'm in a different family." After a visit to the doctor, Gay discovered the growth was malignant, but she refused treatment. "At that point, the Lord had touched me physically a few times and answered my prayers, so we [she and Gerhard] felt that this was a test of our faith. So I prayed, studied the Scripture and helped myself by following the Word."

During the summer, the growth did decrease in size by about 15 percent, but by September, it was larger. "I remember standing in the front of the church one Sunday night and saying, 'Lord, I believe you want to heal me and get glory for it, but if you want to do it another way, by surgery and not supernaturally, then I surrender.'" If it were indeed cancerous—and she had great hopes it wouldn't be—she decided she would face the surgeon's scalpel.

By that time, though, the cancer had spread to the glands under her arms and to her lymph nodes, all of which were cut away, along with one breast. She had a violent reaction to chemotherapy—her colitis flared up—but she underwent some radiation treatment. The incident did not diminish her religious belief; looking back, she feels she was presumptuous and full of pride in challenging God to cure her. Fortunately, she suffered little physical pain with the surgery. She says she was so calm and peaceful in her illness, one of the doctors who treated her "began walking with the Lord."

After Gay's illness, she and Gerhard became ever more dedicated to their faith. In 1984, they joined the Windsor Christian Fellowship, one of the independent, charismatic churches that have become so popular in North America since the 1960s. These believers look to early Christianity for inspiration, before organized conventional churches laid down layers of doctrine. The New Testament scriptures are their one authority and define every aspect of their life. Dreams, visions and talking in tongues are a means of communicating with God. As one scholar puts it, "Ecstatic joy and profound peace are also experiences that they attribute to a divine presence. In exceptional cases, supernatural healing occurs, demons are expelled, and prophecies are uttered. This is the 'stuff' of worship and prayer, not rational discourse."[663]

This philosophy was reflected in how they raised their two daughters. The Wiebes were determined their brand of Christianity would determine the parameters of their children's lives. When they were toddlers, Gerhard had the television removed. Not only was there a lot of junk being shown but he felt Gay was using it as a babysitter. Once, Gerhard found what he considered satanic references in a school reader. He put so much pressure on the teacher that she promised not to use those particular stories and poems in her classes. Gay felt free to read her daughters' private diaries or letters.

Unlike Gay's own upbringing, as her girls grew older, strict curfews were imposed, even into their twenties. They were not allowed to wear makeup and tight pants. Jeans were prohibited for a while because Gerhard considered them a sign of rebellion. School dances were strictly out of bounds; as a teacher, Gerhard knew drinking and drugs were part of the scene. The girls were not allowed to go out with anyone from high school, though chaperoned dates with members of the Church were permitted now and then. "We ran a tight ship here," says Gerhard. "At times, I think now, too tight."

The girls reacted in different ways. Natasha rebelled against the strict regime in her first year of high school, but she quickly realized she couldn't win the battle with her father. "I channelled a lot of my rebellion into becoming the best Christian I could," says Natasha. "I became extremely zealous. I scheduled prayer meetings before school. I was incredibly harsh, too—very blackmailing." She was also a brilliant student, achieving top marks in every subject.

Marina did not break with authority outright; it was more a quiet insurrection. She'd sneak off to the odd dance or, at a girl's sleepover, take the family pickup and go tootling around town till all hours of the morning. "I was known for shooting off my mouth, not being rude, but questioning things, and you weren't supposed to do that. I was basically a rebel in the church, even though in the secular world, I was considered a nun." Marina felt outside both circles: at high school, she was called "a square;" in church circles, a non-conformist. "I came from a perfectionist family and I wasn't up to their standards in school or church." From age 15 to 20, she suffered from anorexia. When her parents finally realized what was wrong, they were deeply shocked.

There was another, happier side to such a rigorous religious life. The church offered young people a rich and secure social setting. "Everything was centred on the church," says Natasha, "all our friends, our social activities, music, everything." There was Christian roller-skating on Tuesday night, organ practice on Thursday evening, the youth group on the weekend. "It really was a wholesome place where a teenage girl could have fun and not feel in any danger," admits Marina. Then suddenly, that secure world was shattered.

In a typical Christian Fellowship church, the pastor is not an ordained minister but someone chosen from the congregation. Natasha says that at Windsor Christian Fellowship, there was a young pastor who had a penchant for getting embroiled in arguments: are Cabbage Patch dolls a good thing, should Christmas trees be permitted, or blue jeans? "He was always jumping from controversy to controversy. Even at my age I thought it was silly and needless," says Marina.

One day, the pastor announced that he and his wife were divorcing. For Gerhard and Gay, the Bible is clear. Mark 10:11–12 reads: "whosoever shall put away his wife, and marry another, committeth adultery against her. And if a woman should put away her husband, and be married to another, she committeth adultery." Others, though, had different interpretations, based on different Scripture. The congregation was suddenly wracked with dissension and debate. After much painful deliberation, the Wiebes finally decided they had to leave the church. It was as hurtful as if they had turned their back on their families. "Everything came crashing down," says Gay. "It shook us all up." Gay's and Gerhard's faith remained as solid as ever, and eventually they returned to the same Pentecostal church where they had begun their spiritual journey 25 years before, but it was a devastating time for the entire family.

They have suffered other spiritual blows. Both their daughters have abandoned their faith. For Natasha, it happened at the University of Windsor, where she studied education. She married a young man from a similar religious background to hers, but he, too, was in the process of rejecting his religious beliefs. "My husband is inclined to believe there is no God, but I'm inclined to think that he/she/it does exist. I'm looking for a new concept in God." After attending college, Marina also rejected her parents' faith. She is married to a man who has never been part of a fundamentalist religion.

What bothers Natasha and Marina the most is the church's attitude towards women. As the Bible stipulates, the man is the head of the household, the woman secondary. "My dad would use language [when talking to Gay] like, 'You obey me, you are being a rebellious wife,'" says Natasha. "I spent the first year of my marriage being furiously angry with that attitude, with my father, because I saw that my life and my mother's could have been so much fuller. Now I realize that's probably too simple."

Despite their differences, the Wiebe family has not splintered apart. Gay has seen to that. Her daughters mean too much to her. "Natasha said to me once, 'I hope you're not disappointed in me.' I said, 'I love both of you very much. I'm very proud of your accomplishments. You both have responsible jobs. You are great kids. I'm disappointed you're not going to church right now, but I know in my heart you'll return.'"

In 1996, Gay was told the cancer had recurred. Doctors surgically removed eight lymph nodes on the other side of her body, one of which was malignant. This time, she underwent a full treatment of chemotherapy. So far, everything is fine and she is back to feeling normal, although she must rest for part of each day. "The Lord is still gracious to me," she says. For Gay, it's all a matter of faith.

Winnie

In the Grade 11 high-school yearbook, there's a photograph of a gang of us at a football game, happily cheering for the home team. Winnie Bron is sitting beside me, and Gay Twiner is not far away. By conventional wisdom, their family lives were exemplary, with a devoted, stay-at-home mom and a hard-working, responsible dad, exactly what the 1950s prescribed, while mine, financially insecure and generally chaotic, was sternly frowned on. Yet both Winnie and Gay suffered emotional breakdowns when they faced the harshness of the real world, while I stepped into adulthood with hardly a nervous twitch.

Winnie Bron's childhood was even more sheltered than Gay Twiner's. Her parents were determined their daughter would never suffer the anxiety and deprivation they had known in their native Holland in the aftermath of World War II. They had emigrated to Canada rather late in life precisely so they could create an idyllic world for their only child.

Winnie's mother Sieta Alssema had already bucked the old European ways. She was born near the northern industrial city of Groningen. At 21, she married a mechanic who turned out to be abusive towards her. After 13 years of marriage, Sieta left her husband, taking Tineke, the couple's only child, with her. Sieta's husband was an elder in the church, and the townspeople, deeply conservative in their religious views, were horrified.

Winnie says her mother had always broke the rules—riding her own motorbike around town, for example, when it was deemed an unladylike thing to do. Before she left her first husband, she had already met her second, another mechanic who worked for her husband's dealership. Siemon Bron was six-foot-five and handsome, with a head of thick, wavy hair, a loving man with a great sense of humour. He was also nine years younger than Sieta, a fact that shocked the community as much as her desertion of her husband. She went ahead and got a divorce anyway, and she and Siemon were married in 1940. Winnie was born two years later.

After the war, Siemon's best friend wrote saying how wonderful Canada was and how glad he was that he had emigrated. By this time, Sieta's first child, Tineke, was married, and the Brons decided to follow Siemon's friend, never mind that Sieta was almost 50 and that, after all the expenses were paid, the family would have exactly $250 to start life in the new land.

When they arrived in Toronto in the spring of 1952, Winnie was ten years old, with long, blonde braids reaching almost to her behind—the proverbial little Dutch girl. She knew not a word of English, so the first months of school were traumatic. "I was just plunked in the deep end," she says. Her lack of English meant she was initially put back several grades, but she advanced as her language improved. By the end of her first year, she was at her age-group level, had plenty of friends and felt very Canadian.

Canada in the 1950s was desperate for mechanics with the kind of experience Siemon Bron had, and a job at British Motors was waiting for him when he arrived. He worked from seven in the morning to seven at night, came home, had his supper and then, in his own garage, worked on other people's cars. Sieta worked in a factory. In less than a year, they had saved enough money for a down payment on a house.

By the time Winnie reached high school, the family was pretty well set financially. Sieta had quit her job to throw herself into housework. "I remember coming home from school at lunch time on Fridays," recalls Winnie, "and she'd have every stick of furniture upside down, waxed and polished. The whole house just shone." Everything was starched. The sheets crackled when you got between them, and Winnie's hair ribbons were so stiff, the bows would stand at attention all day long.

For both Sieta and Siemon, their daughter's well-being was the most important thing in their lives. They never quarrelled, never raised their voices when she was in earshot. Years later, a psychiatrist would deride them for sheltering Winnie too much while she was growing up. Problems or conflicts of any kind were always resolved for her. "I never had to deal with anything," says Winnie. "They told me, 'Just do your work and get good marks and everything will be fine.' And that's what I did."

Her father doted on Winnie and spoiled her, but he was old-fashioned in his attitudes towards the young men in her life. He was always there, waiting in his car, at the dance hall or ice-skating rink, ready to take her home after her date. "I was aware that my parents had all their eggs in one basket, and it was a heavy responsibility. I didn't want to disappoint them, so I just met their expectations."

They didn't suffocate her, though; she had plenty of freedom to enjoy high school. She threw herself into all the activities—tumbling was a favourite sport—grades came easily to her and she had plenty of nice clothes. Her thick, blonde hair, just like her father's, could readily be teased into the ridiculous beehives and Gibson-girl hair-dos that were so popular. Winnie went to every formal dance from Grade 9 onwards. She would soak her crinolines in a solution of water and sugar and plunk them in a corner of her bedroom until they had dried into replicas of armored vehicles. Summers were spent working at the pleasant clerical job her father found for her at British Motors. Most important of all, she found her future husband. Her date at a dance took her coat "and when he came back, he had this gorgeous man in tow. It was love at first sight." To this day, she remembers the exact date of her encounter with Walter Robbins: October 31, 1958. She was 16 years old.

Winnie immediately went on a campaign to snare Walt. "I finagled and connived. I made my girlfriend throw a party and invite him." Two weeks later, the friend phoned. "He's just called asking for your number," she blathered. Winnie shrieked and slammed the receiver down. Seconds later, it rang again. It was Walt, asking Winnie for "the date of her life."

Walt's family, at least the male side, was well educated. Although his grandfather's origins were working class, he had managed to obtain a university degree in botany and taught school. Walt's father was an electrical engineer who was the head of systems planning at Ontario Hydro. Walt, however, hated school. He had a phobia about exams; his mind went blank as soon as he picked up his pen. He stuck with it, though. It took him an extra year, but he got his Grade 13 diploma.

Winnie, on the other hand, always got good grades, and her parents talked about university. Among their large circle of Dutch émigré friends was Dr. Mart Madlener, a dentist and university professor of some renown. Whenever Winnie had her teeth fixed, he would show her the materials and methods he used, which fascinated her. Dr. Madlener urged Winnie to think of dentistry as a career.

She applied "for the fun of it." Since the competition to get into the University of Toronto's School of Dentistry was so fierce, she didn't think she stood a chance, but her Grade 13 exam marks were good, and a letter of acceptance arrived in the mail. "I freaked out, I didn't know what to do." Her parents encouraged her, promising to pay her tuition.

Before entering the professional school, students were required to take a two-year pre-dental course. Winnie found it hard going. There were only six women in a class of 106, which made her feel uncomfortable. The classes were huge, many of the students brilliant and the subjects such as anthropology, physics and zoology were demanding. In the background, Walt Robbins was always urging Winnie to quit. "I was looking for a family and family life ... so I basically gave her a choice. 'Look, honey, you want a career, that's fine, but not with me. I'm looking for a full-time wife.'"

After three months in pre-dentistry, Winnie switched to the much less onerous dental-hygiene course. Her parents were disappointed, but Walt was overjoyed. She found the two-year course a snap compared to pre-dentistry, and spent most of her time in the school's huge clinic, cleaning people's teeth. Winnie found she had a light touch. "I probably would have made a good dentist, after all," she says.

After graduation, she had no trouble finding a well-paying job. Dr. William Denby Patrick Cavanagh, with offices at Yonge and Bloor streets, was one of Toronto's most prominent dentists. He looked after the teeth of the rich and famous, and he taught at the university. He was an older man, sophisticated and charming, and Winnie was utterly in awe of him, although her training had been so good, she felt confident as his assistant and he thought well of her. The problem was the office manager.

A middle-aged woman, she had worked for Dr. Cavanagh for many years and virtually ran the place. She was furious that the wages of the new young assistant were higher than hers. Recalls Winnie, "She was so jealous of the fact that somebody wet behind the ears, fresh out of school was making more than she. She really made my life hell." Three months after she began her job, Winnie suffered a severe nervous breakdown. "My life was full of whispers and shadows. I even believed that Walt had married someone else." She finally became catatonic, totally unable to speak or move. Her father was horrified. "I remember him sitting at the kitchen table, weeping. I had never seen my dad shed a tear before and he was weeping like a child."

Winnie was finally admitted to the Whitby Psychiatric Hospital where she underwent 12 electric-shock treatments. She was tranquilized for all but one. "For some reason the sedation didn't work and I was all there when they did it to me. It was awful. Every fibre of my nervous system was just screaming." Despite this, Winnie feels it was the best treatment for her, certainly better than medication. "It completely obliterates your recent memory. Things came back a little at a time, and I could work them through." After a childhood full of bliss, Winnie had to learn how to resolve conflict.

In three months, she was ready to be discharged from the hospital. She even returned to her job in the same office. The psychiatrist had a long talk with Dr. Cavanagh and he saw to it there was no more bullying from the office manager. In fact, astonishingly, she and Winnie eventually became friends. Winnie continued to see a psychiatrist, but after a few months, it became apparent she no longer needed his help. She has not suffered a relapse since.

Walt helped Winnie through her illness. "Most guys would have said, 'Who needs this? She's in the loony bin. Goodbye.' But he stuck with me." Walt and Winnie were married on July 23, 1965, at Birchcliffe United Church in a candlelight service. "It was beautiful, a dream come true," says Winnie. She wore a full-length, white sheath dress, with a coat trimmed in satin and embroidery over top. Her bridesmaids' dresses were of pastel, printed chiffon. The reception was held at Fantasy Farm, followed by a wonderful honeymoon. Then it was back to the workaday world.

Walt had studied general arts at Carleton University, hoping eventually to become a teacher, but at the end of his first year, he managed to pass only three of his five courses. He decided to stop floundering. He realized he'd be better at learning on the job than in a classroom and he agreed to work without pay for a small company that manufactured precast cement. He put their bookkeeping in order and then began teaching himself how to price construction jobs. He subsequently found work as an estimator and quickly moved into a responsible position in sales.

After their marriage, Walt and Winnie moved into an old cottage on acreage in the Sheppard Avenue and Markham Road area in Scarborough that had been in Walt's family for years. The little house meant a great deal to him. It was located on the same land on which his botanist grandfather had grown his unusual species of roses, Japanese cherry trees and other plants. "It was a tradition that every evening, my grandfather would read his Bible. He was very quiet, never said anything, he'd just sit and read." It's not surprising that it was in this house that Walt, soon after he and Winnie moved in, underwent the most dramatic spiritual encounter of his life.

He woke up one night to discover a beam of light shining down on him. He thought he had left a hole when he was shingling the roof, until he realized this would have been impossible; there were about eight inches of materials from the plaster to the roof board. He was being blinded by the light, so he put his hands over his eyes and sat on the side of his bed, scared to death. "I looked up and there, standing in the air, was a pair of feet [attached] to a being. It was the most beautiful being you could ever imagine, the most majestic male form I have ever seen. He was metallic, a gunmetal blue. There was gold on his feet and a gold cloak over his shoulders.... There was a radiance coming from him. Not tinsel-like, cheap, but a rich lustre. The beauty was so much that I felt like I was filled with maggots. I was rotten in front of this glory.... Then I heard a voice speak in my mind: 'Are you ready yet? Follow me.' I thought, 'I'm in big trouble. I'm being called to judgement,' so I said, 'No I'm not ready yet.' The light collapsed and there was blackness."

At first, Walt thought he had been visited by an angel, but after studying descriptions in the Scriptures, he realized his caller had been the Lord himself. He tried to tell his sister about what he had seen, but she just gave him weird looks and he realized that was how everybody would react. There was no use talking about it. Winnie believed him, though, and for years it was a marvellous secret between them.

The Robbinses' early marriage was typical for an upwardly mobile young couple. There were vacations in Acapulco and ski trips to Quebec and a lot of dinner parties. In 1969, their daughter Jennifer was born, and two years later, a son Bill arrived. "We had two beautiful children, a lovely place in the country, we both had fulfilling careers, lots of high-powered friends," says Winnie. "Life was moving along nicely. And it was so empty."

What was missing for Winnie was religious belief. As a child, she and her mother had attended Warden Woods Mennonite Church. Winnie taught Sunday school, became a counsellor in a Mennonite camp and volunteered in the church library. When she had her nervous breakdown, however, she completely rejected her faith. "The minister came to visit me in hospital," she recalls. "I loved this man, he was so good to me, and I literally rolled over and turned my back on him. I wouldn't even speak to him."

It was Winnie's cleaning lady who led her in the right direction. "She was a single mom, she had been into witchcraft, she'd been abused by men, she'd tried to commit suicide—I mean the whole nine yards. Yet she was radiant, she just shone. I thought, 'Man, you have something I don't have.'" The woman began leaving little notes: "We need some Ajax, and by the way, why don't you read John 16:13?" Finally, she asked Winnie to accompany her to a service at the Stouffville Christian Fellowship.

Winnie remembers this date clearly, too: the Sunday of Thanksgiving weekend, 1977. Featured was a visiting preacher from England, where the roots of this particular Fellowship are found. Winnie had never heard anything like Mr. North, all white hair and twinkling, and she could hardly wait to return the next night. "He said, 'If any one feels in their heart that God is speaking to them, then I invite you to come.' Well, I just about climbed over top of people in order to get to the front. I knew the Lord was speaking to me because he was addressing an issue in my life: the great void. The earth moved that night. God came in such a tangible way. It was powerful. It completely transformed my life."

When Winnie returned home, she was walking on air. Walt thought, "What have these guys done to her head?" but he agreed to accompany her the next evening. He was dubious at first, but he loved the old gospel hymns and the study of Scriptures, so he continued to attend Fellowship meetings. One night, he was driving a member of the congregation, a physically handicapped young woman, to her home in Stouffville when he began hearing strange words going on in his head, a mumble-jumble of sound. He was too embarrassed to say anything to his passenger. He helped her off with her boots and was returning home along the town's main street when he heard the strange sounds again. "It came back again, and it was really powerful. Finally I thought, 'Okay Lord, I will speak.' It was just like something inside me burst open and I split. These words came out of me like a machine gun. It just freaked me out."

He burst in on Winnie at home, shouting that he could talk in tongues. She said, "Oh yeah, let's hear you." He did, and she was amazed. "I was so jealous. His in-filling of the Holy Ghost was so much more dramatic than mine." From that time on, Walt and Winnie's life centred around the Christian Fellowship Church, much as Gerhard and Gay Weibe's had.

Walt says he doesn't know what would have happened if he hadn't embraced the Lord at that particular moment. He was going through one of the most traumatic periods of his life. Over the years, he had worked for several large construction companies and had got to know the precast-cement business well. When, in the mid-'70s, several big outfits went under, including the one he was working for, cement-making machinery became available, valued at ten cents on the dollar. Walt borrowed $10,000 from his father, took a collateral mortgage on his house and went into business for himself.

The first year went well, but then Walt made a fatal mistake; he tendered $120,000 on a job that should have been $200,000. It wasn't a huge amount of money, but he was under-financed to begin with, and the company couldn't withstand the loss. Walt's world came smashing down.

Fortunately for him, his religious faith remained solid. One night while he was sleeping, he heard a heavenly voice say to him, "If you and your wife will humble yourself and pray, I will honour your business situation." In just a few days, the proprietor of another construction company, a young man whom Walt had never much liked before because he considered him a know-it-all, approached Walt. He told him he wanted to experiment with Fiberglas concrete. Walt swallowed his pride and started to listen. "He said he needed a plant, he needed a crew, he needed machinery, he needed some-one to run it. I said, 'I have all those things.'" Bankruptcy was averted and Walt ended up with a job.

In 1990, the pastor of Stouffville Christian Fellowship left for Vancouver and the congregation asked Walt to take his place. "It was a matter of: do I try and maintain my job and take on the ministry, without any training or experience and not being particularly gifted, afraid to talk in front of people." He decided that, to be fair to the congregation, he would become a full-time pastor, even if it meant a big cut in the family's income.

He, Winnie and the two kids moved into the split-level house designated as the pastor's home right next to the church. Winnie, in her own way, became as involved in the ministry as Walt. At any time of the day, her house could be full of guests, including itinerant preachers from all over the world. A lot of very troubled people showed up, looking for someone in whom they could confide. Winnie admits this was hard on her. "I find the seedy side of life really hard to listen to, I guess because it's so far from my frame of refer-ence." Still, she found the job as the pastor wife's gratifying. "It's like giving birth—when you finally see somebody come through to the Lord, you see them baptized and you know that your prayers and your tears and your words have had an effect. You know that the travail of your soul has brought forth a new life in God, and that's wonderful."

In 1994, a fierce controversy split the Stouffville Christian Fellowship, rendering the Robbins family bereft. Walt recounts what happened. "There was one particular guy [in the congregation], John, who was very talented, intelligent. He was very artistic, and I'm straight-line, practical. My preach-ing was too flat, too dull, too boring for him. We just knocked heads."

A vicious whispering campaign started, targeting Winnie and Walt. "A lot of terrible things were said about us," says Winnie, "and we couldn't defend ourselves. We believed you don't try to vindicate yourself. You let God do that for you." Finally, Walt had had enough of malicious gossip. He asked the man, whom he considered the trouble-maker, to leave. Two-thirds of the congregation went with him.

It was an emotionally draining time, horribly so, for the Robbins family. "I was crying all the time," says Winnie. Large patches of her hair fell out. Worst of all, their son Bill, 13 at the time, developed ulcerative colitis. Recalls Winnie, "I finally had to bring him to the hospital in a wheelchair. He couldn't walk, he was in such pain.... That was the ultimate low in a year of grief and difficulty. And, boy, Walt and I had to really hang on to God and each other."

With only a dozen of the faithful remaining, Walt could no longer afford to remain as a full-time preacher. He went back to the same company he had left five years earlier. Bill is still the part-time pastor at Stouffville Christian Fellowship and the church remains important to both him and Winnie.

Winnie's son Bill has remained fervent about his faith. Her daughter has not. Both children attended a fundamentalist Christian school until they reached high school. For Jennifer, the change in environment was too much of a shock. There were years of drugs and drinking and hanging out with, as her mother calls them, "the grubbies." Winnie says, "My daughter and I aren't as close as I wish we were.... Her way of living and her choices have been so contrary to the way I was raised and my ideals in the Christian faith. I found that very difficult to cope with." However, they are not estranged. When Jennifer's marriage split up only a year after the wedding, she moved back in to her parents' home. "Deep down, she knows all the right things and the right decisions and it's going to surface as she gets older." Once she's open to the Lord, Winnie feels, He will surely show her the way. She will re-establish her place as one of the chosen.

The Chosen

Come and adore
Dionysus with dance and song and a thunder of drums!

Euripides, *The Bacchae*, 405 BC

The souls of men and of women are the same and do not differ. The whole difference
between man and woman is in their bodies which Satan made.

Testimony of a shepherd during the Lauragais Inquisition, 1245

God hath put no such difference between the Male and Female as man would make.

Quaker, Margaret Fell, 1666

One year at school, we studied George Bernard Shaw's *Saint Joan*. The grumpy English teacher liked neither the play nor the Maid of Orléans. It was obvious she was crazy, he said, and it was just as well that in 1431, she was burned at the stake as a heretic. A few years later, I saw a summer-stock production that presented such a decidedly feminist slant on the play, one could imagine G. B. S. smiling in his grave. In this production. a rather large-sized Joan, strolling about in a cage of metal armour, nicely put to flight the "goddamn" English. The plump, flesh-faced actress was a perfect Saint Joan: naïve, fervent, compelling and brave. By the end of the night, I would have jumped on my horse and followed her to the ends of the earth. It was my first insight into a remarkable phenomenon: throughout history, certain women have used their charisma, their charm, and their special relationship to God to thwart the restrictions of the conventional patriarchal Church. Others have only been too glad to follow.

I

The whirling dervish of maenads circles around an ornamental mask depicting that great party-boy, Dionysus. Each reveller, her hair dishevelled, her diaphanous robes billowing, is caught up in her own energetic rapture. Several are dancing, a few play musical instruments, all are enjoying themselves immensely. The scene, painted on the base of a cup, c. 490 BC, is the most dramatic depiction extant of maenads enthusiastically worshipping their god.

You might say ancient Greek religion consisted of a number of cults, a system of religious worship and ritual focusing on a single deity, but some gods provoked more obsessive, frantic devotion than others. Stern Zeus seems pretty dull compared to Dionysus. Interestingly, his cult was at its most intense in the early fifth century BC, at a time when women were most suppressed. Why did the Dionysian mysteries appeal so much to women? Historian Ross Shepard Kraemer puts forth this theory: "Greek women, normally devalued by men, restricted to their homes, and limited in the scope of their social interactions, found in the ecstatic worship of Dionysus temporary experiences of community and the expression of critical social and psychological tensions that were sufficient compensation for the inadequacies of their normal lives."[664]

As the Christian era approached, a vast shifting of people, carrying with them foreign and exotic cultures, occurred in the Greco-Roman world. The religions that came with these immigrants attracted a large following among the Greeks and Romans, especially those who were disenfranchised by the state cults: wealthy slaves, freed persons, foreigners and, of course, women. No religious worship spread so quickly, or attracted such a huge number of followers of all ages and both sexes, as the cult of Isis. Indeed, many scholars believe it was the leading contender with Christianity in the struggle for the Roman heart and soul.

Isis was a national deity of ancient Egypt dating back to at least 2500 BC. By the time her cult reached the shores of Italy in the second century BC, her mythological origins were complex and fantastical. Isis was the twin sister of the Egyptian king Osiris; the two apparently fell in love in their mother's womb. Their marriage set the pattern for the brother–sister unions that were so common among ancient Egyptian royalty. Another brother in this family named Set (or Typhon), the god of Darkness, was jealous of Osiris and craved his power. Set tricked his brother into climbing into an ornamental box, which he quickly locked and threw into the Nile. Heartbroken, Isis went searching for the coffin, found it and made love to her dead husband, managing through her own willpower to become pregnant. Shortly after, Set again found the corpse, cut it up into 14 pieces and dumped them all once again into the river. Sailing through the marshes in her papyrus boat, Isis managed to find the various bits of her beloved brother/husband—all except the penis, which had been eaten by a fish—and painstakingly reassembled him. Ultimately, Osiris returned from the underworld.

That a divinity had suffered so much was probably what appealed to Isis's female followers. They could identify with a wife who had lost her husband far more than with the stern, all-perfect state divinities. As well, the fact that Osiris had suffered death and was born again served as hope for their own renewal after their time on earth was finished.[665] As historian Sarah Pomeroy writes, the worship of Isis suited the individualism that was evolving in the Hellenistic and Roman worlds. "Individuals were responsible for their own acts: they could be initiated, rewarded, forgiven, and granted eternal salvation. In contrast, traditional Roman religion was based on a communal responsibility, in which the unchastity of a Vestal jeopardized the entire population."[666] In mourning the death of Osiris every October 28, the ordinary woman was mourning the grief she herself had experienced in a harsh, patriarchal world.

As the cult grew, Isis took on the colouring of many other goddesses including Fortuna, Athena, Aphrodite, Hestia, Hera and Demeter. What was even more amazing was that Isis held powers usually associated with male gods. Not only could she heal the sick but she also had dominion over lightning, winds and storms. As Pomeroy notes, "She is the creator, for she divided earth from heaven, assigned languages to nations, and invented alphabets and astronomy. Aretalogies [miracle tales praising gods or prophets for their extraordinary lives and deeds] surviving from antiquity give long lists of the attributes of the goddess; her epithets are innumerable, her powers limitless."[667]

Isis was also affectionate and merciful, the great, good mother, loving all her children. In the long hymn to Isis dating from the second century AD, found in Oxyrhynchus, Egypt, is this all-important phrase: "she made the power of women equal to that of men." One can only imagine what might have happened if the cult of Isis had prevailed over the male-dominated, hierarchical religions of Judaism and Christianity.

II

If there is a picture that brings into sharp relief the high and late Middle Ages, it is of black-robed religious, each wearing rope sandals and a girdle, shuffling along the dusty roads of Europe, begging and preaching sometimes the most outlandish of doctrines—the equality of the sexes, for example. Strange and heretical religious sects rolled across Europe, attracting disciples from all walks of life. Women made up the majority of these adherents, partly because they were attracted to the asceticism, by the vows of poverty, humility and chastity that these roving preachers talked about, and partly because they were irked with their second-class status in the Catholic Church.

The Guglielmites, for example, believed women were the only hope for the salvation of mankind; only by recognizing the female, as well as the male, in the Godhead could the world be redeemed. Their devotion revolved around Guglielma of Milan (1210–c. 1281), a mysterious figure who may have been the daughter of the King of Bohemia. She supposedly fled her noble family, her little son in tow, to live a life of a Cistercian nun in Milan. Like Hildegard of Bingen and so many other important women religious of the time, Guglielma was a visionary, a prophet and a teacher.[668]

Her devotees believed she was the Holy Spirit, the third person of the Trinity, the female equivalent to Christ. Stigmata on her body proved to them that she was of the same flesh as Jesus, capable of miracles just as he was. In this new religion, the Roman papacy was to be abolished and a church established with female popes and cardinals. Guglielma named the aristocrat Mayfreda de Pirovana as her representative on earth, as Jesus has ordained St. Peter. On her death, her followers were sure, her body would ascend to heaven, if not right away, some time in the future.

When she did die in about 1281, her disciples, both male and female, washed her body with a mixture of wine and water, dressed it in Cistercian garb and reburied her. The liquid used to wash Guglielma's corpse came to be regarded as a miracle cure, especially by the Cistercian monks. Guglielma was eventually buried in consecrated grounds near the monastery of St. Maria di Chiaravalle where she had once been an apostate. An altar was erected there and a fresco painted in her honour. Each year, a festival marking the anniversary of her death was held at the monastery, the abbot of Chiaravalle providing the food and the monks giving thanks for the miracle cures provided by her bath water.[669] Her cult grew quickly, much to the annoyance of the Church establishment.

In 1300, condemned by the Inquisition, three of her disciples, Mayfreda and two monks, were put to death, and Guglielma's remains were exhumed and burned. Her cult petered out, but its ideas rippled under the surface for centuries to come.

The Guglielmites never reached more than a few hundred dedicated souls. A cult that was far more successful, drew far more adherents and was even more ferociously suppressed was the Cathars. Noble women, in particular, were attracted to the sect, which flourished in the 11th century in Langue-doc in the south of France, and by the next century, had spread to Italy, Germany and the Netherlands.

The Cathars' philosophy was rooted in gnosticism, a contrary, ascetic cult that flourished during the early Christian period. Like the Gnostics, the Cathars believed in two supreme forces: an Evil God, symbol of the material, the flesh, and a Good God, who represented the soul. Sexuality and procreation were the Devil's doing, marriage a state for the weak-of-will only. St. Luke 20:34–35 was a much-quoted text: "And Jesus said to them, 'The sons of this age marry and are given in marriage/but those who are considered worthy to attain to that age and the resurrection from the dead, neither marry, nor are given in marriage.'"

The Cathars believed Jesus was pure spirit. Mary had been merely an incubator, contributing no material substance to his being. The Cathars took as gospel the texts of the Bogomils, a tenth-century religious sect that quoted Christ as saying: "Then I descended and entered her by way of her ear and exited by way of her ear."[670] The worship of Mary was downplayed; she was not considered a mediator with God and she played almost no role in Cathar rituals. As historian Shulamith Shahar writes, "Thus there was no feminine element in the celestial world of the Cathars, and woman played no part in the salvation of mankind."[671] The female remained a corrupter and temptress, her soul inferior to the male's.

There was another face of Cathar religious belief, however, which had a markedly androgynous cast to it. Since it was the Devil who had created matter and thus the two sexes, the Holy Father could undo gender difference at the time of salvation. Indeed, souls entering heaven were neither male or female but pure spirit. The hierarchy based on sex would disappear.

As Roman matrons had done during the early Christian period, upper-class women donated substantial amounts of money to the sect, setting up homes for poor widows or girls without dowries that provided workshops, schools and dispensaries. The Cathars' asceticism—they were vegetarian, completely chaste, owned no property and lived humble and simple lives—appealed to women of all classes. Like men, they could become a *perfecti*, a vehicle of the Holy Spirit; only *perfecti* could communicate with God. Like men, they could preach, bless and administer the *consolamentum* (a final act of confession and baptism). And like men, they were the closest to the pure spirit that, upon death, would be embraced by God. (The Cathars believed in reincarnation; Cathari, it was thought, would live many lives, both as males and females, before they became *perfecti*.)

Some Cathars believed the Roman Catholic Church, with its corrupt, hypocritical clergy and its immense wealth, was the agent of Satan and should be renounced. At the beginning of the 13th century, Pope Innocent III, angered by their belief, sent out a call to arms that was promptly answered by powerful lords of northern France, eager to plunder and loot to their own advantage. The Albigensian Crusade, as it was called (1208–1229), laid waste the farmlands of the south and, through unparalleled butchery, suppressed the Cathars and other heretics. Within 50 years, the cult was extinct.

III

The early modern period was marked by a religious revolution against the authority of the pope and the supremacy of the Roman Catholic Church. The Protestant Reformation produced three great churches—Lutheran, Reformed and Anglican—all of which quickly became as patriarchal in structure as the traditional Church had ever been. St. Paul's admonition that women were to be silent, certainly not preachers or teachers, was strictly followed. Dozens of splinter groups, though, interpreted the Scriptures in their own way. The Zwinglians, the Brownists, the Anabaptists, the Moravians, the Independents, the Millenarians, the Familists (member of the Family of Love) and the Ranters were a few. Women flocked to these new faiths, sometimes because the brand of spiritualism appealed to them but often because they felt they were more valued. These were women who believed they were equal to men, at least on the spiritual plain, and they should be allowed to expound their ideas on Biblical text. Some even founded churches for that purpose.

Dorothy Hazzard (c. 1610–1675) for example. The wife of a Bristol grocer, she took over her husband's business when he died. To show her contempt for superstition, she refused to close her shop on Christmas Day, thereby establishing her reputation for nonconformity.[672] She married a minister years younger than she, and turned the rectory of St. Ewin into a shelter for families of Puritans about to leave for New England and for women about to give birth who wanted to avoid church baptismal rituals in which they didn't believe. Dorothy began to have grave qualms about the Book of Common Prayer. Eventually, she left her husband's faith—amazingly, they continued to live together for 30 years—and, along with a farmer, a butcher, a farrier and a young minister whom Dorothy sought out, founded her own church. Three-quarters of the 160-member congregation were women,[673] who spoke out whenever they wanted to.

Of all the divergent sects it was the Quakers who advanced the status of women the most. Founded by shoemaker George Fox (1624–1691), the Society of Friends emphasized human goodness, believing that something of God exists in everyone and everyone is a potential vessel for His word—including women. Fox was unequivocal in his championing of a woman's right to preach and proselytize. The significance of this was profound. As historian Olwen Hufton writes, "He [Fox] based his claims on the scriptures and in so doing exposed many of the contradictions in that random compilation and showed that by comparing alternative quotations ... it was possible to see that the ancient assertion of women's inferiority to keep silence was a purely arbitrary decision on the part of churchmen."[674]

Among Fox's first converts was Margaret Fell, an extraordinary woman whom Fox would eventually marry. Married at age 16 to a man much older than herself, a judge and parliamentarian, in 1658 she was left a wealthy widow. At the time she first met George Fox, she was 38 years old, the mother of seven intelligent daughters, three of whom became Quaker preachers, and one ne'er-do-well son. Margaret and her daughters turned the family estate, Swarthmoor Hall, into a comfortable refuge and gathering place for the Friends. The Fund for the Service of Truth was Margaret's inspiration, and she contributed significantly to it. The money was used to finance travelling preachers and assist their families if they landed in jail, which, in the time of ongoing persecution in Britain, was often the case. Eventually, it would develop into the vast charity work that became a Quaker hallmark.

Margaret Fell fought hard for her faith. She wrote to Oliver Cromwell on many occasions, pleading for more tolerance towards the Friends, and she did everything within her power to get George Fox and other followers released from prison. Because she refused to take the Oath of Allegiance to the King and refused to obey an order forbidding her to hold Quaker meetings, she herself was sentenced to life imprisonment, and spent four long years jailed in Lancaster Castle until the King had her released.

During her first stint in prison, she wrote her famous defence of female preachers, *Women's Speaking*. She summed up her message succinctly: "the seed is one in male and female" and "God hath put no such difference

between the Male and Female as man would make."[675] There was one trav-
esty that particularly angered her. She believed that men, by excluding
women from the pulpit, were attempting to limit the power of the Almighty
by insisting that all-important "inner light," the command to voice their
inspiration, existed only in one-half of the human population.

Margaret Fell was not the only female Quaker who suffered for her faith.
The first convert to the Friends, Elizabeth Hooton, continued to preach
during the whole time she was in jail. Mary Dyer was hanged in Boston.
Elizabeth Williams was publicly flogged for addressing the undergraduates of
Sidney Sussex College, Cambridge.[676] All faced their persecution stoically,
believing if they claimed spiritual equality with men, they must endure the
same harsh punishment.

IV

At the heart of the great religious revivals that swept England and North
America in the early part of the 19th century, the inspiration for their most
eccentric ideas were female prophets. Sects sprang up adhering to the ideals
of these charismatic women that rejected not only the rituals and doctrine of
the traditional churches but just about every other belief society held dear.
What amazement was expressed when these spiritual leaders insisted they
were the reincarnation of Christ, the female part of the godhead! As one
historian wrote, these women realized that "Only as a cultic Goddess, as
Father-Mother God or a female incarnation of Jesus, could women have
significant leadership roles outside the home."[677] In the wake of the criticism
and ridicule that rained down, what is astonishing is how many believers,
both men and women, loyally stuck by these religious trailblazers.

Joanna Southcott (1750–1814) was a domestic servant from Devonshire,
England. At age 42, she began to have fantastic visions; in one she appeared
as the "Woman clothed with the Sun," God's emissary on earth. From that
time on, a voice whom she identified as the Spirit regularly spoke with her.
The revelations resulting from these chats were written down (by a secretary,
because Southcott was so poorly educated, she could barely write) and
published. At the heart of her teachings was a belief in the imminent second
coming of Christ, and that she was the person to herald His arrival. She was
to be the Bride of Christ when He returned to the world.[678] Her writings
were passionate, irreverent and feminist. Often it is Jesus speaking.

They [women] followed me to my Cross, and stood weeping to see me crucified; they were the first at My Sepulchre to see My resurrection.... It was by a
woman I came into the world in the form of a man; and now by a woman I will
reveal Myself unto men....[679]

Much of Joanna Southcott's time was spent on the preaching circuit,
mesmerizing huge crowds all over England and converting believers by the
thousands. In 1803, she began her mission with some 58 supporters; ten years
later, 30,000 believers, more than 60 percent of them women, had pledged
their loyalty. Eventually, a wealthy Englishwoman became a devoted disci-
ple and invited Southcott into her household. Thereafter, she led a life of
relative ease, although unhappily her life ended rather pathetically. In her
65th year, she astonished her followers by announcing that, like Sarah in the
Old Testament, she had been visited by the Spirit, who told her, "This year
the sixty-fifth year of thy age, thou shalt have a SON, by the power of the
most HIGH."[680] The child, named Shiloh, was to be Christ's "pro-consul" on
earth, preparing for the Second Coming.

Southcott invited 25 physicians to examine her. Modesty prohibited vaginal examination, yet 17 of them declared she was pregnant. Accolades and
gifts poured in, and visitors arrived from around the world, but by that time,
Southcott was ill and could not have been pleased with the circus going on
around her. She died shortly afterwards, supposedly during childbirth. An
autopsy revealed not only that there was no baby but, aside from an enlarged
liver, no apparent physical reason for her death. All of this was an embarrassment for her followers, but many remained faithful to her ideas, a chink,
perhaps, in the armour of patriarchal religion.

Jemima Wilkinson (1752–1819) was an American contemporary of Joanna
Southcott's. A daughter of well-to-do Quaker farmers in Rhode Island, she
had suffered a grave illness at age 23 during which, delirious with fever, she
believed she had actually died and was sent back to earth by God as His
Second Incarnation. Thereafter she called herself Publick Universal Friend.
The sect that formed around her ideas used the same name, which emphasized the values of equality and community. Repudiating the material world,
the group moved to a remote part of New York State and there, in the
wilderness, set up a utopian colony, the New Jerusalem.

Their philosophy was a combination of Quaker beliefs and Wilkinson's
own mysticism. War and slavery were condemned, celibacy and simple living

promoted. Plain language and plain dress became the sect's trademark. Despite ridicule and legal harassment, Wilkinson preached for over 40 years, attracting thousands into her community. As historian Carroll Smith-Rosenberg points out, Wilkinson symbolized the amazing power that the revival movement offered women. "In short she turned the religious assumptions of the eighteenth century [and early nineteenth] upside down."[681]

Of all the rebel religious orders that shook the bars of the bourgeois Church, none was so infamous or radical as the Shakers, sometimes known as the United Society of Believers in Christ's Second Appearing. The sect was first heard of in the 1750s in England, but its real flourishing took place in the United States at the time of the Second Great Awakening; by 1826, there were 6,000 adherents living in 18 villages, mostly in New England. No Shaker ever doubted that the inspiration for his or her beliefs flowed from Mother Ann, even though she had died decades before.

Ann Lee (1736–1784) was born in England, the second eldest of eight children, to a family of poor Quaker blacksmiths. She received no schooling, and early in her teenage years, she went to work in a textile factory. At the age of 22, she joined a sect that had split away from the Quakers—the Shakers, so called because of the curious gyrations that dominated their meetings.

Married very young, Ann Lee had four children in quick succession, all of whom died in infancy. During a long illness following her last pregnancy, she suffered a crisis of conscience and came to believe her babies had been taken from her because of her lustfulness. Thereafter she embraced celibacy, and her preaching began to attract a devoted group of followers.

Ann Lee suffered persecution at the hands of the British authorities: she was ridiculed, harassed, beaten and sent to jail for breach of the Sabbath. Finally, in 1774, she and eight followers decided to set out for the New World. In 1776, the first Shaker Village was set up near Albany, New York, attracting many of the same kind of people as her English supporters: poor farmers, artisans and unskilled workers.

Mother Ann, as one historian put it, "preached a gospel that violated virtually every social, economic and theological convention."[682] Forming the foundation of her church was a faith in the equality of all believers; land was owned communally, lives lived in as egalitarian a manner as possible. However, her belief system was full of strange contradictions. Shakers believed, as orthodox Christians did, that sexuality was the root cause of mankind's downfall, that the serpent had "infused into her [Eve's] mind the filthy passion of *lust*." The Shakers' ambition was to transcend their prurient feelings in order to live a life of the spirit. In the villages, men and women lived in separate residences. They were forbidden to speak or walk together, although they worked and ate side by side.[683] Contrasted with this was the sexually charged atmosphere that permeated the meetings. Whatever the spirit dictated was encouraged: singing, dancing, speaking in tongues, wailing prophesies, settling into silent trances, rolling about the ground or spinning about for hours on end. Visions, often with heavy sexual overtones, were relished.

Furthermore, Eve's succumbing to temptation in Eden did not, in the Shakers' eyes, condemn women to a life of inferiority and oppression. The Shaker God was equally male and female, a combination of the Father of Power and the Mother of Wisdom. As God's second incarnation and Christ's equal, Ann Lee was thought to embody the Godhead's female persona.

Three decades after Mother Lee's death, there was a great revival of Shaker spirituality that grew more and more unorthodox. Spirit writing—messages from the "Woman Clothed in Sun" (Joanna Southcott) and Mother Lee— spirit wine, which was particularly exhilarating, and spirit clothing, which enchanted, became part of religious life. The Father of Power, the Mother of Wisdom, Christ and Mother Ann were seen to dance with great joy on Shaker graves. With such excess, it was perhaps a forgone conclusion that the sect would lose its dynamism, and by 1860, it was all but burnt out. However, until the 1980s, there were people who called themselves Shakers, and the legacy of Mother Ann Lee and her radical egalitarian ideals continues to fascinate scholars and lay persons alike.[684]

V

There's something about the 20th century mind that leads it easily astray. The unquestioning patriotism of World War I, the rejection of democracy, the vengeful embrace of fascism in the 1930s, the shattering of progressive ideas during World War II when, in the name of the Final Solution, the lives of human beings were stamped out like so many ants or spiders—all of these required unthinking obedience to a perverse ideology.

Eccentric sects continued to spring up like itchy rashes in the 20th century. Some were liberal in their approach. The Unitarian Universalism Association, for example, has no official statement of faith and does not require its ministers or congregations to subscribe to any particular belief. More typical are those that have gradually evolved into universes unto themselves, with their own hierarchical power structures and unorthodox ideas. In these cases, clashes with authoritarianism, within the cult leadership itself or the outside world, have been marked by terrible tragedy.

On November 18, 1978, over 900 members of the People's Temple, led by Jim Jones, committed suicide in Jonestown, Guyana, by drinking poison. On April 19, 1993, at least 75 members, including 21 children, of the Branch Davidians were either shot or burned to death in their compound near Waco, Texas. On March 23, 1997, five members of the Solar Temple cult died in what was an apparent ritual suicide pact in Quebec. On three successive days beginning on March 23, 1997, groups of a doomsday cult called Heaven's Gate, 21 females and 18 males, packed their bags, put on their new running shoes, turned off their computers and committed suicide.

In all of these extreme cases, women have been a majority among the victims, but they seem to have little to do with the leadership, and while the cults in which women do play a key role are not doomsday, they can be provocative and anti-establishment. They often bring down the wrath of fundamentalist Christians, but at least they are not marked by violence.

In 1972 in Los Angeles, the first coven of feminist witches that practised the "Craft" as a religion began to meet under the leadership of one Zsuzsanna Budapest. It signaled a new religious movement that would loosely encompass neo-paganism, goddess worship and Wicca (from the old English word *wicce*, a wizard). Fundamental to the cult was a belief in a pre-historic Goddess culture, in which female values, particularly nurturing and co-operation, formed the wellspring by which society was organized. As journalist John Allemang writes, "Drawing on pre-Christian rituals and ancient traditions of a nurturing Mother Goddess, Wicca is seen by its followers as an invigorating antidote to guilt-ridden, male-dominated religions of the mainstream."[685]

Wiccans celebrate the female body, in particular its sexuality. The Maiden, the Mother and the Crone make up the Triple Goddess, a metaphor for cyclic time. Witches commemorate eight sabbats or holy days based on the seasonal cycles; Belthane, for example, is a feast of fertility and purification that signals the release of Earth from the season of death, while the sabbat of harvestide takes place at the fall equinox in September. Ritual is important to Wiccans for it is their means to secure a place for women in mythology and therefore in the collective subconscious.

Wendy Griffin is a sociologist who studied two groups involved in the

Wiccan and American Goddess movements first-hand. One August weekend in 1991, she joined a group of 60 women camping in the hills for a weekend of workshops, discussions and rituals. One of these was led by a priestess called Hypatia, who was a follower of Diana (the Roman equivalent of the Greek Artemis), goddess of the hunt. This is what Griffin recorded:

The second night out was a full moon and we waited impatiently for the moon to crest the tall pines so that the ritual could begin. Finally we saw two flames winding down the mountain path. As they neared, we saw that these were torches, held by priestesses in silver gowns which caught the light from the flames and glittered like pieces of the moon herself. The priestesses paused in the south, and then I noticed the enormous shadow thrown against the hill. It is Diana who comes behind them. Rationally, I know it is Hypatia, but I also 'know' it is Diana. A heavy green cape is swept over her shoulders and matches her baggy pants. Her huge breasts are bare, and her chest is crossed with leather straps that hold her cape and the quiver of arrows on her back. She carries a large bow and her face is hidden behind a mask of fur and dried leaves. Deer horns spring from her head. There is no face, not a human one, anyway.... The Goddess pauses between the torches and fits an arrow to the bow. She draws it back and with a 'twang' shoots it into the darkness. The sound is a catalyst. We are released like the arrow and begin to cheer.[686]

It might not be everyone's idea of a church service, but according to Griffin, for most of those who attended, it was a moment of real empowerment. "This is the Diana I want to relate to," said a woman in her twenties. Certainly, it was an affirmation of nature, sexuality and strength—not an obscene denial of life.

6. The Imagination

Adèle

I have one vivid memory of Adèle Hearn. We were taking a Grade 12 art exam, and she had brought no drawing materials at all. I only had a piece of a pencil in the very bottom of my bag. Both of us were too frightened to approach the teacher; it was unheard of to arrive so unprepared. I sketched the bowl of fruit for a few moments, then passed the stub over to Adèle, who frantically scribbled away until it was back to me. As I recall, we managed pretty good marks.

Adèle and I were both disorganized and dishevelled, but it seemed natural to her, for she was such a creative person. Her art work was on display everywhere and her poetry always graced the yearbook.

Adèle hailed from a long line of creative, strong-minded women. Her great-grandmother had been adopted by a respected, old Toronto family. Among other things, Florence Gooderham Heustis was one of the first women to drive an automobile in Toronto. She also sat on committees that introduced pasteurized milk to the city, and she was president of Women's College Hospital. Florence had four daughters, the sprightly Doris, Adèle's grandmother, being one of them.

Doris Heustis went to Havergal Ladies College, a school for the upper crust in Toronto, and she would have gone on to the University of Toronto, but it was thought her health was too fragile to take on a full load of studies. (She lived until age 95.) Instead, she audited courses. Through one of her sisters, she met the talented and handsome W. Gordon Mills. He was not only an up-and-coming young business executive but he wrote divine poetry. Two books of his work would later be published: *Legends of the Mississaugas* and *Timber Line and Other Poems,* edited by Doris.

Doris and Gordon were married just after World War I, and travelled in Toronto's artsy circles. Painter Lawren Harris and his wife were close friends. Doris herself learned to paint under the tutelage of J. E. H. Macdonald and exhibited with the Group of Seven for four years. Eventually though, the marriage soured. Gordon was under tremendous stress in his job as an executive in advertising and personnel for the T. Eaton department store, and his young family paid for it. After 23 years of marriage, Doris decided she wanted out. By that time, she had fallen passionately in love.

In 1934, Doris met J. Murray Speirs at the Royal Ontario Museum, where she was researching the behaviour of birds, particularly the Evening Grosbeak. Murray was a young ornithologist, just obtaining his doctorate. Although he was only 28 and she was in her forties, the two fell in love. After Doris divorced Gordon Mills, she married Murray Speirs in 1939, and they had a long and happy life together, bird-watching all over the world.

Inevitably, though, there were victims in the marriage breakdown. At age 16, Adèle's mother Barbara left home. She dropped out of her prestigious private school and took a job in a boiler factory as a secretary. It wasn't just her family situation that upset her; it was the class system in which she had been raised. "She didn't feel she had benefited by her elitist upbringing," says Adèle. "It hadn't brought much joy." This distaste for the upper classes remained with Barbara for her entire life. When Adèle's grandmother offered to pay her granddaughter's way through Havergal College, Barbara flatly refused. "My daughter is going to school with the plumber's son," she insisted.

Barbara banked at the Temperance Street branch of the Canadian Bank of Commerce. She usually went with a girlfriend, and both noticed one dashing, young clerk-teller—with his devilish good looks, he reminded them of Errol Flynn. The threesome got chatting, and soon Norman asked Barbara out for tea.

Norman Hearn had grown up in the village of Moorlynch in Somerset, England, one of five children of a Church of England minister. The future was not exactly bright in 1930s Britain for the son of a village rector, even if he were well-educated, which Norman was. An uncle had already emigrated to Canada and had managed to launch a successful banking career. He offered to help his nephew find a job. Norman arrived in Canada in 1931 at age 19.

Adèle feels that although her father worked for the Bank of Commerce (later the Canadian Imperial Bank of Commerce) throughout his working life, he was never really comfortable there. With his gift for language and his elegant, articulate way of speaking, he would have made a great teacher of English literature or a Latin scholar, but dealing with finances turned him into a worry-wart. This may have been one reason why he adored Adèle's mother—she was so peppy and energetic. He felt relaxed in her company.

Barbara and Norman were married in a simple wedding in 1941 in Ottawa, where Barbara's father was deputy minister of naval services in Mackenzie

King's defence ministry. Adèle was born in 1943, and, because Norman was overseas, she and Barbara went to live in Doris's lovely house in Ancaster, southwest of Toronto.

Her mother always said she greeted a different man than the one she had waved off to war. As the son of a cleric, Norman had been morally offended in a deeply fundamental way by what he had seen and been forced to do. He became a more rigid, unbending man. Back at the bank, the stress would get to him. His behaviour became unpredictable, and he grew more and more remote from his children.

In 1949, three years after Adèle's brother Miles was born, the Hearns bought a small bungalow on Glenridge Road for $6,000. Money was always a worry during Adèle's childhood. Norman's salary at the bank was small, his advancement slow. Energetic Barbara was always thinking of ways to fatten the family bank account. She typed theses for university students and, more lucrative, she took care of foster children, usually one or two at a time.

Barbara wasn't interested in "blonde, blue-eyed," as she called them. She would take care of babies whom nobody else wanted, those of different racial backgrounds and often with serious health problems: skin diseases, lung difficulties, particularly asthma, or malnutrition. Barbara was often exhausted by looking after these children—she seldom slept through an entire night—and Adèle sometimes had to take time off school to help out. She didn't mind, except when her friends came over. The infants often had digestive problems; the special formula Adèle's mother made stank up the house, and Adèle was embarrassed by that. She was proud, however, when her mother was named one of Toronto's top foster mothers and interviewed on television.

Since Doris was involved in ornithological pursuits around the world and Barbara led a frugal, suburban life, the two women, while not estranged, had only a formal relationship. Adèle remained close to her grandmother, though, whom she called Wendy of Peter Pan fame. Doris was an art collector—on the walls of her house hung not only Group of Seven paintings but also examples of Cubism—and it was she who showed real interest in Adèle's childish sketches and paid for art lessons at the Royal Ontario Museum.

When Adèle was 15, her grandmother and her husband Murray Speirs took her on a grand tour of Europe: England, Finland, Norway, Sweden, Denmark, France, ending up in New York. They visited the Louvre, the Tate, the Guggenheim. They saw the latest Ingmar Bergman films and plays. "It was an overwhelming experience for me," says Adèle.

Her mother, too, was, as Adèle puts it, "a culture vulture." Barbara would drive through a blizzard in order not to miss a Toronto Symphony Orchestra concert. Sunday after church, the family would be handed large mugs full of soup and settled down around the radio to listen to concert and drama reviews.

Still, there was an unhappy strain in the Hearn family. As they grew older, Norman and Barbara began to lead distinctly separate lives. He didn't much like accompanying her to the symphony or theatre she loved so much. They went to different Anglican churches: he low, she high. Their holidays were spent separately: she'd go to Israel with a girlfriend; he'd motor around Ontario for a couple of weeks, stopping at nice hotels and restaurants. There was never any question of divorce or separation, but it made for a disjointed existence for their children.

Adèle flourished at R. H. King Collegiate, but her accomplishments were all in languages—French, English, German and Latin—and visual arts. She couldn't do math or science at all. She'd get 90 percent in English and 30 percent in algebra. With her almost flowery, literate way of speaking—a gift of her father—Adèle was one of the most well liked and admired girls in the class. She won the Nathaniel A. Benson Bluff Award for her creative writing, she was named a prefect and, most prestigious of all, she was the Grade 13 valedictorian.

She was also in and out of love all the way through high school, until, in Grade 12, she met tall, skinny Peter Koehnke, older brother of the glamorous Ursula. "We were all intrigued when the Koehnkes arrived on the scene. Coming from Nashville, they were a different cup of tea," says Adèle. When Peter asked Adèle out, she jumped at the chance. What impressed her the most about him was that he seemed to know exactly what he wanted to do with his life. Adèle, on the other hand, was at a loss.

Even though Norman was now a bank manager and Barbara had a full-time secretarial job at the Borough of Scarborough, they decided they could afford to send only one of their two children to university. Adèle had high marks in Grade 13 and would readily have been accepted into a fine-arts or English-literature program, but it was her brother Miles who was given the opportunity. As the male, it was reasoned, he would eventually have to provide for a family. Perhaps more important, Barbara had always loved classical music, and Miles showed real talent in that direction. Eventually, he became a professional French-horn player. Barbara felt it was more important for dreamy Adèle to "get her feet on the ground."

Adèle's father was so heavily involved in his work, he played almost no role in the important decisions affecting his daughter's life, and Adèle's grandmother, who might have been an advocate for her, was away bird-watching. Says Adèle, "I should have stuck up for myself more. If I had it to do over, I would have worked, saved enough, lived at my grandmother's and gone to school. But I was so passive. I didn't know what my options were."

In the high-school yearbook, Adèle listed her ambition as taking journalism at Ryerson Polytechnical Institute, which would have opened worlds for her, but her mother discovered scholarships worth a year's tuition were available for girls entering the three-year secretarial-science course. Adèle won one, and resigned herself to learning how to be a handmaiden in the world of business. Except for the English-literature course, she hated it. "It wasn't what I wanted to do at all. It was something my mother wanted me to do. I was sick about it." At the end of her first year, she dropped out of college. A few months later, in September 1962, at age 19, she married Peter Koehnke.

Adèle believes she was probably acting out her frustration and resentment. What she wanted more than anything was to get away from home. In fact, both she and Peter were wounded ducks. He had had a difficult time when, at age ten, his family had moved from Germany to Tennessee. He had had trouble adjusting not only to a new language and culture but also to the fact that his elegant father, a senior executive in Germany, had to work pumping gas. In addition, a serious conflict between father and son developed over Peter's performance in school. Ursula says, "I think my father was very hard on my brother, very demanding of him. He was never happy or content with him. My brother must have felt there wasn't anything he could do right. He sort of built this wall to protect himself." Peter may not have lived up to his father's expectations during high school, but he was very clever and ambitious. In only a year, he had obtained his engineering-technologist diploma from the Radio College of Canada and had started his own industrial-electronics business with a man older than himself.

The Koehnkes were married only a year and a half when their first child Jamie arrived. A daughter Tanya followed in 1968. Peter did so well in his business, he and Adèle were soon able to buy their own storey-and-a-half, three-bedroom home in Highland Creek. Adèle remembers some good things about that period in her life. She loved her children dearly. She and Peter had enough money to travel, and they visited Ursula and her husband Whayne in Washington. Adèle got along well with the elder Koehnkes, and enjoyed celebrating German Christmas and other festivities with them.

However, Adèle felt strongly that there was something lacking. "I would have enjoyed everything a lot more if I had had a profession of my own," she admits. It didn't help that, for many years, Peter worked seven days a week and most evenings. When he was home, he was exhausted. Adèle also says she was unreasonably demanding of him. "I lived the role of a wife, I was Mrs. Koehnke. I threw every job in his lap. I couldn't screw a light bulb in. I expected him to be an entertainment committee." In 1973, after 11 years of marriage, Peter asked Adèle for a divorce. He had found someone more compatible. "You are very charming," he told Adèle, "but she is a hard worker."

Friends of Adèle say she is being too hard on herself in blaming herself for the marriage breakdown. Her and Peter's value systems were very different. She is a woman with a highly developed conscience and artistic sensibility, while he will "do what works." Says his sister Ursula, "I think the real problem in his marriage was that he insulated himself to such an extent that he couldn't properly give or receive. I thought it was very sad."

For the first few years, Peter was generous in his alimony payments, so Adèle's financial worries weren't that great, but he and his spouse moved to Calgary just months after the separation. Adèle was left to raise the two children by herself, although she didn't mind much. "I had been alone much of my married life, because my husband worked many hours a week, so I was used to it," she says. "I'm quite used to reading or going for long walks by myself. I can be alone, but I'm never lonely."

She admits, though, that there were times in the raising of her children when she missed not having the support of a husband. When Tanya was 11, it was discovered she had juvenile diabetes, and for years, her health was in jeopardy. "I remember when it was first diagnosed, sitting in the hospital washroom thinking, 'I'm either going to handle this or I'm not.' It was hard on me not to be married at that point, not to have support in helping Tanya control her condition." On the other hand, she genuinely believes she is a better person for having independence thrust on her. "If I had remained married to my chauvinistic but kindly husband, I would never have learned half of what I know now. I have a good accountant and a good mechanic, and I myself am handy with a wrench."

Her real saviour, though, has been her creativity. Shortly after her marriage breakup, she phoned Scarborough Cable and asked who did the on-air storytelling. "Why don't you come and try?" was the response. For ten years, she performed and produced a variety of programs. *Adèle's Stories for Children* was the most famous, but there were also *Spice and Such*, a cooking show, and *Just Off Centre*, a program that she and a man-friend wrote, produced and acted in. "It was a Mike Nichols-Elaine May routine. I was blonde, he smoked a cigar and we did park-bench stuff, mostly ad lib. It was great fun." Adèle went out with her co-performer, a cigar-smoking manager of a Speedy Muffler outlet, on and off for ten years, and for a time he lived with her.

Since she received almost no remuneration from the cable company, she was forced to sell her house to raise capital, and in 1978, she went back to secretarial work. She was fired from her first job because she was such a slow typist, but she rented an old Remington and practised until she was up to speed. After that, she was on the registry of agencies that specialize in temporary placements. Adèle claims she has worked for over 80 different companies. It wasn't very satisfying. "I thought I had reneged on myself by not carrying on with my education," she says. "I began a pattern which, until maybe six or seven years ago, I continued, not exactly being a ne'er-do-well but not really going anywhere either. I kept it up for a long time."

In 1989, Adèle's father became very ill, and she decided to quit work to look after him. "I got to know my father in a totally different ball park—the stress of the bank was gone. I decided, on a Christian basis, that I would honour my father, even though he had often annoyed and saddened me. I started to be kinder to him, to phone him almost every night, and we became great pals." One of the things he told her before he died was that he was sorry he hadn't helped her more when the decision was made for her to go into the secretarial course at Ryerson.

In 1990, Adèle was hired by General Publishing in Toronto. She was doing basic secretarial work again, but while she was there, she was able to carve out a niche for herself that at last used her creative ability. She occasionally wrote book blurbs for the national sales manager, got involved in cut-and-paste design for library-sales materials and did extensive proof-reading. She also assisted the company president as his administrative assistant, overseeing the work of 16 people, including the sales and marketing force. It was a job Adèle loved, but in 1993, the company downsized and she was among the 15 people who were let go. "Maybe I put too much stock in my work, but it hurt to lose that job. It really hurt a lot."

At 50 years old, she found herself unemployed. She was depressed and bruised, but she pulled herself together and took a desktop-publishing course. This, happily, led to a good job. She now works for a company called Inofas, a computer-service bureau. Once again, her artistic talents are being used in a practical fashion. One of her jobs is to recreate and fix computer images. Pictures that have been scanned and look like smashed eggs become clear, even beautiful under Adèle's steady hand.

During all the years of ups and downs, Adèle's creative endeavours have continued to sustain her. Literature, visual arts and music mean a great deal to her. She has written anthems for her church choir, and in 1990, she won first prize in a Scarborough Arts Council poetry contest. "Pink Hat With Feather" is based on the love she had nurtured for her father later in his life. She has continued to paint, and exhibits her work at local galleries, shops and art shows. The $400 or $500 she sometimes receives from sales is a much appreciated supplement to her income. Finally, she is a part-time diploma student at the Toronto School of Art.

If Adèle had one overwhelming goal, it was to ensure that what happened to her would not happen to her daughter. For years, the brass statue that Adèle received for being high-school valedictorian sat in her china cabinet. It became a symbol for both mother and daughter—who is a graduate student in English literature—of what might have been if a talented young girl, brimming with creativity, had got the proper chance in life.

Creativity

The women's intellect is not for invention or creation but sweet ordering, arrangement and decision. Her great function is praise [of men].

John Ruskin, '*Of Queen's Garden*', 1864

As long as women must fight to become human beings, they will never be creators.

Simone de Beauvoir, *The Second Sex*, 1949

I can't remember how the meeting came about—visiting the elderly was not my mother's thing—but one Sunday afternoon, she and I walked to the nearby bungalow of a certain Mrs. Harris. The round-faced old woman served us tea and cookies, we chatted a bit, then she escorted us to her basement. There, spread out before us, was an amazing sight: a virtual universe of dolls. Hundreds of them, all painstakingly created by Mrs. Harris herself, every one with a split personality. There was Little Red Riding Hood, sporting flaxen braids, a red cloak and a long skirt. Flip her over, though, and up popped the big, bad wolf, ferocious teeth and all, his long hunter's jacket now hiding Red Riding Hood. Every doll was like that. A pretty Juliet turned upside down became a handsome Romeo; Papageno turned into Papagena; King Henry VIII was transformed into Anne Boleyn. Even the former Canadian prime minister William Lyon Mackenzie King was represented. When overturned, he became his mother. I found the dolls fascinating and couldn't stop touching them, but once outside Mrs. Harris's emporium, I smirked, "Talk about corn ball!" My mother, quite rightly, pointed out the exquisite workmanship: every sequin, every button, every little flower was perfectly made, perfectly placed. They were completely original

Years later as a young reporter, I was assigned to cover the opening of an important new folk-art exhibit at the Art Gallery of Ontario. There, on display, were a dozen or so of Mrs. Harris's fabulous dolls. She had died years before, but a great-niece had kept the collection intact. The curator of the exhibition didn't hesitate in his assessment: this was the work of a true artist, he wrote.

It was a lesson well learned. Since recorded time, women have been shut out of the world of the Great Masters. Their creativity could only be expressed underground, in kitchens, root cellars and drawing rooms, between baby-feeds and making meals. The art they produced was as original and profound as that of men. It simply went unrecognized.

I

In classical Greece, the only women who could openly demonstrate their artistic talents and who benefited financially from them were prostitutes. Not any prostitute, of course, but that small, select group of beautiful, intelligent, witty females called *hetaerae*. They were most often slaves who were picked from the crowd by a dealer of prostitutes or a brothel-owner, not only for their looks—often they were not raving beauties—but for their personalities and artistic abilities. Their training led to one end: creative and dedicated suppliers of pleasure for men.

Their forum was the famous *symposia*, the drinking parties so beloved by upper-crust men (certainly not by respectable wives and daughters). These usually occurred in private homes, in the men's rooms called the *andron*, often the one stylishly furnished section of the house. The revellers reclined on couches, drank copious amounts of wine mixed with water, ate expensive fish and other delicacies, played games of all sorts—splattering wine on each other being one of the favourites—and conversed, supposedly about important things. Both Plato and Xenophon wrote philosophical works entitled *Symposium*. At the end of the meal, they were entertained, sometimes by lower-class men but also by women: pipe-players, singers, acrobats and dancers, often dressed in animal skins to represent maenads.

These high-class drinking parties are among the most frequently painted scenes on Greek vessels, cups and wine receptacles. In one such depiction, the merry-makers, their heads adorned with the usual garland wreaths, loll about on couches while in front of them stands an actress dressed in a fancy costume, an arm raised as though she is giving a dramatic performance.[687]

Of course, these companions of men were required to do more than sing and dance; they were there to sexually excite and satisfy the symposium gang. Many *hetaerae* were famous for their erotic techniques, so much so that men often became enthralled by them. Some of the women developed into witty and urbane conversationalists, much sought after by the banqueting crowd. With these connections, many were able to raise the money to buy their freedom. They often became wealthy, and were notoriously mercenary.

The most famous *hetaera*, indeed the most famous woman of fifth-century Athens, was Aspasia (c. 470–410 BC), the consort of Pericles, the illustrious Athenian statesman. An immigrant from Miletus in Asia Minor, Aspasia started her career as a *hetaera*, eventually becoming a dealer and handler of prostitutes. As one commentator put it, she "imported large numbers of beautiful women, and all of Greece was filled with her little harlots."[688] Aspasia was known for her great beauty, wit and political savvy. Pericles was so infatuated with her—he would "kiss her warmly both when he left for the marketplace and when he returned home each day"—that he divorced his first wife to marry her, and their house became a gathering spot for the distinguished of Athens. Plutarch, in his *Life of Pericles* (second century AD), writes:

They say that Pericles had high regard for Aspasia as a philosopher and politician. Socrates, in fact, came to see her with his disciples, and his friends brought their wives to hear her, although she ran a disreputable and improper business, because she trained young hetaerae.[689]

Pericles was said to listen to her advice on political matters, and some historians have blamed her for goading him into starting the Peloponnesian War. When his two sons by his first marriage died, Pericles obtained full rights of citizenship for his and Aspasia's boy.

It's important not to paint too rosy a picture of the life of a Greek courtesan, though; Aspasia was an exception. Neaera was another beautiful, intelligent, talented woman who began life as a child-slave prostitute in Corinth and who eventually was able to buy her freedom for 2,000 *drachmae*. Phrynion was the man who gave her most of the money, but when he brought her to Athens as his wife,

… he kept her and lived with her in a most dissolute and reckless way. He took her out to dinner with him wherever he went, where there was drinking; and whenever he made an after-dinner excursion, she always went too. He made love to her openly, anywhere and everywhere he chose, to excite the jealousy of the onlookers at his privilege.[690]

Upper-class prostitutes were given the opportunity to publicly express their artistic and intellectual talents far more than the cloistered wife in the home, but the question that begs to be answered is: at what price? Many lived creative lives, but they were also subjected to the whims of a man who could debase and ridicule them as he saw fit.

II

From the early to late Middle Ages, the hub of female cultural expression was located in the monastery/convent. Take as an example the famous Dominican house at Engelthal, in what would be the future West Germany. The community was founded by a harpist and troubadour who had been a member of Elisabeth of Thuringia's wedding party. This musician gathered together the Beguines scattered in Nuremberg so they could pool their common goods and skills. Eventually, for political reasons, they settled at Engelthal, where a nobleman endowed the community with land and money. A sister called Reichgard was a superb artist, and another, Alheit, was skilled at many crafts, from weaving to embroidery, which she taught to other members of the convent.[691] Engelthal eventually became one of the great Dominican convents, a cultural centre in southern Germany.

After the monasteries were abolished by the Gregorian reform movement of the late 11th century, many female communities found themselves excluded from the hierarchy of the Church, and thus often without funds. Convent-based industries, using the talents of the sisterhood, became their saving grace. Many convents specialized in spinning and weaving, embroidering silk flowers, interlacing gold designs in cloth—any art produced by the hands of women could be put to good use. There were other creative ways to earn a profit. An English Franciscan house was famous for its carefully concocted rose water, which it sold in pretty vials. Nuns copied books, created miniature paintings and beautifully illuminated manuscripts. The first major convent *scriptoria*, or book-making workshops, began with the reign of Charlemagne (742–814). The emperor's sister Gisela established one at the double convent-monastery at Chelles, northeast of Paris. It was the beginning of a long tradition. In the 15th century, the sisters of San Jacopo di Ripoli operated a printing shop, turning out handsome devotional books.[692]

Nuns sometimes became creative entrepreneurs. The relics of saints that a monastery/convent might own, for example, could be put to lucrative use. These pieces of bone or hunks of hair from martyrs or repentant sinners would, on their feast days, attract a crowd of pilgrims. The hospices and taverns that were needed to accommodate them, not to mention the trinkets and handicrafts that could be sold, were excellent money-makers.

A nun's artistic output was not entirely, or even mostly, devoted to making money. The illumination of manuscripts was primarily meant to beautifully express a spiritual idea or vision. While Hildegard of Bingen was not a painter herself, she is believed to have conceived the wonderful design and illustrations in her book *Scivias*.[693] Hildegard's creativity, expressed in the imaginative illustrations that illumined her visions, could only have been created by a woman with the peace, security and freedom from household busyness that a convent provided.

III

In Paris the Hotel de Rambouillet [the town house of the Marquise] was a sort of academy of wit, style, virtue, and learning ... the meeting place of all who were distinguished by rank or merit, a tribunal to be reckoned with and whose decision carried at least as much weight in matters affecting the reputation of people of the court or of high society as it did with regard to books.[694]

What Louis de Rouvroy, Duc de Saint-Simon (1675–1755), the famous French writer of memoirs, is describing here is a salon, the archetype of what became a remarkably important institution, not only in France but in England and Germany as well. Salons were gatherings of men and women of the upper classes who had a passion for conversation—always polite and refined—about love affairs and court intrigues, but also about new scientific ideas, literature, history and philosophy. Enlightenment ideas were hatched and discussed there; the foundation for the French Revolution was laid in the salons of Paris. And it was in salons that women were at last able to exhibit their intellectual finesse: their wit, knowledge and debating prowess. For the upper-class, well-educated Frenchwoman, totally outlawed from the universities and academies that produced artists and intellectuals, the one place her creativity could be given full rein was in the bubbling discourse of the salons.

It was the brilliant, trilingual Marquise de Rambouillet who, in 1618, established the model of the French salon. Her mother was an Italian of culture and intelligence, who saw to it that her daughter was well educated and who married her off to a French aristocrat. The new Marquise was horrified at the slovenly, uncultured court of Henri IV. She developed a chronic illness, probably allergies, and when her husband was disgraced under Cardinal Richelieu, she was only too glad to retire from the court. By transforming her home into an earthly paradise, she made sure the world, or at least those who counted, would come to her. As Gédéon Tallemant des Réaux put it, "... [her salon] was the theatre of all pleasures, the meeting place of the gayest people from the court and the most subtle wits of the century."[695]

Because she was so often ill, Mme de Rambouillet's gathering place had to include a bed, which she tucked away in an alcove. Thereafter, beds—seldom actually used for sleeping and decorated with canopies, curtains, valances, flounces and even pilasters, capped by feathers—became a feature of fashionable salons, as did little nooks and crannies where intimate conversations could take place. The Marquise filled her apartment with *objets d'art*, vases of fresh flowers, porcelain from China, huge mirrors—a great novelty at the time—crystal chandeliers and elaborate candle-holders.[696]

George Sand, in her novel *Horace*, describes a young writer who is about to attend his first salon. He has high hopes about the important contacts he will make there:

... he was anxious not to appear like a bumpkin in Madame de Chailly's salon. He made an entertainment out of what he called 'this game'; he promised himself to observe, investigate, and collect facts for his next novel; and in the meantime he was very nervous about the idea of slipping on a heavily waxed parquet floor, of stepping on the foot of a lapdog, of crashing into a piece of furniture: in a word, of making himself a ridiculous character in a classical comedy.[697]

Many of the hostesses, the *salonnières*, of the 17th century wanted nothing less than to uplift the cultural tone of their entire society. They were feminists of sorts, believing women had special "heart-centred" qualities and should be treated with respect and dignity. They were heartily ridiculed by the male establishment, of course. Molière had great fun caricaturing them in *Les femmes savantes* and *Les précieuses ridicules*. The *précieuses*—the precious ones—were so called because they supposedly attached value to things of false value, including themselves, but in fact, they were far more than 17th-century versions of Miss Manners. They waged war not only on crudity—the word *obscène* entered the French language in the salons of the *précieuses*—but also on pedantic, technical and archaic language. French became the international language of diplomacy partly because of the example set by *précieuses* writers of belles lettres—the wonderful Mme de Sévigné and the early novelist Mlle de Scudéry, for example.[698]

From the upgrading of the vernacular flowed the belief that knowledge itself should no longer be the sole preserve of the university-educated. As historian Claude Dulong puts it, "To make such a claim was to demystify the pretensions of the pendants, who took the challenge very badly indeed. The criticisms that have been heaped on *précieuses* for three hundred years stem largely from the rancorous campaign that these offended pendants waged against them."[699] Even today, some feminist scholars regard *les précieuses* as nothing more than superficial and silly goody-goodies, an unfair assessment.

The important legacy of the *précieuses* was to make the all-important link between emancipation and knowledge. Women could never take their place in society until they had the tools, language and scholarship to fully express their creativity.

IV

The Victorian era was the great age of amateurism. There were exceptions, but usually, women did not head off to collect reptile specimens in the Galapagos Islands or rock samples in the Andes as men hobbyists did. Women's artistic endeavours centred in the home: in the parlour, playing the piano, in the garden, painting lovely scenes, in the study, writing colourful letters to friends. Few bourgeois young girls were *not* exposed to years of music, drawing and dance lessons. None of this was in preparation for a career, though. The aim was to produce cultured, dainty flowers ready to be plucked by a suitor.

Some women spent years, sometimes their entire lives, practising art or music or both. While Jane Austen wrote her novels, her sister Cassandra (1777–1845) sketched a myriad of drawings. These were displayed to admiring friends and relatives, but never put on public display. The same held true for musicians. Suzanne Leenhoff, the wife of Édouard Manet, gave brilliant renditions of Chopin, but her piano was always in the parlour, never in a recital hall.[700]

The work of female amateur artists almost always illustrated domestic life—the angel by the hearth's vested interest. Family members, particularly children, shady walks, vacation spots, flower gardens were considered appropriate subject matter for lady like painters, who most often pulled back from strong emotion. Queen Victoria was one of these; interestingly, among her thousands of pictures, less than a half-dozen were of her beloved husband Albert.[701]

As historian Anne Higonnet points out, this flowering of amateur arts was at first an educational force; the more one attempted to paint like Monet, the more one came to understand his art. In the end, however, it impeded women's progress towards professionalism. Their paintings or sketches, often done on poor-quality paper, were small and fragile. They were lumped together in an album with other objects—pressed flowers, postcards—which often resulted in them being damaged. Amateur paintings often did not stand as subjects by themselves but were only understood in the context of a family story. As Higonnet writes, "None claimed autonomy, each depended on its relationship to other images and knowledge brought to it by a private audience. These amateurs were picture makers rather than authors; they did not strive for recognizable styles or didactic subject matter; nor did they work for a market. Amateur pictures therefore had almost no formal, intellectual or economic value as those values were then defined by high art, and consequently have all but disappeared."[702]

There were some women who were professionally engaged in the arts as concert pianists, ballet dancers, actresses. Clara Schumann, for example, was carefully trained as a musician and pianist from age five by her father Friedrick Wieck. Predictably, though, even these exceptional women, although acclaimed and appreciated, did not receive society's highest accolades. These went to the so-called author—the composer, choreographer and playwright, and almost none of these was female.

The insidious notion that women were simply not creators came to permeate society more and more—even in works by female authors. In Dinah M. Craik's novel *Olive*, written in 1850, Vanburgh, an artist, explains to Olive why only men can aspire to ultimate creativity:

'I said it was impossible for a woman to become an artist—I mean a *great* artist. Have you ever thought what that term implies? Not only a painter but a poet; a man of learning, of reading, of observation. A gentleman—we artists are the friends of kings. A man of stainless virtue. A man of iron will, indomitable daring, and passions strong, yet kept always leashed in his hand. Last and greatest, a man who, feeling within him the divine spirit, with his whole soul worships God!'

Vanburgh lifted off his velvet cap and reverently bared his head; then he continued, 'That is what an artist should *be,* by nature.'[703]

Most women didn't have time to sit around and praise their menfolk; they were out working for a living. They could sometimes find security and an adequate income in artisan trades that were thought to need the feminine touch: painters of miniatures, wallpaper, porcelain and enamel, as well as makers of artificial flowers and designers of textile patterns. Talented milliners and dressmakers were often praised as being great artists by their grateful, upper-class clientele. While these trades gave an aura of gentility and respectability to their practitioners, there was no lasting recognition of the creativity involved.

As it had for centuries, the home remained not only the studio where a woman's contributions to the arts were performed but also the object of the artist's inspiration. A middle-class housewife spent much time making colourful antimacassars, crocheting doilies, painting miniatures. Magazines gave instructions on producing mats, chair seats and sofa backs. Elaborate fringes were all the rage for a while, and in North America, quilt-making became an obsession.

The creativity of the upper-class woman was poured into hosting lavish social events in her home, the last remnants of the salon. These *grandes dames* had great power in society. They determined who was in and who was out, as this advice given in the 1890s by Lady Warwick to the novelist Elinor Glyn illustrates:

Army or naval officers, diplomats or clergymen may be invited to lunch or dinner. The vicar may be invited regularly to Sunday lunch or supper if he is a gentleman. Doctors and solicitors may be invited to garden parties, though never, of course, to lunch or dinner. Anyone engaged in the arts, the stage, trade or commerce, no matter how well connected, cannot be asked to the house at all.[704]

It was Virginia Woolf who, in *Mrs. Dalloway*, painted the most revealing and poignant portrait of a British society woman whose greatest fulfillment comes with her elaborate parties. Mrs. Dalloway is almost too sensitive to the beauty of her surroundings. In effect, she sacrifices herself for the comfort and enjoyment of others:

She made her drawing-room a sort of meeting-place; she had a genius for it. Over and over again he had seen her take some raw youth, twist him, turn him, wake him up; set him going. Infinite numbers of dull people conglomerated round her, of course. But odd unexpected people turned up; an artist sometimes; sometimes a writer; queer fish in that atmosphere. And behind it all was that network of visiting, leaving cards, being kind to people; running about with

bunches of flowers, little presents; So-and-so was going to France—must have
an air cushion; a real drain on her strength; all that interminable traffic that
women of her sort keep up; but she did it genuinely, from a natural instinct.[705]

"Natural instinct"—the mark of a true artist.

V

She masquerades as a Beaux-Arts student, she arms herself with her battery of
brushes; as she sits before her easel, her eye wanders from the white cloth to her
mirror; but the bunch of flowers or the bowl of apples is not going to appear on
the canvas of its own accord. Seated at her desk, turning over vague stories in her
mind, woman enjoys the easy pretense that she is a writer; but she must come to
the actual putting of black marks on white paper, she must give them a meaning
in the eyes of others. Then the cheating is exposed. In order to please, it is
enough to create mirages; but a work of art is not a mirage, it is a solid object; in
order to fashion it, one must know one's business.[706]

Simone de Beauvoir's judgement is a harsh one. Her argument is that until
women take an equal place with men in human society, they will never be
creators of great art. She blames the lack of status on women themselves: their
laziness, their self-absorption, their obsession with the imagery of beauty, of
style, of superficial matters. Where, in the unflattering picture she paints
above, are the babies, the demanding husbands, the boiling pots?

For eons, women have been expected—and, of course, came to expect of
themselves—to neglect the nurturing of their own creative spirits in favour
of their husband and their children. At the same time, critics have blamed
them for not being serious about their work. The male establishment has long
fostered the idea that women could never be great artists, because the status
quo is very much to the male's advantage. Men certainly weren't going to
look after the kids and cook the dinner. Art historian Linda Nochlin theo-
rizes that serious male artists naturally viewed (and perhaps still do) women
as nothing more than dabblers or hobbyists. "For such men, the 'real' work
of women is only that which directly or indirectly serves the family; any
other commitment falls under the rubric of diversion, selfishness, egomania,
or, at the unspoken extreme, castration. The circle is a vicious one, in which
philistinism and frivolity mutually re-enforce each other."[707]

The challenge was to break out of the pernicious men-as-creators,
women-as-procreators mind-set. Slowly but surely, women artists in the 20th

century have done just that. Some chose to turn themselves into highly skilled and dedicated professionals. They flooded into the conservatories, art schools, creative-writing courses, the dance studios, the director's chairs. At last, they were able to join in the apprenticeship of art. Not only were geniuses recognized—previously the only women who could gain a place on the artistic stage—but also those who needed time and encouragement for their talent to blossom.

The visual-art world also opened up to those outside the academy. The folk and ethnic art movements recognized that indigenous creative forms had always existed alongside the Great Masters, and, as is now apparent, were just as important. The best of women's beautifully crafted needlework pictures, woven belts and patchwork have become treasures, fought after by gallery owners, museum curators and folklorists. The experience of a self-taught woman, representing her own life experience in an original manner, had at last become valid.

The primitive artist Ann Harbuz is an example. Ann's parents emigrated to the Canadian Prairies from West Ukraine just months before she was born in July 1908. Her father filed for a homestead near the village of Whitkow, in the northern farm belt of Saskatchewan, and it was there that Ann spent her childhood. To escape a chaotic family situation—her mother had died in childbirth when Ann was 12, and she did not like her stepmother—she married when she was only 16. Although the union produced two sons, it was not a happy marriage, and after 20 years, Ann finally got up enough nerve to walk away. In the late 1940s, she married a second time to Mike Harbuz, a carpenter and cabinet-maker living in North Battleford, Saskatchewan.

Although she had always engaged in crafts—decorating Easter eggs, for example—Ann did not start to paint until 1967 when she was already 59 years old. After that, nothing could stop her. She produced thousands of pieces in a whole variety of media—pen and ink, oil, acrylic—and on any surface she thought suitable, from old vinyl records to birch-bark logs to stretched canvases. Painting after painting reflects the work of women in the Ukrainian community: rock-picking, tending huge vegetable gardens, hauling logs in the winter, milking cows, washing diapers by hand, carrying water from wells. Her own experience is also present: her mother's death in childbirth, her early marriage, her first-hand experience of rearing children.[708] All of this is illustrated in imaginary communities that bustle with life, little villages full of people, animals and houses. The viewer looks down on this strange world as though floating on a cloud.

Ann Harbuz died in 1989, and by that time, her work was being collected by art galleries and private individuals. The debate continues on whether her so-called naïve, primitive work is art or not. Some see it as old-fashioned, old-womanish folk nonsense, but there's no denying her originality, expressed in her wonderful use of colour and her scrutiny of the interior of people's houses and hearts. The writer Jeanette Winterson could have been thinking of Ann Harbuz when she wrote:

It is not necessary to be shut up in one self, to grind through life like an ox at a mill, always treading the same ground. Human beings are capable of powered flight: we can travel across ourselves and find that self multiple and vast. The artist knows this....[709]

Noreen

Noreen Matthews may have been the smallest girl in the class, the shortest, the most petite, but she had boundless ambition. A famous heart surgeon or a research scientist searching for a cure for cancer—as long as it was in medicine, either career would be fine with her. Paradoxically, what she was best at, where her real talent lay, never entered into these grandiose dreams. Music was something she loved, but she thought it sissy stuff, not something you made your name by. Years would go by before she realized how silly a notion this was.

Noreen thinks she may have been influenced by her father, Ross, who was a driven, determined man possibly because he had had to prove himself. He had been sickly as a child, in and out of hospital with respiratory problems. His ongoing illness meant his mother and three siblings babied him, and even when he was a young man, he was still skinny and looked rather peaked.

Ross Matthews went to Malvern Collegiate in Toronto's east end, and there met Noreen's mother, the pretty, vivacious Grace Phillips, who was quite willing to continue the tradition of caring for Ross. They were married in Kew Gardens United Church on April 14, 1938. Grace wasn't sure until the last moment whether her mother would attend the wedding. As an Anglican, Mrs. Phillips didn't approve of her daughter being married in the United Church, and while her background was hardly high society—her husband worked for the railway as a telegrapher—she thought Ross Matthews was not good enough for her daughter.

The war years were hard for the young couple. To Ross's dismay, his history of ill health led to his being rejected by the Canadian Army. He was laid off from several jobs, and money was so tight, he and Grace had to move in with her mother. Finally, though, he found office work at International Waxes Limited, and thereafter thrived. He studied for years for his accountancy exams, and by the time he retired, he was secretary-treasurer of the company.

Grace had worked as a telephone operator and secretary, but had quit as soon as she married. She stayed home and, as Noreen says, "catered to my father." Noreen was born in 1943 and her brother Herbert in 1946. When the Matthewses moved to Scarborough, it didn't take Grace long to become part of the community. Brownie pack leader, home-and-school volunteer, church—she did it all.

Noreen was so petite and cute, everyone made a fuss over her. A favourite maiden aunt liked to take her to the ballet, followed by dinner at the posh Winston's restaurant. Noreen was mesmerized by *Swan Lake* and *The Nutcracker*, and she thinks that's where her love of music might have originated. Although the Matthewses could hardly afford it, she began taking piano lessons when she was only four years old. At her first recital, her teacher had to pick her up and sit her on the stool. Since her legs were so short, her feet couldn't reach the pedals. She went ahead and played the piece nicely, but once she had finished, she was stranded. Thoughtfully considering her dilemma, she finally rolled to the ground like a ball as the stool collapsed on top of her.

The radio was always on in the Matthews house, and Noreen would sing along: "Put another nickel in, in the nickelodeon." There were also the piano lessons. Her mother would drive miles across the city each week to a teacher whom she considered suitable, primarily because he kept telling her how talented Noreen was.

Noreen was bright in school and skipped Grade 6. Since she was born in December, it meant she was a year and half younger than the average kid, and being small for her age, she looked like a little pixie doll. It did not make for a thrilling social life in her first few years of high school. What saved her was her music.

By the time she finished elementary school, she had achieved her Grade 8 at the Royal Conservatory of Music. She finally gave up formally studying the piano because her hands were so small, she did not have the reach necessary for a professional pianist. To this day, though, she plays the piano for her own enjoyment and finds it necessary to achieve a peaceful state of mind.

In her first year at R. H. King, Noreen was assigned the violin, which she happily played in the school orchestra for five years. Her brother, too, was made to take music lessons, and there is a wonderful photograph taken in the mid-1950s of Noreen at the piano, her brother blowing on a trumpet, a cousin on the drums and another playing the violin. (Guitars were not considered appropriate instruments.) Noreen loved rock-and-roll music, although swivel-hips Elvis was strictly out of bounds. Wholesome, gentle-mannered Pat Boone was considered acceptable, and Noreen went to a concert of his at Maple Leaf Gardens.

For the first two years of high school, Noreen was uncomfortable and shy. Her date for Saturday night movies was her mother. She had one friend, and if that girl happened to be away from school, Noreen would panic. Who could she eat lunch with? Who could she walk with from class to class? To be seen alone was a mark of deep disgrace. One classmate she admired for her social éclat was Pat Inglis. One day, Noreen and Pat got talking. "I said, 'How do people like you become so popular?' And she replied, 'Well, you have to learn to really listen a lot, and you have to join things, get involved. Then you meet more people.'" Noreen took the advice to heart, and joined everything going, from the Glee Club to the Classics. Soon her telephone was ringing every night.

Once Noreen switched from being a wallflower to a socialite, boyfriends emerged from the woodwork. In Grade 13, she met her future life partner.

The Matthews had eventually become a two-car family; Grace was the proud owner of a green-and-white Nash Rambler. After Noreen turned 16 and got her driver's licence, she was allowed to borrow the car if her mother weren't using it. One day in the fall of 1961, there was early-morning orchestra practice at R. H. King. Noreen was told she could have the car if she promised to be back at one. When, at 11:40, Noreen went out to get the Nash, someone had parked a great, big, maroon Oldsmobile lengthwise behind it. She found out it was owned by a guy called Leslie Coombs. Noreen ran back to the school and found Les in the cafeteria, eating a sandwich. Noreen asked if he would please move his car. "I'm afraid not," he nonchalantly replied. "I have wrestling practice." Noreen had no choice but to spend the next three-quarters of an hour gently nudging the Nash back and forth until it finally circumvented the Oldsmobile.

What she didn't know was that a whole gaggle of guys was at the school window, watching her and laughing their heads off. It was Les Coombs, notifying Noreen he had taken notice of her. Shortly after, he pretended to break a date—in fact, it was with his cousin—to take Noreen bowling. Noreen went gaga over him. He was, after all, a star wrestler, his name mentioned on the PA system all the time. As for Les, he proudly admits he has dated only one girl in his life: Noreen.

When Les was presented to the Matthewses, he did not make a great impression. He was shy, slouched a lot and the only good thing Noreen could think to say about him was that he was known as Lester Lovely. "Because he was a wrestler, Mom," said Noreen. Grace Matthews was hardly

bowled over, but when she learned he was the son of Queenie Coombs, she
thought he must be a nice boy.

Everybody in the Home and School Association adored Queenie. She had
a great sense of humour and spoke with a wonderful Irish brogue. The
Coombses had arrived from Dublin in 1957. A family clothing business had
gone bust, and economic conditions were so difficult, the Coombses decided,
even though they were in their late forties, that they would have to emigrate.
Les's father got a job right away with an organization that raised funds for
various churches—with his gift of the gab he was great at it—but it meant he
crisscrossed Canada several times a year. While he was away, Les got to drive
his Oldsmobile.

It was rather unfortunate that Noreen's and Les's great romance had to
happen during their last year of high school. He wasn't the best student
anyway, and he became so distracted, he flunked and had to repeat Grade
13. Noreen's grades also plummeted, which proved disastrous for her big
ambition.

Ever since she could remember, she had wanted to go into medicine. "A
doctor had prestige, a doctor had power, a doctor had wealth—everything I
wanted at that point. I would have big words that I could throw around and
impress people with. When you're as short as I am, you have to admit it's the
little person in control." The problem was that to get into pre-medicine, a
student needed excellent grades in a full slate of math and sciences. Noreen's
best subjects were in the arts, particularly music; physics and chemistry were a
struggle for her. She had managed to keep her average high, but in Grade 13,
she failed both subjects, and ended up with only 67 percent. It was too low to
get into a science course, but high enough for admittance to the bachelor of
arts program at the newly formed York University. Noreen decided to take
that route. "I was still thinking science and medicine down the road, but I had
to get this arts degree in order to improve my chances of getting in."

Her year at York turned out to be a disaster. She had just turned 17, and
she believes she was too young. She never got into the swing of studying. For
one thing, her parents expected her to be home an hour after her classes
ended. "I don't think I set foot inside the library the whole year," she admits.
The result was predictable: she failed two out of five subjects and was not
allowed to return the following year.

That September, she began a secretarial course at a business college. Fortunately for her, she was hired as a technician at the Banting & Best Department

of Medical Research at the University of Toronto, a step closer, she thought, to her dream of wearing a white coat. She started out sterilizing instruments, but she proved to be so capable, she was soon assisting the doctors—who, for the most part, were specialists doing a year's research work—perform their experiments, mainly on cats. "I was right in there. I was in my glory." Noreen was so enthusiastic, her father had to tell her that cat guts was not an appropriate topic of conversation at the dinner table. After a year, however, the head of the lab informed her that funding for the program had been cut and she no longer had a job. He suggested she take a medical-technology course, and that seemed to her to be right up her alley.

For the next seven years, Noreen worked at St. Michael's Hospital, first as a student and then as a registered medical technologist. She enjoyed the job as long as she didn't have to deal with patients. "In hematology, you had to take blood. I would go to pick up a tube and would think, 'Oh, the patient must love this.' My hands were shaking. I was so nervous, I couldn't eat breakfast. Every morning, I was sick." Why she continued to want to be a doctor remains a mystery, but her dream was still intact. She thought about applying to dentistry, with the idea of swinging into medicine, and she investigated a university in New Mexico that admitted just about anybody with the right amount of money into their medical program. For one reason or another, mostly to do with Les, these schemes never became a reality.

Meanwhile, music remained the great balm of her life. She had always studied classical music, which didn't exactly make her the life of the party. When her parents gave her a new piano for her 21st birthday, along with Bach and Beethoven she began practising tunes with one hand, chords with the other. Songs like "Hey Good Lookin'" and "Angel Eyes" became part of her repertoire, and her social life blossomed. In the mid-'70s, the Matthewses' house was burnt down by arsonists. Her parents told her that, sadly, there wasn't enough insurance money left over to replace the piano. Noreen pleaded with her father to allow her to purchase another on the installment plan. Buying on credit was one thing Ross Matthews totally disapproved of, but she was so insistent, he finally agreed.

By this time, she had also developed a passion for choral music. It was an interest that would change her life. In the fall of 1966, she met a friend of Queenie Coombs who told her about a wonderful, new experience he was having. He sang for the famous Toronto Mendelssohn Choir. A superb new conductor, Elmer Iseler, had been appointed two years before, and he was breathing new life into what had become a beloved, but rather decrepit, institution. Noreen had sang in church choirs and R. H. King's Glee Club, and the Mendelssohn sounded very appealing.

Interested singers joined in three rehearsals and then auditioned. Noreen found it difficult. "I had never sung in eight parts before. I was an alto, but sometimes I was called a contralto. And here was this conductor, stamping his feet, ranting and raving and speaking in a foreign language. 'Alti at B,' he'd say, or, 'Tutti at C.'" When it was Noreen's turn to try out, she had not thought to bring music. Iseler played several songs on the piano that she didn't know and finally told her to sing a scale. "If you want to come back, yes, do it. Come back," he said. Remembers Noreen, "Elmer had the most amazing sparkling eyes that just zeroed in on you. He had freckles and reddish hair and I thought, 'Oh, aren't you cute.'" She came to worship the conductor. "I developed a real crush on that man. He was able to look around at all 150 people and really make you think he was looking at you, that you were important. He'd say, 'You're all so wonderful, you're all so musical.' I'd think to myself, 'Elmer Iseler thinks I'm musical, so I guess I am.'"

Noreen loved singing with the Mendelssohn Choir and, on occasion, she was invited to join the Festival Singers, a professional choir led by Iseler. Yet by 1968, she realized there was something wrong with her voice. She would open her mouth and this "God-awful" sound would come out. Iseler told her she could no longer be part of the choir. He suggested she take singing lessons, something she had never done before in her life.

The teacher quickly discovered what was wrong. "I was straining and pushing and was totally in my throat. If I had continued to sing like that, I would have ended up with nodules on my vocal chords. I spent a year just bringing the sound forward." Noreen began working towards an ARTC (Associate Royal Conservative Toronto) certificate in voice, which she obtained in 1982. She missed choral singing, though, and her teacher suggested that, although she felt Noreen still wasn't ready to return to the Mendelssohn, she could join another group, the Orpheus Choir. Noreen not only sang with that choir for over 15 years but took on many volunteer jobs. "I ended up virtually running the choir. I was the librarian and then the president. I hired conductors. I did everything." She only bowed out when she felt she was ready for the Mendelssohn once again.

During this time, Noreen was dating Les Coombs, and in 1967, they finally got married in a candlelight service at Kew Beach United Church, where Noreen's parents' wedding had taken place 29 years before. The reception was held at Scarboro Golf and Country Club. Noreen's father said he'd pay for the affair as long as there was no alcohol, so fruit punch was served instead.

After Grade 13, Les had obtained a job with Excelsior Life Insurance, intending to become an underwriter. He liked it at first, but many of his fellow employees were senior to him and the company wasn't expanding. Les realized he had hit a dead end and began thinking of another career. In his younger years, he had been involved with the Scouting movement and had become a leader, so it seemed only logical to go to teacher's college. "It was the first positive situation I had ever had by way of education," he says. Afterwards, he had no trouble finding a job with the Scarborough Board of Education, and he has been there ever since. By everyone's account, he is a superb elementary-school teacher.

Les discovered the Scarborough Board of Education was offering music-specialist courses in the summer, and he urged Noreen to sign up so she, too, could become a teacher. By that time, her medical-technologist job was becoming tedious; her dream of medical school was finally fading. She realized at last that her great talent lay in her music, and teaching might give it full expression.

Noreen did not enjoy her year at teacher's college. By that time, high marks were required to get a job, and she thought there was a lot of game-playing, "sucking up" to this instructor or that. Her music-specialist courses, which she took for two summers, appealed to her far more, and in fact, 30 years later, she would teach these same summer courses to aspiring teachers.

In the fall of 1970, Noreen began teaching at Vradenburg Junior Public School in Scarborough. Although she had a regular class, she also taught instrumental music. "I stayed one lesson ahead of the kids. The consultant would come in and show me how to blow into a flute, and the next day I'd teach the students." Most exciting for her, she organized a school choir.

Both Les and Noreen realized that, to get ahead in their profession, they would need university degrees. Through extension programs, they each took two courses in the winter and three in the summer. Les graduated with a Bachelor of Arts degree from York University in 1977. Noreen worked for two years on a Bachelor of Music degree at the University of Toronto, but then the extension program was closed down. Noreen was furious, but she realized she had to continue working towards some kind of degree. "I decided on sociology. I took sociology of everything going: sociology of education, sociology of religion, even sociology of death." In 1974, she was awarded a Bachelor of Arts degree with a major in sociology and a minor in music.

Early in their marriage, the Coombses had decided they didn't want children. Les worried that it was too much responsibility and Noreen was busy with her musical pursuits. "It was a purely selfish thing with me," she admits. Unexpectedly at age 34, she became pregnant. Brian was born in 1977, and, because Les and Noreen didn't want to raise him as an only child, they had a second son Alan in 1980. "I had an emotional tug with those kids that I had never experienced before and never dreamed would happen. You can't explain it. Nobody can prepare you for it."

When the children arrived, Les insisted Noreen give up teaching, although she continued to work several hours a week as a musical consultant for the Scarborough Board. By the end of four years, she knew that for her own good, she had to go back full time. "But I truly had to force myself. I had grown that close to the kids." She became what is called a vocal music itinerant, travelling from school to school, sometimes as many as six a day. Her job was to demonstrate how to teach music to the classroom teacher, which is done primarily by conducting the class. "Had I not had very positive reinforcement in music all through my life, I would have been squelched," says Noreen. "I'm very conscious when I'm teaching kids that they must never have a negative experience."

After 15 years on the job, Noreen eventually grew tired of the travelling and thought she was getting a little stale. "The same songs kept popping up," she says. In January 1998, she returned to the classroom at Wolburn Junior High, where she teaches Grade 6 English and other core subjects. She is still heavily involved in music, though, teaching singing and instrumental music for the entire school. She says that right now, it's the perfect combination. "I've been exposed to all these fresh, new ideas. Peter Pan and me, we have a lot in common."

It has not only been in the classroom where Noreen has made her mark in instilling a love of music in children. For over 20 years, she has worked with the Scarborough Youth Choir and is currently its co-conductor.

In 1987, Noreen reauditioned for the Mendelssohn Choir and was accepted. "It was something I personally had to do, to see if I was good enough," she says. She was pleased that, after 20 years, her great hero Elmer Iseler remembered her and welcomed her back. Music now consumes a large part of her life. "It amazes me," says her mother, "that she will be at a Scarborough Youth Choir at four, conduct for two and a half hours, and still make it to Roy Thomson Hall downtown for a Mendelssohn rehearsal." Noreen adds, "Look at December and look at the number of *Messiahs* we perform. It totally destroys your social life. It's a real family commitment. Les had to be prepared to do a lot of babysitting and running the boys around."

On the odd night when she has time to relax at home, she'll tune into *ER* or *Chicago Hope* or some other medical drama on television. It still gives her a thrill to see those white coats rushing about. "It's interesting that what was my hobby has become my profession and what I wanted my profession to be has become my hobby."

Noreen knows she is a fine choral singer but not a great soloist. On a scale of one to ten, she rates her singing voice as a seven, the Luciano Pavarottis and Maureen Forresters of the world being nines and tens. She realizes that's far better than the vast majority of people. Singing at the wedding of the daughter of an old school chum, it occurred to her that her grandiose high-school dreams have been displaced by something more satisfying: her very real musical talent.

Musicians

Mademoiselle Diderot ... is one of the finest harpsichord-players in Paris, and, for a lady, possessed of an uncommon portion of knowledge in modulation.

Charles Burney, 1771

Men compose symphonies, women compose babies.

Time magazine, January 10, 1975

The year before we started high school, Elvis Presley exploded onto the North American music scene. By the time we were in Grade 9, the "Hound Dog"/"Don't Be Cruel" single had sold three million copies. We girls were such a bunch of goody-goodies as we watched him on the Milton Berle or Ed Sullivan shows, we were as shocked as our parents. Those heavy, sensuous lips, sultry eyes, gyrating hips—heavens! Soon, though, we came to love his beat, country blended with blues, loved dancing to "Heartbreak Hotel" or "Love Me Tender." However, there was something about him that frightened us, probably because he was everything we weren't. A boy from the dirt-poor hill country of northeast Mississippi, he was uninterested in school, alienated, sullen and entirely original.

Others were less threatening, and maybe that's why we liked their music so much. Little Richard's "Tutti Frutti," Chuck Berry's "Maybellene" and Bill Haley's "Shake Rattle and Roll" had us jiggling, as the principal said, as though we were in the jungle. Swooning over Paul Anka's "You Are My Destiny" was particularly delicious, because he was one of our own—born in Ottawa in 1941. He was too clean-cut and fresh-faced for my liking. I preferred the more dangerous Everly Brothers crooning "Bye-Bye Love."

We had no idea, of course, that this music was signalling the onslaught of the rebellious '60s. Neither did we realize that, paradoxically, the Presleys, the Haleys and the Ankas were a direct reflection of the restrictive 1950s. There was not a female singer among them. Connie Francis came the closest to joining the club, but she didn't appear on the scene until the decade was winding down. Our music world, the beat we danced to in the gym Friday nights, was an entirely masculine phenomenon. We knew music was our life blood—we sang in choirs, played musical instruments, danced until our loafers were worn out. That girls could be the originators, the creators of any type of music never entered our heads.

I

Prince Hector is bringing his bride, Andromache of Thebes, home to Troy. The news is heralded and the entire population gathers along the route of entry into the city. Sappho paints the scene beautifully:

> the sweet-sounding pipe and lyre were mingled
> and the sound of castanets, and maidens
> sang clearly a holy song, and a marvellous echo
> reached the sky[710]

Not only does the poet describe the playing of music but her lyrics would have been sung by musicians themselves. In ancient Greece, poetry was composed not to be read but to be heard, a branch not of literature but of music, often with religious connotations. The gods and goddesses were honoured at their festivals with lyrical poetry in the form of choral chants, almost exclusively sung by women. Sappho led one such chorus on the island of Lesbos towards the end of the seventh century. Under the patronage of Aphrodite, it consisted of young girls and had a educational function, guiding them into adulthood.

There are scores of vase paintings depicting female choruses. One of the most interesting is drawn on a wine vessel from about 460 BC. Around the inside surface is painted a graceful musical scene. At the top is an altar on which a fire is enthusiastically burning. Obviously a sacrifice of some kind is in progress. A woman on the left, facing the flames, plays her *aulos* or reed flute. The remaining seven, holding hands and singing, dance in a circle. As historian François Lissarrague points out, the very word *choros* had layers of meaning for ancient Greeks. It's associated with the verb *chairein*, meaning to rejoice, with the noun *chôros*, a circular space, and with *cheir*, or hand.[711] This scene is a typical joyful festival of women musicians singing and dancing for the pleasure of the gods.

Music played a momentous role in the lives of women of antiquity. The rites of passage for young girls and their ensuing marriages almost always included female choruses, "dancing a lovely dance to the sound of lyres."[712] Women as well as men were well practised in funeral dirges. At the end of Homer's *Iliad,* when Hector has been killed by the Athenians, his funeral is one loud, musical lament:

> They laid the body of Hector in his bed,
> and brought in minstrels, men to lead the dirge.
> While these wailed out, the women answered, moaning.[713]

If Greek society was permeated with music, it was female personae who inspired it. Nine goddesses, a choir of virgin sisters called Muses, were the patrons of artistic creation. Indeed the word music derives from the Greek *mousikë,* the art of the Muses. Poets couldn't stop writing about the Muses. They were depicted on Mount Olympus, singing at the banquet table of the gods. They performed at the wedding of Harmonia and Thetis. They sang lamentations at the funerals of great heroes. Like all gods, they could turn nasty, especially if their talents were challenged. When Thamyris said he could sing better than they could, they rendered him blind and songless. They defeated the Sirens in a contest and deprived them of their wings. As the scholar Robert E. Bell writes, "One did not foolishly match artistic talents with those of the nine sisters."[714]

Obviously, there were great women musicians in antiquity, yet off-key notes sound. In vase paintings depicting musical occasions, men are often seen on stage, performing in front of judges. Winged Nike hovers nearby with her victory wreath. Women are almost always portrayed indoors, playing the flute or lyre, singing or dancing, and always for other women. Eventually, this dichotomy would establish men as professionals, women as amateurs: men the great musicians, women the tinklers, the listeners, the inspiration.

II

Convents in the Middle Ages were hotbeds of talented women composers. Much of their work has been lost to posterity, but enough exists to reveal the rich and original musicality of these women religious.

Kassia, born in about 810, is the most accomplished woman writer of hymns from the Greek Byzantine Empire. She was born to a wealthy Constantinople family connected to the Imperial court. Like other aristocratic young girls, she received private tutoring in her home and was influenced by classical Greek culture. When she came of age, she participated in the bride-show of Theophilos, emperor from 830–842. Historian Edward Gibbon writes that as Theophilos was walking between the two lines of beauties, his eye was caught by the charms of Kassia. Indulging in playful small talk, the prince observed that women, the descendants of Eve, had been the cause of much evil. Kassia supposedly shot back, "And surely, Sir, they have likewise been the occasion of much good [referring to the Virgin Mary]." The Imperial lover was apparently put off by this clever repartee and turned his back on her in disgust.[715]

Realizing no man would appreciate her quick wit, Kassia decided to devote her life to God. In 843, she founded her own monastery, named after her, situated on the seventh hill of Constantinople. There she composed her great hymns and sacred poems, although she also wrote secular epigrams and verse. Her most famous musical composition, which is still sung today, is the hymn about Mary Magdalene, "The Fallen Woman."

Forty-nine liturgical chants are attributed to Kassia. She probably wrote many more, but it is sometimes hard to trace her authorship. The 12th-century historian Theodoros Prodromos, who wrote commentaries on most famous church musicians and music, felt the composer of a major hymn for Holy Saturday should not be female, and therefore gave credit for Kassia's work to another hymnographer, Kosmas, Bishop of Maiouma in Phoenicia.[716] In addition, other male composers, not nearly as talented or original as Kassia, felt free to alter her work over the years.

For Hildegard of Bingen, music was an expression of her mystical experiences and her connection with the Almighty. Her songs, she said, "are revealed to me and give musical forms to divine mysteries." Between 1151 and 1158, she collected 77 of these plainchants into a cycle she called *Symphonia armonie celestium revelactionum* (*Symphony of the Harmony of Heavenly Revelations*). As the title of the work implies, Hildegard's music reflects her predominant belief that the universe is a symmetrical whole and this harmony is revealed through music. As one critic puts it, her songs "contain some of the most unusual, subtle and exciting poetry of the twelfth century."[717] Many were written to honour women, in particular the Virgin Mary and St. Ursula. They were sung within her own convent—all the sisters had trained singing voices—at daily offices or prayers and during mass. It was Hildegard's way of inviting her nuns into the private world of her visions.

One of her most unique pieces, the opera *Ordo Virtutum* (*Play of Virtues*), is the earliest morality play set entirely to music known in the Western world. It is a song-play with roles for 18 females—the Virtues, their Queen, Humility, and the Soul—and a few men, presumably played by friars. Its plot revolves around the Virtues coming to the aid of "a sick and sinning soul" who becomes whole again.

What is striking about Hildegard is how music is entwined through her spiritual life and her work. In the last vision outlined in her book *Scivias*, she so vividly describes heavenly music, one can almost hear it:

Thereupon the sky got very bright, and I heard all the previously mentioned virtues sing in a wondrous manner to various types of music. They persisted strongly in the way of truth as they sang praises of the city of celestial joy. And they persisted in exhorting and encouraging themselves so that they might fight back the snares of the devil and help people gain salvation.[718]

Outside the convent walls, musical expression was considered a dangerous thing, especially in the hands of women. Salome, who, through her beguiling songs and dances, managed to persuade a reluctant King Herod to present her with the head of John the Baptist, was an image that stuck in the craw of Church fathers. The job of a wandering minstrel, a dancer or musician of any sorts was anathema to medieval women. Nevertheless, *trobairitz* or female troubadours did exist. They were usually educated, highly skilled members of the aristocracy who could not suppress their feelings about courtly love any more than the famous male troubadours could. It's interesting to compare the musical writings of Kassia with those of Comtessa de Dia, a *trobairitz* from Catalonia. Kassia's "The Fallen Woman" is full of religious fervor, guilt and repentance. The Comtessa's song, written in the 12th century, is heavy with licentiousness. Interestingly, though, both are sensuous.

> Handsome friend, charming and kind,
> when shall I have you in my power?
> If only I could lie beside you for an hour
> and embrace you lovingly
> know this, that'd give almost anything
> to have you in my husband's place,
> but only under the condition
> that you were to do my bidding.[719]

III

During the early modern period, women of the middle and upper echelons of society were expected to be skilled musicians. As one writer noted, "Every fine young lady, whether or not she has talent, must learn to play the piano or sing ... it is the fashion."[720] Accomplished women read music, danced well and could play at least one musical instrument. Parlour concerts with flutes, harps, dulcimers and bowed instruments became popular.

Engravings of the period are full of female harpsichord or lute players, but they often looked wan, as though they were recuperating from some illness. Music supposedly soothed the passions of the hysterical female, whose humours were aroused on account of her wandering womb. Musicians listened when medical authorities insisted there was a direct connection between the rhythm and tempo of music and the strength of the pulse.[721] The perfectly balanced, four-part harmony that characterized 16th-century music was designed to soothe the savage beast in both men and women.

Exceptional musical talent in women was celebrated. Susanna Perwick (1637–1661), for example, was the daughter of the proprietors of a fashionable school for girls in Hackney, a suburb of London. Early on, she was given lessons by the school's teachers, many of whom were musical luminaries. She quickly showed talent, not only for playing the violin, lute and harpsichord but for composing extemporary variations on a given theme. She was such a prodigy that ambassadors, foreign visitors and the aristocracy took to frequenting Hackney. That she had a sweet, round face and could converse like a *salonnière* was an added bonus. Unfortunately, in 1661, Susanna came down with a raging fever and died at age 24. Her epitaph reads:

> Here Beauties, Odours Musicks Lie
> To shew that such rare things can die ...
> From Heav'n she came with Melodies
> And back again to Heav'n she flies.[722]

Music-making was not confined to the domestic scene. Houses of religion were incubators for the most extraordinary musical talent. The San Vito convent at Ferrara, Italy, for example, was home to a magnificent ensemble of 23 musicians, nuns who not only sang but played a wide variety of musical instruments, wind instruments of all kinds, cornetti and trombones. In his rhetorical dialogue *Il Desiderio,* Hercole Bottrigari leaves this first-hand description of one such concert.

They all enter quietly and approach the table without making the least noise and place themselves in their proper place, and some sit, who must do so in order to use their instruments, and others remain standing. Finally the Maestra of the concert sits down at one end of the table and with a long, slender and well-polished wand (which was placed there ready for her, because I saw it), and when all the other sisters clearly are ready, gives them without noise several signs to begin and then continues by beating the measure of the time that they must obey in singing and playing.[723]

The Maestra referred to was Raphaela Aleotta (c. 1574–1646), the daughter of a famous musical family who trained the ensemble and conducted them. She was also a composer of note. She published a book of motets in 1593 and may have authored others under a different name. What fascinated Bottrigari about the San Vito musicians was that there was not a single male involved, either in their training or performances. "How could they possibly be human, these singing angels?" he asked.

You would certainly think you were either dreaming or seeing one of those imagined incantations of the Sorceress Alcina; or perhaps one of those German dolls which by means of tempered steel strings move along the table playing instruments which have been made by their ingenious fabricators.[724]

In the 17th century, professional opportunities for female musicians abounded. Actresses, who also sang and danced, were important members of the famous *commedia dell'arte* troupes. A few female instrumentalists were hired at Italian courts. Probably the most famous of the female virtuosi, though, were the women who made up the *concerto delle donne* (women's ensemble), which was established by Duke Alfonso II d'Este at Ferrara.

Their job was to sing at the court's chamber-music concerts and with practices, they were required to work anywhere from two to six hours a day. They memorized most of their repertoire, but they could also read polyphonic music, and each played a musical instrument. Members of the *concerto delle donne* were all given excellent salaries, not to mention fringe benefits. One of the best known, Laura Peverara, received a dowry, an apartment in the ducal palace and stipends for her mother and husband.[725]

The great blossoming of opera in the 17th and 18th centuries brought fame and fortune to female soloists. Prior to that, women's roles had been sung by castrati, men who had been made eunuchs, usually at a young age. Their female replacements became great divas, international stars who travelled from London to St. Petersburg, often with a retinue. In 1723, the Italian soprano Faustina Bordoni earned £2,500 for a season, and her fellow artist Francesa Cuzzoni, £2,000, an enormous amount of money in those days.[726]

Adored by the public almost as much were those solo instrumentalists who were part of the newly popular subscription concerts. Many instruments, such as brass, percussion, oboe and bassoon, were considered unladylike and therefore unsuitable for women, but among those deemed appropriate—the harp, the violin, the harpsichord and later, the piano—women were *artistes* of the highest order. Elisabeth-Claude Jacquet de la Guerre (c. 1668–1729) emerged as one of the *première solo virtuosa* of the period. Musicologist Sir John Hawkins, writing in 1776, described her thus:

She ... was ... instructed in the practise of the harpsichord and the art of composition by her father. She was a fine performer, and would sing and accompany herself with so rich and exquisite a flow of harmony as captivated all that heard her. She was also an excellent composer, and, in short, possessed such a degree of skill, as well in the science as the practice of music, that few of her sex have equalled her. An opera of her composition, entitled Céphale et Procris, was represented in the Royal Academy of Paris in 1694 and is extant in print.[727]

In 1691, Jacquet de La Guerre wrote a kind of opera with singing and dancing called *Les Jeux à l'honneur de la victoire*. The following portion of the dedication, written by the composer for Louis XIV, gives an insight into the life of an aristocratic musician:

From the most tender age (this memory will be eternally precious to me), presented to your illustrious court, where I have had the honor to be for several years, I learned, Sire, to consecrate to you all of my waking hours. You deigned at that time to accept the first fruits of my gifts, and it has pleased you to receive several further productions. But these particular marks of my zeal did not suffice for me, and I welcome the happy opportunity to be able to make a public [offering]. That is what led me to write this ballet for the theatre. It is not just today [but earlier] that women have written excellent pieces of poetry, which have had great success. But until now, none has tried to set a whole opera to music; and I take this advantage from my enterprise: that the more extraordinary it is, the

more worthy of you, Sire, and the more it justified the liberty that I take in offering you this work.[728]

In the early modern period, there was a surprisingly large number of female
composers, many producing wonderful work, and yet there were dark,
misogynist forces working against them. Academic musical education was
becoming a male enclave.

Beginning in the 15th century, the *cappella* became an important element
of the musical scene. The *cappella* was made up of singers hired by the court
or Church to create and perform music for important ceremonial and civic
occasions, church services or processions. A youngster who was fortunate
enough to be chosen for the *cappella* was often sent away to a university under
his patron's sponsorship, thereby receiving a first-class liberal education. He
not only learned to sing and play musical instruments but he studied the
foundations of music.[729] It was an important apprenticeship for anyone aspiring to be a composer, and it was totally closed to young female musicians, no
matter if they "sang like angels and played like nymphs." This discrimination
would have dire consequences.

IV

Few periods were more barren for creative female musicians than the 19th
century, the age of symphonic music. Among the giants—Beethoven, Schu-
bert, Mendelssohn, Brahms, Berlioz, Franck, Tchaikovsky—not one
woman's name appears. What was termed pure or absolute music seemed
beyond the grasp of female composers. Many reasons have been expounded
for this sad state of affairs. A woman was expected to sing and play the piano
beautifully, but only in her own parlour. The intricacies of piano concertos
or requiems were considered far beyond her compositional skill. Some musical academies in Europe and North America admitted women, but their
courses always led to performance and teaching, never to composition.
Moreover, as well as the practical limitations of a house-bound female
restricted by the Puritanism and misogyny of her age, there was also the attitude of women themselves. Absolute music was perhaps too impersonal, too
intangible, to have much meaning in their lives. But why?

This was the era of the artist-genius who could transcend the workaday
world and glimpse "the language of the Gods," and this romantic hero was
always male, his muse always female. As the scholar Marcia J. Citron puts it,

"Transcendent implies not only going beyond but also moving toward the ultimate, toward the perfect, toward God, the embodiment of transcendence and perfection. God the creator is the model for man the creator, who is a likeness of God. As exclusive bearer of God's image, only man is validated as a creator, not woman."[730] As the century progressed, women also had to contend with Darwinism, which, in the eyes of some exponents, placed female creativity lower down the evolutionary ladder than the male variety. No wonder egos large and confident enough to create absolute music were rare among female musicians.

This didn't mean women didn't create music at all during the Victorian era. North American magazines were full of their compositions, although there were more by men. Between 1829 and 1832, Mrs. Philip Millard had works published in *Albion, Godey's,* the *Boston Pearl* and the *New York Mirror.* One of her songs, "Alice Grey," was a smash hit.[731] Ballads, songs, duets, hymns accompanied by piano, flute or violin, and dances—polkas, mazurkas, quicksteps and, most important, waltzes—were published in magazines, and often as broadsheets afterwards. They were designed as home entertainment exactly suited for the angel by the hearth. It was graceful and genteel music, replete with love songs—"When Day is Going," "One Kindly Word Before We Part," "Soft Wind that Sigheth"—but never ostentatious, a reflection of how women were expected to conduct themselves. None of this music was terribly demanding. As musical scholar Bonny H. Miller writes, "Although skillfully written melodies abound, the learned areas of counterpoint, instrumentation, and complex forms—considered unfeminine because they displayed musical erudition—were avoided."[732]

Although it was considered de rigueur for girls to be thoroughly trained in singing and playing musical instruments—it was even thought to enhance their marriage prospects—mature women were not to take music seriously. Fathers and husbands forbade even the most talented from playing in public, publishing their work or even taking money for teaching, all of which were felt to deflate the breadwinner's ego.

The few professional female performers were obsessed with their reputations. They had to be seen to be proper ladies at all times. They insisted on being called Mrs. whether they were married or not, and they always had a male manager by their side who signed contracts and did the banking. Despite these efforts, the stigma of being a music professional remained, dark and indelible. Just before her debut, the famous American opera singer Clara

Louise Kellogg (1842–1916) gathered all her friends together. She was going on stage, she said, and if they never spoke to her again, she would understand and forgive them. Years later, a protégée of Kellogg's, Emma Abbott, refused on moral grounds to sing the role of the courtesan Violetta Valéry in Verdi's *La Traviata*, thereby ending her European career.[733]

Even the great pianist Clara Schumann (1819–96) believed her creativity as a composer was restricted by her sex. She was born in Leipzig to Marianne Tromlitz Wieck, a pianist and singer, and Friedrich Wieck, a renowned music scholar. Under her father's guidance, Clara received a superb musical education. He taught her piano, and she also studied theory, harmony, counterpoint and fugue, composition, orchestration and voice with the most illustrious teachers in Leipzig, Dresden and Berlin. At age nine, she made her debut at the Leipzig Gewandhaus, launching a brilliant career as a concert pianist that would last almost 60 years. In 1828, she met the composer Robert Schumann, nine years older than she. A friendship gradually blossomed into love, but even in the flush of romance, Clara realized her music could not play a secondary role her life. In 1837, she wrote to Schumann:

One thing I must say to you, I cannot be yours until circumstances have entirely altered. I do not want horses or diamonds, I am happy in possessing you, but I wish to lead a life free from care, and I see that I shall be unhappy if I cannot always work at my art and that I cannot do if we have to worry over our daily bread.[733a]

After they won a bitter lawsuit launched by Clara's father, who did not approve of the match, the Schumanns married in 1840. During their 14 years together, they attempted to combine Robert's work as a composer and Clara's career as a concert pianist. The problem was that she kept having babies, and her household duties piled up, prohibiting her touring. Nonetheless, her life with Robert Schumann was artistically rich with an exchange of literary and musical ideas. Thanks to his encouragement, she, too, began to compose. Her first group of songs was written as a Christmas present for her husband.

For years, Robert suffered from mental instability, and in 1854, he suffered a final breakdown. He was hospitalized at a sanitarium near Bonn where, two years later, he died. Clara was pregnant with her eighth child at the time. Nevertheless, she set out on the first of many concert tours. She had a large family to provide for—the children were sent to various boarding schools—but more than that, she had an intense need for musical self-expression.

Clara Schumann's compositional oeuvre consists of 70 pieces: songs, choral works, a concerto for piano and orchestra, chamber music with piano and short piano works. All were written with her husband's encouragement and before his death. Yet she was ambivalent about her creative ability. In November 1839, she confided to her diary: "I once thought that I possessed creative talent, but I have given up this idea; a woman must not desire to compose—not one has been able to do it, and why should I expect to? It would be arrogance, though indeed, my father led me into it in earlier days."[734] Thereafter she called herself an interpreter of music first and a composer second, constantly comparing her work with that of her husband and her devoted, lifelong friend Johannes Brahms.

Robert Schumann succinctly summed up not only Clara's dilemma but that of many talented female musicians of the Victorian era. He wrote in their joint diary of 1843:

Clara has written a series of small pieces, which show a musical and tender ingenuity such as she has never attained before. But to have children, and a husband who is always living in the realms of imagination, do not go together with composing. She cannot work at it regularly, and I am often disturbed to think how many profound ideas are lost because she cannot work them out.[735]

V

In the wake of the first wave of feminism, women musicians began to flourish. From 1870 to 1910, the number of females working in music in the United States grew from three percent to 29 percent of the total, and the number of women teachers increased phenomenally, from 41 percent to 81 percent.[736] In 1893, the Boston Symphony Orchestra performed Margaret Ruthven Lang's *Dramatic Overture, Op. 10*, the first time a major American orchestra had played a work by a woman. Amy Cheney's *Gaelic Symphony, Op. 32,* followed in 1897, an important benchmark, since it was the first full symphony by an American woman played anywhere. In Britain, the strong-willed Ethel Smyth (1858–1944) had her opera *The Wreckers* premiered in 1906. Music critic John Fuller Maitland wrote of it, "It is difficult to point to a work of any nationality since Wagner that has a more direct appeal to the emotions, or that is more skillfully planned and carried out."[737]

Yet by 1920, a powerful backlash had set in that would tumble women professionals back into the dark ages. Suddenly romanticism, the musical

heritage on which most female musicians in the United States and Europe
had built their work, was considered effeminate, sissified, weak. In 1919, a
prominent male critic pronounced a recital of music by American composers
as "Soft, mushy stuff most of them were, painfully devoid of virility, strength
and originality."[738] It suddenly became imperative that music be snatched
from the clutches of meddlesome females. As composer-critic Deems Taylor
put it, "Women have undertaken to be the moral guardians of the race ...
their predominance in our musical life aggravates our already exaggerated
tendency to demand that art be edifying."[739]

Male music teachers, who had felt particularly threatened by the onslaught
of women in "their" field, grabbed hold of the effeminacy issue like a life raft.
In 1918, an article in the *Music Supervisors*, a journal published by the Music
Teachers National Association, pointed out how music was quintessentially
male because:

1. All the great *composers* were *men*.
2. The great Symphony Orchestras of the world are composed of *men players*
   and are conducted by *men*....
3. Many *churches* in the larger cities have their music supplied by choirs of *men*
   and *boys* under a *male organist and director*.
4. The *men* who are playing and singing on the Concert stage and in Grand
   Opera have to be and are men of splendid physique and considerable intellectual attainment. They are the *physical equals* of the best football and baseball players.[740]

No wonder women musicians began to leave teaching in droves.
Modernism, the movement that replaced romanticism after 1918, was also
openly hostile to female musicians. As scholar Catherine Parsons Smith writes,
"Antiwoman attitudes achieved or re-established their cultural hegemony,
effectively suppressing the work of women as composers of art music, shutting them out of the modernist movement, or silencing them completely. At
the same time, hostility toward women stimulated and enabled contemporary
male composers."[741] If there were a nemesis in all of this, it was that women
were so alienated by the blatant, cold misogyny of this new form, they also
abandoned the concert halls that they, far more than men, had frequented.

Women professional musicians fought against outright discrimination as
best they could. Since most large orchestras still excluded female players
(except harpists), women set up their own instrumental groups. They banded

together to play popular and light classical pieces, often in the lobbies of hotels or in posh restaurants. This might have made them a little money, but it was not always very satisfying.

In an attempt to provide themselves with some challenging work, many female graduates of music schools in the 1920s and '30s established their own orchestras with a full complement of 80 or so players, dedicated to performing strictly symphonic music. Los Angeles, Portland, Boston, New York, Cleveland, Chicago, Pittsburgh, St. Louis, Minneapolis, Detroit, Montreal and Toronto all had at least one all-women orchestra, and some cities boasted several. Many of the founders were amazing women. Mabel Swint Ewer, for example, who was the chief force behind the Philadelphia Women's Symphony Orchestra, was not only a trumpet player but a mother of eight.[742]

The conductors of these orchestras were, of course, women. One such was Ethel Leginska (1886–1970), a renowned British pianist who, in the 1920s, decided to study composing. Dressed in her standard costume of a black velvet jacket, a white shirt and slim skirt, she appeared as a guest conductor for major orchestras in Paris and Berlin, and with the New York Philharmonic and the Boston Philharmonic, but most of her work was with women musicians. In 1929, she took the Boston Woman's Symphony Orchestra on a tour of 75 American cities. As one critic put it, "Roanoke [Virginia] music lovers gathered to hear a symphony orchestra of women led by a woman. They stayed to hear a symphony orchestra played by a great conductor."[743] Although Ethel Leginska was highly successful for a few years, she realized she was considered a fluke, a novelty. In a 1917 interview, she expressed the frustration she felt as a female musician:

Why are we always being generalized about? And why, why are we so docile and obedient in abiding by our traditions? If only we women would sometimes rebel, … break loose from traditions and go our own way!… We will never be original, do great work, until we get some courage and daring and trust our own way instead of the eternal beaten paths on which we are always asked to poke along.[744]

By the end of World War II, almost all the women's symphonies had been disbanded. Audiences were preoccupied, and it was too hard to raise the money to keep them going. During the oppressive 1950s, interest even in female conductors as novelty items wore off. Ethel Leginska ended up teaching piano in Los Angeles.

There were always women performers of such exceptional talent that they remained the apple of the public's eye: Peggy Lee, Ella Fitzgerald, Billie Holiday, Patsy Cline, Loretta Lynn, to name a few. When the women's movement descended in the 1970s, female artists screeched in rage at what they saw as gross, systematic discrimination. The music world, however, remained stunningly quiet. It was not until the 1980s that scholars, critics and musicians began to look closely at what role gender plays in music. Gradually, the feminist voice is making itself heard, and there are signals that big change is in the wind. Three examples will suffice: in 1997, in the face of international pressure, the Vienna Philharmonic Orchestra dropped its century-and-a-half ban on women instrumentalists. In the United States, the International Alliance for Women In Music was formed, with the express purpose of targeting those musical institutions and orchestras that receive public money but do not support female musicians, including composers. And festivals of music written by women are attracting huge crowds to listen to long-neglected composers such as Hildegard of Bingen. (*The International Encyclopedia of Women Composers* lists 6,200 female composers from some 70 countries.)

But it is in the traditionally bad-boy world of popular music that the unbelievable has happened. The great divas of the day—Canadians Céline Dion, Shania Twain, Sarah MacLachlan and Alanis Morissette, Cuban Gloria Estefan and Americans Whitney Houston, Madonna and Mariah Carey—sell millions of albums, are often nestled at the top of the charts and attract such huge crowds of enraptured fans that they have become global industries unto themselves. Many write or co-write their own songs and impose their own image on their work. As one critic put it, "Most of these women are damn fine singers. They are a link between the great voices of the past (think of Ella Fitzgerald, Ethel Merman, Edith Piaf) and the ears of people who can't get attuned to the howling self-pity of much contemporary rock but aren't ready to give up on pop music."[745]

What is important is not to dig for what is feminine or female in the music of these divas, or in the work of contemporary composers such as Judith Lang Zaimont or Alexina Louie, but rather to shove aside the Beethovens, Tchaikovskys and Coplands just a little in order to finally display the extraordinary talent of women musicians.

Louise

I didn't really get to know Louise Zurosky until the year after high school, when we worked together as bunny girls in downtown bars. She'd been waitressing for the Bo Beep Restaurant, but when I told her about being a cocktail waitress, the idea of serving drinks in the exotic murkiness of the Caravan and the Gas Light seemed far more appealing. Certainly the money was better. We wore black velvet bodices with puffy sleeves of green tartan satin and the same material draped around our hips, fishnet stockings and high-heel shoes. The costumes were hardly revealing—a little décolletage was as daring as it got—but we looked great in them and our tips were correspondingly large. There was something risqué about spending the summer slinging drinks while our friends were counsellors at summer camp or selling shoes at Simpson's, and both of us had the makings of mavericks, even if it had been disguised during high school.

Everyone knew Louise was a born artist. At school open houses, her work was always the most prominently displayed, and she won lots of prizes. In those days, her artistic talent was also expressed in how she dressed. She was a fashion plate, as stylish as her best buddies, the two beauties Lynne Campbell and Daphne Griffin. She was a cheerleader, and one year was crowned Miss Snow Queen. Miss Popularity is what we enviously called her. Few of us realized that in reality, she disliked school intensely and often suffered depression, brought on, in part, by the anxiety of her family life.

Both her mother and father were Ukrainian immigrants. Nestor Zurosky was born in 1905 in a town near Kiev. The family left for Canada when Nestor was six years old. Although his father had been a skilled harness-maker in Ukraine, the only work he could find in the new country was as a lumberjack. The Zuroskys lived in camps all over northern Ontario and Manitoba, and it was in one such place that Nestor's mother died—probably of a botched abortion. His father was a stern, strict man, a hard drinker with a violent temper. Much of the time he was away cutting trees, so Nestor and his two brothers Willy and Nick, both toddlers when their mother passed away, were placed in a Catholic orphanage.

The family was eventually reunited and moved to Toronto, although life didn't improve much. Zurosky senior took to bootlegging, and Nestor sold newspapers to help out and looked after his younger brothers, who were becoming more unruly and delinquent with each birthday. He eventually became a letterpressman, working for the Aberdeen Press and then the Northern Miner Press.

In the same neighbourhood as the Zuroskys lived the Carpenkos. The families hailed from the same Ukrainian village and knew each other. Nestor was 19 and Eva Carpenko 15 when they encountered each other walking along the street. Nestor, in his spats and with his fedora tilted to one side, was movie-star handsome. Eva, too, was an eye-catcher, with her pronounced Slavic cheekbones and deep-set black eyes. They fell deeply in love. When Nestor told his father he was going to marry Eva Carpenko, Zurosky Senior, realizing the main breadwinner of the family would be gone, swung around to hit his son. He missed, and his fist smashed into the door.

After their marriage, the young couple took on the responsibility of caring for Nestor's younger brothers. Although only in their early teens, Nick and Willy were already heavy drinkers and were constantly in trouble with the law. Eva and Nestor spent much of their early married years in court, bailing out one or other of the boys. (Both brothers eventually married, and while their lives were rather tragic, their children all received a solid education and got good jobs.)

Eva Carpenko's background was both similar and different than the Zuroskys'. Her father Peter had been a Cossack in the Russian army. He was a gymnast and a dancer, and had a most beautiful tenor voice. The Carpenkos, though, were peasants who worked on the estate of a wealthy aristocrat. Trying to find a better life, Eva's father and his family eventually emigrated to Canada.

Peter found a job as a stonemason, working on public buildings in Toronto. Always a rebel, he tried to start a union and was promptly fired for his efforts. The Carpenkos then bought a few acres in the Welland, Ontario, area, with the idea of farming, but the land was so poor, about all that could be cultivated were rattlesnakes. It was hardly the prosperity that life in the new world had promised. One day Eva's mother Mary Carpenko, a large-boned woman who had been the mainstay of the family, packed her bags and announced she was walking to Toronto. In the city, she started a rooming house in the St. Patrick Street area that became quite famous as a place where a poor and hungry immigrant could find a hot meal and a bed for the night. Mary never returned to the farm or her husband. Peter Carpenko eventually sold the land and bought a berry farm in Scarborough.

Eva Carpenko moved in with her mother, and it was in the neighbourhood of the boarding house that she met Nestor Zurosky. They were married in 1926, and their son Ken was born in 1937. By that time, Eva had developed severe epilepsy and had suffered grand-mal seizures. The doctors warned that her health could not withstand another pregnancy. Nestor thought he was taking all the precautions, but five years later, she was pregnant again, this time with Louise.

Music was never allowed to be played in the Zurosky house because it triggered Eva's seizures. Indeed, her mother's illness coloured Louise's entire childhood. Louise would never know if she might come home after school to find her mother covered with blood, foaming at the mouth and thrashing on the floor. Despite her condition, Eva's house was always spick and span. She'd rise from her sickbed to have the dinner on the table. Says Louise, "She was so ashamed of being grand-mal epileptic that she wanted to keep everything going, never let down her end."

When Louise was ten years old, her father went into the hospital for a gall-stone operation. Nestor's absence was provoking Eva's seizures, so Louise decided to sleep with her mother to keep an eye on her. One night, she heard a thundering crash and turned on the light. Eva had fallen off the bed, and embedded in her forehead was the knob from the night table. Louise called for her brother, who phoned some adult friends of the Zuroskys and then an ambulance. "I went into the kitchen and got a bowl and filled it with water and I got a clean cloth," recalls Louise. "I remember sitting in the dining room with the water splashing around and saying, 'I can't go in there. I just can't.' My brother replied, 'You have to do it. You have to be strong and go in there.' And I did."

Eva came home a few days later. "She was on the couch in the kitchen. She had this big zigzag thing in her forehead where they had stitched her together. She was yellow in colour, and I looked at her and my heart broke. I couldn't believe how anybody could suffer like that. She looked at me with these adoring eyes, as if to say, 'I'm so sorry I'm sick.' It just broke my heart. I used to think, 'I'll never get over this. I'll never forget.' Looking back, I don't know how my brother and I got through it."

When Eva reached menopause, her seizures suddenly stopped. Her sense of humour returned, she found pleasure again in cooking and she even got a job at Woolworth's Department Store for a while.

Louise's childhood was not all unhappy by any means. "My brother and I were loved enormously. My parents coped as best they could. They worked very hard and shared everything they could with us," she says. They were raised in the house that their grandfather had built on South Woodrow Avenue in Birchcliff Heights, a working-class area of Scarborough, and Louise says the place was exactly what you'd expect of a singing and dancing Cossack. "He went to the dump and found the windows. They didn't really match, well maybe at the front, but certainly not at the back." The garden, though, was magnificent, full of fruit trees, fresh vegetables and a wonderful flower garden. Louise and her brother were expected to help with the upkeep. "There I'd be with my clippers. All of a sudden I'd be down on my elbows and the bleeding hearts would have turned into fairy slippers. All this had a tremendous influence on me, I know."

Nestor Zurosky's ideas about child-rearing reflected his own strict upbringing. When, at age eight, Louise asked if she could take dance lessons, her father answered, "Get a job and then you'll have money for lessons." Toys were considered frivolous. Louise had two dolls that her aunts bought her, but Christmas presents from her parents consisted of practical things such as slippers. Once a month, though, Nestor brought home from work a gift that could not have pleased the artistic Louise more: the press end-cuts, sheets of paper that Louise and Ken would turn into imaginary worlds of their own. "We'd do these huge topographical maps of Treasure Island, for example. The rail system, the underground system would all be there. There'd be buildings with planes and hangars and storage areas. We'd colour the seas, the mountains, the farms. Architecturally, it was fabulous."

Louise went everywhere with her brother; they'd walk for hours through the fields and down the bluffs to the lake. Ken collected plants and animals and made wonderful terrariums (he eventually became a professional naturalist). The Zurosky house was so small that for years, Ken and Louise shared a room. They'd lie on their beds, and Ken would ask, "What colour do you see now?" and Louise would answer, "I see a rainbow colour and it starts at green and moves through to orange." When, years later, Ken was dying of cancer, Louise played a similar game to comfort him.

Louise remembers the day she started kindergarten at Birchcliff Heights Public School. "There were these little coloured disks and pieces of straw and other stuff all waiting to be threaded. It was like, 'Hallelujah, I've hit pay dirt!' Part of it was just being away from the house and the misery of my mother's illness."

All through public school, her talent was recognized. The class would be studying the Laplanders, for instance, and the teacher would say, "Let Louise do it." She'd create the drawings, the tents, the life-size figures. She was allowed to decorate the blackboards with huge murals of the Madonna and Child at Christmas time, and on the coronation of Queen Elizabeth, she drew the beautiful new queen in a fabulous gold coach.

High school was not exactly the creative paradise elementary school had been. Art lessons were held only once or twice a week, and the vast majority of time was spent on academic subjects. Louise got relatively good grades and was popular, joining all kinds of clubs and activities, but by Grade 11, she was suffering real depression. It didn't help that she had developed an allergy to milk, and acne spread on her face. "I couldn't cope with the burden of my emotions. It was all so overwhelming, it's a wonder I didn't kill myself.... I didn't have anyone to direct me or say, 'Gee, you do have talent. Why don't you cultivate it?'" She'd go home after school and watch television until it was time to go to bed. The next morning, she'd get up early and try to complete the mounds of homework. "That type of education, regurgitating back facts, really made me think I was a dummy," she says.

Louise had considered studying art and archeology at the University of Toronto, but she found Grade 13 so difficult, she got so flustered and nervous, she began having stomach problems. "I said to my dad, 'I don't think I can do this. Are you going to see me as a failure?' He said, 'What are you going to do? Shoot yourself? It's not the end of the world.'" Louise says his attitude helped her a lot. Nevertheless, for years she suffered terrible nightmares that she had failed the exams. She didn't fail, and although her marks weren't high enough for the U. of T., they got her into the Ontario College of Art, Canada's largest and oldest art school.

She couldn't have done a better thing. "I thought I had died and gone to heaven. I could apply myself so incredibly to everything that I did. I got great marks and I turned out mature work. To this day, it stands up." The first year, Louise won the E. Harris Company Award for Foundation Studies. In their second year, students selected a specialty—advertising illustration, material arts or weaving and pottery, for example. Louise chose fine arts, drawing and painting. "I lucked into a really great class. There was no doubt in our minds that we were going to be artists. Not commercial artists—painters." Their instructors tended to be artists who taught to keep bread on the table. The landscape painter Carl F. Schaefer, Eric Friefield, a great figure drafts-man, and William Robert, in particular, had an impact on Louise's art.

It wasn't easy being female at the OAC at the time. Louise recalls male instructors would call her sweetie pie, pinches on the bum were not infre-quent and many men believed making babies was a woman's great creative accomplishment, not painting or sculpting. Says Louise, "Fred Hagan, for example, was a hard man to deal with, a chauvinist to the nth degree, brutally honest, brutally cruel. He destroyed a lot of egos, but he also gave you more stuff for your head, more food for your brain, and he taught us the language of art."

There were five women in Louise's class who formed a tightly knit group. "I remember being in the museum and seeing this woman with a scarf on her head and glasses, and this big, Jewish nose sticking out, looking at some work or other," recalls Louise. "I went over and, said, 'Aren't you June Drutz?' and we were friends for 25 years." June and another of the group, Louise Gordon, were 25 years older than students just out of high school like Louise Zurosky. Both were already accomplished artists, June as a painter and Louise Gordon as a sculptor. Louise relished just being in their presence, and was sometimes invited to join them in trips to Chicago and other places to take in important art shows.

By her fourth year, Louise Zurosky had done so well, she was a contender for the prestigious Honours Graduate Travelling Scholarship, along with June Drutz and another male student. Louise backed out because she thought June's work was so much better than hers. Her instructors were furious— they thought her art as good, if not superior.

While Louise was determined to be an accomplished artist, she also knew she had to make a living. Her painting would not yield an income right away, if ever. Just before Louise's graduation, Carl Schaefer, the head of the fine-arts department, recommended her for a job as the curator of a gallery that was part of the public library in Sarnia, an industrial town southwest of Toronto. "I asked him why he had suggested me. He looked at me and said, 'Don't hide your light under a bushel.'"

It was during her two years at Sarnia that Louise first unveiled what is one of her great strengths: her ability to organize. As well as arranging shows for local artists, her job was to bring in travelling exhibits. For these, she would handle all the correspondence, design the brochures and posters, as well as hang the show when it arrived. Louise also organized retrospectives of individuals—printmaker Nicholas Hornyansky and artist John Gould—which turned out to be profound learning experiences in themselves.

Louise's career might have been blossoming, but she was lonely. Sarnia's art patrons, many of them wealthy, simply didn't think of entertaining a 23-year-old. "I started in September after Labour Day [1965] and by Christmas, I hadn't received one invitation to somebody's home for dinner. I went back to this place where I lived and I painted, often until three in the morning."

Since she was only making about $3,000 a year, Louise had to keep her living expenses as low as possible. She moved into an old apartment building on Front Street, and spent her Saturday nights with the superintendents, Buck and Mary, great country-and-western fans. It was a comfortable enough arrangement until Louise was assaulted. An intruder broke into her apartment and would have raped her—possibly even killed her—if she hadn't managed to get the window of the inner well open and started screaming for help. The man tore out of her apartment, but not before he had severely beaten her, blackening her eyes.

In the days ahead, Louise attended several police lineups, but her assailant was never found. She thought she recognized him in a photo of a local band, but for a while, every young man was suspect in her mind. As traumatic as the incident was, she recovered fairly quickly. "It's my Ukrainian ancestry," she says. "I have always had great coping skills."

Her boss, though, insisted she move to a safer neighbourhood and found a room for her in the home of a Polish immigrant. She set up her easel in a small middle room and continued to paint. "I've never had a living room, ever. It's always been turned into a studio," she says. Thinking she might be lonely after her move, friends arranged a blind date that profoundly changed her life.

Peter Gould was recuperating from a near-fatal car accident, so he and Louise had their individual traumas to talk about. He was a tall, gangly guy, a university student who was interested in art, liked gourmet cooking, good wines—everything that appealed to Louise. But it was his voice that made her fall for him. "It was so sweet and gentle, just music to my ears." It also helped that he drove a sports car. "I had to go and visit my parents, and, although I hardly knew him, he offered to drive me all the way to Toronto. He was always doing nice things like that."

Peter had been planning to take time off work to travel through Europe.

"I thought to myself, 'I'm not letting this one go,' so I asked him to marry me." Although he was only 22, and Louise 24, he agreed.

As soon as they told Louise's mother about their engagement, she began planning a big Ukrainian wedding. Peter and Louise quickly put the kibosh on that. It was too bourgeois for their left-wing tastes. Louise's parents were upset because, over the years, they had been invited to huge numbers of Ukrainian celebrations, and it was their turn to reciprocate. Says Louise, "I've forgiven myself for most of my shortcomings, but not for that one.... Mom never said anything, but I know she cried all night." They ended up getting married at City Hall. Afterwards, Louise accidentally threw her bridal bouquet onto the road and a truck ran over it, a foreboding sign, perhaps, of the fate of the marriage itself.

Peter was completing his Bachelor of Arts degree in philosophy at the University of Western Ontario, so on their return from their honeymoon in England, he and Louise moved to London, Ontario. They found a flat above a store, and Louise took a part-time job shelving books at a library. Mostly, though, she painted, inspired by London's flourishing art scene.

Much of it centred around Greg Curnoe (1936–92), the artist, writer and musician who was considered one of Canada's most interesting young painters. There were others, too: Jack Chambers, Tony Urquhart, Paterson Ewen, Ron Martin, Kim Ondaatje. Louise felt very much part of the scene. The 20/20 gallery organized exciting one-man exhibits and the London Regional Art Gallery was importing shows from all over. Louise had no trouble fitting in. "I painted as much as I could. I was a very determined artist, no question in my mind."

Louise experimented in the hard-edged, abstract work that was so popular at the time. "I could not get into my work that kind of classy look, that precision, that lack of emotion. My circles or lines always looked like they were going to get up and start doing the polka or something." Louise returned to a more figurative approach. It was during this period she had her first solo exhibit at a branch of the London Public Library and Art Gallery and was picked up by the Nancy Poole Gallery.

She also got a part-time job at R. H. Beale High School. Louise taught classes there for four years, and later at Fanshawe College, but she did not consider it a career, never imagined that she would be teaching for the rest of her life. "We were working artists. None of us would go to teacher's college and get a certificate. We'd never waste our time on that stuff."

The late '60s and early '70s was a time of rebellion and anarchy in North American universities, and Louise's husband was in the forefront, at least in London, Ontario. Peter Gould joined a Marxist-Leninist group and quickly became enthralled with the movement. Picketing factories, marching in protests, endlessly debating the evils of capitalism over pitchers of beer became part of his daily routine. Louise didn't want to be left at home alone, so she joined in the activities, but she never felt comfortable. "They were just a bunch of upper-middle-class kids who were a hell of a lot richer than I had ever been and who were into serious revolution. We'd go and picket a factory to help the downtrodden workers and these people would look at us as if we were nuts. I'd say to Peter and the others, 'This is fine, do this, but you guys are all living on grants. Why don't you go and get jobs in the factories? Go and get a taste of real work.'"

Louise painted political posters and became the house photographer, recording the marches and other momentous events. Nevertheless, she was constantly criticized; she was a "rotor-toady" for the capitalists, her art and her culture were serving the interests of the bourgeoisie. Her art work was considered immaterial, unimportant. "I'd tell Peter, 'I can't go to the university and sit at the table selling Mao's *Little Red Book*. I want to work in my studio.' He would look at me and I'd think, 'Oh boy, I'm letting him down again.'"

What added even more strain to the relationship was that Louise had an adverse reaction to the Pill. She gained considerable weight, she cried all the time and her temper would flare. "This behaviour was not without reason," says Louise. "Peter would play, whether consciously or not, a cruel game of blackmail." They fought a lot, although Louise maintains they were still very much in love.

"I remember walking along the streets of London in my misery, thinking, 'How can I do this? How can I spend my time making those ludicrous posters?'" Louise finally had to make one of those agonizing decisions that has been a feature of her life. "I had been drawing since I was knee-high to a grasshopper, it's all I ever did. How do you tell a person, 'Just let me be, just let me live'? You start to fight back, and that manifests itself in having to make choices." Louise finally left Peter. For three years, they lived in the same city and saw each other often, but he finally told her to get on with her life, and they parted for good. "It was so traumatic for me. Total grief and heartbreak. It took me years and years to get over it."

There was one positive aspect of Louise's run-in with the Marxist-Leninist movement. She became interested in printmaking, particularly silkscreen. "I felt it would give me more freedom to be more venturesome and be a little political. I was not the same person after my initiation into Communist dogma." She created a series of silkscreen prints called *Society Matrons*, as well as the *Canadian Sucker Series*, both basically anti-capitalist political statements but interesting, skillful ones. She became determined to learn more technique, especially involving the use of film negatives. In 1972, she moved back to Toronto and took a "lackey's job" at Associated Advertising, an arm of the Dairy Products Association. Her task was to prepare the art work for ads proclaiming the wonders of butter and banana splits. "It was a snake pit," says Louise. "It took me six months to get everything I needed. Then I said, 'I'm out of here.'"

By that time, she had been offered a job as a technician in a printmaking shop—lithography and silkscreen—with the University of Guelph's fine-arts department. "The professor would be there for maybe three hours, and I would literally run the print shop for the rest of the time, not only bailing out the students, helping them with the technical, but doing all the shop keep, mixing the browns, making gum arabic, repairing rollers, keeping the presses up, planning for the student art sales." When she finally left, her recommendation letters were glowing.

In Guelph, Louise bought an old, limestone, semi-detached house for $19,000 and fixed it up, taking on most of the work herself, from replacing the mortar to doing the carpentry. This was the first of many such projects she would undertake over the years. Her living environment is as much a product of her artistic creativity as her moveable art work, but she's never had enough money for these renovations. Pinching and scraping became a way of life. In Guelph, her budget didn't even allow a movie or theatre ticket. "Once a month I would buy a bottle of sherry, and that would be it."

Her job as a technician didn't leave her as much room for her own art work, and after two years, Louise quit. She had already found a part-time position teaching silkscreen and etching—she actually put together the printmaking shop—at Seneca College of Applied Arts & Technology, King City campus, near Toronto. When friends offered her the use of a studio in an old, run-down hall on Boulton Avenue in the east end, she decided to move back to the city.

In 1975, her alma mater, the Ontario College of Art, gave her a job teaching lithography in its printmaking department. Her old bugbear chauvinist from college days, Fred Hagan, was head of the department and hired her. Four years later, though, he decided not to renew the contracts of the current crop of instructors, and Louise, along with everyone else, was let go. She became a itinerant teacher, picking up a course here and there in design or watercolour in OCA's fine-arts department and at Sheridan College in Brampton and Oakville, but after Hagan retired, she was rehired to teach printmaking. In 1992, she was named head of the department, a job she held for four years.

Once she returned to Toronto, Louise's own work flourished. For ten years, she worked at the Open Studio Print Workshop, a co-operative funded by the Ontario Arts Council, donor membership and user fees. For a small sum, artists have use of the facilities: the presses, the inks, the paper. In Guelph, Louise had become interested in photo etching from drawings, and she continued with this technique at Open Studio. Her *Dollie Series*, a takeoff on the beauty myth, and another of horses, *Horsey State I*, *State II* and *State III*, were completed at this time. Each involves a female figure and a stallion, the symbol to Louise of male power and authority in traditional society.

By this time, Louise had worked through the whole gamut of printmaking—silkscreen, etching, photo etching—but she considered lithography the Cadillac of graphic arts. For one thing, it was closer to watercolour and painting. "I went through all sorts of technical experiments and images. It was an investigation of what you want to put down and what you're able to achieve." Gradually, Louise began to focus on stone and plate lithography, separately and in combination. One of her most impressive works from this period is called *Stella Suite*, a study of her stepmother.

After Louise's mother died of cancer in 1969, her father had married an old friend of the family's who had been a punch-press operator for years. In Louise's portrait, Stella is sitting at the dining-room table; one of Louise's own watercolours hangs in the background. She is dressed in the zippered, cotton apron that was her work uniform. On the table rests Stella's right hand, swathed in bandages. She'd had an accident; her gloved hand had caught in the punch press and the top of her thumb had been ripped off. Louise saw the scene as a feminist comment: Stella as Soviet woman.

During the 1970s and '80s, Louise returned to watercolours, a medium she had not attempted since art college. The fabulous twin paintings of an old woman called *Grey Lady*, based on E. J. Pratt's poem "The Iron Door," was completed in 1979. She painted many still lifes—she had a penchant for large, luscious mangoes. This work was always snapped up when Louise exhibited it, and is in many private and company collections.

On her return to Toronto, Louise's social life centred around Open Studio, in particular, beer-drinking at the Spadina House. "I loved it. I was one of the boys. I don't know what the women thought of me. I don't think they liked me very much, but I can't blame them. None of the men bothered with the women. And I didn't either." Then she once again fell in love.

"I had had my eye on Paddy Johnson for some time, or should I say, my ear. He has the most amazing voice." He was in the office-furniture business and in between marriages when Louise started going out with him. "It was a nice romance, but I kind of blew the relationship, not in how I behaved but in that again, I made a choice: I would prefer to do my art work without a lot of aggravation." The breakup, as usual, threw Louise for a loop. "I fall in love so rarely and it's such a profound experience for me that I don't get over it easily. It really takes its toll." She lost a lot of weight, became despondent and finally decided she was fed up with lithography. "I thought, 'I never want to do this again. It's taken years of my life, it's so hard and all you get is a bunch of prints.'" She gave her inks away and quit Open Studio.

She continued to paint during this time, but she was always alone, and she soon realized that for her sanity, she had better return to working among people and get back to printmaking. She began working at the Sword Street Press. Begun by two renegades from Open Studio, Sword Street quickly established a reputation for superb-quality lithos; some of Canada top artists had prints of their work published there. Louise began one of her most significant projects, a series of coloured lithographs called the *Salvation Suite*, partly named because her creative energies had been charged up once again.

She convinced a company that dealt in art supplies to give her 500 sheets of the best paper in exchange for a boxed set of 13 prints. Louise saw the horse as the universal condition of mankind and used the animal's image to express this. Each of the prints represented a specific state: love, labour, community, competition, death, extinction. It was a tour de force technically. "In the process, I evolved a teaching-aid package, so I can show the students all of the processes that are involved in coming to the final result. It's just an incredible body of work." Many of the prints were sold, and one of the series hangs in Louise's home/studio to this day.

When Louise first moved to Toronto, she lived in a studio on Boulton

Avenue, but the building was sold and she was forced to move. She found a row house she liked on Clendenan Avenue in Toronto's west end, and while it didn't need too much basic repair, she repainted it and revarnished the floor. She soon discovered, though, that there was a big problem. The walls were so thin, she could hear the children next door scraping the cereal off the side of their bowls. Louise sold the house in 1983 and bought a newly renovated artist studio for $85,000. For her, it was a huge amount of money, but there were lovely tiles, a fireplace, a cat walk and a place to paint.

Louise threw a house-warming party when she moved in. The large network of artist friends she had formed over the years showed up and, as she says, "Boy, were they impressed with me." However, she soon grew tired of the place. She didn't like the neighbourhood, was afraid to go walking alone at night, the house was terribly hot in the summer and she couldn't afford air conditioning. Most important, she noticed signs of shoddy workmanship. Thinking she was protecting her investment, Louise sold it to friends, making a small profit. In a few years, the same studio was placed on the market for $250,000.

By that time, Louise had moved into rental accommodation in the Parkdale area. "I was in the apartment, feeling like crap because everything was not going the way I wanted it to, a terrible slump, and a big love disappointment, and it burned me up that these friends were living in this place that I helped design. I was mad at myself." On the other hand, the wretched apartment was on the top floor and had wonderful light. Louise consoled herself by continuing to paint—her work was strewn all over her living room. She even managed to hold exhibits there.

In 1991, however, she decided she wanted not only out of her confined quarters but out of the city altogether. She began a major search and found what she was looking for in the Mulmur Hills, north of Orangeville. It was a schoolhouse, built in 1936 but in total disrepair. "It was the grossest place I had ever seen. It was all boarded up, all the windows had been broken, and evidence of mice and bats was everywhere." Louise could see the potential, though. For one thing, the property was gorgeous, situated on a hill with a forest of blue spruce. With only a little help from a few tradesmen, electricians and carpenters mostly, Louise rebuilt the place, basically with her own hands, expertly and carefully. All the trim, wainscoting and boards were removed and numbered, then sanded, washed, resanded and put in place. She even replanted the huge trees herself rather than lose them when a septic field was cleared. Louise's Little Red School is now a work of art itself, perhaps one of her greatest creative accomplishments.

Teaching remains an important source of income and inspiration for her. For three months in 1997, she taught at the Florence, Italy campus of the Ontario College of Art and Design (as it is now known). Afterwards, she travelled in France and Italy, and it is these memories that are being reflected in her current work. On a huge, seven-foot-by-nine canvas, she is painting, in acrylics, a lavish, decorative tribute to Claude Monet's glorious garden at Giverny. It is yet another example of a body of work that is insightful, philosophic, progressive, feminist—a reflection, perhaps, of her own life as an artist.

Visual Artists

... I know a woman called Anastaise, who is so skillful and experienced in painting the borders of manuscripts and the backgrounds of miniatures that no one can cite a craftsman in the city of Paris, the centre of the best illuminators on earth, who in these endeavors surpasses her in any way....
                                          Christine de Pisan, *The City of Women*, 1405

Let men of genius conceive of great architectural projects, monumental sculpture, and elevated forms of painting.... Let women occupy themselves with those types of art they have always preferred, such as pastels, portraits or miniatures.
                                          Léon Legrange, *Gazette des Beaux-Arts*, 1860

As they set up their easels next to men in art classes, they began to feel—or at least some of them did—that they could put their concerns, their way of seeing things into their painting without the disguises and defences of previous centuries.
                                          Frances Borzello, *Seeing Ourselves: Women's Self-Portraits*, 1998

In the corner of the high-school art room hung a print that intrigued me. It was called *Nameless and Friendless*, painted by Emily Mary Osborne (1834– c. 1909) and exhibited in 1857 at the summer show of Britain's Royal Academy. The picture depicts a scene in a Victorian art shop. The elderly proprietor, stroking his chin and looking rather dubious, examines a painting. At the counter in front of him waits a young woman, neatly dressed in a cloak and dark-coloured dress—she is obviously a gentlewoman—and beside her stands a boy holding a large portfolio. What is extraordinary about the picture is the expression on the woman's face; she is not only despondent but outright fearful and embarrassed.

For the longest time I couldn't figure out what was being depicted. Whose painting was the shop owner assessing? Her brother's? Her father's? It finally dawned on me that the young woman was an artist, and it was her own picture she was trying to sell. A lamb among the wolves—as they thumb through pornographic prints, two old men sit ogling her—she appears powerless and utterly vulnerable. That a woman had created the picture made it all the more chilling.

I

It was a young maid called Dibutade (daughter of Butades, a potter living in Corinth) who supposedly invented drawing in the Western tradition. She was in love with a young man, "and she, when he was going abroad, drew in outline on the wall the shadow of this face thrown by a lamp."[746] Her father came along, pressed clay on the drawing and turned it into a sculpture.

If the Roman historian Pliny the Elder (AD c. 23–79) can be believed, women of antiquity, at least a few of them, were an integral part of the artistic scene. Timarete, the daughter of an artist, painted an illustrious panel picture of Artemis at the goddess's great temple at Ephesus. Another artist's offspring, Irene, who lived in the city of Eleusis where Demeter's famous sanctuary stood, was also a renowned painter. According to Pliny, her work included "the Maiden at Eleusis, a Calypso, an Old Man and Theodorus, the juggler, and [she] painted also Aleisthenes the Dancer."[747] Olympias was another artist who was not only accomplished in her own right but also taught painting to aspiring male artists.

Perhaps the most famous female painter of ancient Greece was Iaia of Cyzicus, living in the second century BC. She apparently never married, being utterly devoted to her art. She worked both with a brush and with a *cestrum*, an engraver used on ivory. Iaia specialized in portraits of women, and her best known were a large picture on wood of an old woman of Naples, and a self-portrait. Centuries later, Giovanni Boccaccio explained that she managed it, "with the aid of a mirror, preserving the colours and features and expression of the face so completely that none of her contemporaries doubted that it was just like her." Pliny heaps even more praise on Iaia: "No one else had a quicker hand in painting, while her artistic skill was such that in the prices she obtained she far outdid the most celebrated portrait painters of the same period, Sopolis and Dionysius, whose pictures fill the galleries."[748]

There are no historic mentions of women creating the great architecture and sculptures of the Classical Greek period. Considering they were sequestered in the home and, unless their fathers were artists particularly generous with their time, had no access to materials—the potter's wheel, the sculptor's bronze, the painter's colours—or any means of acquiring the skills to perform the work, it's a wonder there's any record of female artists at all.

Aesthetic expression for the vast majority of women was found in their day-to-day occupation of producing textiles. Every female of every age and class spent vast amounts of time spinning and weaving, as well as embroidering. Helen and Penelope of Greek myth were both weaving fanatics. The designs produced in this work permeated society. Scholar Kate McK. Elderkin, for example, maintains the geometric patterns and decorations found in Dorion wool fabrics produced by women in the eighth century BC were copied by male painters.

From the information that has survived, slight as it is, we can surmise that female creativity in the visual arts was woven into Greek and Roman life, even if, as was most often the case, no individual credit was given.

II

In the 14th century, Giovanni Boccaccio (1313–1375), best known for his licentious stories in *The Decameron*, wrote another book, *De claris mulieribus*, in which he profiled some 104 famous women, beginning with Eve. In its illustrations, the book portrays the artistic life of women in Middle Ages. There is a woman busily painting a fresco, another copying a manuscript, a third sculpting the image of a young woman on her tombstone. A fourth is painting a portrait of the Madonna and Child, while, of all things, a male assistant prepares her colours. A fifth is of a woman painting a self-portrait from a mirror.[749]

There is evidence also that women were accomplished goldsmiths and sculptors in the Middle Ages. In the Metropolitan Museum of Art in New York is housed a huge and astonishing ceremonial crucifix. Made of silver with beautifully crafted gold relief figures, it was sculpted in Spain in the 12th century. Woven into the metal of the cross are delicate letters spelling the name of the creator, one Sancia Guidosalvi, and the fact she dedicated her art to the glory of the Redemptor.

The famous Bayeux Tapestry, one of the few remaining masterpieces of medieval needlework, provides another dimension of female artistic expression on a grand scale. Seventy metres long and only 49.5 centimetres wide, the work depicts the saga of the invasion of England by William the Conqueror in 1066. Worked in brightly dyed wool on linen, it is a lively panorama of 1,512 figures and 72 scenes, all identified by Latin inscriptions. Teams of women almost certainly embroidered it but who the designer was—and there seems to have been only one—remains a mystery, although tradition has it that it was the creation of Queen Mathilda, wife of William the Conqueror.

Until the mid-13th century, the production and illumination of sacred books was entirely the franchise of the monasteries and convents. The names of several female manuscript-illuminators, all nuns, have come down through history. The earliest known signed her work "Ende pintrix et Dei adiutrix" and is now known simply as Ende. Among the most interesting illustrations from a manuscript known as the Gerona Apocalypse (it is preserved in the Gerona Cathedral in Spain) is one entitled *Battle of the Dragon with Child of the Woman*, painted around 975. It's a fascinating abstract design, the large, curving shape of the dragons contrasting with the detailed drawings of men, women and children. Its unique feature, as critic Dorothy Miner notes, is "the sensitive play of sharp colours against disarmingly delicate ones...."[750]

In the late 13th century, commercial book-making businesses began to flourish in Europe, especially in university cities such as Bologna and Cologne. Recent scholarship that has examined medieval payment receipts and contracts has revealed there were far more women employed as calligraphers and miniaturists than had previously been assumed. One of the most interesting was an illuminator known as Claricia. We even have an idea of what she looked like. In a 12th-century German Psalter from Augsberg is illumined an elaborate Q. Forming the lower part of the capital letter is a slender, maidenly figure, dressed in an elegant, wide-sleeved dress. Her arms hold the upper portion of the Q; her head is tilted to one side, which allows just enough room for one word to be delicately written—Claricia. This is one of the first self-portraits of a woman artist that is known.

Since female artists rarely signed their names to their work during the Middle Ages, it's hard to gauge how many there were. What we do know is that at least a few were skillful, original and exciting in the execution of their art.

III

Two extraordinary paintings by women artists from the early-modern period are entirely different in their subject matter and attitudes, yet similar in their goals: to guarantee their talent not be forgotten by posterity.

The first, by Artemisia Gentileschi called *Judith Decapitating Holofernes* (c. 1620), evinces a scene of the most hideous violence and blood, and determined female cruelty. The second, by Clara Peeters, *Still Life with Vases*,

Goblets and Shells, is tranquil and rich but with subterfuge rippling under the surface. The work of both artists is a reflection of their life stories.

Like almost all women artists in the early-modern era, Artemisia Gentileschi (c. 1593–c. 1652) was the daughter of a painter. Orazio Gentileschi was deeply influenced by Caravaggio (1573–1610), and taught the famous *chiaroscuro*, dramatic light-and-dark effect, to Artemisia. She was so talented, her father arranged to have her study with Agostino Tassi, a successful artist who specialized in fresco decorations of Rome's aristocratic houses.

When she was only 15, Artemisia was seduced and then raped by Tassi. When it became clear Tassi was a scoundrel who had no intention of marrying his young student, Artemisia's father sued. What followed was an appalling, five-week trial. Tassi set out to prove Artemisia was a libertine before he met her; on the witness stand, she was made to endure the thumbnail torture, the 17th century's idea of a lie-detector test. Tassi spent eight months in jail, but the case was dismissed. Artemisia's reputation, meanwhile, lay in shreds.[751] As Germaine Greer writes, "The abortive trial had left Artemisia nothing but her talent. It also removed the traditional obstacles to the development of that talent. She could no longer hope to live a life of matronly seclusion; she was notorious and she had no chance but to take advantage of the fact."[752]

Not long after her ordeal, Artemisia painted *Judith Decapitating Holofernes*. The subject matter is based on the Old Testament story involving the beautiful and pious Jewish widow Judith. After upbraiding her fellow Israelites for losing their faith in God while under siege, Judith entered the camp of the enemy Assyrians and managed to convince them she was a informer against her own people. Invited to a banquet, she easily managed, with her great beauty and charm, to seduce the Assyrian leader Holofernes. Once he fell into a drunken stupor, Judith, assisted by her maid, unceremoniously cut off his head.

Artemisia Gentileschi was enthralled with the story of Judith and painted at least six different versions. *Judith Decapitating Holofernes* is the most dramatically gruesome. As scholar Françoise Borin has pointed out, the manner in which Holofernes' massive arms are raised makes them look like thighs, and at first glance, this could be a picture of an agonizing birth with two midwives in attendance. At second look, it could be a violent rape of a man by two women.[753] Finally, though, it is a portrait of revenge. The unflinching determination with which Judith wields the sword as she saws away at

Holofernes' head, a maid looking on with equal fortitude, is one of the most grisly and powerful female representations in existence.

Artemisia undertook many other works with Biblical and historic themes—*Esther and Ahasuerus, Rape of Proserpine, Aurora, David and Bathsheba*—and she also became a successful portrait painter in Rome. Today, the most intriguing of these portraits is a picture of a masterful, dedicated, totally absorbed woman artist called *Self-Portrait as the Allegory of Painting*. Through the unladylike violence depicted in her work, and the sheer power of her painting, Artemisia insured oblivion would not be her fate.

Unlike Artemisia Gentileschi, little is known about the background of Clara Peeters (1594–post 1657). She was probably the daughter of an artist, who may have arranged for her to study with Osias Beert, a noted still-life painter in Antwerp. Her sumptuous, tranquil oils such as *Still Life with Flowers, a Goblet, Dried Fruit and Pretzels* place her in the front ranks of the first generation of still-life painters of the Flemish school. Critic Ann Sutherland Harris concludes, "Peeters would appear to be one of the originators of the genre."[754] One of Clara Peeters's favourite themes was the transitory and artificial nature of beautiful, costly objects. In a picture called *Vanitas Self-Portrait* (c. 1610–20), the young and comely Clara sits at a table, while strewn before her are many valuable artifacts: jewellery, coins, a gold fruit dish and a goblet. Peeters herself wears a silk cape with a delicate lace collar, a pearl necklace and a jewelled headband. Also in the picture, floating along, is a large, glossy bubble. The viewer can't help but smile, for Peeters is obviously predicting that not only the objects around her but her own beauty and youth will surely vanish in a pop.

Her masterpiece *Still Life with Vases, Goblets, and Shells*, painted in Karlsruhe in 1612, depicts a collection of curiosities made by man or nature. Near a pottery vase filled with anemones, hyacinths, tulips and lilies stand two tall, elegant, gilt goblets. Between them is a pale green, Chinese bowl. Coins, gold chains and seashells lie about. In each of the seven bosses on the goblet on the right are painted tiny figures. When the light come from the right direction, there stand seven Clara Peeterses in miniature. It's as if she is pleading, "Don't forget. Don't forget me!"

IV

Let men of genius conceive of great architectural projects, monumental sculpture, and elevated forms of painting. In a word, let men busy themselves with all that has to do with great art. Let women occupy themselves with those types of art they have always preferred, such as pastels, portraits or miniatures. Or the painting of flowers, those prodigies of grace and freshness which alone can compete with the grace and freshness of women themselves. To women above all falls the practice of the graphic art, those painstaking arts which correspond so well to the role of abnegation and devotion which the honest woman happily fills here on earth, and which is her religion.[755]

These opinions by the French critic Léon Legrange, published in *Gazette des Beaux-Arts* in 1860, are striking testimony of what professional women artists were up against in the 19th century. Not only was it considered against nature itself for a woman to create great works of art, but the prudery of the time prohibited her from even learning the basic skills of her trade.

From the Renaissance to the 19th century, studying human anatomy was considered essential in creating great sculpture and, the highest realm, history painting. For most of that period, women were prohibited from copying the nude body. As the art student Gertrude Massey wrote in her autobiography, "It was almost a crime to mention the word nude. Although acquainted with our personal anatomies, we were supposed to accept the conventional point of view that women had no legs. They had heads, arms and feet, apparently linked together by clothes."[756]

Students protested, especially those at the newly created, all-female art academies. When educators decided the cow would serve just as nicely as the human form in the study of anatomy, there were howls of outrage. Finally, some schools allowed sketching from the female nude. In a painting entitled *Female Life Class* (c. 1879) by Alice Barber Stevens, the students, all weighted down in their heavy Victorian gowns, some wearing hats, are painting a naked model. Her back, of course, is turned to the viewer—painting frontal nudity was too shocking—but her slender, elegant body stands in refreshing contrast with the dark, encumbered figures around her.

By the end of the 19th century, pioneers such as Thomas Eakins at the Pennsylvania Academy of Fine Arts, an institution that held the most enlightened attitudes about female art students in the United States, made anatomy classes available that were attended by both men and women students. All the same, in 1886, when Eakins had the audacity to remove the loincloth from a male model, the public outrage was so ferocious, he was fired from his job.[757]

In France, the centre of the art world, the important École des Beaux-Arts, a state-run and state-financed institution, was closed to women, although, beginning in 1803, private art schools for females sprung up like mushrooms. By 1869, there were 20 in Paris alone, compared to only seven for men.[758] The problem was that, even in the most serious of these, women received a lesser education. The hours were shorter, anatomy was not taught and the subject matter was invariably domestic. In 1881, the sculptor Léon Bertraux founded the Union des Femmes Peintres et Sculpteurs, and similar lobby groups sprang up throughout Europe. These organizations held their own art exhibitions and campaigned to have women admitted to art schools, including the École des Beaux-Arts. In 1896, this finally became a reality, but mixed life-study classes were still prohibited, and women could not compete for the school's most prestigious prize, the Prix de Rome.[759]

Despite these restrictions, women continued to paint and to exhibit, but even the subjects they portrayed were dictated by society's idea of the feminine. The angel by the hearth was supposed to paint pictures of her children, her garden and her cat, not scenes of the French Revolution.

Fortunately, the great avant-garde artists, the Impressionists, turned away from classical subjects and embraced the modern urban scenes—gardens and parks, ballet dancers, ships at sea. This was a far more congenial atmosphere for female artists. For one thing, they could draw on their bourgeois families for their subject matter. One critic argued that only a woman could practise pure Impressionism, since "The essence of woman is not to bother herself with the deeper relations of things, [but] to apprehend the universe as a graceful, moving surface with an infinite number of nuances, and to give way inwardly to the adorable succession of her fleeting impressions."[760]

However, the work of female Impressionists went much deeper than that condescending assessment. Berthe Morisot (1841–1895) was a founding member of the Impressionist movement. She was born in Bourges, but her upper-middle-class family moved to Paris when Berthe was seven. Both she and her sister took drawing lessons, and Berthe studied under Camille Corot, the famous French landscape painter. In 1868, she met Édouard Manet and, through him, most of the members of the Impressionist group.

Morisot often painted women in their most private moments. *Lady at Her Toilette* wonderfully portrays a young female sitting in front of a mirror in her boudoir, putting the finishing touches to her appearance, while *Wet Nurse and Julie* is not the old Madonna and Child theme but a touching portrait of a woman who works for a living.[761] Some of Morisot's most poignant art was of adolescent girls. In one picture, *Julie Playing the Violin* (1893), her teenage daughter stands intently playing her instrument. On the wall in the background on the right is seen a small slice of a portrait of her father, Manet's younger brother Eugène, by Degas, and on the left is a larger painting of her mother by Manet. What Berthe Morisot seems to be saying is that the connection between the creative spirits, the musician daughter and the artist mother, was of great significance in that family.

Berthe Morisot was no Bohemian. After she married Eugène Manet in 1874, she lived a staid, middle-class life. She once wrote that she gave up painting outdoors because her husband didn't like wind-blown hair. She was perpetually dissatisfied, forever destroying this piece or that. Her mother wrote that when Berthe painted, she had an "anxious, unhappy, almost fierce look.... This existence of hers is like the ordeal of a convict in chains."[762] No one ever doubted, though, that she was utterly devoted to her work.

Another remarkable painter, Mary Cassatt (1844–1926), was born in Alleghany City, Pennsylvania, to a wealthy family. After four years of study at the Pennsylvania Academy of Fine Arts, she decided the Victorian attitude towards woman painters in the United States was hindering her work. She travelled throughout Europe, settling in Paris in 1874, where she, too, became an active member of the Impressionist group. Many scholars believe she is the best American artist of her generation, male or female.[763]

Cassatt is most famous for her glorious paintings of mothers and children, although she also loved to paint women at the opera; the radiant *Lydia in the Loge* (1874), a painting of her sister, is among her most famous. She profiled women in daily activities: at the tapestry frame, picking fruits, playing the banjo. The importance of her work is expressed by the scholars Rozsika Parker and Griselda Pollock: "In her works Cassatt critically analyzed the life of bourgeois women from infancy to old age in such a way that their acquisition of 'femininity' is exposed as a social process, not as the essence of womanliness, ideologically imputed to women as their nature, but a result of their introduction into place in the social order."[764] In 1877, Mary Cassatt's American family joined her in Paris. She never married, but continued to paint until the age of 70, when her eyesight failed.

Both Cassatt's and Morisot's upper-class domestic and social lives were reflected in their art. Although their painting exhibited great skill and insight, it was full of propriety. Rosa Bonheur (1822–1899), on the other hand, undermined all the social traditions.

Rosa Bonheur, who was a well-known painter of horses, was one of the most popular and famous artists of her era, eventually winning the coveted Légion d'Honneur medal. Her father Raymond Bonheur, an impoverished drawing master, was active in the Utopian socialist movement, Saint Simonianism, and believed both women and artists had a special role to play in the new society. Later in her life, Rosa told her biographer:

Why should I not be proud to be a woman? My father ... told me many times that the mission of women was to elevate the human race, to be the Messiah of future centuries. I owe to these doctrines the great and proud ambition I maintain for the sex to which I have the honor to belong.... I am certain that to us belongs the future.[765]

She remained single, although for 40 years, she lived with a female companion, Nathalie Micas, who was also an artist. One writer calls it "a seemingly cloudless, lifelong and apparently Platonic union with a female woman artist who evidently provided her with the companionship and emotional warmth which she needed."[766]

Rosa Bonheur painted animals, both wild and domestic, mostly in the outdoors. Indeed, the huge oil *The Horse Fair* (1853) became one of the most celebrated paintings of the 19th century. It is a study in realism, full of energy—men and the horses strain against each other—but also laced with a violence barely held in check.

Bonheur frequented the slaughterhouses for preliminary studies and sketches, which was the excuse she used to wear trousers and a loose smock. She also wore her hair cropped like a boy's. That didn't mean she abandoned Victorian decorum. She would tell her biographer, "Despite my metamorphoses of costume, there is not a daughter of Eve who appreciates the niceties more than I do; my brusque and even slightly unsociable nature has never prevented my heart from remaining completely feminine."[767] As she pointed out, she always made sure to get permission from the Paris police before she wandered the streets in her masculine attire.

V

The birth of the 20th century saw the emergence of that most exotic, and disturbing of creatures, the female bohemian artist. At last, women began to live their art in the way male artists had been doing for centuries. They left families and even husbands and headed for Paris, the centre of the art universe.

This new boldness, confidence and zest are obvious in the many self-portraits that appear during this time. In Zinaida Serebryakova's *Self-Portrait at the Dressing Table* (1909), the Russian artist sits in front of the mirror combing her long, black hair—the viewer can almost hear the crackle of electricity. Her chemise has fallen off one shoulder, her diamond bracelet sparkles and she smiles with seduction and pleasure, as though to say, "I am female, and I am free."

Four years later, the British painter Laura Knight completed her remarkable *Self-Portrait*. In it, the artist is dressed in a baggy, red sweater and a black fedora. She is painting an elegant female nude, who takes up the entire right-hand portion of the picture. "How holy is the human body when bare of other than the sun," Knight wrote in her autobiography.[768] Her painting seems to be boasting: into the sun, at last, have come female artists.

For some women artists, the realistic female nude was of no interest at all. Caught up in the turbulent world events of the century's first two decades, they used their talents as forces for political change. Often they favoured unorthodox and functional art forms, line engraving or collage, to get their message across. The German expressionist Käthe Kollwitz, for example, restricted herself to the graphic media, drawings and prints in black and white, simply because a print was less expensive than a painting and she wanted to reach as many people as she could. She produced remarkable images of suffering, poverty, death, insurrection. A major cycle, *The Peasant War* (1902–1908), depicts the uprising of German peasants in the 16th century led by a woman, Black Anna. As one critic put it, Kollwitz's work was "more universal and more powerful" than anyone believed was possible of the print medium.[769]

One of the most important missions of the 20th century female artist was to destroy stereotypical ideas of women expressed through images. Many of these artists reconstituted the ideas of the powerful art movements sweeping across Europe and North America for their own use—to undermine the assumptions society had about feminine nature. Hannah Höch, for example, literally cut visual stereotypes of women into pieces and reassembled them in witty, sometimes hilarious photomontages. Höch belonged to the German Dada Movement, a nihilistic protest against all aspects of Western culture, a reaction to the devastation of World War I and the rampant militarism prevalent at the time. The aim of the Dadaist movement was to startle the public into reassessing established values and aesthetics. To achieve this, they used unconventional materials, from urinals to waste paper, sometimes with pictures and words together. Höch's *Pretty Girl* (1920) is a photo montage of ordinary objects absurdly reassembled: a woman's torso with a light bulb for a head, a male hand holding a watch, a wrench, automobile tires, BMW insignias and a coiffured head of hair of a pretty girl. The work is one of the first to spoof the images of women as sex objects in the mass media, a hilarious put-down of mass-produced standards of beauty. At the same time, it is a troubling and, to some people, offensive image. Femininity, it insists, is not a prerogative of nature but a construct of society.

The Dada movement served as inspiration for the Surrealists, and, even though strange ideas about women were part of the baggage, the exploration of dreams and altered states of consciousness appealed to many female artists. As historian Anne Higonnet puts it, "Surrealism gave women licence to reject the way things were or seemed to be and picture other realities to express their own experiences or fantasies."[770] Meret Oppenheim's marvellous *Breakfast in Fur*, a fur-covered cup, saucer and spoon, achieved the Surrealist goal of transforming the familiar into the strange. While it's a humourous image, there is also something hideous and repellent about it.

The same can be said of some of the work of the Mexican painter Frida Kahlo (1907–1954), one of the most well-known artists of the 20th century. All of her paintings are self-portraits, expressions of her extraordinary life. She not only had polio as a child but at age 18, she was in a near-fatal streetcar accident. An iron handrail pierced her back and she suffered multiple fractures, injuries that later forced her to undergo 35 operations. (She died in 1954 at age 47, after a gangrenous leg was amputated.) The pain that she lived with every day did not dampen her passion for life. She had many lovers, Trotsky and several women among them, and was twice married to the Mexican artist and muralist Diego Rivera. The extremes of her life are expressed in her paintings. *Broken Column* (1944), for example, is an excruciating portrait of a woman in mental and physical pain. Through the middle of her body rises a shattered Greek column, representing Kahlo's own broken spine. A white strap circles her naked body, representing the steel corset she was forced to wear to support her back. Nails driven into her flesh, reminiscent of the arrows of St. Sebastian, denote the suffering that never ceased. She is crying copious tears, but her expression is one of great stoicism.

Some critics have seen the tortured history of Mexico itself in Kahlo's martyr images. In fact, she once remarked that she wanted her "work to be a contribution to the struggle for peace and liberty." Her biographer, Hayden Herrera, however, claims Kahlo's paintings "shriek their personal message so passionately that there are no decibels left for propaganda."[771]

In contrast to the unequivocal personal content of Kahlo's pictures is the intriguing metaphorical imagery painted by American artist Georgia O'Keeffe (1887–1986). Her lush, magnified still lifes look very much like what they are supposed to be: flowers, say, or cow's skulls. Yet what else could *Black Iris* (1927) be but a portrait of female genitalia? O'Keeffe always denied the connection between her flowers and female sexuality. "Eroticism! That's something people themselves put in the paintings. They've found things that never entered my mind."[772] Despite her protestations, critics have had a heyday digging out sexual meaning in O'Keeffe's work. Anna Chave, for example, writes, "O'Keeffe portrayed abstractly, but unmistakably, her experience of her own body, not what it looked like to others. The parts of the body she engaged were mainly invisible (and unrepresented) due to interiority, but she offered viewers an ever-expanding catalogue of visual metaphors for those areas, and for the experience of space and penetrability generally."[773] Once the door was opened on this interpretation, it was difficult to shut it again; iris as vulva is seared into the modern mind.

How to portray the female body, if it could be properly portrayed at all, was a preoccupation of the brash feminist art movement of the 1970s. Is a painting of a female nude a beautiful thing in itself or a sexual object? Some feminist artists dealt with the problem by simply eliminating the human form from their work. The Cuban artist Ana Medieta, for example, in her *Untitled. Serie Volcán 2* (1979), created colour photographs in which the female body is represented by potent and troublesome imagery of fire, earth and water.

Other artists attempted to turn the tables: men became sex objects, women the dominant players. The British sculptor Nancy Gossman bound a male figure in leather, straps, buckles and zippers, an image that, as one critic put it, "at once repels and fascinates, causing us to recognize how our perceptions of sexuality are linked to signs of power, both exerted and submitted to."[774]

Sylvia Sleigh's 1971 *Philip Golub Reclining* is the direct reversal of centuries of male artist/female model paintings. A young, good-looking male nude is lying, his back turned to the viewer, in the kind of seductive pose usually reserved for women. He looks into a mirror directly behind him, where a woman is busily working at her easel.

Another way of dealing with the dilemma of the female form was to confront it head on, to break taboos, to introduce bodily parts and functions that formerly had no place in polite society. Judy Chicago's *Red Flag* (1971) is a photo litho of herself from the waist down, withdrawing a bloody tampon. Carol Schneeman, in her performance piece *Interior Scroll* (1975), stands naked except for a kind of loincloth, all the while reading a poem from a scroll that she pulls from her vagina, supposedly an indictment of the male view of female art.

As the century nears its end, many women artists continue to explore feminist themes in their work, although much of it is more subtle and sophisticated than the rage that had hurtled forth in the 1970s. Others do not create overtly provocative feminist statements but rather incorporate their entire life experiences. The work of Newfoundland artist Mary Pratt is an example.

Her subject matter is of mundane daily life—a dining room with a red rug, a baby being bathed, a dead salmon thrown into the kitchen sink—but her homey objects glow with radiance and transcend their earthly functions. These are not pretty pictures of domestic bric-a-brac. As one critic puts it, in Mary Pratt's work can be seen "the creative and procreative, the environmental and the ecumenical, the sexual, the sacrificial and the subversive."[775] *Burning the Rhododendron* (1990), for example, crackles with apocalyptic energy, violence and passion. This is a body of work that reflects the life of a mother of four children, a wife with a long-time troublesome marriage to another well-known artist, Christopher Pratt, a painter who must now cope with disabling arthritis. Mary Pratt once told a reporter, "There are a lot of women who would come up to me [after seeing her work] and just burst into tears. But I'd far rather that reaction than a good review from the art elite."[776] That might serve as an appropriate epitaph for women artists throughout history.

Marjorie

I never realized how far out of the loop I was, how odd my background, how strange my circumstances. My mother was a gay divorcée, and, while I was going to high school, a very poor one. Our poverty was well hidden; none of my school chums had an inkling of it. Our apartment was always artistically furnished, my little brothers and myself nicely turned out, our table laid, if not with gourmet meals, certainly nourishing ones, all a result of my mother's strength of character, her endurance—working at jobs she hated and was totally unsuited for—and her marvellous ability to create anything with her hands.

My mother's education had been aimed at making her a skilled housekeeper and a superb hostess, and she probably would have been both, if it hadn't been for a quirk in her personality. She was an utterly ethical person, would not compromise even the smallest principle, yet she was attracted to tall, dark, handsome men who could dance beautifully but who were either alcoholics or gamblers. This made for stormy times. She was divorced twice, but for years, there were other male "friends" lurking in the background with whom she did constant battle. While she might have aspired to the domesticated middle-class life touted by the magazines, she was a feminist to her core and would not for a moment put up with abusive male behaviour. It had to do, I think, with her upbringing.

My grandfather William May looked so much like Canada's prime minister William Lyon Mackenzie King that people would turn and stare at him. He was a railroad engineer, and proud of it. He was also a confirmed abstainer and a dedicated atheist for his entire life. He was a hard-working, no-nonsense man, but there was a romantic side to him, too. He loved playing the piano and, whenever he was off shift, his house resounded to the strains of Strauss and Gilbert and Sullivan.

My grandmother Nellie Bridget and her sister were refugees from poverty-stricken Ireland. They were proper young women, and took ladylike jobs as a telephone operator and a wig-maker. Nellie teamed up with Bill May, but the marriage was always a little shaky. He prided himself on being the breadwinner and providing a bountiful table. Grandmother was as independent and strong-willed as my mother. She opened a beauty salon on Queen Street East in Toronto's Beaches and was one of the first to install those monstrous machines that fried women's hair into permanent waves.

One day, my grandfather opened a chest in the cellar of her store and found thousands of dollars worth of useless South African gold-mining stock. It wasn't so much the loss of a small fortune that bothered him but rather that my grandmother had invested it without telling him. They separated shortly after, and divorced once their children reached adulthood.

Elizabeth May, my mother, was sent to Loretta Abbey, a private Catholic school for girls. It was an odd choice for an atheist family, but it was thought my mother's unruly temper might be brought under control and she would develop lovely manners. She seemed to have learned little there except how to say "Please pass the butter" in French, of which she was always inordinately proud. Most of her secondary schooling was spent in the art program at Western Technical School.

I believe my mother could have been a magazine or advertising illustrator, and perhaps even a great artist, she had that much talent, but the fortitude needed to break out of the mold that had been cast for her was beyond her. She took decorative arts and domestic science, and learned how to sew as well as a professional seamstress. The tasteful curtains, my fancy dress to the prom, my youngest brother's shepherd costume for the Christmas pageant were all made by her. Through her skill, a patina of respectability was presented to the outside world that helped secure our tenuous hold in the middle class.

My mother met my father at the famous Palais Royale dance hall. Douglas (Ted) Smith was a gorgeous young man, tall and broadly built, with jet-black hair and eyes as blue as cornflowers. My mother thought he looked like Clark Gable, only without the mustache. He was shy, with a sweet, goofy smile. She, too, was striking, with her dramatic black eyebrows, dark eyes and symmetrical features. They were married in 1941, just weeks before he went off to war, and I was born the following year.

That first Christmas after my father's return from the war, my mother turned our duplex on Concord Avenue into a fairyland, beautifully decorated with an extravaganza of a tree. On the way home from the liquor store, my father dropped a case of 24 beer, picked it up, put it on his shoulder and carried it dripping into my mother's beautiful home. He stumbled into the living room and fell into her tree. That was the end of the marriage.

I don't remember being particularly upset or sad; maybe I didn't know him well enough. Indeed, all I remember about my early childhood is that it was filled with happiness. My mother and I remained in the large duplex. Two rooms in the attic were rented out to single women: June and Terry, factory workers, who were there for years. That they were obviously lesbians did not enter my innocent mother's head. This set-up not only provided her with extra income and some company but also with built-in babysitters. Not that I would have stood in the way of her rather exuberant social life. Almost every Friday at five, a taxi pulled up to our front door and whisked me off to my paternal grandparents.

I seldom saw my father after my parents divorced—the last time was when I was 13 years old—but my grandfather and grandmother nicely filled the gap. When I arrived on the weekends, a new doll house or stuffed animal or board game would be sitting on the dining-room table—anything my heart desired.

Russell and Marjorie (I was named after her) Smith lived on the ground floor of a neat little duplex on Glenlake Avenue. Above resided the family of my father's one brother, Stuart (Bud) Smith. My cousin Virginia and I were only a month apart in age and grew up with the emotional rough-and-tumble attachment of sisters. We have remained good friends.

In my grandparents' house there was always talk about illustrious ancestors. Among many worthies, we were supposedly related to that buccaneer Canadian capitalist Sir Henry Pellatt. Now and then, Virginia and I were marched off to inspect the gold faucets in the bathrooms of his gaudy mansion, Casa Loma. I think my gentle, unassuming grandmother was obsessed with time past because the family she had married into had fallen so far. My grandfather owned a little business putting metal strips on the top of calendars, which eked out a living for his family, my father's (he married again and had two children) and his foreman.

The old man suffered from rheumatism—when I was a child, he could hardly walk—and perhaps that's why he was so miserable—to everybody, that is, except me. I was the light of his life, the one who got the first slice of the Sunday roast beef he always carved, the only one who could get him to put his cardigan on when it was chilly. He and I voyaged to the Orient almost every weekend via his gazetteer, while he played "Slow Boat to China" on his record player. By Sunday evenings, though, I felt like someone who had stuffed herself with too much chocolate cake. I was always glad to return to the reality of my mother's home.

She worked as a floor-walker at Eaton's department store. Every evening, I meet her at the Ossington Avenue bus station and she would tell me about the purse-snatchers and stealers of fur coats whom she had nabbed that day. Those stories, along with the hours I spent alone, happily daydreaming in the sunroom that served as my bedroom, provided, I think, the seeds of a writer.

I was a bookish little girl, and Saturday mornings, long before my mother was out of bed, I would wander off to the Dufferin Street Public Library, a walk along many city blocks and through a small park. The thought that bad men might be lurking behind the bushes worried my mother, and for my seventh birthday, I was taken to the Humane Society and told I could chose a pet. It was one of the most thrilling moments of my life. Peter, a skinny, flea-bitten mutt with bad teeth, became my close companion, waiting patiently outside the library while I collected that week's bonanza. My mother's Saturday-morning sleep-ins became even longer.

I must have done well at school because in Grade 1, I was presented with the Best Girl of the Year Award, a goldfish that the teacher was anxious to get rid of over the summer holidays. I could have been named a Rhodes Scholar and my mother would not have been more delighted. Her philosophy of child-rearing was built entirely on optimism. If you did anything that was at all worthwhile, a mark of 60 in math perhaps, you were praised to the skies. I cannot remember her ever saying a cross word to me, except during arguments when I was a teenager and she was under enormous pressure, but these occasions were very few.

Our idyllic life (from my point of view, anyway) came to an end when I was 12 years old and my mother met John Siggins. There were a number of eligible men circling about our duplex, many of them responsible, with good jobs. She chose a man who was tall, dark and handsome and could sing like Frankie Laine. She married him, and in 1954 and 1956 gave birth to my brothers John William and Michael Matthew.

At first, I, too, thought the world of John Siggins. He was full of fun and took us on picnics, something we had never experienced, since we didn't have a car. He was a baseball fanatic, and practised with me so often that I was made catcher for the Sparkle Cleaners team in the girls' softball league. The longer he lived with us, though, the more a weakness in his moral fibre, a corruption of character, became apparent. I think my mother realized what she had gotten her self into when she finally went to visit his sister. The woman lived with her extended family in a rundown Toronto slum. In the back yard was a large pot full of boiling water; we never figured out if they actually cooked in it or simply tried to get the washing whiter. My mother concluded they were Irish gypsies, and nothing would change her mind.

The marriage was a dreadful one—years of ferocious battling that left everyone, including me, badly bruised. It basically ended when a cheque for a loan to fix up the house was made out to the head of the household (my stepfather, of course) and he lost it all betting on a horse. The saddest memory I have of that time was of my baby brothers, my mother and I sitting in the dark eating cheese sandwiches by candlelight. The electricity had been turned off because the bill hadn't been paid.

My mother finally screwed up her courage and got rid of her immoral, irresponsible husband. Since our lovely Concord Avenue apartment, we had moved some six times—one year I had gone to three different schools—and had finally landed in Scarborough. It was the last place my mother wanted to be. She was a city girl who thought the suburbs an ugly wasteland, but a nice, inexpensive, three-bedroom apartment in a government-subsidized building was found for us on Parkette Place, so we remained in exile for my high-school years.

It was not the happiest time for me. Perhaps the years of marital battles had taken a toll, although I didn't think of that then. One thing I knew for sure: I would never rely on a man for status or financial security.

Like my friends Judy Davey and Noreen Matthews, I, too, got it into my head to become a doctor, although how I ever thought I would manage it financially, I don't know. Although generally I was a pretty good student, I was perpetually anxious about my grades. What's interesting to me now is that, although I loved English literature with a passion, it never occurred to me that I might be a writer. Not a spark of what was obviously my natural vocation revealed itself. Yet I remember being fascinated by the poet e. e. cummings, and, under his influence, wrote my Grade 13 English composition exam without using capital letters or punctuation. I flunked, of course, even though it was probably a pretty inventive paper. (The next year, I rewrote the exam, not using an ounce of my imagination, and easily passed.)

By that time, my dream of medical school had thankfully vanished. I decided to take a year off, but it turned out to be a chaotic, troubling time. I had strange jobs—working as a bunny girl, killing mice in the name of insulin quality control at Connaught Laboratories, working in a used-car lot as a Girl Friday—all of which I enjoyed, although I knew deep down they were rather corrupting experiences. My relationships with the opposite sex were also troubling, to say the least.

I'd had a steady boyfriend in high school. A tall, skinny guy with wavy hair, he went to the parochial St. Michael's High School and planned to be a lawyer. Hot and heavy necking was the order of the day, and we indulged. It was the only interesting thing about the relationship. The night my virginity was lost, he was far more sorry than I, but then, he was a devoted Roman Catholic. It was a clumsy, childish affair, and after I saw the movie *South Pacific*, I decided to wash him right out of my hair. I think he was glad to get rid of me, too. I was not the proper Catholic girl his parents had in mind for him. Just the same, the absence of a boyfriend, and in particular his car, was one of the reasons I found Grade 13 such a drudge.

My first year out of school, I started going out with Spiro (I can't remember his last name). He had been a brilliant student in Greece, and was supposedly on his way to MIT (Massachusetts Institute of Technology). While his immigration papers were being processed, he stayed with his relatives in Toronto. He was good-looking, blond with refined, almost feminine features; these days I would think of that sex pot Dionysus. We started dating regularly, and it was through him that I caught my first glimpse of genuine female oppression. We went to visit his mother in Detroit. She could neither read nor write, and because she was elderly, she was the only one of the many women in the family who was allowed to sit down during the meal.

It shocked me so profoundly that all I could think about was getting rid of the guy. The more I spurned him, the more he became convinced I loved him madly. For over two years, he never stopped harassing and threatening me. I was afraid to go home alone—there he'd be, lurking near my door. These days, it would be called stalking and the police would be called. Perhaps it was an educational experience; my feminism became rooted even deeper.

I don't know what prompted her, but it was my mother who sent away for the application form for Journalism School at Ryerson Polytechnical Institute (now Ryerson University). It was the perfect place for me at the time. My entire three years was spent in one outrageous, loud debate; we yelled at each other in philosophy, political science and sociology. We had a critical-reading class in which, to our great amazement, the layers of propaganda in *Time* and *Reader's Digest* were peeled back. English literature was a three-year survey course, beginning with Chaucer and ending with Hemingway. I think I was the only one in the class to read every single assignment.

My classmates were so few, we became a family. We spent hours together, working on the university newspaper, drinking draft beer—I developed a passion for pickled eggs—talking and talking. I had a brief but passionate love affair, but so did everybody else. One thing was sure: for us, journalism was just a stopgap. We were going to be great writers. Ernest Hemingway, after all, had worked at *The Toronto Star*.

The only thing that marred those years was that our house burned down. My mother and I, with my two young brothers in tow, had finally fled Scarborough and moved into a rickety old house on Mutual Street near Maple Leaf Gardens. The man next door was about to sell—his property was worth far more than the house—and, greedy for the insurance, he had set a fire in his basement. It was Hockey Night in Canada, and the cars were so wedged in on our little street that the fire trucks did not arrive until all three row houses were burnt almost to the ground. I was overjoyed that nobody had been hurt, but my mother was devastated, and I now understand how terrible it must have been for her. She lost almost everything: all the antiques she had hauled out of garbage dumps and refurbished, the Irish porcelain her mother had left her, her photographs. Undaunted, she started over.

All four of us moved into a one-bedroom apartment in the posh City Park apartments in the heart of the city; I slept on the chesterfield in the living room. We might have been cramped, but at least the address was right. (Eventually, we would move up in the world to two- and then three-bedroom apartments in similar trendy neighbourhoods.) A scene from that time: I had been dating an intern, a specialist, I think, in kidneys. I thought him dull and self-centred, but my mother urged me on, thinking, she said, of my security (never mind she had never thought of her own). My boyfriend and I were sitting in my living room, chatting away, when a loud rattle sounded and our marmalade-coloured cat sailed in on the skateboard my brothers had taught him to ride. My mother came to say hello, completely forgetting her face was encased in a mud pack and her hair in rollers; she, too, was going on a date. The doctor eventually excused himself, and when he returned, pale-faced, he politely asked what was going on in the washroom. I had to explain that my youngest brother had found a rare species of turtle. In order to get the thing to eat, a certain ritual was carefully followed: both the turtle and a hunk of hamburger were placed in the tub, the shower was turned on, a tape recorder boomed out thunder, the lights were rigged to blink compulsively off and on, all to recreate the beast's natural habitat. The doctor never called me again, but it was weeks before I noticed.

Reporters and editors in those days were in such short supply that any of us who displayed the slightest talent was hired. I was offered a job at the *Toronto Telegram*. The newsroom was a terrifying place for me. It was a huge, intense beehive, full of scowling, mostly male reporters yanking paper from their old typewriters and yelling "Copy" at the top of their voice. Most drank like troopers, told boring stories about past journalistic exploits and, puffed up like adders, announced they were kings of the universe. I was told not to walk by the copy desk before the morning deadline, as I and my mini-skirt might distract the editors. It was a joke, but I didn't know it. For hours, I sat with my legs crossed, too frightened to go to the washroom. In my first byline, a copy editor decided "Marjorie" was old-fashioned while "Maggie" had more spunk. I was too intimidated to protest, and so was stuck with a label I never much liked. (I have always thought that if I had kept my real name, Marjorie May-Smith, I would have ended up writing gardening books or at least murder mysteries that occurred in gardens.)

Fortunately for me, I was not immediately cast into the newsroom but was assigned to "After Four," a weekly section for teenagers. "After Four" was one of those innovations meant to attract readership, in this case the young. To ensure its success, the publisher's son, Johnny F. Bassett, was put in charge. We became such good friends, he arranged dates for me with some of his rich chums—always, however, after all other plans had fallen through. The two I remember were George Eaton and Conrad Black, although there were several others. I thought them all either spoiled brats or boring, stuffed shirts.

Working for "After Four" was a great job. There were tedious chores— "Fashion Tips for Teens," for example, was not exactly my forte—but I was also sent to Detroit to do a piece on the Supremes. I was so thrilled by their sexy, mesmerizing sound, I wrote my first good journalism. "After Four" was a place I could cut my teeth and, most important, develop as a writer.

Soon, however, I was forced out of my safe cocoon and into the hurly-burly of real journalism. I was never a very good reporter. I was always too slow writing things down, and I hated phoning Judge so-and-so at two in the morning to ask if his report on the Mafia were ready. Usually, I simply faked it. Eventually, though, I did find my métier: covering City Hall. In those days, municipal politics were full of the *Sturm und Drang* of citizen protest. I used to brag that even in the utilitarian Public Works Committee, I could find a story with as much drama, pathos and comedy as *Richard the Third*.

All this time, I was still living with my mother and two brothers in the crowded but fashionable apartment. It didn't put a damper on my social life at all; it gave me an excuse not to get too serious. I was still determined, after living my mother's experience, never to marry.

On September 18, 1971, John Bassett announced he was shutting down the *Telegram*. *The Toronto Star* was buying the circulation list for $10-million. For those many employees in their fifties or sixties, the disappearance of the *Tely* was a tragedy, because no other newspaper jobs were available, but for those of us who were young, the closing provided a timely push to do other things.

I signed up to take English literature at the University of Toronto, but didn't make it to one class. Freelance assignments began flowing in, and writing was much more interesting than sitting in lectures talking about writing. I wrote a column for *Toronto Life* magazine on city politics and articles for *Chatelaine*. Presided over by Doris Anderson, *Chatelaine* was a fascinating magazine in the days when the women's movement was heating up. Hidden among the recipes for whipped cream and ads for bras were inflammatory articles that questioned the very basis of society. I wrote a story demanding housewives should be paid for their work through taxes from their husbands' pay cheques. From the outrage that ensued, you might have thought civilization was coming to an end. Articles on the liberalization of divorce, the legalization of abortion and custody rights appeared among the refrigerator ads. These days, sadly, the magazine is a pale imitation of those few glory years.

In the winter of 1972, I was handed a plum: a grant to travel to the capitals of Europe and study their official plans, paid for by the federal government, a spin-off, I suppose, from my writing about municipal politics. I talked to hordes of city planners and local politicians about their old buildings, and produced a booklet called *The Preservation of Historic Sites: A European Perspective*. The most interesting thing about the trip was a romantic encounter with the Irish poet John Montague.

On my return, I accepted, mostly for the monthly pay cheque, the job of city-hall reporter and commentator for CITY-TV, a lively new television station that was about to beam on air. *The City Show*, the program I worked for, was broadcast for two and half hours every weekday evening. We were among the first to use video rather than film cameras, and 20 minutes of boring planning-committee meetings was among the fare offered, but there were also lively debates, especially during elections, along with serious interviews. One of my first coups was an hour-long interview with Mayor David Crombie. My excited family and friends crowded around the TV, the program came on and my mother let out a howl of outrage. I had accidentally worn the pretty yellow blouse she had made me inside-out. Once, when I was receiving an award from a women's group, I wore one ankle-length black boot and one calf-length brown boot. I simply didn't have time to think about what I looked liked.

It seems much longer to me now, but I worked at CITY-TV for just over a year. In 1972, I won a Southam Fellowship for Journalists, which meant a year of study at the University of Toronto. It was a great deal, because most of your salary was paid and you could audit any course you wanted. The Fellows were part of Massey College for graduate students, the academic setting I had craved writ large. Academic robes were obligatory, foul-tasting sherry was a staple and nuts and cigars were served after dinner.

The fall I arrived, Massey had taken a giant step into the modern age by allowing female students to live in residence. The College Master, novelist Robertson Davies, was still in a state of shock over this dastardly deed. Whenever he attended one of the Southam dinners, he spent most of the time talking about pornography and trying to get a rise, I think, out of me. The feminine must have been on Master Davies' mind because his Christmas story that year was a savage, satirical attack on women scholars. I thought it absurd, and wrote a rebuttal for the college newsletter in which all the female names were replaced by males'. I was told the Master didn't like it one bit. I would have enjoyed myself immensely in this pompous academic setting if I hadn't been so distracted. I had finally got involved in a serious relationship.

Ron Haggart was a giant in journalism in Toronto of the 1950s and '60s. He wrote a daily column about the city and its politics that was some of the best muckraking Canada has ever seen. Everyone read him, including my mother. He had left the *Star* after a fight over what he could or couldn't write about Eaton's department store, a big advertiser in all the papers, and had come over to the *Telegram*. I used to watch him with admiration as he strolled through the newspaper, a tall, beautifully dressed man with reddish-blond hair and baby-blue eyes. When the paper folded, Ron joined CITY-TV as news director and it was he who had hired me.

Right from our first meeting, I understood he was interested in having an affair. I knew he had a wife and child—that he had, in fact, been married three times and had a daughter by each wife. I should have rebuffed him, walked out of the job, but shamefully, I didn't. My mother liked men who could dance and sing; I fell for men who were sophisticated, older—in this case, by 15 years—and took me to elegant restaurants. In my defence, it was the pursuit of the hound after a rabbit. When I occasionally went out for dinner with another man, Ron would be sitting at the next table. With the Southam Fellowship, I would no longer be part of his daily life. He decided to leave his wife and child and move in with me.

By this time, my mother had bought a property on Parliament Street, a tall, skinny, loft-like place; a friend said it was like living in a tree house. As usual, she had fixed it up beautifully and was comfortably ensconced there. My brothers were away at college. With a little help from me with the monthly mortgage payments, she could manage on her own. At 30 years old, I was free at last to move out.

Ron and I began life together in a modern apartment that was as boxy and ordinary as any other. After a year or so, we moved to a chi-chi townhouse in Rosedale; we even possessed the dog du jour, a West Highland terrier. The relationship was fine at the beginning. We had a lot in common, much to talk about and he was surprised I could cook.

After the Southam Fellowship, I got a job as a writer-producer for the current-affairs portion of the CBC's local news-hour supper show. Ron also joined the public broadcaster as senior producer of the superb investigative show *fifth estate*. It was a good time to work at the CBC, before vengeful politicians began to bleed it to death by cutting its budget. My boss was Diana Filer, a wonderfully gutsy producer who had originated several of the CBC's most popular radio shows, and she let us do what we wanted as long as we worked hard. I learned about the short documentary, how to quickly milk the drama of any story—a marvellous lesson for a writer. It was not serious writing, though. I was still getting up early in the mornings to work on a short story or an essay, without much success, since there was so little time. I finally decided to quit daily television and try freelancing again.

Perhaps I'd been out of the loop too long, but magazines weren't exactly lining up to give me assignments. It was a disappointing, frustrating time for me. Ron had made it clear he expected I would pay half the household costs, never mind that he made twice as much as me. It was a scramble each month to find enough money, since our standard of living was so high. Then, in January 1977, I became pregnant.

I always assumed I would have at least one child, and as I approached my mid-thirties, it was obviously about time. Ron knew I had gone off the Pill, and we had even celebrated what had turned out to be a false alarm. When I actually became pregnant, however, he didn't say much, and it was obvious he was upset. Again, I think it was a question of money. Although it would hang on for a pathetic five years longer, I knew then that the relationship was dying.

During my pregnancy, I cried a lot, read Edith Wharton novels and tried to write some poetry. Finally, ACTRA, the union for writers and performers, asked me to join a team bargaining with the CBC for a new contract. It was just what I needed. The sessions went on for months, there was some ready cash and something to think about other than myself. One of my co-negotiators was Gerry Sperling, who called himself a journalist but was really a professor of political science at the University of Regina. It was a spontaneous, hilarious meeting of minds. We became not lovers at the time, but fast friends.

Carrie-May Haggart was born on October 3, 1977, three weeks late and weighing over ten pounds. She came into the world laughing, a beautiful, sunny child who was and has remained a joy to anyone who has ever met her.

By this time, we were living in a large home in the Danforth and Broadview area. Cleaning house and looking after a baby were more tedious than I had ever imagined. I found it pure drudgery and, as Ron kept pointing out, I wasn't making any hard cash. Delmena Bryant, a big, husky Jamaican woman, finally arrived to take over the care of the household. I liked her a lot—we used to dance to reggae music in the kitchen—and I adored her cooking: jellied pigs' feet, black peas and rice, curried goat. Ron didn't approve of the hilarity; he felt left out, I think. Another blow to our relationship.

In 1979, I went back to work for CITY-TV. Again, it was a matter of a pay cheque and desperately wanting to get out of the house. This time, I was the producer of a six o'clock news show with the flamboyant name CITY-PULSE NEWS. It certainly wasn't journalism, more a pastiche of images and sensations. Forever conscientious, I put in 12-hour work days, trying to instill some system of news-gathering. With the input of the news director, a whiz kid not long out of film school called Ivan Fecan, our ratings did zoom upwards, but it was all a mad dash, smoke and mirrors, and I quickly got tired of it.

During that frantic period, my first serious book was published. Actually, there had been two others. It took me a weekend to write a silly take-off called *How to Get a Man*, with drawings by cartoonist Ben Wicks. It was published in 1968 and was my daughter's favourite book for years. I had been, for a brief unhappy time, the *Tely*'s ski reporter, and had written an opus called *A Guide to Skiing in Eastern North America*, published by McGraw-Hill in 1969. It's the only book of mine that has rated an advertisement in the *New York Times*. My book that was published in 1979, a biography of the publisher of the *Telegram* entitled *Bassett: John Bassett's forty years in politics, publishing, business and sports*, was a much more serious effort.

John White Hughes Bassett didn't want me to write it. I was a nobody in his eyes, and he would have no control over what was published. Since he and many of his relatives and close associates refused to talk to me—although a surprising number did agree to be interviewed—it was not so much a biography as an exposé. Bassett's life had been full of ferocious business battles, but what had incensed me, what pricked me on to write the book, was the discovery that it hadn't been necessary to shut down the *Telegram*; there had been at least two serious offers to purchase. Bassett had closed it out of pride. If he couldn't run the paper profitably, nobody could. I was always amazed he never sued me for libel.

The book caused a small sensation, but it wasn't the bestseller it should have been. The publisher James Lorimer sold portions of it to any periodical that wanted it—for peanuts. *Toronto Life* boasted of the largest editions in its history, most of it my book. Why would anybody pay money for it?

I left CITY-TV in 1980, once again determined to write. This time, I enjoyed a blossoming freelance career. I wrote television documentaries for CBC, produced election coverage for CITY, but mostly I worked for magazines. For *Toronto Life*, I wrote a political column, which I loved because it involved digging up scandals and uncovering civil-rights infringements. A two-part series on the Jamaican community, I feel, was the best journalism I've ever done.

Nonetheless, it wasn't the happiest of times. My relationship with Ron Haggart had soured. Nothing is worse, I think, than continuing to live with someone when all love and sympathy have withered. When Ron told me I should stay with him for the sake of the child, whom he now adored, my blood ran cold. I did try, though. Although Ron flatly refused even to consider it, I went to a marriage counsellor, only to be told the relationship was obviously over.

In the fall of 1982, I was asked by Gerry Sperling, my old friend from ACTRA negotiating days, to give a seminar on documentary writing at the Yorkton Short Film Festival in Saskatchewan. During that magical weekend—

we stopped at every historical plaque along the byways, and had a hilarious time discussing buffalo hunters and bootleggers—we became lovers. He was everything the other men in my life weren't. He was short and stocky, with a large nose and dark, curly hair. He reminded me of the Jewish boys I had grown up with, and in fact, as it turned out, his childhood home had been located only three blocks away from mine. He was also amazingly gregarious, openly affectionate and funny beyond words. Hugging was as natural to him as breathing. Most important, I sensed that at his core was a rock-solid integrity. He was a humanitarian, a political scrapper, whose ideals were expressed through his Marxism. Our intimacy would blossom into what for me, with my background, is an unbelievably happy marriage. He is the first reader of my writing, the best editor.

One day in April 1983, I packed a few of our belongings and, with my daughter, the housekeeper Delmena and the West Highland terrier, moved out of my matrimonial home into my mother's tree house. (By this time she was living elsewhere.) I have never felt so happy or liberated in my life.

During my memorable trip out west, I had visited the School of Journalism at the University of Regina where Gerry was a part-time professor (he also taught political science). The director of the school, Ron Robbins, asked if I would consider accepting the Max Bell Chair of Journalism the following September. This was a plum job with a small teaching load, a good salary and an ample expense account. It was perfect timing, given my blossoming relationship with Gerry, and I decided to move with my daughter to Regina.

I was not happy leaving my mother, who wasn't well at the time, but it was only a year's appointment. For sure, I'd be back. Toronto, after all, was my city; Gerry would simply have to find himself a job there. As it turned out, I fell in love with the Prairies, and my mother and two brothers ended up moving to Regina.

Although I try hard, I've never been a good teacher. I'm uncomfortable, always sure I'm boring the students to death. As Max Bell Professor, my teaching load was mercifully small. Most of my time was spent advising individual students on what they should do with their professional lives. It was a year, too, of getting used to this pretty but parochial little city with its wretched winter weather. I was finally seduced by the kind, civilized people and the writing community that was so welcoming. To my amazement, I loved walking in a landscape crowded only with geese, ducks, muskrats and beavers.

Most significant of all were the incredible stories. Just six months before I arrived in Regina, around the corner from where Gerry and I lived, JoAnn Wilson, the former wife of Colin Thatcher, scion of a political dynasty, had been brutally murdered in her garage. Rumours of who had committed the horrible crime and why percolated during my time at the university. In May 1984, just as my appointment was ending, Colin Thatcher was arrested and charged with first-degree murder. There was no question I would write a book on the case. It was a fabulous story: a powerful, political family with deep roots in the province, a marriage breakdown, a battle over custody of the children and the property, and a man so self-centred and evil as to believe he could impose his own reality, even if it meant murder.

I signed with Macmillan of Canada because the publisher Doug Gibson offered me a $20,000 advance. Other books were being written, we knew, so it had to come out that fall. With the help of Sandra Bartlett, a wonderful researcher, I interviewed over 80 people, attended all the court appearances, including the three-week trial, and completed the 150,000-word manuscript in 11 months. It was, and remains, the most nerve-wracking and thrilling journalistic experience I've ever had. *A Canadian Tragedy* won the Arthur Ellis Crime Writers Award, and formed the basis of the CBC-TV miniseries *Love and Hate*, which has sold all over the world.

By the time I completed the manuscript, Gerry was already on sabbatical and living in Beijing. He had been a Soviet expert but, in recent years, his interest had shifted to China. When he was offered a job as a polisher for the Xinhua (New China) News Agency, he decided it would be a good way to experience the country's politics first-hand. Adam, Gerry's son, went as well. When I had arrived in the household, Adam was 17 years old and in full revolt against everything. He was sometimes infuriating, but he was also fun-loving, irreverent and good-hearted, and I liked him at once. Taking him to China was the best thing we could have done. He stayed there for five years.

Carrie-May and I arrived in Beijing in June 1985. Initially, we lived at the Friendship Hotel, a large compound for foreign experts, but in a few months, we were moved downtown into what was a remarkably large apartment by Chinese standards: seven rooms and two bathrooms. Many of the people in the complex had been unjustly imprisoned during the Cultural Revolution. Upstairs lived Michael Shapiro, a British Communist and journalist who had come to assist the revolution in 1949, his wife Liu Qinghe, an educator and psychologist who had been educated at an American university, and their two sons, both in their twenties, Solomon and Roger Shapiro. Michael had been imprisoned during the Cultural Revolution for no reason other than he was a foreigner. He was kept in solitary confinement for over three years, and finally, suffering from Parkinson's Disease, was unceremoniously dumped on his wife's doorstep. Gerry used to read pieces from the book *The Joy of Yiddish* to him. He died while we were in China, but we have remained close friends with the rest of the family.

Carrie-May went to an all-Chinese school and was treated as only a blonde, blue-eyed girl could have been. She learned the language in three months, wore the red scarf representing the blood of the Chinese martyrs and was a star on the bean-bag-throwing team. Her walk to school four times a day was along Fuxingmenwei, one of the busiest streets in Beijing. I worried about her until one day, she caught a cold and had to stay home. Within 15 minutes, the newspaper vendor, the sweet-potato salesman and the street-sweeper were at our door. No child, meandering to school, was ever watched so carefully.

I, too, worked at Xinhua News Agency as a polisher until I gagged on the propaganda. Fortunately, I got a job as a part-time journalism professor at the Beijing Broadcast Institute. I had only three graduate students, all of whom spoke English. I think I must have been an influence on them, because all three became involved in the Tiananmen Square student uprising, although eventually, they ended up with important jobs in journalism, in China and abroad. Gerry, too, ended up teaching journalism at the Chinese Academy of Social Sciences.

Gerry loved Beijing. Every day he rode his bike the 30 minutes to his class, greeting every one of the hundreds, no thousands, of people who crossed his path. Chinese came quickly to him, as it did to Carrie. Even though I studied hard, it took me much longer. When the housekeeper arrived, who spoke not a word of English, I was forced into hesitant Mandarin. That eventually I could carry on a crude conversation was something of which I am still inordinately proud.

As a journalist I was a dud in China; I hardly wrote a word. The whole experience was too complex, too overwhelming. I worked away in the archives, talked to people, especially about their experiences during the cultural revolution, visited historic sights. When I returned to Canada in 1987, I wrote a historical novel called *Beijing Embrace Me*. Even as I was finishing it, I knew the rewriting would overwhelm me. To this day, it remains the famous novel-in-the-bottom-of-the-drawer, though I know sooner or later, I will tackle it again.

Truthfully, though, I've never had as much interest in writing fiction as I have in what is called creative nonfiction. Truman Capote supposedly started the trend with *In Cold Blood*, but the genre has flourished for years. To me, it's storytelling at its best. The dramatic imperative is there, the use of rich language and literary devices, the development of character, but all set in a mold of facts. It is a more direct interpretation of reality.

I had first experimented seriously with creative nonfiction in a book called *Brian and the Boys*, published by James Lorimer in 1984. Partly because there had been so much written in feminist literature about sexual aggression, I became interested in why young men can commit horrible crimes and why they often do so in groups. I found the story I wanted in two cases of gang rape, mostly by the same young men, but the book took on a willful life of its own. I began to wonder if crimes had actually been perpetrated: the testimony of both women was suspect, to say the least. When the book came out, I found myself, a strong feminist, having to defend the kind of young man I was afraid of and despised.

I liked the style of that book, though, the attempt to capture the reality of the underbelly of society. When I returned from China, I began searching for another strong story, this time based in that most eccentric of provinces, Saskatchewan. A murder, of course, is the most dramatic, desperate act any human being can commit. It distills the action, concentrates the attention. I became interested in the case of a young man, severely crippled by a farm accident as a child, who in 1989, had shot and killed both his grandparents. What turned out to be fascinating was the backdrop; the farm where the crime had been committed took on a persona of its own. *Revenge of the Land*, published in 1991, is the history of a single section of land. I told the stories of each individual who had owned a piece of it, from the first settler in 1883 to the Eberles, the elderly couple who were murdered. It quickly became obvious the land was indeed extracting revenge for the indignities it suffered: the rough plowing, the denuding, the defrauding of Aboriginals, the greedy speculation.

The book was difficult to research because most of the people involved were not well known and historical detail was hard to come by. Every edition of the *Moose Jaw Times* (later *Times Herald*) from 1883 to 1936 was examined for little tidbits of information. That Mrs. Smith had won the darning-old-socks competition three times at the Moose Jaw Agricultural Fair was a wonderful discovery indeed. In 1992, *Revenge of the Land* won the

Governor-General's Literary Award for nonfiction. Every writer, no matter how modest or how blasé, has to admit to being thrilled at such recognition. (*Revenge of the Land* has also been made into a four-hour mini-series for CBC and CBS, scheduled to be broadcast in the fall of 2000.)

During the research of *Revenge*, I had become interested in aboriginal rights, particularly the monstrous land grab perpetrated on the Métis nation by the federal government in the 19th century. I was playing around with ideas for another book on the topic when Iris Tupholme, the publisher of HarperCollins, phoned and asked if I would be interested in writing a biography of that eccentric Canadian revolutionary Louis Riel. I knew at once that I wanted to do it; I had always been fascinated by Canada's prime rebel.

Riel's collected writings, including a volume of poetry, had been published by the University of Alberta on the centenary of his death. This allowed me easy and direct access to his own words, his own thoughts, and I decided to use these, rather than academic theorizing. I came to admire Riel far more than I had thought I would. He was not a liar or a braggart but a man utterly devoted to the welfare of what he considered were his people—the Métis. Since his death, historians, usually white and male, have conspired to ensure his reputation as a religious nut has been maintained. To back up their claims, they plundered his personal, secret diaries. I wonder how many writers—and he was certainly that—would be judged insane if their unexpurgated and totally candid thoughts were laid bare. I came away from writing that book with great sympathy and admiration for a colourful humanitarian, as well as anger at those academics who have denigrated him for so long. In writing *Riel*, I became even more addicted to the study of history, in print or on film.

My brother Bill had followed me to China, and was working as an English teacher and journalist when he fell in love with the director of a film in which he had a role. Bill and Guo Fangfang fled China at the time of the Tiananmen uprising. They stopped in Regina to visit us, but decided to stay when he was hired as a reporter for CBC Radio. (He later went on to become ACTRA's representative in Saskatchewan.) Fangfang knew only one sentence of English: "I know no English." She had been an up-and-coming feature-film director in China, and after a year or so, it became imperative to find work for her. In 1993, Fangfang, my husband and I started a film company called Four Square Productions; eventually, an experienced producer, Murray Macdonald, joined us. The company has blossomed. I write the documentaries and Fangfang directs them; this year, we will do a feature. After years as head of the political-science department, Gerry retired from the University of Regina, but now, he has a budding film company to run. I sometimes think we are like Virginia and Leonard Woolf, with their own publishing house, except the film business is a roller coaster, crawling up to success one moment and hurtling down to defeat the next.

Writing permeates our family. My stepdaughter Shoshana Sperling is a Toronto performer and writer of her own hilarious, irreverent material. My daughter Carrie-May studies English literature at Concordia University and struggles over whether she should be a poet or a journalist. My stepson Adam's writing involves daily specials, for he is a fine and creative cordon-bleu chef with a successful restaurant of his own.

Researching and writing this book, I have listened to the echoes of women writers down through the centuries. Their words have profoundly affected me. Even when calling out in pain, these are voices of hope. In the darkest times, when misogyny reigned, women could not be completely silenced. Their writings have always been a symbol of individuality, a sign that original thinking was going on, a beacon of a liberated future.

Writers

Greetings wherever you are, lady, greetings as to a god:
for your songs, your immortal daughters, are with us still.

Dioscorides' poem to Sappho, third century BC

To write is to lose half one's nobility....

Madeleine de Scudéry,
France's most popular writer during the 17th century

Jane Austen can in fact get more drama out of mortality than most other writers can get from shipwreck, battle, murder or mayhem.

John Blythe, introduction to *Emma*, 1966

It seems incredible today, in an age when our educators have quite rightly decided the literature our children read should have some relevance to their lives, that in Grade 10, we were assigned the novel *Silas Marner*, by George Eliot. Groans went up when it was handed out. The language seemed so archaic and flowery, the sentiments so old-fashioned.

I, too, found it hard going at first, but pretty quickly got caught up in the story of poor old Silas Marner, the weaver of Ravelop, a dupe of the first order. When, after all those years of unrelenting toil, Silas's money, the only comfort in his life, was stolen, I shed a tear. When dear little blonde Eppie, an abandoned child came into his life, and everything turned out all right, I cheered. I paid little attention to the author, whom I assumed was yet another male from the murky Victorian past. When the teacher told us that George Eliot was a pseudonym for Mary Ann Evans, I remember a thrill running along my spine. I quite liked the novel by then, and the realization that women were just as capable of writing great literature as men was an enormous boost to my teenage ego.

Women writers have always proved the exception to the rule. Quietly but insidiously, they have pecked away at society's presumptions that women were the second sex and by nature inferior. By the very act of writing, they proved this ridiculous hypothesis false.

I

Sappho was the most beloved female poet in Greek and Roman antiquity. The ancients were fortunate; they could relish her words collected by scholars in Alexandria a few centuries after she lived. What is left to us is only a fraction of what she wrote, fragments on worn-out papyrus. Nor is her personal history clear; separating the myth from reality has proved to be impossible.

We do know she was born on the island of Lesbos, probably before 600 BC, to aristocratic parents. She had three brothers, one of whom was a merchant, another in government service (nothing is known of the third). She apparently was married to the wealthy Cercylas, who traded in goods from Andros (although he, too, may be fictitious. He is mentioned in none of her extant poetry and his name can be translated as "The Prick from the Isle of Man"[777]). She probably had a daughter named after her own mother, Cleis. As she wrote:

I have a lovely child, whose form is like
Gold flowers, my heart's one pleasure, Cleis
For whom I'd not give all Lydia, nor fair....[778]

Sappho's poems were addressed to women and were probably most often sung by choruses of young women. Her subjects are not fertility or child-rearing or wifely duties but a celebration of female passion, yearning and desire. She creates a world of wealth and privilege, full of flowers and perfume, beautiful women and the amorous pleasures of the "soft bed"— gratification with the same sex. There is only one complete poem of Sappho's in existence, "Ode To Aphrodite," but the qualities of sensuousness and originality that made her so famous are there. One verse will give a taste of the introspective nature of Sappho's work:

O immortal Aphrodite of the many-colored throne,
child of Zeus, weaver of wiles, I beseech you,
do not overwhelm me in my heart
with anguish and pain, O Mistress[779]

Sappho lived during the Archaic period (c. 700–480 BC), when women seemingly had more freedom and authority than they did in the Classical period, the so-called golden age of Greek culture. Her references to politics in her writings, her licence to criticize an extravagant, wayward brother, indicate she did not live a secluded, restricted life. Certainly, she was given free rein to write of her heart's desire.

In the Classical age that followed, the most important genre for writers was drama: comedy and tragedy, written in poetic form, mostly prepared for the state religious celebrations held twice a year in Athens in honour of Dionysus. Such public activities involving large audiences were not welcoming to women. There is debate about which of these festivities, if any, they were even allowed to attend. Women continued to write lyrical poetry (poetry sung to the lyre), although none we know about lived in Athens or was part of the influential literary scene.

Korinna of Tanagra was a poet from the Boeotia district, writing in the fifth century. Hers was the dialect of her native region, her subject its myths and legends. As she wrote, "But I myself [sing] the excellent deeds/of male and female heroes."[780] It is reported Korinna beat out Pindar, historically regarded as the greatest of Greek lyric poets, in a competition in his native Thebes. One writer claims this occurred five times. (Other commentators claimed she won because of her good looks.) Pindar's response was to call Korinna "a sow."

Another poet, Praxilla, lived in the mid-fifth-century Sikyon, a city noted for its artists and writers located on the Corinthian Gulf. According to her biographer, she was a versatile writer. Popular songs that made her famous in Athens, hymns about various gods and goddesses as well as choral works in honour of Dionysus were all part of her repertoire.[781]

In the Hellenistic period (330–30 BC), poetry became private, written expression, often taking the form of the epigram, a short, descriptive or satirical verse. Naturalism came into vogue; songs about such subjects as maidens, babies and fishermen were popular. These trends favoured women poets, the work becoming a reflection of their own lives. Anyte, a native of Tegea, writing at the beginning of the Hellenistic era, was famous for her epigrams about the death of young women.

> Throwing her arms around her dear father,
> Erato, melting away in moist tears, spoke these last words.

'Father, I am no more; dark black Death
covers my eyes as already I perish.'[782]

Anyte wrote other kinds of poetry as well, especially verse commemorating the dedication of a gift to a god or goddess in return for a favour. Her most famous work, though, was in the Greek pastoral tradition: poems about animals and landscapes. As one critic remarked, "Curiously enough the qualities of [Anyte's] verse are all of the kind that it is usual to call masculine. Simple, vigorous, restrained, she has none of that somewhat florid exuberance which marks the inferior feminine in art...."[783]

Like Sappho, Erinna, who was born on the Dorian island of Telos, was praised to the heavens by other poets. Her death at age 19 only added to her mythology. Her most famous poem, "Distaff" (a device used in spinning), describes a childhood spent in bliss with her best friend Baucis and their separation, first because of Baucis's marriage and then because of her death.

> You leaped from the white horses
> And raced madly into the deep wave—
> But 'I've got you, dear!' I shouted loudly.
> And when you were the Tortoise
> You ran skipping through the yard of the great court.
> These are the things that I lament and
> Sorrow over, my sad Baucis—these are
> Little trails through my heart that are
> Still warm—my remembrances of you.
> For our former delights are ashes now....[784]

Whenever an opportunity presented itself in the male-dominated world of ancient Greece, women wrote, and wrote well. That they were respected, indeed cherished, is made clear in this epigram by Antipater of Thessalonica, written around the first century AD:

> These are women of heavenly voice, reared on songs
> by Helicon and by Pieria, Macedon's crag:
> Praxilla, Moero, Anyte's lips, the female Homer;
> Sappho, the glory of Lesbos's women with beautiful hair;
> Erinna, renowned Telesilla, and you, Corinna,
> who sang of Athena's shield of furious war.
> Nossis of feminine tongue, and Myrtis who sang so sweetly;

all of them crafted pages that live forever.
Nine were the Muses whom Heaven brought forth: nine too
are these, borne by Earth for mortals' undying delight.[785]

II

Throughout the Middle Ages, men—clerics, rhetoricians, ordinary husbands—
railed at women for their wicked, sinful natures. Since, for the medieval female,
the mere act of speaking in public was considered an indulgence and an
outrage—women were burned as witches because of their "cackle and chat-
ter"—for centuries, there was little female response to this never-ending wave
of denigration. Finally, as the end of the era approached, a lone voice dared to
challenge the lunatic ideas of the male elite. Christine de Pisan (1364–c. 1430)
towers as a writer of talent, imagination and above all, courage.

Christine's father Thomas had been a scholar at the prestigious University
of Bologna, but went to work for the Venetian Republic as a salaried counsellor. Christine was born in Venice, but when she was four, the family
moved to Paris, where Thomas de Pisan was appointed as astrologer and
physician—in those days, the two were related—to Charles V of France.
Christine was brought up in the court. As she later wrote, "The foresight of
the good king would not allow any need in his friend's household to go
unfulfilled."[786] Christine would later write a history of Charles V, one of her
major accomplishments. It was probably in the king's library that Christine
first came upon the books she loved. She was a scholarly young girl, a trait
that her father encouraged but her mother did not. Christine was always
resentful of the time she spent spinning rather than studying.

Christine was 15 when she married the man her father had chosen for her.
Étienne de Castel was ten years older, with what seemed a bright future
ahead of him. He had just been made a royal secretary, a lifetime appointment that automatically made him a member of Paris's intellectual elite. The
marriage was a happy one, and Christine gave birth to three children, a
daughter and two sons, one of whom perished in childhood. Thomas de
Pisan died in 1387, and Christine's husband took over as head of the household. Only three years later, he, too, passed away during one of the epidemics
that periodically raged throughout Europe. Christine was left with her children, her mother and a niece to provide for.

Over the next 14 years, Christine engaged in a humiliating legal struggle
for her rightful share of her husband's estate. At one point, four court battles

were raging, all at the same time. Christine was deceived, sneered at, conde-scended to by greedy clerks and other public officials, although she claimed that, because of her difficulties, she became stronger in body and spirit, and more self-confident. By 1392, she was able to pry free some of her property from the legal maw, which she sold to provide some cash. Her major income, though, derived from her job as a copier of legal and other documents. Soon, too, her love poetry became known.

Perhaps the desperation and helplessness she had felt during her legal battles jelled her ideas about the plight of women, for in 1400, she finally spoke out against the hateful misogyny rampant in her society. Her first sally was against Jean de Meun, the author of the second part of the *Romance of the Rose*, a poem that was an infamous mockery and slander of women. In *Cupid's Letter*, Christine's scorn for de Meun was stinging.

> Jean de Meun in his Romance of the Rose,
> What a long affair! What a tiresome pose!
> What sciences profound, both clear and obscure,
> Devised for many a great adventure—
> So many people either begged or bribed,
> Such far-fetched devices sought out and tried—
> All just to seduce an innocent maid,
> Such is the end of this silly charade:
> for frail defense, why such a great assault?[787]

Christine de Pisan became the first woman to assert her identity as an author, to declare her place in the world of letters. "Let no one accuse me of unreason, of arrogance or presumption, for daring, I, a woman, to challenge and answer back to so subtle an author, or for diminishing the praise due his work, when he, one man on his own, has dared to slander and reproach the entire female sex without exception."[788] Christine's declaration led to an exchange of letters by the leading humanists of the day. What followed was three centuries of passionate debate about the nature of women, known as the *Querelle des femmes*.

Christine's most famous and imaginative work was *The Book of the City of Ladies*, written during 1404–1405. In the opening section, she is sitting in her study, ruminating on why men are so hateful to women, "how it happened that so many different men ... are so inclined to express ... so many wicked insults about women.... It seems that they all speak from one and the same mouth."[789] Suddenly, there appear three remarkable female phantoms: Reason, Rectitude and Justice. All are dressed beautifully, with golden crowns on their heads. It is Lady Reason who urges Christine to build the city. She will provide the materials for the foundation. Lady Rectitude will help construct the high walls, the moat, the bastions. Lady Justice will look after the finishing touches: the towers, the palaces, all of which will glitter with gold. It will also be Justice's task to decide who will be ruler of the city and who will live there.

The design of this allegoric city takes shape during a running discussion Christine has with the three female worthies on the nature of women. The mortar for this construction job turns out to be the examples they provide to back up their arguments. When Christine asks if women have a natural sense for politics and government, Lady Reason, for instance, gives her a long list from history, mythology and folklore of brilliant women who ruled countries or estates with skill and diligence.

The book continues in this vein, reciting the accomplishments of one woman after another. Philosophers, poets, scholars, prophetesses, governors were represented. Nobles, bourgeois, peasants were there. As scholar Danielle Régnier-Bohler puts it, "Piling these portraits one on top of another as a mason might build a wall, Christine built the memory of her sex. Dipping her mortar in ink, she made time the property of her sisters past and present."[790]

III

During the early-modern period, the picture that gradually congealed in literature of all kinds was of a world of women independent of men. Female writers were part of this new-found autonomy. It became possible, at least for a few, to make a living by writing, and this opened brave new worlds. Nonetheless, many women writers published either under a man's name, or anonymously. Fame, they claimed, was the last thing a proper, modest female would desire, although if a writer were successful, the notoriety was such that her identity was widely known, no matter what name she used.

Madeleine de Scudéry (1607–1701), France's most popular writer during the 17th century, published her first books under her brother's name, Georges de Scudéry, and when he died, anonymously. "To write is to lose half one's nobility," she insisted, and claimed to only do so because she was hard up for cash.[791]

Madeleine was orphaned at an early age and sent to live with an uncle, who must have been wealthy and cultured for he saw to it that his niece received a superb education. Her French grammar and spelling were impeccable, and she was fluent in Spanish and Italian (although not in Latin). She knew contemporary and ancient history so well, she used them extensively in the plots of her novels.

When her uncle died in 1637, she went to live with her brother, a military man and a playwright of some note. Georges de Scudéry was apparently a famous braggart who squandered his and his sister's money. Despite these flaws, it was he who introduced Madeleine to Parisian literary society. She was just beginning to write.

Mlle de Scudéry became the darling of the *salonnières*. Among her admirers was the formidable Marquise de Rambouillet, whose soirées became a model throughout France. Madeleine slid in and out of the French salons her entire life, picking up wealthy patrons as she went; Louis XIV, for example, awarded her a generous pension. It was these benefices, more than book royalties, that allowed her to enjoy a comfortable lifestyle.

Her work mostly took the form of huge historical romances with incredibly intricate plots and subplots; one epic, called *Clélie*, was ten volumes long. These were *romans à clef*, keyed romances, wherein prominent contemporaries were disguised as historical figures. All you needed was the social register and you could guess who each of the characters were and with whom they were having a love affair—all part of the appeal, of course.

It was often said Madeleine de Scudéry was a plain woman, with a dark complexion and big jaw, but she had such wit and charm that she three times turned down offers of marriage from wealthy men. "One marries," she once wrote, "in order to hate. Hence a true lover must never speak of marriage, because to be a lover is to want to be loved, and to be a husband is to want to be hated."[792] Such sentiments were only possible because she was able to make a living by her pen.

While Madeleine flitted about the sparkling Parisian salon society, the first professional female writer in England was mucking about in Grub Street. Little is known about Aphra Behn's early background except that her father was a Canterbury barber named Johnson and her mother a wet nurse. In her early twenties, she spent a year or two on a plantation in the Dutch colony of Surinam, where she may have gathered intelligence for Charles II's administration. Later, she would write a novella, *Oroonoko or the History of the Royal*

Slave, based in Surinam, which became one of the most popular books of its time. In 1666, she was sent as a spy to Antwerp to find out what she could (which wasn't much) about Dutch plans to invade England. She married a merchant of Dutch extraction and, after he died, ended up in debtor's prison, fortunately only for a short time.

Her professional writing life began in earnest in 1670 when her play *The Forc'd Marriage* premiered at Lincoln's Inn Fields. By the time of her death 16 years later, she would write 19 plays, mounds of poems, prefaces, epithets, translations, short stories and a shocking *roman à clef*, *Love-Letters Between a Nobleman and his Sister*, which lays claim to being the first major novel in the English language.

It was the raffish, licentious world of late Stuart London in which Aphra Behn thrived. Her work was as bold, bawdy and irreverent as any of the male Restoration playwrights. Across her stage marched heroine prostitutes, cross-dressers, cuckolds, bisexuals and lecherous wives who enjoyed sex, although not with their husbands. If there were one message Aphra Behn aimed to get across, it was that men, any man, could not be trusted. The heroine of her play *The Amorous Prince* is warned by her brother not to believe a word her lover will say in bed: "... beware of men for though I myself be one, yet, I have the frailties of my sex, and can dissemble too. Trust none of us, for if thou dost, thou art undone. We make vows to all alike we see, and even the best of men ... is not to be credited in an affair of love." Behn was speaking from personal experience, for although she never married again, she suffered through many affairs of the heart with both men and women.

Aphra Behn's life, while certainly not boring, was not easy. She was constantly lampooned and ridiculed by male journalists and critics; the cruellest jibe was that her plays were written only with the help of her lovers. It was always hard to scrape a living, and as the 1680s approached, her type of comedy fell out of favour with the public. Perhaps fortunately, she died before she experienced the poverty and indignities that were inflicted on many of her contemporaries.

Two centuries later, Virginia Woolf would write of Aphra Behn, "She made, by working very hard, enough to live on. The importance of that fact outweighs anything that she actually wrote, even the splendid, 'A Thousand Martyrs I have made', or 'Love in Fantastic Triumph Sat' for here begins the freedom of the mind, or rather the possibility that in course of time the mind will be free to write what it likes."[793]

Woolf probably would have been amazed that, in the late 20th century, Aphra Behn is regarded as a giant by the academic community. Several biographies have been written, international symposia organized to discuss her work, volumes of her writings published. Her plays have been revived with big-name stars. She's been the subject of a Canadian play (Beth Hirst's *A Women's Comedy*, 1993) and a Scottish novel (Ross Laidlaw's *Aphra Behn: Dispatch'd from Athole*, 1992). According to one critic, her novella *Oroonoko*, about an enslaved African prince sent to South America, is better known among North American undergraduates than any other late-17th century work, including Milton's *Paradise Lost*.[794] Fans flock to Westminster Abbey and drop flowers on her tomb, where they encounter the epitaph: "Here Lies a Proof that Wit can never be/Defence enough against Mortality." What attracts admirers these days is not that she was the first English-speaking female writer to make a living by her pen but that she was one of the best of the Restoration playwrights, poets and novelists. Breaking free of domesticity and childbirth, her talent shone like a star.

IV

She was careful that her occupation should not be suspected by servants, or visitors, or any persons beyond her own family party. She wrote upon small sheets of paper which could easily be put away, or covered with a piece of blotting paper. There was, between the front door and the offices, a swing door which creaked when it was opened; but she objected to having this little inconvenience remedied, because it gave her notice when anyone was coming in.[795]

Jane Austen's biographers insist her nephew's description of her work methods must be farfetched. How could such original, witty, particular work be accomplished if one were being disrupted every time the door opened? Exaggerated or not, this portrayal does give a sense of what the working lives of women writers were like in the 19th century.

The rigid dichotomy of the sexes had herded the upper- and middle-class woman into the home, and if she were to write at all, it would be from that venue. For the best English-language female writers of the era, home was not exhilarating London or New York but obscure, cultural backwaters. Ironically, the seclusion, both physical and intellectual, was probably what nurtured such remarkable, truly original works of art. In a famous letter to her niece, who was an aspiring writer, Jane Austen wrote this advice: "You are now collecting your People delightfully, getting them exactly into such a spot as is the delight of my life;—3 or 4 Families in a Country Village is the very thing to work on."[795a] The great drama she found in this town or that had, as its foundation, the complicated code of ethics played out in everyday life, "human nature in the midland counties," as Jane herself put it.

It wasn't simply the home and hearth that were important to these writers. The routine of domesticity also fuelled their imaginations. As Charlotte Brontë noted, "I am much happier—black-leading the stoves—making beds and sweeping the floor at home, than I should be living like a fine lady anywhere else."

Jane Austen's biographer Claire Tomalin provides this insight: "The same views from the same windows; the same household routines and daily walks in the garden or to the church or the village; the same sounds and silences, all this sameness made a secure environment in which her imagination could work."[796] When, at age 25, Jane Austen was forced by her parents to leave her childhood home at Steventon and move to Bath, she went into a deep, dark slump; Tomalin believes it was an actual depression. The great spouting of creativity went dry, and she fell silent for almost ten years.

On the other hand, domestic drudgery could be a terrible impediment to getting work done. Jane Austen wrote in 1816, late in her career, that she needed "a few days quiet, & exemption from the Thought & contrivances which any sort of company gives…. Composition seems to me Impossible, with a head full of Joints of Mutton & doses of rhubarb."[797] These writers knew that bearing and raising children would be the death knell of literary ambition, and most remained single: Jane Austen, Emily and Anne Brontë, Emily Dickinson. Austen had an almost neurotic fear of pregnancy, probably because she had seen many of her female relatives die in childbirth. She called each of her novels "a darling child" and seemed quite satisfied with that. Charlotte Brontë, who liked black-leading stoves so much, had her independent-minded heroine Jane Eyre remark:

Women are supposed to be very calm generally; but women feel just as men feel; they need exercise for their faculties, and a field for their efforts, as much as their brothers do; they suffer from too rigid a restrain, too absolute a stagnation, precisely as men would suffer; and it is narrow-minded in their more privileged fellow-creatures to say that they ought to confine themselves to making puddings and knitting stockings, to playing the piano and embroidering bags.[798]

Victorian female writers had to contend with societal prejudices so strong that even the most strong-willed among them must have cringed. The Poet Laureate Robert Southey condescendingly spouted the common wisdom. Discussing some verse Charlotte Brontë had sent him, he wrote to her:

Literature cannot be the business of a woman's life: & it ought not to be. The more she is engaged in her proper duties, the less leisure will she have for it, even as an accomplishment & recreation. To those duties you have not yet been called, & when you are you will be less eager for celebrity.[799]

In fact, it was romance—love and men, men and love—that was the vital stuff of their work. Austen's books are mostly about young, single women on the lookout for husbands—or at least their parents are on the lookout for husbands for them. Austen had been criticized for being obsessed with "the hunt," but as biographer Jane Aiken Hodge notes, "Critics who attack Jane Austen for making it [marriage] the main subject of her novels are simply failing to take into account the hard facts of her time. Writing today [1972], would she, I wonder, have enjoyed herself as much describing her heroines' attempts to become prime ministers or efficient principals of women's colleges?"[799a]

Much of the best work of Victorian female writers reflected their own experience and circumstance. The biographer of the Brontë family, Juliet Barker, writes, "Charlotte was a quintessentially feminine writer: her talents for describing repressed emotion and for accurate observation of the minutiae of daily life were those of the passive observer, a role pre-eminently that of the nineteenth-century woman."[800] At the same time, Charlotte's mousy sister Emily, whose health broke down under the strain of boarding school, could conjure up the most unorthodox, erotically charged emotions from the depths of her imagination. In *Wuthering Heights*, published a year before Emily died at age 29, she creates an uncouth, quarrelsome, volatile, passionate hero in Heathcliffe, and in Cathy, the most willful, self-destructive, fascinating, passionate heroine in Victorian literature.

Since it was thought unladylike, if not impossible, for the angel of the hearth to produce great works of art, Victorian women writers often wrote under a male pseudonym: most famously, George Sand, George Eliot, and Anne, Emily and Charlotte Brontë as Acton, Ellis and Currer Bell. It was a necessary deceit, simply so the work would be judged on its own merits. Those who did use their own signatures were careful to link themselves to their domesticity. The novelist Elizabeth Gaskell, for instance, always wrote under the name Mrs. Gaskell. Jane Austen's first book, *Sense and Sensibility*, self-published in 1811, was attributed to Lady A.... When it was finally discovered Jane was the author of this successful first novel, the critics were incredulous, insisting one of her brothers must have written it. As novelist Mary Brunton exclaimed when asked at the time if she would let her own byline stand: "To be pointed at—to be noticed & commented upon—to be suspected of literary airs—to be shunned, as literary women are by the more unpretending of my own sex: & abhorred, as literary women are, by the more pretending of the other!—My dear, I would sooner exhibit as a rope dancer."[801]

Fame was not something with which Emily Dickinson had to contend. Holed up in her father's house in Amherst, Massachusetts, she produced an awesome body of work—1,775 poems, of which fewer than 20 were published during her lifetime. In 1854, at age 24, she wrote to her friend Jane Humphrey: "I have dared to do strange things—bold things, and have asked no advice from any." What Emily Dickinson meant was she had decided to live the secluded, unorthodox, intellectually challenging life of an original and dedicated poet. As historian Gerda Lerner puts it, "She had alternatives and chose her life and did so not in bitterness and delusion but in ecstatic creativity and celebration of her hard-won powers."[802] By turning herself into an eccentric and recluse, by rejecting the never-ending social demands of Victorian society, Emily Dickinson grabbed hold of the time and the freedom she needed to create "a secret, privileged inner self that could observe life to analyze and criticize with complete safety."[803]

> They shut me up in Prose—
> As when a little Girl
> They put me in the Closet
> Because they liked me 'still'—
>
> Still! Could themselves have peeped—
> And seen my Brain go around—
> They might as well have lodged a Bird
> For Treason—in the Pound—
>
> Himself has but to will
> And easy as a Star
> Abolish his Captivity
> And laugh—No more have I—[804]

Dickinson's concern is not with her own personal predicament but with the human condition. That, of course, is what makes her work so precious. From the small room in her father's house, she created the unique cosmos found in her extraordinary poetry.

V

As Virginia Woolf herself understood, her creativity derived from the "sledgehammer" blows that rained down on her, especially in her young life. She became a writer because she could welcome and make valuable the trauma she had experienced. "And so I go on to suppose that the shock-receiving capacity is what makes me a writer."[805] She must come to grips with this trauma, put it down in words, arrange her devastated universe to accommodate it. This production of "order" or "wholeness" out of shocks is, she says, "the strongest pleasure known to me."[806]

Her shocks were very real. In the 11 years between 1895 to 1906, her mother, stepsister, father and brother all died. Her stepbrother George Duckworth is now believed to have sexually molested her during the time her father was dying of cancer; certainly he was abusive and a bully when she was the most vulnerable. Perhaps because of these tragedies, or at least precipitated by them, Virginia Woolf suffered the worst shock of all: her mental illness. For most of her life, she was vulnerable to episodes of one kind or another: days of anxiety and insomnia, weeks of intense depression, moments of panic. Five times (four between the ages of 13 and 33), she suffered severe attacks and attempted to commit suicide. She experienced horrible mental torment, hearing voices, lost in fogs of confusion. Always after she recovered, there followed the terrible anxiety and fear. When would it happen again? Not surprisingly, these bouts of madness enriched her writing. As she explained it:

Once or twice I have felt that odd whir of wings in the head which comes when I am ill so often.... I believe these illnesses are in my case—how shall I express it?—partly mystical. Something happens in my mind. It refuses to go on registering impressions. It shuts itself up. It becomes chrysalis. I lie quite torpid, often with acute physical pain.... Then suddenly something springs ... ideas rush in me; often though this is before I can control my mind or pen.[807]

Whatever the cause of Woolf's illness—probably a combination of genetic, biological and environmental factors—the dramatic political events of her time could not have helped. She suffered one of her worst breakdowns during World War I, and the Depression, the rise of fascism and the Spanish Civil War added to the general turmoil. There was also the added tension of casting off the influence of her Victorian, middle-class upbringing, which she both admired (for its serenity and civility) and despised (for its close-mindedness and attitude towards women). What she called the "Invisible Censor" was the most difficult enemy to overcome:

And the phantom was a woman, and when I came to know her better I called her ... The Angel in the House.... And when I came to write I encountered her with the very first words.... And she made as if to guide my pen.... I turned upon her and caught her by the throat. I did my best to kill her.... Had I not killed her she would have killed me.... She died hard.... She was always creeping back when I thought I had despatched her.[808]

Despite her illnesses and struggles to establish her unique modernist voice, Virginia Woolf had a rich and full life. As well as her nine novels, three books of short stories and biographies, she wrote 40 periodical articles and reviews a year. She enjoyed a fruitful relationship with her sister and fellow artist Vanessa Bell. Among the Bloomsbury Group were affectionate and supportive soul mates. She had close, intimate friendships, perhaps love affairs, with several dynamic women. Although her husband Leonard was a rather bleak and formidable man, pessimistic about human nature, the marriage provided the support and comfort she needed to keep the creative juices flowing. Yet on March 28, 1941, the great author wrote a note, put a large stone in her coat pocket and walked into the River Ouse close to the Woolfs' Sussex home. It took three weeks of search before the body was finally found. She realized mental illness was about to descend on her again, and she could not face the hell she knew was coming.

It's tempting to see in Virginia Woolf only one of a vast army of women writers who, in trying to escape the straightjackets early 20th-century society imposed on them, either inflicted harm on themselves or were victimized by circumstances. Katherine Mansfield (1888–1923), one of the great masters of the short story, first became ill in 1910 with arthritis probably caused by gonorrhea. She died alone, in poverty, of tuberculosis at the age of 35. She was a friend, and perhaps lover, of Virginia Woolf, who wrote of her: "No one felt more seriously the importance of writing than she did. In all the pages of her journal, instinctive, rapid as they are, her attitude to her work is admirable; sane, caustic, and austere. There is no literary gossip; no vanity; no jealousy....[809] Her legacy was insured with the publication of such absorbing stories as "Bliss" and "Prelude."

In 1945, the Canadian Elizabeth Smart (1913–1986) wrote *By Grand Central Station I Sat Down and Wept*, considered a masterpiece of poetic prose. Then there was silence for 35 years. She bore four children by the British poet George Barker, although, since he already had a family, he never married her. She spent decades writing advertising copy and stories for magazines like *House and Garden* to support her children.

Brought up in Southern Rhodesia, Doris Lessing walked away from two marriages that had produced three children and left for England in 1949. In her autobiography, she hardly mentions a word about the sorrow or anxiety that usually comes with leaving children behind. She refers always to her youngest, whom she did take with her, as "the child," never "my son" or "my boy." The resentment of having to care for him drips from every the page. The cruelty with which she treats her mother, the belittling of her father and most others who enter her life, is staggering. A repugnant coldness seeps throughout this accounting of a life, all in the name of shaking free and becoming a writer. Doris Lessing produced a large and important body of work, but one has to ask: at what price to others?

The acclaimed Canadian poet, novelist and playwright Gwendolyn MacEwen (1941–1987) once commented on her own work: "I write basically to communicate joy, mystery, passion, not the joy that naively exists without knowledge of pain, but that joy which arises out of and conquers. I want to construct a myth...."[809a] However, as her biographer writes, she died a poverty-stricken alcoholic, "convinced, at least for long moments, that art was not worth the price of loneliness."[810]

Finally, of course, there is Sylvia Plath (1932–1963), the most famous of all the female martyred writers. She had huge ambition, and described herself as "the Poetess of America," the latest in a long line of distinguished female poets beginning with Sappho, all of whom she saw as rivals. In October 1962, she wrote to her brother and sister-in-law: "The critic of the *Observer* is giving me an afternoon at his home to hear me read all my new poems! He is *the* opinion-maker in poetry over here, A. Alvarez, and says I'm the first woman poet he's taken seriously since Emily Dickinson! Needless to say, I'm delighted."[811] Four weeks later, she committed suicide. She had two young children and had separated from her husband, the poet Ted Hughes. Whatever the psychosis

involved in such destruction—she was obsessed with mental breakdown and
death—she remains a symbol for young women of a brilliant talent caught in
the trap of domesticity.

There were other writers, of course, who did not self-destruct but lived
long, fruitful lives, who struggled with their art even as they fought the patriarchal establishment. Two Americans, both extraordinary poets, are examples: Marianne Moore (1887–1972), the feminist and baseball fan, and
Elizabeth Bishop (1911–1979), noted by Plath for "[her] fine originality,
always surprising, never rigid, flowing, juicier than Marianne Moore, who is
her godmother...."[812] Unlike Plath, however, neither woman desired or
tolerated a life of domesticity, at least in the traditional sense, which might
have been what saved them.

As the women's movement took hold, the cult of self-destruction, of
morbid self-absorption, of imitating the macho writer's life has diminished.
The writer Margaret Atwood (born 1939) seems like a Girl Guide compared
with the neurotic Plath or Woolf. Atwood was blessed with the most wholesome of childhoods: her father was a professional naturalist who took his
family on long sojourns in the Canadian bush; her mother was a creative and
independent person; her education was enriching. She has enjoyed a long
relationship with the writer Graeme Gibson and has raised one child. Literary awards, honorary degrees, national honours (the Companion of the
Order of Canada, for example) pile up.

Margaret Atwood's third book, published in 1976, is a comic novel called
Lady Oracle. Her sharp wit is there, the devastating sting, the enjoyable story,
but throughout the book are hackneyed stereotypes: the wicked mother, the
ineffectual, self-absorbed father, the poor little fat girl who marries the political nerd, the female writer of flamboyant historical romances and ridiculous
poetry. To read the novel, even if the laughs are still there, is to revisit those
early days of the women's movement with its all-too-genuine grievances, its
exhausting intensity, its howling demands.

Atwood's last novel, *Alias Grace,* published in 1996, takes place in 19th-
century Ontario, an environment more imbued with Victorian prudery and
bigotry than the Motherland itself. It is the story of housekeeper-maid Grace
Marks, who is serving a life sentence in Kingston Penitentiary for the murder
years before of her wealthy employer. Grace claims not to be able to remember anything of the dastardly deed, and an ambitious young doctor under-
takes to discover the truth. What emerges from this most intriguing of tales

is a female character who is marvellously complex, very much an individual, far removed from the stereotype of a 19th-century female servant.

Is it far-fetched to see in Atwood's developing craft the influences of a profound sexual revolution? Surely those demoralizing and demeaning stereotypes that have shadowed women like an ugly, black cloud since time immemorial are finally fading. The ridiculous point of view that posits women as morally weak, intellectually inferior, the flibbertigibbets of the ages, is finally being exposed for what it is: a lie, purposely put in place by a patriarchy craving power and control. Having escaped the shadow, women now laugh at the slanders concocted about them, and declare loudly and clearly their rightful place in society. The 21st century will surely belong to them.

Notes

ᵃ Quoted in Jacques Dalarun, "The Clerical Gaze," Arthur Goldhammer, trans., in Christiane Klapisch-Zuber, ed., *A History of Women in the West II: Silences of the Middle Ages* (Harvard University Press, 1992), p. 3.

¹ Quoted in Julia O'Faolain and Lauro Martines, eds., *Not in God's Image* (Temple Smith, 1973), p. 9.

² Sarah B. Pomeroy, *Goddesses, Whores, Wives and Slaves: Women in Classical Antiquity* (Schocken Books, 1975), p. xii.

³ Euripides, *Trojan Women*, pp. 647–657.

⁴ Eva C. Keuls, *The Reign of the Phallus: Sexual Politics in Ancient Athens* (University of California Press, 1985), p. 2.

⁵ Ibid., p. 76.

⁶ Margaret Williamson, *Sappho's Immortal Daughters* (Harvard University Press, 1995), p. 101.

⁷ Keuls, p. 88.

⁸ Virginia Woolf, *A Room of One's Own*, (Flamingo, 1994) p. 49 in a footnote.

⁹ Pomeroy, p. 8.

¹⁰ Quoted in Williamson, p. 126.

¹¹ Plato, *The Symposium*, trans. W. Hamilton (Penguin Books, 1974), p. 62.

¹² Quoted in Williamson, p. 154.

¹³ Quoted in Jacques Dalarun, "The Clerical Gaze," in Klapisch-Zuber, p. 22.

¹⁴ Carla Casagrande, "The Protected Woman," Clarissa Botsford trans., in Klapisch-Zuber, pp. 70–71.

¹⁵ 1 Corinthians 7:1.

¹⁶ Quoted in O'Faolain and Martines, p. 137.

¹⁷ Marina Warner, *Alone of All Her Sex: The Myth and the Cult of the Virgin Mary* (Vintage Books, 1983), p. 153.

¹⁸ J. T. Muckle, *The Story of Abelard's Adversities* (Pontifical Institute of Medieval Studies, 1964), p. 28.

¹⁹ Ibid., p. 33.

²⁰ Georges Duby, "The Courtly Model," Arthur Goldhammer trans., in Klapisch-Zuber, p. 258.

²¹ Octavio Paz, *The Double Flame: Love and Eroticism*, Helen Lane trans. (Harcourt Brace, 1995), p. 113.

²² Sara F. Matthews Grieco, "The Body, Appearance, and Sexuality," in Natalie Zemon Davis and Arlette Farge, eds., *A History of Women in the West III: Renaissance and Enlightenment Paradoxes* (Harvard University Press, 1993), pp. 64–65.

²³ Ibid., p. 65.

[25] Susan Brownmiller, *Femininity* (Fawcett Columbine, 1985), pp. 60–61.

[26] Grieco, in Davis and Farge, pp. 70–71.

[27] Ibid., p. 79.

[28] Quoted in Lee Rainwater, *And the Poor Get Children: Sex, Contraception, and Family Planning in the Working Class* (Quadrangle Books, 1960), p. 528.

[29] Ibid.

[30] Quoted in Bridget Hill, *Women, Work, and Sexual Politics in Eighteenth-Century England* (Basil Blackwell, 1989), p. 179.

[31] Dianne F. Sadoff, "The Clergyman's Daughters: Anne Bronte, Elizabeth Gaskell, and George Eliot," in Lynda E. Boose and Betty S. Flowers, eds., *Daughters and Fathers* (The Johns Hopkins University Press, 1989), p. 303.

[32] Simone de Beauvoir, *The Second Sex,* H. M. Parshley trans. (Vintage Books, 1989), pp. 107–108.

[33] Jane Austen, *Mansfield Park* (Penguin Books, 1966), p. 240.

[34] Erna Olafson Hellerstein, Leslie Parker Hume and Karen M. Offen, eds., *Victorian Women: A Documentary Account of Women's Lives in Nineteenth-Century England, France and the United States* (Stanford University Press, 1991), p. 118.

[35] John Ruskin, *Sesame & Lilies, Unto This last and The Political Economy of Art* (Cassell and Co., 1907), p. 90.

[36] Joan Perkin, *Victorian Women* (New York University Press, 1993), p. 60.

[37] Ibid., p. 64.

[38] In particular Peter Gay, Gertrude Himmelfarb, Michel Foucault and Patricia Anderson.

[39] Patricia Anderson, *When Passion Reigned: Sex and the Victorians* (Basic Books, 1995), p. 8.

[40] Quoted in Perkin, p. 90.

[41] Quoted in D'Emilio and Freedman, p. 214.

[42] Carroll Smith-Rosenberg, *Disorderly Conduct: Visions of Gender in Victorian America* (Oxford University Press, 1985), p. 20.

[43] Ibid., p. 127.

[44] Quoted in D'Emilio and Freedman, p. 224.

[45] See especially Smith-Rosenberg, *Disorderly Conduct.*

[46] Quoted in Carolyn Burke, *Becoming Modern: The Life of Mina Loy* (Farrar, Straus and Giroux, 1996), p. 6.

[47] Prentice *et al.*, p. 302.

[48] Quoted in Prentice, p. 303.

[49] Quoted in D'Emilio and Freedman, p. 269.

[50] Betty Friedan, *The Feminine Mystique* (W. W. Norton & Co., 1963), p. 15.

[51] Lynne Segal, *Straight Sex: The Politics of Pleasure* (University of California Press, 1994), pp. 6–7.

[52] Quoted in D'Emilio and Freedman, p. 304.

[53] Quoted in Segal, pp. 9–10.

[54] Quoted in D'Emilio and Freedman, p. 310.

[54a] Anne Koedt, "The Myth of Vaginal Orgasm" in *Notes from the First Year* (New York: Radical Women Press, 1968), p. 136.

[55] Quoted in Colette, *Earthly Paradise: An Autobiography,* Herma Briffaut, Derek Coltman *et al.* trans. (Farrar, Straus & Giroux, 1966), pp. 22–23.

56 Ibid.

57 Helen P. Foley, ed., *The Homeric Hymn to Demeter: Translation, Commentary, and Interpretive Essays* (Princeton University Press, 1994), p. 2.

58 Ibid., p. 6.

59 Ibid., p. 22.

60 Ibid., p. 80.

61 Quoted in O'Faolain and Martines, p. 169.

62 Shahar, p. 186.

63 Quoted in O'Faolain and Martines, p. 104.

64 Paulette L'Hermite-Leclerq, "The Feudal Order," Arthur Goldhammer trans., in Klapisch-Zuber, p. 209.

65 Vecchio, in Klapisch-Zuber, p. 124.

66 Quoted in O'Faolain and Martines, p. 167.

67 Quoted in Jean Leclerq, *Le marriage vu par des moines au XII siècle* (Les Éditions du Cerf, 1983), p. 66.

68 Ibid., p. 67.

69 L'Hermite-Leclerq, in Klapisch-Zuber, p. 217.

70 Olwen Hufton, *The Prospect Before Her: A History of Women in Western Europe, Volume One: 1500–1800* (HarperCollins, 1995), p. 208.

71 Olwen Hufton, "Women, Work, and Family," in Davis and Farge, p. 41.

72 Ibid., p. 27.

73 Hufton, *The Prospect Before Her*, p. 64.

74 Angeline Goreau, *Reconstructing Aphra: A Social Biography of Aphra Behn* (The Dial Press, 1980), p. 77.

75 Quoted in Hufton, in Davis and Farge, p. 17.

76 Ibid., p. 19.

77 Prentice *et al.*, p. 60.

78 Quoted in Hill, p. 233.

79 Quoted in Hufton, in Davis and Farge, p. 23.

80 Quoted in D'Emilio and Freedman, pp. 12-13.

81 Frances Mossiker, *Madame de Sévigné: A Life and Letters* (Alfred A. Knopf, 1983), p. 23.

82 Ibid., p. 84.

83 Quoted in Mossiker, p. 73.

84 Ibid., p. 162.

85 Mossiker, p. 155.

86 Quoted in Mossiker, p. 498.

87 Quoted in Hellerstein *et al.*, p. 147.

88 Smith-Rosenberg, p. 186.

89 Quoted in Hellerstein *et al.*, pp. 91–92.

90 Ibid.

91 Knibiehler in Geneviève Fraisse and Michelle Perrot (eds.), *A History of Women in the West IV* (Harvard University Press, 1993) p. 335.

92 Prentice *et al.*, p. 127.

93 Quoted in Perkin, p. 171.

94 Quoted in Prentice *et al.*, p. 148.

95 Smith-Rosenberg, p. 32.

[96] Renee Winegarten, *The Double Life of George Sand: Woman and Writer: A Critical Biography* (Basic Books, 1978), p. 81.

[97] Quoted in Perkin, p. 12.

[98] Knibiehler, in Fraisse and Perrot, p. 341.

[99] Quoted in Smith-Rosenberg, pp. 248–249. See also her analysis of Louisa May Alcott's *Little Women*.

[100] Quoted in Lynda E. Boose and Betty St. Flowers, eds. *Daughters and Fathers* (Johns Hopkins University Press, 1989), p. 77.

[101] Quoted in Boose and Flowers, p. 78.

[102] Simone de Beauvoir, *The Second Sex*, H. M. Parshley trans./ed. (Vintage Books, 1989), p. 298.

[103] Virginia Woolf, *The Three Guineas* (Harbinger, 1966), p. 38.

[103a] Virginia Woolf, *To the Lighthouse* (Flamingo, 1995), p. 12.

[104] Candace Falk, *Love, Anarchy, and Emma Goldman* (Rutgers University Press, 1990), p. 16.

[105] Quoted in Carolyn Burke, *Becoming Modern: The Life of Mina Loy* (Farrar, Straus & Giroux, 1996), p. 47.

[105a] Doris Lessing, *Under My Skin* (HarperCollins, 1994), p. 15.

[106] Ibid., p. 30.

[107] Doris Lessing, *Martha Quest* (Flamingo, 1993), p. 331.

[108] De Beauvoir, p. 281.

[109] Adrienne Rich, *Of Woman Born: Motherhood as Experience and Institution* (W. W. Norton, 1995), p. 232.

[110] Quoted in *Time*, July 17, 1995, p. 64.

[111] Isabelle Allende, *Paula*, trans. Margaret Sayers Reden (HarperPerennial, 1996), p. 324.

[112] Keuls, p. 74.

[113] W. K. Lacey, *The Family in Classical Greece* (Cornell University Press, 1968), pp. 157–158.

[114] Philip E. Slater, *The Glory of Hera: Greek Mythology and the Greek Family* (Beacon Press, 1968), p. 7.

[115] Pomeroy, p. 96.

[116] Keuls, p. 74.

[117] Suzanne Dixon, *The Roman Mother* (University of Oklahoma Press, 1988), p. 170.

[118] S. Dixon, p. 181.

[119] Ibid., p. 195.

[120] Richard A. Bauman, *Women and Politics in Ancient Rome* (Routledge, 1992), p. 60.

[121] Ibid., p. 156.

[122] Ibid., p. 182.

[123] Ibid., p. 203.

[124] Quoted in Tacitus, *The Annals of Imperial Rome,* trans. M. Grant (Cassell, 1963), p. 306.

[125] Quoted in Tacitus, p. 307.

[126] Gregory of Tours, *The History of the Franks*, Lewis Thorpe, trans. (Penguin Books, 1974), p. 221.

[127] Ibid., pp. 222–223.

[128] Philippe Ariès, *Centuries of Childhood: A Social History of Family Life*, Robert Baldick trans. (Vintage Books, 1962), p. 38.

[129] Shahar, p. 181.

[130] Ibid., p. 139.

[131] Lawrence Stone, *The Family, Sex and Marriage in England 1500–1800* (Harper & Row, 1977), p. 71.

[132] Shahar, p. 140.

[133] Frances and Joseph Gies, *Marriage and the Family in the Middle Ages* (Harper & Row, 1987), pp. 209–210.

[134] Quoted in Shahar, p. 232.

[135] Gies and Gies, *Marriage and the Family*, p. 213.

[136] Quoted in Gies and Gies, p. 298.

[137] Janet Adelman, *Suffocating Mothers: Fantasies of Maternal Origin in Shakespeare's Plays, Hamlet to The Tempest* (Routledge, 1992), p. 16.

[138] Ibid., p. 16.

[139] Adelman, p. 20.

[140] Debate has always raged over whether Gertrude knew Hamlet's wine was poisoned or not. My view is that she was so involved in the convolutions going on at the time, she must have at least suspected something was amiss.

[141] Quoted in Stone, p. 120.

[142] Ibid., p. 131.

[143] Ibid., p. 127.

[144] Quoted in Stone, p. 280.

[145] Hufton, *Prospect Before Her*, p. 250.

[146] Knibiehler, in Fraisse and Perrot, p. 361.

[147] George Sand, *Indiana* (Oxford University Press, 1994), p. 36.

[148] Ibid., p. 83

[149] Joanna Richardson, *Baudelaire* (John Murray, 1994), pp. 22-23.

[150] Quoted in Perkin, pp. 7–8.

[151] Cynthia Griffin Wolff, *Emily Dickinson* (Addison-Wesley Publishing, 1988), p. 121.

[152] Ibid., p. 170.

[153] Adrienne Rich, *Of Woman Born: Motherhood as Experience and Institution* (W. W. Norton & Co., 1986), pp. 197–198.

[154] D. H. Lawrence, *Sons and Lovers* (Wordsworth Classics, 1993), p. 142.

[155] Ibid., pp. 185–186.

[156] Ibid., p. 342.

[157] Margaret Storch, *Sons and Adversaries: Women in William Blake and D. H. Lawrence* (The University of Tennessee Press, 1990), p. 108.

[158] Mary Graham, "Mamma's Boy," *Canadian Home Journal* (October 1952), pp. 18–19, 37–39.

[159] Betty Friedan, *The Feminine Mystique* (Laurel, 1983), p. 275.

[160] *The Globe and Mail*, 5 October, 1996, p. D5.

[161] Quoted in Mariana Cook, *Mothers [and] Sons in their Own Words*, p. 12.

[162] Gerda Lerner, *The Creation of Patriarchy* (Oxford University Press, 1986), p. 9.

[163] Gerda Lerner, *The Creation of Feminist Consciousness: From the Middle Ages to Eighteen-Seventy* (Oxford University Press, 1993), pp. 89–90.

[164] Lerner, *Creation of Patriarchy*, pp. 121–122.

[165] Pomeroy, p. 64.

[166] Christopher Lasch, *Women and the Common Life: Love, Marriage, and Feminism* (W. W. Norton, 1997), p. xv.

[167] Giulia Sissa, "The Sexual Philosophies of Plato and Aristotle," in Pantel, p. 79.

[168] Yan Thomas, "The Division of the Sexes in Roman Law," in Pantel, p. 103.

[169] Nicole Loraux, "What is a Goddess?" in Pantel, p. 20.

[170] Quoted in O'Faolain and Martines, p. 15.

[171] Ross Shepard Kraemer, *Her Share of the Blessings: Women's Religions Among Pagans, Jews and Christians in the Greco-Roman World* (Oxford University Press, 1992), p. 66.

[172] Stone, p. 70.

[173] Jean H. Hagstrum, *Esteem Enlivened by Desire: The Couple from Homer to Shakespeare* (University of Chicago Press, 1992), p. 221.

[174] L'Hermite-Leclerq, in Klapisch-Zuber, p. 215.

[175] Quoted in Frances and Joseph Gies, *Women in the Middle Ages* (Harper Perennial, 1978), p. 30.

[176] Gies and Gies, *Women in the Middle Ages*, p. 46.

[177] Geoffrey Chaucer, *The Canterbury Tales,* Neville Coghill trans. (Penguin Books, 1961), pp. 284, 295, 296.

[178] Stone, p. 28.

[179] John R. Gillis, *For Better, For Worse: British Marriages, 1600 to the Present* (Oxford University Press, 1985), p. 15.

[180] Hufton, in Davis and Farge, p. 28.

[181] Quoted in Hufton, in Davis and Farge, p. 28.

[182] Hufton, *Prospect Before Her,* p. 38.

[183] Ibid., p. 161.

[184] Robert Abbot, *A Christian Family Builded by God, Directing All Governours of Families how to act* (1653).

[185] Hufton, *Prospect Before Her,* p. 38.

[186] Stone, p. 109.

[186a] Quoted in *Not in God's Image*, Julia O'Faolain and Laura Martines, eds., pp. 196–197.

[187] Quoted in Stone, p. 111.

[188] Quoted in Hufton, *Prospect Before Her,* pp. 36–37.

[189] Quoted in Natalie Zemon Davis, "Women in Politics," in Davis and Farge, p. 183.

[190] Hufton, p. 283.

[191] Perkin, p. 75.

[192] Quoted in Hellerstein *et al.*, p. 137.

[193] Quoted in Freedman *et al.*, p. 118.

[194] Quoted in Prentice *et al.*, pp. 88–89.

[195] Hellerstein *et al.*, p. 4.

[196] Ibid., p. 124.

[197] Perkin, p. 104.

[198] Quoted in Smith-Rosenberg, pp. 124–125.

[199] Carl N. Degler, *At Odds: Women and the Family in America from the Revolution to the Present* (Oxford University Press, 1980), p. 332.

[200] Nicole Arnaud-Duc, "The Law's Contradictions," Arthur Goldhammer trans., in Fraisse and Perrot, p. 108.

[201] Suzanna Danuta Walters, *Lives Together/Worlds Apart: Mothers and Daughters in Popular Culture* (University of California Press, 1992), p. 16.

[201a] Henrik Ibsen, *A Doll's House* (Dover Thrift Editions, 1992), p. 64.

[202] Quoted in Lerner, *The Creation of Patriarchy*, p. 27.

[203] Quoted in Fraisse and Perrot, p. 72.

[204] Quoted in Falk, p. 151.

[205] Quoted in Falk, p. 122.

[206] Thébaud, p. 51.

[207] Quoted in Prentice *et al.*, p. 150.

[208] D'Emilio and Freedman, pp. 173–174.

[209] Nancy F. Cott, *The Grounding of Modern Feminism* (Yale University Press, 1987), p. 156.

[210] Diana Trilling, *The Beginning of the Journey: The Marriage of Diana and Lionel Trilling* (Harcourt, Brace, 1993), p. 108.

[211] Quoted in Gil Troy, *Affairs of State: The Rise and Rejection of the Presidential Couple Since World War II* (The Free Press, 1997), p. 61.

[212] Quoted in Veronica Strong-Boag, "Home Dreams: Women and the Suburban Experiment in Canada, 1945–60," *Canadian Historical Review*, Vol. 72, No. 4 (1991), p. 478.

[213] Quoted in D'Emilio and Freedman, p. 302.

[214] Quoted in D'Emilio and Freedman, p. 303.

[215] D'Emilio and Freedman, p. 435.

[216] Quoted in D'Emilio and Freedman, p. 332.

[217] *The Globe and Mail,* 20 June, 1996, pp. A1, A8.

[218] Michael Ulmer, *The Globe and Mail,* 9 August, 1995, p. A16.

[219] A pseudonym.

[220] Lerner, *Creation of Patriarchy*, pp. 77–78.

[221] Ibid., p. 96.

[222] Pomeroy, p. 194.

[223] Ibid., p. 192.

[224] Ibid., p. 193.

[225] Ibid., p. 200.

[226] Thomas, in Pantel, p. 135.

[227] Opitz, in Klapisch-Zuber, p. 280.

[228] Shahar, p. 129.

[229] Jennifer C. Ward, *English Noblewomen in the Later Middle Ages* (Longman, 1992), p. 50.

[230] Ibid., p. 75.

[231] Casagrande, in Klapisch-Zuber, p. 79.

[232] Shahar, p. 150.

[233] Ibid., p. 150.

[234] Ibid., p. 175.

[235] Ibid., p. 191.

[236] Gies and Gies, *Marriage and the Family in the Middle Ages,* (Harper & Row, 1987), pp. 161–163.

[237] Chaucer, pp. 230–231.

[238] Quoted in Jean-Paul Desaive, "The Ambiguities of Literature," Arthur Goldhammer trans., in Davis and Farge, p. 281.

[239] Quoted in Fraser, *Weaker Vessel*, p. 96.

[240] Quoted in Fraser, p. 96.

[241] Quoted in Fraser, p. 82.

[242] Quoted in Fraser, p. 99.

[243] Hufton, in Davis and Farge, p. 42.

[244] Ibid., p. 43.

[245] Fraser, p. 233.

[246] Hufton, *Prospect Before Her,* p. 234.

[247] Fraser, p. 102.

[248] Jane Austen, *Emma* (Penguin Classics, 1985), p. 54.

[249] Quoted in Friedman *et al.*, p. 45.

[250] Hermione Lee, *Virginia Woolf* (Vintage, 1997), p. 123.

[251] Joanna Trollope, *Britannia's Daughters: Women of the British Empire* (Pimlico, 1983), p. 172.

[252] Hellerstein *et al.*, p. 290.

[253] Ibid., p. 456.

[254] Virginia Woolf, *Mrs. Dalloway* (Flamingo, 1994), pp. 84–85.

[255] D. H. Lawrence, *Sons and Lovers* (Wordsworth Classics, 1993), p. 16.

[256] Thébaud, p. 73.

[257] Walters, p. 27.

[258] E. Ann Kaplan, "Mothering, Feminism and Representation: The Maternal Melodrama and the Women's Film 1910–1940," in Christine Gledhill, ed., *Home is Where the Heart Is: Studies in Melodrama and the Women's Film* (British Film Institute, 1987), p. 133.

[259] Audre Lorde, "Holistic Politics," *Ms.* July/August 1996, p. 62.

[259a] Ellen Pall, *Among the Ginzburgs* (Zoland Books, 1996), p. 63.

[260] Sandra prefers that her married name not be used.

[261] A pseudonym.

[262] Lysias, *Lysias,* trans. W. R. M. Lamb (William Heinemann, 1967), p. 7.

[263] Lacey, p. 115.

[264] Lysias, p. 21.

[265] Aeschines, "Against Timarchus," quoted in O'Faolain and Martines, p. 23.

[266] Keuls, pp. 208–209.

[267] Pomeroy, p. 65.

[268] Plutarch, "Alcibiades," in *Plutarch's Lives*, B. Perrin trans. (William Heinemann, 1959), Vol. 4, p. 9.

[269] Ibid., p. 21.

[270] Suzanne Fonay Wemple, "Women from the Fifth to the Tenth Century," in Klapisch-Zuber, p. 176.

[271] Phillips, p. 3.

[272] Wemple, in Klapisch-Zuber, p. 179.

[273] Shahar, p. 108.

[274] Phillips, p. 14.

[275] Ibid., pp. 13–14.

[276] Ibid., p. 6.

[277] Ibid., p. 71.

[278] Ibid., p. 90.

279 Hufton, *Prospect Before Her,* p. 260.

280 Berkin, p. 31.

281 Ibid., p. 31.

282 Phillips, p. 263.

283 Ibid., p. 263.

284 Hufton, *Prospect Before Her,* p. 363.

285 Ruth P. Dawson, "'And This Shield is Called—Self-Reliance': Emerging Feminist Consciousness in the Late Eighteenth Century." In Ruth-Ellen B. Joeres and Mary Jo Maynes, eds., *German Women in the Eighteenth and Nineteenth Centuries: A Social and Literary History* (Indiana University Press, 1986), p. 162.

286 Phillips, p. 257.

287 Charlotte Brontë, *Jane Eyre* (Bantam Classics, 1981), p. 291.

288 Arnaud-Duc, in Fraisse and Perrot, p. 98.

289 Anderson, p. 127.

290 Perkin, p. 114.

291 Quoted in Perkin, p. 115.

292 Quoted in Hellerstein *et al.*, pp. 258–259.

293 Phillips, p. 421.

294 Letters from the Emily Landry estate (died 1923) given to the author.

295 Phillips, p. 520.

296 Ibid., p. 517.

297 Frederick Lewis Allen, *Only Yesterday: An Informal History of the 1920s* (Harper and Brothers, 1931), p. 116.

298 George Bernard Shaw, *The Intelligent Woman's Guide to Socialism and Capitalism* (Brentano's, 1928), pp. 408–09.

299 Phillips, p. 551.

300 Ibid., p. 558.

300a Doris Lessing, *A Proper Marriage* (Flamingo, 1993), p. 434.

301 Ibid., p. 562

302 Ibid., p. 562

303 Margaret Philip, *The Globe and Mail,* 15 July, 1995, p. A6.

304 Hagstrum, p. 32.

305 Loraux, in Pantel, p. 24.

306 Ibid., p. 24.

307 Ward, p. 16.

308 Opitz, in Klapisch-Zuber, p. 306.

309 Ibid., p. 307.

310 Quoted in Shahar, p. 206.

311 Opitz, in Klapisch-Zuber, p. 302.

312 Ibid., p. 305.

313 Quoted in Antonia Fraser, *The Warrior Queens* (Penguin Books, 1989), p. 208.

314 Ibid., pp. 223–224.

315 Elisja Schulte van Kessel, "Virgins and Mothers between Heaven and Earth," Clarissa Botsford trans., in Davis and Farge, p. 149.

316 Quoted in Lerner, *Feminist Consciousness,* p. 197.

317 Quoted in Perry, p. 146.

[318] Perry, p. 243.

[319] Quoted in Perry, p. 244.

[320] Lee Virginia Chambers-Schiller, *Liberty, A Better Husband: Single Women in America: The Generations of 1780–1840* (Yale University Press, 1984), p. 2.

[321] Jane Austen, *Emma*, p. 109.

[322] Quoted in Trollope, p. 23.

[323] Catharine Maria Sedgwick, "Old Maids," in Susan Koppelman (ed.), *Old Maids: Short Stories by Nineteenth Century U. S. Women Writers* (Pandora Press, 1984), p. 17.

[324] Quoted in Barker, p. 701.

[325] Cécile Dauphin, "Single Women," Arthur Goldhammer trans., in Fraisse and Perrot, p. 434.

[326] Judith R. Walkowitz, "Dangerous Sexualities," in Fraisse and Perrot, p. 394.

[327] Prentice *et al.*, p. 159.

[328] Dauphin, in Fraisse and Perrot, p. 440.

[329] Virginia Woolf, *The Years* (Vintage, 1992), p. 87.

[330] Virginia Woolf, *To The Lighthouse* (Flamingo, 1995), p. 23.

[331] Ibid., pp. 165, 166.

[332] Letters to the author.

[333] Anne-Marie Sohn, "Between the Wars in France and England," Arthur Goldhammer trans., in Thébaud, p. 94.

[334] Prentice *et al.*, p. 236.

[335] Quoted in Prentice *et al.*, p. 303.

[336] Françoise Navailh, "The Soviet Model," Arthur Goldhammer trans., in Thébaud, p. 248.

[337] Dr. Marion Hilliard, "Dr. Marion Hilliard talks to single women," *Chatelaine* (February 1956), pp. 17–18, 50–52.

[338] Nadine Lefaucheur, "Maternity, Family, and the State," Arthur Goldhammer trans., in Thébaud, p. 437.

[339] "All alone? You've got company," *The Globe and Mail,* 25 June, 1998, p. A1.

[340] Euripides, "Hippolytus," in *Alcestis/Hippolytus/Iphigenia in Tarsus*, Philip Vellacott trans. (Penguin Books, 1972), p. 32.

[341] Pomeroy, p. 85.

[342] Nancy Demand, *Birth, Death, and Motherhood in Ancient Greece* (Johns Hopkins University Press, 1994), p. 129.

[343] Louise Bruit Zaidman, "Pandora's Daughters and Rituals in Grecian Cities," in Pantel, p. 367.

[344] Quoted in Rousselle, in Pantel, p. 299.

[345] Quoted in Beryl Rowland, *Medieval Woman's Guide to Health: The First English Gynecological Handbook* (Kent State University Press, 1981), p. 28.

[346] Pomeroy, p. 168.

[347] Quoted in Mary R. Lefkowitz and Maureen B. Fant, *Women's Life in Greece and Rome* (Johns Hopkins University Press, 1982), p. 21.

[348] Joseph and Frances Gies, *Life in a Medieval City* (Harper Perennial, 1981), p. 60.

[349] Quoted in Rowland, p. 34.

[350] Edward Shorter, *Women's Bodies: A Social History of Women's Encounters with Health, Ill-Health, and Medicine* (Transaction Publishers, 1991), p. 55.

[351] Rowland, p. 32.

[352] Opitz, in Klapisch-Zuber, p. 290.

[353] Rowland, p. xiii.

[354] Ibid., p. 91.

[355] Thomasset, in Klapisch-Zuber, p. 66.

[356] Shorter, p. 261.

[357] Grieco, in Davis and Farge, p. 49.

[358] Ibid., p. 49.

[359] Shorter, p. 262.

[360] Quoted in Mossiker, p. 175.

[361] Knibiehler, in Fraisse and Perrot, p. 334.

[362] Shorter, p. 231.

[363] Knibiehler, in Fraisse and Perrot, p. 336.

[364] Ibid., p. 336

[365] Quoted in Hellerstein *et al.*, pp. 111–112.

[366] Anderson, p. 117.

[367] Smith-Rosenberg, p. 208.

[368] Shorter, p. 132.

[369] Ibid., p. 161.

[370] Ibid., p. 161.

[371] Ibid., p. 174.

[372] "Women dying unnecessarily," *The Globe and Mail*, 7 April, 1998, p. A11.

[373] Lefaucheur, in Thébaud, p. 441.

[374] Ibid., p. 441.

[375] Ibid., p. 441.

[376] Demosthenes, "Against Neaera," in *Demosthenes*, A. T. Murray trans. (William Heinemann, 1964), Vol. 6, p. 393.

[377] Quoted in Lefkowitz and Fant, pp. 265–266.

[378] Demand, p. 68.

[379] Ibid., p. 68.

[380] Opitz, in Klapisch-Zuber, p. 299.

[381] Chiara Frugoni, "The Imagined Woman," Clarissa Botsford trans., in Klapisch-Zuber, pp. 387, 390.

[382] Opitz, in Klapisch-Zuber, p. 298.

[383] Shorter, p. 41.

[384] Opitz, in Klapisch-Zuber, p. 300.

[385] Frugoni, in Klapisch-Zuber, p. 384.

[386] Vincent de Paul, *Correspondence*, 13:430.

[387] Hufton, *Prospect Before Her,* p. 382.

[388] Ibid., p. 382.

[389] Jo Ann Kay McNamara, *Sisters in Arms: Catholic Nuns Through Two Millennia* (Harvard University Press, 1996), p. 483.

[390] Ibid., p. 485.

[391] Hufton, *Prospect Before Her,* p. 388.

[392] Ibid., pp. 388–389.

[393] Ibid., p. 389.

[394] Hufton, *Prospect Before Her,* p. 390.

[395] Ibid., p. 392.

[396] Perkin, p. 160.

[397] Charlotte Brontë, *Shirley* (Penguin Classics, 1974), pp. 197–198.

[398] Quoted in Colleen A. Hobbs, *Florence Nightingale* (Twayne Publishers, 1997), p. 6.

[399] Quoted in Hobbs, p. 65.

[400] Ibid., p. 1.

[401] Knibiehler, Fraisse and Perrot, p. 334.

[402] Perkin, p 38.

[403] Ibid., p. 40.

[404] Ibid., p. 39.

[405] Esther Pohl Lovejoy, *Women Doctors of the World* (Macmillan, 1957), p. 277.

[406] Hellerstein *et al.*, p. 289.

[407] Prentice *et al.*, p. 213.

[408] Peter Paret, Beth Irwin Lewis and Paul Paret, *Persuasive Images: Posters of War and Revolution from the Hoover Institution Archives* (Princeton University Press, 1992), p. 60.

[409] Thébaud, in Thébaud, pp. 41–42.

[410] Ibid., p. 45.

[411] Quoted in Prentice *et al.*, pp. 225–226.

[412] Doris Lessing, *Under My Skin,* pp. 5–6.

[413] Prentice *et al.*, p. 226.

[414] Quoted in Lee, *Virginia Woolf,* p. 281.

[415] Cott, p. 221.

[416] Ehrenreich and English, p. 3.

[417] Quoted in Gena Corea, *The Hidden Malpractice: How American Medicine Treats Women As Patients and Professionals* (William Morrow, 1977), pp. 64–65.

[418] Quoted in Sharon Doyle Driedger, "The Nurses," *Maclean's,* 28 April, 1997, p. 24.

[419] Quoted in Jane Gadd, "Nurses to the rescue" *The Globe and Mail,* 17 February, 1996, p. D2.

[420] Much of the material describing the wandering womb syndrome is found in Laurinda S. Dixon, *Perilous Chastity: Women and Illness in Pre-Enlightenment Art and Medicine* (Cornell University Press, 1995), pp. 15–16.

[421] Plato, *Timaeus,* F. M. Cornford trans. (Library of Liberal Arts, 1959), p. 115.

[422] Quoted in Ann Ellis Hanson, "Hippocrates: 'Diseases of Women,'" *Signs: Journal of Women and Culture in Society,* Vol. 1 (1975), pp. 567–582.

[423] Plato, *Timaeus,* p. 115.

[424] Sissa, in Pantel, pp. 65–66.

[425] Martine Rothblatt, *The Apartheid of Sex: A Manifesto on the Freedom of Gender* (Crown Publishers, 1995), pp. 35–36.

[426] Aeschylus, *The Eumenides,* H. Lloyd-Jones trans. (Prentice-Hall, 1970), p. 52.

[427] Aristotle, "De Generatione Animalium," A. Platt trans., in *The Works of Aristotle* (Oxford, 1958), Vol. 5, 775a: 15–17.

[428] Quoted in L. Dixon, p. 19.

[429] Thomas Laqueur, *Making Sex: Body and Gender from the Greeks to Freud* (Harvard University Press, 1990), p. 25.

[430] Thomasset, in Klapisch-Zuber, pp. 46–47.

[431] Ibid., p. 56.

[432] Warner, p. 41.

[433] Quoted in Casagrande, in Klapisch-Zuber, p. 87.

[434] Laqueur, p. 70.

[435] Evelyne Berriot-Salvadore, "The Discourse of Medicine and Science," Arthur Gold-hammer trans., in Davis and Farge, p. 351.

[436] Ibid., p. 353.

[437] Ibid., pp. 353–354.

[438] Thomas Willis, *Dr. Willis's practice of physick, being the whole works of that renowned and famous physician*, trans. Samuel Pordage. London 1683.

[439] Quoted in Berriot-Salvadore, in Davis and Farge, p. 357.

[440] Quoted in Lerner, *Feminist Consciousness*, pp. 151–152.

[441] Berriot-Salvadore, in Davis and Farge, p. 358.

[442] Quoted in L. Dixon, p. 237.

[443] Quoted in Smith-Rosenberg, p. 184.

[444] Quoted in D'Emilio and Freedman, p. 146.

[445] Smith-Rosenberg, p. 184.

[446] Anderson, p. 115.

[447] Ibid., p. 117.

[448] Ibid., p. 118.

[449] Ibid., p. 118.

[450] Quoted in Smith-Rosenberg, p. 236.

[451] Perkin, p. 71.

[452] Lee, p. 183.

[453] Ibid., p. 184.

[454] Virginia Woolf, *Mrs. Dalloway* (Flamingo, 1994), p. 197.

[455] Mary McCarthy, *The Group* (Harcourt Brace, 1963), p. 300.

[456] Dixon, p. 246.

[457] Jocelyn Argue, "Physician tells women to press for proper medical diagnosis," *The Star Phoenix,* 2 October, 1992, p. 1.

[458] Rich, p. 176.

[459] Kirk Makin, "Abortion private issue, poll finds," *The Globe and Mail,* 16 March, 1998

[460] Jane Coutts, "The Case against male-oriented research," *The Globe and Mail,* 18 March, 1995, p. D8.

[461] Allen Guttmann, *Women's Sports: A History* (Columbia University, 1991), p. 20.

[462] Sextus Propertius, *The Poems of Sextus Propertius,* J. P. McCulloch trans. (University of California Press, 1972), p. 174.

[463] Plutarch, "Lycurgus," in *Plutarch's Lives: The "Dryden Plutarch" Revised by Arthur Hugh Clough* (J. M. Dent and Sons, 1916), Vol. 1, pp. 72-73.

[464] Donald G. Kyle, *Athletics in Ancient Athens* (Leiden: E. J. Brill, 1987), p. 46.

[465] Guttmann, p. 48.

[466] William J. Baker, *Sports in the Western World* (Rowman and Littlefield, 1982), p. 48.

[467] Shahar, p. 152.

[468] Jean Verdon, *Les Loisirs en France au Moyen Age* (Tallandier, 1980), pp. 165–66.

[469] Desaive, in Davis and Farge, p. 291.

470 Quoted in Wendy Hilton, *Dance of Court & Theatre: The French Noble Style, 1690–1725,* Caroline Gaynor ed. (Princeton Book Company, 1981), p. 67.

471 Trollope, p. 203.

472 Helen Lenskyj, "Physical Activity for Canadian Women, 1890–1930: Media Views," in J. A. Mangan and Roberta J. Park (eds.), *From "Fair Sex" to Feminism: Sports and the Socialization of Women in the Industrial and Post-Industrial Eras* (Frank Cass, 1987), p. 212.

473 Jennifer Hargreaves, *Sporting Females: Critical Issues in the History and Sociology of Women's Sports* (Routledge, 1994), p. 43.

474 Quoted in Hargreaves, p. 53.

475 Quoted in Prentice *et al.*, p. 152.

476 Lenskyj, in Mangan and Park, p. 210.

477 Quoted in Mangan and Park, p. 211.

478 Quoted in Hargreaves, p. 54.

479 Guttmann, p. 108.

480 Quoted in Lenskyj, in Mangan and Park, p. 214.

481 Susan E. Cayleff, *Babe: The Life and Legend of Babe Didrikson Zaharias* (University of Illinois Press, 1995), p. 42.

482 Guttmann, p. 144.

483 Ibid., p. 158.

484 Quoted in Lenskyj, in Mangan and Park, p. 212.

485 Ibid., p. 226.

486 Susan K. Cahn, *Coming on Strong: Gender and Sexuality in Twentieth-Century Women's Sport* (The Free Press, 1994), p. 54.

487 Quoted in James Christie and Beverley Smith, "Why can't a woman compete like a man?" *The Globe and Mail,* 21 September, 1996, p. D5.

488 Guttman, p. 252.

489 D'Emilio and Freedman, p. 209.

490 Homer, *The Iliad,* Robert Fitzgerald trans. (Anchor Books Doubleday, 1974), p. 70.

491 Ibid., pp. 72-73.

492 Ibid., p. 73.

493 Thucydides, *The Peloponnesian War,* Rex Warner trans. (Penguin Books, 1967), p. 17.

494 Quoted in Monica Brzezinski Potkay and Regula Meyer Evitt, *Minding the Body: Women and Literature in the Middle Ages, 800–1500* (Twayne Publishers), p. 16.

495 Quoted in Diane Owen Hughes, "Regulating Women's Fashion," in Klapisch-Zuber, p. 144.

496 Casagrande, in Klapisch-Zuber, pp. 92-93.

497 Quoted in Casagrande, in Klapisch-Zuber, p. 93.

498 Quoted in Hughes, in Klapisch-Zuber, p. 136.

499 Chaucer, pp. 291–292.

500 Grieco, in Davis and Farge, p. 50.

501 Ibid., p. 51.

502 Ibid., pp. 52-53.

503 Quoted in Grieco, in Davis and Farge, p. 57.

504 Grieco, in Davis and Farge, p. 62.

505 Ibid., p. 62.

[506] Ibid., p. 61.

[507] Quoted in Grieco, in Davis and Farge, p. 61.

[508] Quoted in Carroll Camden, *The Elizabethan Woman: A Panorama of English Woman-hood, 1540 to 1640* (Elsevier Press, 1952), p. 214.

[509] Véronique Nahoum-Grappe, "The Beautiful Woman," Arthur Goldhammer trans., in Davis and Farge, p. 95.

[510] Brownmiller, p. 87.

[511] Perkin, p. 93.

[512] Quoted in Barker, p. 719.

[513] Charlotte Brontë, *Jane Eyre*, p. 246.

[514] Quoted in Burke, p. 89.

[515] Quoted in Knibiehler, in Fraisse and Perrot, p. 331.

[515a] Doris Lessing, *Martha Quest*, p. 143.

[515b] Margaret Drabble, *A Summer Bird-Cage* (Harmondsworth: Penguin, 1967), p. 54.

[516] Not altogether. As late as the mid-'50s, I can remember my grandmother lacing herself into her "garment" that contained her from bosom to thigh. She was a slender woman, but she said it gave her a sense of security.

[517] De Beauvoir, pp. 262–263.

[518] Naomi Wolf, *The Beauty Myth* (Vintage, 1990), p. 241.

[519] Keuls, p. 104.

[520] Plato, *The Republic of Plato*, F. M. Cornford trans. (Oxford University Press, 1966), p. 145.

[521] Pomeroy, p. 133.

[522] Quoted in Lefkowitz and Fant, p. 166.

[523] Quoted in Pomeroy, p. 170.

[524] Quoted in Lefkowitz and Fant, pp. 52–53.

[525] Ian McAuslan and Peter Walcot, eds., *Women in Antiquity* (Oxford University Press, 1996), p. 42.

[526] Juvenal, "Satire VI," lines 434–456.

[527] Lerner, *Feminist Consciousness*, p. 25.

[528] Shahar, p. 50.

[529] McNamara, p. 137.

[530] Wemple, in Klapisch-Zuber, p. 198.

[531] Lerner, *Feminist Consciousness*, p. 26.

[532] Opitz, in Klapisch-Zuber, p. 298.

[533] Quoted in O'Faolain and Martines, p. 167.

[534] Shahar, p. 23.

[535] L'Hermite-Leclerq, in Klapisch-Zuber, p. 213.

[536] Paris, Bibliothèque des Arts Décoratifs, Maclet Collection.

[537] Martine Sonnet, "A Daughter to Educate," Arthur Goldhammer trans., Davis and Farge, p. 122.

[538] Quoted in Fraser, *Weaker Vessel*, p. 328.

[539] Ibid., p. 465.

[540] Sonnet, in Davis and Farge, p. 114.

[540a] Quoted in Lerner, *Feminist Consciousness*, p. 33.

[541] Perry, p. 104.

[542] Fraser, *Weaker Vessel*, p. 137.

[542a] Bathsua Makin, *An Essay to Revive the Ancient Education of Gentlewomen* (Augustan Reprint Society. William Andrews Clark Memorial Library, 1980) p. 24.

[543] Mary Astell, *Some Reflections upon Marriage* (William Parker, 1730), pp. 172–173.

[544] Perry, p. 105.

[545] Quoted in O'Faolain and Martines, p. 247.

[546] Quoted in Claire Tomalin, *The Life and Death of Mary Wollstonecraft* (Penguin Books, 1992), p. 108.

[547] Jane Austen, *Persuasion* (Penguin Popular Classics), p. 235.

[548] Lyndall Gordon, *Virginia Woolf: A Writer's Life* (W. W. Norton & Co., 1984), p. 10.

[549] Marie-Claire Hoock-Demarle, "Reading and Writing in Germany," Arthur Goldhammer trans., in Fraisse and Perrot, p. 151.

[550] Charlotte Brontë, *Villette* (Wordsworth Classics, 1993), p. 47

[551] Quoted in Lerner, *Feminist Consciousness*, p. 214.

[552] Hellerstein *et al.*, p. 61.

[553] Quoted in Hoock-Demarle, in Fraisse and Perrot, p. 149.

[554] Hellerstein *et al.*, p. 17.

[555] Quoted in Wolff, p. 77.

[556] Martha Vicinus, ed., *A Widening Sphere: Changing Roles of Victorian Women* (Indiana University Press, 1977), p. 141.

[557] Quoted in Smith-Rosenberg, pp. 251–252.

[558] Lerner, *Feminist Consciousness*, p. 44.

[559] Quoted in Rose-Marie Lagrave, "A Supervised Emancipation," Arthur Goldhammer trans., in Thébaud, p. 463.

[560] Cott, p. 227.

[561] Ibid., p. 228.

[562] Quoted in Cott, p. 180.

[563] Quoted in James Fenton, "Lady Lazarus," *The New York Review*, 29 May, 1997, p. 12.

[564] Alanna Mitchell, "Women jump to head of class," *The Globe and Mail*, 15 April, 1998, p. A1.

[565] Kevin O'Connor, "Girls lead boys in nearly all high school subjects: study," *Regina Leader Post*, 30 August, 1996, p. 3.

[566] Plato, *Republic*, p. 149.

[567] Quoted in Keuls, p. 104.

[568] Lerner, *Feminist Consciousness*, pp. 10–11.

[569] Marina Warner, *Monuments and Maidens: The Allegory of the Female Form* (Vintage, 1996), p. 102.

[570] Roy B. Chamberlin and Herman Feldman eds., *The Dartmouth Bible* (Houghton Mifflin, 1961), p. 832.

[571] Mary Ellen Waithe, "Finding Bits and Pieces of Hypatia," in Linda Lopez McAlister, ed., *Hypatia's Daughters: Fifteen Hundred years of Women Philosophers* (Indiana University Press, 1996), p. 5.

[572] Mary R. Lefkowitz, *Women in Greek Myth*, (The John Hopkins University Press, 1990), p. 108.

[573] Lefkowitz, *Women in Greek Myth*, p. 109.

[574] Edward Gibbon, *The Decline and Fall of the Roman Empire* (Modern Library, 1932), Vol. 2, pp. 816–817.

[575] Quoted in Potkay and Evitt, p. 20

[576] Lerner, *Feminist Consciousness*, p. 255.

[577] Nye, in McAlister, p. 26.

[578] Quoted in Nye, in McAlister, p. 27.

[579] *The Letters of Abelard and Heloise*, C. K. S. Moncrieff trans. (Alfred A. Knopf, 1933), p. 57.

[580] L. Dixon, p. 205.

[581] Jane Duran, "Anne Viscountess Conway: A Seventeenth-Century Rationalist," in McAlister, p. 105.

[582] Davis, *Women on the Margins*, p. 141.

[583] Lerner, *Feminist Consciousness,* p. 155.

[584] Quoted in Lerner, *Feminist Consciousness,* p. 196.

[585] Lerner, *Feminist Consciousness*, p. 196.

[586] Quoted in Michèle Crampe-Casnabet, "A Sampling of Eighteenth-Century Philosophy," Arthur Goldhammer trans., in Davis and Farge, p. 329.

[587] Quoted in Hellerstein *et al.*, p. 67.

[588] Quoted in Cott, p. 19.

[589] Elizabeth Cady Stanton, *Eighty Years and More* (Northeastern University Press, 1993), pp. 20–21.

[590] Quoted in Elisabeth Griffith, *In Her Own Right: The Life of Elizabeth Cady Stanton* (Oxford University Press, 1984), p. 9.

[591] Quoted in *Elizabeth Cady Stanton, as Revealed in her Letters, Diary and Reminiscences,* T. Stanton and H. Stanton Blatch, eds.(Arno & *The New York Times,* 1969), Vol. 2, pp. 26–27.

[592] Stanton, p. 145.

[593] Quoted in Griffith, p. 51.

[594] Quoted in Hellerstein *et al.*, p. 165.

[595] *The Revolution*, 3 June, 1869.

[596] Quoted in Stanton and Blatch, Vol. 2, p. 60.

[597] Quoted in Françoise Collin, "Philosophical Differences," Arthur Goldhammer trans., in Thébaud, p. 262.

[598] Quoted in Collin, in Thébaud, p. 263.

[599] Ibid., p. 268.

[600] Mary Catherine Baseheart, "Edith Stein's Philosophy of Woman and of Women's Education," in McAlister, p. 273.

[601] Baseheart, in McAlister, p. 275.

[602] Rothblatt, pp. 3–4.

[603] Wendy Kaminer, "Feminism's Identity Crisis," *The Atlantic Monthly*, Oct. 1993, p. 62.

[604] Katha Pollitt, *Reasonable Creatures: Essays on Women and Feminism* (Vintage, 1995), p. 61.

[605] Pomeroy, p. 78.

[606] Zaidman, in Pantel, p. 352.

[607] Ross Shepard Kraemer, *Her Share of the Blessings: Women's Religions Among Pagans, Jews and Christians in the Greco-Roman World* (Oxford University Press, 1992), pp. 30–31.

[608] Pomeroy, p. 208.

[609] Quoted in Sabina Flanagan, *Hildegard of Bingen, 1098–1179: A Visionary Life* (Routledge, 1989), p. 2.

[610] Quoted in Lerner, *Feminist Consciousness*, p. 53.

[611] Flanagan, p. 142.

[612] Quoted in Lerner, *Feminist Consciousness*, p. 60.

[613] Lerner, *Feminist Consciousness,* p. 63.

[614] Quoted in Lerner, *Feminist Consciousness*, p. 90.

[615] Mossiker, p. 4.

[616] Shahar, p. 145.

[617] Quoted in O'Faolain and Martines, p. 202.

[618] Ibid., p. 262.

[619] Hufton, p. 38.

[620] Van Kessel, in Davis and Farge, p. 152.

[621] John Martin, "Out of the Shadow: Heretical and Catholic Women in Renaissance Venice," *Journal of Family History*, Vol. 10, No. 1, (Spring, 1985), p. 26.

[622] Michela De Giorgio, "The Catholic Model," Joan Bond Sax trans., in Fraisse and Perrot, p. 169.

[623] De Giorgio, in Fraisse and Perrot, pp. 185–186.

[624] Quoted in De Giorgio, in Fraisse and Perrot, p. 191.

[625] Prentice *et al.*, p. 145.

[626] De Giorgio, in Fraisse and Perrot, p. 174.

[627] Perkin, p. 111.

[628] Charlotte Brontë, *Shirley*, p. 316.

[629] Barbara Goldsmith, *Other Powers: The Age of Suffrage, Spiritualism, and the Scandalous Victoria Woodhull* (Alfred A. Knopf, 1998), p. 17.

[630] Smith-Rosenberg, p. 130.

[631] Woolf, *Mrs. Dalloway*, p. 134.

[632] De Beauvoir, p. 624.

[633] Mary Daly, *The Church and the Second Sex* (Beacon Press, 1985), p. xii.

[634] Mary Malone, "Mary Malone talks about leaving the church," *Catholic New Times*, 4 February, 1996, p. 3.

[635] Herodotus, *The Histories*, A. de Sélincourt trans. (Penguin Books, 1959), p. 337.

[636] François Lissarrague, "Figures of Women," in Pantel, p. 186.

[637] Kraemer, p. 88.

[638] Quoted in Scheid, in Pantel, p. 382.

[639] Pomeroy, pp. 213–214.

[640] Kraemer, p. 82.

[641] Scheid, in Pantel, p. 401.

[642] Quoted in Scheid, in Pantel, p. 401.

[642a] I Cor. 11: 7–9.

[643] Quoted in Penny Shine Gold, *The Lady and the Virgin:. Image, Attitude, Experience in Twelfth-Century France* (University of Chicago Press, 1985), p. 80.

[644] McNamara, p. 43.

[645] Shahar, p. 27.

[646] Wemple, in Klapisch-Zuber, p. 193.

[647] Lerner, *Feminist Consciousness*, p. 25.

[648] Ibid., p. 81.

[649] Quoted in Hufton, *Prospect Before Her,* p. 358.

[650] Ibid., p. 335.

651 Quoted in Carroll Smith-Rosenberg, *Disorderly Conduct,* p. 125

652 Elizabeth Cady Stanton, Susan B. Anthony, and Matilda Joslyn Gage, eds., *History of Woman Suffrage* (Fowler & Wells, 1881), Vol. 1, p. 285.

653 Quoted in Cullen Murphy, *The Word According to Eve: Women and the Bible in Ancient Times and Our Own* (Houghton Mifflin, 1998), p. 20.

654 Quoted in Murphy, p. 22.

655 Ibid., p. 37.

656 Jean Baubérot, "The Protestant Woman," Arthur Goldhammer trans., in Fraisse and Perrot, p. 212.

657 Quoted in Baubérot, in Fraisse and Perrot, p. 212.

658 Baubérot, in Fraisse and Perrot, p. 212.

659 Katie Sherrod, "First female bishops find warm welcome at Lambeth Conference," *Anglican Communion News Service,* note 1705, 3 August, 1998.

660 Quoted in Marci McDonald, "Is God A Woman?" *Maclean's,* 8 April, 1996, p. 47.

661 Quoted in Janet Somerville, "Colleagues in Canada lament theologian's dismissal," *Catholic New Times,* 28 May, 1995, pp. 16–17.

662 Joanna Manning, "How the Vatican contorts itself in banning women as priests," *The Globe and Mail,* 28 January, 1997, p. A17.

663 Donald E. Miller, *Reinventing American Protestantism: Christianity in the New Millennium* (University of California Press, 1997), p. 23.

664 Kraemer, p. 12.

665 Pomeroy, pp. 220–221.

666 Ibid., p. 220.

667 Ibid., p. 218.

668 Lerner, *Feminist Consciousness,* p. 91.

669 Stephen Wessley, "The Thirteenth-Century Guglielmites: Salvation Through Women," in Derek Baker ed., *Medieval Women: dedicated and presented to Professor Rosalind M. Hill on the occasion of her seventieth birthday* (B. Blackwell, 1978), p. 301.

670 Quoted in Shahar, p. 260.

671 Shahar, p. 261.

672 Hufton, *Prospect Before Her,* p. 411.

673 Ibid., p. 412.

674 Ibid., p. 413.

675 Quoted in Fraser, *Weaker Vessel,* p. 373.

676 Hufton, *Prospect Before Her,* p. 414.

677 Smith-Rosenberg, p. 323.

678 James K. Hopkins, *A Woman to Deliver Her People* (University of Texas Press, 1982), p. 19.

679 Quoted in Lerner, *Feminist Consciousness,* p. 104.

680 Quoted in Hopkins, p. 199.

681 Smith-Rosenberg, p. 131.

682 Ibid., p. 132.

683 D'Emilio and Freedman, p. 117.

684 Smith-Rosenberg, p. 132.

685 Wendy Griffiin, "The Embodied Goddess: Feminist Witchcraft and Female Divinity." *Sociology of Religion,* Vol. 56, no. 1 (Spring 1995), pp. 39-40.

[686] Wendy Griffin, "The Embodied Goddess: Feminist Witchcraft and Female Divinity," *Sociology of Religion*, Vol. 56, no. 1 (Spring 1995), pp. 39–40.

[687] Keuls, pp. 164–165.

[688] Ibid., p. 198.

[689] Quoted in Lefkowitz and Fant, p. 179.

[690] Ibid., p. 75.

[691] McNamara, p. 282.

[692] Ibid. p. 282.

[693] Wendy Slatkin, *Women Artists in History from Antiquity to the 20th Century* (Prentice Hall, 1985), p. 27.

[694] Quoted in O'Faolain and Martines, p. 276.

[695] Ibid. p. 276.

[696] Claude Dulong, "From Conversation to Creation," Arthur Goldhammer trans., in Davis and Farge, p. 402.

[697] George Sand, *Horace*, Zack Rogow trans. (Mercury House, 1995), p. 93.

[698] Dulong, in Davis and Farge, p. 406.

[699] Ibid., p. 409.

[700] Anne Higonnet, "Images—Appearance, Leisure, and Subsistence," in Fraisse and Perrot, p. 250.

[701] Higonnet, in Fraisse and Perrot, p. 251.

[702] Ibid. p. 251.

[701] Quoted in Linda Nochlin, "Why Have There Been No Great Women Artists?" in *Women, Art, and Power and other essays* (Westview Press, 1988), p. 9.

[702] Quoted in Perkin, p. 79.

[703] Virginia Woolf, *Mrs. Dalloway*, p. 85.

[704] De Beauvoir, p. 705.

[705] Linda Nochlin, "Why Have There Been No Great Women Artists?," in *Women, Art, and Power and other essays* (Westview Press, 1988), p. 166.

[706] Joan Borsa, curator/editor, *Ann Harbuz: Inside Community, Outside Convention* (Dunlop Art Gallery, 1997), no page.

[707] Jeanette Winterson, "The Semiotics of Sex," in *Art Objects: Essays on Ecstasy and Effrontery* (Alfred A. Knopf, 1996), p. 116.

[708] Quoted in Williamson, p. 75.

[709] Lissarrague, in Pantel, p. 185.

[710] Williamson, p. 75.

[711] Homer, *Iliad*, Book 24, lines 861–863.

[712] Bell, p. 313.

[713] Quoted in Diane Touliatos, "Kassia," in Martha Furman Schleifer and Sylvia Glickman (eds.), *Women Composers: Music Through the Ages* (G. K. Hall, 1996), Vol. 1, p. 2.

[714] Touliatos, in Schleifer and Glickman, Vol. 1, p. 3.

[715] Peter Dronke, *Poetic Individuality in the Middle Ages: New Departures in Poetry 1000–1150* (Clarendon Press, 1970), p. 151.

[716] Quoted in Marianne Richert Pfau, "Hildegard von Bingen," in Schleifer and Glickman, Vol. 1, p. 27.

[717] Lerner, *Feminist Consciousness*, pp. 169–170.

[718] Rempel, in Spencer, p. 173

[719] L. Dixon, pp. 180–183.

[720] Quoted in Fraser, *Weaker Vessel*, p. 143.

[721] Quoted in Thomasin Lamay, "Vittoria Aleotti/Raphaella Aleotta," in Schleifer and Glickman, Vol. 1, p. 135.

[722] Quoted in Lamay, Schleifer and Glickman, Vol. 1, p. 135.

[723] Karin Pendle, "Women in Music, ca. 1450–1600," in Karin Pendle (ed.), *Women and Music: A History* (Indiana University Press, 1991), p. 41.

[724] Hufton, *Prospect Before Her*, p. 498.

[725] Quoted in Spencer, pp. 176–177.

[726] Quoted in "Elizabeth-Claude Jacquet de La Guerre: Composer and Harpsichordist," in Neuls-Bates, p. 63.

[727] Bernhard Ulrich, *Concerning the Principles of Voice Training During the A Cappella Period And Until the Beginning of Opera (1474–1640)*, (Pro Musica Press, 1973), pp. 4–5.

[728] Marcia J. Citron, "Feminist Approaches to Musicology," in Susan C. Cook and Judy Tsou (eds.), *Cecilia Reclaimed: Feminist Perspectives on Gender and Music* (University of Illinois Press, 1994), p. 22.

[729] Bonny H. Miller, "Ladies' Companion, Ladies' Canon? Women Composers in American Magazines from *Godey's* to the *Ladies' Home Journal*," in Cook and Tsou, p. 163.

[730] Miller, in Cook and Tsou, p. 160.

[731] Adrienne Fried Block, "Women in American Music, 1800–1918," in Pendle, p. 146.

[732] Quoted in Nancy B. Reich, "Clara Schumann," in Jane Bowers and Judith Tick (eds.), *Women Making Music: The Western Art Tradition 1150–1950* (University of Illinois Press, 1986), p. 267.

[733] Ibid., p. 267.

[733a] Ibid., p. 264.

[734] Catherine Parsons Smith, " 'A Distinguishing Virility': Feminism and Modernism in American Art Music," in Cook and Tsou, p. 98.

[735] Quoted in Nancy B. Reich, "European Composers and Musicians, ca. 1800–1918," in Pendle, pp. 139–140.

[736] Smith, in Cook and Tsou, p. 93.

[737] Quoted in Smith, in Cook and Tsou, p. 94

[738] Ibid., p. 94.

[739] Ibid., p. 90.

[740] Carol Neuls-Bates, "Women's Orchestras in the United States, 1925–45," in Bowers and Tick, pp. 350–353.

[741] Quoted in Neuls-Bates, in Bowers and Tick, p. 358.

[742] Ibid., p. 359.

[743] Richard Corliss, "Viva the Divas," *Time*, 12 August, 1996, p. 49.

[744] Pliny, *Natural History*, R. Rackham trans. (William Heinemann, 1961), Vol. 9, pp. 371, 373.

[745] Ibid., pp. 369, 370.

[746] Ibid., 369.

[747] Frugoni, in Klapisch-Zuber, pp. 402–405.

[748] Quoted in Slatkin, p. 29.

[749] Slatkin, p. 49.

[750] Germaine Greer, *The Obstacle Race: The Fortunes of Women Painters and their Works* (Pan Books, 1981), p. 193.

[751] Borin, in Davis and Farge, pp. 234–235.

[752] Quoted in Parker and Pollock, p. 52.

[753] Ibid., p. 13.

[754] Quoted in Burke, p. 42.

[755] Parker and Pollock, p. 35.

[756] Higonnet, in Fraisse and Perrot, p. 255.

[757] Ibid., p. 255.

[758] Quoted in Burke, p. 94.

[759] Nochlin, p. 37.

[760] Quoted in Nochlin, p. 51.

[761] Slatkin, p. 118.

[762] Parker and Pollock, p. 41.

[763] Quoted in Slatkin, p. 112.

[764] Nochlin, p. 173.

[765] Quoted in Nochlin, p. 174.

[766] Quoted in Borzello, p. 131.

[767] Anne Higonnet, "Women, Images, and Representation," in Thébaud, p. 349.

[768] Higonnet, in Thébaud, p. 359.

[769] Quoted in Lucy R. Lippard, *The Pink Glass Swan: Selected Essays on Feminist Art* (The New Press, 1995), p. 213.

[770] Quoted in Lippard, p. 71.

[773] Parker and Pollack, p. 48.

[774] Higonnet, in Thébaud, pp. 386–387.

[775] Robin Laurence, "The Radiant Way," *Canadian Art* (Summer 1994), p. 26.

[776] Brian Bergman, "Maclean's Honor Roll 1997." *Maclean's*, 22 December, 1997, p. 59.

[777] Williamson, p. 2.

[778] Quoted in Pomeroy, p. 54.

[779] Translation from Snyder, pp. 14–15.

[780] Quoted in Snyder, p. 44.

[781] Snyder, pp. 54–55.

[782] Translation from Snyder, p. 68.

[783] Quoted in Snider, p. 77.

[784] Pomeroy, p. 138.

[785] Williamson, p. 17.

[786] Quoted in Charity Cannon Willard, *Christine de Pisan: Her Life and Works* (Persea Books, 1984), p. 23.

[787] Translation from Willard, p. 63.

[788] Quoted in Danielle Régnier-Bohler, "Literary and Mystical Voices," Arthur Goldhammer trans., in Klapisch-Zuber, p. 438.

[789] Christine de Pisan, *The Book of the City of Ladies*, E. J. Richards trans. (Persea, 1982), pp. 3–4.

[790] Régnier-Bohler, in Klapisch-Zuber, p. 441.

[791] Quoted in Dulong, in Davis and Farge, p. 412.

[792] Ibid., p. 406.

[793] Quoted in Fraser, *Weaker Vessel*, p. 70.

[794] Michael Dobson, "She Spy," *London Review of Books*, 8 May, 1997, pp. 27–28.

[795] James-Edward Austen Leigh, *A Memoir of Jane Austen* (Century, 1987), p. 102.

[795a] Tomalin, *Jane Austen*, p. 174.

[796] Quoted in Claire Tomalin, *Jane Austen: A Life* (Viking, 1997), p. 243.

[797] Ibid., p. 257.

[798] Brontë, *Jane Eyre*, p. 326.

[799] Quoted in Barker, p. 262.

[799a] Jane Aiken Hodge, *The Double Life of Jane Austen* (Hodder and Stoughton, 1974), p. 123.

[800] Barker, pp. 500-501.

[801] Quoted in Tomalin, *Jane Austen*, pp. 218-219.

[802] Lerner, *Feminist Consciousness*, p. 182.

[803] Wolff, *Emily Dickinson*, p. 128.

[804] Quoted in Paula Bennett, *Emily Dickinson, Woman Poet*.

[805] Quoted in Lee, p. 192.

[806] Ibid., p. 79.

[807] Cited in Lee, p. 399.

[808] R. J. Stevenson, "Shadow Maker: The Life of Gwendolyn MacEwen," *Herizons*, (Spring 1996), p. 30.

[809] Sylvia Plath, *Letters Home: Correspondence 1950–1963*, selected and edited by Aurelia Schober Plath (Harper and Row, 1975), p. 476.

[809a] Quoted in "MacEwen's Muse," *Second Words: Selected Critical Prose* (Anansi, 1982), p. 76.

[810] Sylvia Plath, *Journals*, Frances McCullough, ed. (Dial Press, 1982), p. 321.

Bibliography

Abelard, Peter, and Heloise. *The Letters of Abelard and Heloise*, C. K. S. Moncrieff trans. Alfred A. Knopf, 1933.

Adelman, Janet. *Suffocating Mothers: Fantasies of Maternal Origin in Shakespeare's Plays,* Hamlet *to* The Tempest. Routledge, 1992.

Aeschylus. *The Eumenides*, H. Lloyd Jones trans. Prentice-Hall, 1970.

Allen, Frederick Lewis. *Only Yesterday: An Informal History of the 1920s*. Harper and Brothers, 1931.

Allende, Isabel. *Paula*, trans, Margaret Sayers Reden. HarperPerennial, 1996.

Anderson, Patricia. *When Passion Reigned: Sex and the Victorians*. Basic Books, 1995.

Andrews, Edward Deming. *The People Called Shakers: A Search for the Perfect Society*. Dover Publications, 1963.

Ariès, Philippe. *Centuries of Childhood: A Social History of Family Life,* Robert Baldick trans. Vintage Books, 1962.

Aristophanes. *Thesmophoriazusae*. In *Plays*, Vol. 2, Patric Dickinson trans. Oxford University Press, 1970.

Aristotle. "De Generatione Animalium," A. Platt trans. In *The Works of Aristotle*, Vol. 5. Oxford University Press, 1958.

Arnaud-Duc, Nicole. "The Law's Contradictions," Arthur Goldhammer trans. In Geneviève Fraisse and Michelle Perrot (eds.). *A History of Women in the West IV: Emerging Feminism from Revolution to World War*. Harvard University Press, 1993, pp. 80–113.

Aronson, Nicole. *Mademoiselle de Scudéry*, Stuart R. Aronson trans. Twayne Publishers, 1978.

Arthur, Marilyn B. "Women and the Family in Ancient Greece." *The Yale Review*, Vol. 71, No. 4, pp. 532–547.

Atwood, Margaret. *Alias Grace*. McClelland & Stewart, 1996.

Austen, Jane. *Emma*. Penguin Classics, 1966.

Austen, Jane. *Mansfield Park*. Penguin Classics, 1966.

Austen, Jane. *Persuasion*. Penguin Popular Classics, 1994.

Austen, Jane. *Pride and Prejudice*. Signet Classic, 1980.

Baker, Derek (ed.). *Medieval Women: dedicated and presented to Professor Rosalind M. Hill on the occasion of her seventieth birthday*. Basil Blackwell, 1978.

Baker, William J. *Sports in the Western World*. Rowman and Littlefield, 1982.

Barker, Juliet. *The Brontës*. Phoenix Giants, 1994.

Baseheart, Mary Catherine. "Edith Stein's Philosophy of Woman and of Women's Education." In Linda Lopez McAlister (ed.). *Hypatia's Daughters: Fifteen Hundred Years of Women Philosophers*. Indiana University Press, 1996, pp. 267–279.

Baubérot, Jean. "The Protestant Woman," Arthur Goldhammer trans. In Geneviève Fraisse and Michelle Perrot (eds.). *A History of Women in the West IV: Emerging Feminism from Revolution to World War*. Harvard University Press, 1993, pp. 198–212.

Bauman, Richard A. *Women and Politics in Ancient Rome*. Routledge, 1992.

Beard, Mary. "The Sexual Status of Vestal Virgins." *Journal of Roman Studies,* Vol. 70 (1980), pp. 12-27.

Bell, Robert E. *Women of Classical Mythology: A Biographical Dictionary.* Oxford University Press, 1991.

Benton, John F. (ed.). *Self and Society in Medieval France: The Memoirs of Abbot Guibert of Nogent.* Harper Torchbooks, 1970.

Berkin, Carol. *First Generations: Women in Colonial America.* Hill and Wang, 1996.

Berriot-Salvadore, Evelyne. "The Discourse of Medicine and Science," Arthur Goldhammer trans. In Natalie Zemon Davis and Arlette Farge (eds.). *A History of Women in the West III: Renaissance and Enlightenment Paradoxes.* Harvard University Press, 1993, pp. 348–388.

Block, Adrienne Fried. "Women in American Music, 1800–1918." In Karin Pendle (ed.). *Women & Music: A History.* Indiana University Press, 1991, pp. 142-172.

Bock, Gisela. "Poverty and Mothers' Rights in the Emerging Welfare States." In Françoise Thébaud (ed.). *A History of Women in the West V: Toward a Cultural Identity in the Twentieth Century.* Harvard University Press, 1994, pp. 402-432.

Bonnefoy, Yves. *Rimbaud,* Paul Schmidt trans. Harper & Row, 1973.

Boose, Lynda E. "The Father's House and the Daughter in It: The Structures of Western Culture's Daughter-Father Relationship." In Lynda E. Boose and Betty S. Flowers (eds.). *Daughters and Fathers.* The Johns Hopkins University Press, 1989, pp. 19–74.

Boose, Lynda E. and Betty S. Flowers (eds.). *Daughters and Fathers.* The Johns Hopkins University Press, 1989.

Borin, Françoise. "Judging by Images," Arthur Goldhammer trans. In Natalie Zemon Davis and Arlette Farge (eds.). *A History of Women in the West, III: Renaissance and Enlightenment Paradoxes.* Harvard University Press, 1993, pp. 189–254.

Borsa, Joan (curator/ed.). *Ann Harbuz: Inside Community, Outside Convention.* Dunlop Art Gallery, 1997.

Borzello, Frances. *Seeing Ourselves: Women's Self-Portraits.* Thames & Hudson, 1998.

Bowers, Jane and Judith Tick, ed. *Women Making Music: The Western Art Tradition 1150–1950.* University of Illinois Press, 1986.

Brightman, Carol, ed. *Between Friends: The Correspondence of Hannah Arendt and Mary McCarthy, 1949–1975.* Harcourt Brace, 1995.

Brontë, Charlotte. *Jane Eyre.* Bantam Classic, 1981.

Brontë, Charlotte. *Shirley.* Penguin Classics, 1974.

Brontë, Charlotte. *Villette.* Wordsworth Classics, 1993.

Brontë, Emily. *Wuthering Heights.* Penguin Classics, 1985.

Bookner, Anita. *Hotel du Lac.* Vintage Contemporaries, 1995.

Brownmiller, Susan. *Femininity.* Fawcett Columbine, 1985.

Burke, Carolyn. *Becoming Modern: The Life of Mina Loy.* Farrar, Straus and Giroux, 1996.

Burney, Frances. *Camilla.* Oxford University Press, 1972.

Cahn, Susan K. *Coming on Strong: Gender and Sexuality in Twentieth-Century Women's Sport.* The Free Press, 1994.

Camden, Carroll. *The Elizabethan Woman: A Panorama of English Womanhood, 1540–1640.* Elsevier Press, 1952.

Casagrande, Carla. "The Protected Woman," Clarissa Botsford trans. In Christiane Klapisch-Zuber (ed.). *A History of Women in the West II: Silences of the Middle Ages.* Harvard University Press, 1992, pp. 70–104.

Cayleff, Susan E. *Babe: The Life and Legend of Babe Didrikson Zaharias.* University of Illinois Press, 1995.

Chamberlin, Roy B. and Herman Feldman (eds.). *The Dartmouth Bible.* Houghton Mifflin, 1961.

Chambers-Schiller, Lee Virginia. *Liberty, A Better Husband: Single Women in America: The Generations of 1780–1840.* Yale University Press, 1984.

Chaucer, Geoffrey. *The Canterbury Tales,* Nevill Coghill trans. Penguin Classics, 1951.

Citron, Marcia J. "Feminist Approaches to Musicology." In Susan C. Cook and Judy Tsou (eds.). *Cecilia Reclaimed: Feminist Perspectives on Gender and Music.* University of Illinois Press, 1994, pp. 15–34.

Clark, Homer H. *Cases and Problems on Domestic Relations.* St. Paul, West Pub., 1974.

Cohen, Greta L. (ed.). *Women in Sport: Issues and Controversies.* Sage Publications, 1993.

Colette. *Earthly Paradise: An Autobiography.* Herma Briffault, Derek Coltman *et al.* trans. Farrar, Straus & Giroux, 1966.

Collin, Françoise. "Philosophical Differences," Arthur Goldhammer trans. In Françoise Thébaud (ed.). *A History of Women in the West V: Toward a Cultural Identity in the Twentieth Century.* Harvard University Press, 1994, pp. 261–296.

Cook, Susan C. and Judy S. Tsou (eds.). *Cecilia Reclaimed: Feminist Perspectives on Gender and Music.* University of Illinois Press, 1994.

Copland, Aaron. *Copland on Music.* Da Capo Press, 1976.

Corea, Gena. *The Hidden Malpractice: How American Medicine Treats Women as Patients and Professionals.* William Morrow, 1977.

Cott, Nancy F. *The Grounding of Modern Feminism.* Yale University Press, 1987.

Crampe-Casnabet, Michèle. "A Sampling of Eighteenth-Century Philosophy," Arthur Goldhammer trans. In Natalie Zemon Davis and Arlette Farge (eds.). *A History of Women in the West III: Renaissance and Enlightenment Paradoxes.* Harvard University Press, 1993, pp. 315–347.

Cross, Claire. "'Great Reasoners in Scripture': The Activities of Women Lollards 1380–1530." In Derek Baker (ed.). *Medieval Women: dedicated and presented to Professor Rosalind M. Hill on the occasion of her seventieth birthday.* Basil Blackwell, 1978, pp. 359–380.

Dalarun, Jacques. "The Clerical Gaze," Arthur Goldhammer trans. In Christiane Klapisch-Zuber (ed.). *A History of Women in the West II: Silences of the Middle Ages.* Harvard University Press, 1992, pp. 15–42.

Daly, Mary. *The Church and the Second Sex.* Beacon Press, 1985.

Dauphin, Cécile. "Single Women," Arthur Goldhammer trans. In Geneviève Fraisse and Michelle Perrot (eds.). *A History of Women in the West IV: Emerging Feminism from Revolution to World War.* Harvard University Press, 1993, pp. 427–442.

Davis, Joanne. *Mademoiselle de Scudéry and the Looking-Glass Self.* Peter Lang, 1993.

Davis, Natalie Zemon. "Women in Politics." In Natalie Zemon Davis and Arlette Farge (eds.). *A History of Women in the West III: Renaissance and Enlightenment Paradoxes.* Harvard University Press, 1993, pp. 167–183.

Davis, Natalie Zemon. *Women on the Margins: Three Seventeenth-Century Lives.* Harvard University Press, 1995.

Davis, Natalie Zemon and Arlette Farge (eds). *A History of Women in the West III: Renaissance and Enlightenment Paradoxes.* Harvard University Press, 1993.

Dawson, Ruth P. "'And This Shield is Called—Self-Reliance': Emerging Feminist Consciousness in the Late Eighteenth Century." In Ruth-Ellen B. Joeres and Mary Jo Maynes (eds.). *German Women in the Eighteenth and Nineteenth Centuries: A Social and Literary History*. Indiana University Press, 1986, pp. 157–173.

De Beauvoir, Simone. *The Second Sex*, H. M. Parshley trans./ed. Vintage Books, 1989.

De Giorgio, Michela. "The Catholic Model," Joan Bond Sax trans. In Geneviève Fraisse and Michelle Perrot (eds.). *A History of Women in the West IV: Emerging Feminism from Revolution to World War*. Harvard University Press, 1993, pp. 166–197.

Degler, Carl N. *At Odds: Women and the Family in America from the Revolution to the Present*. Oxford University Press, 1980.

Demand, Nancy. *Birth, Death, and Motherhood in Classical Greece*. Johns Hopkins University Press, 1994.

D'Emilio, John and Estelle B. Freedman. *Intimate Matters: A History of Sexuality in America*. Perennial Library, Harper & Row, 1988.

Demosthenes. "Against Neaera." In *Demosthenes*, Vol. 6, A. T. Murray trans. William Heinemann, 1964.

Dennis, Barbara. *Elizabeth Barrett Browning: The Hope End Years*. Poetry Wales Press Ltd., 1996.

De Pisan, Christine. *The Book of the City of Ladies*, E. J. Richards trans. Persea, 1982.

Desaive, Jean-Paul. "The Ambiguities of Literature," Arthur Goldhammer trans. In Natalie Zemon Davis and Arlette Farge (eds.). *A History of Women in the West III: Renaissance and Enlightenment Paradoxes*. Harvard University Press, 1993, pp. 261–294.

Dickens, Charles. *Martin Chuzzlewit*. Oxford University Press, 1968.

Dixon, Laurinda S. *Perilous Chastity: Women and Illness in Pre-Enlightenment Art and Medicine*. Cornell University Press, 1995.

Dixon, Suzanne. *The Roman Mother*. University of Oklahoma Press, 1988.

Doriani, Beth Maclay. *Emily Dickinson, Daughter of Prophecy*. University of Massachusetts Press, 1996.

Dow, Leslie Smith. *Adèle Hugo: La Misérable*. Goose Lane, 1993.

Drabble, Margaret. *A Summer Bird-Cage*. Harmondsworth: Penguin, 1967.

Dreher, Diane Elizabeth. *Domination and Defiance: Fathers and Daughters in Shakespeare*. The University Press of Kentucky, 1986.

Dronke, Peter. *Poetic Individuality in the Middle Ages: New Departures in Poetry 1000–1150*. Clarendon Press, 1970.

DuBruck, Edelgard E. (ed.). *New Images of Medieval Women: Essays Toward a Cultural Anthropology*. The Edwin Mellen Press, 1989.

Duby, Georges. "The Courtly Model," Arthur Goldhammer trans. In Christiane Klapisch-Zuber (ed.), *A History of Women in the West II: Silences of the Middle Ages*. Harvard University Press, 1992, pp. 250–266.

Dulong, Claude. "From Conversation to Creation," Arthur Goldhammer trans. In Natalie Zemon Davis and Arlette Farge (eds.). *A History of Women in the West III: Renaissance and Enlightenment Paradoxes*. Harvard University Press, 1993, pp. 396–419.

Duran, Jane. "Anne Viscountess Conway: A Seventeenth-Century Rationalist." In Linda Lopez McAlister (ed.). *Hypatia's Daughters: Fifteen Hundred Years of Women Philosophers*. Indiana University Press, 1996, pp. 92–107.

Edwards, Samuel. *Victor Hugo, A Tumultuous Life*. David McKay, 1971.

Ehrenreich, Barbara and Deirdre English. *Witches, Midwives, and Nurses: A History of Women Healers*. The Feminist Press, 1973.

Einhard, *Vita Karoli Magni: The Life of Charlemagne*, Evelyn S. Firchow trans. University of Miami Press, 1972.

Elderkin, Kate McK. "The Contribution of Women to Ornament in Antiquity." In *Classical studies presented to Edward Capps on his seventieth birthday*. Princeton University Press, 1936.

Elizabeth Cady Stanton, as Revealed in her Letters, Diaries, and Reminiscences, T. Stanton and H. Stanton Blatch (eds.). Harper & Bros., 1922.

"Elizabeth-Claude Jacquet de la Guerre: Composer and Harpsichordist." In Carol Neuls-Bates (ed.). *Women in Music: An Anthology of Source Readings from the Middle Ages to the Present*, revised ed. Northeastern University Press, 1996, pp. 62–64.

Euripides. *Andromache*. In *Orestes and Other Plays*, Philip Vellacott trans. Penguin Books, 1972.

Euripides. *Hippolytus*. In *Alcestis/Hippolytus/Iphigenia in Tarsus*, Philip Vellacott trans. Penguin Books, 1972.

Euripides. *Medea*. In *The Tragedies of Euripides*, Vol. 1, R. Potter trans. W. Baxter, Oxford, 1808.

Faderman, Lillian. *Surpassing the Love of Men: Romantic Friendship and Love Between Women from the Renaissance to the Present*. William Morrow and Company, 1981.

Falk, Candace. *Love, Anarchy, and Emma Goldman*. Rutgers University Press, 1990.

Flanagan, Sabina. *Hildegard of Bingen, 1098–1179: A Visionary Life*. Routledge, 1989.

Foley, Helene P. (ed.). *The Homeric Hymn to Demeter: Translation, Commentary and Interpretive Essays*. Princeton University Press, 1994.

Fowler, Marian. *In a Gilded Cage: From Heiress to Duchess*. Random House of Canada, 1993.

Foxhall, Lin. "Household, Gender and Property in Classical Athens." *The Classical Quarterly*, Vol. 39, new series. Oxford University Press, 1989, pp. 22–44.

Fraisse, Geneviève and Michelle Perrot (eds.). *A History of Women in the West IV: Emerging Feminism from Revolution to World War*. Harvard University Press, 1993.

Fraser, Antonia. *The Warrior Queens*. Penguin Books, 1989.

Fraser, Antonia. *The Weaker Vessel*. Vintage Books, 1985.

Friedan, Betty. *The Feminine Mystique*. Dell, 1983.

Frugoni, Chiara. "The Imagined Woman," Clarissa Botsford trans. In Christiane Klapisch-Zuber (ed.). *A History of Women in the West II: Silences of the Middle Ages*. Harvard University Press, 1992, pp. 336–422.

Gibbon, Edward. *The Decline and Fall of the Roman Empire*. Modern Library, 1932.

Giddens, Anthony. *The Transformation of Intimacy: Sexuality, Love and Eroticism in Modern Societies*. Stanford University Press, 1992.

Gies, Joseph and Frances. *Life in a Medieval City*. Harper Perennial, 1981.

Gies, Frances and Joseph. *Life in a Medieval Village*. Harper Perennial, 1990.

Gies, Frances and Joseph. *Marriage and the Family in the Middle Ages*. Harper & Row, 1987.

Gies, Frances and Joseph. *Women in the Middle Ages*. Harper Perennial, 1978.

Gillis, John R. *For Better, For Worse: British Marriages, 1600 to the Present*. Oxford University Press, 1985.

Gilman, Charlotte Perkins. *Herland*, introduction by Ann J. Lane. The Women's Press, 1979.

Gold, Penny Schine. *The Lady & the Virgin: Image, Attitude and Experience in Twelfth-Century France.* University of Chicago Press, 1985.

Goldsmith, Barbara. *Other Powers: The Age of Suffrage, Spiritualism, and the Scandalous Victoria Woodhull.* Alfred A. Knopf, 1998.

Gordon, Lyndall. *Virginia Woolf: A Writer's Life.* W. W. Norton & Co., 1984.

Goreau, Angeline. *Reconstructing Aphra: A Social Biography of Aphra Behn.* The Dial Press, 1980.

Greer, Germaine. *The Obstacle Race: The Fortunes of Women Painters and their Work.* Pan Books, 1981.

Gregory of Tours. *The History of the Franks,* Lewis Thorpe trans. Penguin Books, 1974.

Grieco, Sarah F. Matthews. "The Body, Appearance, and Sexuality." In Natalie Zemon Davis and Arlette Farge (eds.). *A History of Women in the West III: Renaissance and Enlightenment Paradoxes.* Harvard University Press, 1993.

Griffin, Wendy. "The Embodied Goddess: Feminist Witchcraft and Female Divinity." *Sociology of Religion,* Vol. 56, No. 1 (Spring 1995), pp. 35–49.

Griffith, Elisabeth. *In Her Own Right: The Life of Elizabeth Cady Stanton.* Oxford University Press, 1984.

Guttmann, Allen. *Women's Sports: A History.* Columbia University Press, 1991.

Gutwirth, Madelyn. *Madam de Staël, Novelist: The Emergence of the Artist as Woman.* University of Illinois Press, 1978.

Hagstrum, Jean. H. *Esteem Enlivened by Desire: The Couple From Homer to Shakespeare.* University of Chicago Press, 1992.

Halberstam, David. *The Fifties.* Fawcett Columbine, 1993.

Hanson, Ann Ellis. "Hippocrates: 'Diseases of Women' I." *Signs: Journal of Women and Culture in Society,* Vol. 1 (1975), pp. 567–582.

Hargreaves, Jennifer. *Sporting Females: Critical Issues in the History and Sociology of Women's Sports.* Routledge, 1994.

Hawley, Richard and Barbara Levick (eds.). *Women in Antiquity—New Assessments.* Routledge, 1995.

Hellerstein, Erna Olafson, Leslie Parker Hume and Karen M. Offen (eds.) *Victorian Women: A Documentary Account of Women's Lives in Nineteenth-Century England, France, and the United States.* Stanford University Press, 1981.

Herodotus. *The Histories,* A. De Sélincourt trans. Penguin Books, 1959.

Higonnet, Anne. "Images—Appearance, Leisure, and Subsistence." In Geneviève Fraisse and Michelle Perrot (eds.). *A History of Women in the West IV: Emerging Feminism from Revolution to World War.* Harvard University Press, 1993, pp. 246–261.

Higonnet, Anne. "Women, Images, and Representation." In Françoise Thébaud (ed.). *A History of Women in the West V: Toward a Cultural Identity in the Twentieth Century.* Harvard University Press, 1994, pp. 343–396.

Hill, Bridget. *Women, Work, and Sexual Politics in Eighteenth-Century England.* Basil Blackwell, 1989.

Hilton, Wendy. *Dance of Court and Theatre: The French Noble Style, 1690–1725,* Carolyn Gaynor (ed.). Princeton Book Company, 1981.

Himmelfarb, Gertrude. *The Demoralization of Society: From Victorian Virtues to Modern Values.* Vintage Books, 1996.

Hobbs, Colleen A. *Florence Nightingale*. Twayne Publishers, 1997.

Hodge, Jane Aiken. *The Double Life of Jane Austen*. Hodder and Stoughton, 1972.

Homer. *Iliad*, Robert Fitzgerald trans. Anchor Books Doubleday, 1974.

Hoock-Demarle, Marie-Claire. "Reading and Writing in Germany," Arthur Goldhammer trans. In Geneviève Fraisse and Michelle Perrot (eds.). *A History of Women in the West IV: Emerging Feminism from Revolution to World War*. Harvard University Press, 1993, pp. 145–165.

Hopkins, James K. *A Woman to Deliver Her People: Joanna Southcott and English Millenarianism in an Age of Revolution*. University of Texas Press, 1982.

Hufton, Olwen. *The Prospect Before Her: A History of Women in Western Europe, Vol. One: 1500–1800*. Harper Collins, 1995.

Hufton, Olwen. "Women Without Men: Widows and Spinsters in Britain and France in the Eighteenth Century." *Journal of Family History*, Vol. 9, No. 4 (Winter, 1984), pp. 355–376.

Hufton, Olwen. "Women, Work, and Family." In Natalie Zemon Davis and Arlette Farge (eds.). *A History of Women in the West III: Renaissance and Enlightenment Paradoxes*. Harvard University Press, 1993, pp. 15–45.

Hughes, Diane Owen. "Regulating Women's Fashion." In Christiane Klapisch-Zuber (ed.), *A History of Women in the West II: Silences of the Middle Ages*. Harvard University Press, 1992, pp. 136–158.

Ibsen, Henrik. *Plays: Two. A Doll's House, An Enemy of the People, Hedda Gabler*, Michael Meyer trans. Methuen World Classics, 1980.

Joeres, Ruth-Ellen B. and Mary Jo Maynes (eds.). *German Women in the Eighteenth and Nineteenth Centuries: A Social and Literary History*. Indiana University Press, 1986.

Kaplan, E. Ann. "Mothering, Feminism and Representation: The Maternal Melodrama and the Women's Film 1910–1940." In Christine Gledhill (ed.). *Home is Where the Heart Is: Studies in Melodrama and the Women's Film*. British Film Institute, 1987, pp. 113–137.

Keuls, Eva C. *The Reign of the Phallus: Sexual Politics in Ancient Athens*. University of California Press, 1985.

Kirshner, Julius, and Suzanne F. Wemple (eds.). *Women of the Medieval World: Essays in Honour of John H. Mundy*. Basil Blackwell, 1985.

Klapisch-Zuber, Christiane (ed.). *A History of Women in the West II: Silences of the Middle Ages*. Harvard University Press, 1992.

Knibiehler, Yvonne. "Bodies and Hearts," Arthur Goldhammer trans. In Geneviève Fraisse and Michelle Perrot (eds.). *A History of Women in the West IV: Emerging Feminism from Revolution to World War*. Harvard University Press, 1993, pp. 325–368.

Koedt, Anne. "The Myth of Vaginal Orgasm," in *Notes from the First Year*. New York, Radical Women Press, 1968.

Koppelman, Susan (ed.). *Two Friends and Other Nineteenth-Century Lesbian Stories by American Women Writers*. Meridian Book, 1994.

Kraemer, Ross Shepard. *Her Share of the Blessings: Women's Religions Among Pagans, Jews and Christians in the Greco-Roman World*. Oxford University Press, 1992.

Kurz, Demie. *For Richer, For Poorer: Mothers Confront Divorce*. Routledge, 1995.

Kyle, Donald G. *Athletics in Ancient Athens*. Leiden, E. J. Brill, 1987.

Labarge, Margaret Wade. *Saint Louis: The Life of Louis IX of France*. Macmillan of Canada, 1968.

Lacey, W. K. *The Family in Classical Greece.* Cornell University Press, 1968.

Lagrave, Rose-Marie. "A Supervised Emancipation," Arthur Goldhammer trans. In Françoise Thébaud (ed.). *A History of Women in the West V: Toward a Cultural Identity in the Twentieth Century.* Harvard University Press, 1994, pp. 453–489.

Lamay, Thomasin. "Vittoria Aleotti/Raphaella Aleotta." In Martha Furman Schleifer and Sylvia Glickman (eds.). *Women Composers: Music Through the Ages.* G. K. Hall, 1996, Vol. 1, pp. 135–162.

Laqueur, Thomas. *Making Sex: Body and Gender from the Greeks to Freud.* Harvard University Press, 1990.

Lasch, Christopher. *Women and the Common Life: Love, Marriage and Feminism.* W. W. Norton, 1997.

Lawrence, D. H. *Sons and Lovers.* Wordsworth Classics, 1993.

Leclercq, Jean. *Le marriage vu par des moines au XII siècle.* Les Éditions du Cerf, 1983.

Lee, Hermione. *Virginia Woolf.* Chatto & Windus, 1996.

Lefaucheur, Nadine. "Maternity, Family, and the State," Arthur Goldhammer trans. In Françoise Thébaud (ed.). *A History of Women in the West V: Toward a Cultural Identity in the Twentieth Century.* Harvard University Press, 1994, pp. 433–452.

Lefkowitz, Mary R. and Maureen B. Fant. *Women's Life in Greece and Rome.* The Johns Hopkins University Press, 1982.

Leigh, James Edward Austen. *A Memoir of Jane Austen.* Century, 1987.

Lenskyj, Helen. "Physical Activity for Canadian Women, 1890–1930: Media Views." In J. A. Mangan and Roberta Parks (eds.). *From 'Fair Sex' to Feminism: Sports and the Socialization of Women in the Industrial and Post-Industrial Eras.* Frank Cass, 1987, pp. 208–231.

Lerner, Gerda. *The Creation of Feminist Consciousness: From the Middle Ages to Eighteen-Seventy.* Oxford University Press, 1993.

Lerner, Gerda. *The Creation of Patriarchy.* Oxford University Press, 1986.

Lerner, Gerda. *The Grimké Sisters from South Carolina: Rebels Against Slavery.* Houghton Mifflin, 1967.

Lessing, Doris. *Martha Quest.* Flamingo Modern Classic, 1993.

Lessing, Doris. *A Proper Marriage.* Flamingo, 1993.

Lessing, Doris. *Under My Skin: Volume One of My Autobiography to 1949.* Harper Collins, 1994.

L'Hermite-Leclerq, Paulette. "The Feudal Order," Arthur Goldhammer trans. In Christiane Klapisch-Zuber (ed.). *A History of Women in the West II: Silences of the Middle Ages.* Harvard University Press, 1992, pp. 202-249.

Lippard, Lucy R. *The Pink Glass Swan: Selected Essays on Feminist Art.* The New Press, 1995.

Lissarrague, François. "Figures of Women." In Pauline Schmitt Pantel (ed.) *A History of Women in the West I: From Ancient Goddesses to Christian Saints,* Arthur Goldhammer trans. Harvard University Press, 1992, pp. 139–229.

Livy. *History of Rome,* B. O. Foster trans. William Heinemann Ltd., 1919.

Loraux, Nicole. "What is a Goddess?" In Pauline Schmitt Pantel (ed.). *A History of Women in the West I: From Ancient Goddesses to Christian Saints,* Arthur Goldhammer trans. Harvard University Press, 1992, pp. 11–44.

Lovejoy, Esther Pohl. *Women Doctors of the World.* Macmillan, 1957.

Lysias. *Lysias*, W. R. M. Lamb trans. William Heinemann, 1967.

Mangan, J. A. and Roberta J. Park (eds.). *From 'Fair Sex' to Feminism: Sports and the Socialization of Women in the Industrial and Post-Industrial Eras.* Frank Cass, 1987.

Martin, John. "Out of the Shadow: Heretical and Catholic Women in Renaissance Venice." *Journal of Family History*, Vol. 10, No. 1 (Spring, 1985), pp. 21–33.

McAlister, Linda Lopez (ed.). *Hypatia's Daughters: Fifteen Hundred Years of Women Philosophers.* Indiana University Press, 1996.

McAuslan, Ian and Peter Walcot (eds.). *Women in Antiquity.* Oxford University Press, 1996.

McCarthy, Mary. *The Group.* Harcourt Brace, 1963.

McNamara, Jo Ann Kay. *Sisters in Arms: Catholic Nuns Through Two Millennia.* Harvard University Press, 1996.

Meade, Marion. *Eleanor of Aquitaine: A Biography.* Hawthorn Books, 1977.

Miller, Bonny H. "Ladies' Companion, Ladies' Canon? Women Composers in American Magazines from *Godey's* to the *Ladies' Home Journal.*" In Susan C. Cook and Judy Tsou (eds.). *Cecilia Reclaimed: Feminist Perspectives on Gender and Music.* University of Illinois Press, 1994, pp. 156–182.

Miller, Donald E. *Reinventing American Protestantism: Christianity in the New Millennium.* University of California Press, 1997.

Mitford, Nancy. *Madame de Pompadour.* H. Hamilton, 1954.

Morgan, Elaine. *The Descent of Woman.* Stein and Day, 1972.

Morgan, Robin. *Lady of the Beasts.* Random House, 1976.

Mossiker, Frances. *Madame de Sévigné: A Life and Letters.* Alfred A. Knopf, 1983.

Muckle, J. T. *The Story of Abelard's Adversities.* The Pontifical Institute of Medieval Studies, 1964.

Mundy, John Hine. *Men and Women at Toulouse in the Age of the Cathars.* The Pontifical Institute of Mediaeval Studies, 1990.

Murphy, Cullen. *The Word According to Eve: Women and the Bible in Ancient Times and Our Own.* Houghton Mifflin, 1998.

Nahoum-Grappe, Véronique. "The Beautiful Woman," Arthur Goldhammer trans. In Natalie Zemon Davis and Arlette Farge (eds.). *A History of Women in the West III: Renaissance and Enlightenment Paradoxes.* Harvard University Press, 1993, pp. 85–100.

Navailh, Françoise. "The Soviet Model," Arthur Goldhammer trans. In Françoise Thébaud (ed.). *A History of Women in the West V: Toward a Cultural Identity in the Twentieth Century.* Harvard University Press, 1994, pp. 226–254.

Neuls-Bates, Carol. "Women's Orchestras in the United States, 1925–45." In Jane Bowers and Judith Tick (eds.). *Women Making Music: The Western Art Tradition 1150–1950.* University of Illinois Press, 1986, pp. 349–369.

Neuls-Bates, Carol (ed.). *Women in Music: An Anthology of Source Readings from the Middle Ages to the Present.* Northeastern University Press, 1996.

Nochlin, Linda. *Women, Art, and Power and Other Essays.* Westview Press, 1988.

Nye, Andrea. "A Woman's Thought or a Man's Discipline? The Letters of Abelard and Heloise." In Linda Lopez McAlister (ed.). *Hypatia's Daughters: Fifteen Hundred Years of Women Philosophers.* Indiana University Press, 1996, pp. 25–47.

O'Faolain, Julia and Lauro Martines (eds.). *Not in God's Image.* Temple Smith, 1973.

Opitz, Claudia. "Life in the Middle Ages," Deborah Lucas Schneider trans. In Christiane
    Klapisch-Zuber (ed.). *A History of Women in the West II: Silences of the Middle Ages.*
    Harvard University Press, 1992, pp. 267–317.

Pall, Ellen. *Among the Ginzburgs.* Zoland Books, 1996.

Pantel, Pauline Schmitt (ed.). *A History of Women in the West I: From Ancient Goddesses to
    Christian Saints,* Arthur Goldhammer trans. Harvard University Press, 1992.

Paret Peter and Beth Irwin Lewis. *Persuasive Images: Posters of War and Revolution from the
    Hoover Institution Archives.* Princeton University Press, 1992.

Parker, Rozsika and Griselda Pollock. *Old Mistresses: Women, Art and Ideology.* Pantheon
    Books, 1981.

Paz, Octavio. *The Double Flame: Love and Eroticism,* Helen Lane trans. Harcourt Brace &
    Co., 1995.

Pendle, Karin. "Women in Music, ca. 1450–1660." In Karin Pendle (ed.). *Women &
    Music: A History.* Indiana University Press, 1991, pp. 31–53.

Pendle, Karin (ed.). *Women & Music: A History.* Indiana University Press, 1991.

Perkin, Joan. *Victorian Women.* New York University Press, 1993.

Perry, Ruth. *The Celebrated Mary Astell: An Early English Feminist.* The University of
    Chicago Press, 1986.

Pfau, Marianne Richert. "Hildegard von Bingen." In Martha Furman Schleifer and
    Sylvia Glickman (eds.). *Women Composers: Music Through the Ages.* G. K. Hall, 1996,
    Vol. 1, pp. 25–60.

Phillips, Roderick. *Putting Asunder: A History of Divorce in Western Society.* Cambridge
    University Press, 1988.

Plath, Sylvia. *Journals,* Frances McCullough (ed.). Dial Press, 1982.

Plath, Sylvia. *Letters Home: Correspondence 1950–1963.* Aurelia Schober Plath (ed.). Harper
    and Row, 1975.

Plato. *The Republic of Plato,* Francis MacDonald Cornford trans. Oxford University Press,
    1966.

Plato. "Symposium." In *Great Dialogues of Plato,* W. H. D. Rouse trans., Eric H. Warm-
    ington and Philip G. Rouse (eds.). Mentor Books, 1956.

Plato. *Timaeus,* F. M. Cornford trans. Library of Liberal Arts, 1959.

Pliny. *Natural History,* R. Rackham trans. William Heinemann, 1961.

Plutarch. "Alcibiades." In *Plutarch's Lives,* Vol. 4, B. Perrin trans. William Heinemann,
    1959.

Plutarch. "Lycurgus." In *Plutarch's Lives: The 'Dryden Plutarch' Revised by Arthur Hugh
    Clough,* Vol. 1. J. M. Dent & Sons, 1916.

Pollitt, Katha. *Reasonable Creatures: Essays on Women and Feminism.* Vintage, 1995.

Pomeroy, Sarah B. *Goddesses, Whores, Wives and Slaves: Women in Classical Antiquity.*
    Schocken Books, 1975.

Posgate, Helen B. *Madame de Staël.* Twayne Publishers, 1968.

Potkay, Monica Brzezinski and Regula Meyer Evitt. *Minding the Body: Women and Liter-
    ature in the Middle Ages, 800–1500.* Twayne Publishers, 1997.

Prentice, Alison, Paula Bourne, Gail Cuthbert Brandt, Beth Light, Wendy Mitchinson
    and Naomi Black. *Canadian Women: A History.* Harcourt Brace & Co., 1988.

Rainwater, Lee. *And the Poor Get Children: Sex, Contraception, and Family Planning in the
    Working Class.* Quadrangle Books, 1960.

Rawson, Beryl (ed.). *The Family in Ancient Rome: New Perspectives*. Cornell University Press, 1986.

Rawson, Beryl (ed.). *Marriage, Divorce and Children in Ancient Rome*. Clarendon Press, 1991.

Régnier-Bohler, Danielle. "Literary and Mystical Voices," Arthur Goldhammer trans. In Christiane Klapisch-Zuber (ed.). *A History of Women in the West II: Silences of the Middle Ages*. Harvard University Press, 1992, pp. 427–482.

Reich, Nancy B. "Clara Schumann." In Jane Bowers and Judith Tick (eds.). *Women Making Music: The Western Art Tradition 1150–1950*. University of Illinois Press, 1986, pp. 249–281.

Reich, Nancy B. "European Composers and Musicians, ca. 1800–1890." In Karin Pendle (ed.). *Women & Music: A History*. Indiana University Press, 1991, pp. 97–141.

Rempel, Ursula M. "Women and Music: Ornament of the Profession?" In Samia I. Spencer (ed.). *French Women and the Age of Enlightenment*. Indiana University Press, 1984.

Rich, Adrienne. *Of Woman Born: Motherhood as Experience and Institution*. W. W. Norton & Co., 1986.

Richardson, Joanna. *Baudelaire*. John Murray, 1994.

Richardson, Joanna. *Victor Hugo*. Weidenfeld and Nicolson, 1976.

"The Rise of Women as Virtuoso Singers." In Carol Neuls-Bates (ed.). *Women in Music: An Anthology of Source Readings from the Middle Ages to the Present*, Revised ed. Northeastern University Press, 1996, pp. 50–52.

Rothblatt, Martine. *The Apartheid of Sex: A Manifesto on the Freedom of Gender*. Crown Publishers, 1995.

Rouselle, Aline. "Body Politics in Ancient Rome." In Pauline Schmitt Pantel (ed.). *A History of Women in the West I: From Ancient Goddesses to Christian Saints*, Arthur Goldhammer trans. Harvard University Press, 1992, pp. 296–336.

Rowland, Beryl. *Medieval Woman's Guide to Health—The First English Gynecological Handbook*. The Kent State University Press, 1981.

Sackville-West, V. (ed.). *The Diary of the Lady Anne Clifford*. George H. Doran, 1923.

Sadoff, Dianne F. "The Clergyman's Daughters: Anne Bronte, Elizabeth Gaskell, and George Eliot." In Lynda E. Boose and Betty S. Flowers (eds.). *Daughters and Fathers*. The Johns Hopkins University Press, 1989, pp. 303–325.

Salisbury, Joyce E. *Perpetua's Passion: The Death and Memory of a Young Roman Woman*. Routledge, 1997.

Sand, George. *Horace*, Zack Rogow trans. Mercury House, 1995.

Sand, George. *Indiana*, Sylvia Raphael trans. Oxford University Press, 1994.

Scheid, John. "The Religious Roles of Roman Women." In Pauline Schmitt Pantel (ed.). *A History of Women in the West I: From Ancient Goddesses to Christian Saints*, Arthur Goldhammer trans. Harvard University Press, 1992, pp. 377–408.

Schleifer, Martha Furman and Sylvia Glickman (eds.). *Women Composers: Music Through the Ages*. G. K. Hall, 1996.

Schumann, Clara. "Clara Schumann: Pianist." In Carol Neuls-Bates (ed.). *Women in Music: An Anthology of Source Readings from the Middle Ages to the Present*, Revised ed. Northeastern University Press, 1996, pp. 91–108.

Sedgwick, Catharine Maria. "Old Maids." In Susan Koppelman (ed.). *Old Maids: Short Stories by Nineteenth Century U. S. Women Writers*. Pandora Press, 1984.

Segal, Lynne. *Straight Sex: The Politics of Pleasure*. University of California Press, 1994.

Sextus Propertius. *The Poems of Sextus Propertius*, J. P. McCulloch trans. University of California Press, 1972.

Shahar, Shulamith. *The Fourth Estate: A History of Women in the Middle Ages*, Chaya Galai trans. Routledge, 1983.

Shakespeare, William. *King Lear*. The Arden Shakespeare: Methuen, 1952.

Shakespeare, William. *Othello*. The Arden Shakespeare: Methuen, 1958.

Shaw, George Bernard. *The Intelligent Woman's Guide to Socialism and Capitalism*. Brentano's, 1928.

Shorter, Edward. *Women's Bodies. A Social History of Women's Encounter With Health, Ill-Health and Medicine*. Transaction Publishers, 1991.

Sissa, Giulia. "The Sexual Philosophies of Plato and Aristotle." In Pauline Schmitt Pantel (ed.). *A History of Women in the West I: From Ancient Goddesses to Christian Saints*, Arthur Goldhammer trans. Harvard University Press, 1992, pp. 46–81.

Slater, Philip E. *The Glory of Hera: Greek Mythology and the Greek Family*. Beacon Press, 1968.

Slatkin, Wendy. *Women Artists in History From Antiquity to the 20th Century*. Prentice Hall, 1985.

Smith, Catherine Parsons. "'A Distinguishing Virility': Feminism and Modernism in American Art Music." In Susan C. Cook and Judy Tsou (eds.). *Cecilia Reclaimed: Feminist Perspectives on Gender and Music*. University of Illinois Press, 1994, pp. 90–106.

Smith-Rosenberg, Carroll. *Disorderly Conduct: Visions of Gender in Victorian America*. Oxford University Press, 1985.

Snyder, Jane McIntosh. *The Woman and the Lyre: Women Writers in Classical Greece and Rome*. Southern Illinois University Press, 1989.

Sohn, Ann-Marie. "Between the Wars in France and England," Arthur Goldhammer trans. In Françoise Thébaud (ed.). *A History of Women in the West V: Toward a Cultural Identity in the Twentieth Century*. Harvard University Press, 1994, pp. 92-119.

Somerset, Anne. *Elizabeth I*. Weidenfeld and Nicolson, 1991.

Sonnet, Martine. "A Daughter to Educate," Arthur Goldhammer trans. In Natalie Zemon Davis and Arlette Farge (eds.) *A History of Women in the West III: Renaissance and Enlightenment Paradoxes*. Harvard University Press, 1993, pp. 101–131.

Sophocles. *Antigone, Oedipus the King, Electra*, H.D.F. Kitto trans. The World Classics, Oxford University Press, 1962.

Sophocles. *The Oedipus Plays of Sophocles*, Paul Roche trans. Mentor Books, 1991.

Spencer, Samia I. (ed.). *French Women and the Age of Enlightenment*. Indiana University Press, 1984.

Stanton, Elizabeth Cady. *Eighty Years and More*. Northeastern University Press, 1993.

Stanton, Elizabeth Cady. *The Woman's Bible*. Northeastern University Press, 1993.

Stanton, Elizabeth Cady, Susan B. Anthony and Matilda Joslyn Gage (eds.). *History of Woman Suffrage*. Fowler & Wells, 1881.

Stevenson, R. J. "Shadow Maker: The Life of Gwendolyn MacEwan." *Herizons* (Spring, 1976), pp. PAGE #s MISSING HERE

Stone, Lawrence. *The Family, Sex and Marriage in England 1500–1800*. Harper & Row, 1977.

Stone, Merlin. *When God Was A Woman*. Harcourt Brace & Co., 1976.

Storch, Margaret. *Sons and Adversaries: Women in William Blake and D. H. Lawrence.* The University of Tennessee Press, 1990.

Strong-Boag, Veronica. "Home Dreams: Women and the Suburban Experiment in Canada, 1945–60." *Canadian Historical Review*, Vol. 72, No. 4 (1991), pp. 471–503.

Thébaud, Françoise. "The Great War and the Triumph of Sexual Division," Arthur Goldhammer trans. In Françoise Thébaud (ed.). *A History of Women in the West V: Toward a Cultural Identity in the Twentieth Century.* Harvard University Press, 1994, pp. 21–75.

Thébaud, Françoise (ed.). *A History of Women in the West V: Toward a Cultural Identity in the Twentieth Century.* The Belknap Press of Harvard University Press, 1994.

Thomas, Yan. "The Division of the Sexes in Roman Law." In Pauline Schmitt Pantel (ed.) *A History of Women in the West I: From Ancient Goddesses to Christian Saints*, Arthur Goldhammer trans. Harvard University Press, 1992, pp. 83–137.

Thomasset, Claude. "The Nature of Woman," Arthur Goldhammer trans. In Christiane Klapisch-Zuber (ed.). *A History of Women in the West II: Silences of the Middle Ages.* Harvard University Press, 1992, pp. 43–68.

Thucydides. *The Peloponnesian War*, Rex Warner trans. Penguin Books, 1967.

Tomalin, Claire. *Jane Austen: A Life.* Viking, 1997.

Tomalin, Claire. *The Life and Death of Mary Wollstonecroft.* Weidenfeld and Nicolson, 1974.

Touliatos, Diane. "Kassia." In Martha Furman Schleifer and Sylvia Glickman (eds.). *Women Composers: Music Through the Ages.* G. K. Hall, 1996, Vol. 1, pp. 1–24.

Touliatos-Banker, Diane. "Kassia." In James R. Briscoe (ed.). *Historical Anthology of Music by Women.* Indiana University Press, 1991, pp. 1–5.

Trilling, Diana. *The Beginning of the Journey: The Marriage of Diana and Lionel Trilling.* Harcourt Brace, 1993.

Trollope, Joanna. *Britannia's Daughters: Women of the British Empire.* Pimlico, 1983.

Troy, Gil. *Affairs of State: The Rise and Rejection of the Presidential Couple Since World War II.* The Free Press, 1997.

Tucker, George Holbert. *Jane Austen: The Woman: Some Biographical Insights.* St. Martin's Griffin, 1994.

Van Kessel, Elisja Schulte. "Virgins and Mothers between Heaven and Earth," Clarissa Botsford trans. In Natalie Zemon Davis and Arlette Farge (eds.). *A History of Women in the West III: Renaissance and Enlightenment Paradoxes.* Harvard University Press, 1993, pp. 132-166.

Vecchio, Silvana. "The Good Wife," Clarissa Botsford trans. In Christiane Klapisch-Zuber (ed.). *A History of Women in the West II: Silences of the Middle Ages.* Harvard University Press, 1992, pp. 105–135.

Velleius Paterculus. *Res Gestae Divi Augusti*, Frederick W. Shipley trans. Harvard University Press, 1979.

Verdon, Jean. *Les loisirs en France au Moyen Age.* Tallandier, 1980.

Vicinus, Martha (ed.). *A Widening Sphere: Changing Roles of Victorian Women.* Indiana University Press, 1977.

Waithe, Mary Ellen. "Finding Bits and Pieces of Hypatia." In Linda Lopez McAlister (ed.). *Hypatia's Daughters: Fifteen Hundred Years of Women Philosophers.* Indiana University Press, 1996, pp. 4–15.

Walkowitz, Judith R. "Dangerous Sexualities." In Geneviève Fraisse and Michelle Perrot (eds.). *A History of Women in the West IV: Emerging Feminism from Revolution to World War.* Harvard University Press, 1993, pp. 369–398.

Walters, Suzanna Danuta. *Lives Together/Worlds Apart: Mothers and Daughters in Popular Culture.* University of California Press, 1992.

Ward, Jennifer C. *English Noblewomen in the Later Middle Ages.* Longman, 1992.

Warner, Marina. *Alone of All Her Sex: The Myth And the Cult of the Virgin Mary.* Vintage Books, 1983.

Warner, Marina. *Monuments and Maidens: The Allegory of the Female Form.* Vintage, 1996.

Watkins, Susan Cotts. "Spinsters." *Journal of Family History,* Vol. 9, No. 4 (Winter 1984), pp. 310–325.

Wemple, Suzanne Fonay. "Women from the Fifth to the Tenth Century." In Christiane Klapisch-Zuber (ed.). *A History of Women in the West II: Silences of the Middle Ages.* Harvard University Press, 1992, pp. 169–201.

Wessley, Stephen. "The Thirteenth-Century Guglielmites: Salvation Through Women." In Derek Baker (ed.). *Medieval Women: dedicated and presented to Professor Rosalind M. Hill on the occasion of her seventieth birthday.* Basil Blackwell, 1978, pp. 289–303.

Willard, Charity Cannon. *Christine de Pizan: Her Life and Works.* Persea Books, 1984.

Williamson, Margaret. *Sappho's Immortal Daughters.* Harvard University Press, 1995.

Winegarten, Renee. *The Double Life of George Sand: Woman and Writer: a critical biography.* Basic Books, 1978.

Winterson, Jeanette. *Art Objects: Essays on Ecstasy and Effrontery.* Alfred A. Knopf, 1996.

Wolf, Naomi. *The Beauty Myth.* Vintage, 1990.

Wolff, Cynthia Griffin. *Emily Dickinson.* Addison-Wesley Publishing, 1988.

Woolf, Virginia. *Mrs. Dalloway.* Flamingo, 1994.

Woolf, Virginia. *Three Guineas.* Hogarth Press, 1952.

Woolf, Virginia. *To The Lighthouse.* Flamingo, 1995.

Woolf, Virginia. *The Voyage Out.* Granada, 1978.

Woolf, Virginia. *The Years.* Vintage, 1992.

Wright, Thomas. *The Book of the Knight of La Tour-Landry.* Green Wood Press, 1969.

Zaidman, Louise Bruit. "Pandora's Daughters and Rituals in Grecian Cities." In Pauline Schmitt Pantel (ed). *A History of Women in the West I: From Ancient Goddesses to Christian Saints,* Arthur Goldhammer trans. Harvard University Press, 1992, pp. 338–376.

Zilboorg, Gregory. *A History of Medical Psychology.* W. W. Norton & Co., 1941.

Zwinger, Lynda. *Daughters, Fathers, and the Novel: The Sentimental Romance of Heterosexuality.* The University of Wisconsin Press, 1991.

Permissions

Index

Abbesses in Middle Ages, 483–485
Abbot, Robert, 136
Abbott, Emma, 568
Abdication of Edward VIII, 203–204
Abélard, Peter
  and Héloïse, 24–25, 420–421
  The Story of My Misfortunes, 420
Abortion
  in 19th century, 316–317
  in late 20th century, 319–320
Académie Royale de Danse, 338
Adèle's Stories for Children, by Adèle Koehnke, 535
Adelman, Janet, 101–102
Adonis, mourning ritual, in ancient Greece, 452–453
Adultery
  in ancient Greece, 188–189
  in Middle Ages, 192–193
Advertising
  effect on women, 373
  in 1950s, sex in, 41
Advocate, The, 36, 141
Aeschylus, *Eumenides*, 309
Agrippina the Elder, 96
Agrippina the Younger, 96–97
Ainley, Miss (in *Shirley*), 287–288
Aishinabe, John, 446–447
Alcibiades, 190–191
Alcott, Louisa May
  Jo's Boys, 74
  Little Women, 73–74
Aleotta, Raphaela, 564
Alexander Romance, 335
Alexander, William, *The History of Women*, 31
Alias Grace, by Margaret Atwood, 636–637
"Alice Grey," by Mrs. Philip Millard, 567
Alice in Wonderland, 73
Allemang, John, 524
Allen, Frederick Lewis, 202
Allende, Isabel, *Paula*, 79–80
Amalasuntha, 391–392
Ames, Sherry, *Ministering Angels*, 272
Amherst Academy, 402
Among the Ginzburgs, by Ellen Pall, 176
Amorous Prince, The, by Aphra Behn, 628
Amos, Betty, 178
Amos, Bob, 177–178
Amos, Margaret, 177, 178, 183
Amos, Sandra, 177–186
Anatomy, teaching of in 19th-century art schools, 593
Angel in the House, the, 634
Ann, Mother (Ann Lee), 522–523
Annulment in Middle Ages, 193–194
Anthony, Susan B., 368, 428
Antigone, 224–225
Antipater of Thessalonica, 623–624
Antiseptics, idea of, 266
Anyte, 622–623

Aphra Behn: Dispatch'd from Athole, by Ross Laidlaw, 629
Aphrodite, 21, 128, 357
Aquinas, Saint Thomas, 310
Archery as activity for women in Middle Ages, 336
Ariadne, 127
Ariès, Philippe, 101
  Centuries of Childhood: A Social History of Family Life, 98
Aristotle, 309
Armstrong, Garner Ted, 122
Armstrong, Herbert W., 118–119, 121–122
Art, "great," as male domain
  in 19th century, 544, 566–567, 593, 631
  in early 20th century, 570
Art schools for women in 19th century, 593–594
Artemis, 21, 225, 332
Artists, visual, female, 573–600
  in ancient Greece, 588–589
  in Middle Ages, 588–590
  in early modern era, 590–592
  in 19th century, 592–596
  in 20th century, 597–600
Asclepias, 283
Aspasia, 539
Astell, Mary, 230–231, 398
  A Serious Proposal to the Ladies, 230
Aswald, Gunter, 153
Atalanta, 332–333
Athena, 21, 225, 257, 357, 417
Athena Polias, priestess of, in ancient Greece, 479
Athletes, women, backlash against in 20th century, 342–343
Athletic activity in women. See Physical activity in women
Athletic competition. See Competition, athletic
Athletic festival for girls in ancient Greece, 334
Atthill, Lombe, 266
Atwood, Margaret, 636–637
  Alias Grace, 636–637
  Lady Oracle, 636
Auclert, Hubertine, 172
Audley, Margaret, 226
Augustus, 129–131
Aupick, Major Jacques, 106
Aurelius, Marcus, 95, 161–162
Austen, Cassandra, 543
Austen, Jane, 543, 629–630, 631
  Emma, 170–171, 232
  Mansfield Park, 32
  Northanger Abbey, 425
  Persuasion, 399
  Pride and Prejudice, 138–139
  Sense and Sensibility, 632
Austin, George, 491
Avery, Rachel Foster, 488–489

Bacchus, 127
Bachofen, J. J., *Das Mutterrecht*, 142–143
Baker, William J., 335
Ballet, 337–338
Ballet comique de la reine, 337–338
Barker, George, 635
Barker, Juliet, 631
Bartlett, Dale, 208–214
Bartlett, Norma, 208–210
Bartlett, Sandra, 615
Bartlett, Walter, 208, 209, 210, 211, 212
Baseball, origins in Middle Ages, 335
Basketball, women's
    in 19th century, 340
    in 20th century, 344–345
Bassett: John Bassett's forty years in politics, publishing, business and sports, by Maggie Siggins, 613
Bassett, John White Hughes, 613
Bassett, Johnny F., 608
Bathing in early modern era, 261, 362
Battle of the Dragon with Child of the Woman, 590
Baucis, 623
Baudelaire, Caroline, 105–106
Baudelaire, Charles, relationship with mother, 105–106
Bauman, Richard A., 95, 96
Bayeux Tapestry, 589–590
Baylac, Augustine, 377
Baylac, Jean-Marie, 377
Beatles, 42
Beattie, Elinore, 407, 408
Beattie, Mary, 407–415
Beattie, Norman, 407–408
Beauty in women, 347–374
    in ancient Greece, 356–359
    in Middle Ages, 359–362
    in early modern era, 362–367
    in 19th century, 367–370
    in 20th century, 370–374
Beauty Myth, The, by Naomi Wolf, 373–374
Beauvoir, Simone de, 75, 127, 373, 546
    The Second Sex, 31, 78, 431, 463
Bedford Ladies College, 402
Beginning of the Journey, The, by Diana Rubin, 145
Behn, Aphra, 30, 627–629
    The Amorous Prince, 628
    The Forc'd Marriage, 628
    Love-Letters Between a Nobleman and His Sister, 628
    Oroonoko, or The History of the Royal Slave, 627–628, 629
Bell, Acton, 631
Bell, Currer, 631
Bell, Ellis, 631
Bell, Marilyn, 331–332
Bell, Robert E., 560
Bell, Vanessa, 634
Bernardine of Siena, 284
Bernhardt, Sarah, 44
Berriot-Salvadore, Evelyne, 313
Berry, Dr. James, 290
Bertraux, Léon, 594
Bevin, Edward, 269–270
Bevin, Liz, 269–270
Bicycling as activity for women in 19th century, 339–340
Birth control
    in 19th century, 315–317
    in 1950s, 319
    pill, development and effects, 267–268
    pill, effect on women's sexuality, 43

Bischofsheim Convent, 392–393
Bishop, Elizabeth, 636
Blackstone, William, 132
Blackwell, Elizabeth, 290–291
"Bliss," by Katherine Mansfield, 635
Bloomers in 19th century, 368
Boccaccio, Giovanni, 588
    De claris mulieribus, 589
Bohème, La, by Giacomo Puccini, 255
Bonheur, Rosa, 595–596
    The Horse Fair, 596
Book of Divine Works, The, by Hildegard of Bingen, 455
Book of the City of Ladies, The, by Christine de Pisan, 625–626
Book of the Courtier, The, by Baldassare Castiglione, 363
Bordoni, Faustina, 565
Borin, Françoise, 591
Boston Women's Health Book Collective, *Our Bodies, Ourselves*, 319
Bottrigari, Hercole, *Il Desiderio*, 564
Boys, 81–112
    in ancient Greece, 92–97
    in Middle Ages, 97–101
    in early modern era, 101–104
    in 19th century, 104–107
    in 20th century, 107–112
Bradley, Pat, 344
Brahms, Johannes, 569
Branch Davidians, 524
Brassieres, 371
Brathwaite, Richard, *The English Gentlewoman*, 168
Brentano, Bettina, 400
Brian and the Boys, by Maggie Siggins, 617
Briscoe, Lily (in *To the Lighthouse*), 236
Brodie, Jean (in *The Prime of Miss Jean Brodie*), 388–389
Bron, Siemon, 504–505
Bron, Sieta, 504–505
Bron, Winnie, 504–512
Brontë, Anne, 263, 630, 631
Brontë, Charlotte, 234, 263, 369, 630, 631
    Jane Eyre, 18, 70, 197, 369–370, 630
    Shirley, 287–288, 461
    Villette, 369, 400–401
Brontë, Elizabeth, 263
Brontë, Emily, 263, 630, 631
    Wuthering Heights, 18, 631
Brontë, Maria, 263
Brookner, Anita, *Hotel du Lac*, 239–240
Brown, Arthur, 475
Brown, Helen Gurley, *Sex and the Single Girl*, 43, 146
Browning, Elizabeth Barrett, 314
Browning, Robert, 314
Brownmiller, Susan, 367
Brunton, Mary, 632
Bryn Mawr, 402
Buchanan, Daisy and Tom (in *The Great Gatsby*), 174
Budapest, Zsuzsanna, 524
Bundling, 30
Burney, Fanny, *Camilla*, 365–367
Burns, Walter (in *His Girl Friday*), 223–224
Butler, Josephine, 172
By Grand Central Station I Sat Down and Wept, by Elizabeth Smart, 635
Byrd, William, 66
Bywater, Alicia, 351
Bywater, Christopher, 351–352
Bywater, Lynne, 347–354
Bywater, Roger, 349–351
Bywater, Sarah, 352

Caesarean section, 266
Cahn, Susan K., 343
Calisthenics as activity for women in 19th century, 339
Callias, 190
Calvin, John, 457
Cambridge University, admission of women, 403
Camilla, by Fanny Burney, 365–367
Campanini, Barberina, 338
Campbell, Bernice, 347–348
Campbell, Joseph, 445
Campbell, Leslie, 347–348
Campbell, Lynne, 347–354
Canadian Tragedy, A, by Maggie Siggins, 615
Canterbury Tales, by Geoffrey Chaucer
    "The Nun's Priest's Tale," 166–167
    "The Wife of Bath's Tale," 132–134, 361–362
Care-givers, women as, 269–295
    in ancient Greece, 280–282
    in Middle Ages, 282–284
    in early modern era, 284–287
    in 19th century, 287–291
    in 20th century, 291–295
Careers, sons', control over in early modern era, 103
Carpenko, Mary, 574
Carpenko, Peter, 574
Carter, Elizabeth, 424
Casagrande, Carla, 23, 360
Cassatt, Mary, 595
    The Bath 72
    Lydia in the Loge, 595
Castel, Étienne de, 624
Castiglione, Baldassare, *The Book of the Courtier*, 363
Cathars, 516–518
Catherine de Médicis, 337–338
Catherine of Aragon, 193–194
Catholic Church
    in early modern era, sexual role of women, 29
    in early modern era, women's position in, 458–459
    in 20th century, ordination of women, 492–493
Centuries of Childhood: A Social History of Family Life, by
    Philippe Ariès, 98
Cercylas, 621
Ceres, priestesses of, 480
Certaldo, Paolo da, *Handbook of Good Customs*, 60
Chambers-Schiller, Lee Virginia, 232
Chantal, Baroness Jeanne de, 457
Chaplin, Charlie, 40
Charlemagne, 192
Chaucer, Geoffrey
    "The Nun's Priest's Tale," 166–167
    "The Wife of Bath's Tale," 132–134, 361–362
Chave, Anna, 599
Cheney, Amy, *Gaelic Symphony, Op. 32*, 569
Chesser, Eustace, *Love Without Fear*, 41
Chicago, Judy, *Red Flag*, 600
Child-rearing in early to mid-20th century, 318
Childbirth
    in ancient Greece and Rome, 257–258, 280–282
    in Middle Ages, 258–260
    in 20th century, 266–267
Children. See also Boys; Girls
    attitude toward in Middle Ages, 98–99
    attitude toward in 18th century, 103–104
    effect of divorce on in 20th century, 206
Chilperic, King, 97–98
Chopra, Deepak, 448
Choruses, female, in ancient Greece, 559–560
Christian era, early, women's leadership in religion,
    481–482

Christina, Queen of Sweden, 424
Christine de Pisan. See Pisan, Christine de
Chudleigh, Lady, 395
Church and the Second Sex, The, by Mary Daly, 464
Church of God, International, 122
Circe, 283
Citron, Marcia J., 566–567
Claricia, 590
Class, social, and women, 148–176
    in ancient times, 159–162
    in Middle Ages, 162–167
    in early modern era, 167–170
    in 19th century, 170–172
    in 20th century, 172–176
Cleland, John, *Memoirs of a Woman of Pleasure (Fanny
    Hill)*, 31, 42
Clélie, by Madeleine de Scudéry, 627
Clement VII, Pope, 194
Cleomenes, King of Sparta, 479
Clergy, female, acceptance of in 20th century, 490–492.
    See also Religion, women's involvement in
Clifford, Lady Anne, 167–168
Clothing, women's
    in Middle Ages, 359–362
    in early modern era, 362–363
    in 19th century, 367–368
    in 20th century, 370–373
Clytemnestra, 93, 94
Code of Hammurabi, 126–127
Cohen, Gustave, 404
Colette, *Earthly Paradise*, 57–58
Colette, Sidonie, 57–58
Collin, Françoise, 429
Colombat, Dr. Marc, 70
Cometh up as a Flower, 140
Commedia dell'arte troupes and female performers, 564
Common Sense Book of Baby and Child Care, The, by Dr.
    Benjamin Spock, 318–319
Competition, athletic
    between men and women in 20th century, 345–346
    in ancient Greece, 334–335
    in bicycling in 19th century, 340
Composers, female
    in Middle Ages, 560–562
    in 19th century, 567, 568–569
    in late 20th century, 572
Constantine, 192
Convent schools
    in Middle Ages, 392–393
    in early modern era, 395–396
Convents as places for women's creative expression. See
    also Nuns
    in Middle Ages, 540–541, 560–562
    in early modern era, 563–565
Conway, Anne, Viscountess, *The Principles of the Most
    Ancient and Modern Philosophy*, 422–423
Cook, Mariana, *Mothers [and] Sons in Their Own Words*,
    112
Coombs, Alan, 556
Coombs, Brian, 556
Coombs, Leslie, 551–552, 554–555, 557
Coombs, Noreen, 549–557, 605
Coombs, Queenie, 552
Coriolanus, 95, 453
Cornell University, admission of women, 403
Corsets, 367–368
Cosmopolitan, 42
Cott, Nancy F., 145, 426
Coubertin, Pierre de, 346

Courting game in 18th century, 30–31, 32
Courtly love, 25–27
Craik, Dinah M., *Olive*, 544
Crates, 418
Crawford, Christina, 79
Crawford, Joan, 38, 79
Creative nonfiction, 617
Creativity in women, 529–548
    in ancient Greece, 538–540
    in Middle Ages, 540–541
    in early modern era, 541–543
    in 19th century, 543–546
    in 20th century, 546–548
Crombie, David, 610
Crombie, Lillian, 238
Croquet as activity for women in 19th century, 339
Crucified Woman, 465–466
Cults. See Sects, women in
cummings, e. e., 605
Cupid's Letter, by Christine de Pisan, 625
Curie, Marie, 416–417
Curie, Pierre, 416
Curnoe, Greg, 580
Cuzzoni, Francesca, 565
Cynics, 418
Cyprian, Saint, 23
Cyril of Alexandria, 419–420

Dadaist movement, 597–598
Dallas, Laurel (in *Stella Dallas*), 175
Dallas, Stella (in *Stella Dallas*), 174–175
Dallas, Steven (in *Stella Dallas*), 175
Dalloway, Clarissa (in *Mrs. Dalloway*), 172–173,
    545–546
Daly, Mary, 463–464
    The Church and the Second Sex, 464
Damian, Peter, Saint, 100
Danaus, daughters of, 129
Dancing as activity for women in early modern era,
    336–338
Darwin, Charles, 143
Daughters and mothers, 46–80. See also Girls
Daughters of Charity, 285–287
Davey, John, 297
Davey, Judy, 296–306, 605
Davey, Laurie, 296–297
Davey, Wilf, 297, 298
Davies, Robertson, 610
Davison, Emily Wilding, 370
Day, Doris, 41
De claris mulieribus, by Giovanni Boccaccio, 589
De matrimonio, by Seneca, 258
Dead End, 40
Dean, James, 91–92
Declaration of Sentiments at first women's-rights
    convention, 427
Defoe, Daniel, *Moll Flanders*, 231
Dekker, Thomas, *The Witch of Edmonton*, 485–486
Delphine, by Mme de Staël, 138
Demand, Nancy, 257, 281, 282
Demeter, 21, 59–60
Democritus, 417
Demosthenes, 18–19, 280
Denison, Grace, 340
Desaive, Jean-Paul, 336
Descartes, René, 423
Desdemona (in *Othello*), 194
Desiderio, Il, by Hercole Bottrigari, 564
Dewar, Phyllis, 342

Dia, Comtessa de, 562
Dialogue on Love, by Plutarch, 19
Diana (goddess), 332
    20th-century worship of, 525
Dibutade, 588
Dick and Jane, 405–406
Dickens, Charles, *Martin Chuzzlewit*, 288
Dickinson, Austin, 107
Dickinson, Edward, 107
Dickinson, Emily, 106–107, 402, 630, 632–633
Didrikson, Mildred "Babe," 342, 343
Dietrich, Marlene, 44
Dio, 97
Dionysus, 127, 513–514
Discussion des parties du corps humain, La, by Charles,
    Estienne, 311
Diseases of Women, 282
"Distaff," by Erinna, 623
Divorce, 177–207
    in ancient Greece, 189–191
    in Middle Ages, 191–194
    in early modern era, 196–197
    in 19th century, 197–201
    in 20th century, 201–207
Dixon, Laurinda S., 422
Doll's House, A, by Henrik Ibsen, 141–142
Domitian, 453
Donne, John, 168
Doran, Bob, 271, 272, 273–274, 275, 276–278
Doran, Christina, 275, 278
Doran, Jeffrey, 275
Doran, Lesley, 275
Doran, Pat, 269–278
Dowries, 64–65
Drabble, Margaret, *A Summer Bird-Cage*, 372–373
Dramatic Overture, Op. 10, by Margaret Ruthven Lang,
    569
Drutz, Jane, 578
Duby, Georges, 99
Duchess of Malfi, The, by John Webster, 168–169
Dulong, Claude, 543
Duncan, Isadora, 371
Duran, Jane, 423
Durham Ladies College, 402
Dyer, Mary, 520

Eakins, Thomas, 593
Earhart, Amelia, 38, 342
Earthly Paradise, by Colette, 57–58
East of Eden (film), 91
Eastman, Crystal, 405
Ecclesiasticus, 418
Eddy, Mary Baker, 478–479
Ederle, Gertrude, 38, 342
Edgeworth, Maria, 399
Education for women, 377–406. See also Schools
    in ancient Greece, 389–391
    in Middle Ages, 391–394
    in early modern era, 394–399
    in 19th century, 400–404
    in 20th century, 404–406
Edward VIII, 203–204
Eggley, Anne, 171
Egypt, ancient, perception of female physiology, 308
Ehrenreich, Barbara, 293
Eifert, Christiane, 174
Eighty Years and More, by Elizabeth Cady Stanton, 428
Eisenhower, Mamie, 145–146
Ela, Daniel, 195

Elderkin, Kate, McK., 589
Eliot, George, 631
  Silas Marner, 620
Elizabeth I, 228–229, 261, 337, 362
Elizabeth, Princess of Bohemia, 424
Elliot, Anne (in Persuasion), 399
Ellis, Havelock, 37
  Studies of the Psychology of Sex, 37–38
Emile, by Jean-Jacques Rousseau, 399, 425
Emma, by Jane Austen, 170–171, 232
Ende, 590
Engels, Friedrich, Origins of the Family, Private Property
  and the State, 143
Engelthal convent, 540
Englemann, George J., 313
English, Deirdre, 293
English Gentlewoman, The, by Richard Brathwaite, 168
English Law for Women in the Nineteenth Century, by
  Caroline Sheridan Norton, 200
Epicoene, by Ben Jonson, 364
Epicurus, 390
Epitre d'Othéa, by Christine de Pisan, 283
Equality of Men and Women, The, by Marie le Jars de
  Gournay, 229
Eratosthenes of Oe, 188
Erinna, "Distaff," 623
Erotica and pornography, 28, 31, 35
Espérance, Ode d', 63–64
Este, Duke Alfonso II d', 564
Estes, Clarissa Pinkola, Women Who Run with the
  Wolves, 465
Estienne, Charles, La discussion des parties du corps
  humain, 311
Eugenius III, Pope, 483
Eumenides, by Aeschylus, 309
Euphiletos, 188, 189
Euripides
  Hippolytus, 256
  Medea, 129
  Trojan Women, 19
Eurydice of Hierapolis, 390
Evans, Mary Ann, 620
Eve, 23, 360
Ewer, Mabel Swint, 571

Falconry as activity for women in Middle Ages, 336
"Fallen Woman, The," by Kassia, 561, 562
Family, 115–147
  in ancient Greece, 127–131
  in Middle Ages, 131–134
  in early modern era, 134–138
  in 19th century, 138–142
  in 20th century, 143–147
Fanny Hill (Memoirs of a Woman of Pleasure), by John
  Cleland, 31, 42
Fanshawe, Ginevra (in Villette), 400–401
Farthingales, 361
Fashion
  in Middle Ages, 361
  in early modern era, 362–364
  in 19th century, 367–368
  in 20th century, 370–372
Father Knows Best, 41
Fell, Margaret, 519–520
  Women's Speaking, 519–520
Female Moral Reform Society, 36, 105, 141
Female-only musical ensembles
  in early modern era, 563–564
  in 20th century, 570–571

Feminine Mystique, The, by Betty Friedan, 42, 111, 239
Feminism
  in 19th century, 36–37, 141–142
  in late 20th century and 1960s activism, 43–44
  in late 20th century and beauty, 373–374
  in late 20th century and education, 406
  in late 20th century and female clergy, 491–493
  in late 20th century and gender differences, 431–433
  in late 20th century and medicine, 319–320
  in late 20th century and music world, 572
  in late 20th century and religion, 463–464
  in late 20th century and sects, 524–525
  in late 20th century and social-class issues, 175–176
  in late 20th century, egalitarian, 432
Femmes savantes, Les, by Molière, 542
Ferguson, Elmer, "I Don't Like Amazon Athletes," 343
Fields, W. C., 40
Filer, Diana, 611
Filles de la Charité, Les, 285–287
Finch, John, 422
First Blast of the Trumpet against the monstrous regiment of
  Women, The, by John Knox, 228
First Wives Club, 206–207
Fitzgerald, F. Scott, The Great Gatsby, 174
Flesselles, Phillipe de, 311
Floriana, 258–260
Forc'd Marriage, The, by Aphra Behn, 628
Ford, John, 'Tis a Pity She's a Whore, 364
Fortuna, cults of, in ancient Rome, 453
Fouillée, Augustine, Francinet, 425
Four Square Productions, 618–619
Fox, George, 519
Francinet, by G. Bruno (Augustine Fouillée), 425
Fraser, Antonia, 168, 170
Fredegund, Queen, 97–98
Freed slaves in ancient Rome, 161–162
Freud, Sigmund, 75–76, 107–108
Friedan, Betty, 41–42, 373
  The Feminine Mystique, 42, 111, 239
Frigidity in women in 19th century, 34
Frohock, Jane, 426
Frugoni, Chiara, 284
Fun with Dick and Jane, 405–406

Gaelic Symphony, Op. 32, by Amy Cheney, 569
Gaia, worship of in late 20th century, 464
Galen, 309–310
Galswinth, 97
Gamp, Sarah (in Martin Chuzzlewit), 288
Garbo, Greta, 44
Garçonne, La, by Victor Margueritte, 237
Gaskell, Elizabeth, 632
Gassendi, Pierre, 423
Gatsby, Jay (in The Great Gatsby), 174
Gender differences
  as natural, 425–426, 429–431
  perception in late 20th century, 431–433
Gender differences in education
  in ancient Greece, 389
  in Middle Ages, 393–394
  in early modern era, 394–395, 398
Gentileschi, Artemisia, 590–592
  Aurora, 592
  David and Bathsheba, 592
  Esther and Ahasuerus, 592
  Judith Decapitating Holofernes, 590, 591
  Rape of Proserpine, 592
  Self-Portrait as the Allegory of Painting, 592
Gentleman's Magazine, 66

George, Boy, 44
Gerberga, 483
Gerona Apocalypse, 590
Gertrude (in *Hamlet*), 101–102
Gibbon, Edward, 419, 561
Gibson, Graeme, 636
Giles of Rome, 311
Gillis, John R., 135
Girdles, 371
Girls, 46–80. See also Education for women
    in ancient Greece, 58–60
    in Middle Ages, 60–64
    in early modern era, 64–69
    in 19th century, 69–74, 106–107
    in 20th century, 75–80
Girton College, 403
Glick, Paul, 146
Glorifying the American Girl, 40
Glory of Hera, The, by Philip Slater, 93–94
Glyn, Elinor, 545
Gnosticism, 517
Goddess worship in 20th century, 464, 524–525
Goddesses, Greek
    and marriage, 128–129
    sexual role of, 21
    unmarried, 225
Godly Form of Householde Government, A, 137
Goldman, Emma, 76, 143–144
Goldsmith, Barbara, 461
Gordon, Louise, 578
Gossman, Nancy, 599
Gould, Louise, 573–586
    Canadian Sucker Series, 582
    Dollie Series, 583
    Grey Lady, 583
    Horsey State I, II and III, 583
    Salvation Suite, 584
    Society Matrons, 582
    Stella Suite, 583
Gould, Peter, 579–580, 581
Gournay, Marie le Jars de, 229–230, 424
    Equality of Men and Women, The, 229
    Grief des Dames, 229
Governesses, single women as, 234–235
Graduate, The, 78–79
Grapes of Wrath, The (film), 40
Gray, Harry, 81–82
Gray, Jessie, 81–82, 85
Gray, Mary, 81–90
Greece, ancient
    adultery in, 188–189
    boys in, 92–97
    creativity in women in, 538–540
    divorce in, 189–191
    education for women in, 389–391
    family in, 127–131
    female visual artists in, 588–589
    girls in, 58–60
    goddesses and gods in, 21, 128–129, 225
    homosexuality in, 21–22
    intellectualism in women in, 417–420
    mother-daughter relationships in, 59–60
    mother-son relationships in, 93–97
    perception of female physiology in, 308–309
    physical activity for women in, 332–335
    sexual role of men in, 20
    sexual role of women in, 18–22
    single women in, 224–226
    women and cults in, 513–514

women as care-givers in, 280–282
women as musicians in, 559–560
women writers in, 621–624
women's health issues in, 256–258
women's leadership in religion in, 479
women's spirituality in, 451–453
Greer, Germaine, 591
Gregory of Tours, 97, 98
Grieco, Sara F. Matthews, 261, 362, 363
Grief des Dames, by Marie le Jars de Gournay, 229
Grien, Hans Baldung, *The Weather Witches*, 486
Griffin, Daphne, 46–56
Griffin, Lionel, 46–49, 52
Griffin, Mabel, 46–49, 52
Griffin, Wendy, 524–525
Grignan, Françoise-Marguerite de, and relationship with mother, 67–69
Grimké, Angelina, 487
Grimké, Sarah, 487
Group, The, by Mary McCarthy, 318
Gruchy, Lydia Emilie, 489
Guglielmites, 516
Guide to Skiing in Eastern North America, A, by Maggie Siggins, 613
Guidosalvi, Sancia, 589
Guilds
    in Middle Ages, women in, 165
    in early modern era, treatment of widows, 169
Guo Fangfang, 618
Guttmann, Allen, 333
Gymnastics as activity for women in 19th century, 339
Gynecology, by Soranus, 281
Gynecology in 19th century and perception of women, 313–314

Hades in myth of Persephone, 59–60
Hagan, Fred, 578, 583
Haggart, Carrie-May, 612, 615, 616, 619
Haggart, Ron, 610–612, 613
Hainault, Margot, 336
Hair in early modern era, 364
Hales, Bill, 441–442, 443–444
Hales, Mary, 437–449
Hals, Frans, 134–135
Hamilton, Mary, 467, 468
Hamlet, 101–102
Hammurabi, Code of, 126–127
Handbook of Good Customs, by Paolo da Certaldo, 60
Happy Days, 40
Harbuz, Ann, 547–548
Hargreaves, Jennifer, 339
Harris, Ann Sutherland, 592
Harris, Lawren, 529
Harris, Mrs., and dolls she created, 537–538
Harrison, Jane Ellen, 367
Harvengt, Philippe de, 63
Harvey, William, 168
Haweis, Stephen, 371
Hawkins, Sir John, 565
Hawthorne, Nathaniel, 34–35
Hazzard, Dorothy, 518–519
Health issues, women's, 243–268
    in ancient Greece and Rome, 256–258
    in Middle Ages, 258–261
    in early modern era, 261–263
    in 19th century, 263–265
    in 20th century, 266–268
Health of 19th-century girls, 70–71
Health research, biased testing in late 20th century, 320

Heaney, Geraldine, 346
Hearn, Adèle, 529–536
    Adèle's Stories for Children, 535
    Just Off Centre, 535
    "Pink Hat With Feather," 536
    Spice and Such, 535
Hearn, Barbara, 530–531, 532
Hearn, Miles, 531, 532
Hearn, Norman, 530–531, 532, 533, 535
Heathcliff (in Wuthering Heights), 18
Heaven's Gate, 524
Hecuba, 94
Helen of Troy, 356–359
Helike, Macria, 258
Helmbrecht, 100
Helmer, Nora (in A Doll's House), 142
Helmer, Torvald (in A Doll's House), 142
Héloïse and Peter Abélard, 24–25, 420–421
Henderson, Heather, 294–295
Henri IV, 541
Henry VIII, 193–194
Hephaestus, 21
Hera, 21, 128–129, 334, 357
Heraia, 334
Herodotus, 359
Herrera, Hayden, 599
Hestia, 225
Hetaerae, 538–540
Heustis, Florence Gooderham, 529
Higonnet, Anne, 543–544, 598
Hildebert of Lavardin, 23
Hildegard of Bingen, 259, 454–456, 483–484, 561–562
    The Book of Divine Works, 455
    Ordo Virtutum, 561–562
    Scivias, 541, 562
    Symphonia armonie celestium revelactionum, 561
Hill, Octavia, 171–172
Hilliard, Dr. Marion, 146, 238–239
Hillingham, Lady, 34
Hipparchia, 418
Hipparete, 190–191
Hippolytus, by Euripides, 256
Hirst, Beth, A Women's Comedy, 629
His Girl Friday, 223–224
History of Woman Suffrage, 428
History of Women, The, by William Alexander, 31
Hobbes, Thomas, 138
Hobbs, Colleen A., 289
Höch, Hannah, 597–598
    Pretty Girl, 598
Hockey, women's, in 20th century, 345
Hodge, Jane Aiken, 631
Hogan, Edward, 235
Hokhmah, 418
Hollingsworth, Chris, 120
Hollingsworth, Elizabeth, 115–124
Hollingsworth, Ellery, 117, 118, 119, 120, 121
Hollingsworth, Jeremy, 120
Hollingsworth, Rebecca, 120, 124
Holmes, Bert, 215–216, 219
Holmes, Frances, 215–222
Holmes, Henrietta, 215–216
Homer
    Hymn to Aphrodite, 225
    Hymn to Demeter, 22, 59–60
    The Iliad, 159, 358–359, 560
    The Odyssey, 359
Homosexuality
    in 1980s and 1990s, effect on gender barriers, 44–45

in men, blamed on mothers in 1950s, 111
in men, in ancient Greece, 21
in women, in ancient Greece, 22
in women, perceptions of in early 20th century, 37–38
Hooton, Elizabeth, 520
Hope, Edith (in Hotel du Lac), 239–240
Hôpital Général in early modern era, 286
Hopper, Dennis, 92
Horace, 481
Horace, by George Sand, 542
Horseback-riding as activity for women in Middle Ages, 336
Hospitals in early modern era, 286–287
Hotel Dieu in early modern era, 286
Hotel du Lac, by Anita Brookner, 239–240
How to Get a Man, by Maggie Siggins, 612
Hufton, Olwen, 65, 104, 135, 170, 195, 286, 458, 519
Hughes, Molly, 73
Hughes, Ted, 635
Hume, Leslie Parker, 291
Husserl, Edmund, 430
Huygens, Constantijn, 424
Hymn to Aphrodite, by Homer, 225
Hymn to Demeter, by Homer, 22, 59–60
Hypatia of Alexandria, 419–420
Hysteria
    and the wandering womb, 312
    as disease in 19th century, 264–265

"I Don't Like Amazon Athletes," by Elmer Ferguson, 343
Iago (in Othello), 194
Iaia of Cyzicus, 588
Ibsen, Henrik, A Doll's House, 141–142
Iliad, The, by Homer, 159, 358–359, 560
Illuminators of manuscripts in Middle Ages, 590
Impressionists, female, 594–595
Indiana, by George Sand, 105, 139
Inferiority feelings in girls of 19th century, 69–70
Inglis, Bill, 269, 270, 271
Inglis, Effie, 274
Inglis, Inez, 269, 270, 271–272, 274
Inglis, Pat, 269–278, 551
Intellectualism in women, 407–433
    in ancient times, 417–420
    in Middle Ages, 420–421
    in early modern era, 422–425
    in 19th century, 425–429
    in 20th century, 429–433
Iseler, Elmer, 553–554, 556
Isis, cult of, 514–515

Jackson, Michael, 44
Jacquet de la Guerre, Elisabeth-Claude, 565–566
    Les Jeux à l'honneur de la victoire, 565
James of Vitry, 360
Jane Eyre, by Charlotte Brontë, 18, 70, 197, 630, 369–370
Jazz King, The, 40
Jerome (early Church scholar), 420
Jesus Movement in ancient Rome, 454
Jeux à l'honneur de la victoire, Les, by Elisabeth-Claude Jacquet de la Guerre, 565
Joan of Arc, Saint, 513
John of Salisbury, Policraticus, 336
John Paul II, Pope, Ordinatio Sacerdotalis, 492
Johnson, Hildy (in His Girl Friday), 223–224
Johnson, Paddy, 584

Johnson, Samuel, *The Rambler*, 169
Jointures, 65
Jones, Jim, 524
Jong, Erica, 17
Jonson, Ben, *Epicoene*, 364
Jordan, Betty, 467–477
Jordan, Ken, 470, 471, 473–474
Jordan, Kirk, 472, 473
Jordan, Tanya, 472
Joseph, Saint, 136
Joyce, James, 38
Jo's Boys, by Louisa May Alcott, 74
Juette of Huy, 456
Julian of Norwich, *Revelations of Divine Love*, 456
Jullien, Stéphanie, 69–70
Just Off Centre, by Adèle Koehnke, 535
Justinian I, 192
Jutta of Sponheim, 454
Juvenal, 391, 418

Kabbala, 422, 423
Kahlo, Frida, 598–599
   Broken Column, 598
Kahun Papyrus, 308
Kaplan, E. Ann, 175
Kassia, 560–561
   "The Fallen Woman," 561, 562
Kearsley, Bill, 274
Kellogg, Clara Louise, 567–568
Kennedy, Anthony, Rev., 491
Kennedy, Jacqueline, 373
Kent, Duchess of, and relationship with daughter
   Queen Victoria, 72
Keuls, Eva C., 389
Kilbourn, Elizabeth, 475
Kilman, Miss (in *Mrs. Dalloway*), 463
King, Billy Jean, 344
Kinsey, Alfred, 39
Kirk, Betty, 467–477
Kirk, Eva, 467–468
Kirk, Maurice, 467–468, 469
Klesmorim, 337
Knibiehler, Yvonne, 71, 72, 264, 289, 368
Knight, Laura, *Self-Portrait*, 597
Knox, John, 457
   *The First Blast of the Trumpet against the monstrous
   regiment of Women*, 228
Koedt, Anne, "The Myth of the Vaginal Orgasm," 44
Koehnke, Adèle, 529–536
   Adèle's Stories for Children, 535
   Just Off Centre, 535
   "Pink Hat With Feather," 536
   Spice and Such, 535
Koehnke, Eva, 150
Koehnke, Hans, 148–151, 152
Koehnke, Jamie, 533
Koehnke, Margarethe, 148–151, 152, 153
Koehnke, Peter, 150, 532–533, 534
Koehnke, Tanya, 533, 534, 536
Koehnke, Ursula, 148–157, 533, 534
Kollwitz, Käthe, *The Peasant War*, 597
Korinna of Tanagra, 622
Kraemer, Ross Shepard, 130, 514
Krafft-Ebing, Richard von, *Psychopathia Sexualis*, 37

La Roche, Sophie von, 400
Ladies of Charity, 284, 285
Lady Audley's Secret, 140
Lady Oracle, by Margaret Atwood, 636

Laflueve, Christina, 268
Laidlaw, Ross, *Aphra Behn: Dispatch'd from Athole*, 629
Landry, Emily, 201
Lane, M. E., 388–389
lang, k. d., 44
Lang, Margaret Ruthven, *Dramatic Overture, Op. 10*, 569
Laqueur, Thomas, 310, 311
Lasch, Christopher, 128
Laurens, André du, 312
Lawrence, D. H., 38
   Sons and Lovers, 109–110, 173
Lawson, John, 446–447
Learned Maid, The, or Whether a Maid may be a Scholar,
   by Anna Maria von Schurman, 424
Leave It to Beaver, 41
Leclercq, Jean, 63–64
Leda, 356
Lee, Ann, 522–523
Lee, Carla, 71
Lee, Hermione, 317
Leenhoff, Suzanne, 543
Lefaucheur, Nadine, 268
Leginska, Ethel, 571
Legrange, Léon, 592–593
Leibniz, Gottfried, 423
Leinster, Duchess of, 168
Lenglen, Suzanne, 342
Leo XIII, Pope, 139
Leoba, 392–393
Leporin, Dorothea Christiane, 424
Leprosy, women as carriers of in Middle Ages, 260
Lerner, Gerda, 126, 127, 159, 160, 394, 417, 424, 455,
   456, 632
Lesbianism
   in 1980s and 1990s, effect on gender barriers, 44–45
   in ancient Greece, 22
   perceptions of in early 20th century, 37–38
L'Esperance, David Laurent, 10–13
L'Esperance, Jane, 7–17
Lessing, Doris, 635
   A Proper Marriage, 204
   Martha Quest, 78, 372
   mother's life as nurse, 292
   relationship with mother, 77–78
   Under My Skin, 77
*Letter to the Queen on Lord Chancellor Cramworth's
   Marriage and Divorce Bill, A*, by Caroline Sheridan
   Norton, 200
Lewald, Fanny, 402
L'Hermite-Leclercq, Paulette, 64, 394
Linen in early modern era, 363
Lissarrague, François, 559
Lister, Joseph, 102, 266
Literature as male domain in 19th century, 631
Little Women, by Louisa May Alcott, 73–74
Liu Qinghe, 615
Lives, by Plutarch, 190
Livia, 130
Lockart, Grace Annie, 402
Locke, John, 138
Lomas, Jack, 437, 438
Lomas, John, 437
Lomas, Joyce, 437–438
Lomas, Mary, 437–449
London University, admission of women, 403
Lorde, Audre, 176
Louie, Alexina, 572
Louis XIV, 338
Louyer-Villermay, Jean-Baptiste, 264–265

Love and Hate, 615
Love-Letters Between a Nobleman and His Sister, by Aphra Behn, 628
Love Without Fear, by Eustace Chesser, 41
Lower-class women
    in Middle Ages, 166–167
    in early modern era, widows, 170
    in early 20th century, 172
Loy, Mina, 39, 76–77, 371
Lustful Turk, The, 35
Luther, Martin, 137, 395, 458, 486
Lycurgus, 334
Lye, Bill, 302–303, 304–306
Lye, Judy, 296–306, 605
Lysias, 188

Macdonald, J. E. H., 529
MacEwen, Gwendolyn, 635
MacFadden, Benarr, 341
MacKenzie, Alison (in *Peyton Place*), 187
MacKenzie, Danielle, 377–387
MacKenzie, Don, 382, 383, 384, 387
MacKenzie, Martine, 385
MacKenzie, Monique, 383
MacKenzie, Robert Bruce Alexander, 385
Macleod, Christopher, 440, 443, 448
Macleod, Mary, 437–449
Macleod, Ron, 439–440, 441, 444
Mademoiselle magazine, 158–159
Magritte, René, *The Rape,* 307
Maitland, John Fuller, 569
Maître à danser, Le, by Pierre Rameau, 337
Makejoy, Maude, 336
Makeup in early modern era, 364
Makin, Bathsua Pell, 397–398, 424
Malleus Maleficarum (The Witch Hammer), 486
Malone, Mary, 465
Manet, Édouard, 594
Manet, Eugène, 595
Manning, Joanna, 492–493
Mansfield, Katherine, 634–635
    "Bliss," 635
    "Prelude," 635
Mansfield Park, by Jane Austen, 32
Manuscript illuminators in Middle Ages, 590
March, Jo (in *Little Women*), 73–74
Margueritte, Victor, *La Garçonne,* 237
Marillac, Louise de, 284–287
Marinella, Lucretia, 424
Marital abuse
    in Middle Ages, 132
    in early modern era, 194–196
Marriage, 113–240. See also Divorce
    in ancient times, 59, 126–131
    in Middle Ages, 61–62, 63–64, 131–134
    in early modern era, 102–103, 134–138
    in 19th century, 138–142, 630
    in 20th century, 142–147
Marriage, women's status in
    in ancient Greece, 128–131
    in Middle Ages, 131–134
    in early modern era, 136–138
    in 19th century, 139–143
    in 20th century, 143–147
Martha Quest, by Doris Lessing, 78, 372
Martin Chuzzlewit, by Charles Dickens, 288
Martin, Clara Brett, 140
Martin, Danielle, 377–387
Martin, Henri, 377–379, 386

Martin, John, 458–459
Martin, Yvonne, 377, 378–379, 386
Martyrs, female, in early Christian times, 481
Marx, Karl, 143
Marx Brothers, 40
Mary, Virgin, 460
Mason, Priscilla, 401
Massey, Gertrude,
Mastin, Benjamin, 116
Mastin, Bruce, 115, 117, 118, 119, 122, 124
Mastin, Edna, 116, 118, 121
Mastin, Elizabeth, 115–124
Mastin, Jim, 116, 118, 121, 124
Mastin, Paul, 115, 117, 122–123
Mastin, Sally, 122–123
Mating game in 18th century, 30–31, 32
Matrimonial Causes Act, 200–201
Matthews, Grace, 549, 551
Matthews, Herbert, 549
Matthews, Noreen, 549–557, 605
Matthews, Ross, 549
Matthews, Victoria, 491
May, Elizabeth, 601, 602, 604, 605, 606, 607
May, Nellie, 601–602
May, William, 601–602
May-Smith, Marjorie, 601–619
McCarthy, Mary, *The Group,* 318
McClung, Nellie, 490
McCormick, Katharine, 267
McEnroy, Sister Carmel, 492
McGill University, admission of women, 403
McKnight, Jack, 410
McMillan, Rachel, 287
McNamara, Jo Ann Kay, 482
Medea, 94
Medea, by Euripides, 129
Medical establishment
    and birth control in 19th century, 315–317
    and female physiology in 19th century, 313–315
    and late-20th-century feminism, 319–320
Medical schools, attitude toward women students
    in Middle Ages, 282–283
    in 19th century, 289–291
    in early 20th century, 293
Medical work, women in, 269–295
Medici, Cosimo de', 101
Medieta, Ana, *Untitled. Serie Volcán 2,* 599
Medieval Woman's Guide to Health, 260
Meilanion, 333
Meitner, Lise, 404
Memoirs of a Woman of Pleasure (Fanny Hill), by John Cleland, 31, 42
Menander, *The Shield,* 128
Menelaus, 356–358
Menopause, perception of in 19th century, 315
Menstruation
    perception of in early modern era, 311–312
    perception of in 19th century, 70, 314
Mental illness in early 20th century, 317–318
Merian, Maria Sibylla, *Metamorphosis of the Insects of Suriname,* 423
Metalious, Grace
    No Adam in Eden, 188
    Peyton Place, 187–188
Metamorphosis of the Insects of Suriname, by Maria Sibylla Merian, 423
Meun, Jean de, *Romance of the Rose,* 625
Micas, Nathalie, 596
Michelet, Jules, 459

Middle Ages
    adultery in, 192–193
    attitude toward children in, 98–99
    beauty in women in, 359–362
    boys in, 97–101
    courtly love in, 25–27
    creativity in women in, 540–541
    divorce in, 191–194
    education for women in, 391–394
    family in, 131–134
    female visual artists in, 589–590
    girls in, 60–64
    improvement in women's position in, 27
    intellectualism in women in, 420–421
    mother-son relationships in, 100–101
    perception of female physiology in, 309–311
    physical activity for women in, 335–336
    sexual role of women in, 22–28
    single women in, 226–228
    social class in, 162–167
    women as care-givers in, 282–284
    women as musicians in, 560–562
    women in sects in, 515–518
    women writers in, 624–626
    women's health issues in, 258–261
    women's leadership in religion in, 482–485
    women's spirituality in, 454–457
Middle-class women
    in Middle Ages, 164–165
    in early modern era, widows, 169
    in 19th century, 170–171
    in 20th century, 172
Midwives
    in ancient Greece, 280–281
    in Middle Ages, 283–284
    in 19th century, 289
Millard, Mrs. Philip, "Alice Grey," 567
Millay, Edna St. Vincent, 38
Miller, Bonny H., 567
Mills, Doris, 529–530, 531
Mills, W. Gordon, 529–530
Milton, John, 137
Miner, Dorothy, 590
Minerva, 417–418
Ministering Angels, by Sherry Ames, 272
Mirror of the Simple Soul, by Marguerite Porète, 484
Mode, Bruce, 321–323, 325–326
Mode, Gwen, 321–330
Mode, Ruth, 321–323
Modern era, early
    beauty in women in, 362–367
    boys in, 101–104
    creativity in women in, 541–543
    divorce in, 196–197
    education for women in, 394–399
    family in, 134–138
    female visual artists in, 590–592
    girls in, 64–69
    intellectualism in women in, 422–425
    mother-daughter relationships in, 66–69
    mother-son relationships in, 101–104
    perception of female physiology in, 311–313
    physical activity for women in, 336–338
    sexual role of women in, 28–32
    single women in, 228–232
    social class in, 167–170
    witch hunts in, 485–487
    women as care-givers in, 284–287
    women as musicians in, 563–566

    women in sects in, 518–520
    women writers in, 626–629
    women's health issues in, 261–263
    women's lack of leadership in religion in, 485–487
    women's spirituality in, 457–459
Moerloose, Isabella de, 64
Molière
    Les femmes savantes, 542
    Les précieuses ridicules, 542
Moll Flanders, by Daniel Defoe, 231
Mommie Dearest (film), 79
Monasteries as places for women's creativity in Middle
    Ages, 540–541. See also Convents; Nuns
Monroe, Marilyn, 355–356
Montagu, Elizabeth, 424
Montague, John, 609
Montaigne, Michel de, 229
Moore, Colin, 247, 250, 254
Moore, Don, 245, 246, 248–249
Moore, Gail, 243–254
Moore, Kathy, 248, 249, 250, 251, 254
Moore, Marianne, 636
Moran, Eddy, 323
More, Hannah, 399, 424
More, Henry, 422, 423
Morel, Gertrude (in Sons and Lovers), 109–110, 173
Morel, Walter (in Sons and Lovers), 109, 173
Morisot, Berthe, 594–595
    Julie Playing the Violin, 594
    Lady at Her Toilette, 594
    Wet Nurse and Julie, 594
Mortality rates of women in 20th century, 266
Mossiker, Frances, 67, 68
Mother Right (Das Mutterrecht), by J. J. Bachofen,
    142–143
Mothers and daughters, 46–80. See also Girls
Mothers and sons, 81–112. See also Boys
Mothers as scapegoats in 20th century, 78–79, 107–111
Mothers [and] Sons in Their Own Words, by Mariana
    Cook, 112
Mott, Lucretia, 427
Mount Allison University, admission of women,
    402–403
Mrs. Dalloway, by Virginia Woolf, 172–173, 317–318,
    463, 545–546
Murphy, Frank, 325, 326, 327, 328–329
Murphy, Gwen, 321–330
Murphy, Patrick, 328, 330
Muses in ancient Greece, 560
Music as male domain in early 20th century, 570
Music, popular
    of 1950s, 558–559
    of late 20th century, 572
Music teachers, female in early 20th century, 570
Musical education restricted to men in early modern
    era, 566
Musicians, female, 549–572
    in ancient Greece, 559–560
    in Middle Ages, 560–562
    in early modern era, 563–566
    19th century, 566–569
    20th century, 569–572
Mutterrecht, Das, by J. J. Bachofen, 142–143
"Myth of Vaginal Orgasm, The," by Anne Koedt, 44

Nahoum-Grappe, Véronique, 365
Nattrass, Susan, 345
Natural Claim of a Mother in the Custody of her Child …,
    by Caroline Sheridan Norton, 199

Natural look in 18th century, 365
Neaera, 280, 539
Neglect of girls in 19th century, 69–70
Nero, relationship with mother, 96–97
Neville, Anne, 163
Neville, Philip (in *Hotel du Lac*), 240
Neville, Richard, Earl of Warwick, 163
Newman, Christina McCall, 205
Niboyet, Eugénie, 488
Nichols, Garth, 85–90
Nichols, Kyle, 85–90
Nichols, Mary, 81–90
Nichols, Melissa, 84, 86, 87, 89
Nichols, Steve, 83–89
Nielsen, Dorise, 40
Nightingale, Florence, 287, 288–289, 294
Nightingale School and Home for Nurses, 289
Nineteenth century
    artists, visual, female in, 592–596
    beauty in women in, 367–370
    boys in, 104–107
    creativity in women in, 543–546
    education for women in, 400–404
    family in, 138–142
    girls in, 69–74
    intellectualism in women in, 425–429
    mother-daughter relationships in, 72–74
    mother-son relationships in, 104–106
    perception of female physiology in, 313–317
    physical activity for women in, 338–341
    sexual role of women in, 32–37
    single women in, 232–235
    social class in, 170–172
    women as care-givers in, 287–291
    women as musicians in, 566–569
    women in sects in, 520–523
    women writers in, 629–633
    women's health issues in, 263–265
    women's leadership in religion in, 487–489
    women's spirituality in, 459–462
No Adam in Eden, by Grace Metalious, 188
Nochlin, Linda, 546
Nonfiction, creative, 617
Northanger Abbey, by Jane Austen, 425
Norton, Caroline Sheridan, 198–200
    A Letter to the Queen on Lord Chancellor Cramworth's Marriage and Divorce Bill, 200
    English Law for Women in the Nineteenth Century, 200
    The Natural Claim of a Mother in the Custody of her Child …, 199
Norton, George Bentley, 198–200
Nouvelle Héloïse, La, by Jean-Jacques Rousseau, 138
Nudes and women artists in 19th century, 593
Nuns. See also Convents
    and visual arts in Middle Ages, 590
    as intellectuals in Middle Ages, 420
    cloistering of in early modern era, 458
    creativity of in Middle Ages, 540–541
    leadership roles in religion in Middle Ages, 482–485
"Nun's Priest's Tale, The," by Geoffrey Chaucer, 166–167
Nun's Story, The, 450–451
Nursing
    19th century, 288–289
    effect of World War I on, 291–292
    in late 20th century, 294–295
    schools, 289, 292
Nussey, Ellen, 234
Nutrition in early modern era, 262

Obstetrics in 19th century and perception of women, 313–314
"Ode to Aphrodite," by Sappho, 621
Odyssey, The, by Homer, 359
Oedipus complex, 107–111
Oenopion, 127
Of Woman Born, by Adrienne Rich, 79
Offen, Karen M., 291
O'Keeffe, Georgia, 599
    Black Iris, 599
"Old Maids," by Catharine Maria Sedgwick, 233
Olive, by Dinah M. Craik, 544
Olympias, 588
Omerod, Bill, 50–51, 52, 53
Omerod, Daphne, 46–56
Omerod, Elizabeth, 52, 53, 54–56
Omerod, Shelley, 52, 54, 55, 56
Omerod, Stephanie, 51, 54, 56
On the Apparel of Women, by Tertullian, 359–360
Opera in early modern era and opportunities for female singers, 565
Opitz, Claudia, 162, 282–283
Oppenheim, Meret, *Breakfast in Fur*, 598
Orchestras, all-female, 571
Ordinatio Sacerdotalis, by Pope John Paul II, 492
Ordo Virtutum, by Hildegard of Bingen, 561–562
Origins of the Family, Private Property and the State, by Friedrich Engels, 143
Oroonoko, or The History of the Royal Slave, by Aphra Behn, 627–628, 629
Osborne, Emily Mary, *Nameless and Friendless*, 587–588
Osiris, 514–515
Othello, by William Shakespeare, 194
Our Bodies, Ourselves, by Boston Women's Health Book Collective, 319
Our Dancing Daughters, 38
Ovaries as disabling factor in women's health, 314
Ovology, 34
Oxford University, admission of women, 403

Pall, Ellen, *Among the Ginzburgs*, 176
Pankhurst, Christabel, 143
Pankhurst, Emmeline, 370
Paraclete Convent, 420
Pargiter, Eleanor (in *The Years*), 235–236
Paris (son of king of Troy), 357–358
Parker, Rozsika, 595
Patmore, Coventry, 139
Patriarchal marriage
    in ancient times, 126–131
    in Middle Ages, 131–134
    in early modern era, 136–138
    in 19th century, 139–143
    in 20th century, 143–147
Paul, Saint, 482
Paula, by Isabel Allende, 79–80
Paz, Octavio, 26–27
Pearson, Marilyn, 295
Peeters, Clara
    Still Life with Flowers, a Goblet, Dried Fruit and Pretzels, 592
    Still Life with Vases, Goblets and Shells, 590–591, 592
    Vanitas Self-Portrait, 592
Penis envy, theory of, 75–76
People's Temple, 524
Perfumes in early modern era, 362–363
Pericles, 539
Perkin, Joan, 140–141, 460
Persephone, 59–60, 128

Persuasion, by Jane Austen, 399
Perwick, Susanna, 563
Petites écoles in early modern era, 396–397
Peverara, Laura, 564
Peyton Place, by Grace Metalious, 187–188
Philip, Earl of Pembroke and Montgomery, 167
Philip of Macedon, 390
Philip of Novara, *Les Quatre Ages de l'Homme*, 393–394
Phillips, Roderick, 196
Phrastor of Aegilia, 280
Physical activity in women, 321–346
    in ancient Greece, 332–335
    in Middle Ages, 335–336
    in early modern era, 336–338
    in 19th century, 338–341
    in 20th century, 341–346
Physicians, female
    in 19th century, 290–291
    in 20th century, 292–294
Physicians, male, in ancient Greece, 281–282
Physiology, female, perceptions of
    in ancient Egypt and Greece, 308–309
    in Middle Ages, 309–311
    in early modern era, 311–313
    in 19th century, 313–317
    in 20th century, 317–320
Pickford, Mary, 38
Piercy, Marge, 43
Pillow Talk, 41
Pincus, Gregory Goodwin, 267
"Pink Hat With Feather," by Adèle Koehnke, 536
Pirovana, Mayfreda de, 516
Pisan, Christine de, 62, 624–626
    Cupid's Letter, 625
    Epitre d'Othéa, 283
    The Book of the City of Ladies, 625–626
Pisan, Thomas de, 624
Plath, Sylvia, 635–636
Plato
    Symposium, 22
    The Republic, 389–390, 417
    Timaeus, 308
Playboy, 42
Plebeian Chastity, shrine of, in ancient Rome, 453
Pliny the Elder, 588
Pliny the Younger, 390, 391
Plouffe Family, The, 125–126
Plutarch, 128, 334
    Dialogue on Love, 19
    Lives, 190
Poetry as music in ancient Greece, 559
Policraticus, by John of Salisbury, 336
Pollitt, Katha, 432
Pollock, Griselda, 595
Polyneices, 224
Pomeroy, Sarah, 515
Poor Clares, 397
Porète, Marguerite, 484–485
    Mirror of the Simple Soul, 484
Pornography and erotica, 28, 31, 35
Portnoy's Complaint, by Philip Roth, 111
Powders, use of, in early modern era, 362
Pratt, Christopher, 600
Pratt, Mary, *Burning the Rhododendron*, 600
Praxilla, 622
Précieuses, 542–543
Précieuses ridicules, Les, by Molière, 542
Pregnancy, perception of in 19th century, 315
"Prelude," by Katherine Mansfield, 635

Preservation of Historic Sites: A European Perspective, The,
    by Maggie Siggins, 609
Presley, Elvis, 558
Pride and Prejudice, by Jane Austen, 138–139
Priestesses in ancient Greece and Rome, 479–481
Prime of Miss Jean Brodie, The, by Muriel Spark, 388–389
Primogeniture, 99
Principles of the Most Ancient and Modern Philosophy, The,
    by Anne Viscountess Conway, 422–423
Prodromos, Theodoros, 561
Promiscuity, control of, in ancient Greece, 20
Proper Marriage, A, by Doris Lessing, 204
Propertius, Sextus, 333
Property, ownership by married women in 19th
    century, 141–142
Prophets, female, in 19th century, 520–523
Prostitutes, upper-class, in ancient Greece, 538–540
Prostitution
    in Middle Ages, 226–227
    in 19th century, 35
Protestant churches in early modern era, women's
    position in, 457–458
Protestant sects in early modern era, 518–520
Pseudonyms used by women writers in 19th century,
    631–632
Psychoanalysis and gender differences, 429. See also
    Freud, Sigmund
Psychopathia Sexualis, by Richard von Krafft-Ebing, 37
Puberty, meaning of, for 19th-century girls, 70–71
Publick Universal Friend, 521
Puccini, Giacomo, *La Bohème*, 255
Puritanism and sexual role of women, 28–30
Pythagoras, 390

Quakers, 519–520
Quant, Mary, 43
Quatre Ages de l'Homme, Les, by Philip of Novara,
    393–394
Querelle des femmes, 625
Quin, Gretchen, 155
Quin, Ursula, 148–157, 533, 534
Quin, Whayne, 152, 153–154, 155–156, 533

Radegund, 392
Rader, Stanley R., 122
Rambler, The, by Samuel Johnson, 169
Rambouillet, Marquise de, 541–542, 627
Rameau, Pierre, *Le Maître à danser*, 337
Ramière, Raymon de (in *Indiana*), 105
Ramsay, Agnata, 403
Rape, The, by René Magritte, 307
Rebel Without a Cause, 91–92
Régnier-Bohler, Danielle, 626
Reid, Elizabeth Jesse, 402
Reitman, Ben, 143
Religion
    and divorce in Middle Ages, 191–192
    and ideals of family, 131–132, 136
    feminization of in 19th century, 459–462
    unconventional. See Sects, women in
    women's movement away from in 20th century,
        463–465
Religion, women's involvement in, 437–493
    in ancient Greece and Rome, 451–454, 479–481
    in Middle Ages, 454–457, 481–485
    in early modern era, 457–459, 485–487
    in 19th century, 459–462, 487–489
    in 20th century, 462–466, 489–493

Reproduction, perception of male and female roles in Middle Ages, 310–311
Reproductive system, female
  as disabling factor in women's health, 314–315
  as sole purpose of women, 312–313, 314
  perception of in ancient Egypt and Greece, 308–309
  perception of in Middle Ages, 310
Republic, The, by Plato, 389–390, 417
Research on health issues, bias of, in late 20th century, 320
Revelations of Divine Love, by Julian of Norwich, 456
Revenge of the Land, by Maggie Siggins, 617
Revival movements in 19th century, 461–462, 520–523
Revolution, 428
Rich, Adrienne, 108, 319
  Of Woman Born, 79
Richardson, Joanna, 106
Richardson, Mary, 370
Richelieu, Cardinal, 424
Riel, by Maggie Siggins, 618
Riggs, Bobby, 344
Rivera, Diego, 598
Robbins, Bill, 509, 512
Robbins, Jennifer, 509, 512
Robbins, Walter, 506, 507, 508–509, 510–512
Robbins, Winnie, 504–512
Rochester, Edward (in *Jane Eyre*), 18, 197, 369–370
Rock, Dr. John, 267
Rokeby Venus, by Velázquez, 370
Romance of the Rose, by Jean de Meun, 625
Rome, ancient
  childbirth in, 258
  intellectualism in women in, 417–420
  slavery of women in, 160–161
  women and cults in, 514–515
  women's leadership in religion in, 479–481
  women's spirituality in, 453–454
Roth, Philip, *Portnoy's Complaint,* 111
Rothblatt, Martine, 431
Rousseau, Jean-Jacques, 313
  Emile, 399, 425
  La Nouvelle Héloïse, 138
Rouvroy, Louis de, 541
Rubens, Peter Paul, *Rubens, his wife Helena Fourment and her first-born,* 134, 135
Rubin, Diana, *The Beginning of the Journey,* 145
Rufus, Musonius, 390–391
Ruskin, John, *Sesame and Lilies,* 33
Rykiel, Jean-Philippe, 112
Rykiel, Sonia, 112

Sackville, Richard, Earl of Dorset, 167
Sainte-Croix of Poitiers, 392
Saint Joan, by George Bernard Shaw, 513
Salchow, Ulrich, 345
Salome, 562
Salons in early modern era, 541–543
Sand, George, 72, 368, 631
  Horace, 542
  Indiana, 105, 139
Sanderson, Eleanor, 7–9, 12
Sanderson, Jane, 7–17
Sanderson, Ted, 7, 8, 9, 13
Sanger, Margaret, 267
Sappho, 21, 22, 559, 621–622
  "Ode to Aphrodite," 621
Saturninus, Pompeius, 391
Saunders, Margaret Marshall, 72
Savage, Dr. George, 317

Scheid, John, 481
Schneeman, Carol, *Interior Scroll,* 600
Schools. See also Education for women
  art, in 19th century, 593–594
  convent, in early modern era, 395–396
  convent, in Middle Ages, 392–393
  elementary, in early modern era, 396–397
  elementary, in Middle Ages, 393
  in early modern era, 395–398
  medical, attitudes about women students, 282–283, 289–291, 293
  nursing, 289, 292
  post-secondary, in 19th century, 402–404
  private, in 19th century, 402
  private, in early modern era, 396
  public, in 19th century, 401–402
  secondary, in 19th century, 402
Schorr, Thelma M., 294
Schumann, Clara, 544, 568–569
Schumann, Robert, 568, 569
Scivias, by Hildegard of Bingen, 541, 562
Scriptures, reinterpretation by women in 19th century, 487–489
Scudéry, Georges, de, 626, 627
Scudéry, Madeleine de, 542, 626–627
  Clélie, 627
Second Sex, The, by Simone de Beauvoir, 31, 78, 431, 463
Sects, women in, 494–526
  in ancient Greece and Rome, 513–515
  in Middle Ages, 515–518
  in early modern era, 518–520
  in 19th century, 520–523
  in 20th century, 523–525
Sedgwick, Catharine Maria, "Old Maids," 233
Segal, Lynne, 42
Semen, perception of role in Middle Ages, 311
Seneca, *De matrimonio,* 258
Sense and Sensibility, by Jane Austen, 632
Separation, legal, in Middle Ages, 193
Serebryakova, Zinaida, *Self-Portrait at the Dressing Table,* 597
Serious Proposal to the Ladies, A, by Mary Astell, 230
Servants, work as, for girls in early modern era, 66
Sesame and Lilies, by John Ruskin, 33
Sévigné, Mme de, 542
  and relationship with daughter, 67–69
  illness, 262–263
  widowhood, 167
Sex and the Single Girl, by Helen Gurley Brown, 43, 146
Sex as vile and low
  in Middle Ages, 22
  in early modern era, 28–29
Sex education for 19th-century girls, 72–73
Sexologists in late 19th century, 37–38
Sexual harassment of working girls in early modern era, 66
Sexual relationships, 7–45
Sexual revolution of the 1960s, 42–44
Sexual role of women
  in ancient Greece, 18–22
  in Middle Ages, 22–28
  in early modern era, 28–32
  in 19th century, 32–37
  in 20th century, 37–45
Shahar, Shulamith, 98, 165, 482–483, 517
Shakers, 522–523
Shakespeare, William, *Othello,* 194
Shapiro, Michael, 615–616

Shaw, Anna Howard, 489
Shaw, George Bernard, 202
  Saint Joan, 513
Sheridan, Richard Brinsley, 198
Shield, The, by Menander, 128
Shirley, by Charlotte Brontë, 287–288, 461
Shorter, Edward, 261, 266
Siggins, Elizabeth, 601, 602, 604, 605, 606, 607
Siggins, John, 604–605
Siggins, John William, 604, 618
Siggins, Maggie, 601–619
  Bassett: John Bassett's forty years in politics, publishing,
    business and sports, 613
  Brian and the Boys, 617
  A Canadian Tragedy, 615
  A Guide to Skiing in Eastern North America, 613
  How to Get a Man, 612
  The Preservation of Historic Sites: A European Perspective,
    609
  Revenge of the Land, 617
  Riel, 618
Siggins, Michael Matthew, 604
Silas Marner, by George Eliot, 620
Simmel, George, 429
Simpson, Wallis Warfield, 204
Single women, 215–240
  in ancient Greece, 224–226
  in Middle Ages, 226–228
  in early modern era, 228–232
  in 19th century, 232–235
  in 20th century, 235–240
Sisters of Charity, 285–287
Slater, Philip, The Glory of Hera, 93–94
Slavery of women, 159–161
Sleigh, Sylvia, Philip Golub Reclining, 599
Smart, Elizabeth, By Grand Central Station I Sat Down
  and Wept, 635
Smiley, Sarah, 489
Smith, Catherine Parsons, 570
Smith, Dr. Andrew, 288–289
Smith, Harriet (in Emma), 170
Smith, Marjorie, 603
Smith, Russell, 603
Smith, Septimus Warren (in Mrs. Dalloway), 317–318
Smith, Ted (Douglas), 602
Smith College, 402
Smith-Rosenberg, Carroll, 36, 70, 72, 172, 265, 462,
  522
Smyth, Ethel, The Wreckers, 569
Social reformers in 19th-century upper and middle
  classes, 171–172
Society for the Propagation of Christian Learning, 397
Society of Friends, 519–520
Socrates, 190
Solar Temple, 524
Soloists, female operatic, in early modern era, 565
Solomon, Rebecca, 234
Somerville, Mary, 367
Sons and Lovers, by D. H. Lawrence, 109–110, 173
Sons and mothers, 81–112. See also Boys
Sophia (goddess), 418
Soranus, 258, 309
  Gynecology, 281
Southcott, Joanna, 520–521, 523
Southey, Robert, 631
Spark, Muriel, The Prime of Miss Jean Brodie, 388–389
Sparta, compulsory physical activity for girls, 333–334
Speght, Rachel, 312
Speirs, J. Murray, 529, 531

Sperling, Adam, 619
Sperling, Gerry, 612, 613–614, 615, 616, 619
Sperling, Shoshana, 619
Spice and Such, by Adèle Koehnke, 535
Spirituality, women's, 437–466
Spock, Dr. Benjamin, The Common Sense Book of Baby
  and Child Care, 318–319
Sports, professional, and women in 20th century,
  344–346. See also Physical activity in women
Staël, Mme de, 424
  Delphine, 138
Stafford, Ralph, 226
Stamphorse, William, 236–237
Stanton, Elizabeth Cady, 172, 368, 426–429
  Eighty Years and More, 428
  The Woman's Bible, 428, 488–489
Stanton, Henry, 426–427, 428
Stein, Edith, 430–431
Steinem, Gloria, 239
Steiner, Nancy Hunter, 406
Stella Dallas, 174–175
Stevens, Alice Barber, Female Life Class, 593
Stevenson, Adlai, 406
Stone, Lawrence, 30–31, 99, 102–103, 131, 136–137
Stoolball as activity for girls, 335
Storch, Margaret, 110
Storer, Horatio, 314
Story of My Misfortunes, The, by Peter Abélard, 420
Stubbes, Philip, 28–29
Student Christian Movement, 10
Studies of the Psychology of Sex, by Havelock Ellis, 37–38
Summer Bird-Cage, A, by Margaret Drabble, 372–373
Surrealism, 598
Swift, Jonathan, 104, 396
Swoopes, Cheryl, 345
Syers, Madge, 345
Symphonia armonie celestium revelactionum, by Hildegard
  of Bingen, 561
Symposia in ancient Greece, 538–539
Symposium, by Plato, 22
Syphilis and effect on sexual mores in early modern era,
  29

Tacitus, 96, 454
Talfourd, Serjeant, 199
Tallemant des Réaux, Gédéon, 542
Tassi, Agostino, 591
Teachers, female, in early modern era, 397–398
Teal, Jane, 7–17
Teal, John, 13–14
Tennis as activity for women in 19th century, 340
Tennyson, Lord Alfred, 139–140
Teresa of Avila, 460
Tertullian, On the Apparel of Women, 359–360
Textiles, in ancient Greece, 589
Thackeray, William Makepeace, 369
That Touch of Mink, 41
Thatcher, Colin, 615
Thébaud, Françoise, 291
Theophilos, 561
Thesmophoria, 451–452
Thomas, M. Carey, 73, 403
Thompson, Alan, 414
Thompson, Andrew, 414
Thompson, Carl, 412–413
Thompson, Flora, 106
Thompson, Mary, 407–415
Thompson, Simon, 414
Thrale, Hester, 104, 168, 424

Thucydides, 359
Timaeus, by Plato, 308
Timarete, 588
'Tis a Pity She's a Whore, by John Ford, 364
To the Lighthouse, by Virginia Woolf, 76, 236
Tomalin, Claire, 630
Toronto, University of, admission of women, 403
Towner, Gail, 243–254
Towner, Georgina, 243–244
Towner, Laurence, 243–244
Trilling, Lionel, 145
Trojan Women, by Euripides, 19
Trollope, Joanna, 172
Troubadours, female, in Middle Ages, 562
Trousers on women in 19th century, 368
Troy Female Seminary, 402
Twentieth century
    beauty in women in, 370–374
    boys in, 107–112
    creativity in women in, 546–548
    divorce in, 201–207
    education for women in, 404–406
    family in, 143–147
    female visual artists in, 596–600
    girls in, 75–80
    intellectualism in women in, 429–433
    mother-daughter relationships in, 76–80
    mother-son relationships in, 107–112
    perceptions of female physiology in, 317–320
    physical activity in women in, 341–346
    sexual role of women in, 37–45
    single women in, 235–240
    social class in, 172–176
    women as care-givers in, 291–295
    women as musicians in, 569–572
    women in sects in, 523–525
    women writers in, 633–637
    women's health issues in, 266–268
    women's leadership in religion in, 489–493
    women's spiritual'ty in, 462–466
Twiner, Esmé, 494–495
Twiner, Gay, 494–503
Twiner, Jim, 494–495

Ulmer, Michael, 147
Under My Skin, by Doris Lessing, 77
Unitarian Universalism Association, 523
United Society of Believers in Christ's Second
    Appearing (Shakers), 522–523
Upper-class women
    in Middle Ages, 163–164
    in early modern era, 167–169
    in early 20th century, 172–173, 174
    in 19th century, 170–171
Upshall, Philip, 384, 386–387
Upshall, Wilma, 384
Uterus. See Womb

Valentines of 19th century, 35
Van Helmont, F. M., 422
Vanity in Middle Ages, 361
Vassar, 402
Vasse, Marie, 195–196
Vecchio, Silvana, 62
Velázquez, Diego de Silva, Rokeby Venus, 370
Verney, Edmund, 103
Verwoerd, Gail, 243–254
Verwoerd, Hank, 249–250, 251–253
Vesta, priestesses of, 480–481

Vestal Virgins, 480–481
Victoria, Queen, 72, 543
Victorian era. See Nineteenth century
Villani, Giovanni, 393
Villette, by Charlotte Brontë, 369, 400–401
Vincent de Paul, Saint, 284–286
Vindication of the Rights of Women, by Mary
    Wollstonecraft, 338
Virgin Mary, 23–24
Virginity, importance of
    in ancient Greece, 59
    in Middle Ages, 23–24, 61, 62
Vives, Ludovicus, 102
Von Schurman, Anna Maria, 423–424
    The Learned Maid, or Whether a Maid may be a Scholar,
        424

Walters, Suzanna Danuta, 79
Ward, Jennifer C., 163
Ward, Mary, 397
Warhurst, Bill, 494
Warhurst, May, 494
Warner, Marina, 23–24, 310, 418
Warwick, Lady, 545
Watson, Harry, 14–16
Weather Witches, The, by Hans Baldung Grien, 486
Weber, Max, 482
Webster, John, The Duchess of Malfi, 168–169
Wellesley College, 402
Wemple, Suzanne Fonay, 191
West, Mae, 40
Whitemoon, Alice, 236–237
Whiting, Terry, 209
Wicca, 524
Widowhood in early modern era, 167–170
Wiebe, Gay, 494–503
Wiebe, Gerhard, 496–497, 498, 499, 501
Wiebe, Marina, 498, 501–503
Wiebe, Natasha, 498, 499, 501–503
Wieck, Friedrich, 568
"Wife of Bath's Tale, The," by Geoffrey Chaucer,
    132–134, 361–362
Wife-beating. See Marital abuse
Wilkinson, Jemima, 521–522
Willard, Emma, 402
Willbern, David, 75
Williams, Elizabeth, 520
Williamson, Margaret, 20
Willis, Thomas, 312
Winterson, Jeanette, 548
Wisdom depicted as female, 417–418
Wisdom of Solomon, 418
Witch Hammer, The (Malleus Maleficarum), 486
Witch hunts
    in Middle Ages, 284
    in early modern era, 485–487
Witch of Edmonton, The, by Thomas Dekker, 485–486
Witchcraft in late 20th century, 524
Wolf, Naomi, The Beauty Myth, 373–374
Wolff, Cynthia Griffin, 107
Wollerin, Cecilie, 227
Wollstonecraft, Mary, 399
    Vindication of the Rights of Women, 338
Woman's Bible, The, by Elizabeth Cady Stanton, 428,
    488–489
Womb
    and perception of women in ancient Greece, 256
    and perception of women in early modern era, 262
    wandering, in ancient Egypt and Greece, 308–309

wandering, in early modern era, 312
Women
  and ownership of property, 141–142
  as incomplete men in ancient times, 309
  as slaves, 159–161
  as vile and low in early modern era, 22, 28–29
  images of by female artists in 20th century, 597–600
  sexual objectification of, 373
  single. See Single women
Women Who Run with the Wolves, by Clarissa Pinkola
  Estes, 465
Women's Comedy, A, by Beth Hirst, 629
Women's-rights convention, first, 427
Women's Speaking, by Margaret Fell, 519–520
Woodhouse, Emma (in *Emma*), 170–171
Woodward, Joyce, 324, 326
Woolf, Leonard, 634
Woolf, Virginia, 20–21, 67, 400, 629, 633–635
  and mental illness, 317, 633
  Mrs. Dalloway, 172–173, 317–318, 463, 545–546
  To the Lighthouse, 76, 236
  The Years, 235–236, 292–293
Working women
  in Middle Ages, 165–166
  in early modern era, 66
  in 19th century, 71
World War I, effect of
  on divorce, 201–202
  on girls' lives, 76
  on marriage and family, 144
  on single women, 236–237

World War II, effect of
  on divorce, 204
  on marriage and family, 145–146
  on sexual role of women, 40
  on single women, 238
Worldwide Church of God, 118–119, 121–122
Wreckers, The, by Ethel Smyth, 569
Writers, female, 601–637
  in ancient world, 621–624
  in Middle Ages, 624–626
  in early modern era, 626–629
  in 19th century, 629–633
  in 20th century, 633–637
Wuthering Heights, by Emily Brontë, 18, 631
Wycherley, William, 137

Years, The, by Virginia Woolf, 235–236, 292–293

Zaimont, Judith Lang, 572
Zola, Émile, 371
Zurosky, Eva, 574, 575–576, 583
Zurosky, Ken, 575, 576
Zurosky, Louise, 573–586
  Canadian Sucker Series, 582
  Dollie Series, 583
  Grey Lady, 583
  Horsey State I, II, and III, 583
  Salvation Suite, 584
  Society Matrons, 582
  Stella Suite, 583
Zurosky, Nestor, 573–574, 575, 576, 577, 583